THE NEW
CAMBRIDGE MODERN HISTORY

ADVISORY COMMITTEE

G.N.CLARK J.R.M.BUTLER J.P.T.BURY

THE LATE E.A.BENIANS

VOLUME XI

MATERIAL PROGRESS AND
WORLD-WIDE PROBLEMS

1870–1898

THE NEW
CAMBRIDGE MODERN
HISTORY

VOLUME XI

MATERIAL PROGRESS AND
WORLD-WIDE PROBLEMS
1870–1898

EDITED BY
F. H. HINSLEY

CAMBRIDGE
AT THE UNIVERSITY PRESS
1967

Published by the Syndics of the Cambridge University Press
Bentley House, 200 Euston Road, London, N.W. 1
American Branch: 32 East 57th Street, New York, N.Y. 10022

First Published   1962
Reprinted   1967

Printed in Great Britain
at the University Printing House, Cambridge
(Brooke Crutchley, University Printer)

CONTENTS

v

CONTENTS

CHAPTER V
LITERATURE
By A. K. THORLBY, *Professor in Comparative Literature,
University of Sussex*

CHAPTER VI
ART AND ARCHITECTURE
By NIKOLAUS PEVSNER, *Professor of the History of Art,
Birkbeck College, University of London*

CHAPTER VII
EDUCATION
By A. VICTOR MURRAY, *Emeritus Professor of Education, University of
Hull, and lately President of Cheshunt College, Cambridge*

CHAPTER VIII
THE ARMED FORCES
By M. E. HOWARD, *Professor of War Studies, King's College, University of London*

CONTENTS

CONTENTS

CHAPTER XIII
RUSSIA

By J. L. H. KEEP, *Lecturer in Modern Russian History, School of
Slavonic and East European Studies, University of London*

CHAPTER XIV
GREAT BRITAIN AND THE BRITISH EMPIRE
By PAUL KNAPLUND

CHAPTER XV
INDIA, 1840–1905

By PERCIVAL SPEAR, *Fellow of Selwyn College and Lecturer in History
in the University of Cambridge*

CHAPTER XVI
CHINA

By C. P. FITZGERALD, *Professor of Far Eastern History,
Australian National University, Canberra*

CONTENTS

CONTENTS

CHAPTER XXI

RIVALRIES IN THE MEDITERRANEAN, THE MIDDLE EAST AND EGYPT

By A. P. THORNTON, *Professor of History in the University of Toronto*

CHAPTER XXII

THE PARTITION OF AFRICA

By R. E. ROBINSON, *Fellow of St John's College and Smuts Reader in the University of Cambridge*, and J. GALLAGHER, *Fellow of Balliol College and Beit Professor of the History of the British Commonwealth in the University of Oxford*

CHAPTER XXIII

EXPANSION IN THE PACIFIC AND THE SCRAMBLE FOR CHINA

By F. C. LANGDON, *Lecturer in Economics and Political Science, University of British Columbia*

CONTENTS

CHAPTER I

INTRODUCTION

To ask what were the important developments of the last thirty years of the nineteenth century is to be reminded of the force of continuity in men's affairs and of the rarity of abrupt change. The growth of material power and wealth; of industrialism and urbanisation; of technology and scientific knowledge; of transport, communications and trade; of population and of the movement of population; of centralised government; of democracy; of literacy and education; of public opinion and the press—these prominent developments of the age had been almost as prominent in the generation, if not in the whole century, which ended in 1870; and the same developments are no less central to an understanding of the years which stretch from the beginning of the twentieth century to the present day. If we call this period simply the age of material improvement or of industrial development or of democratic progress we have not said much of value about it. Nor does it help towards sharper definition to reflect upon another characteristic of the time: that these continuing massive developments, or most of them, occurred only in European society and its off-shoots in North America and the other areas of white settlement. This restriction and the consequent predominance of European power and civilisation in the world had existed long before 1870. They were to last beyond 1900, when European monopoly of all this progress was still scarcely touched by changes in Japan, and the discrepancy between the European and less advanced societies had become more acute than it had ever been. In studying this other feature of the time, as in analysing the changes that took place in the more developed areas, the first problem is to allot the period its proper place in a much longer span during which the same forces and relationships were always dominant but never at rest.

A second problem arises. The contradictions between some of the main characteristics of this period are at first sight startling. These were years of enormous material expansion and of economic depression; of vast strides towards the closer integration of the world's economy and yet of sharp reaction against the economics of free trade; of improved living standards but also of poverty and social degradation; of rapid social change but of stagnation in the internal politics of states; of the spread of democracy and yet of the strengthening of government and even of absolutism; of international peace but of armed peace—while intellectually and culturally they produced both work which proclaimed the triumph of enlightenment and work which touched the depths of disillusionment and despair.

But contradictions or apparent contradictions between the developments of any age loom large when it is studied as a whole—until closer study succeeds in explaining or resolving them. The explanation or the resolution of these contradictions is another route to an understanding of the character of the age.

Its character from the economic and material points of view is announced by two facts. It witnessed to a greater extent than any earlier generation the geographical spread of modern industry beyond its countries of origin and the application to industry and agriculture of science and technology; and as a result there was an increase in total industrial and agricultural production on a greater scale—if not at a greater rate—than the world had ever previously experienced. This is not difficult to explain. It is not a feature which distinguishes the age from some others: the increase and spread of material production and the growth of science and technology have been continuous and virtually autonomous processes throughout modern times. Much more distinctive is the second fact. Because material output jumped farther and more sharply in advance of demand than ever before, these years were also years of declining prices, profits and investment yields to an extent that has earned for them the title of 'The Great Depression'.

Only the economies of Great Britain and Belgium could be described as highly industrialised in 1870; even in Great Britain in that year the combined labour force in mining, quarrying, the metal industries, engineering and shipbuilding still did not equal the number of textile and clothing workers or of agricultural labourers or of domestic servants. In the next thirty years industry came to predominate in the economies of the United States and of most countries in western Europe, and developed to a lesser degree in the rest of Europe and in Japan. From the beginning of the period entirely new basic industries were introduced—the electrical and the chemical—in the more industrialised countries. They were the first industries to originate wholly in scientific discovery. Their origin, unprecedented speed of development and immediate effect in increasing and diversifying industrial production—particularly that of electricity, which provided an entirely new source of heat, light and power—are only the most dramatic illustrations of the extent to which, as never before, industry, technology and science were becoming interlocked. The majority of earlier inventions had been the work of practising craftsmen with only a modest knowledge of scientific theory. Now a whole century of slow progress and restatement in pure science—particularly in thermodynamics, electro-magnetism, chemistry and geology—began to meet up with rapid development in practical mechanical engineering—and particularly in the production of machine-tools—and in industrial methods. In a process of interaction between all three which became so cumulative that it is difficult to distinguish cause from effect, not only were new industries developed and new sources of power provided—the internal combustion engine, stemming from progress in thermodynamics theory, being only less important than electricity. Innumerable existing industries—mining and road-building, steel, agriculture, petroleum, rubber, concrete are but a few examples—were transformed and expanded. Innumerable new products—the modern bicycle, the telephone, the typewriter, linoleum, the pneumatic tyre, cheap paper, artificial silk, aluminium, ready-made clothing and shoes—were manufactured and marketed for the first time. It was in this period that mechanisation first became characteristic of industry in general, although traditional, empirical methods were nowhere entirely ousted and in some industries remained dominant, and that the range of industrial products assumed something like its present extent.

The consequent increase in total output was enormous. Between 1870 and 1900 world industrial production increased nearly four times.[1] World production of pig-iron more than tripled—from $12\frac{1}{4}$ to over 37 million tons. It had increased just under threefold—from about 1,600,000 tons to 4,470,000 tons—between 1830 and 1850 and just under threefold—from 4,470,000 tons to $12\frac{1}{4}$ million tons—between 1850 and 1870. The rate of increase between 1870 and 1900 was not as great as between 1830 and 1850 or 1850 and 1870, but the amount of the increase greatly exceeded that of the previous forty years. World production of coal increased by three and a half times—from about 220 million to nearly 800 million tons. It had increased about sevenfold—from 30 to 220 million tons—between 1830 and 1870, at the rate of 60–70 per cent per decade. Thus, again, this earlier rate of increase was not maintained between 1870 and 1900, but the amount of the increase greatly exceeded that of earlier years. The number of cotton spindles almost doubled in Europe as a whole and in the United States, and more than doubled in Germany, Italy and Russia.

If the rate of increase of production declined as industrialisation spread to new areas, it declined most markedly in those countries where industrialisation had had an earlier start. British industrial production about doubled, so that the British share in the world total dropped from about one-third in 1870 to about one-fifth in 1900; it was exceeded by that of the United States in the early 1880's, by Germany's in the 1900's. The output of the French metallurgical industries scarcely increased at all between 1871 and 1895, while in Germany it increased threefold and in the United States fourfold. But in the older areas, and particularly in Great Britain, the process by which the industrial base and society itself were becoming more complex and diversified did much to offset this relative fall. There was an immense expansion of output in newer directions, in the light industries

---

[1] It must be emphasised that almost all quantitative estimates for this period are approximations, subject to a good margin of error, because of the inadequacy or absence of many of the statistics. This should be remembered in connection with all figures quoted.

made possible by the advance of technology and in the production of the consumer goods—soap, chocolate, beef-extract, cheap newspapers—made possible by cheaper distribution methods and rising standards of living, just as there was a great increase in the numbers employed in the distributive, clerical and professional occupations in these most advanced societies.

Aggregate wealth mounted with total production. Capital investment in Great Britain did not increase at the same rate as in the thirty years before 1873, but it still doubled in the next twenty-five years, as it did in France, and it increased by three times in Germany and by more than that in the United States. Real income per head in Great Britain, which had risen by about 30 per cent over the whole period from 1851 to 1878, increased at the rate of between 17 and 25 per cent per decade between 1870 and 1900—a rate that had never previously been sustained for an appreciable period and that was not to be sustained in subsequent years—despite the continued increase in total population. In other industrialising countries, in proportion as heavy investment was still being required in the basic equipment of an industrial society—in railways, docks and towns—the national income grew at a slower rate, but still at a faster rate and to a much greater extent than they had ever before experienced.

This increase in production and wealth was not confined to industry and to the industrialised and industrialising nations. European investments abroad, which even before 1870 had enabled some overseas areas to produce food and raw materials for a world market, continued to grow. British overseas investments, like British domestic investment, did not maintain their earlier rate of increase, but they increased nearly threefold in this period, while in some areas their increase was much greater. In Argentina, for example, they increased ten times between 1870 and 1900. Those of France more than doubled in total amount; Germany's rose from nothing to being one-third of Great Britain's. These rates of increase represented a huge increase in the amount of capital exported. British overseas capital, which had totalled about £200 millions in 1855 and £1050 millions in 1875, amounted to about £1530 millions in 1885, to about £2400 millions in 1900 and to nearly £2700 millions in 1907. Nor was it capital alone that Europe exported.

There was a considerable increase in the movement of European population across the oceans and a vast improvement in Europe's knowledge of the geography and geology of the outside world. Of the 55 million Europeans who emigrated between 1821 and 1924, 21 million emigrated between 1870 and 1900, of whom half went to the United States and half to other areas—to Latin America, Canada, South Africa, Australia and New Zealand. This figure does not take into account the fact that with the improvement of communications perhaps as many as one-third of the emigrants now returned to Europe, and an increasing proportion were people who made a regular practice of temporary and seasonal migration. The exodus was still greater than it had ever been. It was in the same thirty years that most of the undeveloped agricultural areas of the world were opened up and that, with the increase of geological knowledge, though not all were yet exploited, most of the world's great mineral-bearing districts were discovered. Many of the emigrants, particularly among those from Great Britain, were skilled craftsmen who played a significant part in the establishment and spread of industry in their countries of reception. But the opening up of those countries as primary suppliers was the chief effect of this movement, of the transfer of capital that accompanied it and of the simultaneous leap forward in knowledge and in long-distance transport and communications that did so much to stimulate the emigration and the capital export. In no period of history has the world come into possession so quickly of so huge an increase in its natural wealth. And in an age that was inaugurated in 1869 by the opening of the Suez Canal and of the first trans-continental railway in America, as the railway was improved in efficiency and pushed beyond Europe, as world shipping increased from 16 million net tons in 1870 to 30 million net tons in 1900, as the carrying capacity of the world's shipping increased by four times in the same period—the world's steam tonnage came to equal that of sail by the mid-1890's and the carrying service of a steamship was equal to that of a sailing vessel four times its net tonnage—previously peripheral areas began to produce and export on a scale hitherto unimagined, and an ever-increasing flow of food and raw materials reached the old world from new lands. Until the early 1900's the supply was dominated, except in wool, by the United States, but other lands—Australia and New Zealand, South Africa, Argentina and other Latin-American states—were beginning to export on a large scale by the end of the century. At first the increase was mainly in grain, wool and cured foods. Dakota and Argentina, unimportant for wheat in 1880, were exporting 62 and 8 million bushels respectively by 1887. Argentina exported 100 million bushels of wheat and maize in 1897. By 1890, with the development of mining and of the refrigerated ship—the first refrigerated ship left Argentina with mutton in 1877; the first ship-load of New Zealand mutton reached England in 1882—it was involving oil, minerals, meat and dairy products, tropical and sub-tropical fruits, everything but the most bulky and perishable of goods.

Since there was also an expanding demand for European manufactures in these newer lands, where there was a rapid increase in the area of cultivation and in the application of machinery to mining and farming as well as in population, the extra-European areas played a large part, as importers as well as exporters, in stimulating the industrialisation of the more advanced countries. Their development provided new markets both for old products and for newer types of manufactures as well as increasing the wealth and the range of products, and thus the demand for goods, within the older societies themselves. They also took a greater share than ever before in the flow of world trade. The foreign trade of Argentina tripled between 1870 and 1900, the trade between India and Europe more than doubled. Foreign trade, an unimportant element in the economy of many nations in 1860, became indispensable to most nations between 1870 and 1900 as the division of labour between manufacturing countries and primary producers was intensified. This development was especially marked as between the economies of north-west Europe and the United States. But the closer economic integration of a single Atlantic community was not the sole result. There were new specialist developments within Europe itself, notably the expansion of Scandinavian timber and iron production and export. The ring of distant primary producers was widened from North America, Roumania and Russia to tropical and sub-tropical lands and, beyond them, to Australasia and South Africa. Areas and lines of commerce that had previously been self-contained dissolved into a single economy on a world scale. Improvements in banking and financial services and (with the extension of cables and the introduction, at the end of the period, of wireless) in communications were simultaneously knitting the world the more closely together by creating a single multilateral system of international payments. A world market, governed by world prices, emerged for the first time. In the last quarter of the nineteenth century more of the world was more closely interlocked, economically and financially, than at any time before—and perhaps since.

It seems at first sight surprising that in these circumstances—when the spread and diversification of industry and agriculture were increasing the wealth and production of the world and when huge improvements in transport, communications and finance were combining to integrate the world's economy—the rate of increase in the total flow of world trade was not greater than it was. This increased by a larger amount than in any previous generation. In the thirty years after the mid-1870's its gold value probably more than doubled, from about £2800 millions to £5000 millions per annum, and, in view of the fall in prices, its volume may have trebled. Since prices and the amount of trade both rose considerably between 1896 and the mid-1900's, the increase both in value and in volume was less than this over-all figure would suggest, however, between 1873 and 1896, when its value probably rose from about £2800 to £3900 millions and its volume about doubled; and this, though still considerable, was, by value, a smaller increase than that achieved in half the number of years between 1860 and 1872 and, measured by value or by volume, a lower rate of growth than at any time since the 1820's.[1] But this reduced rate of

[1] A. H. Imlah, *Economic Elements in the Pax Britannica* (Harvard, 1958), pp. 189 ff., gives the latest estimates, which can only be approximate. According to these, the increase in value between 1873 and 1896 was by one-third compared with increases of 80 per cent between 1850 and 1860 and of almost 100 per cent between 1860 and 1872. These earlier

increase was a corollary of the spread and improvement of industry and agriculture. These processes took place so rapidly that the world's industrial and agricultural production temporarily mounted in excess of the increase in world demand. After the mid-1890's world trade again increased at the rapid rate that had been experienced before the mid-1870's—its value doubled between 1898 and 1913—but between these dates it was this excess which brought down prices; and lowered prices largely account for the lowered rate of increase in the value of world trade. It was this which also lowered the rate of increase in the volume of trade. Wherever industry spread and industrial production increased in these circumstances, the effect was to supply home markets which had hitherto been supplied from abroad, and thus to increase commercial activity within nations but to reduce the rate of increase in the volume of trade between industrialised nations. Trade between Great Britain and European countries, as a proportion of their total foreign trade, steadily declined after 1880, as did that between Great Britain and the United States after 1890. On account of the same circumstances trade between the industrialised and the new agricultural areas was also hampered by a decisive trend towards national protection for both agriculture and industry.

The effect of the general situation, and of the resort to tariffs in particular, must not be exaggerated. World trade, though it mounted at a slower rate between the mid-1870's and the mid-1890's than before or after, still expanded by an impressive absolute amount. In France alone among the main trading countries were exports smaller in 1895 than in 1875 or 1883. The expansion of production was forcing total trade upwards to a greater extent than it was limiting its rate of increase, and the reversion to protectionism was more than offset by the constantly widening opportunities in international trade. This reversion, moreover, was neither so sharp nor so extensive as is sometimes assumed. Perhaps because it is the natural disposition of nations and businessmen to be protectionist, the earlier trend towards the liberalisation of trade had been slow, and liberalisation was far from complete in the 1870's when the protectionist trend was resumed. The removal of obstacles to international trade had depended on many things, including the ability of countries to afford the loss of customs revenue or to find a substitute at a time when, while other sources of revenue were developing, state expenditure was also mounting. In Europe, too, economic liberalisation and free trade had been associated

periods had been periods of rising prices; but if trade is measured by volume it increased by nearly 300 per cent (7 per cent per annum) between 1800 and 1840 when prices were falling, and increased by nearly 400 per cent (over 13 per cent per annum) between 1840 and 1872 when prices were rising, compared with the 100 per cent (4 per cent per annum) increase between 1873 and 1896, when prices were falling. But between 1898 and 1913 world trade again increased at something like the earlier rate, doubling in value from £3900 to £8360 millions per annum.

with political liberalism, which was anathema to privileged governing classes. There had been a trend towards lower tariffs—in the German Zollverein, in the United States and in France, for example—but only after 1850. Although there had been a discernible tendency to lower import duties, and few cases of tariff increases, after that year, it was only in very rare instances that duties had been removed completely by the 1870's. Even in Great Britain, where the reduction and removal of duties had begun in the 1820's, there were still seventeen dutiable imports in 1870. After the 1870's, on the other hand, some countries resisted the resort to increased tariffs.

Nevertheless, these countries were exceptional and they had special reasons for clinging to free trade. In Great Britain and Belgium industrial and commercial interests outweighed agrarian interests in economic and political importance, and industry was so far advanced that protectionism would have reduced rather than stimulated the foreign and domestic demand on it. In Holland, as in Great Britain and Belgium, commerce was too dominant to make protectionism practicable. Denmark's dependence on agricultural exports necessitated free trade and forced her, instead, to escape the new agricultural competition by specialised farming. In Turkey tariffs could be raised only with the consent of the great powers. Their policy cannot alter the fact that the same developments which were producing an enormous increase in the world's total production and integrating its economy at one level were contributing to a departure from free trade at another, that the age was the age of the tariff as well as of an increasingly integrated world economy—and so much so, that the world economy could not have developed as it did if the exceptional countries, and especially Great Britain, the largest international trader, had not kept their doors open to the imports of all nations at a time when most nations were adopting increasingly protectionist policies.

This was because the changing over-all relationship between supply and demand was not only limiting the rate of increase in total trade but was also taking place, at a time when distances were being slashed, within a changing geographical framework. It was creating the problem of re-adjusting supply and demand between the individual nations, which cannot quickly adopt specialised economies or easily operate an international division of labour. It is tempting to assume that protectionism had a special political attraction for the generation that had issued from the wars of the 1850's and 1860's and now maintained an armed peace. In fact the decision to adopt increased tariffs bore little direct relation to political situation or political goal. While Great Britain clung to free trade in spite of being deeply involved in international politics, American tariffs were higher than any in Europe in spite of the aloofness of the United States from world politics. They rose from 47 per cent in 1869 to 49·5 per cent in 1890 and (after some relaxation) to 57 per cent in 1897. Canada and the other British Dominions, more peripheral politically even than the United States, reared enormous tariff walls. Even in Latin America tariffs were resorted to in the defence of infant industries if, as in Chile, industrial interests became strong enough to demand them. In Europe tariff wars did not always coincide with political rivalries. Germany's barriers against foreign grain were a source of serious complaint in Russia after 1879, when Bismarck was anxious to maintain Russo-German friendship. On the plane of intellectual rationalisation, moreover, political rivalries were rarely urged in defence of protectionism. Men, responding to a changed economic situation, made much the same claim for it, with as much justification or as little, as they had made in the 1850's and 1860's for *laissez-faire*: it would benefit all mankind by enabling some nations to avoid exploitation by others, thus ensuring that all the nations would reach the happy goal of international harmony and material well-being. When this changed situation is considered it becomes difficult to avoid the view that the nations would have reverted to tariffs if they had been wrapped in perfect peace—even as the earlier wars had coincided with a trend towards free trade—and that, except when special economic circumstances countervailed, as they did in the exceptional countries, it was natural enough that men should assume more readily than before that they could not prosper without national protection.

What the problem was emerges especially clearly in connection with agricultural produce. Agricultural prosperity had previously accompanied a country's industrial development almost automatically, since mounting demand had been supplied locally. British agriculture had boomed between the 1840's and the 1870's despite the repeal of the Corn Laws. From the middle of the 1870's, world production, of grains in particular, surged upwards in excess of population growth, and certainly too rapidly for easy absorption in the world's markets at satisfactory prices, as a result of the intensification of agriculture in other parts of the world; and the cheap transport of the produce over long distances, at costs that were no higher between continents than they had once been between provinces, threatened the whole of Europe with agrarian crisis. There was accordingly some protection for agriculture in the earliest European tariff increases of the 1870's, and most of the further increases after 1885 were carried out in the interests of agriculture. Even so, the price of wheat in Europe fell by a half between 1871 and 1895. The object was to preserve a balance in the economy of the kind which Great Britain was losing as a result of her adherence to free trade, but which it was more important to preserve where society, despite industrialisation, was still more agrarian than in Great Britain. Industry also received protection, and here the motives included both the need for safeguards against the consequence of rapid industrialisation elsewhere and the wish to further industrialisation at home. The first modest steps in this direction were taken by countries where industry, though it had made a beginning, was still in its infancy—by the United States in 1875, Russia in 1876, Spain in 1877, Italy in 1878. They were taken when depression conditions in industry, which had set in in 1873, were being aggravated by the dumping of manufactures by more industrialised nations. Subsequent tariff increases for the protection of industry, beginning with the great German tariff of 1879, which applied to industry and to agriculture, still derived from the circumstance that, while industrialisation was spreading, it continued to stand at different levels of development and efficiency as between different industries in different countries. But wherever they were adopted they stimulated industrialisation as well as protecting existing industry. They thus contributed to the continuation of those depression conditions which, in industry as in agriculture, arose from the spread and intensification of production beyond the immediate power of world demand to absorb the results.

Depression conditions were limited, however, to the field of prices, profits and investment yields. The period was not one of economic depression as a whole. By the tests of production, consumption and income, as has already been shown, as opposed to those of prices and profits, it was one of expansion and boom. The fall in prices, moreover, was not wholly a symptom of depression. After rising steadily during the previous generation, prices moved downwards till the early 1890's, when they were generally 40 per cent lower than in 1873, and did not pick up again till 1896. But this decline was due as much to the great reduction in transport costs, the improvement in technology and the increased scale of production as it was to the excess of production over demand. It was improved methods and increased production, combined with the revolution in transport, that forced down the price of food and raw materials. Improved methods and increased production, combined with the fall in raw material costs, are what—to take but one example from industry—reduced the European price of steel rails by 60 per cent between 1872 and 1881 and made it possible to sell American steel rails in 1898 at little more than one-tenth of what they had cost in 1875. In the same way the price of iron had fallen in the previous generation, against the general trend, from £10 per ton in 1825 to £3 per ton in 1866. What had then been exceptional now became the general, though not the universal, trend. And because all these factors were involved, falling prices were not necessarily accompanied by falling profit margins. The advantages of reduced transport costs and raw material prices, of improved methods, of wider markets and increased production, could lead to the opposite result.

Yet profits in general fell as well as prices, and to almost the same extent. Their decline, the central feature of the Great Depression, was due to two causes. It was brought about partly by the element of temporary over-production that was also, though again only partly, the cause of the fall in prices. It followed chiefly from the fact that the advantages of the time were being exploited by an increasing number of competing firms in every market and in every field. The explanation of the reversion to tariffs at a time of widening and increasing exchange is that a growing number of nations took part increasingly in the total exchange; the key to the Great Depression is that, while total production and total profits mounted, the profits of the individual enterprise—though there were exceptions, the consequence of rapid adaptation and initiative in exploiting new fields—in general declined with the proliferation of undertakings and the growth of competition. The world economy as a whole flourished; national economies as a whole flourished, to the extent that they participated in and adjusted to the changing world economy; but times were harder for the rapidly increasing number of individual firms.

The combination of material expansion and growing competition that was producing on the international scale both a more integrated world economy and increased protectionism, both increased output and falling profits, also underlay the changes that were taking place within the more advanced societies. These reflected a pronounced trend from *laissez-faire*: towards combination in economic enterprise, towards collective self-help among wage-earners, towards state regulation in the economic and social fields. Like the movement towards greater material output and like the advance in technology and production methods, processes with which it is intimately connected, the drift towards greater organisation among men, as specialised groups and as total communities, has been virtually continuous and has continually increased in momentum throughout modern times. But it was in the generation after 1870, when the drift was so much accelerated by the interaction of the greater problems and the greater opportunities with which societies were confronted, that those forms and attitudes first took clear shape which exist today.

The problems were not merely those created by the growth of material production and economic competition. Although these asserted themselves within the more advanced societies as well as between nations, they were also arising in increasingly complex and rapidly changing social structures in consequence of the march of industrialisation and urbanisation among expanding populations. Population was growing faster in these countries than at any previous time. Even after allowing for emigration, which drew off 40 per cent of the natural increase, Europe's population increased by over 30 per cent and by 100 millions—from 300 to 400 millions—between 1870 and 1900 compared with an increase of 30 millions—of 11 per cent—between 1850 and 1870. Helped by immigration the population of Europe's overseas frontier in North and South America, Australia, New Zealand and South Africa rose at an even faster rate—and by 60 millions—in the same period. In the most industrialised of these areas the rush to the towns now took place on such a scale that the increase in urban and suburban population equalled this huge increase in total population. In the remainder—in Argentina, Brazil and Chile, in European Russia, Austria and Australasia—the same development still produced large if isolated urban growths, as it did beyond these areas, in India and Japan, where population was also increasing fast but where there was even less industrialisation.[1] Germany, with eight towns of over 100,000 people in 1870, had forty-one in 1900. Except in France—where the population increase was exceptionally low, but where nearly half the total increase in these years, about 800,000 people, accrued to Paris—urbanisation on a similar scale took place throughout western Europe and in the United States. Even in European Russia the number of such towns had risen from six to seventeen by 1900. By that date one-third of the population of the United States lived in manufacturing centres, one-tenth of that of England and Wales had concentrated in London, the percentage of Germans living in towns had risen from 36 in 1870 to 54, and Berlin, Vienna, St Petersburg, Moscow, New York, Chicago, Philadelphia, Buenos Aires, Rio de Janeiro, Tokyo, Osaka and Calcutta had joined London and Paris as cities with more than a million inhabitants. Nor was it simply the case that population was rapidly increasing and that more and more people were being drawn into industry and the urban areas.

The organisation of industry and the conditions of work in industry were becoming more complex. The interrelationship between industry and the total economy, between the urban areas and the society in which they existed, was being transformed. The increased physical difficulties involved in organising industrial production and in disposing of its products, the increasingly complex tasks that must be performed if the industrial conglomerations were to fulfil their role in society as a whole—these jostled with social problems thrown up by the growth of large areas of dense population as well as with the economic problems created by growing competition in industry.

Industrial and other forms of enterprise necessarily responded to these changes. Most of the industrial, commercial and financial expansion of earlier generations had been undertaken in simpler technical and social conditions by the family firm or the small partnership, with unlimited liability for all partners and unlimited freedom for masterful men. The extent of the transition that now took place in business organisation and methods from the small unit and the principle of unlimited liability to the large joint-stock enterprise is easily exaggerated. The joint-stock company

---

[1] The population increase was not world-wide. It took place almost as fast in India and Russia as in more industrialised societies, and so much in advance of other developments there as to produce famine or famine conditions. But in other areas material conditions remained so much worse that population was stationary (as it probably was in Africa) or even declined (as in China, where it is estimated that the population in the lower Yangtse valley was higher in 1850 than in 1950 and that in the 1870's alone the North China famine killed more than 15 millions).

had proved increasingly necessary since the 1840's in the management of public utilities—canals, railways, water and gas supply, banking and docks—and the principles of private incorporation and limited liability had been firmly established in the 1850's. The family business and the small firm still predominated in every country long after 1900: in Germany 93 per cent of industrial enterprise was still conducted by individual proprietors at the beginning of the twentieth century, when one-third of the industrial workers were still employed in establishments employing not more than five people; in Great Britain in 1914 four-fifths of even the 62,762 active joint-stock companies were private companies, family firms and private partnerships in a new guise. Then again, although limited liability was ultimately to be a new means of raising capital for industry through the stock exchange, it was not until after 1890 that it began to be used for this purpose to any great extent. Increasingly after 1870, however, the small firm was replaced by the large limited liability company, which now for the first time entered the manufacturing, commercial and financial fields.

By 1900 a dual economy had appeared in the industrialised countries— a sharp contrast between a large traditional sector hardly touched by organisational change and a limited but economically preponderant modern sector comprising the major industries and a large part of the commercial and financial enterprise, in which the typical unit was a limited liability undertaking on a considerable scale. This had resulted from the growth in the size and capital of larger firms and from the amalgamation of firms. Those processes had been supplemented by the formation of associations of firms for agreements on prices, the creation of trusts in the pursuit of monopolies—the earliest was Rockefeller's Standard Oil (1882)—and the establishment of cartels by which firms in one industry sought to control sections of the associated and subsidiary industries on which they depended. These developments took place on an international scale as well as within countries. In 1883 a market-sharing agreement was reached between the steel companies of Great Britain, Germany and Belgium. It was short-lived, but was followed by many similar arrangements between industrialists and bankers for rationing producers, fixing shipping freights, rebates and fares. Armament manufacturers like Armstrongs, Krupps and Creusot shared foreign markets by agreement. In 1886 Nobel established the first international trust, the Dynamite Trust Ltd. In the 1890's J. and P. Coats Ltd created a virtual world monopoly in cotton thread by amalgamating rival British, continental and American firms. And since these were necessarily discontinuous developments—the kind of development which, once undertaken, could not be repeated or advanced for a considerable time—the late nineteenth century was distinguished not only from earlier periods but also from the generation after 1900 by the extent to which they then took place.

They were the consequence of a rapid increase in the complexity both of enterprise and of the society in which it was being conducted—and of the greater difficulties as well as of the greater opportunities which this was producing. Firms grew with the expansion of production and the application of technology, processes which necessitated greater size and greater amounts of capital. The larger the firm the more easily it could aspire to amalgamate others and, aided by technological break-throughs and the growing integration of society, the more easily could it control prices and achieve monopoly. The fortunes built up by Nobel and Rockefeller and other pioneers of big business are examples of the success that could flow from seizing such opportunities, and it was no doubt these opportunities which Rockefeller, that great individualist, had in mind when he declared that 'the day of combination is here to stay. Individualism has gone, never to return.' But difficulties arose as often as opportunities at a time when firms were multiplying rapidly and when it was becoming a continuous instead of an occasional feature of industrial life for established methods to be rendered obsolete by innovation. Alongside every firm that expanded in size or aspired to amalgamate others there were more than one that, failing to expand or to survive the new competition, became ripe for amalgamation. For every firm that sought association and monopoly in order to expand markets and profits there was another that was led in these directions by its need to conserve them, by the greater concern for security that followed from requiring larger amounts of capital in conditions of increasing competition. This was the major impetus behind the movement towards organisation among agricultural producers. Unable to concentrate and centralise after the fashion of the manufacturer or the financier, these everywhere responded to changed conditions—in France and Denmark from the early 1880's, in Ireland from 1889, elsewhere from the 1890's—by setting up increasing numbers of co-operatives for the provision of credit, for insurance against risks and for the processing and marketing of their produce.

The movement towards organisation and combination was not limited to employers and producers. Among wage-earners and consumers, friendly societies and co-operative stores, protected by new legislation, multiplied all over Great Britain, western Europe and the United States after 1880. Friendly societies were protected by legislation after 1875 in Great Britain, where they had a membership of nearly 7 millions in 1885, of nearly 14 millions in 1910. Co-operative societies were legislated for in Great Britain in 1876, and there were over 1400 co-operative stores in the country in 1900. Much the same growth of both occurred in the United States and in Europe. There was at the same time an increase in trade unions in these countries and a marked change in their character—developments which spread to other areas, to the rest of Europe and to Latin America, after 1890. The unions were also given legal recognition at last, in Belgium, for example, in 1866, Austria in 1870, Great Britain between 1870 and 1876, Spain in 1881, France (after partial recognition in 1864) in 1884, Germany after the collapse of the anti-socialist legislation in 1890—in Russia, however, they remained illegal till 1906. Breach of contract by workmen was removed from the list of criminal offences. From the middle of the 1880's legislation was followed by the 'new unionism'.

The unions had previously been craft organisations, largely confined in their membership to skilled workmen in particular trades and in their function to providing mutual insurance against sickness, accident and death and operating conciliation machinery between employer and employed. The 'new unionism' sought working-class organisation on a national scale and by industries, rather than locally and by crafts, in response to the situation in which, with the improvement of internal communications, districts and jobs once localised were becoming competitive with one another. It enlisted unskilled and semi-skilled labourers as well as skilled artisans in response to the powerful effect of changes in industry and the spread of elementary education in increasing the proportion of semi-skilled workers and the chances of promotion. Compared with the earlier unions the movement was more militant and political in its objects and more closely linked with political creeds, especially socialism, or with social outlooks, as was the case with the Catholic-sponsored unions of France, Austria, Italy, Germany and Belgium and with the anarcho-syndicalist unions of the 1890's in Argentina, Chile and Mexico.

If they began to assume their modern character the unions increased their membership far less in these years than did the friendly and co-operative societies, and far less rapidly than they were to increase it after 1900. Between 1886 and 1900 union membership rose from $1\frac{1}{4}$ million (from about 1 million in 1875) to 2 millions in Great Britain, from 300,000 to 850,000 in Germany, from 50,000 to 250,000 in France. In America the Federation of Labour had only half a million members in 1900. By 1913 membership had risen to 4 millions in Great Britain (where most of the increase, from $2\frac{1}{4}$ to 4 millions, occurred after 1906); to 3 millions in Germany; to 1 million in France. In the United States the A.F.L. had $1\frac{1}{2}$ million members by 1904. They also made little progress before the 1900's in their new functions. These facts are again explained partly by the increased problems and partly by the improving conditions of the age.

The growth of industrialisation and urbanisation, while it made the organisation of working men physically easier, also involved a vast unplanned and unpleasant upheaval in the conditions of living and a new subjection to temporary and cyclical unemployment, the consequence of the more rapid succession of technological change and industrial reorganisation. It is not surprising that in these circumstances the increased possibilities of collective self-help were chiefly applied by the growing numbers of the skilled and semi-skilled, who alone could afford it, to the problem of material provision for family and individual through friendly benefit schemes; or that trade-union membership among the unskilled—potential competitors in several trades who were driven to undercut each other with employers when times were bad—fell away rapidly after the temporary success in organising them into general unions in the 1880's, and did not recover until the 1900's. Both the general unions and the unions which remained strongest, those representing skilled and semi-skilled men in special crafts, continued, moreover, again until after 1900, to negotiate for localities and on behalf of separate trades, in individualistic competition with each other; they made no progress towards collaboration or federation for nation-wide action on behalf of entire industries, let alone for the devising of political programmes and parties for pressure on governments on behalf of working men. And this was not only because the uncertainty of permanent employment induced them to continue to fend for themselves. Progress in these directions required a new consciousness of the status of the worker in society. Despite their inevitable future the unions remained at this time organisations among, rather than of, the masses because public opinion, including that of the workers themselves, with their more immediate preoccupations, was slow to recognise the right of labour to unite for the enforcement of its claims. It was on this account that they developed more rapidly in some newer lands like Australia than they did in Europe.

On the other hand in the United States, almost as new a country, their growth was slower than in Europe, and this was because in both areas, though to a greater extent in the United States than in Europe, their development into a major force in society was also delayed by favourable circumstances. Although these were years of increased temporary unemployment, over-all employment was well sustained despite the large growth of population in the working age-groups. In Great Britain the increase in over-all unemployment was only from 4 or 4½ to 5 per cent despite the fact that the working population increased from 10 millions to about 14½ millions between 1870 and 1901. For all except a minority, chronic under-employment gave way to occasional and limited unemployment. In the United States most notably, but to a marked extent in all industrial countries, they were years of increasing real wages. These rose by about 75 per cent in Great Britain, by more than this in the United States, by rather less in France and Germany, in contrast both to the previous generation in which they had risen much less—the increase between 1873 and 1898 was more than six times greater than the increase between 1853 and 1873 in Great Britain, more than twelve times greater in the United States, more than double in France—and to the years between 1898 and 1914 when they were stationary. This was in consequence of the fall in prices and the steady increase in the proportion of skilled and semi-skilled to unskilled workmen—in the proportion of higher-paid occupa-tions—in most industries. The proportion of skilled workers doubled in Great Britain between 1850 and 1888, and continued to increase at at least the same rate thereafter. The wage differential between skilled and un-skilled workers was also steadily increasing and by 1900 skilled wages were double those of the unskilled workers. Alongside the good level of employment and rising wages there was the increasing range of cheaper consumer products and the reduction that was taking place in the size of the average family—in Great Britain this fell from 5·71 children in 1860–85 to 4·66 in 1880–1905. These were years of improving standards of living in which it became slowly less necessary to put children to work, slowly less necessary for married women to work for a wage, slowly possible to increase voluntary leisure and reduce hours of work.

The biggest share of the increase in the national incomes in all these societies went to a minority—though it was to an enlarged minority and to richer middle classes rather than to the aristocracies. But in addition to the fact that the middle classes were being enlarged by the steady stream of people who were moving out of the wage-earning classes into better-paid occupations, the mass of the wage-earners, relative to their incomes before 1870, improved their position even more than did the middle classes. This relative improvement went on continuously, if slowly, throughout the period. There had probably never been a time when, materially, things had been so good for the bulk of the population; and they were not to remain so good in the generation which followed. A sub-stantial minority did not share in the improvement. It is probable that the very poor became more, not less, miserable with the development of urbanisation and the marketing of less nutritious cheap foods. But they became a smaller proportion of society than at any earlier time, even if there is no reason to believe that they declined in absolute numbers. Better conditions were reconciling most people, and increasing numbers of people, to changes in their living and working conditions. And not less important in delaying the development of the trade unions and working-class political parties, these were the years which saw the first considerable amelioration of the lot of the working classes by the direct action of the state.

In the long history of the modern state—a subject as full of pitfalls as the rise of the middle class, of which in despair it has sometimes been con-cluded that it has always been rising—this much is beyond dispute. It was in the last third of the nineteenth century, wherever it has not been a development of even more recent growth, that governments first under-took the comprehensive regulation of society. Although there had been earlier steps in this direction—all such developments are of long gestation and slow growth—government in this sense existed hardly anywhere in

1870.[1] Wherever government evolved at all after that date, except into decline and collapse, it began to assume this character and to do so at speed. The more advanced countries all witnessed in the next thirty years an unprecedented increase in the powers and functions of government and a fundamental alteration in the relations between government and society —developments which are not rendered less impressive by the fact that these powers and functions have gone on increasing, these relations changing in the same direction, ever since.

Like the movements towards increased organisation within the state—among employers and wage-earners, producers and consumers—the process was the product of the simultaneous appearance of increasingly pressing problems and of improved possibilities of dealing with them. It went farther and faster than those other movements—and its progress was partly responsible for delaying them—because it was one of the central features of these years that while all manner of social problems assumed so technical a character and such complex proportions that collective self-help, despite its advance in the development of the business unit, the friendly and co-operative society and the trade union, was increasingly unable to deal with them, new means arose which only the state was able to exploit. What was true of voluntary private organisation was hardly less true of local government authorities. Although these were improved and reformed, although some of them—Birmingham after 1873, Vienna after 1890—undertook important pioneering work in public planning and control, although other towns, at least in Europe, followed up their work or, more frequently, had it imposed upon them by central government action, they were becoming ineffective without central assistance and control. Every further stage in the internal transport revolution, in the growth of industry, in the movement of population and the growth of urban areas and in the complexity of society increased the inadequacy of local authorities except as agents of the central government—and not least because every advance in scientific and administrative knowledge revealed that nothing less than central action would suffice if the knowledge was to be applied.

This knowledge was also growing apace, in parallel with the problems. It was partly the result of the autonomous development of science, as was

---

[1] Great Britain is the only serious exception to 1870, which must in any case be an approximation, as an important dividing line in this respect. It is generally agreed that the 'nineteenth century revolution in government' was taking place in Britain from about 1830, during the so-called age of *laissez-faire*, and the beginnings of the regulatory state can be pointed to in the creation of the Metropolitan police (1829), the appointment of the first factory inspectors (1833) and of the first emigration officers (1833), the assumption by the state of a share of the responsibility for elementary education (1833), the setting up of the Poor Law Commissioners (1834) and the institution of prison inspection (1835). But even in Great Britain there was much hesitation in, and some retreat from, the collectivist trend between the 1840's and about 1870, and from about 1870 a great advance in the scope and an important change in the tone of legislation.

especially the case in the field of public health. Very little of the enormous progress that was now made in this field would have been possible without the success of the founders of preventive medicine—of Pasteur, Lister, Virchow and Koch—in the ten years after 1867 in establishing that many diseases were caused by microbes and could be avoided by simple precautions and procedures like asepsis and inoculation. It was partly due to the accumulation of practical experience of the new conditions of society by increasing numbers of experts, either self-appointed reformers or officials. The cumulative experience of the inspectors and administrators in regulating factories, mines and public health, as in supervising education, was a most powerful influence in producing government action and in extending government attention to wider and wider fields. But the work of the scientists and the agitation of the individual reformers, like the experience of the official, would have been of little avail if they had not been backed by the power of central government.

If these considerations created the opportunity for governments, as the urbanisation and industrialisation of society created or at least increased the problems, governments now seized the opportunity, as never before, because central action was becoming both more practicable and more necessary. The changes in society which were producing the problems were simultaneously making it more feasible to deal with them. It was easier to insist on the provision of water, sanitation, hospitals and roads among dense populations, and among populations served by fast transport, than it was among scattered and ill-connected communities, and easier also to regulate and supervise such things as working conditions. It was also more essential to do so. Widespread disease, for example, or unhealthy working conditions became preventable—if only by state action—at a time when, in conditions of mass living and mass working, it was a matter of public efficiency and political necessity, rather than of individual need and private conscience, to prevent them. It was for these two reasons that whereas a large part of the history of the nineteenth century before the 1870's is to be explained by the inability or unwillingness of governments to adjust their attitudes and enlarge their activities at the rate required by social change—and perhaps at a rate made possible by the growth of knowledge—the attitudes and activities of some governments now began to draw level with the more pressing problems. Wherever the development of industrialisation, urbanisation and knowledge—or the search for more rapid progress in industrialisation, urbanisation and the use of knowledge—forced government to respond, in Austria as well as in Great Britain, in Japan and Latin America as well as in Europe, to different extents in accordance with the different rates of change within different societies and the varying efficiency of governments, but with little regard to the political complexion of governments, the same increase of government took place. The agents of local authorities began to be joined by, and supervised by, the agents of central governments; increasing numbers of experts and officials pressed upon central governments the need for the proliferation of legislation and the expansion of their own powers; governments began to invoke the most stringent powers of compulsion for social and public ends and 'the grammar of common legislation acquired the novel virtue of the imperative mood'.[1]

The process developed farthest and fastest in four fields in which only the most tentative steps had been taken anywhere by 1870—public health, elementary education, the regulation of working conditions and the government ownership or control of public utilities. In those fields it developed at different rates in different countries.

Throughout western Europe, North America and Australasia in the next thirty years, beginning with the string of Acts on food and drink standards, sanitation, health and housing conditions in England between 1860 and 1875, there was continuous legislation and continuous development of administrative and enforcement machinery on these questions in the cause of public health. The effects were startling, especially in the towns, and not least important among the reasons for the great growth of population in these areas. As early as 1880 the battle was being won against the important killing diseases—plague, typhus, typhoid, smallpox, cholera, scarlet fever—and the city was being made healthier than the countryside for the first time in history. The death-rate in England and Wales, which at 22 per 1000 was as high in 1870 as in 1840, and twice as high for some towns as for the country as a whole, declined in almost every quinquennium after 1870 and was brought down to 18·1 in the 1890's, to 15·2 in the 1900's. The average expectation of life increased by more than ten years during the same period. Similar improvement was achieved throughout these areas. In Russia, by way of contrast, the death-rate was still 35 per 1000 in 1890—the highest in Europe—and beyond Europe it was higher still.

In the same areas—and beyond them, exceptionally, in Japan—rapidly changing economies and societies, with their growing need for skilled and semi-skilled labour and clerical staff and for better training even of the unskilled, also demanded, and were seen to demand, equal attention to the provision of compulsory and free elementary education. From a situation in which in 1870 in Great Britain a substantial part of the child population, in Japan perhaps the whole of it, was still left untouched in a state of ignorance, the development of national education systems proceeded so fast that by 1895, except in rapidly growing towns, there was a school place for every child in Great Britain and for 61 per cent of the child population in Japan, where 95 per cent were at school by 1906. These

---

[1] Dr John Simon, of the English Public Health Act of 1866, quoted by G. Kitson Clark in 'The Modern State and Modern Society', *Proceedings of the Royal Institution of Great Britain*, vol. XXXVII (1959), pp. 561–2.

figures are a measure of the progress made in all the more advanced countries by that date. The education provided was still of the simplest kind. Secondary schooling advanced much more slowly. But the effects of this transformation upon society and on the individual can hardly be overestimated.

The advances in public health and education were accompanied in most of these countries by the extension of state control over working conditions. Factory laws were introduced—in Belgium, the Netherlands, Switzerland in the 1870's, in Austria from 1883, in Italy and Spain from 1886, in France from the 1890's. Where they existed already they were extended, as by the British Factory Acts of 1878, 1886, 1891 and 1901— —the last two of these introduced into England the principle of delegated legislation by permitting the Home Office to make further large changes in regulations without further legislation—to deal with shops and laundries as well as factories, with the working-hours of men as well as of women and children, with the control of occupational diseases as well as with simpler safety regulations. A more novel departure was the introduction of compulsory insurance against accident and sickness for working men. Here the lead was taken by Germany. Bismarck's insurance programmes of 1883–9 were copied in many European countries between 1887 and the end of the century—by Austria in 1887–8, Switzerland in 1890, Denmark in 1891 and 1898, Belgium in 1894 and 1903, Italy in 1898. Where they were not adopted in industrialised countries, as in Great Britain—where the state at least obliged employers to compensate workmen for accidents—and the United States, it was because the earlier development of private enterprise and of a strong liberal tradition had set up resistances to state intervention which could not easily be overcome.

On this account and also because of the rapid expansion of opportunity for the individual that was now taking place, the United States lagged behind Great Britain and western Europe in the development of factory and insurance legislation and of other inroads into the principle of freedom of contract. Even there, however, by way of retaliation, the state was forced by the emphasis on freedom for the individual to attempt to regulate capitalism in the interests of freedom of competition. Although progress was slow before 1900, the Act of 1887 for the supervision of railways and the Sherman anti-trust Act of 1890 led the way in making trusts in restraint of trade illegal and in subjecting the business world to the danger of prosecution by agents of the central government; and even in the United States, despite the federal system, the spoils system and the strongly established opposition to a professional civil service (as being an aristocracy), considerable strides were made in the expansion of the central government's powers and the development of a professional civil service for this and other tasks, particularly after 1883. More work was done by central government and by civil servants than in any previous period in American history, and it necessitated the proliferation of Committees of Congress.

For similar reasons the United States, and, to a lesser extent, Great Britain remained behind in the process by which governments were driven, by the necessity for economic expansion and public efficiency, to nationalise or to control in other ways the more complex public utilities. In Great Britain, because of the earlier development of local authorities and the continuing strength of private enterprise, the taking over of the telegraph and of an increasing proportion of the telephone service was the only important addition to the services provided directly by the central government. In the United States even these remained in private hands; so in both countries did the railways, though they were assisted by public subsidies and subjected to the beginnings of government regulation. In Great Britain, but not in the United States, there was far more extension of the functions of local authorities, assisted by central loans and grants. By 1900 these had compulsorily acquired most of the waterworks and many of the gas, electricity and tramway undertakings of the country. In these later fields, however, private enterprise continued to flourish and some of the largest and most rapidly expanding companies were private and not municipal. In many European states, on the other hand, in Belgium, Norway, Austria, Germany, Italy, Russia, Roumania, Serbia, the telegraph and telephone services and the railways were taken over by the government from the beginning of the period, and the central government allowed less freedom to private enterprise and less discretion to local authorities in the provision of other public utilities. In less developed states, both in Europe and beyond, in Japan and Latin America, in India under its British government—wherever the effort was being made to become more developed—while progress with public health, labour legislation and compulsory education[1] was difficult and negligible on account of the backwardness of the economy and of administration, even greater steps were taken towards central control in these other directions. In India the railways and vast irrigation schemes—developments which had indirect effects in improving public health by eliminating death from starvation in India from 1880 until 1943—in Latin America not only the railways but also gas, electricity, water and other services, in Russia and Japan not only public utilities but also a considerable sector of industry, finance and trade were brought under central ownership or close central regulation.

If health, education, industrial working conditions and public utilities were the problems which called most urgently for attention and which, in these varying degrees and circumstances, received most attention, there

---

[1] But Japan was a large exception here. See pp. 20, 179, 472. Otherwise only slight advance in primary education was made in India and a few Latin-American countries and none elsewhere.

was no neat dividing line for expanding governments in rapidly changing societies between more and less essential tasks. Once it had set in, moreover, the tendency towards 'the constant extension and improvement of the mechanism of government...and the increasing application of a new system of centralisation'[1] became a force in itself, autonomous almost, and it spread as far and as fast as conditions required and as physical difficulties and the resistances thrown up by social habits and political interests would permit. In Russia, in eastern and in parts of southern Europe, in most areas beyond Europe where it began at all, it was limited by backwardness and opposition even in the urgent fields. In the United States, except in education which was regarded as an individual right, it was similarly restricted, but more by established traditions, the federal structure and the buoyancy of private enterprise than by physical difficulties. In Great Britain and western Europe, however, effective state intervention in society, either direct or through the central regulation of local authorities, was established in all these fields and on a broader front: by the provision and inspection of prisons and reformatories, of homes and hospitals, as well as of schools; by the provision of subsidies and the imposition of fixed rents and compensation for improvements on behalf of tenant farmers as well as by the regulation of factory conditions; and, not less important, by the resort to income taxes as a means of meeting the growing expenditure on social services and to the use of taxation itself—of graduated income taxes and capital taxes—as a means of social reform and of controlling wealth.

Until about 1870 in Great Britain most of the revenue of the central government had come from indirect taxes on articles of consumption and more than half of its expenditure had been absorbed by the payment of interest on and the cost of managing the national debt. Its main financial task had been to redistribute a small proportion of the national income from the poor to the rich. In other countries this was the case to an even greater extent. Even though change in the same direction was to proceed at a far more rapid rate from the 1900's, the beginnings of a fundamental change had already taken place in this respect by the end of the century. Income tax had ceased to be regarded in Great Britain— since the 1880's—as an unfortunate emergency device and had been adopted for the first time—since the 1890's—in several European countries: in Germany, Italy, Austria, Norway and Spain. Income taxes, as more came to be required of them, were being graduated so as to fall more heavily on higher incomes and were beginning to be supplemented—in Great Britain after the 1880's and especially after 1894, in France from 1901—by death duties. In Great Britain, apart from the fact that revenue from local rates on property had risen much more proportionately since

[1] A. V. Dicey, *Law and Public Opinion in the Nineteenth Century* (2nd ed., 1914), pp. 306–7.

1870 than revenue from national taxes, the rise in the contribution of income taxes and death duties to total taxation (rates and taxes) had risen from a negligible figure to 30 per cent. In European countries the speed and extent of the change was somewhat lower, and a larger part of the increased expenditure was still met by indirect taxes on consumer goods. Growing expenditure was for some of these governments perhaps as important as the changing world economic situation as a reason for resorting to higher tariffs after the 1870's. But in these countries as well as in Great Britain it was in the last years of the nineteenth century that the first breach was made in the old attitude to taxation and expenditure.

In these countries, indeed, so much had been done by the end of the century that it is important to specify what was not achieved or not yet attempted. The advance in public health had sprung mainly from the control of the physical environment: substantial improvements in medical services and in health practices, which together brought about a further decline in the death-rate, and particularly in the mortality rate for infants and for the old, came only after 1900. Infant mortality rates were as high in 1891–1901 as in the 1840's; the reduction in mortality had been very small for those over 45 and chiefly affected adults below 35. State or municipal provision of working-class housing still lay in the future; it was still on a very small scale in 1914. The extended factory legislation had dealt only with hours of work, age-limits and standards of safety and health; and while hours remained high despite their slight reduction—in Great Britain since 1870 they had fallen from about 60 to about 55 per week—minimum wage-rates had to await a still more socially-minded generation. Their adoption, a major departure from Victorian orthodoxy, was first undertaken in Great Britain in 1909, 1912 and 1914. Insurance against unemployment, as opposed to accident and sickness, and insurance at the expense of the state, as opposed to the employer and the employee, found no place in the various insurance programmes before 1911. Nowhere yet did public social policy concern itself with the problem of poverty, and it was perhaps the greatest failure of the age that poverty was allowed to persist in the midst of plenty, if not to increase. No state yet possessed either the knowledge or the outlook which would together make the regulation of the economy and the avoidance of unemployment a major object of policy in many countries after another fifty years. The provision of universal compulsory elementary education involved huge administrative, building and teacher-training programmes which could only proceed slowly. Hardly anywhere were they completed in 1900, and nowhere had the state, as opposed to individual initiative and private benevolence, provided much assistance towards university and secondary education. Income tax and even graduated income tax had been introduced to meet growing government expenditure, but even in the most advanced of communities an income tax at the rate of 1s. 2d. in the pound was regarded in 1901 as almost unsupportable in time of peace. Income tax in Great Britain rose steadily from 1875 until it reached 8*d.* in 1885. It did not rise above this figure until the outbreak of the Boer War at the end of the century, when it reached 1*s.* 3*d.* After that war it was brought back to 1*s.*, but had got back to 1*s.* 2*d.* between 1910 and 1914. Most states still relied heavily on direct consumer taxes, and notably on tariffs, which fell on poor and rich alike. Nevertheless, the provision of social needs and the control of social problems by central governments, for all these limitations on their scope, had proceeded so far by the beginning of the twentieth century, and in thirty years, at least in the foremost European countries, that—as has been said of the British Local Government Bill of 1888—they had already 'transformed the tissue of. . . .existence' and brought 'the entire range of ordinary life, from birth, or even before birth, to burial,. . .within the ambit of public interest and observation'.[1]

These were policies which, once taken up, could not be reversed or ignored, and if there could be no going back it was equally impossible to stand still. In the more advanced societies from the early years of the twentieth century further progress in the same direction had become the test, applied with increasing impatience, of acceptable government. Before much longer governments in the rest of the world would be faced with the choice of courting political chaos or attempting to follow suit. This was not yet true between 1870 and 1900. In marked contrast with the undercurrents of economic, technical and social change—but also in consequence of them—the period was one of comparative stability in domestic politics, of negligible development in the constitutional sphere, of conservatism in political outlook.

Throughout the hundred years to 1875—and even during the last fifteen of them, which witnessed the American Civil War, the Polish insurrection, the Meiji revolution in Japan, the fall of the Empire in France and the restoration of monarchy in Spain as well as the many readjustments involved in the unification of Germany and Italy—revolutions or attempted revolutions and violent changes of political regime had been common occurrences. Throughout much of the world since 1905 internal politics have been no less unsettled. In the intervening generation, at least in those countries that were caught up in economic and social change, it was otherwise. In old and predominantly monarchical Europe, except that new states—themselves monarchies—were erected in Roumania and Bulgaria on the basis of Balkan nationalism and Ottoman decline; in the New World—predominantly republican—except for the downfall of its only monarchy in Brazil, the overthrow of Spanish rule in Cuba by the combined efforts of local nationalism and American expansion, and the

[1] G. M. Young, *Victorian England: Portrait of an Age*, p. 151.

continuation of civil war and *coup d'état* in the smaller Latin American states which were hardly touched by economic and social change; in Japan with its even newer order; in the other centres of white settlement beyond Europe—in none of these areas were there changes or even attempted changes of political regime. This was the longest period of comparatively unbroken internal stability that they experienced in the nineteenth century—that they have experienced in the past 150 years.

Even within the framework of the established regimes there was little constitutional change. In the constitutions of all these countries except Japan and Russia[1] a parliament of a sort was already established in 1870: none of these parliaments, with the exception of those of Great Britain, Belgium and the United States, had more than nominal powers against the executive. In the next thirty years no new parliament was introduced except in Japan; and in no country except France did the legislature make significant strides towards a system of parliamentary control over the executive comparable to that which Great Britain, Belgium and the United States—but also in an earlier age—had developed. Elsewhere the executive government, whether it was monarchical or republican, easily retained its power and position or enlarged them. Even in Great Britain, Belgium and the United States, while parliamentary control remained firmly established, the legislature entered upon the beginning of a decline in relation to the executive. In the United States the period began with a bid for the supremacy of Congress over the President and the Supreme Court, but ended with Congress in retreat before the development of the powers of the Presidency and a steady increase in the vetoing and interpreting of Congressional Acts by the Court. In Great Britain the golden age of the independent Member of Parliament and of House of Commons initiative in legislation gave way before increasing party organisation and increasing control of the business of the House by the cabinet which controlled the majority party. In Belgium Leopold II succeeded in removing overseas activities and policies from parliamentary surveillance and in particular created, through his International African Association, a personal, not to say a despotic, sovereignty over the Congo Free State.

At another level of politics, because of the continuing and often growing strength of the executive in relation to the legislature, political parties in most states either continued to be coteries of oligarchs and notabilities manœuvring for office and cut off from the public or, if they became mass parties like the Social Democrat party in Germany, remained cut off from political influence or hope of power. At this level the political systems of Great Britain and her self-governing colonies, of the United States and of

---

[1] The only other states without a parliament in the whole of Europe were Montenegro and Mecklenburg-Schwerin and Mecklenburg-Strelitz (which retained medieval estates systems until 1918) and Turkey. Beyond Europe, in the areas mentioned, the more unimportant Latin American countries were the only exceptions apart from Japan.

France were perhaps the only ones which experienced appreciable development from within—organic changes in the complex relations between government and the governed as opposed to the development of new tactics for maintaining old political structures. They bore witness to the prevailing political character of the age by moving towards conservatism in political outlook.

In Great Britain, where republican sentiments were not uncommon in the 1870's and a lengthy Liberal administration was in power between 1880 and 1885, the following twenty years were years of almost unbroken rule by the Conservative party. Between the Civil War and the end of the century the United States, once the beacon of European radicals, moved steadily towards a uniformity behind conservative beliefs; the increasingly conservative Republican party was in the ascendant; radical proposals for political and economic change won less and less support; and even the Populist agitation of the period, which might seem to form an exception to these trends, was in tune with them in being fundamentally a demand for more government—a protest against the fact that, on account of the continuing strength of the *laissez-faire* attitude to government, the country lagged behind western Europe in social reform and industrial legislation after 1880. In France—even in France—divisions and dogmas on constitutional questions, which were almost everywhere losing the force they had once possessed, receded behind the determination of the Opportunist republicans, conservative, empirical and almost uninterruptedly in power from the early 1880's to 1898, to govern by avoiding all contentious measures except those raised by their insistence on social reform.

Conservatism in these Western countries would preserve the great achievements of an earlier liberal era; its practitioners worked within an accepted and continuing liberal ethos. It was to these achievements and to such an ethos that in Russia and Turkey, on the other hand, conservatism became more than ever opposed. Yet those countries also experienced the conservative trend, even if it there took the form of reaction after a period of liberalising measures by authoritarian governments during the 1860's and 1870's. So it was with the other face of that trend, the decline of liberalism. It was a process whose wide extent is obscured only if historians are misled—as men, in Gibbon's phrase, are governed—by names. So-called 'liberal' parties remained in power in several states. Wherever they were in power for any length of time, as in Latin America, Italy, Hungary and Roumania, their outlook and programmes had little in common with those of traditional western European liberalism. In proportion as liberal parties adhered to that outlook and those programmes they were either proscribed, as in Russia and Turkey, or else they lost influence, following and office and underwent those internal divisions, that narrowing of imagination in favour of sectarianism and dogmatic beliefs, which were eventually, in the twentieth century, to complete their decline—a process observable throughout western Europe and in Great Britain, as well as in the United States, where the Democrat party remained more strictly liberal than its Republican opponents.

The varying character of the liberal decline, as of conservative aims, may suggest that it is misleading, even in the cause of necessary generalisation, to argue that such diverse states shared common political trends; even more misleading to explain those trends by the same considerations. What the evidence in fact reveals is that all these states moved in a conservative direction from different points of departure, and what is significant is that, if at different levels, they all moved in the same conservative direction. There was one main reason for this. They were struck by the economic and social changes of the age when they were at different stages of economic development and in possession of different political structures, the product of their different previous histories. They underwent these changes to different extents. But they all experienced the major political consequence of those changes, the beginnings of modern government. If they all experienced as well a period of political stability or stagnation, if liberalism was exhausted in some, distorted in others, frustrated in others, in a general conservative trend, it was primarily because the rise of the modern state, whatever the consequences for the future, at this time buttressed the existing forms of government—whatever those forms might be—by socialising government's attitudes and by increasing government's power.

Whether the outcome was stability or stagnation, whether it arose more from the changed attitudes of a government or from a government's reliance on its increased power, was determined by a network of circumstances, both past and present, in each individual case. In some states—on the whole those of north-western Europe and the English-speaking world which were most politically advanced and which experienced the most rapid social and economic change—it was the change in government attitudes which was crucial. Here the pressure on government for political change was also reduced because economic and technological advance was creating improved real wages and living-standards. This fact, which helped to delay the development of the labour unions and working-class political parties and to keep them from political agitation, also, in conjunction with the fear of the danger of working-class organisation, helped to ally the growing middle classes with conservative governments. It was especially influential in the United States, where there was always some pursuit more profitable than politics, and in Germany, where the Social Democrat party, Marxist in inspiration and in its programmes, nevertheless—though without success in reassuring the middle class—became revisionist in practice, a pressure group which sought a greater share for the workers in the profits of industry rather than the undermining of society or even a greater share for the workers in the government of the state. Nowhere, however, except in the United States where this other process was delayed, was material improvement in itself so influential as the fact that governments were anticipating those discontents that would otherwise have sustained or created the demand for political change. Except in the United States the extension of central control and intervention in the social field had two things in common in all these states. It was benefiting society most at the less-well-to-do levels where improvement was most needed; it was taking place on government initiative and not in consequence of public agitation. In Great Britain it was regarded as a paradox at the time that measures which had so much effect upon society, and which were so widely welcomed when introduced, were preceded by so little public demand.

What was true of the growth of government control of society was also true of the one direct change effected in these years in the political context in which these governments operated, of the democratisation of the suffrage. Although women nowhere got the vote except in Australia and New Zealand before the twentieth century—Finland and Norway led the way elsewhere in 1907—universal equal manhood suffrage, which existed only in the United States (except for the Southern Negroes) and the British self-governing colonies in 1870, was now approached in these countries, and in some it was achieved. It was approached to different extents and at different times in different countries, but the varying extensions of the franchise took place on the initiative of government, not as a concession wrested from government by those who got the vote. There was sometimes opposition to the extension, more than there was to government intervention in social matters; some governments insisted upon it despite this fact. In this matter as in the extension of government functions in society the difference between the motives of these governments, however different their circumstances, is not easy to detect: the initiative was generally taken, as by Disraeli and Bismarck early in the period, from the conviction that an enlarged electorate would be preponderantly conservative. The difference is immense, on the other hand, between this period, with its government initiative and its absence of political agitation, and the age which had held—in Lord Melbourne's phrase—that 'the whole duty of government is to prevent crime and to preserve contracts'; and which had produced in England the struggle for the first Reform Act, Chartism and the repeal of the Corn Laws and in Europe the revolutions of 1830 to 1849. Nor can there be any doubt of the connection between the initiative and the lack of agitation. It was government action in regulating society, introducing direct and graded taxation and extending the franchise which chiefly accounts for the decline of class bitterness and the prevailing political stability of these years.

At the opposite extreme were countries where the suffrage was not extended—Portugal, Sweden, Denmark, Austria, Hungary, Roumania, Serbia and some of the German states retained their highly restricted franchises, although Austria extended its four-class system of indirect representation to include a fifth class for the mass of the population in 1896—or where, as in Russia until after the revolution of 1905 and Turkey until after the revolution of 1908, it remained non-existent. Here the governments relied less on the anticipation of discontent and more on their increasing ability to suppress it. This was especially true in eastern Europe. In this area traditional forms of governments, subjected to little change for many years, coincided with a situation in which economic and social change was producing worsened, not improved, material conditions, and failed to coincide with ethnographical divisions. The same increase of population which made an essential contribution to Germany's industrial revolution outpaced the rate of industrialisation in Russia and eastern Europe, where almost alone in Europe the rural population increased at a greater rate than ever before, creating poverty, land-hunger and widespread economic unrest. This was also true of southern Italy, Spain and Portugal, but on a smaller scale, and emigration was easier from these areas. The same social and economic changes and the same national sentiment which in western Europe reconciled the middle classes to established authority had the effect in this area, in less-developed political structures, of putting some part at any rate of those classes, as in western Europe half a century earlier, against it. In circumstances like these and most markedly in Russia and Turkey, where parliaments did not exist and political parties were still regarded as conspiracies, serious discontent was kept at bay only by the increasing efficiency of the police, army and administration. The absence of political and constitutional change, in some countries chiefly the consequence of a changed attitude on the part of government and a changed relationship between government and society, assisted by improving economic conditions, was here, in circumstances of social and economic deterioration, mainly the consequence of the great increase that was taking place in government power.

In between these extremes there was every variation. In some countries the suffrage was only slightly extended. In Italy the legislation of 1882, the only extension in this period, extended the suffrage to 7 per cent of the population; in Japan the suffrage was granted for the first time by the electoral law of 1890 to about one in ten of the population, chiefly landowners; in India the British government decided to develop representative institutions on Western lines in 1880 and the electoral principle had spread from local to national assemblies, though on a restricted suffrage, by 1892. In others a highly restricted franchise was abruptly abandoned, usually in favour of universal suffrage, only at the end of this period: in Spain in 1890, in Belgium in 1893, in Norway in 1898, in Baden in 1900, in Bavaria and Württemberg in 1906. In some the social activities of government remained more abreast of the public mind, the repressive actions of government less extreme, than they did in others. Centralised enlightened despotism, as in India, or increasingly efficient dictatorships of order and progress which, as in Japan and Latin-American states, clothed their oligarchical and forcible character with social programmes and a veil of constitutionalism were some of the results. But it is impossible to generalise except to say that government in all these cases relied on a mixture of force and reform, in varying proportions but to a greater extent than was the case at the extremes, for the avoidance of discontent and the preservation of order.

It is possible, on the other hand, to exaggerate the differences at the extremes, and to do so would be to obscure some important characteristics of the period in the history of the most advanced states. The embracing of social reform and the extension of the franchise by these governments were not the same thing as the advance of democracy. If the decisions to take these steps were usually administrative rather than political manœuvres—exercises in the use of established authority rather than consequences of a struggle for the possession of authority—neither did they have much effect as yet in altering the composition of the governing classes. In few countries were they accompanied, as they were in Great Britain as a result of the Ballot Act of 1872 and the Redistribution Act of 1885, by secrecy of voting and an equitable distribution of constituencies. Although the extension of the franchise, by creating mass electorates, would one day alter the forms and institutions of politics—would force political parties to transform themselves from oligarchies into mass organisations, with new men as members and new techniques of oratory and journalism for getting the voters to the polls—this transformation, both for this reason and because of the continuing limitation on the powers of parliament as against the executive, was a slow process.

Even in Great Britain, where the power of parliament and secrecy of voting enabled it to set in early, the continuation of plural votes—half a million voters still exercised plural votes after 1885 and some individuals enjoyed as many as nine votes—and the existence of a long-established and recognised governing class delayed it and ensured that democracy would advance at no formidable pace. The social structure of the governing class was slowly changing, as the middle class was increasing: it was from 1885 that the number of industrialists among the peers began to increase significantly. But politically the situation was not seriously different in 1900 from what it had been in the 1870's, when eighty peers had sons in the House of Commons and a third to a half of the members of the cabinet were peers. The German Social Democrat party, the only one outside Great Britain and the United States to develop a mass following despite the handicaps, discovered that the structure of government did not permit party strength to be translated into political influence and power. In the United States, the only country where democracy in this sense had been long established and was at all developed, there was even a sharp reaction against it. The period saw the beginnings of a profound distrust of democracy among intellectuals and the rich, who regretted that a recognised governing class had failed to establish itself. These were the years (1870–1910) when *mariages de convenance* between American heiresses and European noblemen were particularly frequent—a fact which, whatever light it throws on the history of the European nobility, is surely significant of the movement of opinion among the wealthy in the United States. Although universal suffrage was in principle ineradicable, its extension to the Negroes was in practice avoided by evasion of the Constitution, and it was the fear of majority rule by powerful interests, and the consequent wish both to revere the Constitution rather than the Declaration of Independence and to place the Constitution beyond the reach of the electorate, that underlay the increase in the influence of the Supreme Court against that of Congress and of the legislatures of the component states of the Union.

If even in the least authoritarian of states there was little alteration in the composition of the governing class, little advance towards democracy and some reaction against it, it was also the case that, in those states as much as in more authoritarian lands, the strength of authority was steadily increasing—just as there was at least an effort in some of the authoritarian states to regulate and improve society. Of all the expanding governments at this time it may be said that it was not only in the interests of society that they were intervening in the social sphere, and not only in the social sphere that they were adding to their competence and their powers. All, the least as well as the most authoritarian, were improving in executive and administrative efficiency; all relied on this development— on the growth and professionalisation of the bureaucracy, the army and the police; on the vast improvement in weapons and transport; on the increased possibilities of controlling public opinion and securing public loyalty through influence on the press, the widespread adoption of conscription and the provision of state education; on all these causes and consequences of increasing centralisation—for the maintenance of stability. This reliance was in different degrees and assumed different forms according to how far it was modified by inherited political framework and a progressive government attitude. But even in the least authoritarian of states it played a part in maintaining order and political stability which, if indirect, was greater than ever before and only less important than social reform, the extension of the suffrage and the increased confidence between government and society to which these things gave rise.

These facts are central to an understanding of the politics of the age. It was distinguished, even in the least authoritarian of states, as much by the growth of authority as by the extension of democracy; and less by the extension of democracy and the democratisation of government than by an advance towards the democratisation of government policies and of the political context in which governments operated. It is these facts which account for the collapse of liberalism—for its exhaustion in more democratic countries as well as for its frustration in less democratic circumstances and its distortion in situations that were in between.

In the advanced countries of western Europe during the 1870's, when liberalism was at its zenith in its European home, liberal governments, abandoning the liberal opposition to the power of the state and seeing the state as the most effective means of securing the liberal conception of freedom in changed circumstances, accepted the early steps towards the inevitable extension of the functions of government and the use of unprecedented state compulsion on individuals for social ends—embracing the notion of state education, legalising trade unions, justifying public health measures, adopting even insurance and factory legislation. No governments in such countries, whatever their political complexion, could, indeed, have opposed such developments. From the end of the 1870's, however, they were overrun and overturned in those countries by the further progress of those twin forces, the masses and the modern state. Every advance in the role of the state, every new aspect of the social problem, every recognition of the emergence of the masses, every new turn of policy—whether towards protectionism and imperialism or towards social regulation and the extension of the franchise—conflicted with the liberal belief in freedom of contract and of enterprise, in free trade, in individual liberty, in public economy, in the minimum of government interference. Liberalism's great contribution, the constitutional state, and its guiding principles, the freedom of the individual, legal equality and conflict with the Church, were—to the varying extents that they had been already established in these states—taken over by more empirical and conservative politicians. Liberalism became more doctrinaire and more narrowly associated with urban and big business interests—even while industrial organisation itself, with the movement from personal to corporate control, was deserting it. The liberal parties split into moderate (national, social or imperialist) and radical wings on these current issues and lost office. Liberal rule or its equivalent ended in Great Britain in 1885, in Germany in 1878, in Austria and the Netherlands in 1879, in Sweden in 1880, in Belgium in 1884, in France in 1885. In Italy under Depretis and Crispi and in some states beyond western Europe liberal parties remained in power. But, liberal only in name, they embraced protectionism and imperialism, undertook social regulation and retained of the old liberal creed only opposition to the extension of the franchise and to the pretensions of the Church. In these states, as in even more authoritarian countries, authentic liberalism remained a relevant if a weakened basis for opposition to established authority. But even in that role, and even when it was not proscribed by the increased possibilities of repression, it was doomed to frustration by the growth of the need for social regulation and strong government and by the demand for those things by the mass of the population.

Liberalism's decline was reflected after 1880 in the new lease of life acquired by conservative parties and by the formation of new confessional parties in politics—most of which were representative of a catholic-social movement, as were the Centre party in Germany, the Christian Socialist party in Austria, the Clerical parties of Belgium, the Netherlands and Switzerland, 'Liberal Action' in France and 'Popular Action' in Italy, and all of which made a democratic appeal with their devotion to traditional institutions, their criticism of the materialism underlying liberal economic theories and their adoption of social programmes—no less than in the spread of socialist sentiment. The conservative trend was strengthened, indeed, by socialist rivalry. Socialism, liberalism's historical supplanter, was also its logical successor as the critic and antagonist of existing society, and not only because it made its appeal to the masses of men: it would itself use all the powers of modern government and all the resources of modern repression to achieve its ends, even if it believed that when those ends were achieved the need for repression and the state itself would wither away. But socialism as yet created fear more effectively than it won adherence. It was delayed and frustrated in authoritarian states, where it would one day assert itself the more violently on this account, by repression; in more liberal states, where it lost ground in favour of constitutional reform and even of compromise with monarchical authority, by improving economic conditions and the anticipatory actions of the governments; everywhere by the dogmatic quarrels necessarily engendered among its followers by so precise and comprehensive a creed.

It would be war, with its attendant moral and material dislocations and with the attendant loss of faith in some governments and loss of power by others, that would in the event provide socialism with its first opportunity and with much following. But in the last third of the nineteenth century war on any large scale was as conspicuously absent as internal political and constitutional change.

There was an even longer period of peace between the great powers after 1871—it was to last till 1914—than there had been between 1815 and 1854, and the period was not especially disturbed by minor wars. Between 1854 and 1870 there had been five wars involving one or more of the world's leading states, which were all in Europe, in sixteen years: after years of slowly changing relative strength among those states the existing international order—the territorial arrangements and the political assumptions of the 1815 settlement—had ceased to represent the real distribution of power and interests. The latest and most resounding of those conflicts—those which had resulted in the forcible exclusion of Austria from Italy and Germany; in the defeat of France by Prussia; in the seizure of Rome and the papal states by Italy without a declaration of war or the sanction of an international conference; in the seizure of Alsace and Lorraine by Prussia without the sanction of a conference or a plebiscite—proved to be the final moves in a process of readjustment, the end not the beginning of an age. For at least thirty years the new *status quo* in Europe was as unchallenged and as widely accepted as the pre-1854 situation it had replaced. Only in the Balkans were frontiers altered or sovereignty shifted; even these alterations were forced on the reluctant powers rather than engineered by them; not even this Eastern Question seriously endangered the peace, though it dominated European relations because the powers could not escape the complications thrown up by Turkey's collapse but could not solve them by agreeing to Turkey's partition. Beyond Europe, on the contrary, enormous changes both of frontiers and of sovereignty were made, changes more rapid and extensive than in any previous age. They were effected without war or serious risk of war between the major powers. In these circumstances of great fluidity and uncharted courses diplomacy proved no less effective, governments no less cautious, than in the congested and well-trodden paths of the old continent.

Beyond Europe, as within it, this was basically due to the operation of the new balance of power between the major European states. New extra-European powers were arising; they could go to the lengths of formally declaring war upon another state in the pursuit of their interests, as did Japan against China in 1894, the United States against Spain in 1898. But Japan had to be more cautious after her defeat of China, the United States more cautious in the Far East than in the New World, because until the 1900's—until the Spanish-American war itself, from which the United States, with the seizure of the Philippines and the annexation of Hawaii, emerged as a Pacific power, and until Russia's defeat in the Russo-Japanese War of 1904-5—most problems beyond Europe except in special areas like North America, which was sealed off by the Monroe doctrine and the British Fleet on which that doctrine rested, and Latin America, where local balances of power developed between the central and the southern states, were dominated by the European powers. Of those it was only Great Britain, from her special position, who formally declared war even upon a smaller state—as against the Boers; or who—as in the Fashoda crisis—could go to the lengths of openly threatening it against another great power; or who—as by the occupation of Egypt in 1882—could undertake to make a serious alteration in the existing balance of power. Russia declared war against Turkey in the Near Eastern crisis of the 1870's, though professedly with Christian and European and not with selfish objects; neither she nor other continental powers subsequently avoided activity and even fighting beyond Europe. But even in extra-European contexts, still more within Europe itself, all were restrained from rash activity—from fighting each other, from formal war with other states, from gains for themselves which could not be counterbalanced by gains for the others—by the system of relations which prevailed between them.

Berlin had replaced Vienna and Paris as the centre of that system. The new Germany was sufficiently powerful to ensure that neither Austria nor France could change the situation unaided and that neither could get support in changing it. But these two powers despite their defeat, like Russia despite her humiliation in the Crimean War, remained great powers at a time when the gulf between great powers and lesser states had become enormous.[1] There was no obvious obstacle to their recuperation, their potentiality was not short of Germany's, in the eyes of most contemporaries—who long expected a French war of revenge against Germany. If a few contemporaries recognised or feared their relative decline they also accepted or insisted that Germany would not extend such lead as she had obtained without great risk—that an attack on any one of the weakened powers would bring others to its aid. In 1875 Russia and Great Britain, who had been disinterested spectators of the earlier defeat of Austria and France, indicated that they would no more tolerate a repetition of the Franco-Prussian war than they would help to reverse its outcome. Nor was this the only evidence that the recent changes, far from establishing a dangerous degree of German preponderance, had freed Europe from the threat of French domination, which had reappeared with Napoleon III, without putting German predominance in its place. It was not for nothing that Bismarck, for all his threats, insisted that Germany was a satiated state, suffered from nightmares about coalitions and sought the placation of Russia and Austria and the isolation of France; and not for nothing that no power, not excluding France who most resented them, seriously regarded Bismarck's manœuvres, and the shift from Paris to Berlin that made them possible, as being dangerous to the system or to peace.

[1] One has only to list the states to see how great this gap was. In 1871 in Europe alongside Germany, Great Britain, France, Austria-Hungary, Russia and Italy there were eleven lesser powers: Turkey, Spain, Sweden-Norway, Denmark, Portugal, the Netherlands, Switzerland, Belgium, Greece, Serbia and Montenegro. Of these, only Turkey, Spain, Sweden-Norway and Denmark were fully sovereign. Serbia and Montenegro, though autonomous, still belonged legally to the Turkish empire. Greece was pledged to follow the advice of three protecting powers: Russia, Great Britain and France. Belgium was bound by the treaty of neutrality imposed on her by the great powers in 1839. Switzerland and the Netherlands were similarly bound by the Congress of Vienna. Portugal was by tradition allied to Great Britain. Only Roumania (1878) and Bulgaria (1878–86) were added to these states before the end of the century. Outside Europe only the United States could be regarded as of great power rank in 1871, and neither she nor Japan, after her meteoric rise, can be said to have been incorporated in the international system before the end of the century.

It was mainly for these reasons, in a roughly equal distribution of power and in conditions of general balance, that the powers chose peace in preference to war. Their situation came close to, though it could not quite attain, that perfect condition of peace which would exist 'if everywhere in the world strength dwelt side by side with strength and no weak and decadent spot remained'.[1] But this situation did more than encourage them to revert to the self-restraint of the first half of the nineteenth century. It enabled them to continue to subscribe to the principles on which a sense of the collectivity of the powers, of the Concert of Europe, had been based in that earlier period. These principles—that treaties should not be set aside by unilateral action, that gains should not be made by individual powers without general agreement and, normally, without compensation for the others, that the great powers had a common responsibility for the problems of Europe—had inevitably been suspended during the wars of 1854–71. But since they had never been interpreted as applying in time of war—regulations for which were also, and not illogically, part of the accepted public law—they had still limited the objects of those wars while they were in suspense: the significant thing about these wars, for all that it said about the explosive force of the nationalism which partly inspired them, is that the changes they made were deliberately limited. They also survived the wars: the continuing tacit acceptance of them was as much the basis of the wide acceptance of the new *status quo* and the common determination to keep the peace after 1871 as was the self-restraint induced by practical considerations arising from the balance of power, though the two factors buttressed each other. While the balance between the powers checked dangerous activity this other source of self-restraint was what enabled the balance to work.

International relations differed in character, nevertheless, from those of that earlier period of peace after 1815. The balance between the powers, their common interest in avoiding war, these things kept alive inherited notions of a public if primitive law; they did not permit a return to, let alone an extension of, the forms of collaboration in which the Concert had found expression. Meetings and conferences of the powers, like the public law itself, had become unworkable during the period of wars from 1854 to 1871; they were not resorted to for the settlements of 1870–1 as they had been for those of 1856. After 1871 this mechanism was not at once abandoned. Until the mid-1880's the conference method was not only revived; in response to the fears released by the recent wars there were efforts to improve upon the scope it had earlier acquired. The London Conference of 1871 endorsed the Russian denunciation of the Black Sea clauses. It was, however, endorsed, in accordance with the principle that no gains should be made without the general agreement of

[1] F. Meinecke, *Machiavellism*, p. 420.

37

the great powers, and the Conference also issued a reaffirmation of 'the sanctity of treaties'. In the next crisis engendered by the Eastern Question, between 1875 and 1878, Russia profited so long as she conformed to the agreed decisions of the powers. After the Constantinople Conference, when Turkey failed to reform in accordance with its recommendations, no power would move to protect her against Russia's attack. But when Russia departed from this principle underlying the Concert of Europe, imposing the Treaty of San Stefano on Turkey, she forfeited the forbearance of the other powers; and it was Great Britain who, appealing in her turn to the principle that the Eastern Question was the concern of all the powers, obtained the outstanding success at the Congress of Berlin in 1878–9. The Congress of Berlin harked back to the Congress of Vienna in more ways than merely in name. There followed Gladstone's decision to place the affairs of Egypt under the supervision of the Concert, after the British occupation of 1882, and the Berlin Conference on Africa of 1884, which laid down the rules for the effective occupation of uncivilised lands. Despite these efforts, however, the practice of regular meetings between the powers increasingly gave way before an almost universal feeling that each great power must stand on its own feet—and could stand on its own feet without bringing the system to disaster. The Berlin Conference on Africa of 1884 was, except for the abortive Hague Conference of 1899, the last great international gathering on a political subject for more than twenty years. Gladstone alone among statesmen continued to advocate concerted instead of individual action. Bismarck and Lord Salisbury, with their intellectual contempt for Gladstone's ideas, were more representative of the age.

If these were its representative men, alliances were its typical diplomatic means. Agreements between the powers had been imprecise and temporary during the first half of the nineteenth century—understandings rather than alliances. Beginning with the Austro-German Alliance of 1879, there grew up a network of written undertakings of a meticulousness that had gone out with the *ancien régime*. Every major continental power came to give and regularly renew formal pledges to some other. Not even Great Britain, despite her special position, escaped the practice for some years after 1887 when, in the Mediterranean Agreements, she accepted a more binding undertaking than was contained in her agreements with France and Russia twenty years later. These alliances were limited to European contingencies, though they often restrained, sometimes stimulated and always influenced the European rivalries beyond Europe. The extra-European powers were not yet involved. In both respects the Anglo-Japanese alliance of 1902 was the beginning of a new phase in international relations, an intimation that the search for power and equilibrium was becoming world-wide and extending beyond the narrow circle of the European powers.

It was also the first of all the alliances contracted since 1879 which, if only on the Japanese side, was as much concerned with war as with peace, with changing the *status quo* as well as with maintaining it. Until then, if international relations had differed from those of the first half of the nineteenth century, they were also different from those of the eighteenth century. Because of the greater determination on peace and because of the acceptance of a public law with which the eighteenth century had barely been familiar, the new alliances, unlike those of the *ancien régime*—and of the period of wars between 1854 and 1870—were without exception defensive.[1] Most of them were explicitly aimed at preserving the *status quo*; the remainder equally lacked the intention of changing it. Not one of them was an aggressive pact of the kind which had characterised those other periods and whose primary purpose had been to secure the assistance or neutrality of another power in a projected war. They were quite unlike the Pact of Plombières of 1858, 'the first definite war plot of the nineteenth century', which was a Franco-Italian agreement to find a cause of war; or the secret treaty of March 1859 between France and Russia providing for Russian neutrality in the event of a French war with Austria; or the Italo-Prussian Alliance of 1866 which was predicated on the assumption that it would be invalid if war did not break out within three months. There remained an ironical, if perhaps an unavoidable, contradiction between the contracting of even defensive alliances and the insistence of the powers on their autonomy, but of this they were acutely aware. Until

---

[1] The *Three Emperors' League of 1873* began as a Russo-German agreement for mutual aid if one or the other was attacked, and was completed by an Austro-Russian agreement to consult together if aggression threatened.

The *Austro-German Alliance of 1879* was purely defensive, essentially a promise by the two powers to join together against a Russian attack and to provide benevolent neutrality in the event of an attack by any other power unaided by Russia.

The *Three Emperors' Alliance of 1881* was a defensive alliance. In any war other than with Turkey, Germany, Russia and Austria promised each other only benevolent neutrality, while in any war with Turkey they agreed to consult together beforehand and to make no changes in south-east Europe without agreement. In this last respect it was essentially a self-denying ordinance imposed by Germany on reluctant Austria and Russia. Also behind it was the anxiety of all three powers to safeguard existing conquests—Alsace and Lorraine, Bessarabia and Bulgaria, Bosnia and Herzegovina.

The *Triple Alliance of 1882*, an extension of the Austro-German Alliance as a result of the adhesion of Italy, was essentially defensive. If Italy were attacked by France, Germany and Austria would assist her. If Germany were attacked by France, Italy would assist her. If one of the powers were attacked by two or more other powers all would join together. Italy promised to stay neutral in a war between Russia and Austria. Behind this alliance was the anxiety to safeguard existing conquests—Italy's, now joined to those of Germany's and Austria's, being lest those other two powers would support the pope over the papal state.

The *Reinsurance Treaty of 1887* between Germany and Russia was a promise of neutrality by the two powers except in the event of a Russian attack on Austria or a German attack on France, reservations which had always existed and which were now merely formalised.

The *Franco-Russian Alliance of 1892–4* arranged that Russia would employ all her forces against Germany if France were attacked by Germany or by Italy with German support, and that France would attack Germany if Russia were attacked by Germany or by Austria with German support.

the 1890's—in 1891, and prematurely, the Triple Alliance was renewed for twelve years and the Franco-Russian military convention of 1892 which was the basis of the Franco-Russian Alliance was concluded 'to last as long as the Triple Alliance'—the alliances were all made for brief periods, usually three or five years,[1] for the same reason that they dealt meticulously with precise and defensive contingencies: the reluctance of every power to give up its freedom of action.

After 1890, no less than before, reluctance was the keynote of the negotiation of each of them. The reluctance of the powers in concluding the first of the alliances, that between Austria and Germany, is indicated by the fact that, although it was 'secret', the German emperor insisted on sending a copy to Russia to prove its defensive character and Austria notified the British government of its existence. The reluctance of Austria, Italy and Germany to conclude and renew the Triple Alliance varied from time to time and as between the three parties, but it was always a factor in the negotiations. The Franco-Russian Alliance was notoriously an unwelcome bargain between Russia and France—whose reluctance has often been mistakenly attributed merely to the mutual distrust of tsardom and the French Republic. Great Britain at least was most reluctant to conclude the Anglo-Japanese Alliance in 1902, and this would have been an Anglo-German-Japanese Alliance had not Germany been determined to stay free. Partly because of this reluctance, though they were all technically secret alliances, their existence and often their contents were generally known to all the foreign offices.[2] Being precise, short-term and technically secret they left the powers free, as they were intended to do, in all but the stated and narrow contingencies they envisaged. The powers used this freedom. It would be an exaggeration to assert that the system of alliances was a façade, ignored except on ceremonial occasions and by gullible persons. It is certain that its nature cannot be understood unless it is emphasised that it was no barrier either to understandings between

---

[1] Whereas no term had been set to the Three Emperors' League of 1873—which was an understanding of the old style, a revival of the Holy Alliance or, rather, of the understandings of pre-1854—all alliances after 1879 were deliberately short-term—three or five years, and occasionally ten, as in the Austro-Serbian Alliance of 1881—but were renewable.

The *Austro-German Alliance of 1879* was concluded in the first place for five years and renewed at five-year intervals.

The *Three Emperors' Alliance of 1881* was for three years and was renewed in 1884 and expired in 1887.

The *Triple Alliance of 1882* was for five years, and was renewed for five years in 1887; but in 1891, and prematurely, it was renewed for twelve years.

The *Austro-German-Roumanian Alliance of 1883* was for five years and renewed at frequent intervals.

The Reinsurance Treaty of 1887 was for three years. It expired in 1890.

[2] Parts of the Anglo-Japanese Alliance were published—but it had its secret clauses. Until then the alliances had been secret. Insufficient research has as yet been done on the extent to which, despite this fact, their contents were known. It is clear that on the whole they were.

members of opposed alliances—between Austria and Russia, France and Germany, Germany and Russia, Italy and France—or to disagreements between allies—between Italy and Austria, France and Russia, Austria and Germany. Any power tempted to adventure was restrained by its allies as much as by its opponents. Bismarck went far towards contracting incompatible alliances with Austria and Russia, with Italy and Austria. There were times when the British government did not remember that it had signed the Mediterranean Agreements or could not decide whether or not the agreements had lapsed. All the powers sought to be as isolationist in fact as Great Britain was normally able to be. Their alliances testified to their wish for independence as much as to the difficulty of achieving it.

This difficulty was perhaps inherent in the existence of suspicious sovereign states. It was increased by the stupendous development which now took place in the weapons and techniques of war. The Austro-German Alliance took its rise from Bismarck's determination to preserve the advantageous *status quo* of 1871, from his fear that another European war could not be localised and might end in the weakening or dismemberment of Germany. Against this danger he relied on Germany's military preparedness as well as on diplomacy. But just as the first alliance inexorably led to others, so military preparedness increasingly involved the need of an ally. The application of science, technology and industry to the means of war, and of the increasing efficiency and bureaucracy of the state to military organisation, was making continuous readiness, rapid mobilisation, large forces and universal conscription essential for success in resisting an attack with modern transport and modern weapons. All the leading continental states, following Germany's example in these directions, became for the first time nations in arms in time of peace. On the other hand, the greatest single consequence of these developments was that weapon development, which had moved in advance of improvements in locomotion and made tactics increasingly static since the sixteenth century, now moved farther ahead of them than ever before. Weapon ranges, which were ten times greater in 1870 than in the days of the first Napoleon, were forty times greater by 1898. Weapon efficiency similarly shot forward, especially with the development of machine-guns in the 1860's and of Maxim's truly automatic machine-gun in 1889. But mobility and flexibility on the battlefield—as opposed to the increased strategic mobility resulting from the growth of railways—was reduced by the introduction of larger weapons until the subsequent application of the petrol engine to warfare, which did not come before 1914. More than ever before, battlefield mobility and weapon power had become incompatible. This was the great difference between naval and military developments at this time. Navies gained in speed and mobility, as well as in weapon power, because of the much earlier development of propulsion at sea compared with that of automotive power on land—and so much so that the difficulty with them, as was shown in the war of 1914, was becoming that of bringing an enemy fleet to battle at all.

Success in a land attack against a prepared enemy, if not rendered quite impossible, accordingly required an ever-increasing ratio of superiority by the attack over the defence. When all the powers were in any case prepared, when technical developments were constantly increasing the expense and the rate of obsolescence of weapons, when increasingly complex and efficient general staffs planned—as was their habit and, in view of the lack of tactical mobility, to some extent a continuing need—for frontal assaults and—as was their function—for victory and not merely for successful defence, and at a time when governments were also spending increasing amounts on education, welfare and other social measures, the burden became so great, both financially and psychologically, that the powers felt forced to contract alliances. If these all dealt with precise contingencies it was in the details of mutual military aid that they reached the greatest precision. By 1892 this fact had become so pronounced that what in due course became the Franco-Russian Alliance originated in a strictly military convention, made to balance the military forces of the Triple Alliance of Germany, Austria and Italy, between two powers who had no intention of concerting their policies and entered no commitment to concert them.

If only because they were so directly necessitated by the armaments situation, the alliances, while they accentuated the defensive character of the age by presenting the powers with the choice of only a general war or a general peace, did nothing, indeed, to offset the central characteristic of its international dealings—the ultimate self-reliance of each power. Bismarck initiated the alliance network because his alliances, whatever their eventual effect, increased his control of international politics. As the deadlock in Europe grew more complete, and particularly after 1892, it encouraged the powers to search for compensating advantages and leverage effect beyond the continent, thus intensifying their colonial activities. Russia increasingly turned to Persia and north China; France to south China and Africa; Italy to Africa; Austria and Germany in the Turkish direction. These activities occupied forces that were negligible compared with the effort and preoccupation applied to preserving the balance in Europe. As yet, and until Russia overreached herself in the preliminaries to the Russo-Japanese War in 1904, they were always subordinated— though sometimes, and with growing frequency, only after they had produced an international crisis—to the maintenance of that balance and of peace. But they were not subordinated to the wishes or interests of European allies. It was the increase of these independent activities, cutting across alliances which dealt with purely European contingencies, that contributed most to the growing interpenetration of the alliances after 1892. At the end of the period, when they had already introduced—with the Kruger telegram, the Fashoda crisis, the scramble for China—an additional source of stress in international relations, Russia, the first power to find the armaments burden crippling, proposed the Hague Conference for the discussion of excessive armaments and of means to preserve the peace. Though all the invited governments consented to attend, none, in Lord Salisbury's phrase, took the conference 'too seriously' and all agreed with the German emperor that it was 'utopian'. These problems were not seen as problems requiring the revival of the old Concert machinery or—beyond the establishment of a purely voluntary court of arbitration, and even this step all but precipitated the resignation of von Holstein from the key position he had held in the German foreign office—the adoption of any new form of international co-operation. Governments apart, there was a pronounced increase of concern with the problem of war prevention during the 1890's, but the prevailing view, as represented by Nobel, Carnegie, D'Estournelles and Ivan Bloch, was still that progressive governments could solve the problem by concerted action and without the need for that complicated international machinery and that limitation of sovereignty which had been advocated earlier, during the eighteenth century, and was to be advocated again, with appeals to the eighteenth century, in the twentieth century.

This continuing confidence of the powers in their ability to work without machinery was, like the earlier eclipse of the Concert itself, a reflection of the most significant developments of the time. It is all the more noticeable in that it was precisely when they were becoming outmoded in other directions (and by the growth of international administrative dealings as much as by developments within the states) that the principles of *laissez-faire* were reasserted in this way as the basis of international political relations. It is estimated that the numbers of international unions or conventions for such matters increased from twenty between 1878 and 1880, to thirty-one in the 1880's, sixty-one in the 1890's and 108 between 1900 and 1904). It was when freedom and individualism were giving way to regulation and organisation in domestic affairs, and also when the world was necessarily experiencing the first huge proliferation of international legislation and committees on administrative and technical matters of common concern to the states like postage, telegraphs and public health, that the states insisted as never before on autonomy in international politics; that they began to rely as exclusively as possible on the operation of a balance between themselves for control of the international position; that they came to believe that in foreign affairs, as in such matters as tariffs, the maximum liberty for each would automatically produce the best results for all. The same developments which underlay the growth of internal organisation and of international law and administration—the extension of the functions and competence of government and the alteration of the relations of each government to its society—had this apparently contradictory consequence for international relations. They were bringing states into closer and more continuous contact with each other—even as they were making them more similar to each other in organisation—but they were simultaneously emphasising their political individuality and putting a strain on their political solidarity.

The decline of monarchical solidarity was a symptom rather than a cause of this change. Up to the 1870's, however attenuated, this had remained as a general sentiment on which the arch of a Concert system could rest among governments who were all on guard, if in different degrees, against internal dissidence. It now declined, and what took the place of monarchism or dynasticism was not a new loyalty uniting governments but a new conception of the state in accordance with which each government was rather ranged with its own society than with other governments against it. The heightening everywhere of the emotional attachment towards the armed forces as symbols of the national state was only one indication of this process. Nationalism itself underwent a change. Except in central and eastern Europe, which for the time at least became the only considerable area where nationalist feeling was both strong and unsatisfied, loyalty to the nation gave way to loyalty to the state among the general populations. In that area national movements which opposed established governments were now more easily repressed. It had always been true that such movements had usually succeeded only where embraced by a strong government and favoured by other governments; they were now handicapped by the greater resources of state power and by the fact that governments themselves, and not least the governments of Germany and Italy which had previously profited from the national principle, became intensely nationalist in their policies within existing borders. The Congress of Berlin ignored the principle of nationality even more than it had been ignored by the Congress of Vienna. Turkey was deprived of half her European territory; but for the purpose of rounding off the territories of the powers and in the interests of the balance between them, and not in the cause of freeing national minorities. How could there be sympathy, let alone support, for Czechs or Poles or Serbs or Balts when—all other considerations apart—governments within their own states were, with wide popular support, favouring national majorities and making intense efforts to create homogeneous populations by absorbing minorities; when the German government was Germanising Poles and Danes, when centralism in Italy no less than in Austria was ignoring minorities and provincialism, when Russification was as ruthless as Magyarisation and more extensive? Even in England Gladstone was discovering that public sentiment was stubbornly opposed to his plan for Home Rule for Ireland, and even in small states—in Belgium, for example, where the ascendancy of the French over the Flemish element was steadily developed—the governments equally pursued a policy of administrative centralisation and national unification.

This shift, with its accompanying increase in the concern of governments to limit the responsibilities and to guard the security of their own states, made governments reluctant to invoke the conference method even in political disputes which were of interest to them all. It was not only in the Eastern Question and not only by Bismarck that, increasingly after the 1870's, such trouble and risk were regarded as unworthy of the bones of a grenadier. In such an atmosphere it was the more certain that the efforts of men like Gladstone not merely to revive the Concert but to extend it, to convert it back to a Congress system, would only contribute to its collapse. But the problems which Gladstone tried to submit to it— the internal administration of Egypt, the reform or dissolution of the Ottoman empire, the opening-up of Africa—illustrate the importance of another development that was working in the same direction. If governments were more reluctant than before to collaborate in the settlement of even common problems it was also true that an increasing number of international political problems were not of common, or at least of equal, concern to a structure of purely European powers. At the same time, for all the continuing primacy of those powers, some problems were arising which were not the concern of European powers alone. The political problems of this period, to a larger extent than ever before, arose in areas beyond Europe in which, for both of these reasons, the conditions did not exist for the application of a European concert machinery or even— despite the effort to apply them there in the 1884 Conference on Africa and the international guarantee of the status of the Congo Free State— of those general notions of a European public law on which such machinery had once been based.

This second development was the direct consequence of two others. The discrepancy between the developed and the undeveloped parts of the world was becoming acute. It was becoming acute at a time when the world beyond Europe was shrinking with the enormous development of communications, and at a time when the possibilities of exploiting undeveloped areas were being vastly enlarged by this and other technical and organisational developments. On account of the different circumstances and different previous histories of the different parts of the world the industrial and technical revolutions and the rise of the modern state, such prominent features of this period wherever they did occur, did not take place everywhere—any more than, where they did take place, they took place to the same degree and at the same speed—but only in some countries. The effects on international relations were momentous. Not only were new powers emerging for the first time beyond Europe. Not for the first time, for there had been a growing disparity between western Europe and other areas since the eighteenth century, yet more rapidly, more extensively and more directly than before, the more developed states extended, were perhaps unable to avoid extending, their intervention and their control in areas where society and government were still as they had been in the European Middle Ages. This happened in Turkey's European provinces and in Central Asia from about 1870; in Turkey's North African possessions, in the Near East and Persia, in undeveloped Africa and the undeveloped Pacific from about 1880; in China and Korea from about 1885; in the New World, even, from about 1890 as the United States expanded from her continent into the Caribbean, undertook the Panama Canal and asserted her right under the Monroe Doctrine to be the directing power in South as well as in North America. And when none of the problems of this wider world of politics involved all the European powers, when few of them affected even those powers in equal degree, when some of them were more directly the concern of new powers beyond Europe than they were of some European states, it is not to be wondered at that these developments confirmed the impossibility of upholding an older and purely European habit and system of collaboration, or that, notwithstanding the attendance of the United States, Japan, China, Siam and Mexico as well as of European states at the Hague Conference, they also did nothing to encourage the growth of a wider system.

Whatever further elaboration may be needed for a complete analysis, these developments were the sufficient cause of the increase in imperialist activity and imperialist sentiment which marked the last fifteen or twenty years of the century. This imperialism derived much of its character, and no doubt further impetus, from the special economic conditions of the Great Depression and the international situation in Europe on the one hand or from increased humanitarianism and missionary activity on the other. The age was one of constantly growing missionary activity by the Christian churches. This was facilitated by material developments—the growth of transport, the development of cheap printing, the improving control of diseases, the growing wealth in Western countries which gave growing financial assistance to this work—whatever it owed to continuing and perhaps increasing dedication to the work of spreading the gospel and tending the backward. The White Fathers were founded by Lavigerie in the 1870's. The Cambridge University mission to China was inaugurated in 1885. There followed a multiplication of Catholic and Protestant missions all over the world. By 1900 the army of Christian missionaries in Africa, Asia and the Pacific was comparable in size with the overseas military forces of any of the great powers, comprising (including native priests) more than 41,000 Catholics, 18,000 Protestants, 2000 Orthodox. Their activities undoubtedly stimulated imperialist sentiment both by stimulating public interest in overseas expansion and in more direct ways. But if imperialism now surpassed that of earlier periods in intensity, it was mainly because the disparity between the efficient and the undeveloped areas of the world was becoming more pronounced at a time when the possibilities of expansion and exploitation by the efficient areas were growing more rapidly than they had ever grown. Colonial expansion was at least more extensive than before on this account, and was indulged in by a wider circle of powers.

It is tempting to assume that this fact increased, as it is tempting to assume that the armaments preparations, the alliances and the tariff wars of the period increased, the suspicion and strain of international relations. It is equally arguable that suspicion and strain are necessary ingredients in the relations between sovereign states and that imperialism was as much checked as it was accelerated, as these other manifestations were contained as well as encouraged, by the rivalry of the powers. Certainly if international tension was any greater in 1900 than in 1870, a contention which few contemporaries would have accepted, it was so for a more basic reason than the imperialism, the alliances, the armaments and the economic policies of the powers. The balance between the powers was itself changing and with it the objects of their rivalry.

As the period ended, a period which had been distinguished by an obvious and ever-growing disparity between the developed and the undeveloped states, another disparity was becoming acute—a disparity between the more developed states, the powers, themselves. It had been emerging since the 1860's and 1870's. The unification of Germany, the end of the American Civil War, the abolition of serfdom in Russia, the Meiji revolution and, in 1877, the defeat of the last feudal rebellion in Japan, these developments had already laid at that time the foundation of a different international system from that which had so far prevailed in modern times. Until the end of the century—though work was proceeding fast on these foundations, and faster in Germany than elsewhere; though other states, Great Britain and France, who had developed most before 1870, were losing their earlier lead; though others yet, like Austria and Italy, found themselves limited in opportunities and the resources of modern power—the shift in relative strengths had not been rapid or obvious, and it had been overlaid by the checks and balances of the older international order. The older order had still persisted alongside the new. Germany was already stronger than France, the next powerful continental state, in 1870, with more than twice the coal production and nearly twice the output of iron; she was stronger still after her defeat of France in 1871; she had forged steadily ahead of France and the other continental powers thereafter. But until 1890 she had remained below Great Britain in material strength and had not yet passed beyond the resources of a combination of the European powers. By the 1900's, however, Germany was approaching a degree of material primacy within Europe which no continental power had possessed since 1815 and which checks and balances could no longer disguise. For ten years, and especially since the end of depression conditions in 1895-6, she had been rapidly increasing her lead in industrial production over every other European state except Great Britain. With Great Britain she was rapidly drawing level, and in some important respects she had acquired a lead. In steel production, for example, while the United States had replaced Great Britain as the world's greatest producer by the mid-1880's, Germany had taken second place by 1900, when the United States had one-quarter of the world's production, Germany a fifth and Great Britain less than a sixth. Germany produced 7·4 million tons, Great Britain 6 million; France, by contrast, produced 1·9 million tons. By the same date her population had surpassed that of every European state except Russia. On the other hand, while her population stood at 56 millions and her birth-rate, like that of most of western Europe, was beginning to fall, the most significant changes in population since the 1870's were those which had raised Russia from 72 to 116 millions and brought the United States to nearly 80 millions. More serious still, it was in the 1890's that Russia, although still undeveloped, and the United States, after relatively slow advance hitherto, had begun to experience that rate of industrial and technological growth which Germany had experienced for thirty years. Which of these considerations had more weight with her, her present eminence or the thought that the time in which she could use it would be limited, is not easy to decide. What need not be doubted is that she became influenced by both.

Since 1871, despite her lead over some individual powers in some directions, she had been concerned with her immediate weakness. She now began to be alarmed by her ultimate danger and to reflect on her immediate strength. Beginning in the late 1890's her policy, hitherto cautious, began to acquire an erratic and unstable quality, her interests, hitherto focused on Europe and on her army, encouraged her to combine Europe with empire and to add a naval to her military effort. Her policy roused the fears and provoked the retaliation of the other powers—as her growing relative power might alone have done in due course—from the early 1900's. In the ensuing struggle and in a new phase of international history—a phase which was to last till 1945 and in which grave and shifting inequality in the distribution of effective power between the leading states of the world replaced the previous balance between states in Europe—Germany sought the mastery of Europe as no power had sought it for a century, and all the powers at last set aside those principles and that sense of their collectivity which, despite the breakdown of the Concert itself, had helped to restrain them in the last third of the nineteenth century. Despite many subsequent experiments in international organisation, they have not yet been restored.

CHAPTER II

ECONOMIC CONDITIONS

ABRUPT change is not characteristic of the economic process in history. In most respects even the nineteenth-century world was working out, on a much larger scale, the logic of methods inherited from an earlier age. What distinguished the nineteenth century increasingly from earlier centuries and explains the pace, rhythm and scale of its economic growth was the extent to which international trade and investment came to transmit the very means of economic change themselves from the forward to the backward areas. The sale, or more often the loan, of capital equipment—railways, engines, rolling-stock, mining gear, pumps, machinery—accelerated the rate at which the economic arrangements and social structures of the less advanced nations were transformed. As trade came to imply not only the exchange of goods, but the permanent nexus of investment, a new type of politico-economic relationship emerged, rich in material promise and heavy with political risk. Much of the foreign trade of Britain, still the leading economic power in most respects in 1900, rested upon contracts designed (in the most simplified terms) to enable nations which could not afford to pay for capital equipment on current account to borrow it. The supposition underlying these transactions was that the opportunities they created would enable the borrower to pay a return to the lender.

This phenomenon was not new in 1870; but it owed its new prominence to the period of railway building which had begun in continental Europe before the mid-century. This was still going on vigorously in the fourth quarter, both through new construction and the replacement of old iron track by steel. As the leading iron producer and the pioneer of rail technology, Britain had become the leading exporter of men and materials for world construction. The British ironmaster made the track and rolling stock, the British contractor frequently built the road, the British investor lent the money to build it. Sometimes the functions were combined. Nothing illustrates more clearly the nature of the so-called 'emigration of capital' than the willingness of South Wales ironmasters of the mid-century to accept part payment for their export of iron rails to North America in bonds of the railway company that was purchasing the consignment. Only thus could Britain trade with customers full of promise but short of cash. By 1900 Britain's accumulated hoard of capital in the outside world stood at somewhere between two and two and a half billion sterling. Perhaps a fifth of this was represented by North American railway investment. What proportion was held in railways elsewhere—in

India, South America, the Near East in particular—is less certain, but it was undoubtedly very large. The equipment and exploitation of mines, gas, water, tramway and telephone and cable enterprises also played a large role in developing the system of international capital lending.

This system itself and the goods and services it enabled to be lent and borrowed were an increasingly potent force for change. Mercantilist thinkers had never dissembled their anxiety at the results of allowing potential competitors to buy or borrow the tools and machines on which Britain's early industrial—essentially textile—prowess was founded. Yet the railway was a far more powerful agent of change than the spinning-jenny or the steam-loom. Here, in the technology of transport, lay the foundations of material progress and ultimately of social and political change. Its immediate impact was disturbing, not least on the economy of the great universal provider of capital herself. Within a decade or two of 1870, Britain saw her relationships with America and Europe revolutionised by the changes wrought in their economies through the operation of her own capital and inventions.

The United States economy was transformed between 1870 and 1900, as the greatest producer of foodstuffs and raw material became also a manufacturer of the first rank. The percentage of Americans who worked in industry and transport came in these years to exceed the numbers who worked on farms. There were mining towns in West Virginia, engineering towns in New England, iron towns in Pennsylvania. By 1900 one-third of the American people lived in such towns, and their numbers were growing faster than those of the people as a whole. The masters of this new industrial society were the tycoons, the 'robber barons' of American political folk mythology, whose vigorous but often ruthless enterprise has created those ambiguous figures of American folk-lore, half hero, half villain—the Rockefellers, the Harrimans, Hills, Morgans, Carnegies and the rest. It was no accident that many of them made their fantastic fortunes directly or indirectly out of railways, for it was the railway that made the new America possible; nor that J. P. Morgan's career began with his family's London connection and reached its climax through his determination to preserve his firm's reputation with the British investors who owned well over half the six billion dollars' worth of foreign capital invested in the United States. Increasingly after 1873, the North American railway system was made of Bessemer steel. Lake Superior ores, accessible now by rail to furnaces a third of a continent away, were transported to the new converters. By 1886, and with the use of basically British inventions, the United States had replaced Britain as the world's greatest steel producer. American manufacturers of steel, as of so many other products, were showing a willingness to scrap old plant and invest in new in a way that made them as conspicuous a nation of consumers of capital as they were already reputed to be of other commodities.

In Europe too the main railway system was completed by 1870. The Pyrenees had been turned at both ends, the Alps pierced and crossed. Even Russia had built over 10,000 miles of track. During the next two or three decades the process continued, the density of the European rail network increased, and new links were forged—vital tunnels like St Gotthard and Simplon, the long hauls to Constantinople, Salonica, and Vladivostok.[1] The year 1900 marked the completion of the Siberian railway which was begun from the European end in 1891; nearly 4000 miles of track built at a cost of a hundred million pounds by state enterprise. Like that of the Canadian Pacific Railway and the railways of the United States, its function was to link east and west, open a warm-water port, and join Atlantic with Pacific. It was typical that Russia, farthest east and least economically and socially advanced of the major countries, should by the end of the century have been building fastest of all, stimulated not only by the neo-mercantilist aspirations of ministers like Count Witte but by the opposition to Western institutions and ideas that was common to Slavophil and Pan-Slavist, to whom the railway system was a means of freeing Russia from Western ties. By a curious irony, it served only to bind her more closely to her Western neighbours. Their rail systems were likewise expanding. Belgium remained the best-served country in Europe: Italy, Spain, Holland and Switzerland entered the family of railway states. Germany added some 30,000 kilometres of track: France some 25,000.

The German railway system was impressive evidence of the rapid accumulation of capital in Germany. By 1875 a growing population—including labour made redundant by the decay of rural industry—helped to make construction relatively cheap. French misfortune was joined to German thrift. 'You may say', a German economist wrote in 1903, 'that by way of war indemnity France finished off our main railway network for us.' The industrial foundations for this tremendous advance in transport were firmly and rapidly laid in the 1870's and 1880's. More iron and engineering businesses were set up in Prussia in the four boom years that followed Sedan than in all the previous years of the century. But the great leap forward came in the 1880's: and Germany owed it to a young London chemist called Sidney Gilchrist Thomas, who, with his cousin P. C. Gilchrist, discovered a method for eliminating phosphorus from iron used in steel-making. This was the problem that had defeated Bessemer and Siemens. The Gilchrist-Thomas process opened the door to a vast expansion of steel manufacture based on the ores of Alsace-Lorraine, taken from France in 1871 but hitherto unusable because of the phosphorus they contained. Henceforth, an increasing proportion of Europe's iron and steel came from this ore bed and from the coke of the Ruhr. While

---

[1] Increase of length of track in Europe:

	1860	1870	1880	1890	1900
km.	51,900	104,900	169,000	224,000	283,500

4-2

British steel output rose from 3·7 million tons in 1880 to just under 6 million tons in 1900, and French from 1·4 to 1·9 million tons, German output rose from 1·5 to 7·4 million tons and was to rise even more rapidly thereafter. This in turn formed the basis for a superstructure of metallurgical industries of every kind: by 1900 Germany had already constructed for herself a steel-built steam tonnage for her mercantile marine of nearly 1½ million tons. This too was a measure of progress since the 1870's when Germany had less steam tonnage than France or even Spain.

The material progress down to the 1880's had in one respect owed less to the twin technologies of metallurgy and power than has sometimes been supposed. The Golden Age of sail lay in the years between the Great Exhibition of 1851 and the depression of the late 1880's. This, the mid-Victorian boom, was the time of the highest efficiency of the sailing ship, fighting hard to retain its supremacy against the powered ship, still hindered by unsolved technical problems. Even the iron ship was still proving expensive to operate because of the delays imposed on her by the fouling of the ship's bottom and the cost of cleaning it. Accordingly the coppered wooden sailing-ship retained much of her attraction. In 1870 the sailing tonnage of the United Kingdom was still 4½ million tons, as compared with just over a million tons of steam/iron shipping. Sail continued to convey goods of great bulk—iron, coal, jute, rice, wool, wheat, nitrates—on their journeys half-way round the world. Even when the railway had in the 1870's opened up the prairies of the Mid-West nearly all the grain and guano and the return cargoes of coal crossed the Atlantic under sail. In 1882 more than 500 sailing-ships, nearly all British, were carrying grain from the west coast of the United States to Europe, though by this time new designs giving double the cargo space of the 1850's made it economic to build them of iron and equip them with steel masts. From the 1860's, the problems posed by the higher pressures needed in marine engines if these were to compete effectively with sail were being investigated. They were not solved till the later 1870's and early 1880's when improved steel boilers and tubes enabled shipbuilders to construct ships with triple expansion engines that worked at 150 lb. pressure and more. The launching of the S.S. *Aberdeen* at Glasgow in 1881 for the Aberdeen White Star Line marked the beginning of the end of the obstinate rivalry of sail. In 1883, British steam tonnage came to equal that of sail. Ten years later the same was true of world tonnage.

The growing efficiency of the marine engine was aided by other developments. The largest was the Suez Canal which cut the distance from western Europe to China by 3000 miles. Here, as so often, the inspiration and conception was French, though others benefited more than France by the vision and courage of de Lesseps. Sir Charles Dilke's forecast that France would find she had 'spent millions on digging a canal for England's use' proved not far wide of the mark. Seven years after it was opened by the Empress Eugénie in 1869—a triumph for French prestige celebrated by a performance of *Aida*, specially written for the occasion—the British government became the principal shareholder through Disraeli's opportune purchase of the khedive's holding. Thereafter, it was used mainly by British ships until the twentieth century. The great new ships called also for harbour and dock improvements demanding vast capital investment—deeper channels, larger wharves, bigger warehouses, dredgers, cranes and elevators. In 1872 Caland, the Rotterdam engineer, built the New Waterway connecting Rotterdam directly to the North Sea. The Kiel Canal, linking the North Sea with the Baltic, was constructed between 1887 and 1895. The Manchester 'Ship Canal' followed in 1894. These were workaday affairs compared with Suez, but in the life of western Europe they were vital to the task of easing and stimulating the flow of goods.

No less important in the linking of world markets was the submarine cable. Here again the main ownership was British—even in 1900 more than three-fifths of the world's ocean cables were British owned—but the original invention owed as much to Germany as it did to Britain. The leading figure, both scientifically and commercially, was William Siemens, an immigrant German of farming stock from the Harz Mountains, one of the outstanding pupils of the German system of technical education, who came to England in 1843 as agent for the family business. Siemens was one of a number of German scientists who made their mark on the British economy in the nineteenth century. By 1863 he had established his submarine-cable works at Woolwich, and while de Lesseps was opening Suez Siemens was laying his first oceanic cables. In 1871 the Indo-European cable running from Lowestoft under the North Sea to Germany and through the Middle East via Teheran to India was completed. By 1874 five cables had been laid across the Atlantic. By the time Siemens died in 1883 the firm of Siemens Brothers had made and laid nearly 13,000 miles of major submarine cable—enough to go more than half-way round the world.

Invention and technology, especially in the sphere of power and metallurgy; the growth of transport on land and sea with its ancillary systems of communications; and the apparatus of international capital investment—these were the influences that revolutionised the character and volume of world trade. Some of them were at work by the mid-century and even earlier: but it was in the last quarter of the nineteenth century that their combined force was brought to bear upon the economic life of Europe and the world beyond. No single generalisation or statistical cross-cut will convey the full effects of changes that penetrated deeply into the political and social as well as the economic habits of the late-Victorian world. Among the most illuminating are the figures for the increase of international trade. In the thirty years after the mid-1870's the gold value of world trade probably rather more than doubled. Allowing for the fall in prices its volume may well have trebled.

Moreover, the nature of this trade, as well as its volume, was changing. The international trade of the seventeenth and eighteenth centuries had been preponderantly in textiles. Even in 1900, cottons and woollens and other textiles were still the largest single group of items on Britain's export list. But since 1870 they had been declining in value both absolutely and relatively to the export of metals and machinery. To some extent this shift reflected problems peculiar to the British economy—the impact of tariffs and the rivalry of the new industrial nations. But it was also a sign of the times. Germany's exports of iron and steel, and of goods and machinery made of iron and steel, had exceeded Britain's by 1900. The fact was that the new transport had made foreign trade, an unimportant element in the life of most European nations in the first half of the nineteenth century, an indispensable element by 1900. Goods of great bulk could now be moved over great distances with ease. A division of labour had accordingly developed between the central bloc of European manufacturing nations and a distant ring of primary producers—the southern states of the United States, the Mid-West prairies, India, Malaya, China, Australia, New Zealand, and Russia, all contributing supplies of food or raw materials to Europe by the 1880's. France had become dependent on foreign suppliers for one-third of her coal; Germany for very nearly the whole of her raw wool; England for four-fifths of her wheat. All three relied on foreign trade to supply and pay for the whole of their imports of cotton, rubber, jute, rice and practically all their tin, copper and mineral oils. Britain was most dependent on imported food, but France and Germany were following in her wake and even the United States was tending more and more to balance her food exports with food imports. Germany doubled the value of her food imports between the 1880's and the 1890's. There was this difference between Britain and the rest: she bought essential foods—wheat especially—whereas the others bought a larger proportion of luxuries which could, at a pinch, be eliminated. The dependence of Britain, France and Germany on imported raw materials for industry was growing rapidly.

This division of labour between manufacturer and primary producer emphasised increasingly the reliance of the industrialised nations on the tropical and sub-tropical lands. These were no longer peripheral, visited occasionally by the European trader, and dispatching their cargoes to the West only at annual intervals. Just as the annual fair of the Middle Ages had given place to the entrepôt of the seventeenth and eighteenth centuries, so the entrepôt, with its more frequent but still only spasmodic bursts of activity in furs, spices, fine cloths, wine and so on, now yielded to a flow of international trade that was very nearly continuous through the year.

Harvests might still influence prices, and winter dictate the movements of shipping on the rivers and estuaries of Canada and Russia: but in general the flow of trade was no longer governed by Nature as it had once been. Moreover, over a long period, as will be seen, capital investment tended to reduce the gaps between the values of exports and imports, and to induce a high degree of reciprocity which made the problems of international payment easier. The spread of commercial banking, much of it managed from London, reduced the importance of the precious metals as a means of settling obligations. Bullion and coin had come to be very largely the final reserves of the banker: specie flowed in payment of international balances only as a last resort, usually when something had gone radically wrong. When trade was following its normal course and was not upset by war, rumours of war, or urgent crisis, the movement of gold and silver was reduced to a trickle. Increasingly the London banks helped to finance transactions between buyers and sellers half a world away in commodities which never came near Europe.

The rising tide of commodities that flowed in the wake of overseas capital investment and the services that eased its movement, in the provision of both of which, while she continued to lead, Great Britain was now joined by Germany and France, created a new phenomenon: a world market governed by world prices. It also created new problems of payment. Areas of trade previously more or less self-contained—like the Britain–India–China trade—dissolved into a wider world economy as China, India and Japan began to sell in world markets. The central pivot of the world payments mechanism was Britain's ability to maintain a deficit on her visible trade with one half of the world which she balanced by means of a surplus with the other half. From the 1880's her deficit with the United States rose steadily as the rich natural resources of North America were fertilised. America's deficits in Europe and Asia were paid for by Britain; America's growing balances with Canada and the Argentine financed her imports from Brazil and India. Britain had other large deficits in addition to that with the United States. As capital investment fructified and production and exports increased (for example, in the Argentine, which from the 1890's converted its unfavourable balance of trade with Britain into a favourable one), the new nations frequently spent their balances not with Britain but with other manufacturing nations. In turn, as Britain saw her trading surpluses—with North and South America, Europe and the Dominions—disappear, and as tariffs and competition made it more difficult to export British manufactures abroad, she came to rely increasingly on the favourable balances she still maintained with the less developed countries—Turkey, Japan, but above all India— to settle her deficits in Europe and America. It has been said that it was in the last three or four decades before 1914 that Britain made her most vital contribution to the smooth functioning of the world economy by keeping her doors wide open to the imports coming from the rest of the world. The key to Britain's multilateral pattern of world payments came increasingly to lie in her economic relations with India, whose exports to Europe and the United States helped to finance her deficit with Britain. In this way Britain's surplus with India was probably financing as much as two-thirds of Britain's total deficit with other nations by 1900. The value of this multilateral system to world trade was immense and—in spite of a rising demand for tariff reform—its beneficiaries undoubtedly included many British exporting interests: by enabling other industrial nations to obtain their food and raw materials without having to pay for them bilaterally by manufactured exports, it relieved British manufacturers of possible competition in their non-European markets. It could be argued that almost everybody—save only the British farmer—benefited to some degree. The principal mechanism by which the obligations arising from this world trading system were settled was centred in London, which accepted for payment bills drawn on buyers in every continent. Nothing symbolised more vividly the new world economic order than the payment of Peking's war indemnity to Tokyo in 1894 through the Bank of England.

Within the expanding total of world trade, a marked change was taking place in the balance of economic power, especially in the last twenty years of the century. Great Britain experienced a decline from the unchallenged supremacy of 1870 to a primacy, challenged but in many respects maintained, in 1900. Between 1880 and 1900 Britain's share fell from 25 to 21 per cent, France's share from 11 to 8 per cent. Contrariwise, Germany's share rose from 9 to 12 per cent and the United States' share from 10 to 11 per cent. Reckoning the *value* of foreign trade, contemporaries concluded that at the former date, the foreign trade of Britain and her colonies exceeded that of France, Germany and Italy all combined. This had ceased to be true by 1880, though even in 1890 British trade was still larger than that of France and Germany together. In 1900 the combined trade of Germany and France was little, if anything, short of Britain's, and in some categories of business it was greater.

In the United States the frontier was closing: but the attention of American manufacturing industry was still focused primarily on the vast home market, where supplies of raw material and labour, if not of capital, existed in unparalleled abundance. As an exporter the United States remained, down to the turn of the century, principally concerned with the sale of primary commodities and food—cotton, grain, tobacco—to industrial Europe. Her competition was not yet such as to cause serious anxiety to British manufacturers in foreign markets, though the more perceptive British industrialists who travelled in the United States in the 1890's noted with concern the skill and drive that was fast making many

American industries models of modernity, economy and efficiency. The apparently insatiable demand of a vast protected domestic market enabled the masters of the American iron and steel industry to plan their production on a scale not possible in Britain. Output was going up, prices were falling. Steel rails that cost 160 dollars a ton in 1875 cost little more than a tenth of that figure in 1898. The tinplate manufacturers of South Wales saw their orders from the American petroleum and food-canning industries diverted to a vigorous new industry that grew up—with the aid of Welsh technicians—behind the McKinley Tariff of 1890. The factors behind such growth—the enterprise of manufacturers, the optimism of a labour force that spurned ca' canny, the constant application of capital to labour- and cost-saving devices, the exploration and creation of markets through advertising—all these were observed with interest mingled with concern as the century came to a close. But the concern was not yet acute. America had still much to do at home before she turned her attention to the outside world. So long as American ingenuity was concentrated on machines for making boots and shoes, cheap textiles and Mr Ingersoll's famous watches, comment could afford to remain benevolent.

France like the United States was not in the front rank of the competitors for the new expanding markets for manufacturers: but in her case it was because she was industrialising herself at a slower tempo and with marked difficulty. Down to about 1890 the slow growth of powered machinery in industry and the slow increase in output suggest a country accepting only reluctantly the conversion from a rural and individualistic way of life. It was certainly not that the flame of French creative genius was burning less brightly. In the sciences, as in the arts, the evidence of vitality was abundant. The eighteenth-century tradition of inventiveness seemed strong as ever. Were not the underwater periscope, the diesel engine, the photolithographic process, the gyroscope and many other inventions all of French origin? Was not *la houille blanche* that tumbled down the sides of the Alps first harnessed by a Grenoble paper-maker, Bergés, who thus became the pioneer of hydro-electricity? Levassor, a Frenchman, produced the first pattern of the modern motor-car. In the 1880's and 1890's the discoveries of Pasteur and the Curies made France without question the pioneer of the new medicine. France was, indeed, *le pays des grandes découvertes.* Yet the rate at which invention passed into industrial application was much slower than amongst other peoples. The progress towards industrialisation was, down to the mid-1890's, leisurely. Thereafter, it picked up: but the pace remained much slower than in Germany, and at the end of the century French production of steel, at less than 2 million tons a year, was only a third of that of Britain and a quarter that of Germany. Textile output—especially of cotton, worsteds and silks—increased fast with the application of power: and in the 1890's steam power more than doubled in France—from less than a million horse-power to some two million. But, compared with the contemporary gallop of German industry, this was a jog-trot.

While French competition was of a unique and limited kind, and while America was still preoccupied at home, the great rivalry in world markets for manufacturing pre-eminence became that between Britain and Germany. The transformation of Germany from an *Agrarstaat* to the most advanced industrial economy in Europe remains one of the wonders of economic history, a science not accustomed to sudden metamorphosis. As late as 1871 the new German empire was only slightly less rural in character, a trifle more industrialised, than the Prussia of 1816. Then, in the last three decades of the nineteenth century, all the forces stimulating industrial growth made their combined force felt. In those years, while the population increased from 41 to 56 million, the percentage of Germans who lived in towns rose from 36 to 54 per cent in the same period. The figures suggest 'a whole nation rushing to town'[1] and the greatest rush was to the nearest towns. It was not now the attractions of Pennsylvania or the Mid-West but of Berlin, Essen, Dortmund, Düsseldorf, and Leipzig that drew workers and miners from the east, leaving East Prussia, Pomerania and Silesia short of the labour they needed on the farms. This radical adjustment of a whole society imposed social burdens: wages were often low by British or American standards, food and working conditions poor; German workers were the largest consumers in the world of cheap butter substitutes; and relations between capital and labour gave rise to intractable problems. But unquestionably (as Treitschke said) the railways had released the latent energies of the German people.

The startling effects of this release of energy were reflected in coal output figures. Between 1871 and 1900 German output (including lignite) rose from 38 million tons to 150 million tons: British from 118 to 228 million tons: French from 13 to 33 million tons. Here, in combination with the ore beds of Lorraine and Luxembourg, was the basis of an iron and steel industry which, from small beginnings in 1870, overtook that of Britain by 1900. Coal, moreover, supplied an export industry which helped to create business for the rapidly growing mercantile marine of the same period. Not that the Germans were newcomers to the ideas and techniques of industry. On the contrary, rural industries—mainly rough textiles—had been widespread in Germany since the Middle Ages. And who can doubt that there was a continuity between the skills of the toy-makers, clock-makers and weapon-makers of medieval Germany and the new industries that made the engines and machines and drove up the output of the woollen, worsted, silk and cotton industries? Some ancient crafts, moreover, like that of the cutlers of Solingen in the Rhineland, were preserved and strengthened by the prowess of Germany in electrical

[1] J. H. Clapham, *The Economic Development of France and Germany in the Nineteenth Century*, p. 279.

technology which gave the small men light for working and power for operating their lathes, wheels and grindstones.

Statistically, the contribution of Germany's industries to her export trade differed from that of British industries to hers: for while Britain's exports were traditionally based first on textiles, Germany put her affairs in the reverse order. Iron and steel came top, then machinery, then coal, followed by woollens, cottons and other textiles. It was not illogical; for the German textile industries depended largely on foreign raw materials. If Britons depended on foreigners for their food, Germans depended on them for their clothes. But this should not hide the unique character of some of the new processes she was developing through technical education and by forms of industrial organisation peculiar to Germany: the heavy chemical industry and the electrical industry. The material basis of the chemical industry which grew from relatively nothing in the 1860's to the largest contemporary industry of its kind lay in the rich salt and potash deposit of Prussian Saxony. Its scientific basis was the system of state education. It was not unnatural that a country that had produced men like Liebig, Bunsen, Hofmann and many other distinguished chemists should place a high value on scientific education. Long before the dimensions of the German chemical industry were apparent, Henry Roscoe (who had managed only by Herculean personal example to prevent Owens College Manchester from abolishing the Chair of Chemistry to which he had been appointed) told the Select Committee on Scientific Instruction that in Germany 'a love of science and knowledge for its own sake is much more seen in those universities than it is in ours'. For little more than £20 a year, and more cheaply elsewhere, a student at Berlin could provide himself with lectures and laboratory experience. The link with industry was provided by the *technische Hochschulen* where industrial scientists were taught science in an applied form at a higher standard than at the English Mechanics' Institutes. In 1870 Prussia was spending £25,000 a year on them: by 1900, £117,000, and the investment duly produced a steady flow of well trained N.C.O's for the German chemical industry, led by an upper cadre of inventive chemists and engineers from the universities. While in France and Britain chemical manufacturers were increasingly hampered by obsolescent plant—especially the Leblanc soda process which lay at the base of much of the industry—Germany was free to develop new methods, like the Solvay process. German sulphuric acid producers were free to attack the markets for dyestuffs and agricultural fertilisers. In every branch of production there were stupendous increases between 1870 and 1900—output of sulphuric acid and alkali was multiplied eight times, that of dyestuffs about four times. The German fine chemicals and synthetic dyestuffs industry was the shining example of an industry based on British and French invention converted to a virtual monopoly for Germany by education and enterprise. By 1900 the small German firms which had pushed on with the synthesis of chemical dyes were giant concerns that accounted for some 90 per cent of world production of dyes.

The creation of the electrical industry was the greatest single economic achievement of modern Germany. Again, some of the basic inventions were of an earlier date than the period covered by this survey. Werner von Siemens, a thrustful brother of the young German scientist who had landed in England in 1843, designed and constructed six years later the first major electric telegraph in Germany, which in 1849 conveyed to an astonished Berlin the news of the election of the emperor within an hour of the event. Here were the beginnings of the great business of Siemens and Halske, for many years linked to the British business established by William Siemens. 1867 saw Werner's invention of the dynamo. Within a few years of the invention of the telephone in 1861, Germany became the largest user of it. After the dynamo came experiments with the transmission of power and with electric traction and the success of these in turn produced the electric lighting of the German cities and the provision of electric trams. English travellers noted how far ahead Germany was of Britain in such things. A great new industry sprang into existence to supply the generating machinery, the telegraph material, cables and lamps required for the new equipment. In the 1882 census, there was no category for workers employed in the electrical industry: in 1895 it registered 25,000 workers; by 1906–7, 107,000.

Like the chemical industry, the electrical industry illustrated by its concentration (it was dominated by three large firms) the peculiar characteristics which large-scale production and expensive plant were beginning to demand. Much of its market was abroad, in countries like Italy, Switzerland and Scandinavia, now delivered from their natural fuel shortage by hydro-electricity. The plant was often made in Germany which thus manufactured the means of industrial revolution for the third phase of industrialisation in Europe, just as Britain had manufactured the means for the second.

The structure of the German export trade, its emphasis on heavy capital goods, the speed of its advance between 1875 and 1895, the advanced stage of transport and public utility development in the West, all these combined with Germany's geographical situation and her traditional political habits to give German industry a special interest in foreign markets, especially in the Middle East and Far East. But the new German imperialism cannot be laid exclusively—not even primarily—at the door of German industry. The new mercantilism, like the old, was the product of many forces, motives, ambitions, not by any means all economic. Its aspirations were expressed by the so-called 'Historical Economists', led by Gustav Schmoller, Professor at Berlin after 1882. For Schmoller and his school, which had no counterpart in any other country, there were no economic laws valid for all time. Economic theory had a value only in relation to practice, history, and real institutions: and in Germany these demanded that the state intervene and regulate economic affairs in the interests of national power and national wealth, the dual objectives of policy which were always associated. The Navy Law of 1900 had its intellectual roots in doctrines that had been maturing for a quarter of a century. Economic progress was equated with the efficiency of the nation's political institutions: 'it was precisely', Schmoller wrote in 1884, 'those governments which understood how to put the might of their fleets and admiralties, the apparatus of customs laws and navigation laws, with rapidity, boldness and clear purpose at the service of the economic interests of the nation and state, which obtained thereby the lead in the struggle and riches and industrial prosperity'.

The fluctuations of the previous decade had already weakened the faith of the great agrarian interests of the east—normally corn exporters—in free trade. After 1877 Bismarck was listening ever more attentively to the complaints of the manufacturing interest of the west, all the more because his Treasury had also felt the pinch of depression. From 1879 Germany had a planned economy, within which industry, with the approval and co-operation of the state, attempted to achieve stability behind the tariff. German industry was free to plan price agreements, organise its raw material supplies, divide and organise its markets. No traditions of individualism, no suspicions of political autocracy, hindered German industry from forming great combines for self-protection against depression as opinion did in Britain and especially in the United States in the hard times of the 1870's, 1880's, and 1890's. The amount of fixed capital sunk in the new industries meant that markets could not be left to chance: demand as well as supply had to be 'organised'. This theory reached its logical climax in the relations between the engineering and electrical industries and their 'customers'. The 'customers' were themselves companies—consuming companies—formed, with the help of the supplying company, to buy its products. The process only carried one step farther the principle of the vertical combine by which each component firm sold its product to a 'customer' one stage nearer to the ultimate market. And it was merely the extreme example of the 'associations', mainly promoted through the financing banks, which proliferated in late nineteenth-century Germany, outraging all the principles of free competition still dear to British economists if not to all British businessmen. The German industrialist did not differ markedly in outlook from the government servant who administered public affairs. Economics was itself a branch of law and the same training as *Verwaltungsjurist* served for a career in business or the professions. The eighteenth-century *Kameralist*, the servant of the royal treasury, had often in Germany performed functions carried out elsewhere by the private entrepreneur: the tradition was not entirely dead in Bismarck's Germany. Resources were still comparatively meagre and neither statesmen nor economists were prepared to leave their exploitation to the workings of *laissez-faire*. The alliance of Junkers, industrialists, bureaucrats and economists assured their neo-mercantilism undisputed sway: while cartels and trusts had to fight a tough battle against public opinion in America and Britain, no influential section of opinion challenged Germany's need for them. After the crisis of 1900, the Darmstädter Bank observed that 'the community of interests of the great industrial groups, as expressed in cartels, protects industry from expenses and sudden collapses such as happened before their establishment'.

They did more than that. To men like Mevissen, the founder of the Darmstädter Bank, Werner von Siemens, Harkort the engineer and scores of others, the industrial struggle for world markets seemed a mission for German prestige. They felt entitled to the support of the German state— protective tariffs, subsidies, preferential freight rates and the like. The result was that Germany missed the age of free trade, passing 'virtually without a break from the age of Colbert to the age of Dr Schacht'.[1]

The effects of the new mercantilism in Germany have been much debated. Critics held that Germany was constructing in these years a dangerously top-heavy economy, overloaded with artificial and pampered industries, for which Germany had no need and no aptitude, apart from the dictates of autarky and military ambition. Certainly the cost was high, even when fair allowance has been made for the need of infant industries for protection, and the need for time to acquire new skills. Then again, the people of Germany, partly because of the policies of protection, subsidies and 'the community of interests' that promoted uneconomic investments and kept them afloat, were kept down to living standards lower than their skill and labour deserved. Between 1876 and 1900 the average real *per capita* income of the population in Germany rose from £24 to £32 per annum, while that in Britain rose from £28 to £51, increases of 33 and 82 per cent respectively. The slow progress of trade unionism no doubt had something to do with it. Union numbers never reached the million mark in the nineteenth century, and widespread socialism amongst the workers and intense conservatism amongst employers both made it difficult to reach wage agreement by means of collective bargaining. The other criticism of the German economy—that its tendency to overproduce was bound to lead, sooner or later, to the search for outlets by political or military means—is more difficult to assess. There were certainly close relationships between some German industrialists and the political demagogues who began to dominate German politics in the last few years of the century. What their influence was in the course of policy is still a matter of opinion.

Meanwhile, British observers had been noting with growing concern

[1] A. J. P. Taylor, *The Course of German History* (London, 1954), p. 126.

since the 1870's the rising competition of foreign, and especially of German, industry. From the 1870's warnings began to trickle in from British consuls in various foreign lands. The French were beginning to compete for the Italian textiles market. Belgian iron was making its presence felt in Spain. Roumanian peasants were showing a preference for German ploughs. The cloud was still only the size of a man's hand. By the mid-1880's it was decidedly larger. A consul in Greece, lamenting gains—indisputably mostly German by now—at the expense of British exporters, thought that British manufacturers were not moving with the times or consulting at all the tastes and wishes of foreign consumers. The German, contrariwise, had 'no prejudices': if he found that an article of a certain shape would command a ready sale in any particular country, he would make it...'however foreign it may be to his own taste or wants'. This kind of charge continued to be levelled for many years. Rightly or wrongly, the Commission on the Depression in Trade and Industry in 1885 were impressed by the evidence: 'The increasing severity of [German] competition—in every quarter of the world', they wrote, 'the perseverance and enterprise of the Germans, are making themselves felt. In the actual production of commodities we have few, if any, advantages over them; and in a knowledge of the markets of the world, a desire to accommodate themselves to local tastes or idiosyncrasies, a determination to obtain a footing wherever they can, and a tenacity in maintaining it, they appear to be gaining ground on us.'

The British response to these unfavourable comparisons varied according to time and place. The most intelligent businessmen—like Ludwig Mond and his partners in Cheshire, William Lever, next door, or Crosfields of Warrington—recognised the value of German scientific knowledge, and bought or borrowed both it and its practitioners freely. Progressive sections of the chemical industry took full advantage of German experts in these years. Other industries were more complacent. The iron and steel industry was relatively slow to follow up the economies of heat and power made possible in German plant practice by linking the various processes together as continuously as possible. They faced, undoubtedly, some problems not always allowed fair weight. There were, in reality, few areas of British manufacture where genuine 'mass-production' could be said to predominate. Most industries made their products in relatively small batches, often to special orders; processes and factories were still rich in the embarrassment of craftsmen and traditional skills. The nature of 'quality' markets built up slowly—in the case of woollens over the centuries—and the natural individualism of the private business tended to discourage innovations which might reduce costs by damaging quality. Less defensible conservatism was rooted in simple ignorance or insouciance, like that of the Welsh tinplate manufacturer whose response to a new method was to inquire 'whether any other fool had tried it yet'.

When the skies cleared later in the 1880's, the natural optimism of the businessman quickly reasserted itself. The severe slump of 1891–5 brought forth once more protests from Members of Parliament who raged against the purchase of Bavarian pencils by the foreign office, or the importation of cheap brushes made by German convict labour. But the rising trade and employment of the last years of the century seemed to quiet English fears once more. German competition was by now something to be lived with. Protection had little popular support and even those industries most hit by German rivalry were slow to abandon a creed which had taken them so long to learn.

Only Great Britain and the small western European countries remained free-traders. Bismarck's tariff of 1879 was followed, from 1881, by the raising of French tariffs. In 1892 the whole French tariff was raised. Russia raised her tariffs in 1881 and 1882. The McKinley tariff of 1890 and the Dingley tariff of 1897 raised American tariffs until they ranked among the highest. The British colonies adopted tariffs: Canada and Victoria adopted high ones in 1879; in 1900 all Australia went protectionist.

The real victim of continuing free trade in Britain in these circumstances was the British farmer, who was ruined twice over: first in the 1870's and again in the mid-1890's. In industry, within the framework of Great Britain's declining share in the expanding total of trade, the main consequence was a shift in the relative importance of the various manufactures in the export markets.

The largest group of manufactures, accounting for nearly half of the value of British exports in the early 1880's, was textiles and yarn, especially Lancashire cotton. The largest markets were in India and China but by no means unimportant customers, especially for quality goods, were to be found in the United States, Germany, and central Europe. And here was the rub. As tariffs rose in Europe and America, as the economies of backward nations developed—with the aid most often of British capital and British capital goods—the market for British cotton piece goods in those countries ceased to exist. By 1900 British cotton textile exporters were forced back on to the Asiatic markets, and even here the building of cotton mills had begun. Even woollens did little more than hold their own in the last decade of the century. The industrial growth that was going on behind the rising tariff walls called, on the other hand, for coal, iron, steel and machinery to equip and energise the new factories. Hence the stimulus to British industries that provided them. The situation in the last decades of the century emerges clearly from the export figures in the table opposite.

It was difficult to deny that one section of British industry was providing foreign competitors with weapons to be used against other sections of British industry. Much of the automatic machinery by which the United States

The value of the principal British exports (in thousands of £)

	To all countries		To ten principal protected countries	
	1880	1900	1880	1900
Cotton goods	75,564	69,751	15,990	13,840
Woollens and worsteds	21,488	21,806	13,526	11,475
Iron and steel, etc.	32,000	37,638	17,626	15,171
Machinery, etc.	9,264	19,620	5,797	10,892
Coal, coke	8,373	38,620	4,822	23,349

outpaced British competitors was of British invention and some of it of British manufacture. There were not lacking critics of the apparent folly of equipping customers so that they might stop buying from Great Britain. Coal export—as a raw material for potential competitors—was open to a similar objection, though here it might be argued that coal was the necessary outward bulk cargo to economise the operation of Britain's great mercantile fleet that brought in the grain, timber and forage for her industrial millions. The real answer to such critics was that Britain could not possibly hope to hold out against the rising tide of economic nationalism and maintain a monopolistic and dangerously specialised economy. The only remedy was to put the eggs in a larger number of baskets. The process of industrial variegation, even when reflected in the rise of industries which seemed to be sowing dragon's teeth, was therefore part of an ultimate remedy, even though the immediate readjustment was painful.

While manufacturing industry remained the heart of the British economy, methods for marketing and disposing of goods were becoming a more important source of income and the growing yield of earlier lending played an increasing part in the nation's accounts. Ever since the Napoleonic wars the deficit on Britain's visible trade had been growing until, for the years 1871-5, the average yearly deficit was about £65 millions. But Britain's earnings through the commercial services she provided for foreigners—insurance, handling of goods, brokerage, commission trading, and above all shipping—had risen so swiftly that there was still an annual overall surplus of some £23 millions a year, quite apart from an income of some £50 millions a year from Britain's accumulated foreign investments. A striking feature was the earnings from shipping, which had risen since the mid-century from some £18 millions a year to nearly £50 millions. By the first quinquennium of the twentieth century they reached nearly £70 millions a year. Britain continued to hold the lead at sea long after she had lost it on land. Even in the late 1890's the tonnage built by British shipyards for the British flag was only a trifle below the record figures of the early 1890's: that built for foreign flags was bigger than ever before.

The second half of the 1870's saw a fundamental change in the national accounts. The value of imports into Britain rose steeply, so that the deficit on visible trade increased (by about 100 per cent) to some £125 millions a year. Britain's manufactured exports paid—ton for ton—for less than they had done before the slump of 1873. The terms of trade, that is, moved temporarily against the manufacturing country, and Britain's total surplus on visible trade and on services turned in these years to a sizeable annual deficit of £32 millions. For the first time since the battle of Waterloo, the books could be balanced only by the yields from overseas investments—now well over £1000 millions and yielding an annual income to British investors of about £55 millions. From 1881 there was some improvement; the deficit on visible trade dropped as the terms of trade improved. But from 1891 to 1906 there was no year when Britain did not have to rely on her large income from foreign investment to help her to pay her way. And this she was easily able to do, for the income that accrued to her in this way had itself more than doubled—from £50 millions to £112 millions per annum—between 1870 and 1900. Clearly, the balance of Britain's economic interests, and her situation *vis-à-vis* the nations her capital had helped to develop, was changing. But the change can be overdramatised. It is not by any means certain that the period of 'export surplus' was over in 1875 as writers have often suggested. There were, on the contrary, many years between 1880 and 1914 when Britain could still show a surplus on the trade and services she carried on with the rest of the world.

Critics have never been lacking of what has sometimes been called the 'policy' of foreign investment, though whether such a multiplicity of private decisions can correctly be described by a term implying a conscious direction of things is very doubtful. The main objections that have been urged against it are, first, that it was unprofitable; second, that it implied —necessitated even—a new and undesirable interference in the affairs of the countries to which money was lent, in other words, that economic penetration went hand in glove with imperialism; third, that the 'capital' exported would have been better employed at home, and that the migration of capital fostered the growth of a *rentier* class whose main interests lay outside Britain. The most recent investigations suggest that British investors generally placed their money with prudence and profit, especially after 1875. It seems doubtful whether late-Victorian governments supported imperialist policies where earlier governments would not have done so. Mid-Victorian Britain had developed India as an economic colony, Latin America as a sphere of private trade and investment, and there was no sharp change in the late-Victorian period. Investment continued to flow to non-Empire as well as Empire countries. The spectacular late-Victorian entrepreneurs like Cecil Rhodes, Barnato and Beit in Africa, or Cassel in Egypt, were no more 'typical' of overseas enterprise than William Lever or Thomas Lipton were of home industrial enterprise. They were, however, 'characteristic' in that they were opening up new geographical territories, just as the new industrialists were creating new areas of domestic consumption. But it would be wrong to infer that the older areas became in either case less important when in fact they were only, like the underside of the iceberg, less observed. The scramble for Africa after 1888 should not entirely divert the historian's eye from the effects of the earlier fertilisation of India, Latin America and Canada which was now bearing fruit.

Much criticism of the 'export' of capital failed to perceive how deeply and intricately it was entangled with the process of production itself. The export industries would have been unable to find and maintain, much less expand, their markets without the willingness of investors to lend foreign customers the capital with which they purchased these goods. Thus South Wales ironmasters had taken United States railway bonds in part payment for rails; steel-makers of Sheffield, Glasgow and Swansea had invested in the development of iron-ore workings in Spain, which produced half Britain's ore requirements in this period. The connection between the exporting industries and the migration of capital was not always as direct or immediate as this: but the effects were none the less plain. The railway building, the steamships and the reapers brought in the rich harvest of grain—from North America in the late 1870's, from South America after 1885—which was a prime factor in raising the real wages of the British working man in late-Victorian England. That it had promoted exports, and therefore employment; that it had speeded the flow of food and raw-material imports, and therefore raised standards of welfare, health and comfort; these were themselves the partial answer to the charge that Britain would have done better to keep her capital at home. There had, in reality, been no alternative, for neither the private nor public enterprise that might have created an alternative demand for the iron, steel, rolling-stock, telegraphs, machinery and the like, existed in nineteenth-century Britain.

In Britain the general advantages of foreign investment seemed to be dwindling as the nineteenth century turned into the twentieth. It seemed less likely that further investment would reduce the cost of imports, and therefore the cost of living; rather more likely that it might increase foreign competition. The form of capital export which consisted in putting down factories behind the tariff walls of former importing countries was probably the form of capital export least open to criticism: there was, after all, no way to avoid the gradual death by strangulation of such former export trades. As one capitalist put it: 'When the duty exceeds the cost of separate managers and separate plant, then it will be an economy to erect works in the [purchasing] country so that our customers can be more cheaply supplied from them.'[1] Such ventures were common after 1900.

[1] C. Wilson, *History of Unilever* (1954), vol. I, p. 99.

Nor was investment concentrated abroad. It was as a direct result of enterprise at home as well as of investment abroad that there was, from the early 1880's, a many-sided improvement in the British standard of living that was well in advance of anything achieved elsewhere except by the bounding economy of North America. Real wages improved by some 75 per cent between 1860 and 1900, and about one-quarter of this increase took place in the last decade of the century. The rise was due basically to the increased wealth that came from the enterprise and investment of earlier years, its wide scope and downward penetration through society partly to the fall in the cost of living that came from the returning wave of cheaper food and raw-material imports. These in turn were the rewards for earlier overseas investment, especially in railways. It owed something too to the steady pressure of trade unions on employers, to the 'prosperity strikes' of the 1890's and to collective bargaining in all its forms. Lower prices for necessities left more to spare for semi-necessities and even for luxuries. There existed, in short, amongst the 10-million-odd working men and their wives a mass market which caught the imagination of some of the liveliest business minds of the day. They saw, as one observant journalist put it, that 'the factory housewife is saving, cleanly, loquacious and very often extremely shrewd'. It was largely from the pence earned and saved by them that some very large industries were reared in the 1880's and 1890's. National consumption and production of soap was probably running at about 100,000 tons a year in 1860 or double what it had been in 1800. By 1890 it was 260,000 tons, and by 1900 320,000 tons. There were many other industries helping to create higher standards of life and comfort—even entertainment—for the rising artisanate: industries providing processed foods were prominent; chocolate, jams, tea, margarine, beef extract, tinned meat and fish, sausages and so on. Nothing is more typical of these years than the multiple grocery shop that cut its prices by specialising in one or two commodities—butter, margarine, eggs. Thomas Lipton, the first of a long line of entrepreneurs of this kind, started his shops in Glasgow in the 1880's, and came south to London and the home counties in the 1890's. While Lipton took care of their diet, men like Alfred Harmsworth and Arthur Pearson hastened to seize the opportunities created by free education of the masses. They provided the halfpenny papers that relayed news of politics and—equally important—the turf. These new enterprises were competing strongly for the working-class pocket against that older enterprise that had so far provided a large part of working-class diet and not a little of its entertainment: brewing.

Farther up the social scale came another institution typical of the times —the great London general stores that catered for a middle-class market. As an historian of Victorian England has remarked: 'The lead of the great industries was shortening: and, in compensation, capital, labour and intelligence were flowing away to light industry, distribution, salesmanship.'[1] It was here, amongst the new industries, that the natural disciples of Samuel Smiles, the opportunists, the advertisers, were to be found in the largest numbers. Their contribution to industry was different from that of their predecessors whose genius contained a larger element of technical knowledge. Their emphasis was on selling goods and they enormously extended the methods for doing this, widening, incidentally, the gap between themselves and the older industrialists who still looked askance on their devices. 'The whole object of advertising', said one of the new men, 'is to build a halo round the article.' Often of dissenting liberal stock themselves, they frequently represented a kind of social enlightenment that was at once genuine and self-interested, for they knew that the fortunes of their businesses were intimately connected with those of the millions of customers, mainly working class, to whom they sold. The profit-sharing scheme and the model industrial village, Bournville in 1879, Port Sunlight in 1888, were their characteristic contributions to the improvement of industrial relations. What proportion such industries formed of total production it is difficult to say: certainly it was increasing, but they were still 'characteristic' of a changing society rather than 'typical'. The 'basic' industries remained the heart of the economy. The new industries were nevertheless to contribute much to the change in industrial methods and relationships. They had, moreover, one feature that was to be increasingly important: their plant could be established with relative ease wherever there might appear to be a potential market. They could therefore, and did, circumvent tariffs by creating a local production and supply.

Contemporary opinion divided sharply over the health and prospects of this maturing economy. Sir Robert Giffen, the statistician, who exercised a powerful influence on public opinion, was convinced that the British economy was growing rapidly and with special benefit to the working classes. Patience, he thought, would cure most of the evils that arose from its temporary fluctuations, and his faith in *laissez-faire* was in no wise dimmed by the vicissitudes of the 'Great Depression'. Growth in some large industries, he agreed, might be slowing down, but it was going on in less observed places. 'Industry', he wrote in 1887, 'by a natural law is becoming more and more miscellaneous, and as the population develops, the disproportionate growth of the numbers employed in such miscellaneous industries and in what may be called incorporeal functions, such as teachers, artists and the like, prevents the increase of staple products continuing at the former rate.' Others, including Alfred Marshall, were less sure that all was well. There was something to be said for both sides. But at least in some directions, as the historian of the Victorian economy has said, British conservatism had been shaken by the new competition and Britain 'was preparing to prove that she was not decadent,

[1] G. M. Young, *Portrait of an Age* (1949).

though both enemies and friends often said that she was'.[1] The most recent statistical inquiry has likewise concluded that the last thirty years of the nineteenth century saw a period of most rapid sustained growth in the British economy.[2]

The task for the historical imagination in this, more even than in most recent phases of modern history, is to comprehend a process of economic growth that consisted not in a steady expansion but in a series of fluctuations. In this process, some industries were set back, as British farming was; some were actually killed, as many peasant crafts in Europe were. Yet the phase as a whole was one of increasing output, and the aggregate volume of wealth emerged from each cyclical phase not smaller but larger than before. Economic fluctuations were not in themselves new; what was new was their amplitude and pervasiveness. The inquiry into their causes has proved, more than most economic inquiries, a bottomless well. The causation of cycles and the interrelation of the various economic phenomena that composed them remains in many respects a matter of hypothesis. That the incidence of major fluctuations was the result of massive friction between inventions, large-scale manufacture, investment, the supply of money and goods, changes in demand, wars, is merely a truism: but it is worth saying if only to demonstrate that it is, *prima facie*, unlikely that an economy in a condition of rapid and continual change would behave according to a regular rhythm. Markets for heavy capital goods behaved differently from markets for consumer goods. In the depression of the early 1890's, for example, British textile production dropped relatively little, while iron and steel production fell heavily by one-third. In 1885–6—dark years for many industries—the members of the British Soap Makers Association were so prosperous that it was not easy to persuade them of the need to attend meetings. Conversely, they failed to share in the revival of the late 1880's. Their fortunes were linked almost entirely to raw-material prices. The incidence of misfortune varied also between nation and nation: the crisis of the mid-1880's was more severe on England than on Germany: that of 1900 reversed the order of things.

The cyclical progress of these years may be summarised somewhat in this wise: from 1870 to 1873 Europe was at the tail end of a long upward trend of rising prices and profits. Capital was still flowing into railway construction, industry was still expanding to meet these and other needs. Employers, bankers, and farmers shared in the prosperity and *Punch* could publish cartoons of British miners drinking champagne. Then from June 1873 European markets collapsed and there followed nearly a

---

[1] J. H. Clapham, *An Economic History of Modern Britain* (C.U.P. 1938), vol. III, p. 223.
[2] P. Deane, 'Contemporary Estimates of National Income in the Second Half of the Nineteenth Century', *Economic History Review*, 2nd series, IX, no. 3 (1957).

quarter of a century when investment yields were low, price levels low. *Per contra*, the real wages of labour and the standard of living they made possible rose during this phase often known as the Great Depression. Unemployment rose in Britain during specially bad years, particularly in trades connected with the export of capital goods, but well over 90 per cent of the working force was employed at wages that rose by some 2 per cent a year from 1874 to 1900. The so-called Great Depression was a depression of certain business prices and profits, especially severe in the heavy industries that had expanded rapidly during the previous period of buoyancy. Rail prices fell by 60 per cent from 1872 to 1881. This temporary over-expansion in the heavy industries coincided with the growing flood of grain and materials made possible by earlier investment to bring a general collapse of prices. For the moment there was an embarrassment of riches.

New American expansion brought some revival from 1879 to 1882. Gold in South Africa, the Panama Canal plans, and expansion in America and in the British Empire gave new hopes from 1887–90; but this boom also broke in a welter of bankruptcies, repudiations and disappointments. The centre of the storm was the fall of the House of Baring, deeply involved in South American affairs. It was not till 1896 that a new upward trend can again be distinguished. New demand for rails—in Europe, America and the Empire—was its foundation: but now there was new equipment to be supplied for the electrical, chemical, petroleum, motor-car and other new industries, and the new impetus was to last until 1914.

The causes of economic fluctuations might be remote and mysterious; not so their effects. The unfettered competition of the generally prosperous third quarter of the century was altogether too bracing an air for business-men in the 1880's, and in every country they sought shelter from the chill winds not only behind national tariffs, but also behind agreements to restrict what they often called 'cut-throat competition'. These agreements may be divided into two broad categories: those which aimed at maintaining the sovereign independence of the firms which entered into the voluntary contract to restrict competition; and those which aimed at creating a larger business unit by submerging the identity of the existing businesses in that of a larger business. The former method went by many names—*Kartell* (cartel), syndicate, pool, conference, *comptoir*—but it usually portended similar policies. Members of the cartel would agree not to sell their product below a certain price and they might well come to some arrangement for dividing the market, either by geographical area or by a quota system. This might culminate in a central marketing agency. In Britain especially, such arrangements sometimes grew out of much older trade associations whose expressions of general benevolence had usually been as vague as they were pious. Now something more precise and positive was needed. The soap trade, for example, had had such an association for many years but it was not until the 1890's that it began overtly to fix prices, and even at this date such a departure from British *laissez-faire* traditions was enough to provoke the secretary to resign. The persistence of a large number of small businesses meant that the equilibrium of agreements to limit competition was always precarious. As soon as times improved they were torn up. Their threat to the interests of consumers was therefore very limited. Nor did a legal tradition strongly biased against restraint of trade help architects building on what was politely called 'the principle of association'.

British industry in search of stability went therefore rather for the more permanent type of association. Between the crisis of the mid-1880's and the end of the century, a number of very large amalgamations had been formed: the Salt Union, comprising all the Cheshire producers and some others (1888) and the United Alkali Company, comprising all the Le Blanc soda-makers (1891), were the most important. From the mid-1890's came large textile mergers. In 1895 J. and P. Coats, the sewing-thread manufacturers, joined with their four largest rivals. Brunner Mond, the great chemical firm operating the Solvay process, were absorbing competitors after 1895. Then came the Calico Printers, the Yorkshire Wool Combers, the British Cotton and Wool Dyers, and many others. The precise methods by which such unions were achieved—outright purchase by one firm of other firms, exchange of shares or the formation of a new holding company—are less important than the permanent increase in the size of the business unit. Some aimed at greater efficiency, others at quick profits, a few at outright monopoly. In general, success came to those which organised themselves so as to pursue consistent business policies.

Germany was in general more fertile soil than Britain for the new growth. After a Bavarian court in 1873 gave a verdict in favour of the legality of a *Kartell*, their numbers multiplied. In conjunction with the tariff of 1879, they gave German industry substantial protection against that foreign competition which had threatened it so severely in 1873. Three great *Kartells* handled a range of products vital to Germany in this stage of development: the potash syndicate formed in 1879 to combat over-production, the Westphalian coal *Kartells* from 1879 onwards, and the iron and steel *Kartells* from the 1870's. Most of the *Kartells* in Germany dated from the 1880's. They were the offspring of adversity and, like the British trade associations, none too stable in face of prosperity: but in some industries—chemicals for example—they proved to be a forum from which more permanent groupings (*Interessengemeinschaften*) were to emerge. These formed the more easily in Germany because so many firms had common links in the shape of directors appointed by the banks. German industry was knit together by a labyrinthine series of channels that offended against all the dogmas of classical economics but which Germans had come to regard as perfectly normal.

Both German and British promoters of business union alike looked for their model to America; and especially to that Standard Oil Alliance into which, between 1872 and 1881, John D. Rockefeller had brought a very large segment of the American oil industry. Rockefeller in oil, Carnegie and Morgan in steel, Harriman and Hill in railways, created great trusts which achieved their purpose of restricting competition so effectively as to arouse a storm of protest. 'A small number of men', wrote that vigorous opponent of trusts Henry Demarest Lloyd, in 1894, 'are obtaining the power to forbid any but themselves to supply the people with fire in nearly every form known to modern life and industry, from matches to locomotives and electricity.' Liberal fears were partly economic but they were even more political—the fear that America was creating organisations so rich as to be able to corrupt all politics and destroy forever the foundations of a free society. The Sherman anti-Trust Act of 1890 attempted to halt the movement, but little had been done when Roosevelt came to power in 1900. Even Roosevelt's caution was caricatured by Mr Dooley: 'The thrusts', says he, 'are heejous monsthers—on wan hand I would stamp them undher fut; on th'other hand, not so fast.'

Fluctuations in sales and profits brought about amalgamations that were principally of the 'horizontal' type, that is, between firms which sold the same or similar products. Simultaneously technology suggested amalgamations of a 'vertical' kind. By the 1870's Bolckow Vaughan of Middlesbrough owned a dozen collieries, ore mines in Spain and Africa, and a fleet of steamers, employed 10,000 men and were moving from iron into steel manufacturing. This move to secure raw-material supplies was everywhere characteristic of industries which demanded a smooth 'flow' of production. Chemical manufacturers secured their supplies of alkali by buying salt deposits, pottery manufacturers went into china-clay mining, soap-makers operated vegetable-oil mills.

Both types of expansion needed larger capital resources than those available from partnerships or family relationships. In 1875 *The Times* city column was still entitled 'Stocks, Railway and Other Shares'. The 'others' comprised a few telegraph companies and half a dozen industrial concerns. By 1900 they had been joined by South African mines, fourteen large breweries, seven iron and steel firms, chemicals, textiles, and the great London stores and multiple grocery chains. Thus the trade cycle and technology combined to generate size in industry; size demanded capital, capital demanded security, and security demanded combination. Manufacturers were often still genuine believers in a free economy and individualism: but the economies of size could not be ignored. This was to be the recurrent paradox: that competition was always killing competition.

From an early stage, German industry had demonstrated authoritarian and 'collective' tendencies quite unlike the atomistic improvisatory method of Britain, where the fathers of the industrial revolution had been tinkerers like Arkwright and Cartwright. Industrial organisation was profoundly affected by the problems of obtaining capital in a country where wealth was thinly spread. Entrepreneurs in heavy industry had necessarily from the start looked to the banks, and the banks had played an increasing role in the formation of companies after 1870. The joint-stock bank was not merely a credit organisation but a politico-economic agency for converting Germany into an industrial state. Speculative advances of capital were made to the iron and steel industries in the 1880's. Between 1894 and 1900 the Essen *Kreditanstalt* trebled its capital in order to advance capital to the surrounding mining and metal industries. Many of the banks created in the 1870's and 1880's—the Deutsche, Dresdener, and the Reichsbank—performed such functions. This form of financial organisation did not encourage the maximum of competition that economists in Britain and British businessmen (in theory at least) regarded as the healthy norm of an industrial system. The banks appointed directors of industry who could influence its policy, and sometimes even the price of its shares through sales from the banks' portfolios. They themselves were simultaneously undergoing a steady process of amalgamation. The system offered considerable scope for government intervention and control. Nor did German economists in general object to its implications. Capitalist association, from informal agreement on prices via the *Kartell* to the fully integrated *Konzern*, was regarded not as an aberration but as a phenomenon resulting from the normal flow of economic development towards monopoly. Its justification lay in the greater stability it provided against the fluctuations of profits and employment.

Not only goods but services were affected by the trend towards collective self-help. If the nature of an industrial society made trade unionism more necessary, it also made it easier to organise. Men who worked in pits and factories were more likely to feel a community of interest and realise it than men scattered in cottages or small workshops. But there were two conditions of trade-union development. The first was that public opinion, political authority and the law should look favourably on the claim of labour to organise and enforce its rights. Secondly, that the labour force should be a stable body of wage-earners conscious of the permanent status of wage labour. In most countries one or both of these conditions was absent. In France, the restrictions on labour associations were not withdrawn until 1884 and the *Confédération Générale du Travail*, formed in 1895, did nothing to make its doctrines of direct action effective until the next century. Belgium had allowed unions from 1866, but continued to penalise strikers. In Germany, unionism made progress between 1868 and 1875, but after Bismarck declared war on the 'Social Peril' in 1878 more than a hundred unions were suppressed. The bait offered in return was insurance against sickness, accident, incapacity and old age, and politically it was not unsuccessful. The problem in the United States was different: a high degree of mobility, social and geographical, among the workers. If a man did not move up, he could always move out. Such conditions did not make for stable unions. The early, idealistic unions all fell on evil days. Even the Federation of Labour had only about half a million members in 1900. Against these hesitant beginnings the achievement of British labour was impressive. Disraeli's Act of 1875 put an end to the legal doubts of half a century and legalised collective bargaining and its incidents. The 1870's saw vigorous action—both the so-called 'prosperity strikes' of 1871 and the strikes against wage reductions of 1873 and 1875. Encouraged by the great dock strike of 1889, unionism forged ahead in the 1890's, penetrating and organising the labour employed in whole industries instead of merely crafts. By 1900 membership passed the two million mark. It made its strength felt by stoppages and strikes; in 1893 over 30 million days' work was lost. Some large unions, like the Amalgamated Society of Engineers, found themselves faced by countervailing organisations of employers like the Engineering Employers Federation, which fought the bitter battles of 1897–8.

Thus on every side, and in varying degrees, the world of 1900 was slipping away from *laissez-faire* towards collective or state interference. Even allowing that *laissez-faire* had always been in some sense a *Civitas Dei* of the economists whose ideas of perfect freedom and competition had been but dimly reflected in the *Civitas terrena* of statesmen, bureaucrats and businessmen, the change since 1870 was a real one. Yet it is doubtful whether more than a handful of thinkers pondered the larger changes in the economic nature of things. Even those who were paid to think and write on such matters were hardly yet trend-minded. For most people, economic issues were something immediate, to be treated empirically. In Britain, as the century ended, war in South Africa seemed to most people more important than economic prophecy. Gold was coming into the bank, the money market looked more hopeful. In Germany, trade was very satisfactory. There was a shortage of coal wagons. America was prosperous. The Victorians brooded less on economic matters than on many other things and the ending of the most revolutionary century known to mankind provoked few thoughts more profound than these: 'Trade was never better, wages were never so good, nor were there ever fewer workmen unemployed.' So wrote *The Times* on 30 December 1899.

CHAPTER III

SCIENCE AND TECHNOLOGY

SCIENCE and technology were far more closely related between 1870 and 1900 than in any earlier period. In the last three decades of the nineteenth century there were few branches of industry that were not affected by new scientific discoveries, although this is by no means the same as saying that traditional empirical methods were entirely or even largely ousted. Empiricism remained dominant in many industries; in some it remains so to the present day; but after 1870 we can clearly see the beginnings of the scientific industry of the twentieth century. The changed outlook is naturally more apparent in the new industries—such as the electrical industry—that originated wholly in scientific discovery than in those, already long established, in which the application of science resulted to a great extent in improving old processes rather than in creating quite new ones.

While the close relationship between science and technology within this period is evident, it is in many instances exceedingly difficult to distinguish cause from effect. Sometimes a purely scientific discovery, resulting from research with no practical objective in mind, was of such obvious practical importance that its commercial development followed almost as a matter of course. The development of the dyestuffs industry was a conspicuous example: the first coal-tar dye was the result of an unsuccessful—and, as we now know, wholly misguided—attempt to synthesise quinine. Other scientific discoveries, however, became significant primarily because contemporary conditions favoured their application; in different circumstances their historical significance might have been slight, or have been apparent at a much later date. For example, the widespread introduction of the steam-turbine into ships was not directly due to the need of marine engineers for a different kind of motive power. It was due primarily to the fact that the new electrical generating industry required a steam-engine capable of running very much faster than the reciprocating steam-engine.

While this was a period in which science and technology were jointly changing the course of history, both were also advancing separately. In science this was a fruitful period for what is commonly called pure—as opposed to applied—research and many discoveries were made that contributed to the sum of human knowledge but had no immediate effect on the course of events. Mendeléef, for example, formulated his famous periodic table of the elements in 1869 but the profound significance of this, particularly in relationship to the structure of atoms, was discerned only by a later generation: many of his contemporaries, indeed, received his ideas with the greatest scepticism. Organic compounds of silicon were well known and being closely investigated before the close of the century, but it was the military needs of the second World War that made them of practical importance and introduced the term silicone into common usage.

Just as science could advance on its own, so could technology. The internal combustion engine, destined to revolutionise transport on land, was originally developed almost entirely empirically by practical and determined men who had little or no knowledge of current scientific developments. Equally, the new petroleum industry, essential companion to motor-car manufacture, was built up not by scientists but by men with a talent for improvisation and a keen commercial sense.

Since many technological advances resulted from fundamental scientific research it is appropriate to discuss the main lines of scientific progress before considering the profound changes in industry that occurred at the same time. Although we must in the main consider the period 1870–1900 it will also be necessary to consider some earlier events, for this thirty-year period is not of any particular significance so far as the history of science is concerned. These were very active years in science, but many of the important discoveries stemmed from earlier researches. While technological progress was to a considerable extent shaped by events of historical importance in the world at large, it would be fair to say that science on the whole developed in isolation. This state of affairs continued until well past the turn of the century.

In many branches of physics this was a period of intense activity and it is difficult to single out any particular field of research as being of exceptional historical significance. It would be generally agreed, however, that progress in thermodynamics and in electromagnetic theory was of particular importance for the future development of physics generally.

Although it had excited speculation from the earliest times, the true nature of heat and its relationship to mechanical motion began to be clear little more than a century ago. The caloric theory, which visualised heat as some kind of imponderable fluid, still found adherents in the midst of the nineteenth century, just as in chemistry the phlogiston theory of combustion lingered on long after the researches of Lavoisier and others had demonstrated the true nature of the theory of combustion. Such fundamental concepts as the difference between heat and temperature also took a surprisingly long time to establish. By 1870, however, the important principles had been established that heat is a form of energy and that in all ordinary physical processes energy is conserved—that is, if one form of energy disappears an exactly equivalent amount of another form appears. The theory of the conservation of energy was of as much fundamental importance as the earlier theory of the conservation of mass. Until the end of the nineteenth century physics was based on the assumption that conservation of mass and conservation of energy were two universal but separate laws. The unification of these two theories into one of still more fundamental importance—the conservation of mass/energy—belongs to our own century but, as we shall see, the seeds of this profoundly important generalisation were sown within the period with which we are now concerned.

Clarification of ideas on the nature of heat led to the establishment of the laws of thermodynamics, a subject which broadly speaking concerns itself with the laws governing the conversion of heat into work, and *vice versa*. The first law relates to the conservation of energy. The second, formulated in 1851, states that there is a theoretical limit to the efficiency of any heat engine. The third states, in effect, that the more it is transformed the less heat-energy is available for doing useful work. The derivation of these laws and discussion of their application lies far beyond the scope of a general work such as this, where it must suffice to say that these seemingly simple generalisations have been profoundly useful in studying all kinds of processes involving heat energy in any way, whether they relate to steam-engines or chemical reactions. As a scientific tool their importance was very quickly realised—as for example in Willard Gibbs' (1839–1903) formulation in 1876 of the Phase Rule, an exceedingly important physico-chemical generalisation. But their great technological importance was only gradually recognised.

The researches of Michael Faraday (1791–1867) established the relationship between electricity and magnetism which, among its other important consequences, made possible the establishment of the electrical industry. His laws were, however, established empirically, and it was left to James Clerk Maxwell (1831–79) to make the important further step of expressing Faraday's ideas in terms of mathematical theory, and to establish the quantitative relationship between the basic units of electricity and magnetism. He deduced a theoretical value for the velocity of electromagnetic waves and found that this was approximately the same as the velocity of light. From this it could be concluded that light itself is an electromagnetic phenomenon. Maxwell's work, which appears in its fully developed form in his *Electricity and Magnetism* (1873), was at once accepted in Britain, but it was so far removed from current conceptions that on the Continent it attracted much less attention. Its acceptance there was due in large measure to the brilliant researches of Heinrich Hertz (1857–94), who discovered the electric (radio) waves whose existence Maxwell had deduced as a necessary consequence of his theory. Hertz established the essential similarity of electric and light waves and showed that they travelled, within the accuracy of his experiments, at the same speed. The practical importance of Hertz's work in the present century needs no emphasis. The firm establishment of the wave theory of light, for which Young and Fresnel had advanced strong experimental evidence at the beginning of the century, represented the first break in Newtonian physics.

Controversy about the true nature of light did not hinder the experimental study of its properties. Of these its velocity was of particular interest because this proved, as indicated above, to be a physical constant of great importance in electricity. An accurate knowledge of its value was necessary, for example, for the design of submarine cables. Astronomical methods had been used since 1676, but the first determination over relatively short distances on the Earth was made by A. H. L. Fizeau (1819–96) in 1849. Subsequent determinations led to the famous experiment of Michelson, carried out in 1887. This yielded the unexpected result that the observed velocity is independent of the motion of the source. This experiment was of critical importance for the formulation of the restricted theory of relativity advanced by Einstein in 1905. This led in 1915 to his general theory of relativity, which is at the very foundation of atomic physics.

Newton's well-known experiments with glass prisms had established that sunlight, and virtually all other light normally encountered, is in fact composed of light of several different colours. In the latter half of the nineteenth century the spectroscopic analysis of light was very highly developed and used to give detailed information about the nature of the source emitting the light. Notable pioneers were R. W. von Bunsen (1811–99) and G. R. Kirchhoff (1824–87). Their work made possible the detection of many chemical elements even in exceedingly tiny amounts. This method led to the discovery of two new chemical elements, caesium and rubidium. The most striking results, however, were achieved in the astronomical field, for it was clear that detailed spectroscopic analysis of the light emitted by the sun and stars could give a wealth of information about their chemical composition. In 1878 Sir Joseph Lockyer (1836–1920) observed in the green region of the solar spectrum a line corresponding to no element known to occur on earth. With great confidence he and Sir Edward Frankland (1825–99) predicted the presence in the sun of a new element, which they named helium. Their confidence was strikingly vindicated in 1895 when Sir William Ramsay (1852–1916) discovered helium in the mineral cleveite. Within a few years four other unknown gaseous elements had been discovered.

Spectroscopic astronomy became increasingly important. Among those who made notable contributions was Sir William Huggins (1824–1910) who was a pioneer in the application for astronomical research of the well-known Doppler effect. The latter depends upon the fact that when the source of a wave and an observer are in relative motion the observed frequency is different from when they are stationary, the difference being a measure of the relative velocity. In the case of stars, their movement relative to the earth can thus be measured by precise measurements on their spectra. These measurements greatly increased knowledge of stellar motions and form the basis of modern cosmological theory. In 1885 J. J. Balmer (1825–98) for the first time showed that the frequencies of certain spectral lines (those of hydrogen) had a simple mathematical relationship.

Although atomic physics in its modern sense is essentially a development of the twentieth century, its beginnings can be clearly seen in the latter part of the nineteenth. The critically important Michelson experiment on the velocity of light, for example, has already been mentioned. Equally significant was the discovery of X-rays in 1895 by W. K. Roentgen (1845–1923): apart from their medical importance these rays were subsequently used with great effect to determine the atomic structure of crystals. In the following year A. H. Becquerel (1852–1908) discovered that uranium compounds emitted a penetrating radiation, so laying the foundations of the study of radioactivity. In 1898 the Curies isolated radium from pitchblende.

The three final decades of the nineteenth century were no more a well-defined historical period in biology than they were in physics. They were years of great activity, during which important discoveries were made and new ideas were formulated, but all this stemmed from earlier days and continued without a break into the twentieth century. Two developments were of outstanding importance. The theory of organic evolution, first clearly formulated by Charles Darwin (1809–82) and Alfred Russell Wallace (1823–1913) in 1858, became firmly established—thanks in large measure to the brilliant advocacy of T. H. Huxley (1825–95)—after intense controversy. Although his work remained virtually unknown until 1900, Gregor Mendel (1822–89) had discovered the mechanism by which natural evolution worked. Secondly, the doctrine of vitalism became increasingly unfashionable. According to this doctrine the processes of life are not to be explained in terms of the laws that govern the inanimate universe, but demand the existence of some inexplicable 'vital principle'. The exploration of both these lines of thought naturally brought scientists into direct conflict with the Church. The famous dispute between Bishop Wilberforce and Huxley at the British Association meeting in Oxford in 1860 was by no means an isolated incident.

It is not to be supposed, however, that Darwin's theory of organic evolution by natural selection gained the immediate and unqualified support of the scientific world, even though earlier biologists had done much to prepare men's minds for the new ideas. Among them may be mentioned Étienne Saint-Hilaire, Robert Chambers and, better known, Lamarck. It is an interesting example of the cross-fertilisation of ideas, however, that Darwin's main debt to his predecessors was not to a biologist but to an economist. In his autobiography he recorded that it was Malthus' *Essay on Population* (1798) that gave him his first clear conception of how evolution might work.

It was characteristic of the age that although Darwin first conceived his theory in 1838 he made no attempt to publish it, but devoted the next twenty years of his life to the intensive collection of evidence to support or refute it. Even when, in 1858, he received from Wallace a communication containing the gist of his own theory, he was reluctant to claim priority. Eventually joint publication was arranged through the Linnean Society. Darwin then marshalled his vast collection of evidence in his *Origin of Species*, unquestionably one of the greatest contributions to human thought ever written.

The theory of evolution revolutionised biological thought. It not only gave new significance to the vast amount of existing knowledge, but it provided a logical basis for many new lines of inquiry. Among those who benefited notably were the anthropologists, who were enabled to see some pattern in the distribution of the various races of mankind, and the geologists, for whom was provided a logical interpretation of the fossil record.

The doctrine of vitalism has a natural philosophic appeal and, of course, still finds many adherents. Nevertheless, the latter part of the nineteenth century provided much evidence against it. Growing knowledge of the basic principles of physics and chemistry made it possible to explain many vital processes, such as respiration and digestion, in purely physical terms. Belief in spontaneous generation was exploded, notably by the work of Louis Pasteur (1822–95) in France, and it was demonstrated that certain substances, such as urea, that were characteristic of living organisms, could be made in the laboratory. Ferments, such as those in yeast that convert sugar into alcohol, were proved to be active after separation from the living cells in which they normally exist. The law of the conservation of energy was shown to apply to living beings as well as to inanimate ones. When so much could be explained without recourse to vitalism it seemed logical to suppose that all could be so explained. This inevitably brought further conflict between science and the Church. But it was by no means only on religious thought that the theory of evolution had far-reaching repercussions outside science itself. Philosophic, and thence political, thought was also affected in certain important respects. To some, the ultimate logical deduction from the principle of the survival of the fittest was that the basic moral values are not those that make for survival. Friedrich Nietzsche (1844–1900), for example, denounced religion and looked for the creation of a race of supermen as a result of the forcible self-assertion of the strongest. His championing of the 'morals of masters' is generally agreed to have had a considerable influence on the growth in Germany of the attitude of mind that led her into two world wars.

Advocacy of brute strength and selfishness, the view that mankind and all living beings must be remorselessly 'red in tooth and claw', was one consequence of general interest in evolutionary theory. Precisely the opposite view was also derived from it. Moral instincts, it was argued, make for communal stability and thus promote survival: one consequence of natural selection should therefore be to increase and perpetuate moral instincts in human communities.

While the formulation of the theory of evolution was the greatest feature of nineteenth-century biology and caused intense controversy about man's place in the universe, great progress was made in other fields of biology without much assistance from it. Outstandingly important was the work on micro-organisms in which Pasteur was so notable a pioneer. Clarification of ideas about the growth and function of micro-organisms— in which the improvement of the microscope played an important part— had far-reaching consequences.

Pasteur demonstrated that certain diseases, such as anthrax and silkworm disease, were caused by specific micro-organisms. This paved the way for important medical developments. Joseph Lister (1827–1912) found Pasteur's views complementing his own on the possibility of preventing death from infection in surgery and childbirth. Infections were first prevented from developing by antiseptic techniques—the liberal use of bactericidal substances such as carbolic acid. Later, aseptic techniques were introduced in which infective agents were eliminated by extreme cleanliness. These developments came most opportunely, for the earlier discovery and use of anaesthetics had made possible surgical operations that were hitherto impossible, but the effect of this had to a great extent been nullified by the subsequent high mortality from infection. Anaesthesia, coupled with the extensive use of antiseptic and aseptic techniques, effected a revolution in medical practice. The revolution was not achieved without much opposition. Opposition by the Church to one of the most valuable uses of anaesthesia, namely for the relief of pain in childbirth, had only just died down in 1870. The tide had turned only when chloroform was administered to Queen Victoria by John Snow during the birth of Prince Leopold in 1853. Lister's methods escaped the criticism of the Church, but not of his own colleagues, many of whom derided his ideas. By the end of the century, however, the principles of modern surgery had been firmly established.

Increasing knowledge of the nature of disease had other important practical consequences. By the end of the century most of the important pathogenic bacteria had been identified, as well as some of the disease-causing protozoa. The causal agent of malaria, for example, was discovered in 1880 and seventeen years later Sir Ronald Ross identified the *Anopheles* mosquito as the carrier of the disease. In the hands of masters such as Robert Koch (1843–1910) and Paul Ehrlich (1854–1915) the newly developed aniline dyes proved immensely valuable for the identification of bacteria by differential staining methods. Such staining methods were, incidentally, also of great value in the microscopic examination of a wide range of biological material.

This discovery of the differential affinity of various tissues for dyes led to the foundation of the branch of science known as chemotherapy—the conquest of disease within the body by means of chemical agents that are highly toxic to the invading micro-organisms but harmless to the tissues of the patient. Ehrlich conceived the idea of such a 'magic bullet' that would kill the microbes of diseases but leave the body unharmed. Although no notable success was achieved in this field until the discovery of salvarsan in 1909, the foundations of chemotherapy were laid in the last two decades of the nineteenth century. The modern sulphonamides and antibiotics trace their descent from work done then.

By 1876 it was well known that certain of the effects of pathogenic micro-organisms were due to their production of specific toxins, and by 1888 certain of these toxins had been obtained in a purified state. These developments led to much improvement in the techniques of immunisation. Diphtheria toxin, for example, can be introduced into a horse whose tissues will then produce antitoxin. Serum from the blood of a horse so treated can be used to immunise against diphtheria. Pasteur, again, showed that rabies could be prevented by appropriate inoculation.

Certain aspects of chemical discovery have already been referred to, and this is not surprising in view of its position as the most basic of the sciences. Reference has been made, for example, to the use of the spectroscope in chemical analysis, to the elucidation of the chemical nature of the respiratory process, and to the synthesis of chemotherapeutic agents. The whole of chemistry developed enormously during this time, but undoubtedly the most important progress was in organic chemistry, for here a whole new world was unfolded.

As its name implies, organic chemistry was originally concerned with the wide range of substances that can be obtained from plant or animal material, and originally thought to be obtainable only from these sources. Wöhler's discovery in 1828 that he could prepare urea artificially— 'without requiring a kidney or an animal, either man or dog'—opened a new era, in which, however, the old nomenclature was retained. Virtually all the constituents of living matter are compounds of the element carbon: this is generally associated with only a limited number of the other ninety-one elements that occur in nature, the principal ones being nitrogen, oxygen, hydrogen, sulphur and phosphorus. From being specifically concerned with substances present in biological material, organic chemistry gradually came to include also the rapidly increasing number of purely synthetic compounds of carbon that have no natural counterpart. Organic chemistry became in fact the chemistry of one single element, carbon.

From 1828 onwards a large number of new organic substances were synthesised and clear ideas began to emerge about the way in which these, the atoms of carbon, were disposed relative to each other and to the atoms of the other elements. For some forty years research proceeded steadily and by 1870 most of the important principles of modern organic chemistry had been established. In 1856, however, there occurred an event which profoundly affected the development of chemistry, and of the chemical industry, for the remainder of the century and, indeed, up to the present day. In that year William Perkin (1838–1907) was seeking to synthesise the important drug quinine. Not surprisingly he failed, for he was using a method which we now know could have had no hope of success. He did, however, synthesise mauveine, the first synthetic aniline dye, and thereby both created a new industry and gave a great stimulus to organic chemical research.

As has been remarked, Perkin's discovery of mauveine was accidental. So also was the original synthesis of alizarin by Heinrich Caro (1834–1910): he was called away at a critical moment in an experiment, the mixture overheated, and he returned to find a charred residue which had, however, a pink crust of the dye he was seeking. Much of the organic chemistry of the day was in fact semi-empirical, but such a wealth of new substances lay ready for discovery that the acute observer could reap a rich harvest. At the same time, however, important theoretical progress was being made. Of outstanding importance was the elucidation by Friedrich Kekulé (1829–96) of the structure of benzene. This substance is of the most fundamental importance, for from it derive tens of thousands of different chemical substances, the so-called 'aromatics', such as dyes and drugs. The molecule of benzene is very simple, consisting only of six carbon atoms and six hydrogen atoms. For a long time no arrangement of these twelve atoms was conceived that was consistent with the chemical properties of benzene. It was Kekulé who found the right answer: that the six carbon atoms were arranged not in a straight or branched chain but in a circle. This seemingly trifling suggestion—which now seems obvious—transformed chemical thought in the last half of the nineteenth century.

Another important field of theoretical development was that of stereochemistry. The classic researches of Louis Pasteur (1822–95) had established the fundamentally important fact that certain substances, such as tartaric acid, could exist in two forms that were chemically indistinguishable but nevertheless had important physical differences, especially in their effect on polarised light. This difference was commonly manifested by the fact that a crystal of one form was the mirror-image of a crystal of the other: one type of crystal could be looked upon as a left-hand glove and the other as the right-hand member of the same pair. Such scarcely discernible differences might seem of trifling consequence, but in fact they are profoundly important, especially in the chemistry of vital processes. Thus the human body derives much of its energy from one stereoisomer of the sugar 'glucose': the other stereoisomer cannot be so utilised.

The proper interpretation of Pasteur's discovery was due to the work of two young chemists, J. A. Le Bel (1897–1930) and J. H. Van 't Hoff

(1852–1911). They established that this phenomenon arises from the fact that the atoms that make up molecules are arranged according to a strict geometric pattern, and that the valencies of the carbon atom—that is, the bonds by which it is linked to other atoms—are so directed in space that in certain molecules two geometrically different arrangements are possible for the same group of atoms. Van 't Hoff first published his conclusions in 1874: they were first ignored and then ridiculed. More than a year elapsed before the great German chemist Johannes Wislicenns (1835–1902) saw their great importance and lent his support.

The name of Van 't Hoff is also very intimately associated with another important chemical development, that of the theory of solutions. His experiments on osmosis established the fact that when a solid is dissolved in a liquid its particles behave in much the same way as if they were the particles of a gas occupying the same volume as the solution. By this means it is possible, for example, to explain such important botanical phenomena as the uptake of minerals from the soil and the rise of sap in trees. This conception presented major difficulties, however, when applied to solutions of the important substances known as electrolytes, so-called because their aqueous solutions conduct electricity. Typical of such substances is common salt, sodium chloride. To explain the properties of such substances the Swedish chemist Svante Arrhenius (1859–1927) advanced the revolutionary hypothesis that in solution the molecules of such substances dissociate into what are called ions—that is, electrically charged atoms of the components of the molecule. Thus sodium chloride, he said, exists in solution as positively charged atoms of sodium and negatively charged atoms of chlorine. This brilliant hypothesis Arrhenius incorporated, with great misgivings, in his thesis for his doctorate at Uppsala. His misgivings were well founded: his thesis earned him a fourth-class degree, only a shade better than complete failure. The difficulty, as Arrhenius had foreseen, was that chemists of the day could not appreciate that electrically charged atoms might have properties totally different from neutral ones. Sodium was well known to react most violently with water and the suggestion that any form of sodium atom could exist in the presence of water seemed too ridiculous to be entertained. Not until a copy of the thesis reached Wilhelm Ostwald (1853–1932), professor of chemistry at Riga, did it find a reader discerning and influential enough to ensure its serious consideration. Arrhenius ultimately had an opportunity of working with Ostwald, with Van 't Hoff, and with other great European chemists and of perfecting his theory of ionic dissociation in solution. The collaboration with Van 't Hoff was particularly important, for Arrhenius' theory completely explained the anomalous osmotic pressures of solutions of electrolytes. Nevertheless, many chemists still refused to accept the views of the barbarous 'Ionians'. Not until 1890, some seven years after Ostwald had first championed Arrhenius, may the opposition be said to have been finally routed. The circumstances are worth recalling, as a reminder that science is by no means a cold and logical pursuit but is subject, like all other human activities, to human weaknesses. Arrhenius, Ostwald, and Van 't Hoff were invited to expound their theories to a meeting of the British Association in Leeds in 1890, the confident belief being that they would not stand the force of orthodox opinion and would be discredited. In point of fact, precisely the opposite occurred: the views of the 'Ionians' prevailed.

When turning to technology it is worth while to stress once more that the present tendency to look upon it as being synonymous with applied science is altogether wrong, for many branches of technology were highly developed long before science in its modern sense was born. From the seventeenth century onward, science became increasingly important in industry, but even at the end of the nineteenth century many important processes had changed little, if at all, as a result of scientific discovery. Progress there certainly was, but in the main it was achieved empirically through better design, craftsmanship, and managerial enterprise. Where scientific ideas were adopted, this was often done slowly and grudgingly.

Nevertheless, in certain fields scientific discovery had immediate and dramatic effects, creating new industries where none existed before. Most striking in this respect was the electrical industry, which provided entirely new sources of light, heat, power, and communication. This industry is most conveniently considered under three separate headings: generation, distribution and utilisation. Although this is a rather arbitrary separation —for example, the mode of distribution may be determined by the mode of generation—it at least corresponds to a division of effort and interest that still exists in the industry.

In the present context we are concerned, in the main, with the mechanical generation of electricity as opposed to the much older, but still important, production by chemical changes in batteries. The principles of electro-magnetism were established by Michael Faraday (1791–1867), who showed that an electrical potential is produced when a conductor moves in a magnetic field. Although the first mechanical generators of electricity appeared in Paris as early as 1832, the first apparently being by Hippolyte Pixii, it was many years before generators were sufficiently powerful and reliable for the latent practical possibilities of electricity to be realised. The earliest generators were activated by permanent magnets, and the primary current generated was of what is called the alternating type, that is to say, its direction changed or alternated several times a second. This alternation of the current was at first looked upon with disfavour, prob-ably because all the early workers were more familiar with the direct current produced by batteries, and equipment was designed to rectify it or render it uni-directional. The rectifying equipment was, however, a frequent source of trouble and it was gradually realised that for many purposes alternating current was not only quite as useful as direct current but could have certain technical advantages, especially from the point of view of transmission. Alternating generators were displayed in 1881 at the Paris Exhibition and by the end of the century were in widespread use. Controversy over the relative merits of alternating and direct current raged for a long time and was not finally resolved until after the end of the century. Rather earlier than this, there had been another very important departure from the original designs. This was the introduction of the principle of self-excitation. The permanent magnets of the early machines were replaced by electromagnets activated by diverting part of the electricity generated by the machine itself.

The large-scale generation of electricity, whether direct or alternating, was firmly established by the 1880's. The Edison Company's power station at Holborn Viaduct, which came into operation in 1882, was the first to supply private customers. Within a few years a host of power stations had been established, many of them designed to supply one or a few large customers—for example, local authorities, for street-lighting—but also selling to private customers. In the main, these were designed for purely local supply. Among the first to realise that the future of the electrical generating industry lay in much bigger power stations, designed to supply large areas, was Ziani de Ferranti (1864–1930), whose design for the Deptford generating plant was far in advance of its time. This came into full operation in 1891. Most of the early power stations were steam-driven; one of the first big hydro-electric schemes was that at Niagara Falls, begun in 1893.

The development of the electrical generating industry was greatly influenced by the growing problems of distribution to the growing number of consumers. It was this consideration that finally led to the replacement in large measure of direct by alternating current. Transmission losses are much less at high voltages than at low and it is technically easier to generate high-voltage alternating current than high-voltage direct current. High-voltage alternating current can be reduced to the low voltage required for many practical applications by means of the simple non-mechanical devices known as transformers. These came into general use in the power industry in the 1880's. The distribution of large quantities of electricity at high voltages presented many problems in cable design, especially from the point of view of insulation. For the Deptford power station Ferranti introduced the coaxial copper tube.

Among the earliest important applications of electricity was for lighting, especially in lighthouses, where a very bright source was important. Here the most important development was the arc-light, in which an electric spark is struck between two electrodes. Arc-lights were installed in the South Foreland lighthouse in 1858 and at Dungeness four years later.

Even the smallest arc-lamps were too powerful for domestic use, but they were soon widely used for larger installations. Electric lighting was introduced into a mill at Mülhausen in 1875 and a year later was in use at La Chapelle station in France. The first English installation was at the Gaiety Theatre in 1878.

Electric lighting became widespread following the introduction of the incandescent filament lamp, in the early development of which Joseph Swan (1828–1914) and Thomas Edison (1847–1931) were particularly active. The availability of this simple, cheap, and effective source of light rapidly led to the widespread introduction of electric lighting. As early as 1880 Edison was manufacturing at the rate of 5000 lamps per month. Within a very few years, incandescent filament lamps were being widely used in buildings of every type and size. Electric lighting was much superior to gas lighting, which in its day had been so revolutionary, as long as this depended upon fish-tail and similar burners. Gas lighting became competitive again with the introduction of the Welsbach incandescent mantle in 1886.

The electric motor is essentially an electrical generator working in reverse. Although Faraday demonstrated its principle as early as 1821, the first electric motor of practical significance came on the market only in 1873. This was a direct-current machine: alternating-current motors were not available until 1888. The motor found early application for traction. The first electric railway was demonstrated in 1879 in Berlin, and the first electrified London underground railway was built in 1887–90. In 1895 the first main-line railway conversion from steam to electricity took place: this very significant innovation was on the Baltimore and Ohio Railroad. The use of electric traction on the roads depended—except for trams— upon the development of electrical storage batteries, or accumulators, which alone could supply, independently of external connections, the necessary heavy current. The Planté accumulator appeared about 1880 and an electric-tricycle appeared in 1882. A fleet of electric taxi-cabs appeared briefly on London streets between 1897 and 1899 and a variety of electric carriages appeared in the last decade of the century. The limitations of electric storage-batteries severely limited their use, however, and still do.

Technologically the most important application of the electric motor— and perhaps of electricity generally—is in its use as a small, powerful, and mobile power unit for use in the factory. Although the beginning of this application is just discernible at the very end of the nineteenth century, it is in the main a twentieth-century development and as such does not further concern us here. Electric telegraphy and telephony are conveniently considered at this point, although their consumption of electricity is relatively small. The exceptional importance of speedy communication needs no stressing now, and was generally appreciated by 1870. The first telegraph line, between Paddington and West Drayton, had been established in 1839 and by 1870 an extensive network of telegraphic communications existed. Important developments had been the use of rubber as an insulating material for wires, the introduction of relay systems for communication over long distances, and the building of telegraph exchanges. Telegraphic communication between the Old World and the New was first established in 1858, but a satisfactory cable was not laid until 1865. Electric telephony was first demonstrated in 1861, but the introduction of the telephone as a practical instrument was due to Alexander Graham Bell (1847–1922), whose first patent was filed in 1876. Commercial telephony was established in Britain in 1878 and London had its first telephone exchange in the following year. Practical wireless telegraphy was a twentieth-century development, but the basic experiments were carried out before 1900. Heinrich Hertz (1857–94) demonstrated the principle as early as 1887. By 1895 Guglielmo Marconi (1874–1937) had sent and received messages over a distance of a mile, and by 1901 he had bridged the Atlantic: Marconi's Wireless Telegraph Company was founded in 1897.

The electrical industry was directly linked with the chemical industry, at this time expanding rapidly. Some of the chemical effects of electricity had long been known: for example, in 1807 Humphry Davy isolated sodium by the electrolysis of fused caustic soda. The industrial utilisation of these effects had to await the availability of cheap, regular and abundant supplies of electricity. Once this condition was fulfilled, the electrochemical industry grew rapidly. The availability of electricity was the direct cause of the rapid commercial exploitation of a metal, aluminium, that had been known for a great many years but had previously been too expensive for its many valuable properties to be effectively utilised. In the middle years of the nineteenth century aluminium was made by a process involving the reduction of aluminium chloride with sodium, but the high price of sodium and the general difficulties of operating the process made the resulting aluminium so expensive that it could be used only for luxury goods. In the 1880's H. Y. Castner (1858–99) devised a cheaper method for the manufacture of sodium which made commercial aluminium production a feasibility, and a factory for the purpose was established in Birmingham. Almost at once, however, Castner's process was made obsolete by an electrolytic one developed independently in 1886 by C. M. Hall (1863–1914) in America, and by P. L. T. Héroult (1863–1914) in France. In this new process aluminium was made by the electrolysis of bauxite, the commonly occurring oxide of aluminium, dissolved in molten cryolite. Within a very few years aluminium, which for so long had been little more than a scientific curiosity, came into extensive use. The electrical industry and the chemical industry between them together were responsible for making available the first new constructional metal for many years.

As has been mentioned, Castner's process for the manufacture of aluminium became obsolete almost as it was established. The consequence to him at first appeared to be almost fatal, for his sole asset was a cheap method of manufacturing sodium and the necessary market for this had gone. However, he very quickly devised chemical processes to utilise the sodium. Among his products was sodium cyanide, which found a large market in the developing gold fields, in Australia, America, South Africa, and elsewhere. He was so successful in these operations that in a short time he had to extend his sodium-manufacturing capacity. In doing this he turned his attention to manufacture by electrochemical process, and in particular by the electrolysis of fused sodium hydroxide. He found, however, that the best sodium hydroxide that he could buy commercially at that time contained so much impurity as to make the process he finally devised unworkable. Accordingly he set about devising a process for the manufacture of practically pure sodium hydroxide, by the electrolysis of brine. As a result he was able both to meet his own needs and to put on the market sodium hydroxide of almost 100 per cent purity, a product then almost unknown in the alkaline trade. Caustic soda, much stronger than the ordinary domestic variety, is required for many industrial purposes, especially for soap-making. As a by-product of this manufacture large quantities of chlorine were produced, and this was converted into bleaching powder for which the textile industry, among others, had a large demand. The success of the electrolytic process for the manufacture of caustic soda led to its being worked in the United States, and in 1896 a works was built at Niagara, where abundant cheap electricity was available as a result of the big hydro-electric scheme that had been established three years earlier.

These and other electrochemical developments were, however, only some of the big technological changes that took place in the chemical industry in the last three decades of the nineteenth century. Of outstanding importance were the new methods for the manufacture of soda and sulphuric acid, both products of very great industrial importance. For very many years soda had been almost exclusively manufactured, from salt, by the Leblanc process. This had a number of inherent disadvantages. In particular, it was dirty, giving rise to vast quantities of offensive waste whose disposal was difficult: it produced clouds of hydrochloric acid gas: and it required large quantities of fuel. While noteworthy improvements were made in the process, especially in recovering chlorine from the hydrochloric acid and converting it into bleaching powder, increasing attention was paid to an alternative process, called the ammonia-soda process. This, too, started from salt as the basic raw material, but used ammonia as an intermediary. Although very simple in principle, the perfection of the process as a commercial proposition took many years. The first attempts were made in the 1830's, but it was not until 1861 that a

Belgian chemist, Ernest Solvay (1838–1922) lodged the patent on which subsequent industrial operations were built. Even so, it was not until 1867 that the first factory, at Couillet, was working satisfactorily. Further key patents were lodged in 1872. In that year Ludwig Mond (1829–1909) and John Brunner (1842–1919) acquired the British rights and established ammonia-soda works at Winnington, on the Cheshire salt field. Very soon the process was being worked in the United States, Russia, Germany, Austria, Hungary, Spain, Italy and Canada. From then on the fate of the Leblanc process was sealed, though it survived until well into the twentieth century. In 1902 world production of soda was 1,800,000 tons, and of this no less than 1,650,000 tons were made by the Solvay process.

During the last decades of the nineteenth century another very old-established industrial chemical process found its first serious rival. Hitherto sulphuric acid had been manufactured by the lead-chamber process. The process was considerably improved during the nineteenth century, but no fundamental changes were made. As early as 1831 Peregrine Phillips, a Bristol vinegar manufacturer, had lodged a patent for an alternative, and simpler, process. In this, sulphur dioxide was converted directly to sulphur trioxide through the intermediary of a substance, itself unchanged in the operation, known as a catalyst. The resulting sulphur trioxide could be converted into sulphuric acid by direct reaction with water. Not until 1870, however, were all the technical difficulties of the process overcome. A factory for working it was established at Silvertown, and this had a capacity which eventually rose to 1000 tons per week. Within a few years plants for manufacturing sulphuric acid by the contact process had been established in many parts of the world. The rapid expansion of the dyestuffs industry gave a great stimulus because the contact process was able to manufacture a much stronger grade of sulphuric acid than could be obtained by the lead-chamber process. This high-grade sulphuric acid, known as oleum, had previously been obtainable virtually only from works in Bohemia, where it was made from a particular form of local slate, and its cost was very high. The contact process for making sulphuric acid did not kill the older lead-chamber process in the same way as the ammonia-soda process eventually killed the Leblanc, for the two processes were worked side by side.

During this time very large quantities of sulphuric acid were required for the rapidly expanding fertiliser industry, and it was particularly required for the manufacture of superphosphate. Superphosphate was made by treating bones, or later mineral phosphates, with sulphuric acid. Manufacture was first undertaken near Dublin by James Murray (1788–1871) in the early years of the nineteenth century, but it was not until 1843 that John Bennet Lawes (1814–1900) established the first really large superphosphate factory. This was situated near London, and by the 1870's its production was about 40,000 tons annually.

Phosphorus is, of course, only one of the elements required by plants. Another essential element is nitrogen. During the period with which we are here concerned the most important source of this was Chile, where sodium nitrate occurs naturally as caliche. In 1900 world consumption of sodium nitrate was 1,350,000 tons, by far the greater part of it going to the agricultural industry. A third essential element for plants is potassium. Up to approximately 1870 the main source of potassium salts for fertilisers and for manufacturing purposes was the ash of plants. Wood-ash manufacture was particularly important in Canada. In 1871 there were over 500 asheries there, consuming well over 4 million tons of wood a year. By the end of the century, however, the Canadian industry was virtually extinguished owing to the working of the vast natural deposits of potassium salts at Stassfurt.

Earlier mention of the need for oleum for dyestuffs manufacture is an indication of another exceedingly important technological change that took place in the latter part of the nineteenth century. Previously, and indeed up to 1860, almost all dyes used in the textile trade were of natural origin. By the end of the century synthetic dyestuffs had become of very great importance. This revolutionary change dates from 1856 when William Perkin discovered the first aniline dyestuff, mauveine. He soon established its manufacture in Britain, and within a very few years a wide range of other synthetic dyestuffs was available. Some of these new dyes were completely novel, others were synthetic versions of the natural dyes which had been used for many centuries. Among the latter, two discoveries are of particular interest. In 1869 Perkin in England and Heinrich Caro (1834–1910) in Germany almost simultaneously lodged patents for the manufacture of alizarin, the dye present in madder. This development had immediate disastrous effects on the madder industry. Similarly, the manufacture of synthetic indigo, first put on the market in 1897, almost overnight put an end to the indigo plantations in India, where some 200,000 acres of land were then devoted to the crop.

More important, perhaps, than these synthetic versions of natural dyestuffs were the vast range of new synthetic dyes suitable for dying both wool and cotton. The introduction of these had a profound effect on the textile industry generally. Although the synthetic dyestuff industry had its beginning in Great Britain, there very soon began a drift towards Germany, and by the end of the century the German dyestuff industry had secured a dominating position. This was, however, only one example of the rise of German industry at the end of the nineteenth century; others are referred to elsewhere.

Another important new branch of the chemical industry was that concerned with the manufacture of what are now called high-explosives. The highly explosive properties of nitro-glycerine were discovered as early as 1845, but it was many years before safe means of handling this valuable substance were worked out. A pioneer in this field was Alfred Nobel (1833–96), who in the 1860's invented dynamite, a mixture of nitro-glycerine and a fine mineral substance known as kieselguhr. Blasting gelatine came into use in the 1880's. The introduction of safe forms of these very powerful explosives naturally had far-reaching effects in the mining and civil engineering fields. The military consequences were also of very great importance, and the introduction of nitro-glycerine resulted in a complete revolution in all kinds of armaments both on land and at sea. For use as a propellant the two most important forms of nitro-glycerine during this time were ballistite and cordite. In addition to nitro-glycerine one other new high explosive was introduced before the end of the century. This was picric acid, made by the action of nitric acid on phenol. Its suitability for filling shells was demonstrated in 1886.

The electrical and chemical industries have been dealt with at some length because one was a completely new industry and the other underwent revolutionary change during the period in question. Both, moreover, had far-reaching consequences in other branches of technology. At the same time, however, many of the old-established industries showed important changes, many of them resulting from the application of scientific knowledge and scientific method. The metal industry, for example, to which some passing reference has already been made, showed important changes, both in methods of extraction and in methods of working. The introduction of aluminium as a completely new constructional metal was an event of the first importance. In almost all metallurgical processes the first necessary stage is to concentrate the original ore in order to remove unwanted impurities. This process naturally became of increasing importance as the richest and most easily accessible ores were exhausted, and ores of lower quality had of necessity to be used. Three important new processes of ore concentration were introduced. In 1895 the Wilfley process was introduced for concentrating ground ores by agitation in water on a sloping table fitted with riffles. Flotation separation processes, in which the finely ground ore is agitated with a mixture of oil and water, were first suggested in 1860 and commercial operation began at the turn of the century. Both these processes are of the most fundamental importance in modern mining. A third important concentration process resulted from the ready availability of electricity. This is the process of magnetic separation, in which the ground ore is passed between the poles of a powerful electro-magnet.

During this period the demand for copper increased considerably, because its exceptional conducting qualities made it particularly desirable for electrical applications. In the main, the production of copper followed traditional lines, but there was one very important innovation. This was the introduction of methods of electrolytic refining, again a development made possible only as electricity became generally available. Only the purest forms of copper exhibit the desired electrical properties and this highly pure form could easily be obtained only by electrolytic methods. The first electrolytic refinery was established in 1869 in South Wales. Electrolytic refining of copper was introduced on the American continent in 1892.

Another metal that assumed greatly increased importance was nickel. The demand for the metal had been growing slowly since the beginning of the century, but in 1889 it was demonstrated that the addition of nickel greatly increased the toughness of steel, and very soon large quantities of the metal were being used for this purpose. In 1893 an improved process, known as the Orford 'tops and bottoms' process, was announced. The metal resulting from the Orford process was cast into ingots which were used as the anode in a further electrolytic process that gave an exceptionally pure product. In 1890 a completely new process for the extraction of nickel was described by Ludwig Mond. In this the metal was converted into a volatile substance known as nickel carbonyl, which could be decomposed to yield the metal by further heating. By the end of the century the Mond process had been firmly established commercially. The increased importance of nickel caused attention to be directed towards new sources of supply of ore. In 1883 vast deposits were discovered at Sudbury (Ontario) during the construction of the Canadian Pacific Railway: these were on a scale to alleviate all anxiety for many years to come.

The ability of zinc to prevent the rusting of exposed ironwork led to greatly increased production of the metal at the end of the century for galvanising purposes. In 1860 a process was devised for the continuous galvanising of iron wire, and vast quantities of galvanised iron wire were sent to the newly developing territories abroad. Barbed wire was introduced in the United States about 1880, but was not generally accepted in Europe until some years later.

In the working of metals the most striking changes were in the increased mechanisation and, in many branches of the metal industry, in the size of ingots being handled. The increasing power of mechanisation is strikingly indicated by the fact that Nasmyth's original steam-hammer was introduced in 1842: by 1887 a 4000-ton hydraulic press for forging steel ingots had been installed at Sheffield. In the working of copper, plates weighing more than 2 tons were being rolled by 1873.

The increased demand for wire for fencing, for the cables of suspension bridges, and so on, was further stimulated by the rapid extension of electric telegraph systems and of electricity-distribution systems. The first telegraph cables were of iron, but for all electrical work copper very soon began to be almost exclusively used. Wire-making by drawing through a die had been practised for many years, but in 1875 multi-block machines began to appear. To increase output, drawing speeds were increased, and by 1890 speeds of 1000 feet a minute were being achieved.

We have hitherto considered the non-ferrous metals, for the change in the iron and steel industry during this period was so profound as to deserve separate mention. In 1850 Britain, who at that time was the world's greatest producer of ferrous metals, manufactured about $2\frac{1}{2}$ million tons of iron, but no more than 60,000 tons of steel. By 1900 some 28 million tons of steel were being manufactured annually in the world as a whole and the U.S.A. had replaced Great Britain as the principal producer. During this time steel replaced wrought and cast iron for a great many constructional purposes. The principal reason for this development was the discovery that pig-iron could be converted into steel by blowing air through it while it was in the molten state. The technical history of this development is a complicated one, and too detailed and controversial to enter into here, where it must suffice to say that the pioneer worker was Henry Bessemer (1813–98), whose process is known throughout the world. Bessemer converters were built in many countries from the 1860's.

A different process, but one which achieved the same result, was devised by Frederick Siemens (1826–1904). With Siemens was subsequently associated the French steelmaker, Pierre Martin. The Siemens–Martin process became widely adopted, and by the turn of the century was probably more generally used than Bessemer's. Both the Bessemer and the open-hearth process suffered from the fundamental disadvantage, however, that they could not be used with ores containing phosphorus. This was not a matter of very great consequence to Britain, who had large deposits of non-phosphoric ores, but it was a grave disadvantage on the Continent, especially in Belgium, France and Germany. The solution to this problem was found by Sidney Gilchrist Thomas (1850–85) in 1875, although it was some years before his invention was generally adopted. The principle of Thomas' invention was to line the converter with a basic substance made by calcining dolomite. When the lining had become saturated with phosphorus, it was removed and could subsequently be used as a valuable fertiliser. This invention greatly stimulated the German steel industry, which from 1871 had taken over the rich iron-ores of Lorraine. These ores contained much phosphorus and were of little value to Germany until the introduction of the basic process.

Among the many factors that stimulated the steel industry in the last half of the nineteenth century was the enormous extension of the world's railway systems. Up to about 1880 rails were mostly made of iron, but from that time onwards steel rails began to be widely introduced, for they had the great advantage of lasting fifteen to twenty times as long as iron rails. Steel was also increasingly used for many other purposes. Steel plates began to be used for boilers about 1860. Bessemer steel was quickly adopted by shipbuilders and the first steel ship crossed the Atlantic in 1863. Despite its advantages to the shipbuilder, however, a decisive move away from iron ships to steel cannot be discerned before about 1890.

Steel became a constructional material of the first importance. The first bridge constructed entirely of steel was laid across the Firth of Forth in 1883–90. The Eiffel Tower, erected in 1889, was constructed from open-hearth steel made in France. The tall buildings of which American engineers were pioneers were also made largely of steel by the end of the century. An outstandingly important development occurred in 1885, when the Mannesmann process for making seamless steel tubes was introduced.

The enormous increase in steel production was of great importance in the armament industry. By 1861 it had proved possible to roll wrought-iron sheets a foot thick, but even this was inadequate against the high-explosive missiles made possible by the mastery of nitro-glycerine. By 1892 the Royal Navy had adopted steel sheets for armour-plating, and at the turn of the century steel plates of very substantial size were being rolled. At the Krupp works in Germany, for example, steel sheets 12 inches thick and weighing 130 tons could be made.

Some aspects of technological change in connection with transport—for example, the introduction of steel rails and the substitution of steel ships for iron ones—have already been referred to. These were only part of a continuing revolution in transport on both land and sea. On sea, a new type of steam-engine appeared. In 1897 Sir Charles Parsons (1854–1931) created a sensation at the naval review at Spithead with the *Turbinia*, the first ship ever to be propelled by a steam-turbine. It achieved a speed of $34\frac{1}{2}$ knots, then a record speed on water. Curiously enough, Parsons' original interest in the steam-turbine was not in connection with marine propulsion at all. His basic interest was in the then rapidly growing electrical industry in which he saw an urgent need for a steam-engine capable of running at substantially higher speeds than was possible with the conventional reciprocating engine. His first turbo-generator was built in 1884, and by the end of the century the steam-turbine had become established as the most satisfactory form of steam-engine for electrical generation. On the railways, which had established a decisive victory over the canals, the steam-engine was pre-eminent, and had as yet scarcely felt the challenge of electrical and diesel traction. The seeds of effective competition from road transport had, however, been effectively sown by the end of the century. Satisfactory petrol and diesel engines had been constructed by 1900 and, although motor-cars and motor-lorries were still sufficiently rare to excite attention, almost all the essentials of modern vehicles had appeared. It is fair to say that the automobile engineer of 1900 would see few novel features in the cars of today, although he would, of course, see very great changes in design and constructional materials.

Although the demands of road vehicles for oil and petrol were quite small even up to 1900, the petroleum industry was nevertheless very firmly established during this time, for certain of its products were required in substantial quantity for other purposes. The volatile fractions of petroleum were in little demand, but the higher fractions, known as paraffin or kerosene, were used in large quantities for both heating and lighting. Paraffin stoves first became generally known through the great Paris Exhibition of 1878, and within the next decade over half a million were sold. By the end of the century oil was being used extensively for firing ships' boilers, and paraffin-burning lamps were used almost throughout the world. The widespread use of machinery of all kinds led to a great demand for lubricants, many of which were based on mineral petroleum.

The existence of natural petroleum had been known for a great many years, and indeed bitumen was known in ancient Mesopotamia. The modern petroleum industry dates, however, from 1857, when oil-wells were drilled in Hanover. The real centre of the petroleum industry was, however, in the United States, where in 1859 oil was struck at a depth of 70 feet in Pennsylvania. That these oil-wells could be drilled, however, depended upon earlier technological progress in other fields. Although deep drilling had been used in China for centuries, it was not widely used in Europe or in North America until the nineteenth century. The original incentive to improve techniques was the need for water for agricultural purposes and for brine for the chemical industry. The original North American oil-wells were drilled with wrought-iron bits having steel cutting-edges, and the equipment was driven by steam-engines. In 1864, however, a very great improvement resulted from the introduction of diamond-drilling, and as a result, boring to depths of the order of 7000 feet had been achieved by the end of the century. Early methods of refining petroleum were crude and inefficient. The manufacturers were interested primarily in the medium-volatile fraction, paraffin or kerosene. The lighter fraction, known as gasoline or petrol, was dangerously inflammable and until the advent of the petrol-engine was largely allowed to run to waste. Almost until the end of the century, transportation was mainly in wooden barrels or iron drums. Tanker ships and railway tank-cars began to appear about 1870.

An industry greatly affected by the changes in road-transport was the rubber industry, the insulating properties of whose product also made it of great importance to the electrical industry. It was, however, the demand for rubber tyres, first solid and then pneumatic, that led to the expansion of the rubber industry into the vast organisation that exists today. Pneumatic tyres were first used on automobiles in 1895, but before this they were very widely fitted to bicycles, which became widely popular from about 1885. The first Dunlop pneumatic tyre was manufactured in 1900.

Originally the rubber industry made use of wild rubber obtained principally from South America, but even before the advent of the tyre industry this source of supply was proving inadequate. As early as the middle of the century, plans had been put forward for establishing rubber plantations, but it was not until 1870 that such plans began to receive official consideration. In 1873 the India Office obtained *Hevea* seeds from South America and tried to establish plants in Calcutta, but the project was unsuccessful. In 1876 another attempt was made, and this time a considerable proportion of the young plants grew to maturity. From this small beginning arose the now vast plantation rubber industry. By the end of the century substantial quantities of plantation rubber were being offered on the London and other international markets.

In the textile industry one extremely important innovation, the widespread introduction of synthetic dyestuffs, has already been considered in connection with the chemical industry. Although the textile industry was a relatively conservative one, many other changes took place in it during the last three decades of the nineteenth century. In the main, it is fair to describe these as being a tendency towards more and more mechanisation. Almost all the basic processes underwent some considerable improvement. Perhaps the greatest single innovation was the automatic loom, which was devised in America by J. H. Northrop in 1890–4. This was, however, only one example of the application of mechanical methods to weaving. This period saw the triumph of the power-loom over the hand-loom, and the old-fashioned dobbie underwent very great changes. Changing social circumstances created a big demand for floor-covering of all kinds—linoleum was one of the products of the time—and this led to much mechanisation in the carpet industry. The royal Axminster power-loom was developed in the United States in 1876, and was introduced into Britain two years later. The widespread availability of cheap sewing-machines heralded the beginning of the ready-made-clothing industry, and also resulted in the first invasion of the ordinary household by precision machinery. In spinning, the period was marked by a decisive change towards the ring-spinning method which is now so extensively used. Although this method was invented in the United States in 1828, it was not until 1870 that it was widely adopted in the British textile industry. By contrast, the hosiery industry adopted mechanisation rather slowly; even in 1870 most hosiery was made by hand or at least on hand-driven machines. Thereafter mechanisation became increasingly common. An important development occurred in 1890 when an American inventor, R. W. Scott, introduced a knitting-machine which completely made a stocking save for a small seam across the toe.

The great changes of the nineteenth century, and the steadily increasing proportion of literacy in the population, naturally fostered a greatly increased demand for printed matter of all kinds. There were no very great changes in the method of book-production, but there was a tremendous development in methods of producing newspapers, periodicals, and other literature of a cheap and relatively ephemeral kind. The greatly increased demand for newspapers and similar publications demanded extensive mechanisation in order to accelerate and cheapen production. In this field *The Times* newspaper played a leading role. Bruce's type-casting-machine appeared in 1850, but the first really successful machine of this kind was *The Times* rotary caster, patented by Frederick Wicks in 1881. This was capable of casting 60,000 characters an hour, making it unnecessary to break up the type after printing; the type was simply returned to the foundry, melted, and recast. Mechanical type-composing presented an insoluble problem to inventors for a great many years. Between 1822 and 1890 many were designed, but none was wholly satisfactory until the advent of the Linotype machine. This American invention was remarkable in that it required only one operator. The Linotype machine appeared in 1890 and in 1900 was in use all over the world. In London, for example, a score of dailies, and 250 newspapers and periodicals elsewhere, were being set with Linotype machines.

In the realm of printing machines the great development was that of the rotary printing press, which enormously speeded the work. The incentive towards designing satisfactory machines of this kind was greatly increased after 1855 when the newspaper tax was abolished in Britain. As early as 1846, however, a successful rotary press had been devised. The *Philadelphia Enquirer* was printed by a rotary machine in 1865, designed by William Bullock. *The Times* was being printed on a rotary press, the famous Walter press, in 1868. Two years later mechanical cutting and folding of newspapers began.

The mass-production of literature for popular reading made demands on the illustrator. At the beginning of our period wooden blocks were still extensively used, but in 1880 metal blocks began to appear for line drawings; the *Daily Telegraph* used them as early as 1881. The use of half-tone blocks to reproduce photographs dates from 1877, when they were invented in Vienna: in the 1880's they began to be extensively used in newspapers. By 1900 they were common throughout the world. The principles of reproducing illustrations in colour had been established early in the century, but it was not until 1870 that mass-production methods came into general use.

It has been said with a great deal of truth that the essential feature of an industrial revolution is the creation of tools to make tools. While this is perhaps an over-simplification, there is no doubt that the machine-tool industry is of the utmost importance and it is not surprising that there were important developments in it during the last three decades of the nineteenth century, when there was a great industrial expansion in most parts of the world. In so extensive and complicated a field it is very difficult to generalise, but it is probably fair to say that comparatively few new types of machines appeared. The main changes were in design, in constructional material, and in a marked tendency towards automatic working. The latter was particularly apparent in the United States, where a rapidly expanding economy created a shortage of labour and there was in consequence a strong incentive to turn to machinery. In Europe, where new machinery threatened unemployment, the tendency was often exactly the reverse. The fundamental importance of the machine-tool to industry is not difficult to visualise when it is recalled that it was required to make all the products for every branch of mechanical engineering: for the making of railway locomotives, bicycles, typewriters, textile machinery, printing presses, and many other types of machine to which we have already referred.

Automation is commonly looked upon as essentially a feature of the mid-twentieth century. It is therefore worth noting that in fact it was then already a century or so old, for automatic lathes began to appear in the United States soon after the Civil War of 1861–5. During and after the war there was a great shortage of skilled labour, and automatic machinery was in great demand in consequence. The new machines, which were required in such vast numbers, had in many instances to be made with an accuracy considerably greater than had previously been general in the engineering industry. Special attention was given to accuracy, and precise measuring equipment was designed. In this field Sir Joseph Whitworth played a particularly notable part. Accuracy became of steadily increasing importance as the principle of interchangeable parts for machines became widely used.

One of the most important developments—namely, the introduction of much harder steel than had previously been available—has already been noted. This change dates roughly from 1868, when it was discovered that steel containing vanadium and tungsten could cut at 60 feet per minute, compared with 40 feet per minute for the best steel previously available. In 1900 there came another great jump forward when Taylor and White's alloy steels increased cutting speeds to 120 feet per minute, that is to say three times as great as had been possible only thirty years earlier. It was then found that existing machinery was in many cases insufficiently accurate and robust to be able to take advantage of these new cutting materials, and in consequence considerable changes in design took place in the late nineteenth and early twentieth centuries.

CHAPTER IV

SOCIAL AND POLITICAL THOUGHT

A PERIOD inaugurated by Karl Marx's *Das Kapital* (1867), Charles Darwin's *The Descent of Man* (1871), Clerk Maxwell's *Electricity and Magnetism* (1873) and Friedrich Nietzsche's *The Birth of Tragedy* (1872) was unlikely to be devoid of intellectual ferment. The men who exerted the largest influence on social, political and religious thought during the last three decades of the nineteenth century were Marx and Darwin: but the nature of this influence was greatly affected by the changing character of scientific and social thought in general, and by the repercussions of scientific ideas upon social thought. It was also profoundly affected by the rapidly changing condition of society and government, a condition brought about by scientific inventions, industrial expansion and new forms of social and political organisation. In no other period is intellectual history more inseparable from economic and political history—an inevitable consequence of the conquests of science in both thought and action. Under the impact of Marxism and Darwinism on the one hand, of unusually fast-moving social change on the other, adherents of older political philosophies and social faiths had to modify their arguments and outlooks. Utilitarianism, idealism and positivism continued as operative schools of thought. But they survived within a new context of philosophical and religious beliefs, amid a new ethos and new material conditions: and this context coloured their whole development.

Marx's analysis of economic forces in *Das Kapital* was designed to be the massive underpinning of the political doctrines which he and his collaborator, Friedrich Engels, had propounded since they issued the *Communist Manifesto* in 1848. As the avowed 'continuation' of Marx's *Critique of Political Economy* (1859), *Das Kapital* presented detailed evidence of the working of the laws of dialectical materialism. It expounded the economic principles which, in his view, made proletarian revolution inevitable. It was the most systematic attempt hitherto made to interpret industrial civilisation in terms of economic principles and the dynamics of social history. The first volume appeared in German in 1867: the later volumes were published posthumously in 1885 and 1894. When the first volume appeared in English translation in 1886 it attracted little attention. Marxism, as a political theory, was disseminated mainly by the journalistic and polemical activities of Engels and other disciples, especially in France and Germany. Variants of the doctrines, usually denounced as heresies or deviations by Engels, as later by Lenin, had, by the end of the century, moulded the development of social democratic parties and party programmes in most European states.

Darwin's *The Descent of Man and Selection in Relation to Sex* was in effect, as its title implies, two books. Its first seven chapters were a sequel to his *The Origin of Species by Means of Natural Selection* (published, like Marx's *Critique of Political Economy*, in 1859). The *Origin* had demolished the notion of distinct and separately created species of plants and animals, and had presented impressive evidence for the ultimate unity and common origin of all living things. Darwin now marshalled the evidence he had accumulated for holding that man, like all other living creatures, had evolved by natural selection from earlier and simpler forms of life. It was this conclusion, merely hinted at in the *Origin*, that had touched off much of the popular furore about Darwinism in the 1860's. This did not save his more explicit argument from renewed attack and abuse, though it now won readier acceptance among scientists and intellectuals. The other fourteen chapters of the book introduced a certain modification of his original thesis that natural selection, operating through the process of struggle for survival, explained the existence of diverse species. They explored sexual selection as a factor in the evolution of species: a distinct issue, as he emphasised, for whereas natural selection involved success of both sexes in surviving the hazards of life, sexual selection involved the success of certain individuals over others of the same species and even the same sex. Darwin's book, taken together with his earlier masterpiece, constituted, as T. H. Huxley claimed, a 'connected survey of the phenomena of life permeated and vivified by a central idea'.

Much of the remarkable ferment of ideas in the next thirty years in philosophy, theology, and social and political theory, derived from the double yeast of Marxism and Darwinism. The ferment was kept stirred less by the two originators of the theories, for Darwin died in 1882 and Marx in 1883, than by their leading apostles, T. H. Huxley and Friedrich Engels, both of whom lived until 1895. Huxley, more combative than Darwin, had defended his hero since the memorable meeting of the British Association at Oxford in 1860. Thirty years later he was conducting a scarcely less lively controversy with Mr Gladstone about the credibility of the miracle of the Gadarene swine. The very word 'agnostic' was a product of these great battles, in the course of which Huxley made evolutionary concepts part of the whole texture of men's outlook on life. If Huxley was 'Darwin's bulldog', Engels was Marx's. In 1878 Engels produced, in his *Anti-Dühring: Herr Eugen Dühring's Revolution in Science*, a more complete exposition of Marxist political theory than anything written by Marx himself. An intensely polemical book, attacking the claim of Dühring that politics were more fundamental than economics, it developed into an exposition of the meaning of Marxism for socialist political theory. Though Engels further applied Marxist doctrines to social thought in *The Origin of the Family, Private Property and the State* (1884) and *The Peasant Question in France and Germany* (1894), the *Anti-Dühring* remained his most powerful work. Eduard Bernstein avowed it had 'converted' him to Marxism on a first reading.

The philosophical consequences of both Marxism and Darwinism were all the greater because of the affinities between them. Marx and Engels were insistent that their thought flowed in the same direction as Darwin's, and shared its scientific qualities. Marx claimed to be viewing the evolution of society 'as a process of natural history'. He wished to dedicate the first volume of *Das Kapital* to Darwin, though Darwin with characteristic caution declined the honour: and Engels, in his funeral speech at Marx's graveside, asserted that, 'Just as Darwin discovered the law of development of organic nature, so Marx discovered the law of development of human history'. Certainly each thinker had sought and found, beneath a patiently collated mass of detailed fact and observation, great interpretative ideas—unifying and fundamental ideas which illuminated and connected together hitherto disparate facts. Each had found a simple principle of movement and development, a key to the better understanding of change in the whole history of mankind. Each hypothesis was revolutionary, in the sense that it conflicted violently with accepted notions about the nature of man and of human life, and necessitated a rethinking of much that previously had been taken as self-evident. Each theory found the key to change in conflict—in the struggle for existence and in the class war. Each was fundamentalist, in that it explained history in terms of one great single principle, as intelligible as the law of gravitation, and equally capable of being applied plausibly (if often with distortion or by mere analogy) to other fields of thought. Such theories at any time would be disruptive: in combination they were revolutionary.

Two further circumstances, in addition to their coincidence in time, conspired to make Darwinism and Marxism especially potent as intellectual influences. One was the simultaneous advance of scientific thought as a whole; the other was the new political structure of Western civilisation as a whole.

The sciences of chemistry, mechanics and physics had already reached, at this time, a stage of fresh generalisation and integration. The chemical elements were found to fit into a systematic mathematical sequence according to their atomic weights; and in 1871 Dimitri Mendeléef produced his Periodic Table which facilitated the discovery of new elements (gallium in 1871, scandium in 1879, germanium in 1886, helium in 1895). James Joule had established equivalence between heat and the chemical energy or work expended in producing it, and Hermann Helmholtz had extended the principle to the whole realm of nature as the First Law of Thermodynamics, the principle of the conservation of energy. To this Lord Kelvin had added the Second Law of Thermodynamics, the universal conversion of useful energy into dissipated heat. In his *Electricity and Magnetism* (1873) Clerk Maxwell fitted his discoveries in these fields into the new pattern of mechanics and thermodynamics, putting forward the thesis that electricity is matter moving in waves like those of light and radiant heat, and that therefore all energy might be ultimately electro-magnetic energy.

The parallelism between the new physics and the new biology was impressive. Just as physics began with the idea of solid billiard-ball atoms of fixed weight and moved towards a molecular theory linking matter with energy, so biology began with the idea of distinct species and moved towards an evolutionary theory of the interrelation of species. In comparable manner, Marx proposed to replace the rigid economic 'laws' of the classical economists by an all-embracing theory of dialectical materialism, explaining not only economic change, but also politics and culture, by a class theory of society. The discovery of great fundamental principles, unifying various sectors of knowledge and thought into new patterns, was very much in vogue. Marxism, attempting also to explain change, movement and development, had the advantage of seeming to conform with this vogue: it enjoyed the *cachet* of a scientific hypothesis.

The particular impact of Darwinism and Marxism upon social and political thought must also be assessed in relation to the new political structure of Western civilisation in the 1870's. The outcome of the 1860's was a recasting of the political map: new frontiers were fixed, new states created or old ones reconstituted, new systems of government consolidated. The preservation of the American Union by northern victory in the Civil War, the foundation of a united Canada by the British North America Act of 1867 and its full operation by 1873, the preservation of the Habsburg domains in Austria-Hungary by the improvisation of the Dual Monarchy, the political unification of the Italian Kingdom and of the German *Reich*, the frustration of the Irish independence movements and the suppression of the Paris Commune in France, even the assertion of papal ecclesiastical power that culminated in the Vatican Council of 1870: all these events involved the confirmation or the creation of stronger and more centralised authority. The state of the later nineteenth century was to be a bigger, more stable, more active organ of government and administration than the state of earlier generations. Political thinkers were compelled, by facts and conditions as well as by the challenge of new theories, to ponder the ultimate nature of state power and authority, the grounds of political obligation, the new pre-requisites of successful revolutionary action.

Moreover, these new states existed as a result of prolonged conflicts and decisive wars. The American Civil War, the successive wars of Bismarck against Denmark, Austria-Hungary and France, the long fight for Italian unity, the Civil War in France of which Marx wrote so effectively, suggested that violence was a natural accompaniment of modern state-making. The new Europe of the 1870's could be depicted either as the latest manifestation of a Darwinian struggle for survival or, alternatively, as the prelude to a new phase of historic class warfare implicit in the materialist dialectic. Marx, indeed, interpreted the Paris Commune as the beginning of the coming proletarian revolution. Either way, power, conflict and violence were the very stuff of politics. Events communicated something of their brutality and violence to political and social thought.

The keynote of conflict was what first struck the writers who applied Darwinism to political and social theory, and who have been subsequently classed together as 'social Darwinists'. In Britain and the United States Herbert Spencer, already prolific in sociological theorising, became the chief transmitter of 'social Darwinism'. His volumes of *Synthetic Philosophy* appeared during the 1860's. His influential *The Study of Sociology* first appeared in 1872–3, in serial form in the American *Popular Science Monthly* and in the British *Contemporary Review*. Philosophically tinged with determinism and politically with *laissez-faire* individualism, he argued: 'There cannot be more good done than that of letting social progress go on unhindered; yet an immensity of mischief may be done in the way of disturbing, and distorting and repressing, by policies carried out in pursuit of erroneous conceptions.' He pleaded that social and political science must recognise and adopt the 'general truths' of biology, and must not work against the principle of natural selection by 'the artificial preservation of those least able to take care of themselves'.

Such a view was warmly welcomed by conservatives everywhere. Its French counterpart was the welcome given to Alfred Espinas's *Des sociétés animales* (1877). It was welcomed most ardently by conservatives in America after the Civil War, who found in it justification both for *laissez-faire* competition and for their faith in progress. Andrew Carnegie later described the 'light that came as in a flood' when he read Darwin and Spencer: 'Not only had I got rid of theology and the supernatural, but I had found the truth of evolution. "All is well since all grows better" became my motto, my true source of comfort.'[1] It was not surprising that one of the founders of sociological studies in America, William Graham Sumner of Yale, wrote in these years: 'The millionaires are a product of natural selection, acting on the whole body of men to pick out the requirement of certain work to be done....They get high wages and live in luxury, but the bargain is a good one for society.'[2] So could Darwinism buttress complacent pragmatism. As D. G. Ritchie, an English idealist critic of this attitude, pointed out: 'Natural selection implies no further morality than "Nothing succeeds like success".'[3]

[1] *Autobiography of Andrew Carnegie* (Boston, 1920), p. 327.
[2] W. G. Sumner, *The Challenge of Facts and Other Essays* (New Haven, 1913), p. 90.
[3] D. G. Ritchie, *Darwinism and Politics* (London and New York, 1895), p. 13.

That Darwinism was, in important respects, a refutation of Malthus' basic distinction between men (who multiplied in geometrical ratio) and animals or plants (which increased only in arithmetical progression) was a fact noted only by the Marxists. They welcomed Darwinism as anti-Malthusian, as disproving that poverty was inherent in the nature of life, inferring it was inherent only in capitalist society. 'It is remarkable', wrote Marx, 'that Darwin recognises among brutes and plants his English society with its division of labour, competition, opening up of new markets, "inventions" and Malthusian "struggle for existence".'[1]

Beyond the widespread mediation of Spencer, however, the precise significance of Darwinism in political philosophy is complex and difficult to assess. Even Spencer clung to mechanistic ideas (as suggested by his *Social Statics* of 1864 or his *The Man versus the State* of 1881), and was liable to use organic ideas as mere crude analogies. The many other thinkers conventionally grouped into the somewhat misleading category of 'social Darwinists' drew diverse and often contradictory inferences from their applications of biology to society. The sciences of anthropology and geology influenced their outlook as much as the new biology. Men found in Darwinism, even when they understood it accurately, what they wanted to find: and notions of laws of historical development were inherited from pre-Darwinian thinkers such as Hegel or Comte. Darwinian ideas were often used to reinforce or merely to adorn arguments substantially derived from quite other sources.

The English liberal Walter Bagehot and the Austrian sociologist Ludwig Gumplowicz perceived the subtler implications of the new biology and blended with it the new anthropology of E. B. Tylor, L. H. Morgan and W. Wundt. Bagehot's *Physics and Politics* (1872) was a collection of six provocative essays, as pithy as Spencer's works were prolix. Its theme was described in its sub-title: *Thoughts on the Application of the Principles of 'Natural Selection' and 'Inheritance' to Political Society*. His thesis was that whereas political organisations had formerly served to create a 'cake of custom', to hold society together and enable it to survive in the struggle for existence, progress in more modern conditions required that the cake of custom be broken. Flexibility comes above all from intellectual freedom, encouraged by 'the age of discussion' which 'gives a premium to intelligence', and breeds that quality of 'animated moderation' essential to the good conduct of modern government. He thus shifted the emphasis from conservatism to liberalism. Gumplowicz was more deterministic. He held that the state, and indeed all political institutions, originated in conflicts between social groups and the eventual triumph of one group over others. Material, social and even intellectual progress came from the

---

[1] Marx's letter to Engels, 18 June 1862, quoted in R. L. Meek, *Marx and Engels on Malthus* (London, 1953), p. 173. See also F. Engels, *Dialectics of Nature* (1872–82), quoted *ibid.* pp. 185–8.

fact that it was the fittest group that triumphed: and such progress came 'merely through social action and reaction, entirely independent of the initiative and will of individuals, contrary to their ideas and wishes and social striving'. This view of group struggles came close at times to Marxism, though it drew no inspiration from Marxism itself.

In his insistence that the state is 'the organised control of the minority over the majority' Gumplowicz also approached the viewpoint of the *Machtpolitik* school of German thinkers, of whom the most coherent and influential was Heinrich von Treitschke. But Treitschke emphasised the creative will of great leaders in the making of states. He stood in the direct pedigree of Hegelian philosophy, reinforced by the experience of state-making in the 1860's; and indeed, as he himself avowed, in the still older lineage of Machiavelli.

The American sociologist Lester Ward, associated both personally and in philosophical outlook with Gumplowicz, drew from Darwinism inferences directly contrary to Spencer's. He attacked *laissez-faire* doctrines in favour of social planning. He denied that the truths of biology could be simply transferred to the social sciences, that Nature's ways must be man's. 'The fundamental principle of biology', he wrote in 1893, 'is natural selection, that of sociology is artificial selection. The survival of the fittest is simply the survival of the strong, which implies and would better be called the destruction of the weak. If nature progresses through the destruction of the weak, man progresses through the protection of the weak.' Ward accepted Gumplowicz's ideas of group struggles as applicable to race conflicts in the future, but held that in advanced societies rational policy would replace the violence and brutality of the past: a point made by T. H. Huxley in his Romanes Lecture of the same year on *Evolution and Ethics*.[1]

Later racial theorists seized eagerly upon Darwinian ideas, and racialism in these years usually went hand in hand with imperialism. The loudest advocate of American racialism and imperialism, the Rev. Josiah Strong, produced in 1885 his immensely popular book, *Our Country: Its Possible Future and Its Present Crisis*. He triumphantly quoted Darwin's own view, in *The Descent of Man*, that 'There is apparently much truth in the belief that the wonderful progress of the United States, as well as the character of the people, are the results of natural selection; the more energetic, restless, and courageous men from all parts of Europe having emigrated during the last ten or twelve generations to that great country, and having there succeeded best'.[2] Strong saw the next stage of world history as a great struggle for *Lebensraum*, 'the final competition of races

---

[1] T. H. Huxley and J. Huxley, *Evolution and Ethics, 1893–1943* (London, 1947), p. 81: 'Social progress means a checking of the cosmic process at every step and the substitution for it of another, which may be called the ethical process.'

[2] C. Darwin, *The Descent of Man*, vol. I, p. 179.

for which the Anglo-Saxon is being schooled'. The Englishman who became a German, Houston Stewart Chamberlain, published in 1899 a book which was to have great popularity in Germany before 1914 and exerted some influence upon Hitler: *Grundlagen des Neunzehnten Jahrhunderts* (*The Foundations of the Nineteenth Century*). Drawing heavily on all the writings of Darwin, as of other biologists and anthropologists, he argued that 'crossing obliterates character', that racial purity is a prerequisite of progress, that the Germanic peoples must strive for purity and predominance in the world.

Yet racial theory in no way originated either with Darwin, who regarded racial differences as of minor significance, or even with biology in general. It had, as its pioneer exponent, the Frenchman Count Arthur de Gobineau, in 1853; it had its roots deep in traditional prejudices, in the growing contacts between Europeans and non-Europeans throughout the century, in the bias of the school of 'Teutonic' history that included E. A. Freeman and Charles Kingsley; it found highly unscientific expression in such anti-semitic bigots as Édouard Drumont in France, Adolf Stöcker in Germany and Karl Lueger in Vienna; it was reinforced by pseudo-scientific sociologists like Gustave Le Bon in France or Nicholas Danilevsky in Russia. Here, as in other spheres of argument, Darwinism was pressed into service and wildly distorted in the process. Much so-called 'social Darwinism' is mere lip-service or polemical camouflage, not genuine intellectual influence.

To complete the gamut of different uses to which Darwinism was put, mention must be made of two political theories at the opposite pole to racialism and imperialism: English Fabianism and Russian philosophical anarchism. The Fabians of the 1880's took their economic ideas more from Henry George's *Progress and Poverty* (1879) than from Marx: but they found in Darwinian theory justification for belief in the 'inevitability of gradualness'. If an accumulation of minute physical changes could result in the immense variety of living things, surely social transformation, too, could be brought about by a sequence of gradual reforms rather than by violent revolution. This idea lay at the root of evolutionary socialism as it was understood in England. The society's secretary and historian, Edward Pease, rated Darwinism high among the formative intellectual influences on the younger generation in the 1880's. 'Our parents, who read neither Spencer nor Huxley, lived in an intellectual world which bore no relation to our own; and cut adrift as we were from the intellectual moorings of our upbringings...we had to discover somewhere for ourselves what were the true principles of the then recently invented science of sociology.'[1] Sidney Webb, in *Fabian Essays in Socialism* (1889), argued that 'conscious "direct adaptation" steadily supplants the unconscious and wasteful "indirect adaptation" of the earlier form of the

[1] E. R. Pease, *The History of the Fabian Society* (London, 1916), rev. ed. 1925, p. 18.

struggle for existence', and that in current conditions of civilisation 'the units selected from are not individuals, but societies'.[1] In Fabian hands evolutionary Darwinism became an antidote to revolutionary Marxism. Prince Petr Kropotkin, in *Mutual Aid* (1902), also drew upon zoology to argue that social co-operation and helpfulness were instincts as strong as those of combat and struggle He could correctly claim that Darwin had emphasised the evolutionary importance of man's moral sense, and had not regarded conflict between men as in itself a healthy evolutionary force. But his views had more in common with the 'mutualism' of Pierre-Joseph Proudhon than with any other theories.

Must, then, the conclusion be that the influence of Darwinism (and of biology as a whole) on social and political theory was so diverse and diffuse as to be almost without meaning? Its direct and specific influence has often been exaggerated. Its role was, rather, in conjunction with the advance of scientific knowledge and thought in other fields, especially in the physical sciences and in anthropology, to undermine older political assumptions and beliefs, to open the door to more daring speculation and fundamental rethinking of social and political ideas, and to widen further the gulf already separating political philosophy from theology, metaphysics and ethics. Because of the ease with which Darwinian ideas could be transferred to social thought, they reinforced that tendency to seek precise social data and verifiable social 'laws' to which positivist philosophy had given rise: the new biology gave new life to the principles of positivism, just as in some respects it lent support to the advance of Marxism. But its most effective permeation of philosophy came more silently in the twentieth century, through a philosopher such as Henri Bergson, after the thunder of Huxley's battles had ceased.

Meanwhile Marxism, following a roughly parallel course, was also penetrating men's minds and habits of thought. In nearly every European country it won adherents who publicised and propagated its doctrines and formed political parties. After the founding in 1889 of the Second International, these national parties enjoyed a common forum for debate about principles and policies. But since working-class movements and socialist parties in most countries had strong pre-Marxist roots, much of the debate was concerned with theoretical relationships between orthodox revolutionary Marxism and reformist socialism: or with practical working relationships between trade-union organisations and working-class movements on one hand, and the small but missionising groups of militant Marxists on the other. The result was a rich profusion of differing schools of socialist thought: for Marx and Engels, like Darwin and Huxley, found that the Devil can quote scriptures for his own purpose. Marxist orthodoxy found itself engaged in an almost Darwinian struggle for existence. By 1900 it was still far from having found any basis for peaceful

[1] *Fabian Essays in Socialism* (London, 1889), 1920 ed., pp. 57–8.

co-existence with the beliefs of 'evolutionary socialism', so persuasively stated by men like Eduard Bernstein in Germany or Jean Jaurès in France.

In several countries specifically Marxist parties were founded in the late 1870's or 1880's: the 'Parti ouvrier français' of Jules Guesde in 1879, the 'Parti socialiste belge' in the same year; in Britain Henry Hyndman's 'Democratic Federation' of 1881 became, two years later, the 'Social Democratic Federation'; the 'Liberation of Labour Group', formed in Switzerland in 1883 by Plekhanov and Axelrod, was destined for a great historic role as the germ of the future Bolshevik party of Russia. Such parties were founded, however, against a background of prolonged efforts and wrangles in the 1860's and 1870's, connected with the unsuccessful efforts of Marx and Engels to capture the socialist movement in Germany from Ferdinand Lassalle and his disciples, and with the abortive First International of 1864–76. The most important outcome had been the formation of the German Social Democratic party on the basis of the Gotha Programme of 1875. Marx criticised the programme sharply and his critique, subsequently published by Engels in 1891, had considerable influence on Marxist thought. But the even balance between orthodox Marxism and the doctrines of state socialism advanced by Lassalle during the 1860's made the Gotha Programme an admirable basis for the party in Germany. Postulating that 'labour is the source of all wealth and all culture', it demanded 'the promotion of the instruments of labour to the common property of society and the co-operative control of all labour, with application of the product of labour to the common good and its just distribution'. It then demanded the usual democratic rights: a free state, universal suffrage with secret and obligatory voting, a 'people's army in place of the standing armies', abolition of 'all laws which restrict freedom of thought and inquiry', free justice and universal, free, compulsory public education. It also sought social welfare legislation, right of free association, and a single progressive income tax in place of indirect taxes.

Marx attacked the programme phrase by phrase, showing each to be vague, or confused and inconsistent, or based on a failure to understand the materialist dialectic. The gist of his attack was to restate the Marxist dogma: 'Between capitalist and communist society lies the period of the revolutionary transformation of the one into the other. There corresponds to this also a political transition period in which the state can be nothing but *the revolutionary dictatorship of the proletariat*.' Engels, in a letter of the same time to August Bebel, stated Marxist political doctrine even more explicitly: 'As, therefore, the state is only a transitional institution which is used in the struggle, in the revolution, in order to hold down one's adversaries by force, it is pure nonsense to talk of a free people's state: so long as the proletariat still *uses* the state, it does not use it in the interests of freedom but in order to hold down its adversaries, and as soon as it becomes possible to speak of freedom the state as such ceases to exist.'[1] These basically different conceptions of the state underlay the feuds of the Marxists not merely with the followers of Lassalle, but also with reformist socialists of all kinds.

In its Erfurt Programme of 1891 the German Social Democratic party adopted the doctrines of Marx: in particular, the theory of the growing gulf between monopolistic capitalism and the impoverished proletariat, and the need to socialise the main means of production. But it preserved enough Lassallian faith in the power of the state to add: 'The struggle of the working class against capitalistic exploitation is of necessity a political struggle. The working class cannot conduct its economic struggle, and cannot develop its economic organisation, without political rights. It cannot effect the change of the means of production into the possession of the collective society without coming into possession of political power.' This view naturally came to prevail among the growing Social Democratic parties of Europe, seeking power by parliamentary procedures and making themselves the spokesmen of organised labour. Certain political issues flowed from this position—whether socialists should enter into coalitions with liberal parties, at what point they should resist the claims of the nation state in order to uphold those of the workers who 'knew no country', what form of national army they could logically support. These issues haunted the congresses of the Second International and put French socialists at loggerheads with German.

The success of Social Democrats in winning votes, and in establishing contacts with trade unions whose central aim was to promote the immediate material interests of their members, fostered the view that a socialist society might, after all, be built by gradual reforms and constitutional procedures, without the apocalyptic moment of proletarian revolution foretold by Marx. The French Possibilists led by Paul Brousse, the British Labour party, the followers of Eduard Bernstein in Germany, of Victor Adler in Austria, of Filippo Turati in Italy, all moved in this direction. Wherever the electoral franchise was wide enough and parliamentary institutions strong enough to offer socialism a constitutional path to power, extremist Marxism faltered and lost ground. The eloquence of Jean Jaurès appealed to a creed of liberal socialism that was taking shape throughout most of Europe. Until 1914 a convenient distinction between maximum and minimum programmes preserved unity of purpose on paper. The maximum programmes were couched in thorough-going Marxist terms, the minimum were lists of political and social reforms constitutionally attainable within the existing structure of capitalist society. Only in Russia, where even the minimum demands were in substance revolutionary, did Marxist theory as expounded by Lenin dominate the aims of social democracy.

[1] Marx and Engels, *Selected Works* (London, 1950, 2 vols.), vol. II, p. 39.

The practical achievement of Marxism in nineteenth-century Europe was surprisingly small. It won converts in every country, and its international appeal brought socialists from many countries together within the framework of the Second International. It brought a new intellectual rigour and greater depth into socialist thought: but it also brought a dogmatic harshness and greater quarrelsomeness. Men debated the niceties of socialist doctrine and the subtleties of political tactics with scholastic fervour. Shattered by its own internal divisions and by the cataclysm of the First World War, socialism had to be entirely reconstructed after 1918, by which time Marxism as reinterpreted by Lenin had won its first victory—in Russia.

Before 1900 the consequences of Marxism for philosophy and for social thought had not become fully apparent: yet already Marx's ideas had seeped into men's minds and transformed into overtones the old materialistic undertones of nineteenth-century thought. Economics, in particular, could not be the same after Marx, any more than could biology after Darwin. Many who rejected its materialist determinism absorbed something of its materialism, and were compelled to modify their outlook in fundamental ways. The greater attention already beginning to be paid to economic history owed nothing to Marxism, though the rapid progress of the study of economic history in the twentieth century probably did. The new schools of economic theory, the exponents of marginal utility in Britain or the *Kathedersozialisten* ('Socialists of the Chair') in Germany, owed more to Marx's opponents than to Marx. The party of August Bebel and Wilhelm Liebknecht could even assert, in its Eisenach programme of 1869, that 'the social is inseparable from the political question; its solution depends on this, and is possible only in the democratic state'. But for all economists, as for all political socialists, Marxist ideology became, by its very rigidity, an external term of reference, a form of the absolute by which shades of materialism and of determinism could be measured. In this respect it clarified thought, even if its immediate impact was so much confusion—a respect in which it resembled Darwinism. So it appeared, at least, to a boy in Kazán reading the first volume of *Das Kapital*. Lenin compared Marxism to 'a solid block of steel, from which you cannot eliminate even one basic assumption without falling into the arms of a bourgeois-reactionary falsehood'.

Already, however, Marxism was having to fight on two fronts: not only against right-wing socialists sharing the tenets of Bernstein, as expounded in his *Evolutionary Socialism* (1898), but also against a revolutionary syndicalism of the left, evolved in practice by the French trade unions and in theory by Georges Sorel. Sorel adhered to Marx's doctrines of the inevitability of class war and the need for proletarian revolution to bring a classless society. He did not cling to the full gospel of dialectical materialism. He argued for direct action through the natural proletarian formations, the trade unions; for the leadership of an 'audacious minority' planning every strike as a skirmish in the class war and realising the need to use violence to destroy the bourgeois state; for direct action inspired by a 'myth' of proletarian victory through the general strike. Although his main writings and influence belong to the twentieth century he had already, in 1898, formulated some of his basic contentions in *L'Avenir socialiste des syndicats*. Sorel has been called a 'prismatic thinker', in the sense that many beams of intellectual light focus upon him, and radiate from him. If he derived his social and economic insights mainly from Marx, he derived his psychological insights from Friedrich Nietzsche.

Nietzsche is the only other figure of these decades to rank in stature with Darwin and Marx. *The Birth of Tragedy*, his first book, appeared in 1872; he died in 1900. From 1878, until he went insane in 1888, he produced one book each year. His intense, brooding, introspective genius conceived a philosophy of life and death that defied all existing and conventional doctrines. He was probably the most original genius among even the three giants mentioned. Nietzsche perceived psychological truths such as Sigmund Freud, Henri Bergson and Carl Jung were to proclaim after his death: yet neither Bergson nor Freud seems consciously to have owed him any intellectual debt. Georges Sorel was probably the first important heir of his thought. Study of Sorel reveals unexpectedly numerous points of contact between Marx and Nietzsche: like them he is convinced of the decadence of bourgeois society, he believes in violence as the only cure for its evils, he glorifies war, he despises liberal democracy. He blends the two moralities of Marx (proletarian and bourgeois) with the two moralities (master and slave) of Nietzsche.[1] Sorel's intellectual pilgrimage from revolutionary syndicalism to fascism marks the triumph in his philosophy of Nietzschean ingredients over Marxian.

The whole nexus of tendencies of thought that emanated from Darwin, Marx and Nietzsche can be presented as one single attack upon the philosophy of idealism: for though Nietzsche asserted so violently the importance of human will in opposition to the determinism found in Darwin and Marx, it was not the will of rational intelligence, that expression of pure Idea or Mind described by Hegel and his disciples. That idealist thinkers felt to be fundamental this challenge to their view of the world as a partial yet progressive realisation of absolute ideas and values, was expressed by Benedetto Croce, in a brief essay on 'Contrasting political ideals after 1870': 'Foremost is the doctrine of the struggle for existence and of the survival of the fittest, which inspires the political ideology of both communism (with its class struggle and dictatorship of the class powerful in number and expert in the material production of the means of subsistence) and imperialism or nationalism, which transfers the same struggle from social classes to people and states. This doctrine is found in a heroic and

[1] See E. H. Carr, *Studies in Revolution* (London, 1950), pp. 154–7.

aristocratic form in that kind of troubled religion named after Nietzsche, a poet with an anguished heart. Its weakness is revealed in its bitter clash with the moral conscience, to which it is utterly abhorrent.'[1] The clash between the new ideas and the old appears more absolute in retrospect than it seemed at the time: and other schools of political thought, by partial assimilation and adaptation of the new ideas in the ways described, contrived to soften—or at least to postpone—the 'bitter clash with the moral conscience'.

The political theory of an age includes not only the novelties, but also the extensions, elaborations and modifications of older and more familiar schools of thought. The philosophies of utilitarianism, idealism and positivism developed during these years in a curious semi-insulation from the new ferment of Darwinism and Marxism, and still more of Nietzschean thought. It remains to describe briefly the main lines of these developments.

John Stuart Mill, in the *Autobiography* published in the year of his death (1873), gave classical expression to the development and dilemmas of utilitarianism at that date. It includes no mention of either Darwin or Marx. But it reveals how the honest pursuit of truth and a sensitive social conscience led a thinker, steeped in Benthamite orthodoxy, to accept a much greater measure of state activity. 'The social problem of the future we considered to be, how to unite the greatest individual liberty of action, with a common ownership in the raw material of the globe, and an equal participation of all in the benefits of combined labour.'[2] Mill's radicalism flowed into Gladstonian liberalism. So also did the liberal idealism of the man who did most to revive idealist philosophy in England, Thomas Hill Green. Indeed Mill's *Autobiography*, it has been said, 'explains better than any other record why Benthamism failed to satisfy the England of the later nineteenth century, and why, after 1870, T. H. Green took the place of Mill as the most influential writer on matters of social philosophy'.[3] But the traditions of individualistic utilitarian thought lived on. They survived in lawyers like A. V. Dicey, whose *Lectures on the Relation between Law and Public Opinion in England during the Nineteenth Century* (1905) traced specifically 'the debt of collectivism to Benthamism';[4] in Sir J. F. Stephen, whose *Liberty, Equality, Fraternity* (1873) attacked Mill's essay *On Liberty* from the standpoint of older radicalism; in the philosopher Henry Sidgwick, whose *The Elements of Politics* (1891) avowedly 'derived

[1] B. Croce, *Politics and Morals* (London, 1946), pp. 91–2.
[2] J. S. Mill, *Autobiography* (London, 1873), 1924 ed., p. 196.
[3] H. J. Laski, Introduction to *Autobiography* of J. S. Mill (Oxford, 1924), p. x.
[4] Of Dicey's earlier and even more magisterial work, *Introduction to the Study of the Law of the Constitution* (1885) it has been claimed by its modern editor, E. C. S. Wade, that 'to the historian who seeks to appreciate the outlook of a notable adherent of the Whig school of political thought in the later years of Queen Victoria, the merit of the work needs no recommendation' (*ibid.* 9th ed., 1939, p. xiv).

from the writings of Bentham and J. S. Mill', and paid little or no heed to either Darwin of Marx. Bentham's doctrine, that the purpose of legislation should be to promote the greatest happiness of the greatest number, was separable from *laissez-faire* assumptions, and could be used, as Mill and Sidgwick showed, to justify considerable state activity.

For this reason the moderate Hegelianism of Green could find much common ground, in practical politics, with latter-day utilitarianism. Green delivered in Oxford his famous *Lectures on the Principles of Political Obligation* in the winter of 1879–80, three years after his colleague, F. H. Bradley, had published his *Ethical Studies*. In Green the impress of Kant is greater, that of Hegel less, than in Bradley. But together they founded the Oxford school of idealist thinkers which included Bernard Bosanquet, J. H. Muirhead and D. G. Ritchie (whose *Darwinism and Politics* of 1889, and *Darwin and Hegel* of 1893, brought together the streams of idealist and biological thought). Green's non-utilitarian restatement of the meaning of individual freedom, and his formulation of the 'common good' in ethical and spiritual, rather than materialist, terms, provided a more satisfying political theory of liberal reforms in these years than did Benthamite doctrines.

In other countries too, notably in Germany and Italy, idealist philosophy enjoyed a revival. In Germany, indeed, it survived rather than revived, for the cult of Kant and Hegel had never died and positivism had never gained as great a hold as in France or even Italy. Under the shadow of the great Leopold von Ranke (who died in 1886 after six decades of active historiography), German thinkers like Wilhelm Dilthey, Friedrich Meinecke and Ernst Troeltsch strove to make a coherent philosophy out of the study of history on one hand, and the methods and advances of the natural sciences on the other. For this immense labour the structure of Hegelian thought was convenient, and was compounded with Kantian philosophy. Dilthey's *Einleitung in die Geisteswissenschaften* (1883) rested on a distinction between the world of nature studied by the natural sciences, and the world of human activity (history, society, culture), to be studied equally scientifically but by scientific methods basically different from those of natural science. In this sense, he and his colleagues launched a counter-attack against positivism, as against any mere assimilation of man to animals, society to nature. Knowledge in the field of social and cultural science must come through some kind of internal process, through living experience and understanding. In some respects they paved the way for the political ideas of Freudian psychology and the so-called 'irrationalists'. The fruit of their thought was the sociology of Max Weber, with its ingenious attempt to unravel the historical interplay of religion and economics, the spiritual and the material. Weber's famous study of *The Protestant Ethic and the Spirit of Capitalism* (*Die protestantische Ethik und der Geist des Kapitalismus*) first appeared as articles in

1904–5. It became one of the great pioneer works of social thought in the twentieth century. 'Alone of his contemporaries', it has been claimed, 'Weber was able to bridge the chasm between positivism and idealism.'[1]

In Italy, according to Croce, 'Marxian Socialism came to fill the void created in Italian thought and ideals'. It blended with positivism on one hand, with idealism on the other, leaving orthodox Marxism a curiously impoverished movement. Vilfredo Pareto, positivist in the foundations of his thought, widened Marx's concept of class conflicts into a more complex theory of group conflicts: his *Les Systèmes socialistes* (1902) became a classic refutation of Marxian sociology as well as of Marxian economics. Croce himself passed through his curious 'parenthesis' of intensive Marxist study between 1895 and 1899, when he imbibed the doctrines from the only important Italian theorist of Marxism, Antonio Labriola. Then he reverted to his basically idealist philosophy of history and aesthetics. Croce used the materialist interpretation of history as an intellectual whetstone, a means of sharpening his already evolving theory of history and historiography. He made use of Marxism as a stick to beat the positivists and as a corrective to his idealist ideas: then he unceremoniously discarded it. It is to Italian philosophy in these years that we must look to find the clearest interactions of Marxism with both positivism and idealism.

Positivism prevailed even more in France than in Italy. But French positivism, affected partly by the new biology but even more by the anticlericalism of French intellectuals, no longer shared the optimism of its earlier radical, utilitarian stages. It had become a harsher, more impersonal and fatalistic creed. Ernest Renan, indeed, continued to voice an urbane, balanced scientific outlook, and strove to base political thought, like ethics, on a calm and reasoned view of life. His little study of *La Réforme intellectuelle et morale* (1871) was inspired by the turbulent events of the time in France, and sought to find the permanent forces underlying them. In 1890 he published a work originally written in 1849, *L'Avenir de la science*, his fullest exposition of a positivist approach to history and society. His sensitive, critical, undogmatic mind remained, however, sceptical even of positivism. Although he had many readers he attracted no disciples, and spoke for none but himself.

The leading exponent of French positivism, in direct lineage from Comte, was Hippolyte Taine, an almost exact contemporary of Renan. In Taine the characteristic dogmatic, mechanistic, even deterministic features of positivism came to full fruition. 'All human facts, moral as well as physical, being bound up with causes and subject to laws, it follows that all works of man, art, religion, philosophy, literature, moral, political or social phenomena, are but the results of general causes that

[1] H. Stuart Hughes, *Consciousness and Society* (London, 1959), p. 335.

must be determined by scientific method.' So he wrote in 1870:[1] and proceeded to try to reveal these general causes at work in the course of French history. By his rigorous standards of historical research he fostered a more scientific study of historical sources: by its dogmatic conclusions and its intensely nationalistic interpretation, his great study of *Les Origines de la France contemporaine* (1875–85) served as a conservative (but equally nationalistic) antithesis to the influence which Jules Michelet had wielded earlier in the century. French scholarship, through the lexicographer Émile Littré, the literary critic Émile Faguet, the sociologist Émile Durkheim, the social theorist Alfred Fouillée, remained permeated by what might be called a residual positivism. Such thinkers accepted the challenge of Marxism (like Durkheim) or of Darwinism (like Fouillée), and strove to restate the problems of their time in terms of a positivist philosophy adapted to these new ideas.

In England a group of popular rationalist writers based their outlook on Comtian positivism transmitted in part through John Stuart Mill (who in 1865 had written with reserve of *Auguste Comte and Positivism*, and during the 1840's had corresponded with Comte). Frederic Harrison, John Morley, Leslie Stephen and a host of other contributors made the *Fortnightly Review* a powerful organ of later Victorian liberalism. As in France, however, English positivism was now a residual outlook, greatly modified by less mechanistic and more idealistic components. In America, the pragmatism of Charles Pierce and William James represented an extension of positivism in a different philosophical direction.

Christian thought, whether Protestant or Roman Catholic, found itself challenged by all the new ideas and conditions already mentioned. Whilst churches were confronted with the drift away from religious observance and faith, and with the secular power of the new nation states in Italy and Germany, theology was challenged by the new science and by the cult of 'modernism' that sprang from textual criticism of the Bible. The period brought a series of open conflicts between churches and states, such as the battles about education between clericals and anti-clericals in France, the *Kulturkampf* in Germany, and the feud between the Vatican and the new Italian kingdom. This background of political and social conflicts exacerbated the theological controversies of fundamentalists and modernists. In the realm of ideas, and more particularly of political and social thought, two developments loomed large: a trend towards 'good works' in Protestant thought, and a trend towards social Catholicism and Catholic democracy.

In the Protestant world new religious movements appeared. The Salvation Army was formed in England in 1878, and the Christian Science movement grew up in America in the 1870's. Protestant believers turned their energies increasingly to humanitarian, educational, philanthropic

[1] H. Taine, *L'Avenir de l'intelligence* (1870).

and social reforms, and (as did Catholics) to overseas missions. To the many already existing societies in Britain were now added a host of temperance movements, boys' brigades, societies for the protection of children and animals, and movements to alleviate social distress. Protestant theology tended to divide into two rival wings, those who reaffirmed a fundamentalist interpretation of the scriptures, and those who adopted a modernist approach, absorbing into theology the ideas of the new science and adapting their creed to them.

The Roman Church passed through two successive phases. The first, haunted by the loss of the papacy's temporal power in 1870 and by the outcome of the Vatican Council, was marked by intransigent resistance both to liberalism and nationalism. The stormy pontificate of Pius IX ended in 1878. The pope who had published the *Syllabus Errorum* in 1864 had included among the ideas to be condemned the view that 'the Roman Pontiff can and should reconcile himself and reach agreement with "progress", Liberalism and recent departures in civil society'. His successor, Leo XIII, issued a series of encyclicals defining more constructively Roman Catholic doctrines of state and society: especially *Immortale Dei* (1885), *Libertas* (1888) and *Rerum Novarum* (1891). By his revival and extension of Thomism, with its capacity to reconcile faith with reason, theology with science, he formulated the theological basis for the policy of *ralliement* and of adaptation to new conditions which made possible the rise of social Catholicism. The papacy continued to condemn materialism, secularism and agnosticism: but it now accepted (on conditions) democracy and liberalism, with a view to infusing them with Christian doctrines as against the secular ideas of militant nationalism and socialism. In *Rerum Novarum* capitalist exploitation of labour as a commodity was condemned as roundly as Marxist doctrines of class war. The state was accorded both the right and the duty to encourage free associations of workers and to undertake legislation against economic oppression and social distress.

With papal encouragement Catholic trade unions grew up in most western European countries. They rivalled socialist and syndicalist movements on their own grounds of working-class industrial organisation. Compact, if often small, political parties based on social Catholic ideas emerged to rival liberal and socialist parties. Thereby the Church accepted existing regimes as a proper medium of political activity. From these developments sprang much constructive social thinking. In France, on ground already prepared by Montalembert and Lamennais, men like Marc Sangnier in *Le Sillon*, Albert de Mun and René de la Tour du Pin tried to make the *ralliement* proclaimed by Leo XIII a spiritual and intellectual reality as well as a political force. After the accession of Pope Pius X in 1903, relations between church and state again deteriorated, especially in France. But theories and movements of Catholic democracy survived, to bear fruit later in the twentieth century.

In Germany, where social Catholic ideas had been earlier expounded by Adolf Kolping and Bishop von Ketteler, a confessional Centre party was founded in 1870. It emerged from the storms of the *Kulturkampf* invigorated and popularly based, with a complete programme of constructive social reforms. In Austria-Hungary Christian socialism found a powerful advocate in Baron Karl von Vogelsang, whilst in Vienna the formidable Karl Lueger denounced, in the name of Christianity, socialism and capitalism, Marxists and Jews, with equal ferocity. Pan-German nationalism in Austria, inspired especially by Georg von Schönerer, was also violently anti-semitic: and significantly it was Austrian Jewry that gave birth to the movement of Zionism. Theodor Herzl published his *Der Judenstaat* (*The Jewish State*) in 1896, and in the following year he founded the Zionist Congress. The conflict between religious and racial forces seemed to be the key to Austrian politics: so it seemed, at least, to a young down-and-out in the Vienna doss-houses of 1909. Adolf Hitler later recorded, in *Mein Kampf*, the deep impression left on him by the ideas of Schönerer, Lueger and Herzl, and his growing conviction that 'knowledge of the Jews is the only key whereby one may understand the inner nature and therefore the real aims of Social Democracy'. Hitler, like other racialists already mentioned, saw political conflicts in crudely Darwinian terms. 'The idea of struggle is as old as life itself, for life is only preserved because other living things perish through struggle....In this struggle, the stronger, the more able, win, while the less able, the weak, lose.'[1]

The total outcome of the great ferment of ideas during the last generation of the nineteenth century was mixed in character and purport. But here was the great seed-time of the twentieth century. Materialistic philosophy, powerfully reinforced by Marxism and Darwinism, became more pervasive and struck deeper roots in men's minds. Utilitarianism and positivism, so prevalent in Western political thought before 1870, were affected by it. On the other hand idealist and Christian philosophy contrived to assimilate many scientific and sociological ideas without surrendering to materialism. The greatest economist of the twentieth century, John Maynard Keynes, found philosophical basis for his humanistic liberalism in repudiation of both utilitarianism and Marxism. Writing of his coterie at Cambridge at the turn of the century, he declared, 'we were amongst the first of our generation, perhaps alone amongst our generation, to escape from the Benthamite tradition....Moreover, it was this escape from Bentham, joined with the unsurpassable individualism of our philosophy, which has served to protect the whole lot of us from the final *reductio ad absurdum* of Benthamism known as Marxism.'[2]

---

[1] Hitler's speech at Kulmbach, 5 February 1928: quoted in A. Bullock, *Hitler: A Study in Tyranny* (London, 1952), p. 31.
[2] J. M. Keynes, *Two Memoirs* (London, 1949), pp. 96–7.

From the intellectual ferment itself, perhaps more than by any direct derivation from political philosophers, sprang two new tendencies which were to have immense subsequent importance. One was a realisation of the non-rational, subconscious impulses behind the behaviour of men in society: the other was belief in the efficacy of 'direct action', or organised violence, as an agency of social and political change. It is somewhat unreal to identify the former with the philosophy of Nietzsche, the latter with the philosophy of Sorel; or to seek an explanation of these tendencies in the discoveries of Sigmund Freud (whose *The Interpretation of Dreams* appeared in 1899), in the pragmatism of William James, or in the peculiar blend of positivism and anti-intellectualist racialism to be found in Charles Maurras and the *Action française*. The great future exploiters of irrationalism and the practitioners of activism were, indeed, coming to maturity in these years. Lenin was born in 1870, Stalin in 1879, Mussolini in 1883, Hitler in 1889. But it is impossible to separate the intellectual climate of the time from the violent and irrational movements of the time as formative influences upon their minds. The Spanish–American and South African wars, the upheaval of the Dreyfus Affair in France and the Russian revolution of 1905, the excitability of the popular press and of international diplomacy, all provided a lurid background, implicitly challenging the validity of rationalism and hedonism in philosophy. A whole new temper of thought and action—a new ethos—came to prevail by the opening years of the twentieth century.

The herald of the new age, both in thought and action, was Lenin. His pamphlet *What is to be Done?* (1902) may be read as both the epilogue to political philosophy of the previous generation, and the prologue to political action in the next. It contained the basic idea not only of Bolshevism, but of all single-party dictatorships. He contended that 'without a revolutionary theory there can be no revolutionary movement'; that 'political activity has its logic quite apart from the consciousness of those who, with the best intentions, call either for terror or for lending the economic struggle itself a political character'; and that the prerequisite of successful political action was 'a small, compact core, consisting of reliable, experienced and hardened workers, with responsible agents in the principal districts and connected by all the rules of strict secrecy with the organizations of revolutionaries'. When, after 1903, he proceeded to forge such an organisation and led it to victory, politics entered upon a new era.

CHAPTER V

LITERATURE

THE literature of the late nineteenth century shows unmistakable symptoms of decadence. What is decaying is a literary tradition which dates back to the Renaissance, when its basic genres, its conventions for representing the world and giving a valid picture of human experience, were laid down anew. The tradition was largely founded on a belief that the artistic imagination truly mirrors nature, and this belief persisted through all later changes in theme and expression. The great distinction between realism and romanticism, which accounts for most of the major variations in the literature of the earlier nineteenth century, still did not break the tradition. It rather enriched it with a subtler sense of the difference between the world as mirrored in poetry and the world as mirrored in prose, and indicated a fuller awareness of the interesting role played by specifically subjective adventures in thought and feeling. Confidence in the power of art to reflect the true sense and shape of these richer possibilities remained unshaken. Towards the end of the century, however, the reliability, indeed the responsibility, of the imagination in discovering the way things 'really' are and in knowing what they mean began to be seriously questioned. It seemed possible to write about anything in almost any way, to enjoy literally almost any number of views, but this gain in literary scope and freedom was accompanied by a loss of creative certainty about the true image and status of man. Amidst the bewildering assortment of styles and schools, which sprang up at this period, it is possible to find only one common feature; the search for an authentic form of expression. Did it lie in scientific accuracy or pure fantasy? in moral judgement or ironical detachment? in sound ideas or the pure music of words? These are some of the questions of the time, and even the answers bear still the strain of uncertainty. It is this uncertainty which has made later readers feel that in the style and form, language and ideas, of many works of the period there is something not altogether 'sound', something affected, artificial, intellectual: all these epithets have been associated with the term *fin de siècle* in art. The danger for so much of the varied and intelligent writing of these closing decades of the century is to appear dated: the doom always of mere ideas, however brilliant they may be, which do not command the undivided belief of the imagination and which do not therefore enter the flesh and blood of real experience.

Henry James (1843–1916) has good right to pride of place in a survey of late-Victorian literature. He came to Europe as an American in search of a tradition, but although he acquired all its late refinements and sometimes showed an over-subtle aesthetic intelligence, he never lost his native moral vigour. This rare combination of qualities, which were beginning to appear so often mutually exclusive in his contemporaries, produced such masterpieces as *The Portrait of a Lady* (1881) and *The Ambassadors* (1903). James well understood the problem and it provided him with his central theme: the involvement of art, and what he called generally the 'finer consciousness' of a wealthy and ancient culture, in moral corruption and evil. To love, to admire, to know, is to be initiated into pain and suffering, and to possess is to partake in tragedy: this is the purely spiritual structure of James' curiously insubstantial stories about inheritance, discovery and renunciation. His tragedies are not of the conventional kind; the struggle is all between different visions and values, and it is souls, not people, who are murdered. There is little direct contact with violence, either of action or of passion, and even the material scene appears to recede farther and farther into the background. The actual 'subject matter' of *The Wings of the Dove* (1902) and *The Golden Bowl* (1904) amounts to almost no more than an elaborate play of consciousness, in which the characters themselves are all but reduced to a study of inner and largely abstract relationships. Yet the aim of this extraordinary literary manœuvre remains clear: to redeem the wickedness of the world by sheer beauty of spirit. All James' later heroines, beginning with Fleda Vetch in *The Spoils of Poynton* (1897) and including the amazing little girl of *What Maisie Knew* (1897), have the gift of 'making things right'; their love transcends treachery, failure and death. The moral might be taken to be Christian, were it not of the very essence of fine art which, so James believed, alone '*makes* life, makes interest, makes importance'; with the result that the triumphs of his final novels resemble somewhat an eloquent pretence in the face of unspeakable catastrophe, as though 'to recognise was to bring down the avalanche' and consequently 'the specific, in almost any direction, was utterly forbidden'. This criticism, however, is hardly relevant in the case of the earlier novels, like *The American* (1877), *The Princess Casamassima* (1886) and *The Portrait of a Lady*, where the evil eventually does break loose, albeit only into something very like melodrama. James considered the style of these works very imperfect, but their plainer account of the problems of decadence may be preferred in a century which has less confidence in the façade of 'good form'.

Thomas Hardy (1840–1928) stands at an opposite extreme from James in the art of fiction; his style is comparatively simple and his setting rural, his best figures are plain country folk and his tragedies down to earth. His outstanding gift is a sense of dramatic occasion, and he has depicted scenes of a power to earn him comparison with the Elizabethan playwrights. Yet through this same gift he has also incurred criticism, because of his uncertainty about its use and meaning. Hardy knew the danger for the plainly realistic novelist: 'a story must be worth the telling and a good deal of life is not worth any such thing'. Thus he argued that art consisted in a 'disproportioning of reality', at which he showed his own skill by contriving plots and situations of formidable improbability. *A Pair of Blue Eyes* (1873) contains the most fantastic examples, but the habit persists throughout his work, producing also many magnificent effects, and it is the secret of all his best short stories; for example, *The Three Strangers* (1888, from *Wessex Tales*). Hardy did not, however, only exercise this skill to give new life to the perennial tragi-comedy of human affairs; he also used it to explain them in a new way. He tried to establish a theory of accident and malign chance, and thereby exculpate his characters from the full burden of responsibility. In so doing he worked against them and to some extent even against himself as their creator; for all literary interest stems from the recognition of personal destiny in the chaos of events, seizing upon those features of a man's life which make it altogether *his* story. Hardy's philosophy is far less convincing than his characters, who turn the unfortunate coincidences to which they are exposed into their own terrible fate. Hardy only *thought* that the universe was essentially chaotic and senseless, but his imagination spontaneously *felt* that there was drama and some grand suggestion of significance in all those extraordinary happenings and startling scenes which inspired him to write. What this significance is cannot perhaps be formulated theoretically, because it is all but inseparable from the details of what he intuitively knew to be worth telling: glimpses of lyrical beauty and idyllic charm (for instance, in *Under the Greenwood Tree* (1872) and *The Trumpet Major* (1880)), of the mystery of myth and the terror of tragedy (in two of the finest novels, *The Return of the Native* (1878) and *The Mayor of Casterbridge* (1886)), and of heroic strength and eternal folly (in *Far from the Madding Crowd* (1874) and *The Woodlanders* (1887)). Only one thing is lacking: the final coherence of the whole. Hardy's poetic vision is disturbed by prosaic insights, a fault which mars his style and is revealed still more clearly in his poems (*Wessex Poems* (1898)); most of his poetry was written after he had abandoned fiction, and falls outside the period. He might genuinely see cruelty and pathos mingled in every beauty and joy, sense that his beloved nature is compassionless, indifferent; it is all so obvious and true, yet separated from the simplicity of wisdom by his banal protests and theoretical comments. His 'modern' ideas caused a scandal on the publication of *Tess of the D'Urbervilles* (1891) and *Jude the Obscure* (1896); but they are uninspiring platitudes by comparison with the noble suffering of heroine and hero which they are supposed to remedy.

An interest in the remedial use of literature cannot be dismissed as a mere flaw in the case of George Meredith (1828–1909): it is a constant source of his inspiration. Success came to him slowly, but with *Beauchamp's Career* (1876), *The Egoist* (1879), and *Diana of the Crossways*

(1885), he established himself as one of the worthies of the English novel. What exactly his worth is depends less upon conventional merits of story-telling, social realism or simple 'characterisation', where he rarely excels, than upon the value allowed to the philosophical and analytical 'uses' for which he employs fiction. In a famous essay *On the Idea of Comedy* (1877) he explicitly prescribes the 'comic spirit' as a corrective for the world's errors. The idea is as old as the theatre from which it is taken, but it assumes new importance in Meredith's philosophy of life. This purports to be a doctrine of common sense, but is chiefly remarkable for the mystifyingly oracular form in which it is uttered and which is typical of his style. Never can spiritual temperance have been preached to such excess, or plain dealing analysed in such complicated language, as in Meredith's prose and poetry. His ideal is a looking beyond self to see the natural life, but his writing is notoriously full of intellectual conceits and elaborate introspection. This paradox lies at the heart of Meredith's work, and is to be explained, not by elucidating more thoroughly the meaning of what he thought, but by discovering what thinking as such meant to him. It was like mental athletics: real skill at an artificial activity, convulsive exercise in unnecessary difficulties for the sake of spiritual health and beauty. Hence Meredith could claim, for instance, that prayer is psychologically beneficial, even while disbelieving in any god. His style offers a brilliant display of vigour; it is philosophical, epigrammatic, lyrical, by turns; it combines comedy, romance, tragedy, satire; it only does not quite convince that any of these effects is entirely true or neces-sary, that such is the form the subject had to take. Meredith encountered here already the main artistic problem of the twentieth century, the problem of authenticity, and for this reason he has been hailed as a modern writer; but he interpreted it in the more optimistic spirit of his own age, assuming that the language and ideas of an entire tradition were now all available for the purest intellectual sport, and he thereby became, in fact, a virtuoso exponent of the grand manner. Thus his progressive philosophy is made dignified and respectable enough for a Victorian matron, and his satire of the high-born world has the harmless air of superior hobnobbing; he attacks the tyranny imposed on life by human egotism and deluded vanity, yet only to increase the self-assurance of men and women that they can master themselves and the world. Meredith championed the cause of feminine emancipation and this theme recurs in all his last novels, *One of our Conquerors* (1891), *Lord Ormont and his Aminta* (1894), and *The Amazing Marriage* (1895). His claim is not political but psychological; namely, that the differences in mentality and propriety enforced upon women are a sentimental invention designed by men to flatter their own romantic interests. It was a crucial question of the period, and seemed capable of undermining many traditional values in society and literature. Meredith's treatment of it, however, results only in a somewhat artificial mixture of romance and psychology. He works for all the old benefits of charm and chivalry, while giving the comforting illusion that he is freeing the 'sexual' relationship of all vain prejudice and formality.

None of the other novelists of the period was destined to have his work ranked among the national 'classics'. Many, like Mark Rutherford (1831–1913) or Mrs Humphry Ward (1851–1920), are in danger of being forgotten, and the rapidly increasing mass of minor talent can perhaps now only be of interest as a historical phenomenon. More and more intelligent people sought meaning and sanction for their problems and experiences by turning them into 'literature'. The novel especially seems to have emancipated all manner of spiritual energies which were no longer absorbed or satisfied by traditional ways of life and thought. It is not surprising, therefore, to find in the psychology of Sigmund Freud (1856–1939) the suggestion that imaginative writing is meant to compensate for satisfactions which the writer cannot know in reality. There are certainly hints of a disillusioned theologian in Samuel Butler (1835–1902), and of a frustrated scholar in George Gissing (1857–1903). The famous adventure stories of R. L. Stevenson (1850–94) are like daydream fulfilments of a boyish wish for excitement, and even Joseph Conrad (1857–1924) fears the old heroism of the sea is lost and brings back his tales like curios from remote and secret places. From the bright satire of Butler's *Erewhon* novels (1872 and 1901) to the dark tragedy of Conrad's *Lord Jim* (1900) the reader is constantly reminded that the conventional code of manners and outlook is false; but he may also be left either unconvinced or unsure about what then is true. The truth seemingly lies in the very escape from tyrannical convictions and hypocritical assurance—the theme of Butler's *The Way of all Flesh* (1903); it lies in Conrad's thrilled exploration of sinister mysteries, no matter how uncertain their ultimate 'meaning'; it lies, in fact, in a new kind of literary freedom.

The doctrine of 'Art for Art's sake' is the most characteristic invention of the period. Derived originally from the visual arts, it liberates literature too from responsibility to any moral, religious or philosophical idea of truth. It is not necessary to believe, much less to expound, such ideas in art, but only to perceive beauty; and whether the beauty is 'real' no longer matters, since everything depends on the artist's power to perceive beautifully. The importance of this doctrine must be judged against the background of prevailing deadlock between theological and scientific interpretations of the universe. One centre of that most celebrated of all nineteenth-century disputes was Oxford, which presented a generally solid front against materialists and agnostics alike. Here was discovered the only basis on which the cause of the 'spirit' could make any apparent progress: through that cultural alliance of Christianity and Hellenism, that revival of ailing faith with the reassurance of great literature, which

Matthew Arnold had done so much to achieve, which John Ruskin strengthened by his fervent rediscovery of painting and architecture, and which culminated in the work of Walter Pater (1839–94). His *Studies in the History of the Renaissance* (1873) and the philosophical romance *Marius the Epicurean* (1885) are two of the most influential books of the period. His scholarly style is an essay in perfection, reflecting his ideal of 'refining all the instruments of inward and outward intuition' and striving 'towards the vision—the "beatific vision", if we really cared to make it such—of our actual experience'. This is the last romantic apotheosis of genius, promising aesthetic triumph over doubt; life might be no more than meaningless flux, but the beauty of a moment is eternalised in art; even discredited conceptions of the world make lasting sense in poetry. Well might Swinburne declaim (*Songs before Sunrise*, 1871):

> Glory to Man in the highest! for Man is the master of things.

Echoes of Pater's thought are to be discerned in the work of many contemporaries. Conrad uses surprisingly similar language in his preface to *The Nigger of the Narcissus* (1898) and even Gissing observes that 'only as artistic material has human life any consequence'. The extreme realism which insists upon portraying 'as it is' all the ugliness and mediocrity assembled in Gissing's *Demos* (1886), *The Nether World* (1889), or *New Grub Street* (1891), thus owns unexpected kinship with the cult of beauty and brilliance which more obvious aesthetes, like George Moore (1852–1933) and Oscar Wilde (1854–1900), derive directly from Pater. The two tendencies are related by their common attempt to consider as 'pure art' aspects of life in which accepted notions of what is good, beautiful, and true, are more or less subtly denied. Hence the fascination felt in England for French literature with its vaunted immorality, the label which was supposed to guarantee its aesthetic purity. There were, however, to be no English rivals for Flaubert, the brothers Goncourt, Huysmans, or Maupassant. Gissing's writing is neither ironically detached nor exquisitely stylised, it is morally depressing; for his style does not overcome, but indulges, the bitterness of his feelings. Swinburne hails Baudelaire as a brother in *Ave atque Vale* (*Poems and Ballads*, 1866/1878/1889) but he is superficial by comparison; the poetic licence and spiritual defiance he proclaims have the ring rather of rhetorical effects than of real experiences. Moore's youthful extravagances and foreign imitations, analysed in *The Confessions of a Young Man* (1888) have a character of self-conscious affectation; he produced a minor scandal with *Esther Waters* (1894), yet its excursions into forbidden subjects are less striking now than its conventional moral sympathies. Even Wilde's notorious *Picture of Dorian Gray* (1891) is second-rate fiction for all its brilliantly perverse ideas, while his most moving prose work, *De Profundis* (written after 1895 when he was in prison), records the tragedy and virtual renunciation of the aesthetic adventure. The same year saw the end of *The Yellow Book* (1894–7), a periodical in book form which epitomises a minor fashion for the shocking; *The Savoy* (1896), devoted still more outspokenly to the cause of art for art's sake, lasted only eight months. By 1902 Henry James apparently regards aestheticism as past, likening it to 'a queer high-flavoured fruit from overseas' which could never suit English taste.

Wilde's most exotic work, *Salomé*, was characteristically first written in French, banned from production in London, then published and performed in Paris (1893/6). His social comedies proved more acceptable; the immoral hints of *Lady Windermere's Fan* (1892) and *An Ideal Husband* (1894) might be taken as no more than clever jests in a conventional world of make-believe. Wilde's masterpiece, *The Importance of being Earnest* (1895), succeeds in carrying the logic of inverted truth, upon which his wit largely depends, just safely across the threshold into inspired nonsense where criticism would be out of place; the fun lies in seeing how much of recalcitrant normality turns out to make comic sense in its new surroundings.

This was perhaps the only domain in which the English public knew how to enjoy the art for its own sake, having learnt in childhood from Edward Lear (1812–88) and Lewis Carroll (1832–98) and adopted in later years the burlesque operas of Gilbert and Sullivan as a national institution. W. S. Gilbert (1836–1911) had a considerable satiric gift, but his straight plays and, more unjustly, his *Bab Ballads* (1869/73) are now forgotten beside his famous libretti, from *Trial by Jury* (1875) to *The Grand Duke* (1896), in which the satire is transmuted by music and pantomine into innocuous absurdity. His playful mockery of British customs and characteristics soon established itself as a way of celebrating a patriotic affection for them. The younger satirist of the stage, G. B. Shaw (1856–1950), turned his humour to more earnest ends; his comedy at the expense of the military, *Arms and the Man* (1894), contains an ideological element that is absent from, say, *H.M.S. Pinafore* (1878). For Shaw professed a radical attitude towards social problems, partly because he shared (with less consistency) the political views of Sidney Webb, for whom he edited the *Fabian Essays in Socialism* (1889), but partly also because he hoped to find in them the basis of a modern dramatic revival, such as he proclaimed in *The Quintessence of Ibsenism* (1891). Although the greater part of his work lies outside the period, his *Plays Pleasant and Unpleasant* (1898) and *Three Plays for Puritans* (1901) give a fair indication of its foundations and stature. It is clearly not made of the same imaginative stuff as Ibsen's drama. Shaw came into his own as an intellectual of the 1890's, and his wit was trained in that school of modish paradox at which Wilde and Max Beerbohm excelled. A practised critic of music and literature, he expects art 'to cultivate and refine our senses and faculties until seeing, hearing, feeling, smelling and tasting become highly conscious and critical acts with us, protesting vehemently against ugliness, noise, discordant speech, frowsy clothing and foul air'. This sounds like Pater again, prescribed as a programme of social improvement. Inevitably, reviewers of Shaw have questioned his use of art for moral purposes: 'his ideas are good, but his characters and plots artificial', has been the common objection. In fact, Shaw's genius is at its best in deriving genuine possibilities of dramatic dialogue and comic scene from radical ideas; it is rather the ideas which become artificial in the process, and his play with moral purposes for the sake of art, for literary effects and intellectual brilliance, which is most questionable.

Over against the artistic intellectualism of the period must be set instances of straightforward belief in empire and the manly virtues, such as may be found in writers like Rudyard Kipling (1865–1936) or the barely remembered William Henley (1849–1903). Kipling's *Barrack Room Ballads* (1892) and *The Seven Seas* (1896) have been dismissed as mere 'verse', but he hit upon an important poetic problem, if not upon much important poetry, in his effort to rescue lyrical themes and language from that romantic dreamland full of rhetorical echoes which proved so alluring to many Victorian poets. Kipling's solution is to use dialect and vulgar speech, and to insist on the romance of actual places and material things; above all he fights for a sense of community and publicly shared experiences, which had steadily faded from poetry since the eighteenth century. In his short stories (*Plain Tales from the Hills, Soldiers Three*, etc., 1888) he is not the subtle novelist of character but the raconteur, who has witnessed some stirring adventure out in India, where Englishmen are exposed to elementary lessons in real life from which they are protected in their effetely civilised home. Kipling is the natural enemy of liberals and aesthetes alike; unfortunately, he is less intelligent than they, and too uncritically allies himself with the less defensible aspects of imperial success. He has neither the brilliance of Shaw nor the ingenuity of H. G. Wells (1866–1946), yet he senses an abiding order of things to which wonder and courage provide the only key; and perhaps for this reason his work, though rarely profound and sometimes distasteful, seems nearer than theirs to the traditional springs of poetry.

To regain the source of fully expressive language, of words which both mean something significant and are something significant, becomes the crucial task for the future of the poetic tradition. Gerard Manley Hopkins (1844–89) and William Butler Yeats (1865–1939) are decisively affected by it and, whether what they have accomplished is in the nature of a new beginning or a final experiment, they are still regarded as the greatest modern English poets. Hopkins' brief work, some 1400 lines of poetry, was published only in 1918, while Yeats' earlier collections (*Crossways*, 1889; *The Rose*, 1893; *The Wind among the Reeds*, 1899) give only slight indication of his later achievement in *The Tower* (1928), to which he owes his fame. Nevertheless, some discussion of their style is proper here because of its affinities, the more striking in the case of Hopkins for being free of foreign influence, with a poetic movement which begins to emerge in Europe generally during the latter part of the nineteenth century. This movement is as extensive, though not so clearly defined, as its 'Romantic' predecessor; to call it 'Symbolist' is to refer to its chief characteristic rather than its accepted title. The common feature of its many forms is a loosening of the reins of metaphor. Traditionally, the images of poetry have been held in close obedience to meaning; symbolism springs from a distrust and partial loss of such conventional guidance. What a symbol 'means' in modern poetry is usually not stated and may never become very clear; in extreme cases it does not even seem to matter. The mental picture and the verbal sound are thrown into new artistic relief by being thrown out of ordinary intellectual context. Thus Hopkins has attempted all kinds of syntactical irregularities, while Yeats makes use of an esoteric and frequently unexplained series of ideas.

Since the aim of the symbolist writer is to raise the status of poetic expression, he turns away from discursive or descriptive style, such as produced 'the decorative landscape and still life', as Yeats called it, of his early poems, a phrase that might also serve for what little remains of Hopkins' immature manner. No symbolist is content, in fact, merely to write 'about' something; any mere impassioned dressing up of thoughts and feelings 'about' a subject leads, he suspects, only to rhetoric, a convention as unacceptable now as realism in painting. Poetic language has to fulfil, for Yeats, an almost religious function, though in quite the reverse sense from preaching a sermon. Great poetry is like a 'church, where there is an altar but no pulpit', in that it celebrates mysteries beside which moral comment is superficial. Hence Yeats' interest in Celtic myths, mystical symbols, 'visionary' writing, and apocalyptic movements of history. Most of these themes have had to be also elucidated in prose; the poems endeavour in some way to enact or evoke them, as though the words themselves were playing a part in a ritualistic cult. This is why Yeats so admired Blake, who 'announced the religion of art', and why, looking back to the age of Spenser when 'the earth had still its sheltering sacredness', he so deeply laments the loss to poetry of this sense of holy patronage. Hopkins actually became a priest in the Society of Jesus, a decision which at first caused him to give up writing as falling altogether below the demands of devotion and divine service. When eventually he made a fresh start with *The Wreck of the Deutschland* (1876), he achieved his finest and truly distinctive work through a supreme effort to infuse language, which had grown tired in the service of secular ends and profane conventions, with the intensity of his faith, and thereby turn it into an act of praise.

As a literary term 'symbolism' originates in France, where it was first introduced by Jean Moréas (1856–1910) in 1885; although only minor poets then publicly adhered to it as a school, it has since been taken to include the work of Arthur Rimbaud (1854–91), Stéphane Mallarmé (1842–98) and Paul Verlaine (1844–96). Rimbaud's literary career lasted barely more than three years. He produced his first poems while still a schoolboy in 1870, and with an unprecedented display of early genius showed himself able to master and equal anything that nineteenth-century French poetry had yet accomplished, rivalling even Baudelaire in power or Gautier in technical skill. In his *Illuminations*, published only in 1886 by Verlaine, after he himself had renounced writing, he explored the limits of whatever was likely still to be attained by symbolism. His collected work can, indeed, be regarded as a symbolic history of the modern poetic mind, culminating in the strange and tragic document, *Une Saison en enfer* (1873), which records its ultimate despair. From what region of the soul do the images of poetry arise? Do words have the magic power to evoke any experience, or are they the beginning of hallucination? These are the questions which Rimbaud has explored, not philosophically but by experimenting with every emotional and intellectual possibility that imagination can conceive, even systematically deranging his normal senses to 'reach the unknown'. Lured by the 'alchemy of language' which promised poetry from spiritual chaos, he appears at times to have cut himself off from the real world entirely, and at times again to be in a state of pure awareness of material things. He combines the two extremes of contemporary sensibility, the poetry which is all of the mind, and the realism which is its disgusted denial. He sees visions of fantastic beauty, yet feels himself to be in hell and knows that it is 'Satan...who loves in a writer the absence of any descriptive or instructive faculties'. The shadow of some terrible damnation falls across the brief work of this prince of symbolists, who thought to remake the universe in poetic splendour beyond good and evil, and almost emptied it at a stroke of any certain meaning.

Mallarmé's personality is pale by comparison. The slender volume of his poetry is no less rich in obscurity, though not the work of any so sudden, compelling inspiration; it bears the meticulous marks of elaborate intellectual construction over a period of nearly forty years. In his prose (*Pages*, 1891; *La Musique et les lettres*, 1894; *Divagations*, 1897) and in occasional lines in his poems Mallarmé has communicated his ideal of music as the ultimate secret of words, rejecting as an illusion what he oddly considered the only alternative: namely, 'the claim to enclose in language the material reality of things'. This is the echo of an ancient philosophic debate, in which a symbolist poet now reopens the case against realism, taking his stand by a concept of art with pretensions to great psychological subtlety. A statement is true in poetry by virtue of its suggestiveness, by its power to evoke a dream-like state, by the emotional satisfaction of its cadence, and by its artificial stimulation of the imaginative senses. The result purports to be some kind of pure spiritual pleasure, as remote from reality as music. Yet pure remoteness from ordinary experience alone offers no criterion for the greatness of art, nor are emotions necessarily pure for being of the spirit instead of 'real', as Mallarmé might have discovered from the example of Rimbaud, or even heard in the music of Wagner to whom he wrote his *Hommage*. What his poetry actually achieves is a blend of abstraction and sensuality, where almost meaningless images act like irritants on the nerves, and inscrutable snatches of thought are coupled with confused desires. *L'Apres-midi d'un faune* (1876) and *Hérodiade* (1899) are more or less explicitly erotic reveries; the latter, with its theme of narcissistic virginity, obsessed Mallarmé throughout his life, and both reveal the same effete refinement of any real emotion into 'pure' aesthetic sensations. *Un Coup de dès jamais n'abolira le hasard* (1897) is neither prose nor poetry, but a composition of phrases irregularly spaced across the page, to render Mallarmé's only 'real' experience: the experience of words. For him the perfect phrase, indeed the magic word, came before the completed sentence, and might never arrive at a rationally comprehensible theme. The traditional idea of beauty or significance as necessarily attributes of some coherent whole seems to have all but disappeared in a neurotic obsession with the parts. Mallarmé can commit himself to no more than the single image, the exquisite combination of several sounds. This is his 'absolute', for of this alone is he sure. Yet he knows too that such thoughts are no more than 'throws of a dice' and ever at the mercy of 'chance': the vulgar universe of mere accident which lies beyond the narrow confines of his mind.

Verlaine's symbolism is of a far simpler order and presents the reader with few problems in understanding. Though his *Art poétique* (1884) denounces conventional rhetoric and speaks of words as if they were colours or musical effects, he actually uses them to write 'about' easily recognisable experiences, and is unorthodox mainly in his metrical innovations. These are designed to assist in the production of a mood, which is the predominant characteristic of his poetry, and which a minor contemporary poet, Tristan Corbière, described as an 'impure mixture of everything'. Verlaine employs a rich variety of images, only to achieve a remarkable sameness of tone. To judge from *Pauvre Lelian*, a commentary on his own work which he wrote for his collection of essays on *Les Poètes maudits* (1884/8), this was a considered ideal. He desires, 'since Man, mystic yet sensual, remains still an intellectual creature', the same response to either extreme of human experience, for they are each only 'varied manifestations of a single thought with its ups and downs'. Thus, the wisdom of taking the good with the bad becomes a technique for taking both as a poetic sensation; even the sense of sin appears to be a refinement of aesthetic pleasure. Verlaine's skill lies in evoking the emotional and almost physical charm of his spiritual interludes, and in detecting some ethereal or sentimental tremor in his more earthy adventures. Between an early work like *La Bonne Chanson* (1870) and *Parallèlement* (1888) his themes undoubtedly grow more serious; but his skill remains unchanged, the interchanges between the soul and the flesh varying the artistic effects rather than lending them moral interest, until in the end the play upon mood and verbal music seems merely monotonous. Verlaine's temperament is too passive for true greatness; equally ready for self-abandon in debauch or piety, he cultivates sorrows that are blurred with pleasurable indulgence, and degradations that are languid with regret.

The aesthetic exploitation of life and the symbolist exploration of imagery both imply an attitude of profound disdain or disbelief towards the once common values and experiences which men shared in the world. It may take the form characterised by Pater in his epicurean of ideas and creeds, or by Paul Valéry (1871–1945) in *La Soirée avec Monsieur Teste* (1896), the writer who is amost reduced to silence because he finds even language too grossly real to express the pure processes of the intellect. The most notorious aesthetes of the period are the Duke Des Esseintes and Count Axel of Auersburg, fictitious aristocrats of man's inner estate. The former is the hero of *À rebours* (1884), a novel by J.-K. Huysmans (1848–1907); he is shown in his solitary 'paradise', an indoor world well stocked with stimulants for his curious senses and with a library of decadent literature. Here he retires from all contact with society, is convinced that even 'nature has had its day' as a subject worthy of interest, and finds it unnecessary now to make any journeys into a world which he can far better enjoy in his reading and his imagination. *Axel* (1890) is a dramatic poem in prose by Villiers de l'Isle-Adam (1838–89); it conveys a still more exalted, and questionable, message of spiritual ascendancy in luxurious tones and emotionally voluptuous scenes, which may have been intended to produce effects of Wagnerian grandeur, but which read rather like an invention of Edgar Allen Poe. In the depths of the Black Forest, in an ancient castle, Count Axel studies the hermetic philosophy of the alchemists. He has no desire for the vast wealth which could be his, and kills the self-styled representative of 'real life' who comes to disturb his inner peace. A beautiful girl tempts him with romantic dreams of all the wide world offers them, but again he resists. In their imagination they have 'exhausted the future', the reality would be nothing by comparison: 'Live? our servants will do that for us.' And in the fullest pride of youth, with magnificent treasures at their feet, they commit suicide in an ecstasy of unrealised love.

Villiers' Catholic conscience was troubled by the morality of such an ending, which yet appealed so deeply to his imaginative instincts. More is involved than the particular transgressions in the plot or even Axel's heretical philosophising. Huysmans in his later novels (*Là-bas*, 1891; *La Cathédrale*, 1898; *L'Oblat*, 1903) writes increasingly in harmony with Christian doctrine, yet leaves similar doubts in the mind. For such other-worldliness as delights the decadent imagination of so many late nine-teenth-century writers is the inevitable prey of the psychologist who sees in it the expression of some perverse inner need rather than of any external or 'real' truth. To understand the nature of this distinction is to understand the seriously divided mind of the period. For, obviously, many values and ideas to which society or individuals are attached could be explained away as indirect gratifications ('sublimations' is the psychologist's word) of subconscious motives, if once an explanation of this sort is felt to be decisive. It had long been toyed with: for instance, by satirists bent on exposing hypocrisy; only gradually did it acquire the weight of an apparently crushing blow at almost all 'pretensions' to civilised living and thinking. Such a psychology, which aims at reducing every spiritual phenomenon to some more material cause, is clearly modelled on a scientific concept of truth, but is itself at best a pseudo-science, incapable of establishing proof; it might more accurately be described as a state of mind influenced by science.

One of the more frequently repeated clichés of the time is that know-ledge must be based on facts; but what are the facts in the case of a religious belief, a moral standard, or an artistic form? Earlier in the nineteenth century it had been supposed that they were environmental and operated from without, a scheme of things borrowed from the physical sciences. The next step was prompted by the later development of the biological sciences: environment is no more than a conditioning factor, and what really underlies the activities of consciousness is some vital force, manifesting itself as emotional energy, which operates from within. Such theories make great show of being factual, but much will depend on what is counted as evidence, and even more on what interpretation is put upon it. One tendency, which was particularly strong in France, reaches its extreme in Flaubert's last novel, *Bouvard et Pécuchet* (1881): it is almost fanatically nihilistic in its exposure of all intellectual and emotional en-deavour as illusory and farcical. A similar tendency is expressed in various countries and genres by the naturalist movement, which includes some of the shabbiest and most hopeless views of man ever taken. These are not, however, the only possible interpretation. For their starting-point is vague and ambiguous; it amounts to the general notion that whatever ideals a man may cherish, whether religious, moral, practical, or artistic, they are likely to be 'only true psychologically'; and this idea can be interpreted in the opposite, the proudest, sense—the sense of the symbolists and aesthetes. For them poetry *need* only be true psychologically; the mind is free to create its own satisfactions and fabricate what pleasures, what knowledge it will; the imagination can engineer even religious exultation by playing on the right emotions. Wagner was the master-builder of this inner world, and towards the end of the century his music was treated almost as a cult to celebrate the conquest of the soul. Despite his incomparably greater genius, however, the same suspicion now falls on the mystical celebrations of *Parsifal* (1882) as upon *Axel*. This is not to doubt the virtue of man's ancient striving to transcend material things, but only the manner in which it has been represented. And the doubt is perhaps justified to the extent to which Wagner and Villiers, Huysmans, and indeed many other 'artists of the spirit', were themselves psychologists rather than believers, and were sometimes led by their tastes and talent to find in the search for spiritual purity a pretext for subtle aesthetic orgies.

Naturalism had originated in France during the 1860's with the novels produced in collaboration by Edmond de Goncourt (1822–96) and his brother Jules (1830–70). A commentary on its origins and theory is provided by their *Journal* of the time, published later, with considerable additions, by Edmond between 1887 and 1896. Not for the first time a new departure in art is inspired by the feeling that past conventions have been unnatural, that literature is not sufficiently like life; but instead of a return to nature and feeling, naturalism demands a more scientific record of behaviour. Émile Zola (1840–1902), the greatest novelist of the new school, expounds the same ideal in *Le Roman expérimental* (1880), and he also adopted the method of making a careful compilation of notes and facts for every novel. In an early lecture on Balzac (1866), whom he claims as a precursor, he likens the writer to a surgeon or chemist, able impartially to dissect or establish laws of cause and effect in the human organism. It is Zola's favourite comparison and typifies the naturalist movement; it would have been endorsed by the Goncourts, who similarly speak of 'clinical' analysis in fiction, and probably also by Flaubert.

The obvious problem for the naturalist writer is that a novel can hardly be, in any literal sense, an experiment or a record; everything in it is invented, or at least selected, then arranged and given stylistic utterance, in accordance with quite non-scientific requirements of scene and story, suspense and resolution, pathos and tragedy. This is why Edmond de Goncourt claimed that their works 'had tried, above all else, to kill the plot in the novel'; and why Flaubert, equally aware of a discrepancy between scientific purpose and artistic execution, attempted extraordinary stylistic manœuvres to overcome it. Zola seems only rarely to have considered the difficulty, and wrote in a style which has about it little to suggest scientific detachment. He is a quite unscrupulous manipulator of literary effects, who stops at nothing to evoke a strong emotional response in the reader; with the result that his writing has been called lurid, obscene, coarse, vulgar. For all this (and excepting passages which are merely dull), it is difficult to deny its power. This is of a peculiar, possibly unique, kind: it works, if such a distinction can be made, on the literary senses rather than on the literary intelligence, sustaining them with a pleasure so uncritical that it scarcely varies, even where the subject is horrible and sad. Its chief danger, therefore, is to produce a surfeit; but where it does not, then the imagination eagerly awaits more sensations, not in the form of complex adventures, but from continued contact with physical impressions: such as might well pass for the very raw material of life, but for the fact, of course, that the whole experience is manufactured out of words. Zola's true artistic affinities are perhaps less with such fastidious and intelligent social portraitists as the Goncourts, than with the musician who composed his operas on the same massive scale, and exploited similar effects of sheer emotional power in professed service of a high-minded truth: Richard Wagner.

Between 1871 and 1893 Zola published twenty novels, planned as a series under the general title of *Les Rougon-Macquart* and giving 'the social and natural history of a family during the Second Empire'. The particular truth he wishes to establish is the deterministic influence of heredity upon all the 'instinctive manifestations of human character, which produce what convention knows as virtues and vices'. The congenital tendency of the Rougon-Macquart is, however, nothing more specific than an 'overflowing of the natural appetites', which Zola anyway considers typical of an age altogether bent upon physical enjoyments. The family so distributes itself that he has an opportunity to portray all sections of the national life; he succeeds best with the Parisian working class (*L'Assommoir*, 1877), the downtrodden poor of a mining village (*Germinal*, 1885), and the doomed army of the Franco-Prussian war (*La Débâcle*, 1892), the culminating disaster of which he says, revealingly, that he 'needed it as an artist'. In his later novels, *Les Trois Villes* (1894/8), and *Les Quatre Évangiles* (1899–1903), Zola became the prophet of some brave, new humanity, denouncing religious superstition and proclaiming the gospel of Fecundity, Work, Truth and Justice. During the last years of his life he even achieved the glory of a martyr, and temporary exile, through his famous articles in defence of Dreyfus (*J'accuse*). His political and philosophical ideas present, however, the weakest aspect of his work, and the weakness extends in some measure also to his understanding of character, if this is judged by the high intellectual standards of the nineteenth-century novel. Zola's justification is hinted at in his preface to *Thérèse Raquin* (2nd ed. 1868): 'My intention has been to study temperaments not characters.' In practice this came to mean that his own imaginative temperament played the dominant role in his characters' experiences, the practice less of a literary scientist than of a poet. With the result that, where his imagination is engaged most passionately, Zola seems to carry the whole vast fatalistic scheme of vice and degradation beyond reach or need of psychological analysis or social explanation. He makes descriptions of simple emotions and physical things sound like a mythological celebration of elemental mysteries, surrounding them with an air of demonic intensity which is out of any scientific proportion to the real wretchedness of the actual actors and action and scene.

In 1880 naturalism established itself publicly as a literary school through a joint publication, *Les Soirées de Médan*, prefaced by an aggressive declaration of principles, containing short stories by six authors; these were Zola, Huysmans (who only later found his true medium in aesthetic and religious fiction), three minor novelists: Paul Alexis (1851–1901), Henri Céard (1851–1924), and Léon Hennique (1851–1935), and finally Guy de Maupassant (1850–93). In the judgement of Flaubert, who for a time had been teacher to Maupassant, the contribution of his pupil, *Boule de suif*, entirely 'crushed' the others. The results of this tuition were long apparent in the ironical factuality and terse exactitude of Maupassant's style. He shows a far finer, though less powerful, talent than Zola, excelling above all in his short stories, of which he produced more than three hundred, many of them masterpieces; *La Maison Tellier* (together with *En famille*, 1881), *Mlle Fifi* (1883), *Miss Harriett* (together with *Le Baptême*), *Yvette*, and *M. Parent* (1884) are among the best. Maupassant's naturalism quickly won him notoriety and success; by his high skill with low subjects, his brilliant exposure of shabby gentility, his literary nicety in recounting crude or carnal behaviour, he blended vulgarity with extreme sophistication in a way to suit contemporary tastes tired of more solemn realism. He is persistently pessimistic, yet in a manner which frequently tends towards the thin acerbity of witty cynicism; and for all his wide range of observation and invention, he gives the impression now of having greatly diminished life's potentialities. In the preface to his most substantial novel, *Pierre et Jean* (1888), he comments that 'everyone forms for himself an illusion of the world, which is poetic, or sentimental, or joyful, or melancholy, or unclean, or dismal, according to his nature. The writer's only task is to reproduce this illusion faithfully....' The danger for such a writer is that this psychological insight is likely to reduce virtually all experience to one category, the category of illusion and disillusion, to be represented in an endless variety of instances but always fundamentally the same. The effect might be tedious were not Maupassant's artistry so great in being able to concentrate his whole point into a single scene, a place, a person, an anecdote. He is the master of the fleeting charm, the tell-tale moment, the cruel accident, but his resources seem not quite adequate sometimes to account, at novel length, for the energy inspiring a whole career (*Bel Ami*, 1885) or the shape of a whole life (*Une Vie*, 1883). The only realities in Maupassant's world of illusions are, of course, the senses; variously gratified or frustrated, they inexplicably lure life onward, colouring it sometimes brightly, sometimes sombrely. They represent for naturalism the irreducible phenomenon, 'la joie de vivre' of Zola's bitter novel by that name, physical existence asserting itself in a spiritual void. Such a vision of mortal futility stirs on occasions even in Maupassant's humorous and detached mind a sentiment of pity, though it is mingled with nausea and horrified fascination.

The sentiment is purer, being founded on a genuine affection for man and beast, in the work of Alphonse Daudet (1840–97). Though he was closely associated with the leaders of the naturalist movement, practised their method of keeping notebooks on all he witnessed or heard, and could produce such pieces of painful documentation as *Femmes d'artistes* (1874) or grim details of war and slums in some of the *Contes du lundi* (1873), it is for the fantasy and charm of his stories about the Midi (*Lettres de mon moulin*, 1869), and above all for *Tartarin de Tarascon* (1872), one of the great comic creations of French literature, that he will be remembered. If many of Daudet's novels have declined from their once considerable popularity (*Fromont jeune et Risler aîné*, 1874; *Le Nabab*, 1877; *Numa Roumestan*, 1881) this may be due to a certain unevenness in his later technique and style. For he only half assimilated the influences of naturalism, and half remained the writer of indulgent feeling whose first subject had been his own childhood (*Le Petit chose*, 1868). Though he dedicated his account of religious mania in *l'Évangéliste* (1883) to the famous neurologist Charcot, and earned Zola's praise for his analysis of a degrading passion in *Sapho* (1884), Daudet's 'naturalistic' psychology is weak by comparison with his power of sympathy. This easily degenerates into sentimentality, the inherent flaw in that vein of pathetic sensibility which runs through all his work, but at its best it inspires in him a fond attachment for people and places, and a compassion for humble misfortune, that has suggested to many readers a likeness to Dickens.

The limitations of a concise history are particularly unjust in the case of French literature, where many distinguished names must be dismissed with only a brief mention. The extreme opposition of literary schools in the period helps at least to place certain minor poets clearly within the symbolist tradition, such as Albert Samain, Gustave Kahn, and René Ghil, together with the American-born Stuart Merrill and Francis Viélé-Griffin; and it further conveniently distinguishes between, on the one hand, the naturalistic drama produced by André Antoine at his Théâtre Libre, where adaptations of Zola and original plays by Henri Becque were eventually eclipsed by Ibsen, and on the other hand, Lugné-Poe's Théâtre de l'Œuvre, which first experimented with the symbolist pieces of Maurice Maeterlinck (1862–1949). The early work of this Belgian playwright-philosopher, although it often betrays too glib a use of vaguely portentous symbols, has yet proved rich in suggestive hints for other writers (Pirandello and Yeats were both influenced by him), for stage and, later, film producers, and for Debussy whose music has probably saved his *Pelléas et Mélisande* (1892) from oblivion. Maeterlinck was to achieve greater fame, however, with his scientific and metaphysical writings (the famous series on insect life begins in 1901 with *La Vie des abeilles*); although such works as *Le Trésor des humbles* (1896) have been praised for their beauty of style, and his poet's sense for the essential mysteriousness of life has been of greater literary than philosophical importance, the story of his lifelong inquiry into its meaning belongs rather to the history of thought.

Restlessness of mind, the search for new forms of expression, reliable ideas, and some authentic attitude to life, drove many writers of the time from one style or philosophy or experiment to another, and thus make it impossible to classify them in this school or that. The four poets elected to the Académie Française during the period—Sully Prudhomme (1881), François Coppée (1884), Leconte de Lisle (1886), and J.-M. de Heredia (1894)—alone preserved some measure of continuity with older conventions, affirming a 'parnassian' tradition of style and sentiment; but the more interesting developments were less academic. Jean Moréas, the symbolist, turned away from that movement to found an 'École romane', a neo-classical reaction from overly intellectual and introverted poetry in favour of a Mediterranean ideal of plastic simplicity, wherein he met a distinguished ally in Charles Maurras, a former disciple of Mistral. Frédéric Mistral (1830–1914) is the only remembered poet of a Provençal revival, typical of various attempts during the last hundred years to discover in ancient local traditions (here that of the troubadours) a way of living, and certainly of writing about life, more colourfully and fully than seemed possible in contemporary urban civilisation. Only the Belgian Émile Verhaeren (1855–1916) succeeded in winning occasionally great poetry from this unpromising scene, using symbolist techniques developed in more personal volumes that culminate in *Les Flambeaux noirs* (1890), to convey the socialist indignation, fraternal pity, and visionary criticism inspired in him by the sight of the modern human condition. For Henri de Régnier (1864–1936) man's departed glory could be caught at best in elegiac echoes of the past or dreamy fantasies, while for the still younger poets Paul Claudel and Charles Péguy it had to be regained through a return to the Catholic faith, from which they believed the subtleties of poetic sensibility might alone recover some real purpose and meaning. Claudel's earliest inspiration was intimately connected with his discovery of Rimbaud's *Illuminations*, and he claimed to see in the infernal light of that apparently disruptive and disrupted imagination the possibility (or was it simply a dire need?) of a divine order; certainly, not to find it left poetry too easily inclined towards mere ironic celebrations of disorder, such as mark the work of Jules Laforgue (1860–87).

A considerable Catholic and conservative revival is also one of the more striking tendencies among writers of prose, whether fiction, criticism or philosophy, towards the end of the century; and this tendency coincided with a general reaction against the spiritual emptiness of naturalism, first expressed critically by Brunetière (*Le Roman naturaliste*, 1883). Paul Bourget (1852–1935), whose sense of responsibility for youth at the mercy of pernicious intellectual influences inspired *Le Disciple* (1889), and who tried to analyse the mental components of the age in *Essais de psychologie contemporaine* (1883/5), began a series of religious novels with *L'Étape* (1903), in which he exposed the inadequacies of a materialistic democracy. Maurice Barrès (1862–1923), though by nature a wanderer and an aesthete, outgrew his purely anarchical concern with the inner individual alone, to search for the secret of the good life within a still uncorrupted community: and this meant for him the provincial, conservative society of Lorraine (not Paris, which he condemns in *Les Déracinés*, 1897), and came also to mean a Catholic society, as still later novels show. There were, of course, other solutions, other distractions, of which two examples must suffice by way of conclusion: Pierre Loti (1850–1923), the *nom de plume* of a naval officer, who enjoyed a great success with his sentimental stories and descriptions of distant lands, his glimpses of simpler people and a more natural way of life (*Pêcheur d'Islande*, 1886); and Anatole France (1844–1924), who captured that section of the intellectually-minded public which wanted ideas dealt with in an elegantly cultured and rationally reassuring manner, and was prepared to follow him in his anti-clerical socialism.

To turn from the variously opposed extremes to which French poets and novelists were pushing their exploration of the modern mind and world, to the fiction of their contemporaries writing in German (*Dichter*, as they may be called in that language without regard to an absolute distinction between poetry and prose) is to enter a different realm of the imagination. It is also, apparently, to turn back in time. Besides such obvious pointers as the use of historical themes by Conrad Ferdinand Meyer (1825–98) and to a lesser extent by Theodor Fontane (1819–98), or more subtle hints of bygone romanticism in the nostalgic reminiscences of Theodor Storm (1817–88) and of some altogether older fashion in the stories of Gottfried Keller (1819–90), which seem to have no temporal location at all, there is a common link between each of these otherwise dissimilar writers and the past: their style. This is known as 'poetic realism', and it maintains and develops an artistic tradition of language, a classic manner, which dates back to the period of literary renaissance in Germany at the beginning of the century.

Was it the unique accomplishment of that late cultural revival, with its romantic music and philosophies of art, or some accident of national temperament or political disunity, even backwardness, that German literature remained for so long largely out of touch with the unpoetic realities of the increasingly industrial and scientific age? Explanations are idle beside the fact that the imagination of so many German writers continued to inhabit an ideal world—ideal not because it is morally perfect but because it fulfils certain literary conventions—at a time when in other countries conventional limitations were being drastically revised. Thus, when Fontane writes about the Berlin and Prussian provinces of his day, he sets and describes his scenes (such as excursions into the country or formal visits) in a way which would allow them to take their place in a narrative by Goethe or Stifter. The case is similar with C. F. Meyer: his heroic idyll (*Hutten*, 1871), his novel about the wild and tragic Swiss patriot Jürg Jenatsch (1876) which he first attempted as a drama, his tales of great heroes and criminals and events of the past packed with psychological 'moments' of extreme pathos (from *Der Heilige*, 1879, to *Pescara*, 1887, and *Angela Borgia*, 1891), together with his belief that 'art alone raises us above the trivialities of existence', his admiration of Schiller, and his revulsion from the 'brutal actuality of contemporary subjects': everything suggests a disappointed candidate for the classical German theatre rather than a late nineteenth-century novelist.

The other Swiss representative of poetic realism, Gottfried Keller, is undoubtedly one of the finest and most original writers in the language, but if his humour is all his own, his use of literature for moral enlightenment, his lasting concern over his 'educational novel', *Der grüne Heinrich* (1854/79: the changes in style and form in the second version are designed to bring out more clearly the true *lesson* of experience), and above all his ideal of *Humanität*, that untranslatable concept which is the cornerstone of German classicism, uniting humanitarian and aesthetic virtues in a noble vision of the good life: all this is again traditional. And how unlike any other places in European fiction are the Seldwyla and Zürich depicted in Keller's two collections of stories, *Die Leute von Seldwyla* (1856, continued 1874) and *Die Züricher Novellen* (1878)! The facts about life in the provinces probably do not vary so decisively from country to country, yet Keller has transformed them into the stuff of ballad and legend, humorously bestowing upon domestic episode now epic dignity, now lyrical feeling, and with such perfect naturalness that it is hard to believe that Flaubert or George Eliot were his contemporaries as students of the provincial scene. Keller is also the foremost poet among this group of novelists, who are further remarkable for the amount and excellence of their poetry; even Fontane, who comes closest to conventional realism in his novels, is the author of several beautiful poems. Theodor Storm's popularity has been chiefly established by his song-like poetry in the German romantic style; his career as a realist shows a gradual development from such entirely lyrical stories as *Immensee* (1852) to *Der Schimmelreiter* (1888), his nearest approach to a novel. Opinion is divided over this last work as over Keller's *Martin Salamander* (1886); by their scope and substance they exceed the ideal limits of the 'poetic' tradition (better suited to the form of the *Novelle*, or long story) and enter the wider world of the European novel; here their danger is so to loosen the close spell of imaginative interest that they appear, after all, merely provincial.

Fontane just escapes this fault, while yet extending the tradition to include at least one of the subjects more widely recognised as realistic: the social and psychological problems of marriage and infidelity. In all his better works (*Schach von Wuthenow*, 1883; *L'Adultera*, 1882; *Graf Petöfy*, 1884; *Irrungen, Wirrungen*, 1887; *Stine*, 1890; *Unwiederbringlich*, 1891) he shows love in conflict with the conventions of a society where belief in the moral law on which they were founded is beginning to decline. What is left is ironical acceptance and the dignity even of undeserved suffering. It is this, rather than the actual nature of passion, which concerns Fontane, and which distinguishes his best novel, *Effi Briest* (1895), from its greater rivals on the same theme, Flaubert's *Madame Bovary* and Tolstoy's *Anna Karenina*. That it has not enjoyed their degree of international fame may be due partly to the importance of its stylistic virtues which do not easily survive translation. For a realist Fontane is astonishingly discreet and indirect; many of what might be supposed extremely relevant facts and feelings in a love story seem to receive too little attention, while apparently incidental details and, above all, conversations are rendered skilfully and at length. The explanation lies in a kind of artistic tact, which suggests to Fontane that certain things are not meant to be brought to the conscious attention of language. He has, in fact, for a novelist, a perhaps overdeveloped sense that not all aspects of life may legitimately be made articulate. Hence his predilection for dialogue, which it is always fitting to record, and his interest, at the opposite extreme, in little symbolic details of scene which can be left to speak for themselves. The mood of gentle irony in Fontane's novels stems from the contrast between what his characters are capable of saying and all that, by the merest hints, they are shown to experience and feel.

Any less ironical or less talented acceptance of the noble conventions of 'literature', as opposed to the untractable reality of 'life', easily deteriorates into the kind of literary productions which were the real favourites of the German-speaking public during the period. It is possible that Marie von Ebner-Eschenbach (1830–1916), in whose work the desire for a finer world expresses itself with natural nobility and the authority of the born educator, will continue to command respect; but few readers will now take seriously the massive celebrations of the teutonic past in Felix Dahn's and Julius Wolff's novels, Ernest von Wildenbruch's epic attempts at reconciling the aggressive virtues of modern Prussia with the classical ideal of *Humanität*, or Paul Heyse's 'stylistically pure' heroics of love. At the bottom, but best-selling, end of the scale come Marlitt's sentimental visions of class distinction overcome in the embraces of young aristocrats and daughters of the middle classes. This was the 'state of German literature' against which a naturalist movement, having its headquarters in Berlin and Munich, reacted with doctrines learned from Zola and Ibsen.

Although it ventured into every genre of literature, naturalism had a decisive effect in Germany only upon the drama, reinvigorating it with revolutionary gusto, and drawing large audiences to club theatres (such as the celebrated 'Freie Bühne' in Berlin) which were sheltered from censorship and yet enjoyed the noisiest publicity. It fostered a generation of ingenious stage-producers, whose art exploited new opportunities for working on the imagination, left vacant by the absence of poetry; Otto Brahm and, later, Max Reinhardt were outstanding representatives of this class of artistic entrepreneurs, who only now came into their own. There also grew up a style of 'naturalistic' acting, the remarkable accomplishments of which rendered many good actors incapable of ever again mastering the gestures and rhythms of classical drama, but prepared them for the demands that were soon to be made upon them by the cinema. This kind of performance had already been encouraged to some extent in the plays of the Austrian dramatist Ludwig Anzengruber (1839–89), which were written in peasant idiom and further pretended to frank realism by their themes, their earthy wisdom and coarse humour. Moreover, when the naturalist fashion was at its height, other minor, but technically competent, playwrights like Hermann Sudermann (1857–1928) and Max Halbe (1865–1944), who were not closely associated with the movement, profited from the established taste for the world of the Petty Assizes, as well as from the naturalist technique of acting.

Except for Gerhart Hauptmann (1862–1946) the movement is more famous than its members: Heinrich Hart (1855–1906) and his brother Julius (1857–1930), editors of *Kritische Waffengänge*; M. G. Conrad (1846–1927), editor of *Die Gesellschaft*; Arno Holz (1863–1929) and Johannes Schlaf (1862–1941), joint authors of *Papa Hamlet* (1889) and *Die Familie Selicke* (1890). Their literary ambition now seems in many ways paradoxical: to show man as the victim of environment and heredity, and yet to believe in optimistic ideals of social progress; to unearth the cruder details of human nature with the apparent assurance that this grisly spectacle must liberate and exalt the mind as though in contemplation of a magnificent truth; to arrange cunning and daring 'naturalistic' effects on the stage and yet to justify these artistic refinements by claiming that they were the 'real thing'. Fontane, admiring the works of the young Gerhart Hauptmann for an achievement which he himself could not emulate, points out that 'what seems to the layman a mere recording of life represents a degree of sheer artistry which can scarcely be surpassed'. Such high praise would certainly be excessive with regard to the other German naturalists; their molestations of the tragic muse with indelicate banalities is likely to remain no more than a sensational experiment.

While they amused or 'interestingly' scandalised their audiences by trying to accustom them to the aesthetic enjoyment of what Hermann Conradi, one of the most eloquent spokesmen of the school, called the true emanation of the world: the aroma of uncleanliness, Gerhart Hauptmann succeeded in creating moments of pure and deeply moving tragedy out of the rawest material. This is true above all of *Die Weber* (1892), a play that has no hero and hardly a plot, and yet invades the mind with pity and terror, and persuades through its meticulous thematic coherence. Its one protagonist is a village of Silesian weavers, wretched and exploited creatures who are barely articulate, but who convey in their native dialect the pathos of human misery. If Hauptmann's tumultuously successful first play, *Vor Sonnenaufgang* (1889), was still marred by the rhetoric of ideological convictions, prophecies of the 'dawn of a new age', and too blatant rattling of such fashionable skeletons in the cupboard as hereditary alcoholism, *Die Weber* has no message. Society here is not the large abstraction of the social reformer, but a real and ineradicable pattern of human greed, suffering, unreasoning hope and insensible self-deception. The proclamations of a young rebel are not more affirmed than the Christian resignation of an old man, and even the small-town tycoon is as much a victim as a villain. Such is the poetic justice by which Hauptmann, in a series of naturalist plays, including masterpieces like *Fuhrmann Henschel* (1898) and *Rose Bernd* (1903), bestows the dignity of character and fate upon figures who are small if measured by the traditional standards of tragedy.

That Hauptmann's imagination was not bound to any programme is further demonstrated by his mixture of poetry and prose in *Hanneles Himmelfahrt* (1893). The subject and setting of this short drama could not be more 'naturalistic': the last hours in a poor-house of an innocent little girl who has been driven to suicide by the brutalities of a drunkard foster-father; yet Hauptmann's feelings are stirred to genuine lyricism, which finally dominates the drama in a poetic vision of ministering angels. Though he grafts the poetic on to the real by that most dubious of devices, a hallucinatory transformation of ordinary characters into spiritual beings, he avoids the obvious dangers of sentimentality by sheer effectiveness of language. Hauptmann experimented at greater length, if less successfully, with poetic drama in *Die versunkene Glocke* (1896), a composition in which light and darkness, spiritual freedom and demonic bondage, fight their ancient battles through somewhat confused and confusing symbolic representatives. His later career as a dramatist is characterised by variations between naturalistic and traditionally poetic subjects.

Just as German naturalism was influenced by its French counterpart, so the symbolist poetry of Stefan George (1868–1933) was indebted to Mallarmé and Baudelaire. The closed circle of poets who contributed to George's *Die Blätter für die Kunst* (1892–1919: a German *Yellow Book* in which the high earnestness of initiates takes the place of dandy exclusiveness) also believed that 'the worth of a poem is determined not by the meaning...but by the form'. Yet their aestheticism differed from the French in having about it the air of some militant, quasi-religious cult, of which George was the high priest. Thus, he and his disciples further believed that to preserve and serve the 'pure spirit' of poetry, called for an élite of wise, disciplined men, who should be strong enough in soul not only to resist the corruption of the age—its materialism, its spiritual laziness, its sentimentality—but actually to regenerate the nation. Inevitably, perhaps, George's tendency to assume the role of prophet, together with his insistence on leadership and loyalty, have been misinterpreted as betraying fascist yearnings, but he is guilty, if at all, only of not realising that the impulse towards 'regeneration', which he sought to arouse, might be capable of crude political exploitation. The cultural longing expressed in his poetry is not for any modern country rejoicing in nationalistic arrays of power, but rather for that idealised state of Hellenic perfection of which the German poetic imagination has dreamt in so many forms. The disturbing difference in George's case lies in a change of tone from the traditional harmonies of classical serenity to the aggressively superior accents of Nietzsche's superman. The prophetic note is not, however, typical of all, or even the best, of George's work. Though his poems form a sequence which devotees revere as a kind of spiritual pilgrimage—beginning with the early *Hymnen* (1890) and *Pilgerfahrten* (1891), then travelling through the various domains of art (Arcadian, medieval, oriental, Renaissance: *Algabal*, 1892; *Die Bücher der Hirten und Preisgedichte*, etc., 1895) and exploring the seasonal moods of the soul (*Das Jahr der Seele*, 1897) in order to arrive at last at the revelations contained in *Der Teppich des Lebens* (1899) and a number of later volumes— they are all short lyrical pieces, and the finest stand alone as independent masterpieces without regard to their pretentious context. To give an idea of George by reference to some near English contemporaries, it might be said that certain of his doctrines (such as the 'synthesis of mind, soul and body') are as vague and dated as those of Meredith, which they sometimes resemble; that his fads about printing suggest the craft-revivalism of William Morris; but that his vivid use of symbolism and his determination to avoid the clichés of conventional sentiment or expression rank him with Yeats.

The measure of George's achievement is more easily taken in Germany by a glance at the work of his minor rivals, Detlev von Liliencron (1844–1909), Richard Dehmel (1863–1920), or Max Dauthendey (1867–1918). Their problem is manifestly that of late-comers in a tradition, who struggle for originality in a language ringing with unwanted echoes. Dehmel's typographical devices, meaningless syllables, ingenious images and forced reflections reveal only a more self-conscious awareness of the dilemma than the 'impressionism' of Liliencron and Dauthendey, which pretends to capture a new freshness direct from things by a studied technique of detailed touches and glimpses. Against this background, where striking or felicitous phrases abound but great poems are rare, George's style stands out with firm distinction: a pattern imposed, it is felt, upon words by the same authoritative mind, and shaped by the same assertive will as inspired his lifelong crusade against decadence and his search for a high, godlike standard to affirm.

A more telling contrast is provided, however, by the poetry of Hugo von Hofmannsthal (1874–1929). The author in later years of libretti for the operas of Richard Strauss, he had displayed by the age of twenty-five a lyrical genius of the first order in a brief collection of poems, to which he never again added and which therefore properly belong to the period (unlike the work of Germany's greatest modern poet, Rainer Maria Rilke (1875–1926), who had accomplished nothing to warrant any similar, sudden rise to fame during the late 1890's). The correspondence between George and this young Viennese aristocrat reveals a striking antithesis of artistic temperament, despite their concern over common problems and occasional agreement in theory. Hofmannsthal's nature seems by comparison altogether passive, almost feminine, and although he too is a symbolist, the pure discipline of art is for him the very reverse of a discipline of character; it is as if his imagination were adrift along an endless shore, where he feels drawn to each thing as it passes, but never sets foot. From the first his inspiration is deeply associated with a sense of disintegration, which culminates in the famous 'Letter' (*Ein Brief*, 1902) explaining, through the fictitious character of Lord Chandos, why he has given up writing poetry. He describes a state of mind in which conventional ideas and ways of thinking, indeed the conventional medium of language, appear suddenly devoid of coherence and meaning: leaving the poet with odd bits and pieces of the world that fascinate his attention as though they contained, despite their inarticulate and fragmentary irrelevance, all the vanished meaning of the whole. This is one of the most illuminating commentaries on the mysterious origin and significance of much contemporary symbolism; and it complements a theme repeated and varied in several of Hofmannsthal's poems and short dramatic pieces (*Der Tor und der Tod*, 1893; *Das Bergwerk zu Falun*, 1899): that the pursuit of poetry in this subtle modern form, for all that it may create the illusion of infinite possibilities and profundities of imaginative vision, loses touch with the simple reality of life. The charm of Hofmannsthal's early work lies in his feeling for what has been lost, which inspires its incomparable lyric strain compounded of melancholy resignation and some deep fear half dissolved in sadness.

The many bewildering voices of the period are dominated at last by one who speaks with true authority, having the power to resolve its sophisticated problems into dramas which touch again the perennial springs of human motive and reveal the unalterable shape of man's predicament: it is the Norwegian poet and playwright, Henrik Ibsen (1828–1906). If he is the 'father of the modern theatre', he has begotten no equals. His plays were variously hailed or denounced throughout Europe as revolutionary manifestos, which seemed to make him the ally, if not the founder, of progressive movements for literary or social reform. His name has already been mentioned in connection with naturalism, but he might with equal justification be regarded as a symbolist, or simply as the latest and most gifted writer of 'bourgeois tragedy'. For he does not, even in *Ghosts* (1881), his play involving hereditary disease, merely exploit the sensational horrors which naturalists pretended to consider the sole reality. What is above all real to Ibsen is the salvation of souls, the conflict of good and evil on the psychological, not the material plane. To read *A Doll's House* (1879) merely as a plea for feminine emancipation is to ignore the indications of an inescapably tragic dilemma in its love story. If there is any reform which Ibsen thinks necessary, it must take place within the individual, engaging him in that ancient struggle through which he comes to terms with his destiny; this may indeed have tragic necessity, but no solution.

It has been sufficiently illustrated how uncertain and problematical was the literary character of the age. This is no mere matter of historical generalisation, but reflects a real predicament in the lives of so many individuals. Enjoying unprecedented freedom and knowledge, the contemporary mind is so various that it is in danger of no longer knowing what it really wants or is. Only this problem of establishing for itself a character might possibly be considered still truly 'universal', and in concentrating upon it in the lives of his heroes, Ibsen gave to his work that broadly representative quality, superior to questions of school, which distinguishes the greatest authors. The theme is most beautifully stated in *Peer Gynt* (1867) a masterpiece acknowledged internationally despite the damage done to its poetry by translation. Its hero is the usually comic figure of the braggart, and he comes to typify something in the nature of all mankind as surely as Don Quixote or Falstaff. What is he really? Has he done, has he been, anything worthy the name of man? It is not necessarily evidence of real goodness that is needed for his justification; real badness would do as well: only to *have* a moral character, a soul worth saving or damning, this is for Ibsen the crucial issue. For the danger is not evil, but nothingness, a state of humanity so pointless that it deserves merely to be thrown back into the melting-pot, obliterated without trace. Is this not the deepest worry of the present day—and intimately connected with its proudest boasts? Ibsen insists that it is a matter of spiritual integrity, which must be preserved against sheer dissipation not only of the flesh, but of the imagination and the mind; while the ultimate enemy is a mysterious force which thwarts the soul in its sporadic efforts at self-assertion, and makes it lose its substance in the toils of circumstance. Salvation comes, if at all, through the tragic suffering of love.

The need, amounting to a driving passion, to be a 'real' person provides the central idea for two of Ibsen's finest plays, *Hedda Gabler* (1890) and *John Gabriel Borkman* (1896); and his entire work explores different aspects of the same struggle of the individual for self-realisation. The centres of conflict lie where the modern world has chiefly tried to satisfy its urge for meaning: in its desire to get at some 'real truth' which it suspects must lurk behind the comfortable conventions of the past; in its curiosity, therefore, about the hidden psychology of sex; and in its absolute claims for art. The 'revolutionary' plays, *Pillars of Society* (1877) and *An Enemy of the People* (1882), do not depend for their interest on the selected examples of social hypocrisy and corruption; their underlying concern is with the tragic conflict encountered by an idealistic passion for truth. The conflict would be merely melodramatic were it just a stand-up fight against falsehood; in fact, it is an inner test of character and entangled with personal affections and loyalties. This theme finds its final and best expression in *The Wild Duck* (1884), where Gregor Werle's ruthless insistence upon living in full knowledge of the truth is partly motivated by a deep resentment against his father, and causes nothing but havoc in the lives of his friends whose existence is inseparable from cherished illusions, affectionate complicity and innocent love.

Another version of the theme preoccupied Ibsen from *Brand* (1866) to the later 'symbolic' dramas, *The Master Builder* (1892) and *When We Dead Awaken* (1899). Here it is the artist's need to be true to his inspiration, and to live up to almost inhuman demands upon his integrity, which is put to the test. Ibsen's insight reaches farthest (and borders at times on obscurity) in his effort to understand the ambiguous nature of the artistic character. It aspires to the highest standards yet its motives are questionable; its glory draws near to vainglory, to a glorification of the mind at the expense of love; and when it is tempted into the service of life, it ceases to be true to itself. Ibsen reveals the inevitable paradox of art in a period in which there is no basis in reality for its ideals, and truth no longer conforms to instinctive feelings and beliefs. Then idealism is bound to be charged with heroic perversity, and only a miraculous hope can sustain it from collapse. Ibsen possessed this hope, although it is rarely more than hinted at or expressed indirectly by symbols and metaphors. The hint is always the same: that through suffering, and above all through love, with its ineradicable moral roots in guilt and sacrifice (*Rosmersholm*, 1886; *Little Eyolf*, 1894), the soul will be 'awakened'.

How great is the difference made by this metaphorical hint may be seen from the plays of Ibsen's younger Swedish contemporary, August Strindberg (1849–1912). His characters are irretrievably in hell, which is 'described with a realism that seems to preclude all thought of metaphors, poetical or otherwise'. So it appears, in *The Dance of Death* (1901), to a newcomer to the infernal scene, which, as always in Strindberg's earlier dramas, imprisons within its narrow circle a human couple condemned to mutual destruction. As the play progresses he will learn more about this hell which is the apparent denial of all that has ever been meant by poetry. Here everything is 'translated', as it is called, into evil. The secret of this translation is, in fact, a perversion of man's most creative gift: the power to 'carry over' the things of real experience into a world of spiritual meaning. The power has become satanic because it is now used to destroy, to undermine the pretences of the soul with some demonic interpretation of savage purpose or malign significance. Before this psychology of the jungle, where soul preys upon soul, luring its victim with promises, lulling it with sentiment, nothing is holy. The external action in Strindberg's plays is of secondary importance, resembling so many sham manœuvres which precede the kill; and once the illusions upon which life depends have been broken, the death-blow need hardly be delivered. Thus, *Creditors* (1889) presents what must surely be the most accomplished display of slow spiritual torture in literature. A similar, though cruder, technique is used in *The Father* (1887) where defeat is acknowledged with the words: 'A fatal reality would have called forth resistance, nerved life and soul to action; but now my thoughts dissolve into air, and my brain grinds a void until it is on fire.'

There is no escape for Strindberg's men and women, who are 'bound together by guilt and crime' (*The Ghost Sonata*, 1907); yet neither is there any conventional poetic justice in their doom, as *There are Crimes and Crimes* (1899) ironically demonstrates with its story of a young dramatist who believes 'it is quite simple to figure out a fourth act once you have three known ones to start from'. Driven by past misdeeds to a desperate choice between suicide and religious expiation, the last act finds his conscience happy enough again because of an unexpected theatrical success. The inconsequence does not have the reassuring form of comedy, but rather calls into question, like so much else in Strindberg's dramatic technique, the very conventions upon which traditional drama has been founded. The integrity of character and moral coherence of plot, for which Ibsen had striven, disintegrate into something like a nightmare vision of existence, where subjective delusions are inextricable from objective fact; and from this state there is no awakening, because the mind is cut off from any external standard, any background of reliable truth, against which experience might, even metaphorically, be judged. Thus, Strindberg's 'naturalist' style develops into the 'symbolist' manner of his later dream plays with no more than a change of emphasis. He goes beyond the limits of either school and reaches a point where the assumption, which they had developed to an extreme of difference, that there are entirely separate spheres of reality and consciousness, begins to dissolve. His affinities are less with Zola or Maeterlinck than with the Expressionist drama of the next century.

In one of Strindberg's most famous plays, *Miss Julia* (1888), the highly strung, almost neurotic daughter of a land-owning family succumbs to the valet, whose cruder and stronger nature is not weakened by any 'life-endangering superstitions about honour'. The perception that refinement of mind and manners may be helplessly decadent in the struggle for life appears frequently in the literature of the period; it was felt with particular keenness in Russia, where the upper classes were seen to have lost all contact with the plain concerns and energies of the people. Anton Chekhov (1860–1904) in his last and finest play, *The Cherry Orchard* (1904), also depicts a ruthless servant, the insensitive self-made man of the future, who supplants a landed family grown incapable of managing its affairs; and he might have endorsed Strindberg's view that 'for happiness strong and sound races are required'. Occasionally in his stories and plays speeches are made that look forward to a brighter and better condition of humanity, yet no critic has ever been sure to what extent Chekhov himself believed in it. He was a doctor and a liberal, prepared to journey to Sakhalin to report on prison conditions, and moved to genuine compassion by suffering; but he was also an artist of his time, as detached and ironical in his psychological observation as Maupassant. It is scarcely possible to decide even whether *The Cherry Orchard* is intended as a comedy or a tragedy, and similar doubts exist over the other plays: *The Seagull* (1896), *Uncle Vanya* (1899), and *The Three Sisters* (1901). Chekhov is saved from Strindberg's exaggerations by innate sympathy and humour, but his characters are no less disastrously isolated from one another, no less victims of a situation which they are powerless to control; in fact, none of the traditional forms of drama remains intact. Dialogue, for instance, seems often composed of disconnected remarks, and what takes place resembles rather a sequence of moods and minor episodes than a plot.

Nothing is more easily ruined on the stage; yet Chekhov was fortunate in finding in Stanislavsky, the great producer of the Moscow Art Theatre, an interpreter able to sense and exploit the undercurrent of emotion in each modest phrase, the 'atmospheric' changes which mark the development of a scene. For his art depends on a contrast between commonplace appearances, what people actually do and say or seem to be, and some deeper meaning. It is an old contrast and has surely been known to every philosopher and artist in some form; what is remarkable in Chekhov is his sense that the meaning is of a kind which cannot truthfully be rendered by building up a conventional plot and assigning roles and characters and consecutive speeches. This would be to give life a coherence which it does not really possess—except, of course, in philosophy, or in art. Chekhov was acutely conscious of the familiar paradox, which seems to limit a writer, determined to be faithful to 'what really is', to an ironical attitude towards everything. This irony haunts the philosophisings that are so dear to his characters both in the plays and many of the short stories, but it never deteriorates into cynicism; it gently touches upon the personal frailty in their thoughts, catches the note of pathos in their memories and hopes, and sets into grave relief their eccentricities, their follies and their cruelties. Chekhov well understands the limitation of such an attitude; when his moral conscience asks for a less aesthetic, a plainer meaning, then he must reply like the famous scholar of *A Dreary Story* (1889) that he does not know—though he does know that the 'condition' of human happiness necessitates an answer. For 'if a man has not within himself something which is stronger and greater than all external circumstances, then a bad cold will be enough to upset his peace of mind, and all his pessimism and his optimism, his big and his little thoughts, have no other significance than as symptoms'. This knowledge makes Chekhov the most restrained and sympathetic of the naturalist writers; and although he is a master at detecting details symptomatic of a decadent society, he does not insist on any aggressive naturalistic philosophy. His diagnosis can be as grimly disturbing as anything by Zola or Strindberg (*Ward No. 6* (1892)), but it is softened by real humanity, because he sees that his art does not reveal the truth, only at best the sad awareness of its lack.

To make literature give an answer, to render truths which have a moral meaning, this was the major concern of Count Leo Tolstoy (1828–1910) during the last thirty years of his life. By the end of the century he was venerated as no man of letters had been since Goethe; 'pilgrims' from all over Europe went to Yasnaya Polyana to see the novelist-prophet who dressed like a peasant in the blouse which is now called a 'tolstovka'; and though it was a police offence to be in possession of certain of his pamphlets denouncing the iniquities of the regime, the government no longer dared to interfere with their world-famous author. His fame now largely rests upon *War and Peace* (1869)[1] and *Anna Karenina* (1877), although he himself felt compelled to repudiate them after the spiritual crisis which he has recorded in *My Confession* (1879), one of the most intense and moving autobiographical documents ever written and a turning-point in Tolstoy's career. It was followed by a series of essays in which he developed his unorthodox Christian views (*What I Believe*, 1883, contains the essentials), and a number of simple didactic tales like *What Men Live By* (1882) and *How Much Land Does a Man Need?* (1886). Although he returned to fiction again with *Resurrection* (1898) and *Hadji Murat* (1904), wrote several short stories including the notorious *Kreutzer Sonata* (1886) and the masterpiece *Master and Man* (1895), and

[1] See vol. x, chap. vii.

attempted satirical dramas like *Fruits of Enlightenment* (1889) as well as more serious 'problem plays' like *The Power of Darkness* (1886), all his later work is influenced by the upheaval which had taken place in his life and thought.

Tolstoy had been interested in moral and philosophical questions from the first, less as matters of intellectual theory than in their bearing on the way people live. Such an early story as *The Cossacks* (1862) is clearly inspired by an idea which is the dominant theme in his writing until the end: that a simple, a 'natural' way of life brings people closer to the secret of goodness—and this invariably means for Tolstoy also the secret of happiness—than all the resources of society, culture or civilisation. Both Prince Andrew and Pierre in *War and Peace* are led by devious routes to aspects of the same wisdom, and the vast scheme of the novel is held together by a conviction that the great issues of history and heroism are an illusion beside the real values of homely existence. The moral structure of *Anna Karenina* is even plainer, where the gradual catastrophe of a romantic passion, which consumes the souls of the ever more abandoned and isolated lovers, is matched against the struggle of Levin and Kitty to find their true selves, and one another, and their place in a genuine community. Yet before Tolstoy had completed this novel the tension of moral and religious crisis was beginning to mount; he never properly revised the book, and in the end he renounced it. It is not altogether easy to see why, for the actual content of his ideas underwent little change. What seems to have been involved was the quality of Tolstoy's belief in them, his belief in them as a writer and as a man. He had made fiction out of moral problems, exploited them as part, but no more than a part, of the whole panorama of life, which he loved above all things in his imagination, 'both its darkness and its light'; he had traced the psychology of spiritual awakening and spiritual downfall, enjoyed its excitements and sorrows, and indulged in the sublime artistic pleasure of winning resolution out of tragedy. Yet did he really believe in the truths he told so beautifully, so wisely? Did they make any difference to him, whose experience was that of a writer throughout, or to the public which merely read? It was, after all, only a work of imagination, only art.

'What is Art?' This question was almost drowned at first by Tolstoy's personal confession of faith, but it inevitably emerged again with his later writing and was treated systematically in an essay with that title in 1897. This has shocked by its radical judgements, and was obviously out of keeping with the 'aesthetic' views of the time, although it tries to avoid the narrow argument over didacticism by considering generally with what kind of sympathies and emotions a work 'infects' the reader. Can the imagination dwell safely upon the adventures of evil—with all their colourful detail and fascinating psychology—even if ostensibly they are condemned? For if they are well written they must surely capture its interest. Tolstoy so formulates the problem that even Shakespeare is rejected, while the biblical story of Joseph remains as a model. It is a difficult distinction, yet more telling than is usually allowed by critics outraged by more obviously unacceptable examples. Admittedly, the essay makes sense only against the background of Tolstoy's religious convictions; but from their extreme standpoint it is possible to see that there may be something morally questionable about the glorification of vanity and error. There have been Puritanical objections to art in the past, though not as a rule from artists. Had Tolstoy simply struggled to put aside the unrealities of literature for the realities about which he wrote, his story would have had the admirable simplicity which he admired; but he did not. He struggled to 'convert' his imagination and his art, and he was never a more scrupulous stylist than when he was writing his *Confession*.

Biographers have given many hints that Tolstoy never found the inner serenity which he preached, and have noted occasionally self-destructive elements in his attacks on social evils. These continued to provide him with his subjects and his satisfactions (at the time of writing *Resurrection* he remarks a return of the creative exhilaration of *War and Peace*), yet also with doubts that had to be overcome. *Notes of a Madman* (1881) gives a striking account of the fear of death which was so profoundly connected with his religious crisis and with his obsessive vision of evil devouring every aspect of contemporary life. *The Kreutzer Sonata* or *The Devil* (1889) are as fearful in their exposure of marriage as anything by Strindberg, though they differ by their claim to moral, not merely psychological, significance. Tolstoy's absolute condemnation of civilised society, his intolerance of everything which fell short of his particular ideal, turned even Chekhov against him, who could not accept these damning philosophies that pretended to offer salvation. Now that the myth of Tolstoy the prophet has passed, it is less easy to perceive his pride, the hubris of his genius, which suggested to him that he could and must save the world. Evil may be overcome by saints, but can it be overcome by writers?

The sentence: 'Vengeance is mine; I will repay, saith the Lord', is written above the first chapter of *Anna Karenina*, which begins with the words: 'Every happy family is happy in the same way; every unhappy family is unhappy after its own fashion.' Together they contain Tolstoy's dilemma in a nutshell. There can be no great literature without the story of man's wandering, without his fall; but equally there can be no fall without an order of good and evil which is immutably in the hands of God. Tolstoy was deeply troubled by an inability, typical of the age, to be convinced by the orthodox assurance of final redemption and rectification. The biblical quotation may have been intended only as a rebuke to bigots eager to rejoice at the doom of an adulteress; but the truth it contains began to appear to him later as a shelving of moral responsibility. The evil might be left to the hereafter, but what of the injustice, the misery, the wrong-living here and now? As a writer he needed the unhappiness, but there came a moment when he could not bear it; it had to be condemned, it had to be overcome and put right. And so the struggle with himself and with the wicked world ensued, from which have emerged such victorious endings as are portrayed in *The Death of Ivan Ilyich* (1886), *Master and Man* and *Resurrection*. The irony of Tolstoy's dilemma is reflected in the criticism levelled above all at the last novel, that it is spoiled by its insistence on a solution; and if it is redeemed then it is, after all, by the imaginative sympathy which it shows for weakness and suffering. The proclamation of a state of happiness, designed to rectify moral iniquity and the burden of immemorial guilt, does not make for great literature; and if it is not realised in saintliness, it can only make for revolution.

CHAPTER VI

ART AND ARCHITECTURE

I T is the fault of most writing on the history of art in the nineteenth century that art and architecture are kept separate. Admittedly, it is not easy to see a unity of style between Scott's St Pancras of 1868 and Monet's St Lazare of 1877. Moreover, one is discouraged from any efforts at formulating such a unity by the crashing drop in aesthetic quality directly one moves from the most familiar works of painting to the most familiar works of architecture. No one can deny the truth of this value judgement, but there is also a fallacy involved. One tends to forget official painting and non-official architecture, the one as bad as any insurance company headquarters, the other not as good, but occasionally nearly as good, as Monet and Seurat. If one is aware of the whole evidence, a treatment can be attempted doing justice to all its aspects. The only difficulty which remains is that the layman—and in this respect nearly everybody is a layman—knows much about the Impressionists and Post-Impressionists, but near to nothing about Philip Webb and Norman Shaw, H. H. Richardson and Stanford White, and indeed Antoni Gaudí.

This is one reason why painting is taken first in this chapter. Another is that the nineteenth century was indeed a century of the dominance of painting, aesthetically as well as socially. The dominance had been established before the year 1870. Socially speaking the patron of 1870 was no longer the patron of 1770. About 1770 the social situation of art had still been that of the Middle Ages, the Renaissance and the Baroque. The Church, the courts, the nobility were the patrons, even if the occasional merchant, banker, brewer ought not to be discounted. Patrons were on the whole men of leisure, and their education had included some appreciation of architecture, craftsmanship and the fine arts. A hundred years later architects built hundreds of churches for mean suburbs; speculators, in the absence of architects sufficiently interested, built so as to make these vast new suburbs mean; the nobility had receded or was receding, and the new commercial and industrial class of patrons had neither had the chance of an introduction to matters aesthetic nor the leisure to master them later in life. That determined their attitude not only to the buildings for which they paid but also to the painting they chose for their houses. But while an architect cannot build without a patron, a painter, if he is prepared to starve, can paint without one. The starving painter appears first in the history of art in Holland in the seventeenth century—that is, in the first middle-class republic. He becomes the prototype of the worth-while painter in the nineteenth century. Millet sold six drawings for a pair of shoes. Renoir in 1869 wrote: 'We don't eat every day' and Monet in the same year: 'Here I am, at a halt, for lack of paints.' Painters ready to live in this way can wait for the rare patron to turn up who understands them. So the most convinced of the painters could keep up an aesthetic integrity and an enthusiasm for exploration which architects had no hope of matching.

Impressionism is usually seen as starting with Edouard Manet (1832–83) and such paintings as his *Déjeuner sur l'herbe* and *Olympia* of 1863. But they qualify only with reservations. What shocked critics and the public in them was more a matter of subject than of treatment. Men in their normal clothes out for a picnic and a naked girl with them, or a young woman posing in the Titian tradition but appearing not so much as a nude than as stripped—Courbet had done as much and worse. Worse in that he, demonstrative and obtrusive realist that he was, wanted his nudes to be suggestive, while Manet's were especially irritating because without doubt painted with full aesthetic detachment. Courbet in fact was shocked by *Olympia* too, but for its lack of realism. He called her a playing-card, and here something new was indeed involved. If she looks flat, it is because strong light is focused direct on her, eliminating the nuances of undulating surfaces. Velasquez had done likewise in the seventeenth century, but no one else, and it is understandable that Manet called Velasquez 'the painter of painters', when he visited Spain in 1865. This interest in direct sunlight and its effect on bodies became one of the chief concerns of the Impressionists. Another—less novel but equally important—is that of contemporary, everyday subject-matter. A third comes out in Manet's *Concert in the Tuileries Gardens* of 1862: the problem of painting a crowd convincingly by letting the frame cut arbitrarily into the composition and even more by rapid, forceful, sketchy brushwork, indicating movement of figures by movement of the brush.

Manet was attacked violently. Rossetti called his (and Courbet's) art 'putrescence', Jules Claretie 'jokes or parodies'. And so the best of the young began to rally round him. They were Edgar Degas (1834–1917), Claude Monet (1840–1926) and Auguste Renoir (1840–1919). If Camille Pissarro (1830–1903) and Alfred Sisley (1839–99) are added to these, the principal Impressionists have been named. The word was coined somewhat later; but *impression* had been used occasionally to convey the intention of landscape painters even of the School of Barbizon and their contemporaries, that is, painters born before 1820. One critic said of Jongkind that 'everything with him lies in the impression', another called Daubigny in 1865 'chief of the school of the impression'. Of the five men just referred to, who were all born between 1830 and 1840, three were indeed landscape painters, and Renoir was at least partly a landscape painter. Only Degas kept to the figure. All had been impressed by Manet (and by Courbet), but in one way they soon went beyond him and in their turn influenced him. In 1869 both Monet and Renoir painted the *Grenouillère* near Bougival on the Seine, and these were open-air pictures, in the sense that the momentary, rapidly passing effects of sunlight on foliage and rippled water were caught directly and not filtered through studio adjustments. *Plein air* painting became one of the cornerstones of Impressionism. The others are the 'impression', that is the rendering of what meets the eye as it meets the eye, the translation of movement on to the still plane of the canvas, and the everyday subject, whether landscape or still-life or portrait or genre, the latter in the sense of rendering contemporary events of no significance beyond their just taking place. It is true that Manet in 1864 painted the battle between the *Kearsarge* and the *Alabama*, an episode in the American Civil War which had taken place off the French coast, and in 1867 the Emperor Maximilian of Mexico before the firing squad; but they are exceptions in his *œuvre*, and in any case, just like the *Olympia*, not yet fully Impressionist. Degas was the master of the everyday occurrence. Vicomte Lepic and his little daughters out for a walk in the Place de la Concorde (*c.* 1873)—they are in the foreground and the frame cuts off their legs. Another gentleman appears on the left, but we see only half of him because the frame cuts him vertically. The houses and trees around the square are only lightly sketched in. There is hardly anything else. Yet this is eventful compared with Degas' *Repasseuses* busy ironing or stretching their limbs and yawning, his girls washing their bodies in a tub, observed in such unselfconscious and hence such alluringly graceless movements, 'as if you looked through a keyhole' (so he said himself), and his innumerable *Ballet Dancers* rehearsing or performing—all, in spite of their accidental looking poses, composed on the canvas with wit and an exquisite taste sharpened by a study of Japanese woodcuts.

Japonisme had begun in the 1850's and gathered momentum from the time of the International Exhibition in London in 1862. It means different things to different people—to Manet, who placed a Japanese woodcut behind Zola in his portrait of 1868, shadowless clear and light colours; to Degas a *piquant* asymmetrical arrangement of figures; to Whistler, to Gauguin, to van Gogh qualities we shall have to examine later.

In the five years after 1869 the group, now all men of round about thirty-five, consolidated itself, and in 1874 a first exhibition was held, necessary because the official *Salon* kept its doors closed to most of their works. In the exhibition there was Monet's *Boulevard des Capucines* with the crowd boldly brushed in as patterns of vertical strokes, the trees as a hazy mass, except for the branches of those closest to us, and the houses again only indicated through the cold mist. The distance is a sea of greys and blues into which the street merges. Renoir had *La Loge*, that brilliant portrait of a couple in a theatre box, a test example of how the Impressionist focuses on the central motif, in this case the face of the young woman, and turns more and more sketchy the further he moves away from the centre. The colours are black and white—early-Renoir colours—with his unmistakable roses and greyish pinks in the background. Renoir also showed his exquisite young *Ballet Dancer*, the tulle of the dress the airiest greyish white with just a touch of light blue in the ribbons, brown hair and a piquant black bracelet. The background is here also left entirely without definition. There were ten Degas, five Pissarros and five Sisleys. Among Monet's five, incidentally, one was called 'Impression, sunrise', and from that title *Charivari* took the idea of discussing the whole group as Impressionists. This gave them their name for good.

The public and the press still remained hostile for a long time. *Figaro* playfully called their second exhibition, held at Durand Ruel's in the rue le Peletier, off the Boulevard des Italiens, a disaster second in magnitude only to the recent fire at the Opera. But allies began to appear. Zola had written in their favour already in 1866, prophesying a place in the Louvre for Manet and also praising Monet and Pissarro, and now, in 1878, Théodore Duret published his book on *Les Peintres Impressionistes*. In terms of income the painters themselves, however, did not profit at once from this change of opinion. They tried to follow their first two exhibitions by sales of fifty to seventy pictures but did not succeed in obtaining more than an average of about 160 francs. In 1878 another sale took place. The average for Monet was 185 francs, for Sisley 115. It was different when Duret had to sell his collection in 1894. Some of the major works of Manet then fetched prices between 5000 and 11,000 francs. Among the first consistent buyers were Americans such as Henry O. Havemeyer.

The change from hostility to appreciation of a new style in art is always a change of mind. In the case of the Impressionists it was also a change of optic habits. When Ruskin called Whistler's *Cremorne Gardens* 'flinging a pot of paint in the public's face', we may grant him that perhaps he really could not recognise what was represented on the insulted canvas. Yet for today's laymen the Impressionists have become the easiest to enjoy of all works of painting, easier by far than the Old Masters. This is not so surprising; for the Impressionists were not revolutionaries although their technique made them seem so. They stand at the end of a golden age of painting, not at the beginning of a new age of doubtful, untried aesthetic values. Titian in his later works, Velasquez, Rembrandt, Goya, Constable, all are their ancestors, as all painted the impressions they received and not images distilled into permanence from many impressions as Raphael or Poussin or Ingres had done. It is characteristic of Impressionism that one remembers many familiar pictures yet is unable to single out a few as representative of all. One Monet landscape, one is tempted to say, is as good as another, one ballet study by Degas as good as another. One has one's favourites, and there are of course outstanding successes and indifferent products of routine; but the skill is breathtaking throughout and the pleasure in all that the eye can take in never ceases to be infectious. Camille Pissarro, a little older than the others and more of a thinker, recommended to students when he was about sixty-five that the motif ought to be 'observed more for shape and colour than for drawing', that one ought not to the end 'lose the first impression', that 'precise drawing hampers the impression' and that 'perceptions must be put down immediately'. Renoir, incapable of systematic thought, wrote: 'I have no theories. I paint for the sake of painting.' Monet, not a theorist either, wrote late in life that he did not claim more than 'the merit of having painted direct from nature, trying to convey my impressions in the presence of the most fugitive effects'. In another context he said that he could wish 'he had been born blind and then suddenly regained sight so that he could paint what he saw without knowing what the objects were'. This fanaticism of mere seeing and rendering what had been seen forced Monet immediately after the death of his wife to notice the various tones of death on her face.

If death could become reduced to a visual experience, it is obvious that Impressionists would not be interested in the intellectual values of subject matter. No *Adoration of the Shepherds* for them, no *Perseus and Andromeda*, no *Uncle Toby and Widow Wadman*, no *Slave Market*. The field of the painter is infinite, but it is most strictly the visual field. The intellectual field is closed to him. There is a limitation here which was soon to be felt. Monet had the courage to draw the ultimate consequences. In 1891 he exhibited fifteen pictures of the same haystack painted in different light (and sold them at 3000 to 4000 francs each). Let no one, his argument ran, be distracted from my artistry by irrelevant thought on the subject of these paintings. Just look and admire the truth of my vision. Realism thus remained valid as radically as in the days when Courbet had been proud of being 'sans idéal et sans religion', as he had put it in his cruder way, but it was now a realism evaporating into the immaterial reality of air and light.

Impressionism in the end spread to all countries and became the vernacular of the academies, but the spread took time. In England the change belongs to the generation of Walter Sickert (1860–1942), in Germany to Max Liebermann (1847–1935). Liebermann had been in Paris in 1874, Sickert in 1883; an Italian, Giuseppe de Nittis (1846–84) had gone even earlier, in 1867. He would have to be considered the earliest foreign convert to Impressionism, if it were not for the Americans who now begin to appear on the European stage not only as spectacular buyers of paintings but as spectacular painters—and none was more spectacular than James McN. Whistler (1834–1903), who reached Paris as early as 1855 and decided to live in London in 1859. In the years following the *Déjeuner sur l'herbe* and the *Olympia* and leading to the *Grenouillères* he was not therefore a member of the group which was taking shape, and if his *At the*

Piano of 1859, his *White Girl* of 1862 and his *Valparaiso Harbour* of 1866 strike one as Impressionist or akin to Impressionism, the reason must lie in Whistler's own, unaided endeavour. The dissolution of everything solid into a blueish-grey haze in the painting of the sea outside Valparaiso does indeed go beyond anything then attempted by the young Parisians, and when Whistler started to formulate his views publicly—which was more than a decade later—a number of them were pure Impressionism. To quote only one, he commented on a snow-scene of his with one single black figure: 'I care nothing for the past, present, or future of the black figure, placed there because the black was wanted at that spot.'

But other and more significant views of Whistler's contradict the doctrine of the Impressionists in a direction already indicated by such early paintings as *At the Piano*, which is a composition, as self-conscious as those that Degas worked on during these early years, that is, before he ever turned to contemporary subjects. So while Degas was still tied to the mythology of the art schools Whistler tried to make use of delicately calculated arrangements of people of his own day for non-academic purposes. They culminate in his most famous portraits, those of his mother (1872) and of Carlyle (1874). Moreover, Whistler called his landscapes not humbly Impressions but more presumptuously Harmonies, Symphonies or Nocturnes—Symphony in grey and green, Nocturne in grey and gold, and so on—and with that introduced connotations of musical—that is, abstract—relevance and of mood, and such connotations were forbidden to the Impressionists, captives as they were in the territory of the visible. One would not expect to find Monet or Renoir saying, as Whistler did, that in the twilight 'tall chimneys become campanili', and in the night 'the warehouses are palaces', or that 'painting [is] the poetry of sight, as music is the poetry of sound', or more sweepingly, that 'Nature is usually wrong'.

Whistler liked to shock, as did his disciple Oscar Wilde. It is easy to be funny about Oscar Wilde's lily and Whistler's cane and eyeglass, in fact about all the trappings of the *fin-de-siècle* aesthete and dandy, but there is also something positive and forward-pointing in Whistler's belief in the supremacy of art over life. The Impressionists, as far as we can see from photographs, had no taste in their own houses. They painted, and that is where their relation to art ended. Whistler's house, the White House in Tite Street, Chelsea, designed by his friend Edward Godwin (1833–86) in 1878, was a challenge to the historicism of nineteenth-century architecture and to the ponderous forms and sombre colours in fashion. The façade was white, the windows and doorway were placed in piquant arbitrariness, and the rooms inside were sparsely furnished and painted in white and pure rich yellow. The walls in Whistler's first one-man show had been grey, and there had been blue and white Chinese porcelain to set off the pictures. Whistler, in his taste in interior decoration, was no doubt guided by Godwin who had, as early as 1862, painted the rooms of his house at Bristol in plain colours and decorated them with a few selected pieces of antique furniture, some Persian rugs on bare floors and a number of Japanese woodcuts. Whistler also was fascinated by Japanese art and painted his *Princesse du pays de la porcelaine* (*Rose and Silver*) as early as 1865. It formed the focal-point of the celebrated Peacock Room which he decorated with peacocks in dark blue and gold in luxuriantly oriental convolutions for F. R. Leyland, the Liverpool shipping magnate, in London in 1877. In the same year Comyns Carr opened the Grosvenor Gallery for the display of modern art, and Gilbert's 'greenery-yallery, Grosvenor Gallery' will be understandable to readers now.

At the same time it is interesting to note that Godwin must have looked to Japan for pure, clear colours and delicacy and sparseness of furnishing —he designed for the furniture trade quite a number of somewhat spindly pieces in the mid-1870's—and that Whistler's admiration for Japan must have included the same qualities but also the unfailing sense of exquisitely dainty composition which delighted Degas at the same time.

The importance of Whistler in our present context lies in his turn from refined realism to refined decoration, and from the gloom of Victorian furnishing to the light colours of the post-Victorian style. In this he and Godwin went beyond the otherwise much more influential work in the field of the decorative arts which was done during the same years by a greater man: William Morris (1834–96). Morris had gone to Oxford to read divinity, but turned to architecture and then, dissatisfied with work at the drawing-board, to painting. He studied for a while under Rossetti; and the Pre-Raphaelites and their defender, John Ruskin, became his heroes. From the writings of Ruskin he learned to love the art of the Gothic Middle Ages, to respect their craftsmanship, and to develop an ardent faith in craftsmanship as such. The art of the Pre-Raphaelites— still young and unsullied—gave Morris in addition an equally fervent faith in accurate and yet decorative line. Ruskin had preached craftsman-ship on the one hand, social reform on the other. Morris united the two and, moreover, endowed them with a burning energy, a robust aggressive-ness and an artistic genius that had all been lacking in Ruskin. So Morris got together with his Pre-Raphaelite friends and especially his closest friend, the architect Philip Webb (1831–1915), and decided in 1861 to found a firm of, as he called them, 'Fine Art Workmen in painting, carving, furniture, and the metals'. They designed furniture, tiles, wall-paper, stained glass windows, in a style totally different from what was then current. Furniture, instead of being pretentious, bulgy and in the so-called Free or Mixed Renaissance—that is, crowded with motifs inspired by anything from Cinquecento to Jacobean and the various Louis—was simple, angular, and indebted to the English cottage.

Stained glass, instead of being realistic painting applied to glass, returned to simple flat shapes in pure, glowing colours and with the leading between the individual quarries judiciously used. Wallpaper, instead of favouring bunches of naturalistically drawn and painted flowers or landscapes in three dimensions or both together, concentrated on simple floral motifs, developed in two dimensions so as to demonstrate acceptance of the surface of the wall to be covered by wallpaper, just as Morris glass accepted the glass surface.

This return to functional fundamentals was a revolution in decoration, and Morris's own designs stand out from those of his age as unchallenged as do the paintings of the Impressionists. The revolution had begun as early as 1859, when Morris had got married and had Red House designed for himself and his wife by Philip Webb. The house, at Bexley Heath to the south-east of London, is unpretentious and informal, not a copy of any one style of the past, and furnished inside with pieces in which the Morris doctrine is already fully exposed. There is in particular one fireplace, inscribed 'Ars Longa, Vita Brevis', which is so completely independent of history, so completely devoid of ornamental enrichment and so functionally designed that it must rank as the earliest defeat of historicism. It has all the freshness and daring which Godwin's rooms of 1862 must have possessed, and more of these qualities than Morris's own work of the 1870's and 1880's.

Yet these are the years in which, by lecturing and writing, Morris formulated his theory of artistic and social reform and thus achieved universal fame and made converts of artists and architects in England, on the Continent and in America. His two points of departure were that the art of our time must be sick, since it is only the self-expression of great individuals, however valuable, and that architecture and design must be sick also, since all they produce is 'tons and tons of unutterable rubbish' in people's houses, and houses themselves which are 'simply blackguardly' for the rich, 'hideous hovels' for the poor. In the Middle Ages, the small towns had been beautiful and everything made by man had been beautiful. Why was that so? Morris's answer is that every artist had been a craftsman and every craftsman an artist. 'Art is the expression by man of his pleasure in labour.' This must be recovered if art is to survive. The machine is an enemy, industry is an enemy, the designer for industry is no more than a 'squinter at a sheet of paper'. Morris himself was of course a designer, but he was also a fanatical maker.

The fact that socialism became his creed, followed, as he himself once wrote, out of 'the study of history and the love and practice of art', art in his mind never being the great individual painting, but design, that is, the making of things useful as well as beautiful, and making them for everybody. 'I do not want art for a few', he said, 'any more than I want education for a few or freedom for a few.' And as he also did not believe in inspiration but was convinced that there was a craftsman in every man, art in the end was both work done as 'a happiness to the maker and the user', and work done—'by the people, for the people'.

Morris never fully made up his mind how this return to a healthy condition of art and life might come about. Sometimes he took the radical line of Spengler; for instance when he wrote: 'Maybe, man may, after some terrible cataclysm, learn to strive towards a healthy animalism, may grow from a tolerable animal into a savage, from a savage into a barbarian, and so on, and some thousands of years hence he may be beginning once more those arts which we have now lost.' At other times he took a more evolutionary view and recommended that we 'do our best to the end of preparing for the change and so softening the shock of it'. In any case he was much too active a man to sit back and wait for his catastrophe. He lectured, he wrote his poetry and he ran his shop, and he had also recommendations for useful action to those who were not producers but consumers. What he told them has remained topical to this day: fight the smoke of factory and domestic chimneys, don't throw away litter, don't fell trees before beginning to build houses and so on. And 'don't have anything in your houses that you do not know to be useful or believe to be beautiful'. Anyone accepting this principle will find that he can (or must) give up many things. Morris himself may be believed when he said that he would prefer 'living in a tent in the Persian desert or a turf-hut on the Icelandic hill-side' to living in the houses built today for 'ignorant, purse-proud, digesting-machines'.

But there runs a flaw through the doctrine of Morris. Although he was a fanatical craftsman, most of what he did and what made him famous—notably his chintzes and wallpapers—were in fact only designed by him but made in factories. Moreover, his furnishing business was not aiming at tents and turf-huts but at the creation of very civilised, very self-consciously contrived surroundings. So what Morris produced did often not entail 'pleasure in labour', and it was certainly never 'for the people'. In short, his was an expensive shop. He knew this. He said once, when asked on a job what he was doing, that he was 'serving the swinish luxury of the rich', and another time he said more elaborately that 'all art costs time, trouble and thought,...and money is only a counter to represent these things'.

So Morris's was more an aesthetic than a social revolution. It is true that he convinced a number of talented young men to turn to craft as a job for life, and that the Arts and Crafts movement in Britain in its early days produced much honest and thoughtful and beautiful work. It is also true that the aesthetic reform in design would not have had sufficient impetus if, at the beginning, it had not been in the hands of makers rather than designers for factories. Yet in the end it was the designer who profited most, and if the twentieth century achieved at its very beginning an original, functional style, the credit must go largely to Morris and his efforts to make people see that everyday products matter more than easel pictures.

Morris was exclusively a designer in two dimensions. When it came to furniture, Philip Webb (1831–1915) designed for the firm. Webb was in addition one of the two most important English architects of his generation. His Red House had been the first of a large number of informal, comfortable houses designed by a large number of architects. The whole movement became known as the Domestic Revival—a term which of course includes Morris's work. Webb did not build much. He was always honest, never modish, and could be daring in his use of materials and his blending of motifs from widely different styles. Richard Norman Shaw (1831–1912) had a livelier imagination and a lighter hand. His houses of the 1870's, mostly in Hampstead and Chelsea and for artists, are of brick, with motifs from the Dutch and English seventeenth century elegantly and picturesquely mixed. Queen Anne was the name given, not quite accurately, to this style. Elements of it appear already in Webb's Red House. Ten years later its possibilities began to be seen by others. Eden Nesfield built a lodge at Kew Gardens in Queen Anne in 1868, J. J. Stevenson the Red House in the Bayswater Road in 1871. Norman Shaw after having left an early partnership with Nesfield discovered it for himself in 1872. It was he who made it the fashion for the sensitive and the 'artistic'. By 1881 Gilbert could write in *Patience* 'that the reign of Good Queen Anne was Culture's palmiest day'. Whatever the real elements of the so-called Queen Anne, and they were the Dutch seventeenth century and the English William and Mary styles, the result was a domestic architecture of a refinement in full contrast to the grossness of the High Victorian decades. It is this refinement that links Impressionism in France with the Domestic Revival in England. Courbet's realism had been as gross as High Victorian architecture. Now delicacy, subtlety, the light touch, became the ideals. Concurrently, in political and social history the unquestioning optimism of the mid-century declined.

It is never possible to fix an exact date for the beginning of a style. Red House is Late Victorian, not High Victorian, though it was designed nearly five years before so High Victorian an effort as Scott's St Pancras Station. Late Victorian also are Morris's designs, Godwin's buildings and designs and Norman Shaw's houses. There is always a time-lag between the first pioneer work and the consolidation of a style. The 1870's must be regarded as the centre-piece of the Domestic Revival, as it is the centre-piece of Impressionism. Norman Shaw's New Zealand Chambers, his house, now the Royal Geographical Society, near the Albert Hall, his own house in Ellerdale Road, Hampstead, Swan House, Chelsea—all of 1872–6—are among the best examples, unrivalled at the time anywhere in Europe and of infinitely greater value and historical significance than his own late work in a Neo-English Baroque. Socially the most interesting job of Norman Shaw's is the design done in 1875 for Bedford Park, Turnham Green, London, commissioned by Comyns Carr's brother Jonathan Carr. This is the first of all garden suburbs and the pattern on which—with a typical twist from catering for a cultured middle class to catering for the working class—Port Sunlight and Bournville were designed in the 1890's. From them it was only a step to the independent garden city, complete with its own industrial and civic buildings, and this step was taken in theory by Ebenezer Howard in his *Garden Cities of Tomorrow*, published in 1898, and finally in practice by Barry Parker and Raymond Unwin's Letchworth, begun in 1903.

All this had a great influence abroad. *Cités jardins*, or *città giardini*, began to appear in France and Italy, the Prussian government in 1896 sent Hermann Muthesius to London for a number of years to study the Domestic Revival, Morris was translated into many languages, Edmond de Goncourt in 1896 called the new style of decoration by the English name Yachting Style, the Grand Duke of Hesse commissioned English architects to design for his palace at Darmstadt, and artists began to turn craftsmen on the Continent as they had done in England. However, the movement remained on the intimate scale of the private house and its furnishings. Official architecture stayed grand, just as official and highly paid painting in all countries had remained unaffected by Impressionism. To remember this, it is sufficient to thumb the illustrated souvenirs of the Paris Salons or to follow the purchases of the Royal Academy in London under the Chantrey Bequest—prices of £2000 and £3000 being paid for the works by Millais and Lord Leighton. Edwin Long's *Babylonian Marriage Market* was bought in 1875 for £1700 and changed hands in 1881 for £6615.

Architecture outside Britain before the turn of the century had nothing to compare with the Domestic Revival in Britain. It is Neo-Baroque unashamedly, whether one goes to Rome to see the Monument to Victor Emanuel II begun in 1884 and the Ministry of Justice begun in 1888, or to Berlin to see the Houses of Parliament begun in 1884 and the Cathedral begun in 1894.

Only the United States form an exception. Here at least as much of importance took place in architecture as in Britain. For the moment only the domestic aspects of the reform concern us—houses of the 1880's by Henry Hobson Richardson (1838–86) and Stanford White (1853–1906), as freely improvising on motifs of the past as Webb and Shaw and their partisans, and not uninfluenced by them. These American houses, like the paintings of Whistler, mark the moment when America jumped forward from a provincial back seat into the front row of Western art which she was henceforth not to leave. Even in official architecture the United States now assumed a distinction beyond other nations. McKim, Mead and White, the firm to which Stanford White belonged, turned, again in the 1880's, to an imitation Italian Renaissance (Public Library, Boston, 1888–92) and later, together with others, to a Classical Re-Revival, more restrained and more disciplined than the Neo-Baroque of Europe (Pennsylvania Station, New York, 1906–10).

It is in these works of the Americans that one must look for the parallel to that noble Classicism which, in opposition to Impressionism, appears in France in the cool grey murals of Pierre Puvis de Chavannes (1824–98) and culminates in Germany in the mysterious, sombre and technically naïve paintings of Hans von Marées (1837–87). In these paintings vaguely mythological figures, placed frontally or in profile, stand or move silently in sacred groves. Compositions keep to the most elementary axes. Marées, though only once in his life commissioned to execute mural paintings, always thought in their terms. In this and everything else the contrast to the principles of Impressionism is complete. Marées reached his position from the traditions of classicism and not in any conscious opposition to an Impressionism which was hardly noticed by him.

In France a comparable position was established during Marées' last years by Georges Seurat (1859–91). His subjects are as different from Marées' as can be, his colour is different, his handling of the brush is extremely different, but faith in strict simplification and axiality connects Seurat and Marées. Seurat was more discussed during the few years of his maturity, that is, between 1884 and 1891, for his system of coloration than for his composition. Yet the latter is more novel and must have been more baffling than the former. Seurat's was a clear logical mind and a cool temperament. He became interested in the optical treatises of Chevreul and others and found that if one reduced one's palette to a limited number of clear, bright, unmixed colours and applied them to the canvas in dots unmixed the eye would perform the 'optical mixture' and a greater truth to colour in nature would be achieved. Seurat's scientific technique made converts at once, Paul Signac (1863–1935) first, and then others, some Frenchmen and almost immediately some Belgians (including Henri van de Velde). Signac wrote in 1887: 'Our formula is certain and demonstrable, our paintings are logical, and no longer done haphazardly.'

This group, called for their technique 'divisionists' or 'pointillists', but better known as Neo-Impressionists, was so set on the science of painting that they took an interest also in rules of composition, directions of lines and their emotional meanings, especially in conjunction with the emotional meanings of colours. Once this move was made, however, the result was not greater exactitude in representing nature but a radical departure from this principle. There is a portrait of Félix Fénéon by Signac which has a background of circles, stars, bright vortexes, wavy lines in parallel formations and other, somewhat Celtic looking, shapes. Fénéon had been the first to write on Neo-Impressionism. Such an abstract background, heralding Italian Futurism of about 1910–15, was a compliment to him who had said that Signac 'sacrifices the anecdote to the arabesque'. However, the figure juxtaposed to abstract shapes remained a rarity. Seurat never went so far. All the same, his figure-scenes are just as artificial and stylised, painted not to catch a passing moment but to establish a sense of permanence. The Impressionists, as Fénéon put it, had been fascinated by the 'changes from second to second [of] sky, water, foliage' and had endeavoured to catch 'one of these fugitive aspects on the canvas'. In Seurat's *Afternoon on the Grande Jatte Island* of 1884–6 everybody seems to be fixed in one position. The figures are like wooden toys, simplified in their outlines, stiff, mostly frontal or in profile and making only the most elementary gestures. The bright colours and the close dots which form the surface are the right accompaniment to this self-consciously naïve, child-like or childish treatment of a scene. In his later *Circus* and *Chahut* Seurat went even farther in grotesque and bizarre stylisation.

If one recognises Seurat as a master of stylisation forcing nature into elementary patterns (as indeed, for instance, van de Velde did when he singled out Seurat as the artist who 'returned to style'), it becomes possible to see him as a complementary figure to Paul Cézanne (1839–1906), whom Pissarro, the wisest of the Impressionists and the only one to understand their later opponents as well, had called 'this refined savage'. Cézanne ever since about 1870 had worked tenaciously on the simplification of the 'motif', the ordering of the planes in a landscape, the cubic firmness of houses, the apple-like solidity of a woman's face. In all these patient researches he yet never lost sight of nature. Seurat's compositions seem a short-cut compared with Cézanne's. If the elementary and the essential is the aim, Seurat's world of dolls cannot be the answer. Yet he, like Cézanne, believed in simple geometry as a remedy against the impermanence of the Impressionist vision. Cézanne in an often-quoted letter to Émile Bernard wrote: 'All in nature is formed by the cylinder, the sphere, and the cone.' Cézanne's art is much more than that, and he continues this letter indeed by emphasising at once that for the painter all drawing is colour and all modelling is colour. So his landscapes, still-lifes and portraits have in the end a calm, reposeful nobility in which no sign of the effort of concentration was allowed to remain. All the same, if one principle can be singled out as underlying all these efforts it is faith in geometry as the ordering force of the cosmos.

Émile Bernard (1868–1941), the recipient of the Cézanne letter just quoted, was also a correspondent of van Gogh and a disciple of Gauguin. Bernard for a few years steps into the limelight of history with a few religious paintings and with work in the decorative arts. They belong to the years 1888–90 when Bernard spent much time with Gauguin in Brittany. Bernard was not a strong character, and he sought inspiration from those more powerful than himself. He lives on more as the listener to Cézanne and van Gogh than as an artist in his own right. Yet, although Bernard's designing for appliqué and embroidery and for stained glass was no doubt encouraged by Paul Gauguin (1845–1903), who in the same years made crude vessels of earthenware and carved reliefs in wood, Bernard's religious painting rather inspired Gauguin than the other way round. Bernard's *Deposition* of 1890 has excessively attenuated figures in attitudes of high tension, influenced by medieval tapestry and stained glass, but the painting as such lacks tension. However, although the quality of Bernard's pictures may be vastly inferior to that of Gauguin's, the return to subject-matter of emotional value remains a fact of great significance. In Gauguin's own religious pictures, the *Jacob wrestling with the Angel*, the *Yellow Christ* and the *Deposition*, the intensity of form and colour matches the subjects—and does so although Gauguin's sincerity was unquestionably less than Bernard's. Could he otherwise have painted that embarrassing *Christ in the Garden*, where he made Christ a portrait of himself? In the *Jacob wrestling with the Angel*, painted in 1888, the ground on which they stand is a violent red, an early case of colour chosen in opposition to what he called 'that damned nature', and purely for emotional reasons. Gauguin spent his summers in Brittany because it gave him, after Paris, the sensation of 'wildness and primitiveness'. The peasant women praying to the vision of Jacob wrestling with the angel or to the Crucifixus in the *Yellow Christ*—copied incidentally from a piece of medieval Breton wood-carving—also signify earthy primitiveness. The search for a primitive, an elementary, life was foremost in Gauguin's mind during these years. It took him for a year to Martinique in 1887, and then in 1891 to Tahiti. He returned again in 1893, but went for good in 1895. In the tropics he found what he had been longing for, satisfaction for his senses, a rich generous landscape, and women and girls (he did not often paint men) blossoming like flowers in this landscape. The modelling is summary, the colour warm, not hot, the gestures and the settings are reduced to essentials. The titles of these pictures from Tahiti are painted on in the native language and are often symbolic in their meaning: *The Spirit of the Dead watches* or *Whence do we come, where are we, whither are we going?* The compositions are reminiscent of those of tapestries, with landscape backgrounds boldly flattened and simplified and figures quietly standing, sitting or lying, in frieze-like arrangement. It was Seurat who had spoken a little earlier of 'people moving about in friezes, stripped to their essentials'. But Gauguin's world is not the toy world of Seurat. It has greater weight and nobility and in this allows comparison with the nobly ordered universe of Cézanne. The direct emotional appeal on the other hand connects Gauguin with van Gogh. He accepted inspiration from Cézanne while he was in Brittany, because he saw that it could be of use to him, but he was not influenced by van Gogh although the two men spent a few ill-fated months together at Arles at the end of 1888.

The idea of attempting such a companionship had been van Gogh's, who believed in 'groups of men gathered together to execute ideas held in common' as the redemption for the solitariness of the artist in the nineteenth century. Gauguin only toyed with Christian themes for a time and soon settled down to enjoy his pagan world; Vincent van Gogh (1853–90) was profoundly religious and essentially Christian. He had for a short time been a lay-preacher before he became a painter. Van Gogh must be the least talented of all great painters. Drawing and painting came to him only after years of stubborn, unpromising efforts. Their intensity remained the intensity of his life and his work during the short three or four years of achievement. What is called intensity here was already before these years occasionally called madness by those who knew him. That van Gogh did go mad at the end of 1888, that he had a number of further attacks after this first and that he finally killed himself, giving up the battle against insanity which he had conducted with perfect sanity, concerns us only marginally. His art is not mad—not madder than that of Grünewald; his illness only broke down the obstacles in his own protestant mind which before the year 1888 had prevented his art from coming to full fruition. There is less than a year between the end of his time in Paris, when he still learned, and the day when he rushed forward to kill Gauguin in their room at Arles. The early months at Arles are the months of his happiest pictures, fully released at last and not yet obscured by the knowledge of the heavy price he had to pay for his release. In Paris in 1886–8 van Gogh had discovered the Impressionists, then the Neo-Impressionists, and Japan as well. If he painted the first dealer who helped him, le père Tanguy, against a background of Japanese prints, that meant to him again something different from what it had meant to Manet, to Whistler, to Degas and to Gauguin. To him it was shadowless clarity of colour and incisively drawn outline, and so he could write: 'All my work is in a way founded on Japanese art.' As he moved from Paris to Arles, he wrote home to his brother: 'I feel I am in Japan.' Even there, however, there is nothing of the daintiness, the delicate balancing of values, as the Japanese evolved them; all is impetuous, the result of frantic work in the southern sun. He painted for twelve hours and slept for twelve hours; every so often he forgot to eat; he worked 'like one possessed', like a reaper 'fighting in the midst of the heat', with 'a terrible lucidity', 'wrung with enthusiasm...like a Greek oracle on the tripod'.

Gauguin went to the tropics to find this absorption in elementary passion, and van Gogh agreed with him so much that he could write (obligingly): 'The future of painting is certainly in the tropics.' But he did not go himself, nor did he feel compelled to search for allegorical, symbolic or indeed religious themes to express it. Gauguin, whose ruthless force and boisterous vitality he envied and admired, influenced him only for a short moment. He objected to what he called the 'abstraction' of Gauguin and his circle and insisted that he at least had to keep to the motif in nature to set off his mind. One Gethsemane he had painted, but he destroyed it. He wrote to his brother: 'They drive me mad with their Christs in the Garden, where nothing is observed', and he warned Bernard that his religious pictures might be 'an affectation', a 'mystification'. Can one honestly try, he asked, to bring back the tapestry of the Middle Ages?

Instead van Gogh made it his job to paint the landscape that surrounded him, the interiors he saw every day, still-lifes of humble objects and the portraits of his few friends, but he painted them with a burning sense of religious mission. He wanted to represent ordinary men and women 'with that something of the eternal which the halo used to symbolise', 'portraits of saints and holy women from life...', and they would be middle-class women of today and yet would have something in common with the early Christians'; and he wanted to paint them in an interpretation and technique 'as simple as those coarse engravings that you find in country almanacs'. Van Gogh was a much truer symbolist than the self-conscious symbolists of Paris and Brittany were. Whatever he drew and painted has a meaning beyond itself. The elements of composition and even more the choice of colours are heavy with emotion. When he painted a café at night he made it, by means of 'soft Louis XV green and malachite contrasting with yellow green and hard blue greens...in an atmosphere of pale sulphur...', a place where one can ruin oneself, run mad or commit suicide'. When he painted a book-shop in the evening 'with the front yellow and rose' it became literally and figuratively 'a focus of light'. He describes in a letter how he paints a friend, a poet, and how, after first having obtained a likeness, he set out to 'exaggerate the fairness of his hair' in 'orange, chromes and pale yellow', to replace the back wall of the ordinary room by 'infinity' in 'the richest, intensest blue' and so in the end to achieve the expression of all 'the love that I have for him'. And in the portrait of Madame Roulin, better known as *La Berceuse*, he meant to paint something 'that would make sailors, who are at the same time children and martyrs, seeing it in the cabin of their boat...feel the old sense of rocking come over them'.

But while his portraits aim at peace, his mature landscapes are turbulent throughout—exalted in 1888, of a furious force of perpetual creation later, and at the end sometimes the expression of 'the extreme of loneliness'. Nature to van Gogh was not order as it was to Cézanne nor grandiosely rich and enchanting fertility as to Gauguin; it was chaos. You cannot, he wrote to Bernard, 'force chaos into a vessel; for it is chaotic just because it cannot be forced into any vessel of our calibre. But what we can do is...to paint one atom of the chaos, a horse, a portrait, your grandmother, apples, a landscape'. That is why, when he was faced with any motif outdoors or indoors, his pen strokes or brush strokes forged ahead, dashing, whipping, hammering, and his colours, put on broad and thick, glowed or burned, as pure as those of Seurat but never applied with scientific reasoning. What he owed to the Neo-Impressionists is patent, but it is not the essentials of his art. He knew already when he arrived at Arles that he wanted 'to exaggerate the essential' (Gauguin had already said the same in 1885: 'There is salvation only in the extreme') and achieve colours 'like stained glass windows'.

Bernard at the same time, as has been mentioned before, did a stained-glass panel of Breton women, the same composition he used for the piece of *appliqué* also already referred to. The rational consideration which at this time led to the Arts and Crafts movement in England—the English Arts and Crafts Exhibition Society had been established in 1888—led these French artists less self-consciously in the identical direction. One universal principle, though one hesitates to use the word in relation to Cézanne and van Gogh, is the decorative. Yet compared with the ethereal naturalism of the Impressionists Cézanne's surfaces, solid as the facing slabs of a wall, and van Gogh's mighty brush-strokes, applied in parallel lines often curved or turning in on themselves, flaming or forming whirlpools, are as much decoration as Gauguin's and Seurat's 'friezes'.

These are indeed the two principal aspects of the change in the later 1880's: from realism to a new faith in subject-matter and expression, and to a new faith in decoration; that is, to a conception of the painted canvas as an organism of an intrinsic value other than that of representing something seen in nature. 'A picture', wrote Maurice Denis at the start of his earliest article, 'is essentially a flat surface covered with colours in a certain order.' Even Renoir underwent this change for a short time. After a journey to Italy he experimented with a strengthening of his outlines in an attempt to emulate Raphael and Ingres. The principal outcome is the exquisite group of *Bathers* of 1884–7. Nor were the French alone in desiring to return to expression and decoration. Mystical subjects and long, disembodied, swaying figures appear in the paintings of the Dutchman Jan Toorop (1859–1928; *Faith Giving Way*, 1891, etc.); sharply drawn, more realistic figures in the forced, excessive attitudes of ritual dancers in Ferdinand Hodler's large allegorical panels (1853–1918: *The Night*, 1890, etc.); subjects of elementary passion such as *Despair*, *The Kiss*, *The Cry*, the *Morning After* in Edvard Munch's (1863–1944) paintings, lithographs and woodcuts. The lines may be overcharged with meaning—sperms actually in the frame of Munch's *Madonna* of 1895—or they may represent just a vague yearning; they always undulate and they always tell of a tension.

Here lies the parallel to the most interesting movement in purely decorative art of the last decade of the nineteenth century, the movement known in English and French as *Art Nouveau*, in German as *Jugendstil*, in Italian as *Stile Liberty*. It is characteristic that Jugendstil is named after a magazine, for the artists of book decoration were the first and most enthusiastic to turn to Art Nouveau, and that Stile Liberty is named after the London shop of Liberty's, which at first dealt largely in Far Eastern goods and was connected with the British revival of decorative art. Britain was indeed earliest in the field, and the title-page of *Wren's City Churches* by Arthur H. Mackmurdo (1851–1942), with its writhing, twisting stalks and leaves and the two excessively elongated cockerels squeezed against the left and right sides of the frame, is now internationally recognised as the first work in the Art Nouveau style. Its date is 1883. Its sources lie no doubt in the Pre-Raphaelites, the Arts and Crafts, Morris wallpapers and certain decoration of the English Gothic Revival. A parallel of the second half of the 1880's is the bronze sculpture and decoration of Alfred Gilbert (1854–1934), best known as the sculptor of the Eros Fountain in Piccadilly Circus (1887–93). The ornamental elements here and in other contemporary works of Gilbert's are as original as Mackmurdo's and as undulating, but they are three-dimensional and have a doughy, lava-ish quality derived from other sources: probably Italian sculpture of Mannerism and Dutch ornament of the seventeenth century. But Gilbert's three-dimensional work found no echo, whereas Mackmurdo's in two dimensions was taken up early by illustrators and other graphic artists, especially Aubrey Beardsley (1872–98). He, for instance, in his *Morte d'Arthur* of 1892, brewed of the same elements an exceedingly highly seasoned and not at all healthy potion, intoxicating continental addicts even more than English.

Beardsley's work was illustrated in volume one of *The Studio*. *The Studio* started in 1893 and at once assumed the leadership in the propaganda for the English decorative and architectural revival. Similar magazines followed in France and Germany within less than five years. They fought, not always in a narrow partisan manner, for the Impressionists as much as the Post-Impressionists, for the sane Arts and Crafts and the exquisite decadence of the Aesthetes, for a revival of folk-art and an understanding of the subtleties of Japanese art. Magazines were backed by exhibitions, those of the Arts and Crafts Exhibition Society already referred to, those of the Independents in Paris and the equally important ones of Les Vingt in Brussels (both founded in 1884). At Brussels in 1892 the exhibition included for the first time stained glass, embroidery and ceramics—four years after Gauguin and Bernard had turned their attention to the applied arts. As a result of influences from the English Arts and Crafts and this little French group the Neo-Impressionist painter Henri van de Velde (1863–1958) turned away from painting and moved towards design and architecture. His illustrations of 1892 (*Dominical*) reflect the sinuous or resilient lines of Mackmurdo but interpret them in an abstract way, without recourse to nature. Art Nouveau decoration can indeed be vegetal or abstract. The former is seen especially in the glass of Émile Gallé (1846–1904) and the furniture, etc., of the school of Nancy to which he belonged, and also in the German book art of Otto Eckmann (1865–1902), the latter in van de Velde, the Belgian architect Victor Horta (1861–1946), the French architect Hector Guimard (1867–1942) and the great Scotsman Charles Rennie Mackintosh (1868–1928). But whether in natural or abstract terms, the line of Art Nouveau always undulates. It is reminiscent of whip-lash or flower-stalk, of coral or gristle, of filaments or serpents, of flames or foam.

Its field is predominantly the surface, its job decoration, just as William Morris's had been. So Art Nouveau is strongest in the graphic arts, where it caused a major revolution affecting not only illustration but also typography and the poster. Here the best work was that of Henri de Toulouse-Lautrec (1864–1901) and the Beggarstaff Brothers (Sir William Nicholson, 1872–1949, and James Pryde, 1866–1941). Toulouse-Lautrec, painter and draughtsman in the wake of Degas but appreciative friend of the Post-Impressionists as well as of William Morris, whom he once called 'the answer to all questions' about the revival of the art of the book and of all art for everyday use, draws his stars of the cabaret with all the gusto and piquancy of Art Nouveau. The Beggarstaffs keep to a soberer, indeed more functional, style of bold flat surfaces. To textiles Mackmurdo had already in the mid-1880's applied the style of his title-page of 1883. He also designed furniture, remarkable not only for Art Nouveau decoration in panels, but also for long slender posts with a flat, shallow, projecting cornice put on top like a hat. Slender shapes instead of the ponderous ones of the High Victorian taste had, as we have seen, already appeared in the Art Furniture designed by Godwin under Japanese influence. Van de Velde in the furniture for his own house at Uccle near Brussels (1895–6) also used light, transparent forms. Soon, however, he and most of the other decorators of Art Nouveau turned to ampler, more richly curved shapes. Once more the English, from Mackmurdo to the best of the younger craftsmen and designers of the Arts and Crafts such as Ernest Gimson (1864–1919), remained saner and more functional, and thus indeed outside Art Nouveau. The pattern is complicated but must be understood to appreciate the European situation in decorative art about 1900. England had heralded Art Nouveau in the 1880's. The fashion on the Continent belongs to the 1890's, by which time England had turned away from it towards a more rational, less *outré*, style out of which the style of the twentieth century could grow.

England—not Scotland; for Glasgow possessed, in Mackintosh, the most brilliant of all Art Nouveau inventors, and the only one to combine the rationalism of the disciplined rectangular shapes of English Arts and Crafts panelling and furniture with the most original abstract decoration. The colours are sophisticated—white, mother of pearl, pale lilac, pale pink, —but the structure to which they are applied is sound. Between 1895 and 1900 Mackintosh and his wife and her sister, the two Macdonalds, and a number of others made Glasgow suddenly one of the centres of European art. In 1900 they exhibited in Vienna and there strongly influenced the young architect-designers who had combined in 1898 to found the *Sezession*.

The Glasgow school worked in wood, in glass, in metal. Art Nouveau glass outside Britain is best known in the persons of Gallé, already mentioned, and of the American Louis C. Tiffany (1848–1933). For Art Nouveau metalwork one thinks at once of the fantastical iron decoration of Horta's house in the rue Paul-Émile Janson (1892–3). The role of iron in the architectural movements of the late nineteenth century is manifold. For the moment we are still concerned only with its decorative aspect. Side by side with Horta's work the wild iron decoration of the Paris Métro stations (1900) and the block of flats known as the Castel Béranger (1894–8), both by Guimard, must be remembered.

The exterior of the Castel Béranger may be weird, with its oriels and gables and its total asymmetry, but it is angular and lacking in those very qualities of curvaceous tension which characterise Art Nouveau. The same is true to a lesser degree of Horta's exterior of the house in the rue Paul-Émile Janson, and even of Mackintosh's country houses near Glasgow, however original and pointedly asymmetrical their compositions may be. The building, however, which established Mackintosh's short-lived professional success, the School of Art at Glasgow (1897–9), combines in its façade features of Art Nouveau as creatively with features of a bold functionalism as do Mackintosh's designs for interior decoration. The large studio windows with their unmoulded frames, mullions and transoms are contrasted against the middle bay—not placed in the middle —which has an eccentric grouping of motifs, curved and angular, light and heavy. There is nothing left here of historicism. Again, incidentally, in the defeat of historicism, Mackmurdo was ahead of Mackintosh. The front of an exhibition stand he made in 1886 for the Century Guild, his guild of craftsmen and designers, has not a motif that reflects styles of the past. It is all exceedingly thin posts with the flat hats already described and a heavy flat attic, again with short posts with hats on as its cresting. But Mackmurdo soon became more moderate in his architecture.

The credit of having demonstrated radically and ruthlessly that Art Nouveau was possible in architecture can go to only one man, an architect working in a marginal country and exceptional circumstances: Antoni Gaudí (1852–1926). He lived at Barcelona and there started with the crazy Morisco-Gothic Casa Vicens of 1878–80, wild in its angular forms, wild in its patterns of surfaces, wild in its spiky ironwork, the latter already amazingly close to Art Nouveau. From here Gaudí's originality and daring shot up to higher and higher summits of utterly unfunctional genius. The Palau Güell was followed by the chapel for the Colonia Güell, the Parque Güell and finally two blocks of flats in Barcelona of 1905–7 and the later parts of the grand unfinished church of the Sagrada

Familia. Columns lean, pinnacles look like antediluvian monsters or termite-heaps, coloured surfaces are made up of broken cups and saucers and tiles, not only façades but even the shapes of the rooms in the flats undulate, and stonework is like molten lava.

There can be no way beyond Gaudí and any attempt to imitate him must lead to disaster. But is not the same also true of the more sophisticated extremes of Art Nouveau decoration, of Guimard's and Horta's ironwork, of Beardsley's illustrations, even of van de Velde's desks? That is the ambivalence of Art Nouveau. In so far as it was made for the aesthetes by the aesthetes it still belonged to the nineteenth century; for the nineteenth century had been the century of art removed from the fulfilment of needs, of art as the extreme skill of the individual, of art appreciated only by the connoisseur. But in its break with period imitation, in its re-establishment of originality, Art Nouveau heralds the twentieth century. Admittedly the turn from historicism had begun with Norman Shaw and H. H. Richardson, but only Art Nouveau presented it radically. Such radicalism is alien to the English temper. Charles F. Annesley Voysey (1857–1941) continued where Shaw and early Mackmurdo had left off, but his charmingly simple and intimate country houses are Tudor in derivation, however simplified the general shapes and details have become. Voysey's buildings and even more his fresh and pretty designs for textiles and furniture once again impressed the Continent, but as an argument against Art Nouveau rather than for it. Perhaps the radicalism of Art Nouveau was needed if ultimately the greater, more comprehensive radicalism of the twentieth century was to be reached. Because Voysey kept his sympathy for the Tudor style and Shaw, in his later years, discovered his for the Baroque of Wren, England in the first quarter of the twentieth century went into compromises and dropped out of the group of countries working for new solutions.

These solutions, wherever they were found, were found in reaction against, not as a continuation of, Art Nouveau. The very radicalism of Art Nouveau, necessary as it had been, defeated it after hardly more than ten years. The more flamboyant a style the shorter will be its duration. Fatigue sets in and even nausea. Thus it happened in Viennese Art Nouveau, and the outcome was the strictly cubic style of the early twentieth century inspired by Mackintosh and handled so superbly by Josef Hoffmann and Adolf Loos. Thus also it happened in Berlin in the weightier style of Peter Behrens who was equally influential as an architect and an industrial designer. He built factories and office buildings— no longer private houses—and he designed electric kettles, electric fans, arc-lamps and the like—no longer domestic furniture, textiles and wallpapers. Rationalism, functionalism and a social purpose, all preached by Morris, made their appearance here just as they did in Auguste Perret's early concrete buildings in Paris and the rectangularity and the open plans of Frank Lloyd Wright's prairie houses around Chicago and in the commercial architecture of Chicago as well.

From the point of view of the twentieth century—that is, not strictly for its significance within its own period—the commercial architecture of Chicago is indeed the most interesting event of the 1880's and 1890's. The architect who saw its problems most clearly and handled it with the greatest aesthetic mastery was Frank Lloyd Wright's 'lieber Meister', Louis Sullivan (1856–1924). Because of the high prices of the ground but also because of publicity America had invented the skyscraper. It was at first simply a high masonry building, but in 1884, at Chicago, iron frame construction was applied to it, with stanchions and beams carrying the building and allowing the interstices to be made of glass or other light materials. As masters of iron and glass European engineers had preceded the Americans. The Crystal Palace had been put up in 1851, all of its 1850 feet put up in five months, and the train-shed at St Pancras Station in London, of 1863–5, had the widest span (240 feet) achieved up to that time. It was outdone by the Galerie des Machines of the International Exhibition in Paris in 1889 which spanned 385 feet in the most elegant construction. For the same exhibition Gustave Eiffel constructed the Eiffel Tower, the highest building ever erected by man.

But these were not the works of architects. Architects of reputation had kept characteristically aloof from this development. Morris, it will be remembered, hated the machine and the effects of industry. Ruskin had hated the Crystal Palace. Sir George Gilbert Scott, the most successful English architect of the High Victorian decades, had paid lip-service to the possibilities of metallic construction but never made use of them himself. By far the most brilliant High Victorian building in which iron and glass play a predominant part, Oriel Chambers at Liverpool of 1864, was designed by a scarcely known architect, Peter Ellis. The first architect of genius to get hold of the new technical possibilities and find a congenial architectural form for them was Sullivan. His Wainwright Building at St Louis of 1890–1 is a grid, emphasising in its rigidity the cellular construction and the cellular use. Sullivan was not strictly adverse to ornament; on the contrary he had in 1888, inside an early building, the Auditorium, used a very original version of feathery leaf ornament that heralds Art Nouveau almost as much as Gaudí's ornament at the same time. But he recommended his contemporaries to 'refrain entirely from the use of ornament for a period of years in order that our thought might concentrate acutely upon the production of buildings comely in the nude'. That is precisely what happened in the twentieth century.

The thirty years here described in terms of art and architecture are indeed the beginning of a new age as they are the end of an old. Impressionism had been the ultimate refinement of realism. Cézanne and van Gogh, Gauguin and Seurat, Toorop and Munch all turned away from realism, and the twentieth century continued into Expressionism and Cubism and abstract art. Webb and Norman Shaw and H. H. Richardson had been the ultimate refinement of historicism. Sullivan, Mackintosh, Gaudí broke with history. So did the decorators of Art Nouveau.

But the twentieth century, inheriting from the painters as well as the architects, inherited a curse as well as a blessing. Architecture and design were enabled by the legacy they had received to work out a style which expressed the new century and could be understood and accepted by all. Painting and sculpture were driven instead into even greater loneliness than that which had been the fate of Cézanne, Gauguin and van Gogh. Abstraction had made architecture a universal tool; it made painting and sculpture an expression so personal that it could hardly any longer be communicated with certainty. The art and architecture of the first third of the twentieth century, though they cannot be treated here, have to be discussed in terms of this antinomy.

CHAPTER VII

EDUCATION

EDUCATION during these thirty years exhibited certain similar characteristics all over the world which enables us to view them together across the national boundaries. Accordingly we shall be concerned not with the various nations one by one, but with aspects of education illustrated from time to time by some particular nation.

The study of the development and content of education cannot but be ecological. Systems do not flourish in the air. They affect and are affected by the social, political, intellectual and religious structure as well as by the movements of their time. Of no period was this more true than of the last third of the nineteenth century. This was a period of the aftermath of wars in Europe, in America, in China and the Far East. It was a period of vast industrial expansion and of the rise into importance of the working class. It was a period of the expansion of Europe into Africa and elsewhere. And above all it was a period of secularisation. The Church, even in Catholic countries, was losing its grip on one department of life and thought after another. In education it saw the emergence of education as a civil right and as the concern of the whole community as such, instead of being merely a private or sectional concern.

One of the earliest aims of education, an aim as old as Plato, was the training of a social élite in the art of government. This attitude to education, which assumed that ability went with status, was but slowly replaced. It was not until the nineteenth century that an *educational* élite was recognised anywhere as an alternative to one that was purely social. Even after 1870 the movement away from a social to an educational élite made only slow strides.

There is probably no better example of this than the English 'public' school.[1] These had taken on a new lease of life with the reforms of Thomas Arnold (1795–1842) at Rugby, but the development of science and the growing criticism of endowments that marked the middle of the century drew attention to their deficiencies. The Clarendon Commission (1861–4) was therefore set up to investigate nine of the larger schools and it reported that there was nothing really wrong with them. Indeed, 'it is not easy to estimate the degree in which the English people are indebted to these schools for the qualities on which they pique themselves most,—

[1] In the English sense a 'public' school is one in which the governors are not owners but trustees and any profit made goes back into the school. Other qualifications have been added to this, the original definition, but this is the justification for the use of the term 'public'.

for their capacity to govern others and control themselves, their aptitude for combining freedom with order, their public spirit, their vigour and manliness of character, their strong but not slavish respect for public opinion, their love of healthy sport and exercise...they have had perhaps the largest share in moulding the character of an English gentleman.' These lyrical sentiments were duly recognised in the Public Schools Act of 1868 which, however, dealt with the trust deeds of only seven out of the nine schools, made no arrangements for inspection or supervision, and left the head of the school in a completely autocratic position as against the assistant masters.

Seven schools were not very many when one considers the large number of endowed grammar schools in England in 1864, some of which dated as far back as the eleventh century. Accordingly another commission was set up in 1864 'to inquire into the education given in schools not comprised within Her Majesty's two former Commissions' (Newcastle, 1859, and Clarendon, 1861). The report of this extremely important Commission (variously known as the Taunton or the Schools Inquiry Commission) was issued in twenty volumes and represents an investigation into over 800 endowed schools and the examination of 147 witnesses. Although the commissioners were concerned mainly with the use of endowments they nevertheless sketched out a scheme of national education which had in it the germ of later developments and which also recognised the urgency of the case for modern as against classical studies. To implement their suggestions they advocated the setting up of a central authority and a system of local authorities. All schools should be inspected and examined, and teachers should be trained after the manner of French teachers in the École Normale. So far, at least, had the commissioners got away from the idea of training a social élite.

Although, since the Revolution, the élite in which the French believed had been intellectual rather than social, this idea of the élite was a feature of French education even more than of the English. Perhaps this was due to the existence of a central educational authority which could organise all grades of education, whereas in England such a central authority did not appear until the Board of Education was set up in 1900. In France there were no educational endowments. They had all been swept away by the Revolution, and so private schools were almost all in the hands of the Church, which ran schools for the poor and also for the well-to-do. When the state came in it perpetuated the system of segregation, and secondary education in France was a different kind of thing altogether from elementary education. There was no crossing over from the lower level to the higher.

The German plans for the education of an élite were worked out somewhat differently from the French. They were linked up with university entrance. Only students from the *Gymnasium* were free to enter the universities in any faculty that they chose. Those from the *Realgymnasium* were barred from the theological faculty, and those from the *Oberrealschule* from medicine as well as from theology.

Apart from the inevitable exclusiveness of schools for an élite, maintained through high fees and a social *cachet*, the classical curriculum created a further barrier which everywhere cut them off from the new interests of the world outside. An increasing urge towards modern studies was being exerted by changing industrial and social conditions, but here again change was slow in coming. In England the Clarendon Commissioners seemed almost oblivious of the changed times for they oozed sentimentality about the advantages to the soul of man from the study of Greek and Latin. When Edward Bowen (1836–1901) established at Harrow in 1869 the first 'modern side' in an English public school he was thought to be lowering his status in the scholastic world. In France this emphasis was even more noticeable than in England for it was not complicated as in England by social considerations. It was a matter of conviction that even in a democracy the tradition of philosophy and politics required an élite nourished on the classics. 'Modern studies' were utilitarian and materialistic, necessary, no doubt, for business and industry but of a lower order than the classics. The Ribot Commission of 1890, however, while justifying the classical curriculum, entered a word of protest against this inequality as 'sheer injustice'.

In the Far East there were more decisive movements against the old idea of training a merely social élite. In India the education given was that of the governing (British) class and it was given in English—a policy which separated the élite from the mass of the people—until the 1870's. Then a new type of élite emerged, not social, not educational, but nationalistic. The Arya Somaj was founded about 1875 and the first Indian national congress met in Bombay in 1885. In Bengal national schools, wholly Indian, were founded, and the basis of the curriculum was Indian history, literature and religion. In Japan there was no alien government to complicate matters and after the fall of the Shogunate in 1867 the country turned with enthusiasm to education on Western lines. The emperor declared that henceforth the administration would look for men of ability whatever their rank in society. The new élite was to be based on educational grounds. China, too, turned to the West in this period. Up to the end of the nineteenth century the Chinese educational system was based on the Chinese classics, but from 1861 when two modern colleges were started, one in Peking and one in Canton, there was a steady movement towards Western education stimulated very largely by Americans. After China's defeat by Japan, which was attributed to the Westernisation of Japan, the Viceroy Chang Chih-tung wrote a book, *China's Only Hope* (1895), which strongly supported this movement.

Nowhere was there to be found a better illustration of the educational philosophy of Europeans than in those areas in Africa in which their governments could act without opposition. The policy, if it can be called a policy, of the nineteenth century was to turn the more educable of the native peoples into Europeans, although different governments interpreted this in different ways. At Fourah Bay College, for instance, in Sierra Leone, there was a long tradition of higher education on classical lines sponsored by Durham University. Elsewhere, as in Mozambique, the aim was simply to produce efficient and amenable servants for the white man. French colonial policy went far beyond the British in West Africa and opened the door of opportunity much more widely. The pick of the native schools in the French territories were sent to Paris to complete their education and the avowed aim was to turn this élite into African civil servants. Similarly, the Belgians sent their most promising pupils from the Congo to Brussels.

The aims of the education of colonial peoples thus varied between the association of an African élite with the European government and the production of a more efficient labour corps. For the most part primary education and the training of teachers were in the hands of the missions and other religious bodies while such higher education as existed was subsidised by the state. It was not until after the great missionary conference at Edinburgh in 1910 that the various colonial nations began to accept the aim of education as the moral, physical and spiritual development of the native people themselves.

The growth of new universities of a modern type in most countries of the world and the reform of the old ones after 1850 was part of the slow movement away from a social to an educational élite.

The two old universities of England were eulogised by John Henry Newman (1800–90) in his *Discourses on University Education* for their tutorial and residential system, which was modelled on the old craft guild. But Oxford and Cambridge were not quite so perfect as he imagined them to be. They were heavily clerical and Anglican, and governed by a close corporation of celibate heads of colleges. The royal commissions of 1854 and 1856 resulted in a more democratic constitution for both of them. The Test Act of 1871 swept away all religious tests except for a degree in theology; even these have now disappeared. But the old universities still failed to satisfy some minds.

In the nineteenth century the master-and-apprentice relation of the craft guild was giving way to the employer–employed relationship. This change was paralleled in education by the development of the attitude that education was a commodity to be bought and sold. London University represented the new spirit. The virtual founder of it, Lord Brougham—the 'learned friend' of Peacock's novels—was a Scot who saw to it that the University should be as different as possible from Oxford and Cambridge.

It was to have no religious tests, it was to have the lecture system rather than the tutorial, and it was not to be residential. After a very stormy existence it was reorganised in 1858, when it became little more than an examining body giving degrees, the colleges being cut adrift and made responsible for their own teaching. Two further royal commissions in 1889 and 1894 resulted in the Act of 1900, which in typically English fashion chose both of the alternatives open to it. The university became both internal and external, giving internal and external degrees, and at the same time being a teaching university. Despite the curiously commercial attitude that marked its early years London University did an enormous service to English and even to world-wide higher education. Most of the modern English universities began as colleges preparing for the London external degrees and thus were able to start with a ready-made recognised standard. Even colleges as far away as Montreal and Ceylon were also able to benefit by their association with London.

Most of the new university colleges in England belong to the period after 1870 and the spirit of the founders may be indicated by the aims of Josiah Mason who established his college in Birmingham in 1880. It was 'to promote thorough systematic education and instruction adapted to the practical, mechanical and artistic requirements of the manufactures and industrial pursuits of the Midland district...to the exclusion of *mere* literary education and instruction, and of all teaching of theology'. In 1881 the colleges in Manchester, Leeds and Liverpool combined to form the federal Victoria University, but after Joseph Chamberlain had turned the Birmingham college into a university on its own—the first 'civic' university in Britain—Victoria was defederalised, and since then all later university colleges have obtained status as single universities.

Federation continued to be the plan of the University of Wales for a special reason. Wales is a bilingual country but one of its languages, unlike those of Switzerland, is spoken only within the country itself. There is also, as elsewhere, a marked difference between north and south, while the mountainous terrain divides it up into still smaller and strongly individualistic units. The Church of England and the Nonconformists represented a further division and within Nonconformity there was another division between Independents and Calvinistic Methodists. In such a situation the only bond of union could be patriotism for Wales itself, and the campaign resulting in the establishment of a College at Aberystwyth in 1872 gave it an objective. Colleges followed at Cardiff in 1883 and Bangor in 1893, and in 1893 under the inspiration of Viriamu Jones the three colleges were federated into the University of Wales which immediately became a rallying point for Welsh nationalism.

While England and Wales were developing new universities and colleges the needs of Scotland were being satisfied by the four ancient foundations, St Andrews (1411), Glasgow (1450), Aberdeen (1494) and Edinburgh

(1582). These from the beginning were fashioned on the continental pattern rather than that of Oxford and Cambridge, perhaps because of the affinities of the Scots with France. One notable feature, however, of the Scottish university system which marked it off from the continental system was its close connection with the schools of the people. In the German system the university was the determining body for all higher education. It laid down the terms on which it would receive pupils and the *Volksschule* was ignored. Similarly in France elementary and secondary education went along parallel lines which never met. The Scottish universities were integrated into the school system, and just as there was no specialised education for an élite at the school level so there was no block in the way of the child of the village working his way up to a university. A large number of university entrants came direct from the primary schools.

The influence of German universities was also felt in England. Mark Pattison (1813–84), the rector of Lincoln College, Oxford, wrote two notable essays (1868 and 1876) on university reform, emphasising the importance of research and condemning the current practice of treating a university as a mere continuation school for grown-up schoolboys cramming for examinations. A university should aim at 'a breadth of cultivation, a scientific formation of mind, a concert of the intellectual faculties'.

In the United States private enterprise was evident in higher education and particularly in the universities. The outstanding university foundation of this period was Cornell, which was due to the collaboration of Ezra Cornell and Andrew D. White, its first president. In a notable speech White made three points which justified the new venture. First, that as regards primary education the state policy should be diffusion of resources, but as regards university education it should be concentration of resources. Secondly, that sectarian colleges are not adequate for the work required. Thirdly, that any institution for higher education should be part of the whole system of public instruction. To ensure the integration of the university with the school system White had written into the charter the provision of four 'state scholarships' for each of the hundred and twenty-eight assembly districts.

After the Civil War existing American universities took on a new lease of life. The revival was due first of all to a remarkable group of presidents of whom White was one. Others were Noah Porter of Yale (1871), C. W. Eliot of Harvard (1869), James McCosh of Princeton (1868), J. B. Angell of Michigan (1871), and D. G. Gilman of Johns Hopkins (1875). Secondly, there was the Young Yale Movement, the aim of which was a liberalising of the studies and the association of the alumni with the control of the college (not always a happy arrangement). Thirdly, there was the Morrill Act of 1862 under which institutions for agriculture and engineering were set up through the assistance of land grants. Agriculture had to fight its way from a merely rule of thumb practice to a scientific status and in this Cornell, under Isaac P. Roberts (1874–1903), led the way. Engineering had a better start, and the Massachusetts Institute of Technology had been established before the war. The Land Grant colleges, however, were not confined to these subjects, nor were they confined to male students only. The growth of these colleges went on despite the panic of 1873, and the curriculum was widened. Asa Gray, Louis Agassiz, Clarence King, J. W. Powell and Lewis Morgan, though not altogether in the first flight of scientists, established science as a major subject of university education.

University education developed considerably in most countries of the world at this time. Existing universities moved in the direction of greater freedom of control or of secularisation (which usually came to the same thing) and towards a technical curriculum. New universities were established in response to local demand. At the same time many colleges, such as that at Zürich, which began as technical institutes developed on university lines. In 1873 Trinity College, Dublin, followed the example of Oxford in 1871 by abolishing doctrinal tests. In 1879 the Royal University of Ireland was established with which the Queen's colleges of Belfast, Cork and Galway became associated, but in the new century another university was established in Dublin and a new university in Belfast. In Switzerland the famous academy in Geneva became a university in 1876 and the theological college of Lausanne followed in 1891. A new university was founded at Fribourg in 1889, specially intended for the canton of that name. This association of a university with a particular region marks a change from the earlier idea and was perhaps most notable in the 'civic' universities of England. On the other hand the universities in Scandinavia—Lund, Uppsala, Christiania and Copenhagen—continued to be closely attached to the Lutheran state church. Racial and religious factors were prominent in the development of universities in Belgium, although not so much in Holland where the new university of Amsterdam was founded in 1877. Considerations of sectarian scruples not only as between Catholics and Protestants but also within Protestantism itself affected university development in Canada where the university of Toronto, for example, had to make allowance in the constitution for Methodists, Presbyterians and both 'high church' and 'low church' Anglicans. This was similar to the 'church related colleges' which are such a marked feature of American education. In South Africa the Dutch Reformed College at Stellenbosch was on the road to becoming a purely Afrikaans University. The London pattern was followed in the University of the Cape in 1874 which gave degrees irrespective of the college from which the students came, and by the University of Sydney which, however, in 1884 began to grant degrees to students of affiliated colleges. The University of New Zealand, founded in 1870, affiliated to itself colleges in Auckland, Christchurch and Otago.

Education as a civil right is enrolled in the Declaration of Human Rights of the United Nations. This is the culmination of a process which began in the nineteenth century, namely the gradual secularisation of education and its liberation from the control of religious and philanthropic bodies. At the same time the idea of 'the state', so often used in a pejorative sense and meaning usually 'the government', has begun to give way to the more organic conception of the state as the whole community acting through its chosen officers. Thus the objection that was current in this period that state education is the education of 'other people's children' was gradually seen to be false.

In England in addition to the 'public schools' and the many private schools for the upper and middle classes there were schools for the labouring classes. These were the outcome of philanthropy and were for the most part Church of England schools belonging to the National Society (1810), and undenominational schools belonging to the British and Foreign Schools Society (1808). State 'interference' in education began in 1833 and was limited to the subsidising of these two societies, although the official in charge, Sir James Kay-Shuttleworth, managed to make the grants a means of raising the whole standard of education. The revised Education Code of 1862, however, made the grants dependent on the results of an examination, failures in which entailed loss of grant by the school. This was the system of payment by results, which continued in England until 1895. Education was obviously a commodity and measurable as such.

The Elementary Education Act of 1870 gave the education societies a year in which to establish more elementary schools if they could. Where this was impossible a School Board was to be set up by the ratepayers to establish a Board School, supported by a rate of threepence in the £. By an Act of 1880 attendance at either Board or voluntary schools was made compulsory. The Act of 1870 marked the first appearance in England of a statutory authority for the provision of education and the weakening of Church and voluntary control. This was not because of any anti-religious feeling but simply because the money could not be found privately. The 'secular solution', as it was called, aimed at the disappearance of clerical *control* and only in the second place had it anything to do with religion in the curriculum. It was one of the most convinced believers in the secular solution—T. H. Huxley—who most strenuously insisted on the Bible in the schools. The clerical party, however, objected to religious teaching being given by laymen, and Disraeli in the debates accused the government of setting up 'a new sacerdotal class', namely the teachers.

The slowness of the development of state control in England was due to a variety of causes. First there was the compromising English temperament. Secondly, there was the rooted belief of the Victorians in the divine origin of class distinctions. Thirdly, there was the belated recognition of the inevitable result of education, which is the demand for more. No one can call a halt and say 'Thus far and no farther'. Fourthly, the belief, almost ineradicable, that education is a private concern and parents' rights in this regard should be inviolate. Fifthly, the absence of adequate local government units and the dislike of the English for *ad hoc* authorities. Not until 1888 when the County Councils were set up by Act of Parliament did there arrive a suitable local authority.

The Churches were not the only parties opposed to the development of elementary education. The employers of labour put up a continual fight against popular education which made itself felt in the recognition by law of half-time employment. An Act of 1876 forbade regular employment under ten and fixed the full-time age at thirteen. In 1901 the half-time age was raised to twelve. In 1918 the compulsory full-time schooling period was fixed at 14, and all regular employment before that age was forbidden. In the same year all fees were abolished.

It is interesting at this point to compare England with Scotland. As far back as the sixteenth century every kirk or parish in Scotland was expected to set up a school for elementary subjects and for Latin, from which the more competent children, rich and poor alike, should be able to go on to colleges of higher education 'until the commonwealth have profit of them'. This truly 'political' aim was included also in the educational aims of the Church, but in so far as it was accepted it was bound in the long run to lead to the secularisation of control. The towns in particular grew restive under clerical authority. The absence of class distinctions made education the concern of everybody and it is interesting that in the Scottish Education Act of 1872 the word 'elementary' was dropped from the title as savouring too much of English snobbery. The teaching of young children was not looked upon as almost a menial occupation as it was in England. The benefits of Trusts such as the Dick Bequest (1828) were put in the way of even the humblest village schools.

Scotland was a more homogeneous country than England in religion and in social life, and even clerical control was not identified with a governing class as in England. Nevertheless, the Act of 1872 took from the presbyteries their long-standing right of visitation, the Burgh and Parochial Schools Act of 1861 having already abolished the requirement of the teachers' subscription to a doctrinal statement. Scotland, moreover, was one of the earliest countries to form an association of teachers, a necessary step towards professional status. The Educational Institute of Scotland was founded in 1847 and received its charter in 1851. Teachers' associations introduced a third factor into the struggle for educational control. Having a professional interest such associations were aligned with neither Church nor state, although their existence helped the trend towards secularisation.

Similar teachers' associations were founded in Denmark, France and

Switzerland. In England the College of Preceptors founded in 1856 was a more academic body, but the National Union of Teachers founded in 1870 did not disdain the use of political pressure on behalf of teachers as a class. In the United States Horace Mann and Henry Barnard founded the National Association of the Friends of Education in 1849, which after various internal changes became in 1870 the National Education Association. This did not prevent individual states from having their own associations, one of the earliest of which was founded in Rhode Island in 1847.

The secularisation of education took different forms according to local conditions. In the United States, where separation of Church and state is written into the Constitution and where in consequence there is no established Church, the relation of Church and state in education has been concerned much more with the cost of education than with its control. In this there has been a marked difference between the North and the South as well as between one state and another.

In the South before the Civil War, patriarchal and rural education was looked upon as the private concern of parents and churches. The Civil War shattered this primitive system. Moreover, the slaves from being a very considerable asset were now a serious liability and state action of some sort was badly needed. Yet all attempts by the Federal government to help education in the South were bitterly resented, although the Southerners did not disdain help from private sources like the Peabody Education Fund, established in 1867. The freedom given to four million Negroes who were mainly illiterate and the political equality which followed from it created a difficult and dangerous situation. The Freedman's Bureau set up by the government to help the Negro was very unpopular in the South because it was run by Northerners. Moreover, it began to help those at the top end of the educational ladder instead of those at the bottom, and its first act was to found Atlanta University in 1867. Fisk University was founded in Nashville in 1890. This policy was popular with the more ambitious of the freedmen to whom education in Greek and Latin was the badge of equality with the whites, but the more far-seeing of the leaders such as Booker T. Washington (1858–1915) believed that above all the Negro needed economic emancipation, and that the way to this was by creating wealth, and wealth could be created only through training in industry and agriculture. Washington himself had been trained at General Armstrong's agricultural institute at Hampton, Virginia, and he became principal of a corresponding institution at Tuskegee in Alabama in 1881. The Negro intellectuals looked down on these institutions on the ground that they restricted the Negro to manual labour but it was clear that both types of development were necessary, for the black South was no more homogeneous than the white South.

In the Northern states general associations for the promotion of education sprang up everywhere. Here, as in the South, there was a marked difference between urban and rural areas. It was the urban areas that wished for education to be tax-supported, publicly controlled, non-sectarian, compulsory and free. Here therefore the state had to wrestle not with the Federal authorities but with hundreds of little communities each wanting to go its own way. However, as elsewhere, financial needs finally determined where the control should lie. New York was the first state to have a state superintendent of common schools. By 1861 twenty-eight states out of thirty-four had put education into state hands. Church authorities were gradually squeezed out from the state system and with the exception of West Virginia no state admitted to the Union after 1858 made any provision in its constitution for denominational schools.

This movement towards secularisation was felt all over the world. The Australian colonies which had begun, like England, by giving subsidies to denominational societies, brought the system to an end in New South Wales in 1858 and throughout the continent by 1863. In Denmark education from the seventeenth century had been essentially a state affair. Holberg (1684–1754), who was the real founder of Danish popular education, had declared that 'children must become persons before they become Christians'.

The situation in France was complicated by the fact that a Catholic country owed its educational system to the Republic, which believed in a system of lay education given by laymen. The Republicans wanted education to be compulsory, secular and free, teaching a morality independent of the Church. On the other hand, the right wing stood for the rights of the Church in this as in other spheres. Control, subsidies, curriculum and the status of teachers were thus affected by the see-saw of French politics. However, one result of the French defeat in the war of 1871 was that more money was spent on schools, and under Jules Ferry (1832–93) as minister of public instruction elementary education became secular, free and compulsory. In 1901 all religious bodies had to apply for state permission to carry on teaching, and under Combes in 1904 all teaching by religious brotherhoods under clerical direction was suppressed.

Switzerland, after a series of violent political convulsions, tackled this question of Church and state in education, and in 1874 the canton Bern secured the supremacy of the state over the Church, while Geneva demanded of the clergy an oath of loyalty to the Constitution. Article 27 of the Constitution of 1874 put education exclusively under the civil authority, and the Confederation was empowered to take the necessary measures against cantons that did not fulfil their obligations.

In Germany the movement towards secularisation had a long history. In all the states education had made vigorous progress in the heyday of the Romantic revival and this new humanism was opposed to clerical control. The revolution of 1848, however, in Germany as elsewhere resulted in violent reaction, and the new regulations for schools took as their norm the little rural school from which no breath of revolutionary fervour was ever likely to come. Frederick William IV of Prussia (1840–61) introduced into the political situation an aura of mysticism which had very serious results. He was a believer in the divine right of kings, and in his eyes the state and not merely the Church was the handmaid of God. Every elementary school in the country was thus drawn into politics. Nevertheless, in the reorganisation of the educational system by Falk between 1872 and 1879 responsibility was put squarely on the shoulders of the state. The right of supervision of elementary education by the Church was taken away and the work was given to superintendents who were officers of the state. This affected the curriculum also. The Emperor William II in opening an educational conference in 1890 came out strongly in favour of modern studies in opposition not only to the ancient classics but even to the classics of Germany. Classical studies, he said, had produced an educated proletariate which was not at all what was needed by the new empire. Goethe's idea of national character gave place to Bismarck's view of the individual in subservience to the state.

Relations between Church and state in Germany present, therefore, an aspect unique among the countries of Europe. It is difficult to call it simply secularisation except that control was taken from the Church as such, for as the state was now a mystical divine 'person' control by the state was as much a religious concern as political. This was indicated by the emphasis on patriotism and by the large part played by compulsory military service whereby every male teacher in every school became a representative of the armed might of the state.

In the more backward European countries primary education at least continued to be either directly or indirectly under the Church. In Russia, for instance, primary education, such as it was, came under the Holy Synod and the local priests. No teaching certificate was required of the teachers and the priests were so fully occupied with their parochial duties that they allowed the schools to fall into neglect. Such education was almost entirely vocational. Secondary and university education were confined to the wealthier classes and were characterised by a strong suspicion of natural science and of Western political ideas. It was not until after the revolution of 1905, which followed the defeat of Russia by Japan, that there was any general development in education. Even in Belgium, although the state took over all communal schools in 1878, the clergy resisted and refused absolution to teachers in the 'godless' schools. In 1884 a Catholic government came into power and reversed the action of its predecessor. In Spain a law of 1857 made primary education compulsory but this remained so much a dead letter that in the early years of the twentieth century the great majority of the people were still illiterate. In 1902 the Liberal government under Sagasta passed a law requiring all private schools and colleges to be licensed by the state and to submit to inspection, but after the accession of Alfonso XIII Church influence again prevailed. Similar influences were at work in Portugal where at an even earlier date, 1844, education of children from 7 to 15 was declared compulsory. This law also was a dead letter and the purpose of it was lost in the struggle of Church and state.

In his report to the Newcastle commissioners in 1861 Matthew Arnold took the opportunity to draw their attention to wider issues which for most people had not yet appeared above the horizon: 'The Education Commissioners would excite, I am convinced, in thousands of hearts a gratitude of which they little dream, if, in presenting the result of their labours on primary instruction they were at the same time to say to the Government "Regard the necessities of a not distant future, and organise your secondary instruction".' This became a slogan for the reformers.

The situation, however, was complicated by the fact that in most countries there was already in existence a system of secondary education in private hands and on a class basis. England had its so-called 'public schools' for a limited class of people. In France secondary schools were unconnected with the primary school system. Parents decided whether their children should go into the secondary or into the primary and, once settled, there was no crossing over. In Scotland there was already a direct road from the parish school to the university, so that secondary education, when it came to be provided by the state, was a movement from the universities downwards quite as much as a movement from the elementary school upwards. The secondary schools, when they arrived, took their place at once alongside the academies and burgh schools because the same class of children were to be found in both.

There was another difficulty. What was to be the aim of secondary education? Was it an extension of elementary education, a little more of what the doctor ordered, or should it be a different thing altogether, different in form as well as in content? Ought it to be a preparation for the university? Was it to be determined by the class to which a person belonged and if so ought it to educate him to fit into that class or should it help him to rise out of that class?

The Elementary Education Act of 1870 producedin England a cra ving for further education, and in areas where the wishes of the parents were sufficiently insistent the Board schools themselves grafted higher classes on to the elementary schools while the London and some other school boards even built 'higher grade schools'. All this of course was strictly illegal, for public money was being used for wider purposes than those sanctioned by the Education Acts. The parents, however, were not the only group concerned. The training colleges for teachers were beginning to realise the need for a higher standard of entrance than that given by the elementary schools. Meanwhile it was discovered that children were seeking entrance to training colleges as one of the means of securing a higher education whether they went on to teaching or not. The establishment of university colleges again showed the need for secondary education as a groundwork, especially in the teaching of science. All these influences combined to put pressure on the government.

Sir Robert Morant, an official of the education department, supplied the facts of the school board situation to Cockerton, the government auditor, who thereupon surcharged the members of the London School Board with the cost of the education which they had provided for children beyond the compulsory age. The Board lost on appeal and the 'Cockerton Judgement', as it was called, became a test case.

This precipitated legislation. The action of the London School Board had to be legalised but this could be done only within the framework of a larger scheme. One difficulty, of course, was that a school board, except in large cities, was too small a unit to handle anything beyond elementary education. In 1888, however, new units of local government had been established, namely the county councils, and, as we have seen, these new bodies were almost immediately given powers over technical education in their area, subsidised out of the surplus of the tax on whisky. Secondary education, however, was too big a problem to be dealt with in this piecemeal fashion, and the Bryce Commission was appointed in 1894 to consider the matter. On its recommendation the county councils in 1902 were made the effective unit for all types of education in their area, and a Board of Education was established in 1900 to be the central authority under parliament for education. In 1944 the Board was turned into a Ministry and thus given status parallel with that of other Ministries.

The organisation of secondary education in Wales was difficult because of its widely scattered rural population. In 1889 the Intermediate Education Act was passed which provided for a new type of day school not quite so ambitious as the three existing grammar schools at Brecon, Bangor and Llandovery. Thirty such schools had been founded by 1895. The county was not then felt to be a suitable body to control this new venture and although Sir John Rhys and Viriamu Jones wished that it should be controlled by the university a separate Central Welsh Board was set up in 1896. This was a curious body, quite remote from its constituents and therefore tending to emphasise examination results. These objections were got rid of when the Act of 1899 set up the Board of Education for England and Wales and the Act of 1902 promised a more realistic unit for secondary education.

In Scotland school boards had also been established, but these were not abolished till 1918. Scotland indeed had long had a national system of education from the parish school to the university. But secondary schools under state auspices were also very much needed, and the Argyll Commission (1864–8) was appointed to inquire into all the schools of Scotland, including secondary. Of all these schools only five in all Scotland were properly secondary schools, for all the others presented 'a confusion of infant, primary and secondary schools combined in one'. The 'burgh schools' were strongly classical in their curriculum whereas the 'academies' had begun by introducing science and commercial subjects, although by 1864 there was not very much to distinguish them from the burgh or grammar schools. As we have seen, the Act of 1872 established school boards and allowed them a year's grace to provide for all the educational needs of their area, after which the voluntary bodies were to be given the opportunity to make good any deficiency and to receive grants for the purpose. In England the arrangements were the other way round, for the voluntary bodies were given the first chance and were given no building grants to help them.

From the beginning the Scottish school boards took a wider view of their duties, but the Revised Code of 1862 had a somewhat unfortunate effect on the parish schools. There was a falling off of advanced subjects, although Scotland was never so much demoralised by the Revised Code as England. Accordingly the Colebrooke Commission was appointed to inquire into all educational endowments in Scotland. Its deliberations resulted in the Endowed Institutions Act of 1878 which authorised the setting up of a permanent commission of seven to determine the uses to be made of endowments, with a special concern for higher education.

The development of secondary education in Germany was along middle-class lines, but was influenced by politics much more than in almost any other country. The *Realschule* had become a permanent alternative institution in German secondary education alongside the *Gymnasium*. It was a symbol of the emancipation of the middle classes from both clerical and aristocratic control. Meanwhile, at a lower level the *Mittelschule*, which was really a higher primary school rather than a secondary school, arose out of the *Volksschule* just as in England the Higher Grade School arose out of the elementary school. By a ruling of 1872 children could be transferred to it at the age of 9 and stay until they were 15. It had a higher social value than the primary school. Tuition fees were charged but they were only half those of the secondary schools. So the *Mittelschule* made the same appeal to parents in Germany as the private schools did to parents in England. They were unable to pay the fees for the highest type of school but on the other hand they were higher in the social scale because their education was not free. In all there were six types of secondary school—three with a nine-year course, that is, the *Gymnasium*, the *Real-gymnasium*, and the *Oberrealschule*; and those with a six-year course, that is, the *Progymnasium*, the *Real-progymnasium* and the *Realschule*.

In France Victor Duruy (1811–94) in his policy of liberalising education established in 1865 what he called *enseignement sécondaire spécial*, which after the war of 1870 was developed by the Republic along three lines—higher elementary schools, *cours complémentaires*, and technical schools for agriculture, handicrafts and commerce. It was not, however, till 1880 that the organisation of a definite secondary system under state auspices was begun. There were founded the *conseil supérieur* and the *conseils académiques*. These were almost entirely elected bodies, and admission was limited to members of learned societies and the teaching profession. This was a decided innovation in educational administration for it put the teachers on a level with university professors and politicians. French education has always been strongly centralised, ever since Napoleon in 1808 joined together all the various grades of education into a single system called the University of France. This principle, which had as its central idea the creation of a lay body of opinion over against the Church, survived both the Revolution of 1848 and the Franco-Prussian War. Hence the University determined the nature of secondary education, rather than secondary education being a development from below.

The higher primary schools were not unlike the intermediate schools in Wales or the *Mittelschulen* in Germany. Two types of examinations were arranged for the pupils—one leading to the normal schools for primary school teachers, and the other with the paradoxical title of *certificat d'études primaires supérieurs*, which was a general certificate. School hours were from 8 to 12 and 1 to 4, and were a dull grind leading to a high degree of merely mechanical efficiency. The schools also suffered from being over-inspected—a fault which was carried over into the normal schools for teachers which were established in each 'department' from the year 1879. It is not surprising that there was a great dissatisfaction with these schools, and this led to an examination of the whole of the French education system. M. Ribot declared to a parliamentary commission in 1899 that 'all over the world one hears complaints about secondary education'.

Secondary education was given by the state in *lycées*, and by the communes in *collèges*, while allowing for private institutions as well. The career open to talent was for pupils from these alone, for secondary education had this class bias. There was an extraordinary similarity of type in all these institutions and one of the aims of the Ribot commissioners was to break down this monotony. In the case of the *lycées* they wished the boarders to be distributed among approved families instead of being shut up in an institution. It is interesting that this was the opposite to the plan of Dr Arnold, who took his boys away from lodgings and put them into school 'houses'. Yet there was also a tendency in the other direction, as in Demolin's book *A quoi tient la supériorité des Anglo-Saxons?* (1897), which led to the establishment of five boarding schools on English lines. The commission resulted in a reorganisation of French secondary education in 1902, the same year as the English Education Act. The curriculum of the *lycées* was to lead up to an examination for the *Baccalauréat* which normally acted as the entrance qualification for a university. The colleges were of a lower grade and had their own certificate instead of the *Baccalauréat*. Private secondary schools were to be inspected by the state. Their teachers must not belong to any religious order and they must have a teacher's diploma. There were *lycées* for girls as well as boys and a training college for women secondary teachers was established at Sèvres.

The earlier years of the nineteenth century had witnessed a notable development in educational theory and a willingness to put it into practice. The three great names in this connection were those of Pestalozzi (1746–1827), Froebel (1782–1852), and Herbart (1776–1841). The writings of each influenced education far beyond the lands of their origin and showed a remarkable capacity for revival long after the first enthusiasm for their works had died away. Pestalozzi had insisted that education comes through things rather than through books and that education ought to follow the development of the child's mind. From Pestalozzi's belief that the chief teacher is experience Herbart had developed a theory of the importance of the 'many-sided interest' for character formation, while from the conviction that all development is from within Froebel developed his theory of self-activity—'the child has the right to be at each stage what that stage requires'.

Froebel's ideas came into England in 1854 and were advocated by Charles Dickens. The word 'kindergarten' became naturalised in English as a description of Froebelian schools. But the schools established at this time were private schools for the wealthier classes and it was not until 1874 that Froebel's principles began to affect the infant schools everywhere. The first kindergarten in the United States was established in Boston by Elizabeth Peabody in 1860, and under the influence of Dr W. H. Harris and Susan Blow it became part of the public school system in St Louis in 1873.

Froebel's ideas did not pass, however, without criticism, at any rate in England. Miss Charlotte M. Mason founded the Parents' National Education Union in 1887 and she criticised the curriculum of the kindergarten for a certain spirit of condescension which had crept in. Miss Mason felt it to be a mistake to shut children off from reading and she declared that 'no education seems to be worth the name which has not made children at home in the world of books'.

If Pestalozzi and Froebel were particularly influential in primary and infant schools Herbart's influence was mainly felt at the higher stage. Ziller (1817–82) developed from Herbart's doctrines what is called the 'Culture Stages Theory'. He believed that the material of the curriculum should be chosen according to the psychological stages of the child's growth, and that these stages correspond to the development of the race. When Herbartianism reached America it was this aspect which interested G. Stanley Hall (1844–1924), and his great book *Adolescence, its Psychology and its relation to Physiology, Anthropology, Sociology, Science and Education* indicated in its very title the Herbartian 'many-sided interest' and was based on an acceptance of the Culture Stages theory. A still greater name in America was that of William James (1842–1910), physician, physiologist, psychologist and philosopher. He was concerned with both religion and science, and therefore with both experience and instruction. His *Principles of Psychology* (1890), one of the classics on the subject, claimed the right of psychology to be a special science, not a mere annex of physiology or of philosophy. His chatty popular style and his gift of the telling phrase and illustration helped to apply common sense not only to psychology but also to education, and emphasised the connection of both with living people rather than with mere theory. His *Talks to Teachers on Psychology* has probably had a greater influence on educational practice than any other book of its kind.

Thus in America in the 1890's Herbartianism gave rise to contrary schools of thought which were long in collision. It provided on the one hand a rational logical explanation of the process of learning and therefore fitted in with the scientific temper of the age. On the other hand, by its stress on literature and history as the two most character-forming subjects it was out of step with the popular enthusiasm for science and mathematics. Herbartianism provided assistance both to the rationalists, who were inclined to identify encyclopaedism with virtue, and to the other side, to whom education was a matter of cultivated imagination and emotion.

England has never been strong on the theoretical side of education, but the scientific movement in the later years of the nineteenth century produced a very notable book as a counter-blast to the classical monopoly in the schools and on behalf of the educational value of the new 'modern' subjects. This was Herbert Spencer's book on *Education, Intellectual, Moral and Physical* (1860). Spencer (1820–1903) had already provided a slogan for the Darwinian doctrine of evolution—'the survival of the fittest'. He was in the thick of the new scientific movement, and he was a strong believer in knowledge in the sense of information. He divided knowledge under five headings in a descending order of importance, beginning with physiology and ending (a long way down the list) with literature and the fine arts which, 'as they occupy the leisure part of life, so should they occupy the leisure part of education'.

Spencer's book was not particularly original, but it set going an interest in science as a subject of education and as an alternative to the classics. A contemporary of his, Thomas Henry Huxley (1825–95), combined a training in science with a truly humanistic outlook on life. He saw more clearly than any of his generation that the Darwinian theory applied to many other aspects of life besides that of natural science. That theory, put in its simplest form, came down to this, that the nature and purpose of an organism are to be discovered in its development. Every institution had to be understood through the way in which it had developed. How did it arise and what have been the stages through which it has passed? Is there any justification for its continuance? The same questions were relevant about the Bible, theology, the franchise, the status of the labouring classes and the subjection of women. To serve on all these institutions a writ of *Quo Warranto?* and make them stand and deliver was a heartening exercise for the young and the adventurous, and it is not surprising that Huxley felt himself to be at the head of a band of young crusaders.

Huxley's influence on education was enormous. He believed in the value of science as a liberal education, but he was perfectly well aware that its value depended on how it was taught. And he himself knew how to teach it—and to write it. Education, he said, 'is the instruction of the intellect in the laws of nature, under which name I include not merely things and their forces but men and their ways, and the fashioning of the affections and the will into an earnest and loving desire to move in harmony with those laws'. For the people of his generation Huxley was the greatest scientist of his time, but what was forgotten, if indeed noticed, was his concern for literature and the Bible. At the newly formed London School Board (of which he was a member) it was his advocacy that retained the Bible in the schools at a time when it was actually proposed to drop it.

Science in education, however, followed the line of Spencer rather than that of Huxley. It had gone to men's heads, and they talked and thought and dreamt science. Cheerfulness, of course, kept breaking through, for science had given amateurs something to play with. John Henry Pepper— the inventor of 'Pepper's Ghost'—showed even in the titles of his widely circulated books what fun could be got out of science—*The Playbook of Metals, Scientific Amusements for Young People*, and *Cyclopaedic Science Simplified*. But as far as the schools were concerned science was looked upon partly as a discipline but mainly as a means of getting on in the world. 'Knowledge is power' was a favourite maxim and knowledge meant scientific knowledge.

After 1872 organised science schools alternative to the elementary schools sprang up. They were under the Science and Art Department, which had been founded at South Kensington in 1853 as a result of the enthusiasm for industry created by the Great Exhibition of 1851. (It was under the Privy Council and so had a status parallel to that of the Education Department. Both were absorbed into the Board of Education in 1900.) They began by teaching nothing but science, and represented an attempt to introduce into England something like the German *Realschulen* but with no literary studies. Huxley, however, soon saw the science schools as mere cramming shops, and it became clear that a specialised education here as everywhere else required a good general education as a basis. Hence the organised science schools added literary subjects to their curriculum at the same time as the schools labouring under 'payment by results' were being modified by the influence of science grants from South Kensington.

Meanwhile science made for itself an enclave in higher education. The London School of Mines became in 1881 the Royal School of Mines and in 1890 the Royal College of Science. And in the 1880's 'science' came to mean more and more applied science, so that technical education became specialised within the general field of scientific endeavour. In 1884 a royal commission inquired into the provision of technical education and in 1889 the Technical Instruction Act gave the newly established county councils a fund for technical and scientific instruction. The newly established university colleges were all concerned with science. Leeds had a department of dyeing before it had a department of English.

The situation in Germany was not dissimilar from that in England. Just over the border in Switzerland there had been established in 1854 the great Polytechnic at Zürich. It became a model for institutions of similar sort in Germany which later were to turn themselves into universities. At the school level, however, the preparation for scientific and technical education had long been laid in the *Realschulen* which dated from the end of the eighteenth century. In 1870 boys who had completed a full course of nine years at a *Realschule* were admitted to the university for studies in mathematics, natural science and modern languages, even though the *Realschule* was still looked upon as the sort of school to which the less intelligent members of the community were sent. Nevertheless, the recognition and development of modern studies showed an awareness that we live in a competitive world and that an industrial and commercial society requires for the younger generation the kind of education which will enable them to hold their own within it. From the time of the Conference of 1890 (see p. 188) scientific and technical education came in for popular approval because it was in keeping with German ambitions in industry and commerce.

The scientific movement which characterised this period under review was apt to be a new form of scholasticism. Only the content of education was new. It was a long time before the *educational* importance of science was realised, for this required an understanding of the characteristic ways of teaching it, and as yet there was no great difference in method between the teaching of science and the teaching of any literary subject. Indeed, H. G. Wells was believed to have taken his B.Sc. without ever having seen inside a laboratory. Professor H. E. Armstrong was a pioneer in new methods of teaching science (1884) to which he gave the name 'heuristic' or 'the art of making children discover things for themselves'. This was a fancy name for the use of experiment in teaching science, a method so obvious nowadays that it is extraordinary that it took so long to discover. The application of scientific method to child study had to wait till the turn of the century when Binet outlined his method of testing intelligence.

At no point does the dependence of education on social structure and on current movements of thought become so evident as in the education of women. It is interesting that a class distinction here cut across the sex distinction. On the whole girls of the working classes everywhere received the same education as boys and sex made no difference. This was due not to any sense of the equality of the sexes but rather to the belief that such girls as well as boys were destined to a life of manual labour. Accordingly, when we speak of girls' education as a separate subject we are not including girls of the working class.

In England it was in the middle and upper classes that girls' education was so poor and it was here that sex distinction meant everything. The girls were taught either at home under ill-qualified governesses or in private schools the aim of which was to train in 'accomplishments' of a very superficial kind. The higher education of women was handicapped by this lack of school education, and in England the pioneers of women's education saw that they must tackle the schools as well as the universities. The Schools Inquiry (Taunton) Commission in 1864 exposed the poverty of girls' education and even the Victorian commissioners were induced to recognise the importance of secondary schools for girls and their urgent need for support and endowment.

Some progress had already been made. Dorothea Beale had become the principal of Cheltenham Ladies' College in 1858, a post which she held till her death in 1906. Under her the school developed in various directions, with a residential training college for secondary women teachers at one end and at the other a kindergarten class preparatory to the main school. Associated with her name was that of Frances Mary Buss (1827–94) who had been with Miss Beale at Queen's College in Harley Street. In 1850 Miss Buss opened the North London Collegiate School for girls, which in 1871 was turned into a school administered by trustees. She was noted for her unusual views about hygiene and about study, and she put an end to the then fashionable habit of swooning by dashing cold water into the face of the patient!

The problem of higher education for women involved an attack on the universities. In regard to women's degrees the United States, Switzerland and the Scandinavian countries were ahead of Britain, but in 1878 the University of London admitted women to degrees. From the start the Victoria University was open to both sexes and so too was the Royal

University of Ireland. In 1892 the four Scottish universities were opened to women.

The real bastions of male privilege, however, were Oxford and Cambridge, and the attack on these seats of learning illustrates at least one fundamental principle of social and educational progress. The two leaders in this campaign were Miss Davies and Miss Clough. Emily Davies, the founder of Girton College, started first at Hitchin, some distance from Cambridge, and only moved to the outskirts of Cambridge in 1870. She wanted for her girls full equality with men in taking university courses and examinations. Anne Jemima Clough was a Liverpool woman who had already established courses of lectures for governesses. Encouraged by Professor Henry Sidgwick she transferred her activities to Cambridge and in 1874 she established Newnham College, which was placed right in the heart of Cambridge because Miss Clough was concerned not about examinations but about lectures. When the two colleges were well established it was quite easy for Girton to ask to be admitted to lectures and Newnham to ask to be admitted to examinations, and they gained their point.

This, however, was only half-way. The question of degrees remained. At this stage the University of Cambridge offered to establish for women a parallel university, somewhat on the lines on which Radcliffe is the women's university parallel to Harvard. Miss Clough would willingly have accepted it but Miss Davies rejected it out of hand. She saw clearly the principle involved, namely that if you get differentiation before you get equality you will never get equality. The men must be met on their own ground and beaten on their own ground before there can be any talk of difference. Accordingly in 1887 it happened that Agnata Ramsey of Girton gained the highest first class in the Classical Tripos, but even this achievement was thrown into the shade when in 1890 Philippa Fawcett of Newnham entered the holy of holies and was graded above the senior wrangler in the Mathematical Tripos. After this there was less talk about the alleged intellectual inferiority of women.

In 1871 Mrs Maria Grey established a National Union for the Improvement of the Education of Women of All Classes, and next year the Girls' Public Day School Company was founded. Oxford and Cambridge instituted local examinations to which girls were admitted. Women educationists threw their weight on the side of day schools rather than boarding schools, and as they were not bound by centuries of tradition like the boys' public schools they were free to experiment both in teaching methods and in discipline. Moreover, the fact that the schools were day schools made them accessible to parents of modest means. The schools were not all of one pattern. Day schools were the most approved but three boarding schools were founded after the pattern of the boys' public schools— St Leonards (1877), Roedean (1885) and Wycombe Abbey (1896).

The growth of girls' schools led to a movement for co-education. This had always been followed in some Quaker Schools, thus following the rule of the equality of the sexes in that body, but now it became advocated as a principle in itself. The passing of the Welsh Intermediate Act in 1889 led to the establishment of numbers of mixed secondary day schools. Bedales School was founded as a boys' school, and after seven years became co-educational in 1900. In Scotland the co-education of boys and girls was for centuries not uncommon in the burgh schools. In the eastern states of America co-education became the rule. It was strengthened by the widespread influence of Pestalozzi in America and his view that schools should be established on the family model. It thus became general in the United States, although there are boys' public schools after the English pattern such as Groton, and schools for girls such as Farringtons.

After the war of 1870 teachers from all over Germany met at Weimar to demand education for girls, and in 1872 there was founded an 'Association for the Higher Education of Women' which represented in education the aims of the *Allgemeine Deutsche Frauenverein* founded in 1865. This connection with the general movement for the emancipation of women stepped up the agitation for girls' schools. From 1888 to 1898 Helene Lange was the leader of both movements. She put forward in 1887 a scheme for the reform of girls' education, and in 1889 founded in Berlin a *Realkurse für Frauen*. In 1893 a 'gymnasium' for girls was founded in Karlsruhe. In many states the high schools for boys were opened to girls also, although for university education many women still went across the border into Switzerland. Private enterprise as usual stirred the official bodies to action, and in Baden and Bavaria the male heads of girls' schools were replaced by women who had qualified by passing the *Abiturientenexamen*. The persistence of the connection of German education with the Church was shown in 1902 when the Minister of Public Worship and Education laid down the general principles of girls' education—namely those of the family and of the belief that women's proper place is the home and so no special training was needed. But this was met with opposition from those who wanted equality with the men up to the university stage, and in 1908 there was organised a system of girls' schools beginning with the *Lyzeum* for children of 9 to 16, followed by the *Oberlyzeum* giving either a two-year general course or a four-year teacher training course for teachers in elementary and lower secondary schools. At 13, however, girls as well as boys who wanted a secondary school course could transfer to the *Studienanstalt*, which provided three courses leading to the university, namely classical, semi-classical and modern. It was noteworthy that the Prussian government found itself unable to break with tradition in the case of boys' education, but was quite ready to inaugurate far-reaching reforms in the education of girls who were 'politically negligible'.

In France it was not until 1867 under the influence of Victor Duruy that girls' education was looked upon as at all important. Here again private enterprise and agitation preceded state action and there was formed an Association for Girls' Secondary Education which organised secondary courses for three years leading to a diploma. Some of these later became colleges and even *lycées*. Camille Sée (1827–1919) reorganised girls' education in 1877 and three years later state secondary schools were established. Their fees were lower than those of boys' schools and their curriculum was entirely modern, with no Latin, and there was nothing like the same overwork from which the boys' schools suffered. As in Germany male heads of girls' schools were replaced by women, a contrast to the situation in Switzerland where in spite of its reputation for democratic government all teachers in girls' schools were males. The spirit of the girls' schools was much more free than that of the boys' schools, and the foundation of the normal school by Sée at Sèvres in 1883 ensured a high standard of work. The aim of girls' education from 12 to 17 was stated by Ernest Legouvé as *l'égalité dans la différence*, and it is interesting to notice how this principle compares with that of Emily Davies.

In this period the Scandinavian countries became notable for their development of education beyond school and college age. In the nature of things adult education was concerned chiefly with the working classes although its reference varied from country to country.

Denmark was first in the field. The work of Grundtvig (1783–1872) and Kristen Kold (1816–70) in establishing the Danish folk high schools was encouraged by the disastrous war of 1864 when Denmark lost the provinces of Schleswig-Holstein to Germany. Like Fichte after the battle of Jena and Robert E. Lee after Appomattox and Victor Duruy after Sedan, Grundtvig's attitude was 'What has been lost without must be won within'. This was a call to advance in education. Denmark turned to the folk high schools as nationalist institutions which no military defeat could harm. The movement grew apace. The original school at Rødding was moved across the new boundary line to Askov where it flourished under Ludwig Schroeder. In return the effect of the schools on the psychology of the people helped Denmark to recover from the next blow. She had been a wheat-growing country and exported grain, chiefly to England, but now the opening up of the vast wheat fields of Canada and the Ukraine made it quite impossible for Denmark to compete in the markets of the world. However, so much had the folk high schools sharpened the intelligence of the peasant farmers that within ten years Denmark had changed over from an economy based on wheat to an economy based on dairy farming. The Askov school under Schroeder and Paul le Cour combined an attachment to Norse mythology with an equal concern for a model farm. After 1876 the course was extended to two years and after 1885 it became co-educational. Its curriculum was very extensive, including physics, chemistry, agriculture, history, mythology, church history and psychology. The city of Copenhagen began to take notice of the movement and in 1890 opened a non-residential folk high school.

Meanwhile adult education was being developed on the strictly vocational side. High schools for agricultural and other industrial workers dated from 1867. The most notable of these were founded by the 'Inner Mission' in the Lutheran Church and had among their adherents Søren Kierkegaard. They got hold of the industrial workers who had been hardly touched at all by Grundtvig.

The movement spread to all Scandinavian countries. Norway began to establish folk high schools from 1864, which were Grundtvigian in character, Christian, co-educational and almost entirely rural. In Sweden the movement coincided with political movements for the extension of the franchise, and became the concern of the Swedish Liberal party. The schools in Sweden were more utilitarian, and the spiritual impulse of Grundtvig was little felt. Swedish practicality showed itself in the elementary schools also, where manual training under the name of *Sloyd* became an important part of the curriculum.

In Finland the Folk High School movement was, as in Denmark, part of a nationalist movement. It was aimed against Russian influence and helped to unite the working classes who spoke Finnish with the highly cultured minority who spoke Swedish. Finland also followed Sweden in developing 'workers' academies', which were evening classes under the municipal authorities, and were started in 1889.

A distinction has to be made here between 'adult' education and 'further' education. The second was an extension of schooling and it was this type that appealed to the Germans. In Germany adult education was concerned mainly with the technical side, although for the full development of this type of education we had to wait until the present century when Kerschensteiner's continuation school at Munich became famous all over Europe. Vocational adult education in Germany, as elsewhere, gradually displaced apprenticeship, although in Germany guilds of apprentices were formed the functions of which were laid down by a law of 1887. Among these was the fostering of good relations between employers and employed. The special vocational schools that were established for the chief industries were an addition to apprenticeship and not, as in France, a substitute for it.

The great centre of adult technical education in Switzerland was Zürich. The Confederation owned the Technical University and by the Acts of 1884, 1885 and 1895 it gave federal aid to vocational education. This included schools for music, art, silk weaving, veterinary studies, training colleges for teachers, a school for artisans and a school of industry, and a highly specialised horological school at Geneva and one for wood carving at Brienz.

After the Civil War the Northern states of America developed into a highly industrialised community. Hitherto agriculture had occupied the attention of educationists and in 1862 the Federal government by the Morrill Act had set up the 'land grant' colleges of agriculture in each state. In 1865, however, the Massachusetts Institute of Technology was set up in recognition of the need for education in industry. It corresponded in the New World to the Zürich Polytechnic in Europe. Nevertheless, vocational education was late in starting and it was not until after the Spanish-American War of 1898 that any nation-wide effort was made, and it was not until 1912 that a national commission on vocational education was set up. This delay was partly due to the enormous influence of John Dewey (1859–1952), who believed that no special schools were needed, since every school should be a vocational school and thereby a training ground for democracy.

The question of adult education on the cultural side was made acute in the United States by reason of the emancipation of the Negroes, and by the vast inflow of foreign immigrants, but the provision thus made was strictly limited and utilitarian. The chief agency, however, of adult education in America was the Church. The constitutional separation of Church and state laid upon the churches a heavy but not unwelcome burden. All sorts of voluntary societies were started, beginning with the Lyceum lectures which after 1874 gave way to the Chatauqua. The first aim of these institutions was to train Sunday-school teachers but they soon catered for a wider public. Yet the fact that a very large proportion of Americans attended some high school or college before settling down to business made the appeal of adult education relatively slight.

In England the distinction between the vocational and the cultural side of adult education became very pronounced in this period. The Livery Companies of London in 1880 established the City and Guilds of London Institute as an examining body to standardise technical education, with Sir Philip Magnus as the head. In 1884 it established a college of its own which became part of the University of London. Interest in technical education produced some very strange bed-fellows. Ruskin, for instance, was misled by the original Greek of the word 'technical' and believed that he was supporting creative craftmanship when he lent his support to the movement. The leaders were thinking very little about this but rather of means to beat the Germans and the Americans in the world markets.

Adult education on the cultural side has always illustrated the fact that it is the people who have had some education who most appreciate it and want more. In England movements started primarily for working men became attractive to clerks and teachers and apprentices, and when these came in the working men went out. Nevertheless, Chartism, which was a genuine working-men's movement, was later associated with the Christian Socialist Movement from which sprang the Working Men's College in

1854. This was the first contact between the older universities and adult popular education and it attracted to itself a brilliant set of lecturers who gave their services free. The Y.M.C.A. and the Royal Institution were popular agencies of adult education, while all over the country were Mutual Improvement Societies, sometimes run by the churches, sometimes independently.

The connection of university men with working-class movements was shown again in the university extension movement started in Liverpool by Miss A. J. Clough with James Stuart as the first lecturer. The weakness was that the audiences were too large for discussion, but these defects were remedied in the Workers' Educational Association founded in 1903, which was organised on a basis not of lectures but of 'tutorial classes'. The various university settlements in London were another outcome of the very fruitful association of university men and working folk. The first of these was named Toynbee Hall after Arnold Toynbee (1852–83), a brilliant young Balliol don. Of a different kind of institution were the polytechnics, of which the first was founded by Quintin Hogg in 1880 in Regent Street. In its very first year it catered for 6800 members. In 1883 the Parochial Charities of London Act permitted some of the charitable funds to be used for establishing polytechnics. One which benefited in this way was the People's Palace, which became the East London College and still later Queen Mary College and part of the University of London.

Meanwhile the trade unions began to move on their own account. In 1899 they established in Oxford Ruskin College, which was intended to be a training ground for trade-union leaders. Its settlement in Oxford was significant. So too was the split ten years later which caused the Marxist section to hive off and after a short time in Oxford to establish itself in South Wales as the Central Labour College.

CHAPTER VIII

THE ARMED FORCES

THE last thirty years of the nineteenth century were for the peoples of western Europe, if not for those of the world as a whole, an era of virtually unbroken peace. In western Europe there was an interval between the Wars of Unification which had shattered the pattern of the Vienna Settlement and the conflicts over the lands of the disintegrating Turkish empire which were to develop into the first World War. Even outside this area there were only three instances where two major powers were involved in mutual conflict—the Russo-Turkish War of 1877–8, the Sino-Japanese War of 1894 and the Spanish-American War of 1898—and these quarrels, either by their nature or from the agreed policy of the great powers, were kept strictly within local bounds. European powers protecting or extending their interests in Africa and Asia were constantly engaged in minor conflicts, and Great Britain in 1899 became involved in a struggle with the Boer Republics of South Africa which assumed proportions transcending the category of 'small wars'; but within Europe itself, outside the Balkan Peninsula, the Peace of Frankfurt signed between France and the victorious German empire in 1871 ushered in forty-three years of uninterrupted peace.

Yet during these years the great powers, particularly those of Europe, were preparing for war with a diligence for which modern history had hitherto offered no parallel. Engines of war, maritime and military, were multiplied prodigiously in number, complexity, and cost. Defence preparations received an ever-swelling allocation in national budgets; and the male populations of the mainland states of Europe became bound to military service from the end of their adolescence until the onset of later middle age. Since the preparations which each state made for its defence were seen by its neighbours as a threat to their own security, the great powers found themselves involved in an apparently inescapable competition which bore increasingly heavily upon public finance, inflamed mutual fear and suspicion, and was to play a considerable part—many historians would say the major part—in preparing the catastrophe of the first World War.

The tensions which underlay the apparent peace of Europe during these years had political, social and psychological causes which are considered elsewhere in this volume. But in part at least they can be attributed to a virtually autonomous and automatic development in weapons and techniques of war which the industrial and scientific improvements of the age for the first time rendered possible. Superiority in armament now gave to the nations which possessed it an overwhelming advantage. The collapse of France in 1870, even more than that of Austria in 1866, made clear the fate which lay in store for the powers which had not learned how to train and deploy mass armies armed with modern weapons; and the states of Europe were faced with the alternatives of acquiescing in the hegemony which these techniques gave to the new German empire, or of acquiring them themselves. An adequate defence system, in the new age, involved not only the military training of the entire adult male population and the acquisition of expensive and rapidly obsolescent weapons. It involved also expenditure on strategic railways; the accumulation of huge stocks of war supplies; and the maintenance of a high birth-rate, of a high level of education, and of an up-to-date industrial potential. Every state which wished to safeguard its independence had to be, even during the time of profoundest peace, a Nation in Arms, capable of deploying armies hundreds of thousands strong within a matter of days, on pain of being itself caught unprepared and totally overthrown.

Such a state of affairs was bound to instil into international relations an element of tension and mistrust; and matters were made yet worse by the speed of technological change which compelled governments to contemplate a total re-equipment of their armies on an average once every two decades, and confronted navies with still vaster problems of expense. Change on such a scale, moreover, brought all professional assessments of strategy and tactics into question. An extensive literature, professional and amateur, ranging from massive military dictionaries and multi-volume studies through periodicals to innumerable occasional and quasi-political pamphlets, came into being in which the changes brought about in the art of war by each new political and technical development were subjected to a continuous and microscopic examination. The General Staffs of Europe created historical sections which published detailed analyses of past and of contemporary wars; while their Intelligence and Topographical departments compiled equally detailed accounts of the resources and the forces of their potential allies and adversaries; assisted in the process by systems of espionage whose contribution, it may be hazarded, was greater to imaginative literature and political *causes célèbres* than to the sum of real military knowledge. The eventual result of their investigations was always the same: the need for greater military expenditure. This, coming as it did at a time when pressure no less great was building up on state budgets for expenditure on education and welfare services, created new political tensions. The military 'interest' regarded itself as responsible for the security of the state and chafed at the limitations imposed on it by democratic control. The growing liberal and socialist movements saw in this obsession with security and the consequent competition in armaments an equally short-sighted 'militarism' which coincided—in the central powers particularly—with the social position and political outlook of a military caste, to be combated not only by representative assemblies but if need be by the weapon of the general strike. In internal affairs no less than external the problems of defence were to exacerbate the difficulties with which the states of Europe had to contend.

During the period under review the conflicts of the powers of Europe were still decisive for the destinies of the world; and since the military preoccupations of these powers were predominantly concerned with land rather than naval warfare, it is proposed here to reverse the customary British order of priorities, and to deal with the former first. Until the last decade of the century the problems of the creation, armament and deployment of armies obsessed the powers of Europe; only then were the writings of Mahan to remind them that their destinies had been settled in the past not simply by their ability to defend their frontiers, but also by their ability to maintain those links with the outside world on which they had for long relied for their wealth and on which they were rapidly becoming dependent for their very existence. Until then Berlin, Vienna and Paris set the fashion in military thought, and were uncritically copied by such peripheral powers as Turkey, Japan, the United States and Great Britain itself. Only as the century ended were naval rivalries to acquire parity with military among the problems of European peace. Both were to be considered together at the Hague Conference in 1899: but although the nature and the gravity of the problem was apparent to the statesmen, if not to the soldiers, of Europe by the turn of the century—as the summoning of that conference bears witness—it was one beyond the power of any of them to solve.

It was only to be expected that the technological revolution of the nineteenth century should make itself felt as much in the military as in any other sphere. Already by 1870 progress in metallurgy had made possible the transformation of the smooth-bore muzzle-loading muskets and artillery of the Napoleonic era, with ranges averaging 100 and 700 yards, into the rifled breech-loading weapons, with ranges nearly ten times as great, with which the contending forces were armed in the Franco-Prussian War. The introduction of metal cartridges in the early 1870's was another considerable advance, as was found by the Turkish army which in 1877 was armed with them while the bulk of the Russian army was not; but in the latter half of the century it was to be chemical discoveries, perfecting ever more powerful explosives, which were to take pride of place. The gunpowder traditionally used as a propellant, compounded of saltpetre, sulphur and charcoal, was a wasteful as well as an unpleasant substance to use. Less than half of it was transformed into gas: the rest remained as a thick deposit fouling the weapon or as a cloud of that dense white smoke which had shrouded battlefields since firearms had first made their appearance five hundred years before. The greater rate of fire of breech-loading weapons increased also, proportionately, the extent of these disadvantages, and the potentialities of other forms of explosive were therefore industriously explored. Alfred Nobel had perfected nitro-glycerine in 1861, but many years passed before it could be put to practical military use. When it was, the transformation both of small-arms and of artillery was as far-reaching as that effected by the introduction of rifling forty years earlier. Combustion in the new explosives was virtually complete: the explosion was in consequence more violent, and the smoke produced negligible. Not only were ranges doubled but, since a greater explosive capacity could be obtained from a lesser quantity of explosive material, the size of the round, both small-arms and artillery, could be reduced. So could the calibre of the weapon from which it was fired; and small-calibre weapons possessed not simply greater range and penetrative power, but, thanks to the low trajectory of the projectile which the improved propellant made possible, increased lethal effectiveness. Small-calibre rifles firing cartridges charged with smokeless powder were, in 1898, considered lethal up to 4000 yards, while the introduction of magazine-loading correspondingly improved their rate of fire. The French army led the way with the Lebel rifle and 'poudre B' in 1886; Germany and Austria followed in 1888 and within the next four years most of the remaining European powers had followed suit.

The tactical effectiveness of the new weapons was so evident that for a time it seemed as if the superiority of artillery over small-arms which the Prussian gunners had demonstrated in 1870 had been decisively displaced. The guns with which the Prussians had outshot the *chassepots* of the French infantry at Sedan would have been at the mercy of riflemen armed with the Lebel. But artillery was undergoing a simultaneous transformation. The debate over the respective merits of bronze and iron for the manufacture of guns had been settled in favour of the latter, and later of steel; in consequence they were now capable of standing up to a yet greater explosive force. The muzzle velocity of guns, as of small-arms, could therefore be increased by the introduction of smokeless powder and by improvement in shell construction. Moreover, recoil-absorbing carriages made it possible to develop quick-firing guns which did not need to be re-sighted after each shot, and by the end of the century field-guns were in service in European armies with a maximum range of 9000 yards and an effective range between 3000 and 6000. Yet even these ranges were dwarfed by the development in siege artillery, in which Germany, anxious for quick results in any future war, took the lead. By 1898 the armies of Europe were armed with heavy guns, howitzers and mortars with a normal range of 10 km.; and their melinite explosive content gave them a comparably increased penetrative power.

Improvement in small-arms made necessary improvement in guns;

equally, improvement in guns demanded improvement in fortification. The introduction of rifled guns in the 1850's had already made it necessary for fortresses to build outlying forts to carry on the fire-fight, as Issy, Vanves and Montrouge had at Paris, and shield the fortress itself from bombardment. But her forts did not save Paris from direct bombardment by Krupps' 21-cm. mortars in 1871. Forts had to be pushed ever farther out from their parent fortress until by 1898 a minimum diameter of 18 km. for the fortress area was considered mandatory. Masonry everywhere gave place to concrete. But even this gave inadequate protection; and during the 1890's military engineers throughout Europe, General Brialmont of Belgium at their head, were seeking new solutions to an apparently insoluble problem. Brialmont himself urged the replacement of fortresses by large fortified areas; there was increasing recourse to subterranean works, and the development of the rising cupola made it possible for the entire fortification system to be placed underground. By the turn of the century such historic fortresses as Antwerp, Verdun, Posen and Lemberg were the centres of spider's webs of works, to a great extent subterranean and invisible, covering hundreds of square miles, and making, for their construction and upkeep, ever heavier demands on national budgets.

Yet the most famous defence of any fortress in the period under review did not depend on complex and expensive permanent fortifications. In 1877 Osman Pasha barred the Russian advance into Bulgaria at Plevna for five months by means of field-works dug on the spot; and the casualties which the Russians suffered in that assault—in one attack 18,000 out of 60,000 men—could not be entirely blamed on faulty leadership and tactics. Plevna taught the Russian army that the effective answer to the breech-loading rifle was the spade, and by the end of the war the whole of their infantry carried entrenching tools. The other armies of Europe copied them. By the end of the century it was accepted as normal that infantry should entrench itself when in the defence, and it became usual for infantrymen to carry not only a personal entrenching tool but picks and shovels in large quantities as well. Artillerymen in their turn, seeing that the Russians even with a fourfold superiority in guns had made no impression on the earthworks of Plevna with high explosive shells, had to devise means to ferret them out. If the spade was the answer to the rifle, shrapnel, howitzers and mortars were the gunner's answer to the spade. But no artillery developments could counteract the enormous advantage which spade and rifle gave to the infantry in defence—an advantage which long antedated even the advent of Maxim's belt-firing machine-gun, a weapon whose high consumption of ammunition and early technical flaws caused it to be viewed with mistrust by European armies until the advent of the first World War. The difficulty of attacking infantry armed even with the primitive breech-loaders of the 1860's had perplexed tacticians and been made evident at such slaughters as Nachod and Gravelotte. Now the destructive range was reckoned to be almost four times as great as that of the *chassepot*, and infantry assaulting defensive positions, even if it passed intact through the 3000 yard belt where shellfire was at its most effective, had another 2000 yards to cross in which it would be mown down by the rifles of an entrenched and invisible enemy. It was thus generally agreed that no assault was possible until the assailants had gained fire supremacy: as one tactician put it, 'the infantry attack has become a moving line of fire'. The skirmishing line which had been gaining in importance over the attacking column since the Napoleonic wars had now ousted it altogether in the text-books, as in 1866–70 it had in fact. To sceptics who demanded whether entrenched infantry was ever likely to be sufficiently worn down by the fire of opponents advancing in the open to be vulnerable to an assault, two official answers were given. One was that of the German infantry regulations, which saw the answer in an approach so slow, patient and well prepared that it might occupy several days and resemble rather a siege operation than a manœuvre in the open field. The other was that of the French, who were prepared to rely on the traditional morale and *élan* of their infantry to overcome all obstacles—a view which the Russian army, under the influence of General Dragomiroff, very largely shared. The French Regulations for Infantry of 1894 abandoned dispersed formations for the assault in favour of close lines of companies marching elbow to elbow, on the grounds that only such formations could maintain the morale of the assaulters and keep up an adequate volume of fire. Thinkers such as Colonel Colin and General Négrier who denounced these tactics as suicidal were persistently ignored, and the French General Staff paid increasing attention to the sustaining of morale to enable its forces to overcome the formidable obstacles which they were likely to encounter in any future war.

Such lack of realism began to distinguish all armies during the 1890's, as the memories of 1870 and 1877 grew dim and the maintenance of enthusiasm in a peacetime force demanded more attention to the ardent and less to the discouraging aspects of war. Nowhere was it more apparent than in the training of the cavalry. In some respects the new developments in weapons made the task of the cavalry more important, if more arduous, than it had ever been before. As yet the internal combustion engine was not sufficiently developed for application to military purposes, and though other inventions were taken up and exploited with enthusiasm—every army had its bicycle and observation-balloon units, and the successful experiments which the French army conducted with dirigible balloons in 1884 pointed the way to a new category of developments transcending any that had gone before—all were marginal in importance compared with the cavalry as the indispensable mobile arm. Never had the importance, and the difficulty, of liaison and reconnaissance been so great as on the wide battlefields of the new mass armies, and scientific breeding was producing strains of bloodstock capable of an unprecedented degree of exertion. But reconnaissance and liaison were minor functions. The traditional tasks of the cavalry lay on the battlefield: the charge which gave the *coup de grâce* to shaken infantry, and the pursuit which could turn retreat into rout; and in spite of the massacres in 1870 at Morsbronn and Vionville and Floing, official cavalry doctrine nowhere accepted the conclusion that there was no place for cavalry on a battlefield dominated by modern firearms. The role of cavalry was considered to be basically the same as it had been in the days of Napoleon I. In the German army cavalry regulations continued to be based on those of Frederick the Great. It was argued that on the new battlefield the cavalry could operate to far greater effect, since smokeless powder would enable it to judge better when the enemy infantry was disintegrating and becoming susceptible to the charge, besides adding to the moral effect of the charge itself.

It is tempting to see in this obstinate adherence to invalid theories the rationalisation of a social prejudice deeply rooted in the class structure of nineteenth-century Europe. The emotional vested interests of the cavalry, especially in the aristocratic-monarchical states of central Europe, were undeniably powerful, and an attack on the effectiveness of cavalry on the battlefield had implications which transcended the purely military sphere. Yet apart from its role as an instrument of shock, there was no reason to suppose that cavalry had outlived its usefulness. Not only were there the greatly extended reconnaissance functions considered above, but the possibility of deep cavalry raids to interrupt enemy communications on the model of the great rides in the American War of Secession was widely canvassed. In the Russian army the prospect of such raids assumed a major part in the national strategy. It was hoped that by massing cavalry units on the German and Austrian frontiers and launching them on missions of road, railway and telegraph destruction as soon as war broke out, it would be possible to diminish the advantage which the central powers gained by their more rapid mobilisation arrangements. Other armies experimented with the restoration of cavalry to the status of mobile infantry, for the conduct of outflanking attacks; and it was to facilitate movements of this sort that the German army, in 1898, first armed cavalry units with the machine-gun, considering it a mobile form of firepower for the attack rather than an additional source of strength for the defence. But such experiments and speculations were eccentric and suspect. Cavalry continued to dominate armies and manœuvres, and no orthodox thinker openly doubted that it would dominate the battlefield as well.

The tactical lessons of the war of 1870 were thus only partially learned. It was in the field of strategy and general military policy that the German victories made their most lasting impression. The most evident explanation for the catastrophe to the French army had been its inability to muster enough men in time—to oppose more than 240,000 to the 370,000 with which Moltke crossed the frontier during the first week of August.

The immediate cause of this was the technical inadequacy of the French arrangements for mobilization and concentration—the recall and embodiment of reservists and the dispatch of the complete formations to the battle area. But the long-term cause lay in the superiority of the entire Prussian system of military organisation—of universal short-term military service over the long-serving professional army which had developed in post-Napoleonic France. The French belief that quality counted more than quantity, that a small but resolute force could defeat conscript masses, was cruelly belied. So also was the creed of the French republicans, that the ardour of an untrained People in Arms was in itself an adequate defence. France after her defeat set herself to copy the institutions of the victor as closely as possible, and the remaining powers of Europe followed to a greater or lesser degree.

The importance of rapid mobilisation derived not only from the advisability of putting to immediate effect the trained manpower which conscription provided, in order to be able to strike—or to ward off—the first and possibly lethal blow. It arose partly also from the nature of the battlefield itself—from the difficulty of frontal attack, the need for outflanking and envelopment and the consequent need for numbers to make this possible. Even in the battles of 1870 victory had never been won by frontal attack; it had been achieved by a numerically superior army lapping round its opponent's flanks. But such outflanking movements demanded an elasticity of which European armies were decreasingly capable. The development of railways had made it possible for forces of unprecedented size to be brought to the battlefield, or to the concentration area behind the battlefield. Once they were there, however, these forces remained completely dependent on the railway for their supplies, and their movements were limited, if not dictated, in consequence. The superior mobility of the German railway system had been a powerful factor in her victories in 1870, and it was clearly the disposition as well as the mileage of a national railway system which would henceforth determine a nation's military effectiveness. The considerable development in the German railways running towards the Belgian frontier during the 1890's—four lines capable of handling three army corps—already gave the German General Staff the capacity to undertake the violation of Belgian territory to avoid a frontal attack on the frontier-fortresses of France.

The development of railways therefore was seen as a necessity for national defence no less compelling than the development of modern armament. As General Derrécagaix wrote in 1890 in *La Guerre moderne* (I, 165), 'the first care of a nation which has to organise the defence of its frontiers will not be to envelop itself with a girdle of fortresses, but to cover its territory with a network of railways which will ensure the most rapid possible concentration'; and General Bronsart von Schellendorff declared in his book, *The Duties of the General Staff*, that it was one of the primary duties of the General Staff 'to examine, in peace, the precise resources of the railway system of the country with a view to the concentration of the army on the different frontiers, and carefully compare the results obtained in each case with the facilities for concentration possessed by the neighbouring country or countries'; 'when any disadvantages of this description had been recognised beforehand', he added, 'they may be remedied by the simple process of extending the railway system at the public expense'. Railway detachments became an intrinsic part of every army; mixed civil/military commissions prepared the lines for military use; and the movement of troops by rail became an exactly calculable science. An army corps, for example, which was reckoned by the Germans to need 117 trains to transport it with all its supplies, took eleven days to dispatch along a single line and five days along a double and could move, on a double-track railway, 900 km. in 9 days—a distance which would have taken it two months to march. But the less the distance the smaller was the advantage in using railways. To cover 112 km., for instance, took 8 days by railway and only 5 by road. Railways thus provided a strategic rather than a tactical advantage—armoured trains were used in the defence of Paris in 1870 and in the Boer War, without any great effect—but this strategic importance was overwhelming. France and Austria followed the lead set by the German empire in developing their networks; between 1870 and 1913 French lines leading to their eastern frontier had increased from three to ten, and the German lines leading to the west from nine to sixteen; while on her eastern frontiers Germany and to a lesser degree her Austrian ally developed a series of lines which the Russians could not hope to match.

Russian backwardness in railway development was one of the main problems which faced the Russian General Staff and that of their allies. To mitigate it the Russians constructed their lines on a broader gauge than those of Europe—5 feet instead of 4 feet 8½ inches—so that her adversaries would at least be unable to exploit her own network in the event of an invasion; but it was a precaution which recoiled on her own head when she herself invaded Bulgaria in 1877 and had to transfer all her forces—200,000 men and 1200 guns—to different rolling stock on arrival at the Roumanian frontier. The inadequacy of the single-track Trans-Siberian railway, constructed between 1891 and 1898, was to be made evident in the Russo-Japanese War, at the outset of which only three trains of sixty axles could run a day—and that at a maximum speed of 11 miles an hour—and it took 40 days to reach Mukden from Warsaw. Yet the fact that the Russians were able to concentrate an army of a million men on their Pacific coast at all was something of a portent, and their railway capacity was being zealously developed, with the aid of French capital, up till the outbreak of the first World War. It was a development which the German General Staff watched with the very gravest anxiety.

Railways thus provided one essential condition of victory in modern war, but no less important was a smoothly organised mobilisation machine. 'In principle,' to quote General Derrécagaix again (I, 363), 'an army which cannot be ready first cannot think of directing the war, but only of suffering it.' The problems of mobilisation were vast, and increased with the size of war establishments. Mobilisation was no mere matter of recalling reservists to their old regiments: it involved the creation of new formations, of new administrative and medical services, of fully staffed commands, and of a network of line-of-communication services which had no peacetime existence at all. The method adopted by every state outside Russia was that which Prussia had developed during the 1860's—the decentralisation of mobilisation, as of other administrative arrangements, on to territorial commands, each of which was responsible for raising, equipping and dispatching to the concentration area one army corps. In each command lists of reservists were kept up to date and stocks of clothing, equipment and ammunition were stored ready for use. Reservists were summoned, either by personal telegram or by public announcement, as soon as instructions came from the Ministry of War; and in the Ministry the necessary telegrams lay ready, needing only the insertion of a date to make them valid.

Thanks to constant improvement and practice the Germans reckoned by the turn of the century that their forces would be ready to begin hostilities in less than two weeks from the day that mobilisation began. The French with their forces calculated approximately the same. Poorer communications and administrative facilities hampered the states of eastern Europe, and when Feldzeugmeister Beck became chief of the Austrian General Staff in 1881 he found to his horror that whereas German forces would be ready to march against Russia in 20 days, the time needed for the Austrians was 45, so that 'we will enter the theatre of war as a sort of Reserve Army after a *fait accompli*. . . .I do not believe that this would be in our political or military interests. If our army goes to war it needs victories, and decisive victories': and so effectively did he work that by 1890 the time the Austrian army needed for concentration had been reduced to 19 days.

This the Russians could not begin to match. Mobilisation itself, thanks to the reforms which Milyutin introduced after the experiences of 1876–7, they hoped to complete in 16 days, owing very largely to their maintenance in peacetime of many of the headquarters and administrative units which other states would have to create in the war. But the concentration of their forces, the transportation of units from the Urals and the Ukraine and Siberia and the Caucasus over their inadequate railway system, was another matter altogether; and the handicap which Russia suffered thereby could be counterbalanced only by the maintenance of a large permanent covering force on her western frontiers. In 1893, according to one calculation, Russia had 442,293 men concentrated in Poland, including a large force of cavalry ready to raid deep into Prussia, Silesia and Galicia: nearly half her total peacetime strength. Yet the maintenance of this covering force slowed down mobilisation and concentration arrangement yet further. The defence of the frontiers could not be entrusted to troops recruited from the unreliable Polish frontier provinces: the covering force had to consist of regiments from the interior, whose reservists in the event of mobilisation would take weeks to join them; while Polish units, employed on garrison duties within Russia where they could do no harm, suffered from the same drawback. Under such circumstances the decentralisation of mobilisation arrangements to area commands was out of the question, and in Russia alone among the major powers of Europe the Ministry of War retained detailed responsibility for mobilising the army— an arrangement which did not in itself make for speed.

Austria-Hungary, a multi-racial empire riddled with nationalist discontent, was liable to suffer even more seriously than Russia from the 'territorialisation' of its army. But in the interests of speedy mobilisation this was a risk which Beck was prepared to run. The army attempted to remain, as it had in the days of Radetzky, an institution above race, with a *dépaysé* officer corps and a uniform German *Dienstsprache*; but the recognition in army documents of eleven other tongues gives an alarming indication of the complexity of administration within the *Kaiserliche und Königliche Heer*. It was hoped that the homogeneous corps of Czechs, Ruthenians, Italians, Croats and Galicians would become impregnated with the *schwarz-gelb* spirit of the army; but although in the regular cadres this hope was to a large extent fulfilled, it could not apply to conscripts and reservists who rejoined the colours after a stretch of civil life; and once the cadres were swept away in the early battles of the first World War the full unreliability of the units which remained stood revealed. In this respect as in many others—the fostering of universal education and the increase in state medical services, for example—military requirements played a leading part in breaking down that old pattern of society which paradoxically enough the military castes more than any other element felt pledged to defend.

Conscription itself had been denounced by Thiers as 'putting a rifle on the shoulder of every socialist'; but after 1870 the military necessity of the measure seemed so self-evident that that objection was overruled. The German pattern of conscription was taken as a model by all continental powers, and the legislation of the Second Reich was itself modelled on that introduced in Prussia by Boyen in 1814 and into the North German

Federation by Roon in 1867. Every German was, by Article 57 of the Reich Constitution, made liable to service from the age of twenty, for three years with the colours and four with the reserve; and then with the *Landwehr*—a body which since 1862 had been so closely integrated with the regular army as to form a regular second-line reserve—until the age of thirty-nine. But this apparently inescapable obligation was softened by concessions to non-military considerations. In the first place, the interests of the professional and wealthy classes were safeguarded by the institution of 'one-year volunteers'—also a legacy from the Wars of Liberation. Young men who had attained a certain educational standard and who were able to provide their own equipment and uniform served only for a year under exceptionally easy conditions, and then qualified as officers in the *Landwehr* or reserve. A reserve commission, in the Second Reich, became an indispensable passport to social acceptability. Secondly, an upper limit to the size of the army was set by the Reichstag's budgetary control—and a political storm invariably broke when it came up for reconsideration. Finally, the Ministry of War had, in a society in which socialism was rapidly spreading, to weigh the military desirability of a numerically strong army against the political need to ensure that that army should consist only of politically reliable elements. Thus the Ministry of War was selective in the demands it made on the different districts of the Reich; and within those districts mixed civil-military commissions selected recruits on a basis of 'worth, fitness and civilian circumstances'.

Austria-Hungary followed the Prussian example by introducing compulsory universal service in 1868, in a law drafted by the victor of Custozza, Archduke Albert, who was to guide the destinies of the army until 1894. There also service with the colours was for three years, with consequent service in the reserve or the *Landwehr*. There also the upper limit was set by the legislature, conscripts were selected by mixed local commissions, and the educated and wealthy could serve as one-year volunteers. Certain landowners indeed, farming their own estates, were exempted from service altogether, as were schoolmasters and seminarists. But conscription found out the weaknesses of the Austro-Hungarian state. It was difficult to enforce on the Ruthenian and Transylvanian peasantry, many of whom were anyhow emigrating in increasing numbers; while even by the end of the century the proportion of conscripts found fit for service was little more than a quarter. In Russia the same problems were even more acute. There universal service on the German model had been introduced as part of Milyutin's widespread army reforms in 1874, service being for five years with the colours and thirteen with the reserve; but it was applied only with considerable modifications to the Cossacks and the Finns, and not at all in Transcaucasia, Turkestan, and several other districts where local susceptibilities were accounted too tender. Moreover, family considerations were given far greater attention than in western

Europe in the selection of conscripts—a vital matter in a nation of peasants working their own land. Finally, the German 'one-year volunteer' system was adopted in an extended form, students being exempted from military service in proportion to their educational attainments. Every European power indeed reckoned that an educated and satisfied professional class was at least as necessary an element to the welfare of the state as was a large army; and found its own compromise in order to preserve both.

The French also, in their military reforms of 1872–3, hastened to imitate their victors, instituting universal service without substitution, and adopting the system of one-year volunteers. But the traditionalists were still strong enough to prevent a total renunciation of the pattern of a long-serving professional army and an unequivocal acceptance of the German conception of the Nation in Arms. Long service was still held to be necessary, both to fashion true soldiers and to create a body which could be relied on in face of the ever threatening *péril intérieur*. A compromise measure was adopted, whereby part of the annual contingents served for five years, and the rest was called up for six to twelve months; the distinction being made partly on compassionate grounds and partly by lot. Only the short-service troops were organised on a regional basis, after the Prussian pattern: the rest of the army was kept *dépaysé*—and indeed the exigencies of African service made it virtually impossible to avoid this. Those who secured exemption from conscription altogether—and budgetary stringency made this at times a quarter of the annual contingent—received no training, though some form of organisation for them was several times projected. Even the organisation and the training of the territorial army had to wait until Charles de Freycinet took over the Ministry of War between 1889 and 1893. Such inequality of service was under constant attack from the more radical republicans, who objected to a measure which not only preserved an *armée au coup d'état* but which exempted clergy and theological students from service altogether. In 1889 a project to equalise service on a three-year basis was voted by the Chamber of Deputies but was mutilated by the Senate; and it was not until 1905 that the republicans, as part of their general assault on the citadels of reaction whose power had been made so evident during the Dreyfus affair, drove through a law enforcing universal service without exemptions for two years. The example of the Germans was powerful, who had introduced two-year service eight years earlier, in 1893; in the interests neither of equality nor of humanitarianism, but simply to increase the rate of training of their manpower in face of the combined Franco-Russian threat which had crystallised the year before. In face of such a menace from beyond the Rhine the soldiers acquiesced; but many grumbled with General Gallifet that it was plain that France wanted neither a Church nor an army.

Thanks to the adoption of conscription by all the major powers of Europe, with the exception only of Great Britain, the number of trained men available for service steadily rose. In 1874 Germany had a regular army 420,000 strong and a war establishment of 1,300,000: in 1897 the regular army had increased only by a third, to 545,000, but the war establishment, at 3,400,000, had nearly trebled. Within the same period the French war establishment increased from 1,750,000 to 3,500,000; the Austrian from 1,137,000 to 2,600,000; and the Russian from 1,700,000 to 4,000,000; while Russia's mobilisation difficulties led her to keep under arms a regular army of about a million men. Altogether, the number of men which the great powers of Europe could put into the field increased during this period by nearly ten million, and it was evident that any future conflict would be on a scale so gigantic that, problems of strategy apart, it was doubtful whether any power would be able to stand up to the sheer economic strain of keeping such forces in the field. This was one reason the more that set Count Schlieffen, Chief of the German General Staff from 1891 to 1905, searching for a war plan which would avoid the long attrition of frontal attack and secure that rapid victory which alone could avert internal collapse.

In organisation, as in armament, the European armies grew to resemble each other more closely as the conduct of military affairs approximated more and more to an exact science. The protagonists of tradition scored some successes in their fight against scientific uniformity: German cavalry adopted the lance as a universal weapon; the French infantry retained their historic red trousers; but there was an ever-widening gap between the dazzling differences which European armies displayed in their parade uniforms and the drab anonymity to which they were compelled by necessity of war. In hierarchical organisation the differences were ones of detail. Everywhere the army corps, some 30,000 fighting men strong, was the smallest unit self-sufficient in all arms and ancillary services; and its size was definitely limited by the impossibility of deploying a larger number of men on the head of a column in the course of a single day. In most European states, as we have seen, the army corps was linked to a definite territorial area from which it drew all recruits and reservists. The corps commander was thus not only responsible for the organisation and conduct of the units under his command, but he had also (except in Russia and Great Britain) considerable responsibility for the administration of military policy in time of peace and for the carrying out of mobilisation on the outbreak of war. A typical corps would consist of two infantry divisions, each containing one cavalry and two infantry brigades—which themselves were composed of two regiments—and a regiment of field artillery; with, under direct corps command, a regiment of heavy artillery. Armament by the turn of the century was equally uniform, infantry being armed with 8 or 9 mm. magazine-rifles, field artillery with 8 cm. steel guns, and the siege and heavy artillery with guns, mortars and howitzers 15 cm. and 21 cm. in calibre. Under corps also came engineering and supply services, constantly increasing in complexity; medical services; telegraph units; railway detachments responsible not only for the maintenance of existing lines but for the creation of new ones—particularly necessary for a campaign in Poland; balloon detachments, cyclists, bridge trains, and the huge administrative services needed to keep armies of such size in the field.

In the control and administration of these great organisms there was little room for the untrained amateur. Staff work became more exacting and laborious, as much in the administration and training of the army in peacetime as in its conduct in war. The German General Staff, with its orderly subdivisions, its stereotyped yet flexible procedure, its control over military training and its omnipotent Chief became a model for other armies to follow. The Chief of the General Staff everywhere became an influential figure—though rarely did he achieve the stature of the great von Moltke. In Russia the Staff remained subordinate to the Ministry of War; in Austria-Hungary the activity and strong views of the Archduke Albert limited the scope of such Chiefs as Beck, and it was only after the death of that prince that a strong Chief, Conrad von Hötzendorf, was able to assert his supremacy. In France the post was until 1888 a political appointment changing with the Ministry and was in any case linked not to the command of the armies in the field but to the Ministry of War; while in England the post was not created until after the Esher reforms of 1904. Everywhere, however, the prestige and importance of General Staffs increased; and everywhere the military education of officers received a growing amount of attention. Military academies and staff colleges had existed, though they had rarely flourished, long before 1870. The Maria Theresa Academy in Austria, the Nicholas General Staff Academy in St Petersburg, the Staff College at Camberley, all existed side by side with the Prussian War Academy, and training colleges for the officers of the different arms were numerous. But after 1870 the lackadaisical atmosphere which had characterised these institutions in the first part of the century disappeared: entrance requirements became higher, syllabuses fuller, competition more intense. The army became a profession as well as a vocation; the officer less of a knight, more of an engineer.

The growing size of the armies of Europe meant that officers could no longer be drawn entirely from the upper classes which in the eighteenth century had virtually monopolised commissioned rank. In Russia less than anywhere was this possible: the bulk of the officers for her great standing army had to be drawn from the Junkers—cadets normally promoted from the ranks—whose level of education and social standing was far below that of the graduates from cadet schools whose ambition was a commission in the Imperial Guards. The same distinction was apparent in the French army, where the upper classes had had no monopoly of commissioned rank since the Revolution. After 1815 the aristocracy had turned away from the military career, and only during the regime of the Second Empire did they begin to turn back. Under the Third Republic the French officer corps became increasingly aristocratic and *bien pensant* in character as members of the upper classes were driven from their estates by the agrarian depression of the 1870's and found that entry into other professions—civil service, law, politics—was barred by the prejudice or the policy of the new republican masters of France. Thus the French army came to acquire, between 1880 and 1900, many of those characteristics of an aristocratic caste, socially if not politically oriented, which the Prussian officer corps had always possessed and which it was now struggling hard to retain.

In Germany, as the army expanded, men of the middle classes had to be admitted in growing numbers, not merely to the specialist arms or as officers of the reserve, but to the regular army itself. In 1890 William II openly appealed to the *Adel der Gesinnung*, the nobility of temperament, to come forward to help the nobility of birth to supply the army with its officers. The results were not so disastrous as the conservatives feared. Not only did the middle-class recruits bring a new degree of military efficiency, but they aped the manners and outlook of the gentry with whom it was now their privilege to consort. The works of Sybel, Treitschke and Bernhardi, the proud traditions of 1870, all made it easier for the German middle classes to accept a degree of militarisation unthinkable before 1860. As for the Austrians, the problems raised for the army by expansion were ones of nationality rather than of class. Of the four traditional bulwarks of the Habsburg monarchy—Church, nobility, bureaucracy and army—the effectiveness of the first two steadily waned as the century drew to its close, and the importance of the army in consequence increased. Its officers were repeatedly reminded of their special position above class and nationality, as the immediate supporters of the imperial throne; and within their ranks a *camaraderie* existed which contrasted sharply with the rigid subordination characteristic of the German army. But all three empires of Europe—Russia, Austria and Germany— shared this common characteristic in their military policy: conscription, by bringing the mass of the population under the control and instruction of a loyal officer corps, could be used as an instrument to combat the growth of democracy and radicalism which threatened the very foundations on which their social structure was based. And in France, where there was no monarchy to enshrine the ideals of order, tradition and hierarchy, the army felt an even greater obligation to guard them itself.

Thus although military leaders—except perhaps in Spain and Latin America, where military pronunciamentos had shaped national destinies since the collapse of the Spanish empire—everywhere professed their indifference to and dislike of politics, pressure on them to enter the political arena was considerable. The growth of dissident nationalism in Austria-Hungary, of social democracy in Germany, of radical republicanism in France, all had repercussions within the ranks of the armies, and military leaders appeared to have good professional reasons—in addition, often, to strong personal inclinations—to throw the full weight of their influence against them. In Russia the situation was exceptional. There a substantial element of the General Staff threw in its lot with the liberal, 'Westernising' elements which were pressing for greater industrialisation, universal education and all the social and economic changes necessary if they were to have literate recruits, adequate armaments and railways. Such military liberalism is not unusual in industrially backward states whose military efficiency depends on the rapidity of technical and educational development: Turkey and the successor states to the Ottoman empire were to show much the same tendencies during the following century; and even within Germany a division grew, towards the end of the nineteenth century, between the General Staff which had committed itself to Schlieffen's conception of an army numbered in millions, with all its social and economic consequences, and the Imperial Military Cabinet, which as the body responsible for appointments and promotions wished to keep the army, so far as was possible, to a size which could be officered in the main by nobility and the old regular N.C.O's.

In France and Germany the object of the military leaders was not so much to interfere in politics as to ensure that politicians did not meddle in military affairs. In part this was the reluctance of specialists to have their provisions questioned by amateurs. When in 1874 the Reichstag attempted to reduce or vary the size of the army demanded by the government von Moltke warned them that 'through fluctuations in this figure you bring uncertainty into all the many comprehensive preparations which must be made long in advance and worked out to the last detail'. Everywhere, as on the one hand technical developments increased the cost of an efficient weapons-system and, on the other, universal suffrage brought into power governments pledged to greater expenditure on education and the social services, the conflicts within National Assemblies and cabinets grew sharper. In 1887 Bismarck dissolved the Reichstag rather than yield to its demands that the size of the army should be debated, not every seven years, but every three; and in 1894 the swollen Naval Estimates played a substantial part in causing the collapse of Gladstone's last cabinet.

The size and equipment of the armed forces was only one of the points of issue between the civil and the military. In an increasingly liberal society the whole apparatus of military justice, subordination and discipline came under searching criticism and attack. In Germany the attempts of the officer corps to maintain old Prussian traditions of *Kadavergehorsamkeit* in a mass army, and the military arrogance which, under the patronage of William II, spread beyond the ranks of the regular army to infect every bourgeois reservist who could sport a uniform, awoke violent reactions in socialist and liberal circles, as the files of such satirical journals as *Simplicissimus* clearly show. The mounting anti-military feeling in the Reichstag led the German army to seek to withdraw military matters from parliamentary control altogether by subtracting the most important parts of its administration from the control of the Minister of War—the only official whom the Reichstag could hold responsible for the conduct of military affairs. Such attempts to evade control were all the easier, since in Germany—as indeed in Austria, Russia and, to a considerable extent, Great Britain—the armed forces were still felt to be the peculiar province of the Crown, to be kept intact and apart from the democratic influence which was invading other areas of society. The emperor in Germany controlled military appointments through his own military cabinet, the emperor of Austria through his military chancery, and their Chiefs of Staff were directly responsible to them. Officers stood to their sovereign in a special relationship of quasi-feudal loyalty very different from the normal obedience owed by the citizen to the head of the state. Interference with the internal affairs of the armed forces was thus held to be as sacrilegious as interference in affairs of the royal household—of which the army was virtually an extension.

It is, however, hard to avoid the conclusion that loyalty was as much a cover as a reason for the *esprit de corps* of the armies of Europe. In the French army, there was no focus for such loyalty. There was simply hierarchical obedience to the Minister of War who, himself a soldier although of political appointment, sat in the Ministry more as the ambassador of the army than as an instrument of democratic control. Yet the *esprit de corps* of the French army yielded nothing to that of the German or the Austrian. Perhaps even more than these did it pride itself on its purity from the defiling spirit of the age. After 1870 there had been a long honeymoon period when the French middle classes and peasantry looked on the army, not only as the predestined instrument of national revenge but as the palladium of social order; while a substantial proportion of French thinkers and statesmen saw in it the school which might teach the nation the moral virtues of patriotism, self sacrifice and respect for authority which the collapse of 1870 had revealed it so conspicuously to lack. The military prints of Détaille commanded wide sales, popular songs fêted the army, and when the unfortunate General Boulanger found himself cast in the role of national saviour his supporters came at least as much from the left wing, where Déroulède and the 'Ligue des Patriotes' kept Jacobin military traditions aflame, as they did from the royalists and dissident conservatives on the right. But by the end of the 1880's the honeymoon was drawing to a close. There was a wave of anti-military literature; Détaille gave way to Caran d'Ache, and the imperfections of the army began to come under the close examination of hostile and intelligent eyes. Like their German colleagues the French military leaders considered such criticism to be not merely ill-informed, but positively harmful to national security and morale; and when rumours began to circulate about the circumstances in which Captain Dreyfus had been condemned for espionage in 1894, their first reaction was to declare it to be a purely internal matter, their second to resist any attempt at re-examining the case, and their third to conclude that, since the reputation of the army now depended on Dreyfus' guilt and national security rested on the reputation of the army, neither perjury nor forgery should be disdained in establishing that guilt as certain.

Yet perhaps the most significant aspect of the Dreyfus affair was not so much the lengths to which the French army was prepared to go to maintain its independence and national prestige, as the degree of public support which it retained in doing so. The *affaire* split society from top to bottom, and anti-Dreyfusards were to be found in all walks of life and of most shades of political opinion. The army was a national symbol which must be held sacred at all costs. In Germany such a feeling was even more intense; in Austria-Hungary and Russia it was qualified only by a yet greater degree of loyalty evoked by the persons of the emperor and the tsar; while in Great Britain the Royal Navy by the end of the century had become surrounded by publicists with an intensity of emotional fervour which would have been unthinkable some thirty years earlier. To examine the causes of this heightening of the emotional attachment in European states towards the symbols and instruments of national sovereignty—the flags, the armed forces, the sovereigns themselves—would be to trespass far beyond the bounds of this chapter. Here it must suffice to note that military—and naval—leaders did not represent simply a professional group-interest in their struggles for larger forces and for the autonomous conduct of those forces: in their role as the guardians of national security they could command a degree of public support which was sometimes denied to the civil leaders with whom they contended; and there can be little doubt that the consciousness of such support provided an additional incentive for the more able among them—Waldersee in Germany, Fisher in Great Britain, Conrad in Austria, Skobolev in Russia—to attempt to influence national policy.

The influence of the military on internal policy was always likely to be marginal. Too many other interests, social, cultural and economic, had to be taken into account. But in the shaping of foreign policy careful attention had to be given to the considerations urged by naval and military advisers as the minimum requirements of security. The terms of the Peace of Frankfurt were to a large extent shaped by the insistence of Moltke and the General Staff on possessing the two fortresses of Metz and Strassburg, and only with some reluctance did they forgo the possession of Belfort as well. British naval and military advisers were so insistent in their demands for overseas bases to protect supply lines that Lord Salisbury declared that 'if they were allowed full scope they would insist on the importance of the moon to protect us from Mars'. From demands for the acquisition of protective bases it was easy to pass to demands for the waging of preventive war. Two of the most notorious examples of this—Fisher's unofficial suggestion of the 'Copenhagening' of the German Fleet, and the steady pressure exercised on the Austrian government by Conrad von Hötzendorf for the elimination of Serbia—lie outside our field of study. The activities of the Austrian and German military authorities with regard to Russia, however, lie very definitely within it.

Like Bismarck in the diplomatic field, Moltke, who remained Chief of the German General Staff until 1888, was far more conscious of the weakness of the new German empire than of its strength. He watched the revival of French military strength with concern, and that concern was intensified when in 1876–8 France covered her north-eastern frontiers with a great belt of fortifications which apparently made impossible any repetition of the rapid victory of 1870. For Moltke was equally concerned about the prospects of war with Russia, and with the growing military effectiveness of that power as Milyutin's reforms made their effects felt. A war on two fronts only promised success if a rapid victory could be expected on one of them; and since the French fortifications seemed to destroy all hope of this in the west, Moltke resolved to stand on the defensive there in his newly won territory west of the Rhine and turn his attention to the eastern front. This decision coincided not only with the conclusion of the Dual Alliance between the German and Austro-Hungarian empires in 1879, but with the Russian decision, after the revelation of the imperfections in her mobilisation plans in 1876–7, to maintain on foot in her western military areas a force which the German and Austrian staffs calculated at 600,000 men. Such an adversary could be dealt with only jointly, and in 1882 planning between the two staffs began without the formal authorisation of either government. Moltke indeed, when asked what the attitude of Bismarck might be to these conversations, proudly replied: 'My position is such that I do not depend on the Foreign Office.' By 1887, when the growing tension in the Balkans had culminated in the Bulgarian crisis, the probability of war seemed so great that to the staffs of Germany and Austria safety seemed to lie only in attacking first, and Waldersee, Moltke's assistant and successor, drafted with Beck a military convention whereby a preventive attack was to be launched against Russia in 1888. This was too much even for Moltke. Bismarck had decisively to intervene and disown the impatient soldiers. But he shortly had to deal with an impatient emperor as well: for in 1889 William II, shaking himself free of Bismarck's restraint, promised Beck 'for whatever reason you mobilise, whether Bulgaria or not, the day of your mobilisation is also the day of the mobilisation of my army, and the Chancellor can say what he will'. A year later the Chancellor had gone, and the soldiers in Vienna openly expressed their satisfaction.

It was premature. In 1891 Waldersee himself was displaced, and his successor, Schlieffen, soon abandoned his policy. Redeployment of Russian forces and the strengthening of fortifications on the Narew and the Niemen made a rapid victory on that front seem equally improbable; Schlieffen in any case mistrusted the capacity of the Austrian army to fulfil its part in any agreed strategy; and before the century ended he had turned his attention back to the western front and begun to draft the famous projects for a great sweep through Belgium, outflanking the French army and fortifications alike, which were to culminate in the notorious *Aufmarsch* of 1914.

Throughout the last quarter of the century German military planners worked on the assumption that France and Russia would be allies in any future war. Perhaps it is not coincidental that the man who reversed Bismarck's pacific policy by allowing the Reinsurance Treaty with Russia to lapse, the Count Caprivi, should have been a professional soldier. In any case it was only after Bismarck's retirement that the Franco-Russian Entente which he had dreaded and which the General Staff accepted as inevitable took shape, and then it originated as a military convention. It was an agreement which was brought about by several factors other than common fear of Germany. Hostility to Great Britain was also a powerful cause, and it was natural enough for Russia to look to France for the capital and the industrial aid which she needed to develop her railways and military resources and which Germany was increasingly unwilling to provide. The civil authorities of both states—Giers in Russia, Ribot and Freycinet in France—showed themselves reluctant to enter into any specific military agreements. French statesmen were as averse to going to war over Constantinople as were the Russians over Alsace-Lorraine. But during the exploratory conversations which General de Boisdeffre, Vice-Chief of the French General Staff, held with his Russian opposite number during the goodwill visit of the French Fleet to Kronstadt in 1891, it became clear that nothing less than instantaneous mobilisation in mutual support could have any military value. The French knew that they could not sustain the onslaught of the entire German army unless the Russians created an immediate diversion; the Russians were no less anxious about the exposed position of their forward troops in Poland against which Austria and Germany, thanks to their superior railway facilities, would be able to concentrate overwhelmingly superior forces; and in 1892 the military specialists, with the powerful support of Tsar Alexander III, overruled civilian hesitations and signed a Convention, whereby the two powers agreed not only to support each other in the event of a German attack on either party, but to mobilise in the event of a mobilisation by any member of the Triple Alliance. Ratification of the Convention still hung fire until the following year; but then the German introduction of two-year military service, and the consequent increase in the trained manpower of that nation, was enough to quell the last doubts.

So far we have confined our attention to the affairs of Europe, for in spite of their increasing interest in and dependence on the world overseas the military policy and organisation of the powers was at this epoch contrived to meet purely European threats. The central powers, with the exception of a small section of the German army equipped for operations in Africa, could devote their military energies entirely to planning for European war. But the colonial empires of the western seaboard, France, Spain, and above all Great Britain, had to plan for other military contingencies than invasion by a neighbour. Their widespread commitments overseas involved them in frontier wars against adversaries who, though usually in a pre-industrial stage of civilisation, showed qualities of skill and courage sufficient to impose a considerable strain on the limited forces available to deal with them—a strain greatly increased as modern rifles became available in the markets of the world. In South Africa indeed, in 1881 and 1899, the British found in the Boer Republics an enemy whose skill and equipment were initially superior to their own; and in 1898 the United States, emerging from their isolation to contest the European monopoly of imperial pretensions, introduced a new element into world politics: a fully industrialised extra-European power.

The defence of overseas territories involved more than the protection or extension of frontiers: it was necessary also to pacify the territories within these frontiers, and this could be done only where military repression was accompanied by enlightened administration and profound measures of social and economic reform. Thus there are two archetypal military figures of the late nineteenth century. One is the European staff officer, skilled in the complexities of weapon development, supply, railway movements, and the administration of large units. The other is the soldier-administrator, the Kitchener or the Lyautey, solitary, many-sided, concerned with civil as much as with military organisation, with the administration of justice as much as with the elimination of opposition, imperial pro-consuls of the classic type. Units of the British and French armies serving overseas—and indeed those of the Russian armies in the Caucasus and central Asia—were employed on projects of building, improvement of communications, and famine relief which were military only in the very widest sense of the word. Within the French army, in Indo-China, Madagascar and Morocco, such highly literate commanders as Galliéni and Lyautey developed a military doctrine whereby the methods of conquest were dictated less by military considerations than by the subsequent needs of pacification and administration; and in the British army the same doctrine, if nowhere so precisely formulated, was in practice usually put into effect.

For the armies of the mainland powers, even that of France, colonial campaigning was a comparatively minor consideration in comparison with the need to guarantee the homeland against invasion by a European neighbour. For Great Britain on the other hand such campaigning was the army's *raison d'être*: and for a force which was constantly scattered in garrisons over the face of the globe the principle of short-term military service adopted by all other major European powers was of doubtful relevance, even if it had been politically feasible—which in mid-Victorian England it was not. Nevertheless, the impact of the Prussian victories of 1866 and 1870 was felt in Great Britain as elsewhere in Europe, and it hastened a movement of military reform which was already well under way. Ever since the fiasco of the Crimean campaign fifteen years earlier the worst anomalies of an army in which eighteenth-century principles of military organisation had remained intact were being slowly eliminated; and the process was speeded up when in 1868 Edward Cardwell brought to the War Office that zeal for economy and reform with which Gladstone's ministry was transforming the entire administration, judicature and educational system of England. In his quest for efficiency and economy Cardwell had to demolish two pillars of the old order: the dichotomy whereby control of the army was divided between a royal Commander-in-Chief responsible to the sovereign and a Secretary of State for War responsible to parliament; and the purchase system, which ensured that control of the armed forces remained in the hands of the propertied classes. These anomalies, justifiable only in terms of the problems and passions of a bygone age, were duly eliminated. The status of the Commander-in-Chief was reduced to that of 'Military Adviser to the Secretary of State'; and Cardwell was able to override parliamentary protests at the abolition of purchase by the argument that the matter was one solely within the jurisdiction of the Crown, and so carry the reform through by use of royal warrant. In addition the army itself was reshaped. The growing ease and rapidity of ocean transport made it no longer necessary to keep large garrisons locked up for years in overseas stations, while the larger overseas settlements—Australia, New Zealand, Canada and South Africa—were able to provide for their own defence. By reducing the number of troops stationed abroad Cardwell was able to build up cadres at home which, established in depots in each of sixty-six newly created military districts, both acted as sister-battalions to units serving overseas and supervised the training of the forces of the local militia; while the latter were removed from the control of the Lords Lieutenant, who had exercised it ever since the Restoration, and came once more under that of the Crown. Cardwell thus introduced a modified form of the German 'Corps Area' in so far as every army unit was linked to a territorial district from which it drew recruits, regular reinforcements and trained reserves. Reduction in length of overseas duty made it possible also to introduce a modified form of continental short service, and the Army Enlistment Act of 1870 enabled recruits to enlist for twelve years only—six with the colours, six with the reserve. And, for the first time, the army became selective in the men it chose. Bounties on enlistment were abolished; men of bad character were discharged; and under the influence of its last two Commanders-in-Chief, Sir Garnet Wolseley and Sir Frederick Roberts, the British army devoted an increasing amount of attention to the comfort, welfare and education of its men. Army and nation could not, in the absence of conscription, become identified to the same extent as in continental powers; but the soldier was no longer a social pariah bound for life to a trade which civilians at once neglected and despised; and by the end of the century, assisted by the activities of writers such as Rudyard Kipling, Spenser Wilkinson and Sir Charles Dilke, the British army was acquiring an unprecedented measure of popular affection and respect.

There was, however, a great deal of room for further reform. The office of the Commander-in-Chief was quite unable to handle the complex problems of military administration which on the Continent were the concern of the growing General Staffs. In 1888 a commission under Lord Hartington recommended the abolition of the office altogether, and its replacement by an Army Council on the lines of the Board of Admiralty and by a Chief of Staff on the German model. Queen Victoria was outraged by this 'really abominable' report, and its recommendations were crippled by compromises. Not until after the Boer War were they given effect; and the Boer War showed other weaknesses as well which urgently needed remedy. Cardwell's army was organised to provide a constant stream of reinforcements for imperial garrisons, a force for home defence, and a small strategic reserve. It could not provide a large force, ready organised with supplies, staff and services, to take part in a prolonged overseas campaign against a 'civilised' enemy. All this had to be improvised; and by 1901 it was clear that if the British army was to be an effective instrument of national policy administrative reforms were still necessary at least as sweeping as any made by Cardwell. Nor were the needed reforms purely ones of administration. The tactics, training, and standard of professional leadership in the army were shown by the ten months of campaigning between October 1899 and August 1900 to be entirely inadequate to the requirements of modern war; while the many problems, naval as well as military, involved in the redeployment of the imperial forces necessary to conduct a distant campaign made evident the need for some central planning organisation whose scope would transcend the purely military and deal with the long-term problems of imperial defence. The need for such a body had been frequently felt, and stressed, during the previous quarter of the century. The Hartington Commission had recommended the establishment of a joint naval and military council under the presidency of the Prime Minister, and Lord Salisbury established a Defence Committee of the Cabinet in 1895; but it was only in 1902 that a specific Committee of Imperial Defence was constituted, whose task it was to 'survey as a whole the strategical military needs of the Empire', and whose membership, apart from the Prime Minister and the Secretariat, was to be kept so fluid that not only naval and military experts but specialists in the economic, financial, diplomatic and political fields might be summoned as occasion required. For a power with commitments so widespread as Great Britain's, in an age when conflicts were to be on a global scale, such a body was as vital to military planning as was, on the smaller scale of European warfare, the German Great General Staff.

For Britain, naturally enough, war was visualised primarily in naval terms. Indeed it is tempting for the historian—especially a British historian—to condemn the parochialism of the continental strategists whose vision was limited to the exploits of a Napoleon or a Moltke and who gave no consideration whatever to the part played in warfare by command of the sea; but it is a judgement which a nation with no vulnerable land frontiers cannot justly make. For Britain, among the powers of Europe, naval affairs were vital; for France and Italy they were secondary; for Germany and Russia they were marginal. The naval superiority of the French postponed defeat in 1870, but could not avert it. Yet by the turn of the century the problems of naval armament and warfare were arousing concern even among the continental states of Europe and in the principal extra-European powers, the United States of America and Japan; and it is to the technical and political problems involved in this form of defence that our attention must now be turned.

In 1870 the revolution in shipbuilding brought about by the introduction of steam and iron and by developments in the science of gun-making had already effected its most sweeping changes. Since the middle of the 1850's steam had replaced sail as the principal means of propulsion for men-of-war, and the indispensability of armour, evident enough since the destruction of the wooden Turkish Fleet by Russian shells at Sinope in 1853, had been placed beyond doubt by the exploits of the Confederate iron-clad *Merrimac* in Hampton Roads in March 1862, when only the providential appearance of the Federal *Monitor* had saved the Union Fleet from destruction by gunfire and ram. The iron-clad steamer, pioneered so boldly by Napoleon III and Dupuy de Lôme when they launched the *Gloire* and her sister-ships in 1859, had come to stay, and the vessels which had fought at Trafalgar were, as one Victorian publicist put it, 'as out of date as the trireme'. Only two more steps were needed to complete the breach with the past: the abandonment of wood as the prime material for naval construction, and the abandonment even of auxiliary sail. Britain had already taken the first step. Iron had its disadvantages, especially for long voyages—iron bottoms fouled more easily than copper-sheathed wood. But it made possible the construction of vessels of far greater size; and, for an industrial nation, it was cheap. Iron was indigenous to England and wood in adequate quantities was not. In the *Warrior* of 1859 Britain launched her first iron-built man-of-war. Italy followed in 1861 and Russia in 1864, but France was slower to abandon the iron-clad wooden vessels which she had introduced and which served her more limited purposes quite adequately. Not till 1872, in her first post-war naval construction programme, did she also adopt iron as the material at once most economical and giving the greatest scope for increase in size. Thereafter wood was virtually abandoned by European naval architects, and the growing metallurgical industries of the Continent throve on shipbuilding contracts.

The second step, and one no less far-reaching in its effects, was taken by the British Admiralty after the catastrophe of 8 September 1870, when the full-rigged iron-clad steamer *Captain* capsized and sank with nearly all her crew. There was an understandable reluctance on the part of all navies to abandon sail, with all the inestimable increment it provided in cruising capacity; but the preservation of full-rig was not compatible with the other considerations which were affecting naval construction. Of these, the chief was the need to present the smallest possible targets to the powerful new guns of the enemy, and in consequence the reduction of freeboard to the minimum above the water-line. It was this combination of low freeboard—a bare six feet—with full-rigged masts that caused the disaster to the *Captain*. But low freeboard meant also the abandonment of the traditional broadside of guns—a step to which two other factors contributed. One was the desire to mount guns capable of firing forward over the bows as the vessel charged and rammed her adversary. It was generally accepted that the new possibilities of controlled movement opened up by the replacement of sail by steam would result in naval battles being fought at close quarters, with ramming and perhaps boarding; as the *Merrimac* had rammed its victims at Hampton Roads and the Austrian admiral Tegetthoff had the Italian flagship at the battle of Lissa in 1866; two actions whose results determined naval thinking for the best part of fifty years. Thus the ram and the forward-firing battery became essential parts of naval armament. The second factor was the increase in the size and weight of naval ordnance. From five tons the weight of naval guns had increased, by the 1870's, to eighty. Increased explosive charges first made necessary a great strengthening of the breech; then slow-burning powders were introduced which needed a greater length of barrel to develop their full explosive power—a development which forced the British Admiralty to abandon the muzzle-loaders to which they clung until 1880. Such monsters could only be mounted centrally; and the old gun-port gave way to the turret, the central battery, or the barbette.

Thus the iron-clad of the 1870's took the form of an armoured platform, low in the water, from which rose the heavily armoured central battery containing the heavy guns, surrounded by unarmoured quarters for the crew. Such were the *Devastation* and the *Inflexible* in England, the *Redoutable* in France, the *Duilio* in Italy. But these vessels had their disadvantages. With all the guns concentrated in one area of the ship the smoke of one blinded all; and as the penetrating power of the shells increased, it became impossible adequately to armour all the vital points— in particular the water-line and the central battery. The vitals of the *Inflexible* of 1874, for example, had to be protected by up to 24 inches of iron armour-plating. The French abandoned the central battery altogether, and in the *Amiral Duperre* of 1876 they armoured only the water-line and mounted their guns on barbettes fore and aft. The British were not prepared to follow in a course which seemed ruthlessly to sacrifice protection of the crew to the protection of the vessel. Science soon came to their rescue. Harvey in America and Bessemer in England were perfecting new processes of chilling and hardening steel, and during the 1880's a new form of armour-plating became available, light, thin and tough, which made possible not only the abandonment of the massive iron strait-jackets to which the vessels of the 1870's were condemned but the armouring of cruisers, which no longer needed to sacrifice protection to speed. With the *Royal Sovereign* of 1890 and the *Majestic* of 1895 the British Navy returned to high freeboard, with all the improvements which that meant in comfort and speed; and foreign naval architects rapidly did the same. The central battery finally disappeared, and the heavy guns in their turret mountings were reinforced by the smaller, quick-firing 12-, 6- and 3-pounder guns down to machine-guns devised by Hotchkiss and Nordenfeldt. By the turn of the century battleships were some 14,000 to 15,000 tons in displacement; capable of steaming at 18 knots; and mounting 12- or 13-inch guns with a muzzle velocity of something over 2000 feet per second.

It was evident that battles between these great gun-carriers would differ in kind as well as in degree from those fought between the men-of-war of Nelson's day. Then the chances of wind and weather might favour a skilfully handled weaker fleet. By keeping to windward and shooting down the enemy's rigging, as the French had learnt to do in the eighteenth century, one might cripple a stronger adversary and escape unscathed. But now against more powerful engines and bigger guns neither luck nor seamanship could provide salvation. The weaker fleet, once located, could not even keep the seas; and once guns developed an effective range of 4000 yards or so it could no longer compensate for its weakness by provoking a mêlée. In 1894 the Japanese defeated a numerically superior

Chinese fleet off the Yalu through gunfire alone, never closing to ram or board, and four years later American squadrons at Manila and Santiago were to drive the same lesson home. The faster, better-armoured, more powerfully gunned and better-drilled vessels would win. In land warfare, the outcome of future battles seemed to lie in long-prepared conscription policies and mobilisation plans; in naval warfare supremacy was seen to rest more and more in the hands of designers and naval construction engineers. Fear of activity in French and Russian shipyards drove on the British. Fear of German and Italian activity drove on the French. Fear of being outclassed in power and prestige drove on the Americans and the Japanese. Spurred by rival national policies, the size of the battleship and its guns steadily grew.

Yet there were other weapons being developed by naval designers as well as the battleship. Moored explosive mines had been used effectively by the Russians during the Crimean War, and ten years after the conclusion of that conflict Arthur Whitehead patented the first of his automobile torpedoes. The first models were slow, erratic, limited in range and exceedingly difficult to launch; but by 1877 the Russians were able to use them effectively against stationary Turkish ships, and torpedo warfare rapidly became a new and important part of the naval repertoire. Torpedo-boats not only became an intrinsic part of coastal defence, making any close blockade doubtfully possible, but they added another element to the naval battle. They were visualised as a sort of maritime cavalry. 'It is not likely', wrote a British specialist, H. W. Wilson, in *Ironclads in Action* (1898), 'that torpedo boats will be sent against intact battleships, whose quick-firers are in good order and whose gunners are unshaken. The boats' time will come towards the close of the battle, when the fighting has left great masses of iron wreckage; when the targets have lost their power of movement; when their crews are diminished in number and wearied by the intense strain of action.' By the end of the century certainly doubts were growing about the ability of these craft to penetrate the curtain of fire with which it was believed that battleships could surround themselves, especially now that ships were no longer swathed in the thick cloud of old-fashioned gunpowder smoke; but already in the submarine a craft was being developed which might more safely take their place.

Like so many other military innovations, the submarine in its origins dated back to the American War of Secession; but the primitive models then employed, with indifferent success, had since been improved, first by Holland's invention in 1877 of the horizontal rudder, which made possible the controlled dive, and secondly by the development of the accumulator battery which made it possible to store electrical power. The French navy acted as pioneers in this as in most other major naval developments of the age. By 1899 they had developed, in the *Gustave Zédé*, a vessel capable of 8 knots at a depth of 60 feet; perhaps the first submarine to be practicable as a weapon of war. Two years later, by placing an order for twenty-three of these vessels, in addition to her existing eight, France made herself stronger in them than all the remaining powers combined. In 1901 the British Admiralty tentatively commissioned five, stating in their memorandum on the Estimates, 'what the future value of these boats may be in naval warfare can only be a matter of conjecture'. It was to be five years before the German navy took any steps to follow. With some reason Admiral Sir John Fisher was to write in 1904: 'It is astounding to me, *perfectly astounding*, how the very best among us fail to realise the vast impending revolution in naval warfare and naval strategy that the submarine will accomplish.'

It was no accident that submarine warfare should have been first developed by the French. In the French navy the memory of the *guerre de course* waged by their great corsairs upon English trade during the wars of Louis XIV had never faded; and in the eyes of some of their theorists the naval and economic developments of the nineteenth century gave their seamen the opportunity, if they could but grasp it, of surpassing the achievements of Duguay-Trouin and Jean-Bart. Great Britain, pointed out the spokesman of this *Jeune École*, was now as never before dependent on her overseas trade not only for her livelihood but for her very existence; its interruption would cause not only commercial panic and industrial unemployment, but starvation. Even the limited activities of Confederate commerce raiders in the American War of Secession had shown how much could be achieved by a few daring and well-found vessels. Now the age of steam gave the commerce raider a new advantage. Limitations of fuel meant that merchantmen were to be found along a few well-frequented shipping lanes instead of being able to cruise safely in the immensity of the ocean; while armed cruisers could be constructed of a speed with which laden merchant vessels could never hope to compete. Such writers as Gabriel Charmes, writing in the 1880's, urged that Britain's command of the seas was a thing of the past. Torpedo-boats would make her weapon of close blockade unusable, while such damage could be inflicted on her merchant shipping by armed commerce raiders, striking if need be with no consideration for existing rules of war, that she could quickly be brought to her knees. 'Others may protest; for ourselves we accept in these new methods of destruction the development of that law of progress in which we have a firm faith, and the final result would be to put an end to war altogether.' Thus, with fashionable Darwinism, wrote Admiral Théophile Aube, who at the Ministry of Marine during the 1880's was able to put much of the teaching of the *Jeune École* into effect. The French navy began to concentrate on torpedo-boat and cruiser warfare, and greeted with enthusiasm the potentialities of the submarine. In the *Gustave Zédé* lay the answer to Fashoda; and at least one enthusiast, d'Armor, in his book *Les Sous-marins et la guerre contre L'Angleterre*

(1899), urged that France should abandon battleship construction altogether, rely on armoured cruisers for the destruction of enemy commerce and on submarines for the elimination of the enemy fleet.

But the *Jeune École* did not get its way entirely even in France. The French Ministry of Marine accepted the cruiser, the torpedo-boat and the submarine as auxiliaries to the battleship, but never as substitutes. When in 1900 it adopted a seven-year programme for building six 15,000-ton battleships and five 12,500-ton armoured cruisers, the explanation of the Minister relied on the orthodox argument which British naval thinkers had never abandoned. It was above all necessary, he declared, to float the most powerful possible gun. This could be done only on a large and stable platform; and when to this platform was added the necessary qualities of armour and speed, the result was the battleship. Comparative naval strength was ultimately calculated in terms of ships of the line.

Certainly the British thought in these terms when, during the 1880's, they became aware of the inadequacy of their naval power if their two principal rivals, France and Russia, should ever join forces. If the German General Staff was haunted by calculations of the combined French and Russian manpower, British naval thinkers were no less worried by the sum of French and Russian ships. Not only was friction with both these powers increasing throughout the decade, as Britain came in repeated conflict with them in Africa and Asia, but the Bulgarian crisis of 1885, over which war seemed a distinct possibility, revealed that the Royal Navy's mobilisation and training arrangements were as inadequate as was its striking power. A campaign in press and parliament culminated in the official adoption of the Two-Power Standard. The Royal Navy was to be kept at a strength in battleships equivalent to that of the combined fleets of the next two major naval powers. It was to implement this policy that the Naval Defence Act was passed in 1889—a step which set on foot an armaments race of an entirely new intensity. Britain committed herself to a naval construction programme, costing £21·5 million and involving the construction within the next three years of ten battleships—eight of them of the new *Royal Sovereign* class, over 14,000 tons burden—together with nine large cruisers and thirty-three smaller ones, to deal with the vessels of the *Jeune École*. This was only the beginning. The twin goads of Franco-Russian competition—seen as particularly menacing after the fulsome demonstrations of naval amity between these two powers in 1891—and the rapid obsolescence of naval units, forced the British to visualise the construction of forty-two battleships and forty-five armoured cruisers by 1904, and to lay down, between 1893 and 1904, an average of seven capital ships a year. Conservatives, Radicals, Liberal Imperialists co-operated, under the stimulus of the newly founded Navy League, in forcing the pace. Only Mr Gladstone declared that the demands of the Admiralty were 'mad! mad! mad!' and he resigned rather than endorse a policy which he considered fatal to the interests both of economy and of peace.

The logic of technical development and the fears bred by traditional colonial rivalries were thus in themselves enough to account for the naval race with which the twentieth century began. The race involved more than merely ships. The abandonment of sail even as auxiliary motive power reduced all vessels to complete dependence on the availability of coaling stations at sufficiently frequent intervals along their routes; and for men-of-war more than fuel would be necessary if they were to be, and remain, fit for action in distant waters. They would need ammunition and food supplies, dockyard facilities, naval barracks and hospitals; all the facilities of a complete naval base. Thus if governments were to give their commerce the protection to which it was traditionally entitled they needed to establish naval bases all over the world from which this could be done. Those bases would themselves need protection; so would the lines of communication connecting them; and yet more vessels and expenditure would be required. Thus the demand for naval expansion came not only from the military circles concerned with questions of security; it was swollen also by the multiple commercial and financial interests of western Europe and the United States which were dependent on the survival and expansion of a prosperous world trade; and the great shipbuilding, metallurgical and armaments industries which boomed on government contracts would have shown a degree of saintly unworldliness if they had not added their moral and financial support to Navy Leagues which were founded throughout Europe and America to agitate for the continuation and increase of a policy which was not only vital for the protection of national interests but highly profitable in itself.

As Jean-Jacques Rousseau crystallised and expressed the general revolt of sensibility and individualism against the formalism of the eighteenth century, so did this new 'navalism' find its apostle in the person of Captain Alfred Thayer Mahan of the United States Navy. In 1890 Mahan published the lectures on the *Influence of Sea Power on History* which he had given at the United States Naval College. For the most part these consisted of a close analysis of the tactics and strategy of naval warfare in the seventeenth and eighteenth centuries; but they contained generalisations about the nature and constituent elements of sea-power and the relationship of sea-power to national prosperity which summed up all that the 'Navalists' were coming to believe. 'For the first time', wrote Sir Julian Corbett, 'naval history was placed on a philosophical basis.' Such a judgement does less than justice to the thinking going on in Corbett's own country, especially that of Rear Admiral Philip Colomb, whose great analytic work on *Naval Warfare* appeared at the same time as Mahan's masterpiece. But Mahan's pronouncements had a magisterial and convincing ring which made them quotable—and translatable—in a way that Colomb's careful technicalities were not; and in a series of books and articles he continued, until his death in 1914, to expound a coherent teaching about naval power and policy which became accepted doctrine for every naval power in the world. Sea-power, commerce and colonies, he maintained, all these were inseparably connected, and they were the indispensable foundations for national wealth and prosperity. 'In these three things', he wrote, 'production, with the necessity of exchanging products, shipping, whereby the exchange is carried on, and colonies, which facilitate and enlarge the operations of shipping and tend to protect it by multiplying points of safety—is to be found a key to much of the history, as well as of the policy, of nations bordering on the sea.' Moreover, sea-power not only protected commerce; it derived strength from it. Sea-power, he wrote, 'includes not only the military strength afloat, that rules the sea or any part of it by force of arms, but also the peaceful commerce and shipping from which alone a military fleet naturally and healthfully springs, and on which its security rests'. Without commerce, no navy; without a navy, no commerce. And commerce and navy both needed overseas bases. 'Control of the seas...is the chief among the merely material elements in the power and prosperity of nations', wrote Mahan in 1893. '...From this necessarily follows the principle that, as subsidiary to such control, it is imperative to take possession, when it can be done righteously, of such maritime positions as contribute to secure command.'

Mahan's teaching rather gave emphasis to existing policies than created new ones. The *Jeune École* was already in decline when his critiques of the whole policy of *guerre de course* appeared, and the scramble for overseas bases was well under way. He could only urge his own countrymen to join in. The United States, he maintained, must occupy, first, positions which would give them control over the Panamanian isthmus, through which commercial and strategic considerations were making it imperative that a canal should soon be built; and secondly, bases in the Pacific to protect United States interests in the Far East, where the old rivals, Britain, France and Russia, were joined by three new expanding and mutually suspicious powers, Japan, Germany and the United States: all countries whose rulers were fervent disciples of Mahan.

Germany's advent as a great naval power involved a complete break with her national tradition. Individual German vessels or squadrons had been showing the imperial flag and protecting commerce ever since the foundation of the Reich: at Haiti in 1872, to exact compensation for damage to German traders; in the China seas in 1876, in a joint *démarche* with the other European powers to suppress piracy; at Angra Pequena in 1883, and Zanzibar in 1885. But these activities were marginal to German naval policy. Ever since its foundation by Albrecht von Roon in 1867, the German Navy had been a step-child of the War Office, administered by soldiers who, efficiently though they cared for their charge, regarded its function as being primarily to free the army from the obligations of coastal defence. Apart from the unarmoured corvettes and gunboats allotted to trade protection, and a handful of iron-clad frigates, the German fleet consisted primarily of a force of torpedo-boats and coastal craft—and one sufficiently formidable to alarm the French, against whose coasts and harbours it was quite capable of being used in time of war. This was the strait-jacket imposed by Bismarck's policy of limited liability in foreign affairs, and one which began during the 1880's to chafe. Already in 1884 a memorandum from the Ministry of Marine to the Reichstag complained that the unarmoured vessels on which Germany relied for trade protection would be valueless in war time; and such an argument appealed to those growing commercial and industrial classes whose representatives in the Reichstag grudged, as much from political as from economic motives, the increasingly vast sums gobbled up by the Ministry of War. A great navy could not only gain for Germany the place in the world to which her industry, talents and destiny entitled her; it would do so without increasing the influence of the Junkers who still monopolised more than their share of power. Bismarck's fall removed the main obstacle to a navalist policy in Germany. It was significant that the new emperor should have inaugurated the new era with the creation of an independent Admiralty and with a naval metaphor: 'The ship's orders remain the same: full steam ahead!'

William II was not the man to be left behind by the latest developments in world thought. He 'devoured' Mahan, and had translations placed aboard every vessel in the German navy; and in 1892 he gave to his Chief of Naval Staff, Admiral von Tirpitz, the right of direct access already enjoyed by his principal military adviser. Tirpitz had risen to eminence as a torpedo-boat commander, but in his view the German Navy had a part to play far more significant than that of purely coastal defence. 'National world commerce,' he wrote in 1894, 'world industry, and to a certain extent fishing on the high seas, world intercourse and colonies are impossible without a fleet capable of taking the offensive.' Not only that: Tirpitz went a step beyond Mahan, and saw the value of a strong 'fleet in being' even in peacetime, to add strength and meaning to diplomatic negotiations—an argument which particularly appealed to his emperor. But a strong fleet meant battleships, and battleships in sufficient quantity —if they were to be used other than purely defensively—to make an impression on the British. It was to meet this last point that Tirpitz developed his celebrated 'risk' theory. The German fleet should be at least strong enough to be able, if it clashed with the British, to inflict such damage that the Royal Navy would no longer be able to hold its own against its French and Russian rivals. The risk involved in trying conclusions with the German Navy would thus deter the British from attacking it as effectively as would any vast increase in size. It was a bid for sea-power on the cheap, and Tirpitz's measures when he became Minister of Marine, 1897, were relatively modest: the construction of seven new battleships—largely explicable as replacements of obsolete units—to bring the German total to nineteen.

Even the first Navy Law of 1898 could be seen as a measure of rational-isation and standardisation as much as one of expansion, fixing the strength of the navy at nineteen battleships and twelve large cruisers and setting an upper limit on expenditure. But two years later the tone had changed. Tirpitz found himself out-distanced by the enthusiasm of his emperor and of the *Flottenverein* which he had done so much to found. Great Britain no longer appeared a naval power of such strength that she could be dealt with only on a basis of risks and balances. The Boer War revealed not only her military inadequacies but her diplomatic isolation; and impressive as had been the Jubilee review of the Fleet at Spithead in 1897, it was evident that British overseas commitments were so extensive that it was by no means unthinkable for the German navy to achieve parity with the force left available to the Royal Navy in home waters. The opening of the Kiel Canal in 1896 had significantly increased German potential strength in the North Sea, and new large docks were under con-struction at Emden and Wilhelmshaven. The Navy Law of 1900 provided for the doubling of the number of capital ships in the German navy; and when concessions had to be made to protests in the Reichstag against the increase in expenditure involved, it was not capital ships but cruisers which were thrown to the wolves. The twentieth century thus opened with the German decision to construct a formidable fighting fleet, and the British could not for long avoid the conclusion that it was directed primarily against them.

The United States, unlike Germany, did not feel it necessary to adopt British naval strength as an exact criterion in assessing the optimum size for their fleet. But, like the German, American naval policy had by the end of the century swung far away from the simple reliance on coastal fortifications and commerce-raiding which had characterised it since the War of Secession, and come into line with the doctrines so pertinaciously spread in public and in private by Captain Mahan. Until the 1880's the United States felt no need or impulse to join in the expensive competition in ironclads which obsessed the powers of Europe. Absence of overseas interests, reliance on the isolating power of distance, obsession with internal affairs, all contributed to arrest American naval development. Until 1883 the United States navy consisted of wooden vessels; even the three steel ships laid down that year were commerce-raiding cruisers carrying full rig. That so cautious a policy was inadequate even for the barest needs of defence became obvious when the republics of South America began to acquire modern vessels from European shipyards which could blow the whole United States fleet out of the water. The Americans began to experiment cautiously with battleship construction; and in 1889 the Secretary of the Navy, Benjamin F. Tracy, boldly set a new course. The defence of American coasts, he declared in his Annual Report of that year, could be undertaken only by vessels capable of defeating the enemy on the high seas. 'To meet the attack of ironclads, ironclads are indispensable', he claimed. 'The country needs a navy that will exempt it from war, but the only navy that will accomplish this is a navy that can wage war.' Such a force he estimated at twenty battleships and forty modern cruisers. The demand was too extreme for Congress, and Tracy got only three battleships. But it was a beginning. Next year *The Influence of Sea Power* was published, and the arguments which had already won over the Navy Department quickly converted the industrialists who would receive the government contracts, the businessmen opening up markets in the Far East, and a general public becoming conscious of America's manifest destiny as a great power. Tracy's successor, Hilary Herbert, laid it down that the navy must be kept 'in such a condition of efficiency as to give weight and power to whatever policy it may be thought wise on the part of our government to assume'. That policy could not be purely defensive. The navy must 'afford unquestionable protection to our citizens in foreign lands, render efficient aid to our diplomacy, and maintain under all circumstances our national honour'. Under such pressure Congressional hesitancy evaporated. The conflict with Spain, brief as it was, provided the final incentive. In 1898 the United States navy possessed five battleships; in 1901, when Theodore Roosevelt entered the White House, it had a total, afloat or building, of seventeen.

A powerful fleet and a thriving commerce were two elements in Mahan's trinity. Overseas bases was the third; and Mahan, as we have seen, turned the attention of his countrymen to two areas where such bases should be established: the Caribbean, to guard Atlantic commerce, and the Pacific, to protect the growing intercourse with China and Japan; and, by natural progression, to the isthmus between the two seas—a passage through would not only increase the potentialities of American commerce, but would ease the difficulty of protecting it. Now in both of these areas the American eye encountered the spectacle of a European power in decay, slothfully misgoverning the last relics of a once great empire. The Cuban revolt against Spanish rule was a matter almost of domestic concern to the United States, and the mysterious destruction of U.S.S. *Maine* in Havana harbour in February 1898 only provided the occasion for a conflict into which the United States government was swept by an overwhelming clamour of public opinion. The Americans could hardly have found a better adversary on whom to cut their teeth. The Spanish navy had one battleship to the United States' five; its vessels were dilapidated and its crews untrained. Dewey annihilated the Pacific fleet at Manila on

1 May, Sampson the Atlantic fleet at Santiago on 3 July, and the capture of the Philippines and Cuba, their garrisons isolated from their homeland and their native populations in revolt, followed as a matter of course. Mahan's doctrines of sea-power seemed most triumphantly justified.

But the Spanish-American War was not entirely a matter of naval conflict. A landing in Cuba was planned and, after a fashion, executed, and the problems of organisation and fighting which this involved made it clear to the Americans, as similar problems in the Boer War were to make it clear to the British a year later, that if conflicts were to be pressed through to final victory sea-power by itself was not enough. In 1898 the United States army was as ill-equipped to wage war as the navy had been ten years before. Its 28,000 men were scattered throughout the land in small detachments which never came together for training. The National Guard provided another 114,000 men, and guarded its independence from the regular army with a jealousy which reacted sadly on its military effectiveness. Volunteers brought the total number of men which the war department had to administer to 225,000, and its complete inability to feed, clothe, or house them adequately caused even greater public concern than did the failure of the forces which did land in Cuba to force the Spanish lines before Santiago. In July 1899 Elihu Root became Secretary of War, with the task of straightening out the confusion and ensuring that it did not recur; and in his first Annual Report he sketched out the lines on which the army must be reorganised. 28,000 men would no longer suffice for America's new colonial responsibilities. Her peacetime strength must be increased to 100,000, and all steps must be taken to render this force capable of immediate expansion in time of war. Root demanded for the United States all the military institutions now so long familiar in Europe: an expanded War Department, a General Staff, a National War College, and a system of trained reserves. It was a programme popular neither with the old regular army which it was to transform nor with the legislature which was to pay the bill; but during the first years of the new century, the American people gradually reconciled themselves to its necessity. America, no less than the powers of Europe, had to transform itself into a Nation in Arms.

So also had the emerging Asiatic power of Japan. Imitation of western military and naval patterns was a major element in the process by which the Japanese, awakened from their isolation, were fitting themselves to compete as equals with the states of Europe. In 1866 the Sho-gun had invited a military mission from France and a naval mission from Britain to lay the foundations of the new Japanese armed forces. The work of these missions was interrupted by the rebellion which established the personal authority of the emperor; but in 1872 they returned, and found their pupils adaptable and industrious. In 1875 the emperor destroyed the *samurai* monopoly of arms with a proclamation which aligned Japan with the powers of Europe in its adoption of universal military service. 'In future', he declared, 'I wish the army to be the entire nation.' Ten years later the French military mission was followed by one from the German empire, and Japanese military training and organisation became yet more closely modelled on the German pattern. Three-year compulsory service with the colours and four with the reserve; a territorial force modelled on the *Landwehr*; territorial military districts; one-year volunteers; all were established or confirmed by the legislation of 1889.

Neither the Sino-Japanese War of 1894 nor the punitive expedition of 1900 in which the Japanese collaborated with the western powers gave the world more than a foretaste of the military efficiency which was to prove so devastating in 1904–5 in the war with Russia. But 1894 gave the Japanese navy a greater opportunity to show how much it had imbibed from its British tutors. In development it had lagged far behind the army. In 1894 it still possessed only three armoured vessels, twenty-year-old ironclads of totally obsolete pattern, and its main strength lay in three unarmoured cruisers mounting heavy battleship guns. But in seamanship, training and gunnery the Japanese showed themselves infinitely superior to their more powerfully equipped rivals, and at the battle of the Yalu they won that command of the sea which alone made a victory on the mainland possible. Thereafter the Japanese government worked hard to strengthen a force whose usefulness had been so signally proved. In 1895 a building programme was set on foot which involved the construction of four 15,000 ton battleships and four 7500 ton armoured cruisers—one of the former and two of the latter to be built in Japan itself, in the dockyards whose expansion and re-equipment constituted a major part of the new programme. In 1904 the Japanese navy was to meet the Russians with six first-class battleships and eight armoured cruisers, and establish a supremacy in Pacific waters which was to have profound effects on the balance of power.

According to Bloch's estimate in his book *La Guerre Moderne* (IV, 280) the total expenditure on defence of the principal European powers increased between 1874 and 1896 by slightly over 50 per cent. The expenditure of the German empire during this period rose by 79 per cent, and that of Russia by 75 per cent, while Britain, France and Austria-Hungary followed with 47 per cent, 43 per cent and 21 per cent respectively. For the states of western Europe the burden was not crippling: their economies were expanding and great interests of labour as well as of capital were vested in the thriving shipyards and in the great, sometimes interlocking, concerns of Armstrong, Schneider, Skoda and Krupp. But Russia was less able to sustain the burden. Between 1883 and 1897 Russian military expenditure rose from 201,564,621 roubles to 284,379,994 —this excluding the considerable cost of strategic railways; and the whole sum had to be found out of a state budget which totalled only 1414 million roubles. There can be little doubt that the strain of keeping up in an armaments race which it was ill able to afford was a powerful, if not the decisive factor in impelling the imperial Russian government in August 1898 to propose that the powers should confer on 'the most effective means of ensuring to all peoples the benefits of a real and durable peace and, above all, of putting an end to the progressive development of the present armaments'.

The imperial circular was received by the powers with much the same sceptical politeness as had been shown towards the apocalyptic suggestions which came from the same quarter after the Napoleonic wars; but all the states invited—which included Luxembourg, Montenegro and Siam in addition to the powers diplomatically represented at St Petersburg—sent representatives to the conference which opened at the Hague on 18 May 1899. So far as disarmament was concerned the conference was a failure. The Russian proposals included a five-year moratorium on military budgets and the size of peacetime armies, and a restriction on the adoption of explosives more powerful or armaments more effective than those at present in use. These proposals were almost unanimously rejected. The disarmament subcommittee reported 'that it would be very difficult to fix, even for a period of five years, the number of effectives, without regulating at the same time other elements of national defence; [and] it would be no less difficult to regulate by international agreement the elements of this defence, organised in every country upon a different principle'. As to the restriction on further inventions, the representative of the United States flatly declared that his government 'did not consider limitations in regard to the use of military inventions to be conducive to the peace of the world'. Eventually the conference voted only three restrictions on armaments. One was on the 'throwing of projectiles from balloons'—for five years only, since by the end of that period some method of discriminate bombing might have been devised; and the others were on the use of soft-nosed bullets and asphyxiating gases—both voted over the protests of the United States and Great Britain.

Yet in two respects the achievements of the Hague Conference were considerable. First, it took two further steps in the direction of the humanising of war which would do much to soften the terrible struggles of the twentieth century. The Geneva Convention of 1864, with its provisions for neutralising medical personnel and establishments and for ensuring impartial attention to all wounded, was extended to naval warfare, and all powers which had not yet signed the Convention now did so. At the same time the Declaration Concerning the Laws and Customs of War which had been drawn up at the Brussels Conference in 1874 was overhauled and embodied in a new Convention defining the status of belligerents, the correct treatment of spies and prisoners of war, the limitations to be observed by armies conducting operations or occupying hostile territory, and the protocol to be observed for truces and armistices. Secondly, the powers represented, recognising that arbitration was 'the most efficacious and at the same time the most equitable' manner of settling international differences of a juridical character, undertook to organise a permanent Court of Arbitration, with the necessary secretariat, to sit at The Hague. Like later and more ambitious attempts at the creation of international organisations, the Hague Court could only provide machinery for powers with sufficient goodwill and self-restraint to use it; and the restraints enjoined by the Hague Convention could have no sanction save the humanity and the enlightened self-interest of the belligerent powers. These were slender threads to bind powerful sovereign states fighting for their survival with increasingly destructive implements of war.

CHAPTER IX

POLITICAL AND SOCIAL DEVELOPMENTS IN EUROPE

ABOUT the year 1870 Europe entered upon a new phase in its history with the final achievement of the nation-state in Germany and Italy. The emergence of two nation-states in central Europe marked the sole great change within the European system of states during the century between the Congress of Vienna and the first World War. It was a change that transformed the system without disrupting it. Two predominant features of the nineteenth century, liberal constitutionalism and the principle of nationality, characterised this event; the third dynamic of the age, socialism, did not make its advent till the revolt of the Commune in 1871.

In the 1870's liberalism was at the zenith of its historical course. In most of the countries of Europe it had brought into existence written constitutions with parliaments, a widening franchise, and constitutional guarantees of personal freedom. The last relics of legal inequality and bondage were removed by the Revolution of 1848 and Russia's abolition of serfdom in 1861. Equality before the law and personal freedom had practically everywhere become principles in law, despite strong opposition from both the feudal aristocracy and the bourgeoisie. Liberalism had thus achieved its civil programme; but the liberals' constitutional aims, an executive controlled by parliament and a legislature with unlimited powers, had been realised only partially and in differing degrees in the various countries. From about the mid-1870's the liberal parties, hitherto drawn from notabilities in the middle classes, became more and more involved in difficulties that raised problems of form and organisation. Towards the close of the century the social problem of the working class brought liberalism everywhere face to face with the task of translating legal freedom into real freedom within the social pattern. This seemed impossible without offending such radical liberal principles as the rejection of state interference in the social or economic field; thus social liberalism could never launch out whole-heartedly.

The principle of nationality achieved its greatest triumph of the century in Germany and Italy, culminating in the foundation of states by Bismarck and Cavour; yet these were the very states which raised a bulwark against any further upsurge of nationalism. It is true that in Italy this bulwark was soon breached by the impetus of irredentism, but the foundation of the German empire by Bismarck long served to halt the advance of nationalism, in particular in the south-east, in Austria. For the time being in the areas of mixed nationality in eastern Europe the movement towards the nation-state gained ground only in European Turkey, where by the close of the century Bulgaria and Roumania had achieved autonomy.

The conservative forces and parties sought to hold their ground in the trial of strength with the thrusting forces of the age, in particular with democratic and national ideas; in England the Conservative party developed along the lines of 'democratic Toryism', and in Prussia and Germany it took over the representation of agrarian interests. Almost everywhere constitutional democracy with its parliamentary groupings was still compatible with influential monarchical institutions, as it was in Great Britain. In Spain after the Carlist wars the monarchy again (in 1875) overcame the republic; the German empire and Italy, the new nation-states of central Europe, were united and held together by strong monarchies; and within the Turkish empire the new states of Bulgaria and Roumania were headed by monarchs. In France the republican form of government set up after the collapse of the Second Empire survived, though even here there were repeated attempts to restore the monarchy. In Austria-Hungary and in Russia, with their powerful monarchical systems, the process of democratisation had for various reasons made the least headway. In Germany, where the imperial authority set up in 1871 was subject to federal rather than parliamentary restraint, an evolution towards 'personal rule' by the emperor began after 1890, though this was never ratified in the constitution. At the close of the century Europe was still predominantly monarchical; and it was obvious in almost every European state except France and republican Switzerland on the one hand and Russia on the other that the middle classes, at any rate for the time being, preferred monarchical to republican forms of government.

At the same time, although foreign treaties, as for instance the Triple Alliance between the German empire, Austria-Hungary and Italy, were still sometimes concluded with the aim of strengthening the principle of monarchy, monarchism had lost all autonomous historical force and now existed only in conjunction with more powerful contemporary influences such as constitutionalism, giving these indeed in many cases effective support but at the same time being limited and repressed by them. The industrial workers' associations and their political organisations, moreover, almost all supported the principle of a democratic republic; and it was mainly they who brought about the fall of the great monarchies in central and eastern Europe at the end of the first World War. The alliance between the monarchy and the working class, the social kingship dreamed of by many and proclaimed particularly in Germany by writers from Lorenz Stein to Friedrich Naumann, never became a reality anywhere.

In the three decades from the Franco-Prussian War to the turn of the century the acute tension between the monarchy and the middle classes that had occupied the states of Europe during the first half of the century was relaxed, except in the case of Russia. What was left of the revolutionary tradition passed to the working-class movement; but this still lacked the ideological and political momentum to launch a decisive attack. This explains why the decades between the revolt of the Commune in Paris and the first Russian revolution in 1905 form the longest period in the century up to the first World War without any revolutionary upheaval.

These decades also saw an unprecedented extension and increase in the power of the state both within and beyond its frontiers, a power growing alive to the resources and potentialities of technical science and the industrial system. The social community mobilised by the industrial revolution became a dynamic force whose impetus overran every state frontier; increase in population, its concentration, its movements, occurred in all states and were only partially under the control of the states. And further, the urge felt by this mobilised community seized the states themselves; they flooded out beyond Europe and rounded off centuries of discovery and colonisation abroad with a breathless surge of political expansion. The imperialism that characterised the new epoch was simply the outlet for internal changes and transformations, the political aspect, one might say, of the process by which the industrial revolution which had started in Europe went on to embrace the whole world.

The continuous increase in the population of Europe forms the background to every nineteenth-century political and social development; and this increase slightly exceeded the growth of population in the world as a whole, where the proportion of Europeans rose from 22·4 per cent about 1800 to 25·9 per cent about 1900. The population of Europe increased from roughly 187 millions in about 1800 to 266 millions by 1850 and 401 millions by 1900; in other words it more than doubled itself within a century. This curve of growth no longer represented an increase in the number of births, for in almost every European country this had passed its peak by 1890 and in certain countries, for instance in France and in Norway and Sweden, its gradual decrease had been going on much longer.[1]

[1] The curve of live births per thousand of population reached its zenith as follows:

1861–70	England and Wales	35·2
	Belgium	31·6
	The Netherlands	35·3
	Russia	50·0
1871–80	The German empire	39·1
	Austria	41·8
	Scotland	35·1
	Ireland	30·2
	Denmark	34·0
1881–90	Hungary	44·0
	Italy	37·8

Bulgaria and Roumania alone reached their zenith at a later date. The figures for European Russia are not entirely reliable, but despite a higher actual peak they reveal a slow decline from the 1860's. (From J. Conrad's *Grundriss zum Studium der politischen Ökonomie*, 1923.)

The increase arose mainly as a result of the decline in the death-rate; so the maximum excess of births over deaths usually occurred later than the highest birth-rate figures. (The clearest examples here were Germany with its excess of 14·4 per 1000 in the yearly average for 1901–5, Italy with 12·0 for 1903–13, and Austria-Hungary with 11·2 for 1901–5.)

The population of the European states increased at different rates in the last three decades of the century. France showed the least change (in 1872, 36·1 millions; in 1901, 38·7 millions); Great Britain and Ireland rose from 31·5 millions (1871) to 41·5 millions (1901), Germany from 40·8 millions to 56·7 millions (1870–1900), Italy from 26·8 millions (1871) to 32·5 millions (1901), Austria-Hungary from 35·9 millions (1869) to 45·4 millions (1900). But, as these figures show, no important shift was established in the balance between any one European power and another; and besides they were seeking compensation overseas. Only European Russia's increase (72·2 millions in 1867 to 115·9 millions in 1897) fore-shadowed a significant shift, in favour of the Slav peoples.

But the whole great process of increase in population should be looked at not so much from the state or national point of view as in the light of the expansion of industry in Europe which was then taking place. The surplus among the peoples of Europe now crowded together in the great industrial regions, above all in the lower Rhine area and on both sides of the English Channel. The Ruhr district outstripped others at this time in its growth, but the older industrial areas, such as the English Midlands, Saxony, the Bohemian frontier districts, shared in the upsurge, though their sharpest percentage rise in population came before 1870. After that date the process of urbanisation gathered speed everywhere and it determined the future patterns of living and the framework of the European industrial community. The larger the towns the greater their increase; in Germany there were eight cities of over 100,000 inhabitants in 1871; in 1900 there were thirty-three. For the rural population on the other hand the percentage remained static or even decreased. This tendency was most clearly seen in England after 1870. Eastern Germany, the region where the greatest increase in rural population had followed Freiherr von Stein's emancipation of the peasants, showed a check from the mid-1880's onwards. Only in European Russia, affected by the emancipation of the serfs in 1861, and in south-eastern Europe, did the rural population now begin to show its greatest increase.

The growing concentrations of industrial population were chiefly the result of migratory movements with a constantly widening radius. The industrial cities thus began by filling up the nearer and farther rural fringe; the influx of settlers from eastern Germany into the Ruhr district represented a more distant migration forming a considerable element—in some places virtually the essential one—in the growth of the industrial population. Special conditions have always governed the confluence of these millions into the capitals of Europe; one can seldom define the areas drawn upon, though this is possible for instance for Berlin.

This movement of the masses during the final decades of industrial expansion left the national framework of the European community in the main unaltered. Only at isolated points did the migrations set in motion by the economic revolution cross the European state frontiers. The first instance was France, where the increase in population came earliest to a halt and a considerable influx, mainly from Italy, can be noted; and Polish agricultural labourers, at first mainly on seasonal work, penetrated eastern Germany. But emigration overseas from most countries of Europe during the last thirty years of the nineteenth century was still considerably strengthening and extending the white man's area of settlement in the world, in particular in North America. Between 1871 and 1900 the emigration from Europe to the United States reached the figure of 10·5 millions, the proportions among the nations of Europe differing widely at different times (see ch. xxiv for details). As many again went to other overseas areas. The motives for this emigration were seldom political or religious as they had been in the first half of the century, except perhaps in the large states of eastern Europe and in Ireland; they were chiefly economic and social. But emigration was also an indication of the greater ease of transport and of the progressive growth of the world into one economic whole; within Europe national differences have never been abandoned, but in the new lands national barriers fell more easily. The new community in the United States grew to be as much a melting-pot of the nations as of the orders and classes.

The emigration from Europe was a sign that economic and technical development there was not keeping pace with the growth in population. And yet, especially in the last three decades of the century, industrialisation made enormous strides, and the expansion of industrial methods of production over all the countries of Europe and then over the areas of settlement in North America, the increased production of commodities, the improvement of transport and the growing exchange of merchandise gradually brought into being a universal system, delicately harmonised and reacting extremely sensitively to agitation at any point, a comprehensive economic system that was directed technically, financially and politically by Europe and that was the economic counterpart to developments in world politics. Liberal economists during the middle years of the century had seen the world economy that was now beginning to take definite shape as an organic system that would put one uniform community in the place of the traditional pluralism of nations and states. International free trade as proclaimed in that model agreement of economic liberalism, the Cobden Treaty of 1860 between England and France, was to bring about the threefold harmony of world trade, world unity and world peace. But events moved in other directions; the world economic crisis of 1873, whose effects were still felt up to the mid-1890's, shook the naïve belief in continuous progress, and free trade, which had been adopted by practically every state but the United States and Russia, was ending. Between the late 1870's and the 1890's most of the countries of Europe went over to protection except Great Britain, the Netherlands, Denmark and Turkey, which for different reasons kept to free trade. This predominance of protectionism in economic matters was a symptom of the intensification of state control that marked this period and was to take other forms, for instance, state intervention in the socio-political field and colonial imperialism. International commerce changed into an economic struggle between rival competing states, the momentum behind actions governing trade and economics shifted indirectly to the political field, and this was overshadowed by the profound hostility felt by the powers, urged on by their own economic interests, for each other.

The great convulsions that changed central Europe by the formation of the Kingdom of Italy and the German empire did not completely upset the order set up in 1815; they simply modified its structure at certain important points. The idea of the nation-state had prevailed in those regions where the Congress of Vienna had wished to prevent its appearance; but after 1870 it seemed essential that the progress of the nation-state idea should be limited to what had been achieved by the wars that had set up the German and Italian nation-states. From 1882 onwards Italian irredentism was held in check by the alliance between Austria-Hungary and Germany, and did not develop fully. Bismarck described the German empire he had brought into being as 'satiated', and held aloof from any sort of national irredentism, even from any intervention on the part of the empire in favour of the German groups in Austria and Russia's Baltic provinces. And Bismarck's successors held to this course; the members of the pan-German (*alldeutsche*) organisations formed after 1890 belonged to an Opposition that was hostile to official German policy, and their influence on it was negligible.

In the whole of eastern Europe the internal problem facing the great empires remained that of nationality; and this affected their policy towards one another. In Russia the influence of a nationalism nourished on pan-Slav ideas increased, and it helped to weaken those who looked in supranational and federal directions, and to transform the country into a nation-state comprising Great Russia. In the Baltic provinces (Alexander III on his accession in 1881 had been the first tsar not to ratify their traditional privileges) the 1880's were a period of intensified russianisation, especially in the schools. The close of the century witnessed the crippling of the Grand-Duchy of Finland's autonomous constitution. After the Polish revolt of 1863 Russia's portion of Poland had lost the last remnants of independence and now also felt the increasing weight of a policy of russianisation. In Germany the position of the Poles and Danes, those non-German minorities in the east and north, was radically altered after the founding of the German empire in 1871; for the state had then in theory accepted the principle of the German nation and in practice had adapted itself to it. The German empire and Austria agreed in 1878 to waive Article V of the Prague Treaty of 1866 which would have given the inhabitants of northern Schleswig a free plebiscite on union with Denmark. The attempt of the Magyars, in control in Hungary, to create a Magyar nation-state out of the eastern half of the Habsburg Dual Monarchy had effects still felt in much later years. While these events were taking place Gladstone was trying in vain to introduce his Home Rule Bill into parliament, a bill to end the subjection of the Irish people and to give them self-government.

During this period the governments of the great powers decided almost without exception in favour of the national majorities from which they drew their support and which they tried to render as homogeneous as possible in language and national feeling. In the political system of the classic nation-state there was scarcely room for the privileges of minorities. It was only in Turkey, a feeble and decadent state, that the nations continued to move towards autonomy and new states, as for instance Roumania (1878) and Bulgaria (1878, 1887), came into being. In the case of Bulgaria it took only a few years for a national movement to annul (in 1887) the decision taken by the Berlin Congress to divide the country into two states in the interests of the balance of power. The movement towards national independence was evident in northern Europe also, where it grew increasingly obvious that the union of Sweden with Norway could not last. Norway eventually dissolved it in 1905. And in states of multinational structure, for instance in the Cis-leithan half of the Dual Monarchy of Austria-Hungary, the national problem came to affect both organisation and constitution. After 1870 more than one attempt was made to relax the centralisation introduced by Joseph II and based on the dominance of the Austro-Germanic element, and to place the nations and languages of Bohemia and Moravia, those centres of national contention, on an equal footing. These attempts touched the traditional hegemony of the Austro-Germans on a sensitive spot (see the efforts of the Hohenwarth Ministry in 1871 to adjust German–Czech differences, and Badeni's Languages Decree of 1897). While within this region it was possible only at one or two points to dull the keen edge of nationalist antagonism, as in the Moravian settlement of 1905, Switzerland kept its position outside the storm-zone of national strife. The constitutional reform of 1874 ratified the federal system of government which showed itself the most effective instrument for neutralising multi-lingual nationalism.

The nation-state, now predominant in Europe, took on very different forms. France, where the great Revolution had destroyed the old historic provinces, still held even under the Third Republic to a type of centralisation. There were no links connecting the centralised administrative and political organisation with the very vigorous political life of the local regions, in particular of the constituencies. Italy's national monarchy followed this French pattern and emulated France and Belgium in creating a centralised administration with new provinces which obliterated the frontiers of the former Italian states. Such a system was the outcome of a national revolutionary uprising against the existence of separate states controlled by foreign dynasties; but it was quite out of touch both with the rich historical and cultural inheritance of Italy's different provinces and with their varied economic and social structure; and it met, particularly in the south, with violent opposition. Despite criticism levelled at the 'Piedmontism' of the new administration of Italy, the frequent demands for decentralisation, for self-government in the provinces, went unsatisfied. The German nation-state of 1871, unlike that of Italy, was founded as a federation of monarchies, a league of sovereigns and free cities. The constitution firmly established Prussian hegemony, though mingling it in its own way with federal and centralising traits. Towards the end of Bismarck's term of power, as the author of the Constitution came more and more into conflict with the Reichstag, he considered dissolving the alliance of 1870–1 and organising a *coup d'état* to bring a new one into being, with the national-democratic institution of the Reichstag weakened or even eliminated. After Bismarck's fall in 1890 came the 'personal rule' of the emperor; this had no foundation in the Constitution, but it undoubtedly expanded the imperial dignity into a far more impressive symbol of national unity than anything provided for at the creation of the empire.

Great Britain differed from the countries of the Continent in that the keynote of its constitution was neither centralisation nor federal alliance but union; its traditional component countries were retained by, were fused in, the unity of the joint state and its institutions, in particular its parliament. In Catholic Ireland alone this system was always felt to be one of oppression, of force, and was resisted; for there the issues were national and not merely constitutional. When the first efforts towards Home Rule for Ireland were made in 1886 and 1893, they were defeated by an intense and violent opposition from many sources. But the significance of the Irish Question went far beyond the struggle for Home Rule and lies in the conception of self-government which was then modifying the whole British empire. For during the age of imperialism the greatest administrative and constitutional problems no longer concerned the development of the nation-states but the structure of the great imperial complexes.

At this stage colonial expansion everywhere clearly took place under the aegis of the state and led to some kind of official annexation, though sometimes this was no more than a protective superstructure on top of the existing local or native authority. The nation-states of Europe thus expanded into organs of world-wide dominion at a time when conceptions of policy appropriate to a nation-state still governed their constitution and administration. The classic example here is the British empire, which had gained such a start in colonial expansion that none of the other powers was able to draw level with it. British imperialism was now directing its energies chiefly towards Africa; it was in Africa that it developed great schemes of expansion and control and a political programme; it was also in Africa that it became most involved (from the intervention in Egypt in 1882 to the Boer War) in both political and military problems. But if this last great phase of expansion undoubtedly lent urgency to the problem of organising a world-empire which, in Seeley's well-known phrase, had originated 'in a fit of absentmindedness', two of the fundamental ideas which arose sprang from the political tradition of the mother-country. These were the idea of responsible self-government and the notion of trusteeship. The position of the great settlement areas in the empire— Canada, Australia, New Zealand and South Africa—was radically transformed by the extension of self-government. In the other types of colony— the old Crown colonies, the Malay states, Cyprus and various regions in Africa—the conception of trusteeship on behalf of the native peoples took on a new significance. In theory, even if theory was not always fully in harmony with the somewhat harsher realities, it now affirmed rather than questioned the principle of colonial sovereignty. Stress was similarly laid on India's existence as a separate political unit within the empire when Disraeli conferred on the Queen in 1876 the title of 'Empress of India'.

With the British empire, as with the smaller Habsburg empire on the Continent, the increasing organisation of its member-units at once raised the question of the organisation of the empire as a whole. This is where a third idea, that of federation, became an active force. This idea could not be borrowed from the modern constitutional structure of the United Kingdom with its centre in a mother-country; it clearly went back to the United States pattern which had influenced the federally based constitutions of the Dominions. The United States, too, disproved the old prejudice that self-government must necessarily lead to the dispersion of an empire's component parts. Disraeli had first declared this to be an error in his famous Crystal Palace speech of 1872. From Seeley onwards the view gained ground that federation is rather a form of expansion. The Imperial Federation League, founded in 1884, advocated federation for the empire. But the dream of reorganisation as a grouping of federated states was soon at an end, for the two colonial conferences of 1887 and 1897 failed to reach agreement on this. The Dominions did not support Joseph Chamberlain when as colonial secretary he termed the Federal Council 'our ultimate ideal'. The institution of imperial conferences and a rudimentary military and economic organisation were the sole results. The federal idea, evolved in continental empires in America and Europe, could not dogmatically be applied to anything of so totally different a structure as the British empire. Its unity has always depended on a loose attachment and not on a formal constitution.

Among the European continental powers colonial expansion did not alter the structure of the entire state to anything like the degree that was the case with Great Britain. With Italy and the German empire the colonial acquisitions were in any case not extensive enough to be of great importance. The bold colonial aspirations of Italy's Crispi era reached their climax in the Treaty of Ucciali (1889) and in the establishment of a protectorate over the Negus's empire, but collapsed with the defeat at Adowa in Ethiopia (1896). The German empire's colonial policy, launched in 1884 under Bismarck, at first aimed neither at direct imperial colonies nor at a colonial empire but exclusively at 'protected' regions to be governed by trading companies. This system proved a failure everywhere, and most clearly so in East Africa (1888) and in New Guinea (1898), and by the Act of 1900 the 'protected' regions came under the direct suzerainty of the empire, that is, the emperor, as up till then the imperial territory of Alsace-Lorraine alone had been. In Germany's case colonial expansion had helped to strengthen the central power in the mother-country, and this was characteristic of most of the continental states of Europe. The most interesting example here is that of France. The French colonial regime which during the last quarter of the nineteenth century controlled a large colonial empire (1875–89, French Equatorial Africa; 1885–96, Madagascar; 1881, Tunis; 1883–4, Tongking and Annam) was based entirely on the centralisation also prevalent in France itself, and constituted simply an offshoot of the French state. The French colonial administration, up till 1889 a branch of the Ministry of Naval Affairs and later transferred to the Ministry of Commerce, did not acquire its own department in the shape of a Ministry for the Colonies till 1894; its aim from the beginning was to make the colonies, though in a geographical sense and in standards of living far removed from one another, into 'une masse homogène soumise à un régime uniforme'. The acquisition of many new colonial territories with no cultural or historical link with France placed limits to this aim, and towards the turn of the century the Act of 13 April 1900 led to some decentralisation in colonial administration. Despite influences derived from the English colonial system, the principles of colonial self-government were, however, never applied anywhere; likewise in the protectorates, the French administration was far more in evidence than that of the British in theirs.

On the whole, the political structure of the continental states of Europe was altered very little by colonial imperialism. The disintegration of Europe, which the stressing of nationalism had brought and was still bringing about, was helped rather than hindered by their indulgence in nationalist imperialist enterprises. But they did not always and everywhere meet as competitors and rivals in the colonial territories; to a certain degree the era of colonialism increased the general awareness of the need to base inter-state relations on standards of international law and to fix them in established institutions. Vast new areas came not merely under the suzerainty of European powers, but also under the international law evolved in Europe. A strange result of a combination on the one side of expediency on the part of European powers and on the other of both humanitarian and economic motives was the founding of the independent Congo State under Leopold II of Belgium and his *Association internationale africaine*, recognised by the Berlin Congo Conference of 1884/5. The Congo Act of 1885 declared the furthering of trade and civilisation in central Africa to be the basic aim of the foundation of the Congo State and of the signatories to it. It proclaimed complete freedom of commerce, prohibited the slave trade, and established the neutrality of the Congo Basin. Here Belgium's own neutral position in Europe was mirrored in the African continent, and here too it obstructed the rivalry between the larger powers. The powers announced in the Act that the bringing of civilisation to underdeveloped areas as a kind of secular missionary task was the purpose of colonisation, though in the case of the Congo state this programme was not fully carried through.

The tension between self-interest and co-operation in the policies of the states was not limited to colonial affairs; it pervaded all inter-state relations during the era of imperialism, which with its increasing ease and speed of communication brought states nearer to each other at the same time as their growing national consciousness estranged them. By the end of the nineteenth century every vestige of the former limitation of state sovereignty, every memory of solidarity among the states of Europe, had been obliterated. The great congresses like that in Berlin in 1878 or the Congo Conference of 1884/5 were now the only sign that the community of states and not merely its isolated members was still in existence. And yet this community now expanded beyond Europe, and began to spread over the whole world. The Congo Conference, in which the United States of America took part, most clearly showed this. Nor were congresses convened *ad hoc* any longer adequate to consolidate political and economic links and to bring the nations into a closer unity in all branches of technical and commercial intercourse. To meet the need new forms of co-operation emerged; administrative unions and agreements between states, for specific purposes, increased in every decade from 1870 onwards—from twenty in 1870–80, to thirty-one in 1880–90, sixty-one in 1890–1900, 108 in 1900–4. A network of international organisations and inter-state treaties grew up, aimed at matching the political and individual nationalism of each state with a kind of technical and legal internationalism. This sought to extend as far as possible the legal security created within the individual states and the effective range of technical achievement to the whole community of states. So these specific conventions in the first place decided questions of traffic and communication, uniform standards, the exchange of goods and ideas. For instance the Berne Treaty of 1874 and the World Postal Treaty of 1878 brought the World Postal Union into being, and in 1875 the Weights and Measures Union with the *Bureau international des Poids et Mesures* in St. Cloud were set up to control the metric system. In 1886 there followed the Berne Convention, signed by ten states for the protection of works of literature and art, and ten years later the Private International Law Agreement, concerned mainly with defining the forms of legal aid in inter-state relations.

What had been applied to certain regions and for special purposes began to be attempted for the political intercourse between states, for the settlement of the great vital questions of war and peace. This was first tried at the Hague peace conferences of 1899 and 1907. True, several tactical considerations affected the convening of these conferences, which was initiated by the tsar; but this fact did not obscure the impression that the conferences, where three continents were represented, were making a determined move to set up standards of justice above the individual states in the effort to arrest the decay of inter-state solidarity. The hope that the end of all war would result from a fully developed and firmly established international law was not to be realised; but acknowledged legal bounds were being set to inter-state relations in war and peace during a period when state sovereignty was making greatly increased claims and great wars could work unparalleled destruction. The Brussels Declaration of 1874 was followed by a convention on the laws and customs of war on land, and this in the form it acquired at the Hague Conference of 1907, the Hague Regulations governing War on Land, is still considered valid. It has a definite code for the different branches of international military law (belligerents, the rights of armies of occupation, the position of prisoners of war, are all defined). The idea of an international court of arbitration, further developed after the first World War, took shape with the setting up of a *Cour permanente d'arbitrage* at the Hague. This was not at this stage a permanent court of justice but an institute to facilitate the formation of tribunals to arbitrate in special cases. It represented the first tentative move to provide the community of nations with institutions which would uphold its principles of justice.

Despite all the estrangement in foreign policy, moreover, the individual state systems and the constitutions of the states were drawing closer to one another. There were still profound differences of historical and national origin between the political and social structures, and these differences were later to break through once more in the first World War; but the age as a whole tended towards greater uniformity of constitutional patterns and social systems. In particular, the democratic principle made headway in various forms; powerful forces still opposed it, especially in Russia, but everywhere these had been driven intellectually and politically on to the defensive.

Two problems clearly illustrate the constitutional development of these decades; these concern the types of parliamentary system and the progressive extension of the franchise. By now all the states except Russia possessed parliaments varying in importance and scope. But among the great powers England and France alone had a genuinely parliamentary system of government; and especially in these two countries the last decades of the nineteenth century were a period of significant change and development. In England decisive steps were taken to realise by gradual reform the ideal of a universal franchise. The Reform Acts of 1867 and 1868 had considerably widened the franchise in the towns and had admitted a large proportion of the workers to it; and by the Third Reform Bill of 1884 the Gladstone ministry brought representation in the country districts into line with that in the towns. The Redistribution Act of 1885 brought uniformity to the electoral districts and introduced the principle by which each constituency returned one member only. Not only did these reforms almost double the electorate; they entailed very considerable consequences for the entire structure of the constitution, where the principle underlying the plebiscite now became clearly established. Gladstone's famous Midlothian campaign (1879–80) showed an important swing towards this appeal to the masses of the electorate, a democratisation in even the conduct of politics, now finally breaking with aristocratic tradition. The political parties joined in this process of democratisation; this was the period when they created nation-wide organisations and transformed themselves into democratic mass-organisations. And this in turn affected the functioning of the parliamentary system; it was no longer the practice for ministers when defeated in the election to resign without first meeting parliament again. This is what Disraeli did in December 1868 and in April 1880, and Gladstone in 1874; but Salisbury in the summer of 1892 waited until after his defeat in parliament. On the other hand a defeat in the Lower House and the ensuing change of government now usually led to the proclamation of an election; this is how Salisbury acted as the new head of the government after the fall of Gladstone's second cabinet in 1885 and so did Gladstone himself when, on his defeat in the Lower House in the summer of 1886, he asked for an immediate election. The appeal to the electorate, although an integral part of the English constitutional system and fully in accord with the democratisation of the franchise, was in conflict with the undisputed right of the Crown to call in a government, in particular to nominate its head. But this right was decaying, except in unusual circumstances, with the rise of parties and of a recognised leader of the opposition, as was discovered in 1880 when Queen Victoria tried to prevent the appointment of Gladstone. The functioning of the classic English parliamentary system which developed during the last decades of the nineteenth century rests upon a balance between different elements in the constitution: the Crown, the parliament, the people as a democratic body of electors. But it also rests upon the classic form of the two-party system, even though this may at times be disturbed, as it was by the emergence of Parnell's Irish party in the elections late in 1885 or by the split of the Liberal party in the summer of 1886.

The constitutional system of France's Third Republic was radically unlike the English. Established in the three *Lois Constitutionelles* of 1875, it took on its final form in the main during the political crisis of 1877. The sovereignty of the people as an idea was realised in the supremacy of parliament, the *gouvernement d'Assemblée*, and there was nothing to counterbalance it, no provision for a plebiscite or for authoritative presidential control. Article V of the Constitution Act of 25 February 1875 foresaw the possibility that the president might order the dissolution of the Chamber but conditioned it by requiring the consent of the Senate. When in 1877 Marshal MacMahon as President of the Republic came into conflict with the Chamber and dissolved it, his action was in fact constitutional but it amounted to a *coup d'état*. After that occasion the President's right to dissolve the Chamber actually ceased to be used. As the Boulanger crisis only a few years later was to show, it was considered to have monarchical tendencies rather than to be a principle of plebiscitary democracy.

The absolute supremacy of parliament in the Third Republic was matched by a poorly developed and pluralistic system of political parties lacking any definite organisation, any 'party machine'. This led to cliques within parliament. Fluctuating majorities in the Chamber meant that coalitions of different groups became the only possible mode of government. This practice appeared to conform closely to the idea of a liberal representative constitution, to which however, given the marked independence of parliament, it was in fact radically opposed. The system nevertheless contained considerable general stability despite frequent changes of government; and it satisfied both the need for security and the ideals of freedom felt by the mass of Frenchmen, who recognised this oligarchic parliamentary regime as the best expression for them of the democratic principle. The strongly individualistic trait in French life operated against a more rigid party organisation and in favour of the authority of the *député* nominated and elected on local grounds.

Belgium was the European country whose constitution came nearest to the English type, while Italy's constitutional policy was subject to strange fluctuations. It was based on the 1848 *Statuto* of the Kingdom of Piedmont-

Sardinia which the process of unification had made applicable to the rest of the new Italian nation-state. The strong position occupied by the monarchy in the Piedmont constitution of 1848 in theory extended to the whole Italian nation-state, but it was weakened from the start because the House of Savoy lacked any roots outside its own dynastic territories. So the monarchy could not provide any effective counterbalance to parliament. Nor could any democratic expression of popular opinion; for the masses of the Italian people had not become politically conscious enough and, besides, the system of franchise in force till 1882 incorporated a relatively high tax qualification limiting the electorate to some 600,000. A reform of the franchise in 1882 considerably lowered this and reduced the existing educational qualification to the completion of obligatory elementary schooling. The electorate rose to over two million and came near to universal franchise, though the comparatively high figure of illiterates continued to restrict it. The monarchical and democratic elements being comparatively weak, the accent in Italian constitutional policy fell on the Chamber of Deputies. Its political structure had considerably changed since the foundation of the Italian nation-state; up till 1876 the Destra party, then in power, had had the Sinistra in opposition. The English two-party system seemed a possible model, but after the fall of the right-wing ministry in March 1876 it was soon apparent how feebly rooted this system was. Though a Sinistra government (Depretis, Crispi) now succeeded the Destra, it no longer represented a clear alternative opposition. The parties dissolved; Italy became the 'classic country of no parties'; parliamentary groupings and cliques with personal or regional ties, like those in France but more exclusive in tone, replaced clear-cut party conditions; the governments consisted of the personal followers of individual statesmen and no longer expressed any definite political trends. Anti-parliamentary criticism and ideology throve in this political climate. Political instability became a principle embodied in the expression *trasformismo*.

While Italy tended towards parliamentary supremacy after the French pattern, in the German empire, the other new nation-state, parliament was restricted to purely legislative duties, and the constitution did not guarantee it any direct influence on the government. By the complicated constitution built up between 1866 and 1871 by Otto von Bismarck the Reichstag, democratic and national in character and based on universal suffrage, was to offset the particularist attitude expected from the individual states and their rulers. It was designed to partner the other organ of the constitution, the *Bundesrat* or Federal Council, which was not an Upper House but a kind of collective government of the 'Allied Governments' (*Verbündete Regierungen*). The liberals failed at the inauguration of the constitution, and again in the 1878–9 crisis, to create imperial ministries responsible to the Reichstag; the Imperial Chancellor bore sole political responsibility for imperial policy and it was not essential for him to enjoy the confidence of the Reichstag. Every chancellor of the German empire owed his position to the confidence of the emperor and lost it when this was forfeited. Yet the Reichstag was not wholly without political influence over the dismissal of this responsible imperial statesman; this was true even of the chancellor-crisis of 1890 in which Bismarck fell. And a clearer case is that of Chancellor von Bülow's dismissal in 1909. Parliament might be said to be gradually assuming control in the imperial constitution.

The constitutional system in Germany might be called a constitutional monarchy of a federal type, and it had two weaknesses. The first of these was the lack of constitutional homogeneity as between the empire and its leading state, Prussia; though universal suffrage had been introduced in the empire, Prussia retained to the end her unequal three-class system. The second weakness was the disproportion between the extensive suffrage on which the Reichstag was based and the limited powers of that assembly. Universal suffrage favoured the rise of parties of the masses and from the late 1870's onwards these concentrated mostly on representing social interests; yet at the same time there was no means for those in command of these parties to succeed to public appointment. Only a few party leaders, the National-Liberal Johann Miquel, for instance, who rose to be Prussia's Finance Minister, managed to secure government posts. There was a great gulf fixed between the organised German party system and the state. The democratic element which the constitution contained was confined to a few spheres only; a strange 'separation of powers' developed, for side by side there stood parliament, government and the emperor, the last not as the representative of the presidency in the federal state but as the holder of a special military command.

The constitution of the Swiss Confederacy, revised in 1874, represented an entirely different type of federal constitution. It was an alliance not of individual monarchies but of cantons based on ancient people's law and in the end was better able to resist excess of federal authority than were the monarchies of the German federal state. This authority was exercised through a federal assembly made up of the National Council (*Nationalrat*) based on universal suffrage and the Council of the States (*Ständerat*) representing the cantons. The ascendancy of these parliamentary organs reduced the federal government, the Federal Assembly (*Bundesrat*) of seven members, to the level of a managing committee uninfluenced by parliamentary majorities. Moreover, Article 89 of the revision of 1874 introduced a plebiscitary element, namely the referendum over federal laws, which has since had important effects. It must be remembered that this constitution was designed for a multi-lingual country and that, though this is not very obvious in the constitution itself, a compromise between the language groups was among the aims of this confederated system. Though elsewhere democratisation almost always led to an increase of nationalist tension, the Swiss democracy—not least because of its federal structure—remains an exception.

The Dual Monarchy, Austria-Hungary, on the other hand, its existence menaced by both the national and democratic tendencies of the age, failed to develop any constitutional policy that would have brought this threat under control. The constitution was based on the *Ausgleich* of 1867 which reconstructed the kingdom of Hungary and then set up arrangements and organs common to Hungary and the empire's western half. Three joint ministries, of War, Foreign Affairs and Finance, and bodies representative of both halves of the empire, consisting of delegations from the two separate parliaments, made up the framework of the Dual Monarchy, whose only actual link, however, was in the person of the emperor-king. The 'dualism' of the monarchy appeared to favour the majority-peoples in both the halves of the empire, but in reality it was only the Magyars who fully benefited, while the lead held by the Germans in the western half of the empire crumbled away piecemeal. In both western and eastern portions of the empire any yielding to democratisation in the franchise and the powers of the parliaments meant also a gain for the nationalist elements among the rest of the nations and nationalities. In the last decades of the century all sorts of attempts were made to find some way out of this dilemma, among them the idea of a tri-partite system with a special place for the domains of the Bohemian Crown; and attempts were made in different territories, especially in Bohemia and Moravia, to relieve tension among the nationalities. These efforts succeeded only in Moravia (the Moravian Settlement of 1905) and in the Bukovina. In the western half of the empire, in addition to the existing particular class franchise, a general franchise was introduced in 1896 to include all citizens over twenty-four, empowered to elect, however, only 72 of the 425 members. Universal suffrage was not introduced in the Cis-leithan kingdom till 1907 and did not extend to Hungary till the first World War.

It is hardly possible to speak of any constitutional system for the Dual Monarchy as a whole, because of the different development of the two halves of the empire. In both halves the parliaments were tardy in carrying out the principle of democratic representation. In the Cis-leithan kingdom in particular political fluctuations were a matter less of parties and party power than of the influence of the different nationalities, and it was questions of nationality which in fact brought about changes of government.

None of the great countries of the continent of Europe produced anything like the English system of parliamentary control; in Germany this was prevented by elements in the constitution favouring monarchical absolutism and federalism, in Austria-Hungary by the state's complicated multi-national structure, in France and Italy by the weakness of the political parties. But it is possible for the two-party system to be in operation and yet mean something quite different from what it does in England; we see this in the countries of the Iberian peninsula and in the Balkans. Here, in Greece and Roumania, in Spain and Portugal, we have a dual-party system with in each case a progressive-liberal and a conservative group of parties, and yet these parties were cliques and personal coteries with no deep roots in the country. The parliamentary regime often changed abruptly, and the lack of political continuity made important political decisions impossible. This was especially clear in Spain after the Bourbon restoration of 1875–6, where the alternation between liberal and liberal-conservative ministries in no way expressed any constant interplay between great rival popular forces but was merely manipulated from above; each government on reaching power manœuvred the voting to secure a parliamentary majority. In Portugal, as in Italy, the principal parties, progressives and conservatives, wore themselves out by frequent changes from government to opposition and in the end one could hardly call the system there a two-party one at all.

In Europe as a whole the close of the nineteenth century was a period of dwindling constitutional development; the idea of the constitution rarely had any force of its own but was now associated with the founding of new states, with the principle of nationality. Only in France and Great Britain did the structure of the state exhibit evolution from within, and only in Russia, which still lacked any constitutional form of government, was constitutionalism a revolutionary element. Especially in the smaller countries (Switzerland in 1874, Belgium in 1893, the Netherlands in 1887) constitutional amendments of a technical nature took place, but these were not felt to be radical alterations in the structure of the government. During this period no attempt whatsoever was made anywhere to settle the question of how the workers' political movements would affect states whose constitutions had been framed in the main by the middle classes. The political and ideological leaders of the workers tried to expose the liberal constitutional system as a disguise for middle-class dominance, and this remained a tenet of revolutionary socialism. But in reality constitutional democracy began to make headway against the workers' social revolutionary movement.

This process was furthered by the most important event of these decades in constitutional development, namely the democratisation of the franchise which in most countries brought nearer universal suffrage for all male citizens and in some indeed had already achieved it. Universal equal suffrage without important qualifications existed *de jure* (by Article 20 of the Imperial Constitution) in the German empire from 1867 to 1871 (but not in its individual states except Baden, 1904); in France from 1870 to 1875, Spain 1890, Switzerland 1874, Greece 1864, Bulgaria 1879, Norway 1898. Almost purely nominal property qualifications still remained, for instance, in Great Britain (till 1884), Italy (1882), the Netherlands (1896); the franchise was universal but not equal in Roumania (the three-class system, by the Constitution of 1866) and in Belgium (plural voting, by the Constitution of 1893). The suffrage, one of the most important bonds linking government and community, now began to develop energy of its own and to alter the forms and institutions of politics. This was especially true of the political parties; in most countries these now developed from being clubs of the notabilities in society, with a loose organisation usually apparent only at election-time, into parties of the masses with a fixed nucleus and roots spreading out all over the country. This is seen most clearly in the case of the English Liberals; from 1867 onwards, at first in the Birmingham constituency, they set up well-disciplined organisations modelled on the American Caucus and brought politics to the masses. In other countries, however, the liberal parties were among the most resistant to any form of democratisation and retained longest their character as groups drawn from leading individuals. The continental socialists, on the other hand, beginning with the Social-Democratic party in Germany, which went this way from the 1890's, after the era of the Socialist Acts, created parties of the masses under united leadership and supported and financed by a wide following; and through their systems of organisation these parties penetrated every department of cultural, social and economic life. The socialists had a socially homogeneous following; but a different type of modern mass party was recruited from denominational Church groups—especially the Roman Catholics—for instance, in Belgium after 1869 (*Fédération des Cercles d'Associations Catholiques*), in Switzerland, in the Netherlands, in Austria-Hungary, in Germany from 1870 to 1871 onwards, and eventually in Italy where, to begin with, the pope's veto had prevented any entry into parliament. The form of organisation that these denominational parties took is most clearly seen in the structure of the German Centre party, which had no real party machinery but was based on Church unions such as the People's Union for Catholic Germany (*Volksverein für das katholische Deutschland*) and on denominational guilds. Such a party was not a firmly articulated mass organisation but a loose structure, a focus for the interests of various groups. The Catholic parties in other countries were organised along similar federative lines.

A similar or identical structure among the parties of various European countries must not blind us to their very different function in the different national communities. Politics had still barely begun to reach the masses, for instance, in the Balkan countries and in Spain and Portugal; the middle classes were weak, and so the parties were able to retain their character as cliques even though under the terms of the constitution they might have considerable opportunities for expanding their influence. Elsewhere, as in France, the strongly individualistic and regional tone in public life hampered their full development, and in Russia, with its total lack of any constitution, the forming of any party still counted as a revolutionary conspiracy. The German example shows that energy in organising a party is not necessarily the same thing as political influence within a country. Traditional patterns and forms of national life sometimes had their influence within the parties; in England, for instance, there were the religious sectarian movements with their home-mission programmes reaching out to the masses, and in Germany the doctrinaire and dogmatic elements in a Church bounded by state limits and later in the Philosophic School. In almost every country the parties had now become preserves from which those giving the lead in politics were drawn, though feudal traditions and modes of advancement still held their own. This process of recruiting those giving the lead in politics from among the parties had gone farthest in the Romance countries, France and Italy; in Great Britain, too, of course, it had gone a long way, though here a strong aristocratic influence was still effective, as for instance in the Foreign Service. The misfortune of the German parties lay in the impossibility of rising from party politics to any public office or appointment.

At the close of the nineteenth century liberalism still occupied a dominant position among the great political movements; but its political function, its social sphere of influence and in part its stock of ideas had undergone considerable change since the mid-century. European liberalism's past great achievement had lain in creating and developing the liberal state, with its constitutionalism and rule of law, and in insisting on certain political guiding principles adopted later by all kinds of non-liberal movements and parties, denominational, socialist, aristocratic, and sometimes even conservative. It had lain further in the decisive influence which liberals had exerted, particularly in Germany and Italy but also in eastern Europe and the Balkan countries, on the development of the nation and the nation-state. The constitutional state that liberalism demanded had even come into being, if only with the help of nationalism, in those countries where, as in Italy, the anti-liberal forces entrenched themselves behind particularism. The unification of Italy is the classic example of a nation-state being formed by the extension of a constitution, in this case the Piedmontese *Statuto*, to a much wider area. The third great field of liberal influence had been that of economic policy and the impetus given to it for instance by the Manchester School.

After 1870 liberalism was confronted by a series of fresh problems. The most vital was the social problem which for the liberals had two aspects. The first was the question, what was the liberal parties' sphere of action in society to be in an age when beside the middle class there was growing up a new, steadily increasing class, organising itself along strict lines—the workers? The second question concerned the role of the state in the social crises which had followed from the industrial revolution and which were obviously not to be solved if the non-intervention policy of the Manchester School was to prevail. Liberalism did not arrive at any uniform answer to these questions, and it was radically divided in its attitude to the contemporary political movement which was carrying forward the policy of the nation-state—to imperialism. The attitude of liberalism to this question is another of the great general themes governing its policy during these decades. And there is yet another, where the traditions of older liberalism were even stronger: the relation between state and Church or rather between the states imbued with liberal ideas and institutions, in particular the Roman Catholic Church since the Vatican Council, which opposed the liberalist spirit of the age.

What was the attitude and what were the resources of European liberalism as it entered this phase of its history? In almost every country it was organised into parties sharing in, or alone directing, the government. The English liberal party under W. E. Gladstone, the most important liberal statesman of his day, alternated in office with conservative cabinets and four times took over the government (1868–74, 1880–5, 1886, 1892–4). It adapted its organisation to the realities of mass democracy and in its policy fused Whig traditions with the radicalism that had grown up outside parliament. Italy and France had unstable cabinets whose composition merely reflected different nuances of liberalism. This was true of Italy's *trasformismo* period after 1876 and of French politics between MacMahon's resignation (1879) and the Dreyfus crisis. In France at that time the republican party was in power, its different groups supporting a republican, anti-plebiscitary, parliamentary liberalism. Later (after 1899) the Radical Social party gained the lead. In Germany between 1867 and 1878 the National Liberals were the party in power in the Reichstag, but Bismarck's attempt to bring them directly into the government (by the candidature of Rudolf von Bennigsen as Minister in 1878) failed because of the Chancellor's and the National Liberals' conflicting aims. The liberal left wing in Germany was unwaveringly in opposition from 1874 onwards; its right wing never managed to abandon an inherently ambivalent position between opposition and support, though on the whole after 1884 it sided increasingly with the government. In Russia before 1905, while there was as yet no constitution, no liberal party could come into being, though the organs of local self-government, the 'Zemstvos' (Beseda), were the first step in that direction. Liberalism here was still occupied with the struggle for a constitution and constitutional institutions, and was almost considered a revolutionary political activity. And roughly the same was true of Turkey.

Apart from the exceptional case of England, the liberal parties were loosely organised. They retained their character of clubs for the upper and middle classes and never achieved any contact with the mass-democratic trend of the times. Nowhere, not even in England for any length of time, did the liberal parties manage to penetrate the working classes; in every case these were organised by socialist parties. In some countries, the Netherlands after 1888 for instance, and Belgium, one can see the beginnings of the process of contraction to which the liberal parties have succumbed since this century opened. But at this period men and ideas of liberal mould were still to be found at the centre of contemporary events; in some countries (Hungary and Roumania) liberal parties were consistently in power. And yet some flagging of energy was noticeable in the increasing tendency of political liberalism to fragmentation; this process was especially obvious in Germany and Italy; and in England too the liberal party split in 1886 over the Irish Home Rule question. By the close of the century liberalism, grown more opportunist, had lost any solidarity in face of the great questions of the day, the questions of protectionism, state intervention in social problems, and imperialism, which was bound up with these other two.

The transition to protectionism, to the policy of tariffs, did arouse violent liberal opposition. In Germany it led indeed to a rupture between the government and the National Liberals, who up till then had supported it. But their rejection of tariffs was far from complete; a group favouring protectionism at once split off from the National Liberal party. Only the liberal left wing which represented financial interests remained throughout faithful to a free trade policy.

Interventionism in the social field, to which most governments, liberal and conservative, were committed at this period, was a much more complicated question. In view of the radical transformation in social conditions liberal theory could not always remain true to the doctrine of the Manchester School; it proclaimed the right of the state to intervene where the freedom of the individual was being threatened by the unhindered course of economic evolution. In England T. H. Green and Francis C. Montague expressed this view; in his essay on *The Limits of Individual Liberty* published in 1885 Montague even wrote: 'In countries in which individuals have neither the capital nor the qualities requisite for a plentiful production of wealth, the State has to undertake many industrial enterprises which are absolutely indispensable to this production.' Liberalism was very hesitant and uneasy over putting the policy of intervention into practice—not least in England. Yet England provided an example of liberal initiative. Gladstone's Land Act of 1881 was a bold step towards giving the Irish tenant-farmer some means of reducing his rents by fixing them officially. It was a conservative government, that of Bismarck, that first tackled the great socio-political task of bringing some security into the workers' precarious existence. The German Imperial Chancellor brought in Insurance Acts against sickness (1883), accident (1884) and old age (1889). The German liberals regarded this legislation with mixed feelings. The liberal left wing remained radically opposed to Bismarck's state socialism even though it embodied the conclusions of the liberal parties' own social tendencies. Only after Bismarck's dismissal did this group fall into step and try to improve the system of compulsory insurance by introducing greater flexibility. The National Liberals, on the right, tried to rid the government proposals of their background of both state socialism and corporative ideas, but in the end they voted almost unanimously for the Acts. Similar conflicts arose when the influence of German social legislation caused a first wave of debate on accident insurance Acts in many other European countries (Austria 1887; Norway 1894; England, 'Workmen's Compensation Act', 1897; France, Italy, Denmark 1898; Spain and the Netherlands 1900; Sweden 1901; Belgium and Russia 1903). The impetus imparted by social liberalism was considerable; but it is impossible to say that the driving force in social policy at the close of the nineteenth century was to be found exclusively or even predominantly with liberals or liberal ideas. The new social liberalism despite its merits failed to achieve as much as liberalism in its early days and its prime had done in constitutional matters.

Protectionism, state intervention and imperialism essentially made up one whole; and towards imperialistic policy, too, liberalism presented a divided front. This was especially true of British liberals; their views were still affected by Cobden and the Manchester theorists who held that a radical exercise of free trade would lead to relaxation and dissolution within the empire and would bring more economic profit to the mother-country than the defence of the older colonies and the acquisition of new ones. The radicals and moderate liberals asked doubtfully whether a democracy and an empire were compatible and some, like Lord Derby, the fifteenth earl, concluded that 'kings and aristocracies can govern empire, but one people cannot govern another people'. But there were also liberals among the early supporters of imperial expansion, for instance in the 1880's outstanding men such as Dilke, author of *Greater Britain* (1868), and Joseph Chamberlain. From 1895 onwards the classic phase of British imperial policy is linked with Chamberlain's name, and this policy sought to make the empire into a federated alliance and at the same time a customs union with protective duties.

The problem of imperialism profoundly troubled German liberals also, though the majority approved Germany's entry into world politics and only the social democrats had any anti-imperialist leanings. Liberals such as Friedrich Naumann and Max Weber saw in Germany's participation in the course of world politics the great destiny that alone could train the German people to become a politically conscious nation and fuse the working class with that nation. To them it presented not so much an alternative to social reform as a prerequisite for it. In Italy, President Francesco Crispi (1887–91, 1893–6) provided a typical example of a great imperialist and of colonial policy undertaken in the spirit of a democratic liberalism strongly infused with nationalism. On its catastrophic collapse in 1896 pacifist elements for a time invaded Italian liberalism, but on the whole national irredentism took over what was left from the wreck of imperialism.

Interventionism in the social field and imperialism were trends of the day which had little or nothing to do with traditional liberal ideas even if in course of time they became imbued with the liberal spirit. Liberalism played a much more prominent part in the genesis of the crisis that developed during these decades between state and Church. Three things led up to this crisis. There was the advance of secularised laicised education seeing its ultimate philosophical basis in a kind of scientific monism. With this there went a marked antipathy to clergy and church, typical of radical liberals and, on their left, of socialists. Even English radicalism was not free of it, though English liberalism was characterised by its connection with the nonconformist sects. In the second place there was the vast increase in the power and authority of the state, which took place once the conception of the nation-state had triumphed in Europe and when the state began to spread its active influence over almost every department of social and intellectual life. Liberalism had first appeared as a force opposing this growth in the power of the state; then, taking a Hegelian view and seeing the state as the most effective means of achieving freedom, liberalism contributed materially towards the state's increase of power. If freedom and enlightenment came through the state, however, then the Churches might become the real hindrance that many liberals saw them to be, in particular the Roman Catholic Church which because of its structure stood in an entirely different relationship to the state authorities from any state-church system. Thirdly, the Roman Catholic Church, threatened by the temper and events of the times, in particular in Italy, countered the inroads on her temporal power with an intensification of her papal system, and by the 'spiritualisation of Canon Law' (Vatican Council of 1870).

From these three directions the ground was made ready for a conflict; and this broke out on the highest level in Italy, where the occupation of the Roman papal states and their incorporation in the Italian nation-state was the beginning of an antagonism between the Curia and the Italian state that lasted for nearly sixty years. The Vatican refused to accept the Italian Law of Guarantees of 13 May 1871 (*Legge delle Guarentigie*), assuring to the pope his independent and sovereign status in Rome, and rejected it as a unilateral pronouncement. This law also proclaimed once more the separation of Church and state (*libera chiesa in libero stato*) which was an inheritance from Piedmontese-Sardinian liberalism. It meant that Italy's domestic policy was now anti-ecclesiastical; civil marriage and state schools with religious instruction as an optional subject were introduced. Public life in Italy was coloured by an anti-clerical liberalism controlled by laymen; and Catholicism could not develop any opposing force in politics, since a Papal Decree of 1874 (*Non expedit*) forbade the faithful to take any part in the elections, a prohibition not relaxed till 1905.

In the German empire, where soon after its foundation the *Kulturkampf* broke out, the state and in particular the Prussian state upheld a stringent policy *vis-à-vis* the Roman Catholic Church; by the May Laws of 1873 it sought to limit the rights of the Church to a considerable extent and to bring it under state control. Further enactments threatened heavy penalties for infringement of these Acts; bishops and priests were dismissed, imprisoned and sentenced. Bismarck had provided the first incentive for this action, for quite un-liberal reasons of state, but it was mainly the work of a liberal bureaucrat, namely Falk, Prussian Minister of Education. The liberals in parliament, and especially the left wing, did not remain passive in this struggle; it was they who spread the slogans and supplied the conflict with basic arguments going far beyond Bismarck's aims. Rudolf Virchow, who first used the expression *Kulturkampf*, traced the liberal line of argument when he spoke of the struggle against the hierarchy which had assumed 'the peculiar character of Ultramontanism' and also of intervention 'for the emancipation, the secularisation of the state'. In the *Kulturkampf* the liberals were defending the liberal nation-state; but they could not prevent it when Bismarck, pursuing his own ends, made his peace with the Curia over their heads. The final outcome of the *Kulturkampf* was not a victory for the liberal state over a narrow-minded Church, but at most a fresh demarcation of what Bismarck called 'priests' rule' as distinct from 'king's rule'.

This result did not go so far as what was determined in France during the Third Republic in the field of ecclesiastical policy. Here, too, 1877 was an important year; the defeat of the monarchists and the victory of the republicans meant at the same time a victory for anti-clerical secularism over the combined supporters of the Church and of the Restoration. The republican state now proceeded to extend the jurisdiction of the state at the expense of the Church and its organisations, indeed to prepare for complete separation of Church and state. A school law of 1882 established the principle of laicised state schools from which any kind of religious instruction was excluded; and in 1886 the clergy were debarred from teaching in state schools. There was a phase, known as the *Ralliement*, during which the Roman Catholic Church and the Republic drew somewhat closer, but the conflict flared up again after the turn of the century. In June 1904 a law was brought into force making education in the secular state schools obligatory and excluding the religious orders from any kind of instruction; finally, in 1905 the law 'de séparation de l'église et de l'état' achieved a break-through in favour of a radical state controlled by laymen. In other countries, too, and at the moment when compulsory school attendance had just become established, the schools developed into the battlegrounds between the ecclesiastical-denominational and the secularist-liberal outlook. In almost every case liberalism tried to use the obligatory state schools as an instrument to further its ideal of a free, autonomous education not bound by any dogma. This same struggle went on in Belgium between laicised state schools (Act of 1879) and parish schools under denominational guidance (Act of 1884). In the Netherlands (1889) the denominational schools held their ground beside the state ones and in Austria, where the Concordat had been suspended in 1870 and a liberal ecclesiastical policy inaugurated with the Church Acts of 1874, denominational schools were restored in 1883. Liberals all over Europe were carrying out a similar policy, but the attitude of English liberalism revealed a more complex dilemma. While liberalism, especially in the radical wing, included a strong free-thinking, agnostic element, its relationship to Nonconformity, to the Dissenters, and thereby to the opposition between these bodies and the Established Church, was no less important. Large sections of English liberalism— here Gladstone is the most striking example—were much more concerned than was continental liberalism with religious, denominational questions. This is clearly illustrated, for instance, in the attitude of English liberalism to the state Church. Free-thinking radicals and nonconformists could agree in opposing it, but not in their reasons for doing so. The idea of disestablishing the state Church therefore never really permeated English liberalism; Gladstone, who for special reasons had moved the disestablishment of the Church of Ireland, held fast to the state Church in England despite numerous currents running against it. The Education Act of 1870, dating from Gladstone's first period as Prime Minister, did not simply set up a secularist state school system after the continental pattern but retained the Church schools under the Establishment side by side with the new state schools. In spite of violent criticism from the liberals no changes were made in this arrangement even under the Education Act of 1902.

Croce has called the period between 1871 and 1914 the 'liberal era'. This term is applicable in the sense that public life and political and social institutions were imbued during this period with liberal ideas; and yet liberalism was no longer alone in setting its seal on the age. For socialism in its various degrees and nuances now at last became a political force. It appeared in political parties, in revolutionary movements, in workers' associations, in international unions, and it stimulated politics by rousing states and governments to counteraction, to economic and socio-political measures and reform. The theoretical framework of 'scientific socialism' provided by Karl Marx and Friedrich Engels was already in existence by about 1870, but many ideas were added to it in the 1880's and 1890's, when Engels published the second and third volumes of Marx's *Das*

Kapital (1885 and 1894) as well as the most important of his own writings. About the turn of the century Marxist doctrine developed along two lines; one was the so-called 'Revisionism' introduced by Eduard Bernstein in his work *Die Voraussetzungen des Sozialismus und die Aufgabe des Sozialdemokratie* (1889) which was later published in English with the title *Evolutionary Socialism*. Its evolutionist tone was taken in part from the ideas of the English Fabian Society, active in theory and practice from 1883 onwards. The other line, the concentration and intensification of revolutionary elements in Marx's doctrine, was followed in particular by Vladimir Ilyitch Lenin in Russia. This divergence between a democratic-social reform movement and an impetus towards social revolution, already implicit in Marx's dual conception of revolution, was debated with the utmost fervour during the last decades of the century. Consciousness of the theoretical issues involved was very much stronger on the part of the workers than it had been at the time of the earlier bourgeois revolutions; indeed action sometimes threatened to be lost in the maze of speculative deliberation. To prevent this there were only the concrete economic interests of the workers, as represented by their trade unions, and the ambition of practical revolutionaries; among them Lenin emerged, adopting any theoretical view simply as a technical means towards revolution. The period up to 1870 had been occupied with the struggle for the theoretical bases of socialism; from now on the development of theory and its practical application went hand in hand.

Even the forms in which the socialist workers' movement took shape were in the main considered to spring from tactical considerations, to serve a period of transition; yet they involved fundamental decisions affecting the future. Marx had played a decisive part at the founding of an International Workers' Union in London in 1864, in which the workers' organisations from the individual countries were to count as subdivisions and in no sense as independent party-like groups. These organisations were all directed by the General Council as the highest executive body, and in this Marx himself had a determining influence. This First International was crippled not only by the conflict between the extremes it contained, a conflict which subsided only after the expulsion of the Anarchists under Bakunin at the Hague Congress of 1872; from the very beginning it also suffered from its lack of close touch with the workers' movements in the individual countries. When the General Council on expelling Bakunin moved at Marx's instigation to New York, it was simply floating in a vacuum until its dissolution in 1876. Partly because of legal difficulties it was impossible fully to bring out the international character of the socialist workers' movement in any organised form; but Marx saw that it was retained as a vital ideological postulate assumed by most of the national workers' parties. The very varying political and social conditions in the individual countries, the workers' differing share in the suffrage and so in parliament, the unequal political activity of the working class—all these led to the foundation of socialist parties of very diverse nature, but they still had much more contact with each other than did the liberal-national parties. In their revolutionary strategy and tactics they exemplified every trend from the most ardent revolutionary zeal to a leaning towards reform through evolution, as seen in the Fabians in England or the 'Possibilistes' in France. In spite of numerous syndicalist influences pressing for exclusively economic action such as strikes, and also despite occasional contacts with anarchism, the socialist workers' movement almost always made use of the liberal constitutional state with its leanings towards an extension of the suffrage, and its parliaments and parties, as the gateway to political responsibility. Only Russia was a special case, its absolutist police-state making for very different conditions; here affairs took an entirely different turn even after the granting of some liberal institutions in 1905.

The three decades between 1870 and 1900 saw the founding and first growth of socialist parties—in Germany 1869–75, Denmark 1878, France 1881, Italy 1882–92, Belgium 1885, Norway 1887, Austria 1888, Sweden 1889, Great Britain 1893–1903, the Netherlands 1894. In Germany, France and other countries they on occasions felt the full impact of the state against them. In the beginning various trends and groups—syndicalist, anarchist, Marxist—worked in association, later either fusing into a whole or separating again. The political and sociological conditions of the workers, who usually still lacked full political rights, certainly strengthened the need to unite and checked the tendency to split except over major decisions in revolutionary policy, though these were generally fought out with the greatest bitterness. But the violent expression of radical differences, for instance the question of revolution or evolution as the basis for social policy, often obscures the process of constant adaptation to new circumstances that was going on within the workers' parties. The German social democrats, for instance, officially condemned revisionism more than once, in the party rallies of 1899, 1901 and 1903, and yet their practice approximated to it more and more. The actual work of forming a party, taking up a role in parliament, sharing in the political problems of the day—all this demanded from the socialist parties a considerable degree of tactical ability and willingness to compromise, and this is not always apparent behind the façade of revolutionary speeches. This must be kept in mind when studying the formative phase of the socialist parties; it reaches far back beyond 1870, especially in France, Germany and England.

The German socialists were the first to assume the lead. They had been divided into on the one hand the supporters of Ferdinand Lassalle and his Universal German Workers' Union of 1863, and on the other the 'Social Democrats', August Bebel and Wilhelm Liebknecht for instance, who came from the lower middle-class liberal left and took up Karl Marx's ideas. Both branches met over the Gotha Programme of 1875, a compromise uniting elements of Lassalle's State Socialism with Marx's Internationalism. In 1878 the first rise of the young Social Democratic party was checked by the measures introduced against it under the 'Exceptional Law' which sought 'to control the universally dangerous aims of Social Democracy' (*Gesetz gegen die gemeingefährlichen Bestrebungen der Sozialdemokratie*). The party was only able to evolve and expand after the repeal of these laws in 1890. At the Erfurt Party Congress it brought out a new programme, this time strongly Marxist in character, developed and centralised its organisation and increased its membership and still more its electorate. It became the strongest socialist party of all, its indirect influence on the socialist organisations of other countries was considerable, it played a leading part in the committees of the international workers' congresses that the Second International revived after 1889 as a confederation of national workers' parties. German social democracy was a typical democratic party of the masses, with power to integrate its organisation and its ideology as well. Gradually—and from 1891 on completely—it took over the Marxist doctrine as the ideological basis of its policy, to the exclusion of what had come from either Lassalle or the Anarchists. And yet, without relinquishing the Marxist theory of the dictatorship of the proletariat, it shifted its ground to democratic electoral contests and a policy of parliamentary opposition and obstruction which made no use of any revolutionary or terrorist technique. The reformist trait in its policy was strengthened after the close of the century, despite ideological opposition, by the movement within the trade unions.

German social democracy possessed penetrating power, thanks to its discipline and its relatively compact ideology. In this it was superior to most other socialist parties. In France, where socialist and specifically revolutionary traditions are oldest, divisions dating from before 1870 split the workers' movement and could not, or at least could not yet, be bridged. This showed at once when in the later 1870's the fierce and bloody persecution of those who had fought with the Commune abated and there was a chance that socialist organisations might be built up again by the communards who were returning. Within ten years there were a Marxist group (*Parti Ouvrier Français*), a group following the revolutionary-activist tradition of 1789–1871 and based on L. A. Blanqui's ideas (*Parti Socialiste Révolutionnaire*), a third group (*Parti Ouvrier Socialiste*) in which syndicalist ideas ('Revolution of the Folded Arms') lived on, and finally the *Fédération des Travailleurs Socialistes de France* which put forward a programme of social reform described as 'politique des possibilités'. Étienne Alexandre Millerand, an independent socialist, tried to rally French socialism under the banner of a social reform programme with moderate demands for socialisation and a national-patriotic accent (The Programme of St Mandé, 1896), and this appealed to tradesmen and small farmers alike. Millerand took office in the Waldeck–Rousseau cabinet of June 1899—an important date in European socialism. But this step led to fresh divisions, so that the twentieth century opened with a more intransigent group of Marxists and Blanquists and a more moderate reformist one under Jean Jaurès and Millerand. What really prevented a complete victory for the Marxist branch was France's sociological structure, the local loyalties in French politics, the nationalist element in French democratic republicanism.

Great Britain presents a complete contrast to the Continent; it was impossible here for any workers' party looking to socialist revolution and based on class warfare and the dictatorship of the proletariat to develop at all. English Radicalism, which had played so great a part in the regeneration of the liberal party, provided a kind of intellectual reservoir for ideas and ideals of social reform that could also be drawn upon to strengthen the political will of the workers. There was something of this in the Fabian Society which from 1883 was promoting the idea of gradual peaceful social reform. And there were the trade unions, of immense importance for the practical improvement of working conditions in industry, and thus exercising considerable influence on the development of the political parties—very much more than did any continental unions, even the German ones. Different elements worked together, then, to form a workers' party in England: the reformist socialism of small groups of the intelligentsia, isolated political units like the Independent Labour party of 1893, the practical social policy of the trade unions and finally the need for direct representation of the workers' interests in parliament. This last in particular led to the formation in 1900 of the Labour Representation Committee which adopted the name Labour party in 1903 though for a while it remained more a rallying point than an independent party.

If the formation of the British Labour party marked a complete victory for the ideas of social reform, Russia offered an example of radical social-revolutionary theory and practice taking shape. Socialism sprang here from the revolt of the intelligentsia against the autocratic despotism of the tsarist regime. A planned system of terror became an integral element in this revolutionary movement, which lacked any legitimate means of expression. Marxist ideas passed into the movement and the social revolutionaries began to wonder whether Russia's evolution into a capitalist state was a prerequisite for any victory for the social revolution, or whether the socialist movement could not link up with original communist elements in Russia's traditional agricultural system—a question to which Marx had had no definite answer. Lenin, who headed the Bolsheviks, the majority in the socialist party, left this question completely on one side and evolved a programme adapted to conditions in Russia: a revolutionary outbreak before capitalism in Russia had created any class-conscious proletariat; mobilisation of revolutionary energies among the peasantry; the organisation of a revolutionary action-party with a general staff of professional revolutionaries to work towards a revolution by force.

Among the socialist parties of the other European countries there were many variations on the great alignments and conflicts that we have seen in the four largest states. In Italy a revisionist type of Marxism had to overcome strong currents of revolutionary anarchism and democratic Mazzinianism. In Austria it proved impossible to maintain social democracy above national distinctions in a party of socialists drawn from all the nationalities; a Czech party split off, and in 1897 the whole party dissolved into six national organisations which grew more and more independent. In the Scandinavian countries the socialist parties were soon following the English pattern of social reformism. By the turn of the century the phase of organisation and ideological consolidation was everywhere at an end, and socialist votes began to increase with the extension of the suffrage. Isolated socialist parties, especially the German one, were soon among the most forceful groups in their parliaments. The question arose of some share in the government, in the operations of parliament, in political responsibility altogether.

Liberalism was able to influence contemporary thought directly and in different ways through the guiding principles laid down in parliamentary constitutions and through its share in political responsibility. Not so socialism; it could only arouse opposition and sting its antagonists into taking the initiative in social policies. The great insurance Acts of the 1880's of Bismarck's empire, the model for similar undertakings in many countries of Europe, are an illustration of this kind of cause and effect. Yet there were also many instances of state socialism at this time which did not arise out of reaction to socialist demands. Many states for instance, even before the close of the century, had begun to nationalise their railways; Prussia (after the failure to establish the imperial railway system Bismarck had wanted) did so; and so did Belgium, Switzerland, Norway, Serbia, Roumania and in 1905 Italy. These were the first signs that in economics the shape of things to come would not keep the traditional outlines of classic liberalism but would also owe some of its features to socialism.

CHAPTER X

THE GERMAN EMPIRE

THE Franco-German War of 1870–1 completed the political move-ment which had aimed at bringing the unity of a national state to both Italians and Germans. In both cases the state had had to gain control over a national revolutionary movement which had come to grief when it opposed the states in 1848. In Italy this movement had done more than in Germany towards consolidating the nation into a whole; but in Germany too, led politically by middle-class liberals, it had supplied the chief stimulus in the great cause, even though representatives of the liberal movement had been denied any appreciable share in the actual foundation of the empire. At decisive moments in his trial of strength with Austria even Bismarck had not hesitated to employ national revolution as a political means; in 1866, if arms had not brought quick results, he would have mobilised it with a call to the Germans—as also to the Czechs, Magyars and other nationalities—within the Habsburg monarchy. But the rapid and complete victory of Königgrätz meant that diplomatic and military activity largely obscured the share that national revolution had had in the founding of the empire. This had been precisely Bismarck's design: he meant to make use of liberal and democratic leanings only in so far as they helped him to overcome the conservative and particularist forces opposing him in Germany. The less Bismarck needed popular support, the more he could and indeed had to consider the principalities which in Germany, unlike in Italy, remained a constituent element of the national state. The final decision brought about by the battle of Sedan (1870) had confirmed and strengthened this characteristic feature of German unification. By their annual celebration of Sedan, 2 September, as their National Day, the Germans of the Second Empire showed plainly that the empire owed its foundation to the military victory over France, that the German princes had united under the Hohenzollerns for this purpose and that the nation's principal contribution had been a military one. The original national movement towards unification, defeated in 1848 and revived again in the 1860's, gradually receded behind all that was expressed in the commemoration of the Day of Sedan.

From 1871 onwards the problems of Germany's domestic and foreign policy, as of Italy's, were bound together in a new way by the existence of the national state. If the European system of states, temporarily dis-turbed by the events in Germany and Italy, quickly adapted itself to the new situation, it was because it was reaffirmed by the conscious avoidance of any further disturbance of Europe on the part of the two new national states. In 1871 Bismarck declared the new empire to be 'satiated'. He was talking here of resistance to any kind of revolution that might alter frontiers in response to national feeling or allow internal social pressure within the states of Europe to unsettle the existing political order. He set out to curb the national uneasiness among Germans with which, though only up to a certain point, he had formerly allied himself. And his decision meant that the principle of the national state was not to be applied to Austria-Hungary. He desired the assured continuance of this monarchy and therefore held that the different nationalities there must remain linked as before in a manner independent of nationality. On more than one occasion he indicated to the Germans in Austria that any attempt towards a 'Germania Irredenta' would be inappropriate. The Chancellor needed stability within Europe in order not to endanger his young empire; he therefore consistently set his face against any movements towards a 'Greater Germany' though these had followed naturally from the wish to build up a national state comprising all territories predominantly German in population. Bismarck was prepared to confine the German nation politically within a 'Lesser Germany' in order to check the advance of national revolution in Europe; and he was ready to make use of the eight million Germans within Austria-Hungary to neutralise her non-German peoples who were four times their number.

An internal policy of halting every democratic trend was the counterpart to this restriction of German centrifugal forces. At home as well as within Europe Bismarck sought to control the spirits he himself had called up when he was carrying on his hazardous policy of bringing a united empire into being. He had to find a middle course between on the one hand the forces of tradition, still powerful and demanding restraint, and on the other hand those of nationalism and democracy, pressing in the direction of change. This characterised Bismarck's whole policy between 1871 and 1890. His *cauchemar des coalitions* united with his fear of revolution. With brave pessimism Bismarck attempted to control them both, coalitions and revolution; and in the end both defeated his successors between 1890 and 1918. From the foundation of the empire to the first World War the domestic history of Germany—always closely knit with her foreign policy—thus takes the form of an unremitting tension between conservative rigidity and national dynamism. But while stressing this we must not forget that, given the forces at work about 1870 within Germany and Europe, no other solution which could have resolved the tension would seem to have been feasible. It was hard for Bismarck to steer his course; he had to consider the European powers, the particularist interests of the German princes, the Prussian conservatism of his own King William I and of his own colleagues of the aristocracy, as well as the divergent party sympathies of the great mass of the people now growing increasingly politically minded.

The Imperial Constitution, modelled in all respects on that of the North German Confederation which he had personally designed and shaped, was an expression of Bismarck's perilous course among the reefs. It was not fashioned in accordance with any logically constructed system; it was suited to existing conditions in being a compromise between unification and federation and between the monarchist principle and the sovereignty of the people. It made the empire an alliance of constitutional monarchs and also in itself a constitutional monarchy, its apex the German emperor (the 'Praesidium of the Confederation', the *Bundespräsidium*). The empire possessed no comprehensively detailed written constitution, as did the separate German states; for much was withheld from the competence of the empire and remained the concern of the states. Further, to humour these states, especially Prussia and the departmental egoism of her ministers, the creation of imperial ministries was intentionally avoided. In place of ministries the Federal Council (*Bundesrat*), the body representing the federated governments, might have been given not only legislative powers but also through committees some control over branches of the imperial administration. Though Prussia held no absolute majority in this Federal Council, she could in fact scarcely be outvoted. This was the intention of those federalists who were consistent thinkers. According to a contrary view, the imperial administration should have been carried on by Prussian ministries. This kind of 'Greater Prussian' solution would have been in line with the wishes of the Prussian *Staatsministerium*, or cabinet of Prussian ministers. Bismarck did not expressly reject either solution, for he knew how far-reaching were the concessions he must make. Some sections of the imperial administration were made over to Prussian ministries which thereby—especially the War Office—became quasi-imperial ministries. But in reality Bismarck's intention was neither ultra-federal nor along Greater Prussian lines. From the autumn of 1866 onwards he was secretly aiming at his own administration for the empire, as extensive as possible and under the leadership of a single responsible Minister of State who should be none other than himself. By playing off the allied state governments, the Prussian king and the Prussian cabinet against each other, as he had done in the North German Reichstag of 1867, Bismarck achieved what he had sought—the solution which afforded scope for his own will. He became Federal Chancellor, from 1871 onwards Imperial Chancellor, and thereby the responsible head of a monocratic government rather than the head of a plural executive composed of equal colleagues. True, the expression 'imperial direction' (*Reichsleitung*), not 'imperial government' (*Reichsregierung*), was the one officially used. Bismarck remained at the same time Prussian Minister-President, that is to say *primus inter pares* in the Prussian cabinet, and for the moment also Prussian Foreign Minister. Although on 1 January 1870 the Prussian Ministry of the

Exterior became the Foreign Office of the North German Confederation (and from 1871, of the German empire), it always remained exclusively Bismarck's own ministry. In the 1870's the imperial administration was rapidly extended in accordance with Bismarck's design, by the formation of one 'imperial department' (*Reichsamt*)—not 'imperial ministry' (*Reichsministerium*)—after another. Each imperial department, for instance the Postal Services, the Navy, Justice, the Interior, was under a Secretary of State without ministerial responsibility.

The 'responsibility' of the Imperial Chancellor according to section 17 of the Imperial Constitution was a political and moral conception, and it expressed the Chancellor's authoritative position, as Bismarck saw it, in relation to the emperor's presidency. There was no responsibility towards the Reichstag. Bismarck had no wish to be restricted by a parliament any more than by a body of fellow-ministers. And so the German empire and its separate states remained true to the typical nineteenth-century form of constitution in Germany, a constitutional monarchy ruling without parliamentary control of the executive. According to the Imperial Constitution the emperor was free to nominate and dismiss the Chancellor in complete independence of the Reichstag. The Reichstag possessed legislative powers in conjunction with the Federal Council; its position was thus a limited one. It was inevitably granted some importance, however, for the laws of the empire had to be newly created and the legislature had control over the Budget, including the Army Estimates.

A constitutional monarchy was certainly the form of government that suited the Germany of 1870. But the tide was running towards democracy; this clearly meant that both the Reichstag and the parliaments of the separate states would in time strengthen their position and would determine the formation of the government. One of the greatest obstacles to the alliance of democracy and imperial authority in a parliamentary monarchy (apart from strong traditional opposition) was the multiplicity of the German political parties, confusing clear-cut parliamentary decisions and preventing the formation of any stable government majority. For this reason it was not possible simply to transfer the English type of constitution to Germany; even the National Liberals, the advocates of the parliamentary constitution, recognised this directly the empire had come into being. But the chief hindrance to development along democratic parliamentary lines lay in the fact that, as the preamble to the Imperial Constitution declared, the empire was an alliance of sovereigns. Any strengthening of the Reichstag would inevitably have favoured the unitary character of the empire—something that the sovereigns and governments of the separate states were not prepared to tolerate. Bismarck had been obliged to yield to federal pressure. As a counterbalance, however, to federalism, which endangered the unity of the empire, he made use of the Reichstag, which he found most apt for this purpose, and also of the fact of Prussia's hegemony: she had 65 per cent of the area and 61 per cent of the population of the empire as well as its three principal centres of heavy industry in the Saar, the Ruhr, and Upper Silesia, besides many and various very close personal and institutional links with the empire.

German constitutional history up to the first World War shows how successfully Bismarck adjusted the balance of his Imperial Constitution, particularly in relation to federalism. The difficulties with the states in the North German Confederation were overcome in 1867, and Bavaria and Württemberg were granted additional special privileges, above all in military and postal affairs, in 1870; and from then on the history of the empire contains no serious differences between the empire and the several states. The Federal Council always supported imperial unity; and this unity was not endangered by the particularist interests of the several states because, after the shock that followed his annexation of Hanover, Hesse (Hesse-Cassel and Hesse-Nassau), Frankfurt and Schleswig-Holstein, Bismarck was consciously forbearing in his treatment of the states.

A more difficult relationship developed as time went on between the imperial leadership and the Reichstag. The latter was elected at first every three and later every five years by universal suffrage, equal, secret and direct, a method which in the 1860's Bismarck had considered a suitable weapon against the liberals. As a result of the plurality of parties, their programmes dictated by mutually exclusive ideologies, most sessions yielded variable negative majorities against the policy adopted by the imperial administration, which was obliged to seek a separate majority for each bill it proposed. In the first Reichstag, 1871, the National Liberal party, the party that had supported the founding of the empire, led by the Hanoverian county squire von Bennigsen, even when joined by other pro-imperial liberals and the 'Free Conservatives' who supported Bismarck, controlled only a bare half of the seats (168 out of 382). Even this majority was lost as early as 1874; and towards the end of the 1870's Bismarck dissolved his alliance with the steadily declining National Liberal party and turned instead first to the Centre and the conservatives and later to the conservatives and those National Liberals who had severed themselves from their left wing. With these he achieved an absolute government majority at the Reichstag election of 1887, for the first and last time.

Since 1867 the National Liberals had been the leading national party in Germany; they had separated from the anti-government left-wing liberals, represented in Prussia from 1860 onwards by the Progressives, in order to end the conflict between king and parliament, to effect a compromise with the government in accordance with 'political realism' and to bring the national empire into being. The National Liberals almost invariably held to this line of loyalty to the empire, though to the end of the 1870's their left wing, led by parliamentarians of note, in particular the Jewish lawyer Lasker, kept liberal parliamentary demands alert and sharpened their antagonism to Bismarck to the point of defection from the party in 1880.

Left-wing liberalism, long under the undisputed leadership of Eugen Richter (from the Westphalian industrial town of Hagen), had a varied history of disruption and fusion. It scarcely ever achieved a positive attitude to imperial policy and exhausted itself in mostly negative opposition. Yet even this party grew accustomed to things as they were and, apart from late proposals made for instance by Friedrich Naumann, it never did anything positive to further the political aim of a monarchy under the control of parliament.

The fact that Bismarck prevented the full realisation of liberal hopes for the Constitution and that the liberals, once divided, were out-played by the Chancellor, has led to talk of the 'tragedy of German liberalism'. But to understand this tragedy aright we cannot be content merely to trace the political and ideological struggle between Bismarck and liberalism; we must take into account the social-economic trend towards organisation and democracy on a scale embracing the masses. What wrecked the liberals and their ideals was not only a powerful government but the development towards an increasingly democratic society which they vainly tried to resist, for instance by opposing universal, equal suffrage. It was not until the turn of the century that serious and moderately successful attempts were made to bring about a not very popular alliance between liberalism and democracy, and to organise the liberal parties more effectively. Friedrich Naumann, Lujo Brentano, and Max Weber—this last with the sharp precision of his political theories—come to mind in this connection.

The Conservatives were split into two main parties. The old Prussian Conservatives expressed their devotion to the Prussian state and their aversion from National Liberalism by remaining at first sullenly aloof in their displeasure at the foundation of the empire. After the reforming of the party in 1876 (now the 'German Conservative party') they followed the example of the other conservative party, the 'Free Conservative party' (*Reichspartei*), by turning towards Bismarck. From then on they increasingly supported imperial policy which was swinging to the right—without, however, having any intention of renouncing their specifically Prussian characteristics. Their voting strength was drawn almost exclusively from the agrarian territories to the east of the Elbe. Their political leaders sprang for the most part from among the Prussian aristocracy of the eastern provinces. Thus from the 1880's onwards, in the course of the general trend by which most of the German parties became influenced by economic interests, they became the party representing agrarian interests and adopted the aims of the 'Landowners' League', founded in 1893. As a result of the 'Three-Class' system of voting in force in Prussia up to 1918, the party occupied a much stronger position in the Prussian chamber of deputies than in the German Reichstag with its democratic system of voting. After the 1880's, when Bismarck allowed von Putt-kamer, the Prussian Minister of the Interior, to carry out his anti-liberal policy, this party gained and kept power in Prussia, above all controlling appointment to office. After the liberal era came to an end, offices in the higher branches of the administration in Prussia were reserved in the main for the sons of the aristocracy, or possibly for middle-class lawyers who, by virtue of their conservative political outlook, their membership of some distinguished Students' Corps, and their commissions in the Reserve, were classed with the Prussian aristocracy. Prussia and the empire were so closely interwoven that the latter was naturally affected by this kind of personal policy in a bureaucracy which, for all its professional and moral excellence, could not be called, on an average, politically far-sighted. Prussian 'bureaucratic rule' had been specifically liberal in the tradition of Stein and Hardenberg up to the middle of the century and partly again in the 1860's and 1870's; from the 1880's onwards it grew increasingly rigid in its conservatism. Tension between the monarchy, allied with the aristocratically led society, and the middle-class and proletarian sections of the community, striving for political responsibility, grew more and more acute up to the first World War. The justiciary on the other hand remained politically independent and was more successful in keeping alert a liberal outlook.

The political and social tension of the times was expressed most clearly in the growth of the Social Democrats, who became a unified party after the Gotha Congress of 1875. Their number increased from election to election in spite of their having been declared 'enemies of the empire' by Bismarck in the Exceptional Law of 1878 on account of their revolu-tionary programme and their refusal to come to terms with the state. In 1871 they amounted to only 2 per cent of the electorate and had only one member in the Reichstag; but at the last Reichstag election of the empire, in 1912, they had increased to 29 per cent of all electors and 28 per cent of the seats in the Reichstag. This rapid increase was due above all to the fact that they managed to enlist the new recruits to politics; besides those workers who were already socialistically minded when the empire was founded, Social Democracy drew its strength largely from the lower stratum of people who had left the rural for the industrial areas and who before they became industrial workers had made no use of their right to vote. In the end, then, Bismarck was deceived in his hope that universal equal suffrage would result in loyalist masses supporting the government and outvoting resistant liberalism.

From 1890 onwards the 'Social Democratic Party of Germany' (SPD), its ideologicai basis the popular Marxist Programme of Erfurt

(1891), became the rapidly increasing party of the masses with a large membership (just before the first World War close on one million registered members and four million voters) and a highly developed organisation. In this and in its closely integrated control over its members it differed from the so-called middle-class parties, which lagged far behind the SPD in the efficiency of their organisation, discipline and success in attracting new members. But with the growth in numbers and in the strength of the organisation came a slackening in revolutionary zeal for action. Marxist ideology and politico-social reality were obviously at odds, a fact from which the 'Revisionists' under the intellectual leadership of Eduard Bernstein drew their conclusions. These were not accepted by the party committee and were rejected at the party congress in Dresden in 1903. Bebel, the party's head, and his followers wanted officially to retain the revolutionary doctrine because they felt that it still had force enough to succeed in the not very distant future. But no revolutionary strategy or tactics emerged such as those which later characterised the communism of Lenin. On the contrary, in the *Social-Democratic Catechism* of 1893 the authoritative party ideologist, Karl Kautsky, wrote of the 'democratic-proletarian...so-called peaceful method of class warfare' which he recommended for the party. The SPD was 'a revolutionary party, but not a party that makes revolutions'. This laid down the party line for the whole period from 1890 to 1918.

Organised, 'peaceful' class warfare was carried on with success from 1890 by the trade unions, in complete independence of the SPD, in the favourable atmosphere of a rapidly developing industrial economy. The German workers, though ready enough to believe the socialist ideology and to be conscious of themselves as a class, were in practice more interested in raising their living-standard and in strengthening their political influence than in revolution. It was much easier to accept things as they were. In spite of the strength of organised socialism among the workers, the Germany of 1914 was not on the verge of revolution, though the voting in the Reichstag, especially in that of 1912, unmistakably revealed a potentially explosive situation. During the stable conditions of the pre-war years, no outburst could have taken place; it needed the growing disasters of the war in its final phase in 1917 to 1918 to bring this about.

The Catholic party, the 'Centre', gives us a particularly clear picture of the special nature of a German political party. As far back as the old German Reichstag before 1806 the religious Confessions, the *itio in partes*, had had some independent existence, and had in special cases broken through the curial system of the Estates. Since that date opposition between the Confessions had been sharpened in connection with social movements. The Centre party, founded in 1870, derived from the Catholic fraction of the German Frankfurt Parliament of 1848 and the Prussian

Diet of the 1850's and 1860's. It considered itself pledged to conduct a policy based on the Catholic doctrine of the state and of society, and in particular to apply it in the sharply strained situation prevailing in 1870. The general conflict between the Catholic Church and revolution in all its forms, above all liberalism, mounted to a climax in the 1860's, and the Catholic Church's readiness to fight was emphatically expressed at the Vatican Council of 1870. But it was the situation in Germany, in particular from 1866 onwards, that Catholic politicians saw as most dangerous. Their aim had been a federal Greater Germany. Instead of this, after the exclusion of Catholic Austria they saw themselves relegated to a minority first in the North German Confederation and then in the German empire under a Protestant king and emperor, and further forced into the defensive by the powerful influence of the National Liberals. The Centre saw it as their mission to oppose every effort towards unification within the empire in favour of a federalism as far-reaching as would be compatible with a minimum of imperial authority, to insist on adherence to the provisions of the Prussian Constitution concerning the protection of the Church, and to promote the adoption of the relevant paragraphs in the text of the Imperial Constitution. They had already met with some success in the elections of 1871, but the number of their members in the Reichstag rose considerably in 1874 as a result of the *Kulturkampf*, and from then to the end of the empire the seats held by the party remained constant at 100. In other words, about 25 per cent of the German Reichstag members belonged to the Catholic party, just 37 per cent of the total population of the empire being Catholic.

Finally, another characteristic of the German system of parties was the emphasis on a resistant separatism in sharpest contrast to the German national state. The former kingdom of Hanover had recently become a Prussian province; and here the Guelf party was a rallying-ground for all those who wished to voice their protests at Prussia's annexation of the kingdom. This, however, was only a dwindling minority among the inhabitants. The people of Alsace and Lorraine, whose chosen representatives had protested in the French National Assembly at Bordeaux against annexation by the German empire, in a great majority elected strongly regionalistic members to the Reichstag. These members maintained a separatist attitude and so gave proof of a basic conception of regional autonomy which rejected any unifying national state under either German or French control. In addition there were always one or two Danish members from North Schleswig, where, since the plebiscite provided for by the Peace of Prague (1866) had not been held, the northern frontier strip by Hadersleben showed a Danish majority. The Polish 'fraction' was of greater importance. This usually consisted of from fifteen to twenty members, and up to the end of the century the number of voters rose gradually to just 250,000; but in the three Reichstag elections of 1903, 1907 and 1912 it soared abruptly to 350,000, 450,000 and 440,000. The main reason for this sharp rise in the decade before the first World War was the success of Polish agitation among a section of the Catholic Polish-speaking inhabitants of Upper Silesia; having belonged to the Holy Roman Empire for the past 700 years, they had been moulded by Austria, and then since 1740 by Prussia. These regionalist party groups taken together always amounted to about 5 per cent of all electors and from 5 to 10 per cent of the seats in the Reichstag.

The system of voting for the Reichstag did not reflect the will of the electors in exact proportion, for it was a personal vote with the possibility of a second ballot in cases where no candidate in the constituency had secured a majority at the first. Furthermore, the constituencies for the Reichstag elections, remaining unchanged, ignored the shift of the population from the rural areas to the industrial districts. If instead of the seats in the Reichstag we study the votes at every election from 1871 to 1912, we come on the remarkable fact that the percentage cast for all the so-called middle-class party groups—despite considerable fluctuation in individual elections—remained constant. For instance, the conservative parties (including smaller sympathetic splinter groups which after the 1870's were weak, with only some 10 per cent of the electorate) kept to a medium strength with 14–15 per cent of all electors—these and the following percentages apply to *all* electors, including those who did not take advantage of their right to vote—while the right and left Liberals, apart from a period of special weakness between 1893 and 1903, remained fairly constant at 23 per cent. After the considerable preponderance of National Liberals earlier on, and the fluctuations of the 1880's, the two liberal groups were for the most part equally matched (in 1912, 12 per cent and 10 per cent). The Centre with a bare 15 per cent of the electorate and the Separatist parties with their 5 per cent showed a more constant and consistent representation than did the Conservatives and Liberals. Contrast with these relatively stable electoral results the rise of the SPD from 2 per cent to 29 per cent, which closely corresponded to a decline in the non-voting population from 48 per cent to 16 per cent. The increase in political awareness measured in terms of the poll corresponded very nearly with the growth of Social Democracy. Where the decline in nonvoters exceeded the increase of Social Democracy, it was the Centre party that benefited; between 1871 and 1874 it rose from 9 per cent to 16 per cent of the electorate and, as we have seen, it maintained this level.

Thus the parties of the Right, that is, Conservatives and National Liberals—since the mid-1880's fairly consistently 'loyal to the empire' and supporting imperial government policy—together amounted to no more than a good quarter of all electors, their share of the votes cast declining in proportion as the poll favoured the Social Democrats and, in 1874, the Centre. In the first year of the empire the three parties of the Right still held 57 per cent of all votes cast, though admittedly they did not go politically hand in hand; but in the 1870's and 1880's, except for their electoral defeat in 1884, they had only 47–48 per cent and from 1890 sank gradually to 30 per cent in 1912. And their proportion of seats within the Reichstag, though usually slightly higher, corresponded to the proportion of votes. But the Centre too, once the *Kulturkampf* had died down, increasingly developed after 1879 into a party ready for collaboration with the government: under the empire it was already advancing towards the stabilising role it has played in Germany since 1918. Ranged against these the Socialists and Separatists, consistent in an opposition based on principle, increased during the period 1871–1912 from 8 per cent to 34 per cent of the electorate and from 6 per cent to 37 per cent of the seats in the Reichstag. If we add to these the left-wing Liberals (in 1912, 10 per cent of the electorate and 11 per cent of the Reichstag seats) almost half the voters and members at the end of the empire must be described not only as in opposition to but as rejecting the Constitution on principle. This somewhat alarming condition loses some of its political gravity, however, when we remember two things. In the first place many varied paths led to and fro between the more pro-imperial and anti-imperial parties so that shifting combinations were possible; and secondly, the ostensibly 'anti-imperial' parties were all to a large extent accustomed to things as they were and, *rebus sic stantibus*, were not in a position to carry on any active and constructive policy of opposition. It was not until the first World War that the German parties other than the Conservatives did anything positive towards political constitutional reform—in particular towards altering the suffrage in Prussia and stressing the role of the parliament in the German Imperial Constitution.

The political condition of Germany, one of traditional rigidity strangely compounded with social unrest, corresponded to the process of social transformation, and this process and economic development acted and reacted upon one another. The founding of the empire in 1871 marks no fresh start in this respect. From the economic point of view it is the period from 1850 to 1914, not from 1871 to the first World War, that must be regarded as a whole. This was the period of vast industrialisation in Germany, the first rapid rise coming shortly before the mid-century and lasting till the great slump of 1873, the end of the 'Promoters' Boom'. The revolution of 1848 had come as the climax to many years of crises and at the end of a period of acute hunger; the Bismarckian empire was founded at a peak of industrial growth and economic prosperity. The Greater German revolution had come to grief in a period of austerity; the Lesser German empire was founded in prosperity. There followed after 1873 twenty years in which industry, after periods of sharp depression, grew more slowly. But from the mid-1890's a further vigorous upward movement began, and this was maintained, apart from minor crises, till the outbreak of the first World War rudely interrupted it. By then Germany, which half a century before had been relatively poor though extremely active, had taken her place beside the United States and Great Britain as a leading economic great power. In 1913, 190 million tons of coal (excluding lignite) and 19·3 million tons of pig-iron were produced.

Germany's great coal supplies were amply sufficient and attracted pig-iron from within the country and from abroad, mostly Sweden, to build up heavy industry, the main basis of Germany's economic and military power at that period. Up till the end of the nineteenth century German economy was based chiefly on the association of coal and iron; but later, in the rapid advance after the mid-1890's, electricity, chemistry and the internal combustion engine, with their accompanying industries, also played a part.

The following fundamental facts in connection with German industry during the period of the German empire were of capital importance in the political sphere.

Agriculture roughly doubled its yield between 1871 and 1914. This meant that with strict restraint Germany could just manage to feed herself without imports for a while. After the mid-1870's, however, dependence on agricultural imports continued to increase; for growing urbanisation and a rising standard of living brought new and greater demands in the matter of food; and after the late 1870's agriculture, in particular the corn market, felt the pressure of import prices from overseas and Russia.

Up to the middle of the century Germany had still lacked capital. This state of affairs altered rapidly during the period of industrial promotion. Bank stock and industrial capital, closely linked and expanding fast, were mutually dependent to a very high degree. Opportunities were quickly sought for investing capital abroad. Germany, till the 1880's an importer of capital, now began to export it. In 1913 investment of German capital abroad was estimated at about 30 milliard Marks. German foreign trade developed slowly up to 1890, then more quickly up to 1900, and between 1900 and 1914 with a sharp rise; and largely because of capital reserves abroad it could be maintained at the same level. The vigorous development of industry and its share in this foreign trade are expressed in the proportion of industrial finished goods in the total exports; in 1872 this was only about a third, but by 1913 it amounted to about two-thirds. This rise corresponded to the rapid decline in German emigration, which took place when the long period of prosperity began in the mid-1890's. Despite the rapid growth of the population during the empire (1871–1914) from 40 to 67 million, it was possible from the mid-1890's onwards to absorb this increase within the country and gradually to raise the general standard of living at the same time.

The optimism caused by the rising curve of economic expansion found expression in this increase in the population. From the 1880's onwards Germany experienced the slowly onsetting decline in the birth-rate that is typical of all industrial countries. But it was not till the last decade before 1914 that the birth-rate dropped more steeply to 28 per 1000 (the death-rate being 16 per 1000). In the years immediately before 1910 the population of the empire increased annually by over 800,000; each year the army's annual intake was more than double that of France. This was the period of maximum increase in Germany's population, and in the first years of the century its components were particularly favourable: 32 per cent of the population were young people under 14, only just over 4 per cent old people over 65. In addition, the population during the decades of the empire was extraordinarily mobile. More intensive and rational methods in agriculture caused a shift of the surplus population from the rural districts (not only of the eastern provinces) to the congested industrial centres with their growing demand for labour.

The number and the percentage employed in agriculture sank: in 1882 it was 19·2 million or 42·5 per cent; in 1907 17·7 million or 28·6 per cent. In other words, from the foundation of the empire to the first World War the proportion of the population employed in agriculture sank from one-half to one-quarter. Thus the decades of the empire came in the middle of the so-called 'flight from the land', that great impulse that began exactly at the economic turning-point in about 1850 and has by today brought about almost the lowest possible figure of approximately 15 per cent of the population employed in agriculture. The numbers of those employed in industry show a corresponding rise for the years 1882–1907 (16·1 million or 35·5 per cent to 26·4 million or 42·8 per cent), and so do those in commerce and transport (4·5 million or 10 per cent to 8·3 million or 13·4 per cent). The great demand for workers made by industry and other sections of the economy besides primary production could easily be met during that period out of the surplus streaming in from rural districts, over-populated till then, or out of the great natural accretion. All this growth was not only a matter of population; it distinguished every branch of the national economy, raised individual standards of living and produced the beginnings of nation-wide organisation in trade, society and culture. And with it came a robustly optimistic way of life which, especially after the 1890's when the educated middle classes began a lively criticism of society and culture, was often characterised as materialistic.

The confidence inspired by this rising curve experienced its first severe shock earlier than this, however, in the great economic crisis of 1873, and prevailing conditions in the two following decades did little to sustain it. It is important to stress that Bismarck with his constant burden of troubles at home was the guiding force in imperial policy for the most part during years of depression and stagnation, whereas William II's chancellors profited by the great economic upsurge. It was a movement which, while simplifying their domestic policy (despite the rise of social democracy), also endangered it by creating the temptation to make light of unsolved problems.

Bismarck's domestic policy from 1871 to 1890 can, like his foreign policy, be traced back to one single guiding principle, namely, to make the empire secure; for its founder was more directly conscious of what endangered it than were most Germans. They soon grew to regard their national state, their aim for two whole generations, as an asset to be taken for granted. Bismarck knew that he waged a constant defensive war, both within and without, on all 'enemies of the empire'. It is well known that in the domain of foreign policy he was always employing novel, bold methods of diplomacy and alliance for this defensive purpose. He even toyed with preventive war; but he always remained aware of how unreliable this was, and in contrast to Count Moltke, Chief of the General Staff, and to Count Waldersee, he never seriously wished to make use of it. His methods for meeting internal political discord were analogous and this analogy certainly reveals Bismarck's limitations as a domestic politician. It is true that, much more than critics then or since will allow, he had a high sense of his responsibility, which was most deeply rooted in his Lutheran faith: he was a statesman in the service of a righteous state and stood above any and every party. But in practice he found himself continually so hard pressed, fighting on several fronts, that he was always being forced to take measures which have been justly described in terms of a 'domestic preventive war'.

This is particularly true of his fateful decision, in the very year when the empire was founded and when there was special need for reconciliation between the denominations, to cross swords with the Centre and so with the Catholic Church in Prussia. Bismarck, however, had no wish to mingle in the philosophical warfare of the Liberals with the Catholics, and the idea of the *Kulturkampf* was in no way in the spirit of his thought. (The name *Kulturkampf* was first used by Professor Rudolf Virchow, one of the most convinced parliamentarians among the Progressives.) The Chancellor's aim was rather to obviate the danger of an alliance of all Catholic powers, both within and without, against his empire—in other words a union between Austria, France, where a restoration was possible, and the Centre and its tactical allies, the Poles and the Guelf party, in Germany. It exasperated him that political Catholicism, hostile to the foundation of the empire along Lesser German lines and allied to the ancient enemy, Austria, had formed in the Centre party a sort of spearhead in domestic politics. For a Christian denomination to organise itself into a party seemed to him as disruptive as that one stratum of the population, the workers, should form itself into a class and organise a political party. In this way the Centre and the Social Democrats, though so opposed, were classed together by Bismarck as 'enemies of the empire'. In the interests of the state Bismarck abhorred any mass organisation claiming autonomy and an international outlook.

His aims in the *Kulturkampf* were the most radical separation possible of state and Church, and so of Church and education, and the strengthening of state control over Church and clergy. These were common tendencies in Europe at the time. Their unusual and exacerbating feature in Prussia was the aggressive legislation culminating in prohibition and penal laws. When the clergy resisted the May Laws of 1873, in particular the 'Law governing the Training and Appointment of the Clergy', proceedings were taken against bishops and priests. In 1876 every Prussian bishop was in prison or had left the country, and very many parishes were vacant.

Bismarck realised that he had let himself be driven into a hopeless conflict. He had believed himself obliged in the interests of the state to take it up. The same interests led him to look for ways to allay it, after the 1870's, when he no longer felt any necessity for it. On the contrary; as he began in 1878–9 to draw away from the National Liberals and to aim at an alliance with Austria-Hungary, Europe's chief Catholic power, he sought the support of the Centre as his confederates. The succession of a new pope in 1878 favoured this design. Direct negotiations with Pope Leo XIII, whom Bismarck manœuvred to separate from the Centre, led to an ebbing of the strife. In 1879 the Centre gave its support to Bismarck's financial and protectionist policy. But it was not till 1887 that the conflict came officially to an end, after the controversial laws had been repealed; and even then important changes such as state inspection of schools and civil marriage were retained. The quarrel had not ended unfavourably for Bismarck. But it had its effect on people's minds for a long time after. The political Catholicism of the Centre party emerged from the struggle both confirmed and strengthened.

Bismarck's preventive war against the Social Democrats failed in a similar way. After two attempts on the life of the Emperor William I—though these had nothing to do with the Social Democratic party—Bismarck ushered in the conflict by presenting a bill 'Against the dangerous activities of the Social Democrats' in 1878. This measure led to grave dissension among the National Liberals who, though the keenest opponents of the Social Democrats, had scruples on principle about any Exceptional Law. It was not until after a dissolution and their electoral defeat that in the new Reichstag of 1878 they gave their support and the Exceptional Law was therefore approved. This considerably restricted the scope of Social Democratic agitation. Meetings and publications were banned, proceedings were taken against party officials and they were expelled. But elections and political activity were still sanctioned; and though the police in carrying out the law were strict enough to create difficulties and cause bitterness, there can be no comparison with the harsher repressive measures of modern totalitarian states. At the same time the twelve years of the anti-Socialist Act brought greater firmness and clarity within the Social Democrat party. The period of repression lived on in the socialists' memory as a 'heroic age' (Kautsky). In spite of the Law their numbers rose, and in 1890 the great increase began that was to make them the party of the millions.

It would be wrong to think of Bismarck's actions in regard to the SPD as showing simply a lack of social responsibility. As early as the 1860's he had become convinced that socialist demands could not be ignored and that the state was in duty bound to tackle the social question. Tactical considerations had not been the only reason for his brief connection with Lassalle. In Bismarck's view the state's own task of social reform was linked together with the struggle against the socialists in their refusal to come to terms with the state. His conception of the state as a 'continuing personality' above all groups and parties is shown most clearly in his social policy.

Bismarck embarked on a state system of social insurance in the three famous laws covering sickness (1883), accidents (1884), and old age and disability (1889). His principle was one of corporate self-help through insurance contributions by employers and employees, with additional financial help from the state, which should also make this insurance compulsory by law. He found himself accused of 'state socialism' by his liberal opponents, who rejected any kind of state compulsion or subsidy. The Chancellor took up the expression and avowed it, prophesying for the future an increase in inevitable trends towards state socialism. He was not even averse from some form of nationalisation for the mines. But these decided steps towards founding the modern state system of insurance and pensions contrast with Bismarck's extraordinary reluctance to make any attempt to protect workers by the prohibition of Sunday work and the restriction of hours of work for women and children and of working hours generally. In this Bismarck's experience as a landowner accustomed to rural conditions of work kept him faithful to tradition, and he believed that in this he was not opposing the real interest of the families of workers themselves.

Both the anti-Socialist Act and the social policy of the state are related to Bismarck's political antagonism to liberalism. Here we touch upon the great combination of influences at work in 1879. This year must be seen as the decisive turning-point in the economic and domestic policy of the empire, one which basically determined the whole age of William II. The immediate occasion for it arose from economic necessity in a double sense. In the Constitution the imperial finances had received unsatisfactory and only provisional treatment. The empire could not impose any taxes. Even in its first years its meagre revenue, largely derived from the Department of Posts and Telegraphs, was insufficient in view of the expanding imperial administration, so that the empire became as it were the 'boarder of the states', dependent on their contributions; and even these were not enough. A reform of the imperial finances was therefore urgently needed. Bismarck tried to raise revenue from indirect taxation and customs dues. For this reason his plans for the imperial finances were closely bound up with the dispute on free trade or protection which began in Germany in the mid-1870's when the economic depression invited criticism of free-trade theory and practice. Under the influence of Carey's theory the leader of the Free Conservatives, Wilhelm von Kardorff, whose own business interests were both agrarian and industrial, wrote his pamphlet *Against the Current* and in 1876 founded the 'Central Alliance of German Industrialists for the Promotion and Preservation of National Labour'. Kardorff had a decisive influence on Bismarck, who determined in 1878 to follow the example of almost every other industrial country except Great Britain by abandoning free trade and introducing fairly high tariffs. He was all the more determined because, for the first time, not only the iron and steel industry but agriculture too was calling for protective duties; with its relatively high production costs it could no longer compete with the low prices of America and Russia. This was especially unfortunate since in the mid-1870's Germany had become an importer of corn, whereas up till then the economy of the eastern provinces had been built up on the export of agricultural products. As the export of corn continued to decline, landowners were extremely anxious to secure a guaranteed home price. In 1878–9 corn and iron entered into an economic alliance under the slogan 'Protection of National Labour'. The objection that the consumers suffered from the rise in prices brought about by protective tariffs was met by Bismarck with the argument that it was only through state help that commerce could recover at all, and so once again afford a basis for employment and increased purchasing power. He further expressed the hope that the individual states would be able to lower their direct taxation once it was possible to discontinue or to reduce their contributions to the empire because the empire had at its disposal a revenue of its own sufficient to its needs.

Bismarck skilfully made long-term preparations for his tariff and financial reforms. He first made sure of his finance minister, then of the Federal Council and finally of the Reichstag, where towards the end of 1878 the 'National Economic Union' of protectionist members cut across almost every party. The Centre was won over. While the National Liberals split over this question, a completely new one to them, the majority of them sided with Bismarck despite their liberal tenets. This gave him an assured majority which lasted through the debates and divisions on the tariff in the summer of 1879. His dependence on the Centre did however jeopardise his chief object, which was that the tariff question should be effectively bound up with financial reforms. A motion put forward by the Centre was adopted by which all imperial revenue exceeding 130 million Marks was annually to be handed over to the several states and by which the states were bound as occasion demanded to the payment of contributions to the empire. In this way financial federalism was saved, despite Bismarck's intentions, as was parliamentary control of a large proportion of the imperial revenue. Bismarck had thus won a half-victory only. The financial constitution of the empire always remained a particularly sore point. Rising expenditure involved increasing dependence on the several states and a growing debt on the part of the empire.

After 1879, corresponding to the general trend that was affecting most of Europe, German agriculture remained dependent on guaranteed prices, while in industry cartels were formed to protect the new foreign-trade policy. At the same time the various trade associations grew steadily more influential, especially those of heavy industry and of the landowners to the east of the Elbe, whose interests were merged in 1879 though they subsequently often clashed.

Although Bismarck's protectionist policy, in a situation allowing him no choice, had arisen from his economic aims, the consequences in domestic and party politics were equally important for him. He had been able half to win over the Centre; the National Liberals, after he had split their ranks, lost their authoritative influence; and he saw this as a significant triumph. Besides, it brought about the ultimate rejection of the parliamentary system of government which had again been the subject of negotiations between Bismarck and Bennigsen in 1877. Bismarck's aversion from parliament and parliamentarians, of which he made no secret, dates from 1879, and in the sittings between 1881 and 1884, with majorities against him, Bismarck again and again found himself frustrated by the refractory character of the Reichstag. His feelings even led him to consider (though never very seriously) an alteration in the Constitution in the direction of corporative representation.

Taken as a whole, the 1880's even more than the 1870's were for Bismarck years of hostility and exacerbating friction. There were many causes for this. There was no reliable majority in the Reichstag, split as it was into many parties. The European balance, as Bismarck wished to preserve it, was continually being threatened. Other most important factors were the wastage of power resulting from the Chancellor's often unfortunate personal policy and the strife between the different generations of the Hohenzollern dynasty. All this told on Bismarck's health, which was always sorely tried and which he himself made worse. He tormented himself and all who had anything to do with him by his testy rudeness, his intransigence, his suspicion. His actions were based on the determination never to become dependent upon anyone. He carried this to such extremes that intimate friendship became impossible for him. He wanted to be in sole command of circumstances, though he well knew the limited power of a helmsman in these waves—a metaphor he sometimes used, as for instance in the motto '*Fert unda nec regitur*'. As the tension continued he more than once let himself be carried away into using measures that thwarted his own aims. These included not only instances of lack of personal consideration in which, ostensibly for reasons of state interest, he showed contempt either for right or justice, but also basic decisions of his policy.

It is well to look at Bismarck's colonial policy in this light. The brief unheralded era during which Germany acquired her colonies resulted indirectly from the 1879 turning-point in commercial policy. In 1882 the German Colonial Union was founded, in 1884 the Association for German Colonisation, and by 1884–5 the acquisitions in Africa and the South Pacific were virtually completed. These were made thanks to a few enterprising businessmen and to bankers of the Berlin Discount Company, acting against a background of colonial propaganda that was rapidly diffused among the middle classes. The imperial administration did nothing beyond following up private initiative. At first Bismarck held aloof, for he wished to avoid any international entanglements for this European empire of his. Next he tried to limit the empire to exercising only protective authority over the trading companies holding colonial territory. But this sort of reserve was opposed to the general trend of the times towards colonisation, in which Germany felt that, even as a late-comer, she was still entitled to a share. So Bismarck let himself be carried by the tide, came indeed to do so consciously and deliberately, so that he could use a national rallying-cry to make his difficult position in domestic politics somewhat more secure. But he never intended to inaugurate an imperialist international policy for Germany through the foundation of colonies. He feared the association of colonial and naval power, which in fact irresistibly prevailed from the 1890's onwards.

Even the idea of 'home colonisation' in combination with the spread of German peasant settlement in the areas of mixed German-Polish population in the eastern provinces—an idea along national-liberal lines—came to Bismarck from others, and he only accepted it with some reluctance. For he still held to the old idea that, though the Polish aristocracy and their confederates, the Polish clergy, were enemies of the Prussian-German state, the Polish population, in particular the Polish peasantry, had always shown themselves to be loyal subjects, as they had recently done as soldiers in the wars between 1864 and 1871. In yielding to the Germanising tendencies, which were strengthened after 1894 by the 'German Association of the Eastern Marches', Bismarck once again accepted a popular national movement he had originally opposed. In this movement Poles as well as Germans were now caught up. Since the *Kulturkampf* there had been a hard struggle over language and education, in which the Poles had been forbidden the use of their mother tongue; and since 1886, when the Prussian 'Settlement Commission' was set up, there was also the fight for the land. The Poles countered German state aid with their communal co-operative system, and by keen purchase and settlement of the land they successfully kept up the struggle down to the end of the empire.

Towards the end of William I's reign Bismarck scored another great success in domestic policy with the so-called Septennate Elections of 1887. Once again home and foreign policy were closely interwoven after the typical Bismarckian fashion. The military question was the actual and urgent starting-point. Since the Bulgarian crisis of 1885–6, and in view of the intensified *revanche* spirit in France under Boulanger as Minister of War, Bismarck had been worried by the realisation that in Germany the build-up of the armed forces lagged behind that of France. France spent far more than Germany and her conscription was far more rigorous, with the result that despite a much smaller population her peace strength in 1886 exceeded that of Germany. Bismarck therefore felt obliged to present a bill for a 10 per cent increase in the army; like previous army bills it was to run for seven years, as a 'Septennate'. The matter itself was serious enough, but Bismarck's chief motive was a tactical one of internal policy in relation to the Reichstag. The Reichstag rejected the Septennate, though not the increase in the strength of the army altogether; and this was what Bismarck wanted. It gave him a favourable pretext for dissolving the Reichstag and also a slogan for the new elections: 'The Fatherland is in danger.' It was a great success. The three parties of the right, Conservatives, Free Conservatives and National Liberals, who united to form the 'Cartel', won an absolute majority of 220 of the 397 seats, to a large extent by mobilising a high proportion of previous non-voters. It brought considerable relief to Bismarck, though this was short-lived, as the Cartel broke up in 1890.

A double change in the succession to the throne introduced a new situation for Bismarck and for the empire in 1888. The Chancellor lost in William I the royal master to whom he had been bound by what one might term the loyalty of a vassal, though in decisive situations Bismarck had always imposed his own superior will. He feared that the liberal-minded Emperor Frederick III and his ardently political consort Victoria, Queen Victoria's daughter and Bismarck's great opponent, would govern through a sort of 'Gladstone ministry', too anglophile abroad and too liberal at home, under Freiherr von Roggenbach, a native of Baden. But the emperor, already mortally ill, died only three months later without having exerted any appreciable influence. The attitude of his twenty-nine year old son, the Emperor William II, had been one of sharp opposition to his parents. In spite of his nimble mind and versatile interests, the dangerous aspects of his character at once became apparent: unrest and a hunger for appreciation, a leaning towards an autocrat's 'personal rule' and, further, an overestimation of things military and a military tone in society which reflected his training in a Potsdam regiment of Guards.

The optimistic young monarch, yearning to achieve great things, was eager for independence. He could not tolerate the old Chancellor, who was accustomed to his own sole responsibility. This was the fundamental reason for Bismarck's dismissal on 20 March 1890. The court chaplain, Stöcker, head of the Christian-Social anti-semitic movement, and Count Waldersee, Chief of the General Staff, who in contrast to Bismarck was working for a preventive war with Russia, were the leading figures in the intrigues against him. Following a great strike of mineworkers in the Ruhr (1889) the clash came early in 1890 over questions of social policy, which the emperor wished to base on measures for the protection of the workers, and over a dispute about the anti-Socialist Act; Bismarck wished to extend this in a more acute form while William II hoped to be able to work towards a reconciliation by repealing it. The Reichstag rejected an extension of the law; the Cartel of the three parties of the right disintegrated. The new elections in February that followed the dissolution of the Reichstag brought a clear defeat for Bismarck and considerable success for the Social-Democrats and left-wing Liberals. This fact certainly played an important part during the altercations between emperor and Chancellor. Bismarck was determined to resist the Reichstag; that is to say, he was clearly bent for the present on repeated dissolutions of parliament and, if need arose, would not have shrunk from an alteration in the electoral franchise and the imposition of a new constitution. Such a drastic line of action was in complete contrast to William II's views at that period; and so, amid bitter and provocative exchanges, Bismarck tendered his resignation and the emperor accepted it with relief.

It is well known that Bismarck's dismissal marks in some ways the end of an epoch in foreign policy: Russia who was seeking an extension of the 'Reinsurance Treaty' of 1887 met with a refusal; and above all Bismarck's artfully contrived diplomacy, denounced by Privy Councillor Holstein as too subtle (*Finassieren*), was radically replaced by a policy of 'simplification'. But in home affairs, too, the departure of the man who had shaped the Imperial Constitution to his own requirements was of far-reaching significance. None of his successors was of Bismarck's stature; none of them could fill the position, so dangerously comprehensive, that had been his within the Constitution. The relationship of the Chancellor's 'responsibility' to the autocracy claimed by the emperor, who was in fact far from capable of 'personal rule', remained undecided. The Reichstag increased its importance. And most important of all, from now on the political leadership of the Chancellor on the one hand and on the other of the departments of the army and the navy, each quite independent, became more than before completely disconnected, linked solely now—and most imperfectly—in the person of the emperor.

Judging after the event one could justify Bismarck's dismissal by saying that not only social but also constitutional reforms were overdue, and that William II, the 'social emperor' of so many hopes, might have carried them out. In view of the latent constitutional crisis, was there not an alternative to the anti-parliamentarian *coup d'état* considered by Bismarck, namely an alteration in the Constitution towards democratic parliamentary control? This would certainly have involved a political risk, with the party system as it then was; but it would have been more suited to the trend of the times than any anti-democratic course. In the event William II evaded any constitutional decision. Social reform was half-hearted; and no move at all was risked in constitutional policy. It was not many years after Bismarck's departure that William II was himself considering *coups d'état*; and in a speech in Königsberg on 6 September 1894 he launched the rallying-cry, ill-timed in the romanticism of its sounding rhetoric, 'For religion, for morality and sound order, against the parties of destruction'—the plural being used to show that not only the Social-Democrat enemies of the empire were meant. And so the illusions about a 'new deal' soon passed away; and in any case this would have been beyond the powers of von Caprivi, Bismarck's worthy successor as Imperial Chancellor, a model of Old Prussian single-mindedness. The emperor and his men did not take any notice of critics such as the sociologist Max Weber, who in his inaugural address at Freiburg University in 1895 spoke in favour of a powerful national state with an expanding economy and also made a stern, pessimistic forecast about internal policy. Friedrich Naumann's publication with its platform-title *Democracy and the Imperial Dignity*, though it made a stir, was not seriously heeded. Despite his open attitude to modern technology, navigation, artistic and cultural movements, in his conception of the state and of society the emperor shut himself off as if at some feudal court, impervious to the changed social conditions among his own people.

After von Caprivi's fall in 1894 Prince Chlodwig von Hohenlohe-Schillingsfürst, a Bavarian noble and a liberal Catholic, an elderly man unable to take the lead, was Imperial Chancellor for six years. Though Hohenlohe did not contribute to this result, these were the years that decided the course the Germany of William II would follow. The economic boom had started vigorously and had begun to have effect. The emperor wanted first to deal with the naval question, in order to adapt Germany's position to new conditions. Germany's foreign trade was already second in Europe after that of Great Britain, but her navy was still far behind Britain's and those of France, Russia, and Italy as well. Now Germany, belatedly enough, was to join the general trend of 'new navalism'. It seemed impossible also to stand aloof from 'world politics' as Bismarck had done, now that, in view of the growing foreign trade and the colonial footholds newly won, in China and the South Pacific, Germany's maritime interests claimed attention. The interrelation of foreign trade, sea-power and international politics guided the emperor's whole statecraft, and his dearest wish came to be to have a powerful German navy. In this he consciously abandoned Bismarck's European policy of a 'satiated' empire. If we rightly consider economic facts and the spirit of the times, we cannot call William II's decision an instance of irresponsible pride; it was a recognition of the urgent needs of a new and rapidly expanding industrial nation by means usual in that day. Germany was obliged to go beyond the Bismarck scale. But the point was to find among the new conditions some new scale, and to control the consequences (in particular with relation to Great Britain) that followed from Germany's geographical key-position by land and sea. The generation of William II, schooled politically by such an advocate of the strong national state and of active international policy as the historian Heinrich von Treitschke, was inclined in its optimistic consciousness of power to underestimate this basic problem of German politics.

At first it was difficult to carry through this naval policy at home. The Foreign Office, often subjected to criticism as 'anglophile', acted obstructively. The imperial chancellor gave way only to the emperor. The Conservatives, with their largely agrarian interests, remained aloof and suspicious. Eugen Richter's Progressives and the Social Democrats naturally opposed the burden of a large naval programme. And so at the Reichstag naval debate in the spring of 1897 the emperor's aims miscarried. William II had thoughts of staging a *coup d'état*. But instead of this doubtful step he tried a change of ministers in order to bring about what he wanted. He appointed Admiral von Tirpitz Secretary of State to the Navy Office and Count (later Prince) von Bülow as Secretary of State for Foreign Affairs (1897). Later, in 1900, Bülow also became Imperial Chancellor.

Naval policy developed rapidly after Tirpitz's appointment and became a constant source of violent disputes in domestic politics. The industries concerned supported the Navy League which became extremely active, inspiriting the Right while it exacerbated the Left. It often made much wider demands than either Tirpitz of Bülow welcomed. With its large membership, rising to over half a million, it was the most effective of the political 'pressure groups' which were a counterpart among the middle classes to the proletarian organisations, the trade unions and the SPD. The political organisation of the right-wing middle class can be studied in these associations. Besides the Navy League there were the German Colonial Union, the Imperial League against Social Democracy, the German Association of the Eastern Marches, and the Defence League, which was not founded till a few years before the war. This last worked not only for an increase in the army but in practice for its reform along the lines of national democracy; for the army through its leaders had maintained an aristocratic reserve and in this could be said to lag behind the navy. There was talk of the 'people in arms', its duty to wage a 'to be or not to be' struggle and, in the event of an emergency, to fight for its existence and national honour. This spirit was foreign and suspect to the body of high-ranking officers, steeped in Old Prussian tradition, and even to such a 'soldier pure and simple' as General von Schlieffen, Chief of the General Staff from 1891 to 1905. The 'Pan-German League', though relatively small in membership (before the first World War it never much exceeded 20,000) was the most extreme of these bodies. In the unbridled demands of its comprehensive nationalism, to which were added elements of a political Darwinism that was not confined to Germany, this association was already clearly developing the medley of 'popular' ideologies that later characterised National Socialism. The Pan-Germanists exerted appreciable influence through Reichstag deputies of the right, to a lesser degree through professors at the universities, and through cross-connections within commerce and the bureaucracy. The imperial administration under Bülow and still more under his successor Bethmann Hollweg (1909–17) saw its agitation as a disturbing element but was unable to avoid its influence.

We touch here on the central question of the extent to which Germany before 1914 was impelled by forces leading to war and encouraging the development of war aims. Certain features in official German foreign policy show clearly that it had not succeeded in adjusting itself firmly to the new international political situation in the so-called imperialist age; and here the emperor's occasional outbursts of fantastic behaviour were not without their effects. But in spite of commercial expansion, naval policy and undertakings such as the Baghdad Railway, there was no real intention to alter the *status quo*, let alone to disrupt it violently. To that extent it was still official policy to regard the empire as what Bismarck had termed 'satiated'. It was not the leadership in the government or the army but a national middle-class movement that provided the motive power and the dangerous explosive material that were driving the country beyond this point. In this movement the idealism of the era of classical liberalism joined with the ambition of successfully expanding commerce to produce an exaggerated national consciousness and will-power, and—as it is with suddenly aspiring, 'awaking' peoples—this will was so strong as to involve the danger that sense of principle and proportion would be lost. This wave of national exuberance broke over even the Catholic Centre and the parties of the left, though it was often resisted both by them and at times also, and with firmness, by the old Prussian conservatives.

The year 1906 thus led to a situation in internal politics in some ways resembling the Cartel elections of 1887. The Imperial Chancellor von Bülow, who up till then had managed the parties with some adroitness but without any real over-all plan, dissolved the Reichstag at the end of 1906, after the Centre as well as the Social Democrats had refused a supplementary estimate for the expenses of the colonial war in German South-west Africa, and launched against the Centre and the Social Democrats his electoral slogan of the 'Conservative spirit matched with the Liberal spirit'. The 'block' of the conservative and liberal parties, joined after Eugen Richter's death by even the left-wing Liberals, secured half the seats in the Reichstag at the next election. At long last a combination comparable to a government coalition had come into being in the Reichstag.

The so-called 'Daily Telegraph Affair' revealed how much the Reichstag had by then grown beyond the role assigned to it in the Constitution. The occasion was an article in the London *Daily Telegraph* of 20 October 1908, entitled 'The German Emperor in England', which quoted remarks made by William II to the Englishman Colonel Stuart Wortley. The emperor had expressed his friendly attitude towards Great Britain but in doing so had tactlessly revived memories of the Boer War. The article at once raised a great stir, less in England than in Germany. The emperor had been satisfied with the published text but had shifted the onus by sending on the text to Bülow for approval. Without reading the article, Bülow passed it on to the Foreign Office for their attention and then, after only minor changes, let it go for publication in Germany, still unread by himself. Here the Chancellor, who happened to be on holiday at the coast and was preoccupied by the outbreak of the Bosnian crisis, had acted with very great negligence. The full responsibility was his, as he was the responsible director of foreign policy alongside the emperor. But after the first few days public opinion became much more critical of William II and his misuse of his 'personal rule' than of the Chancellor. And Bülow, though he was conscious of being to blame, dissociated himself from William II as much as possible in his explanations to the Reichstag. His chief desire was to extricate himself from the affair with unblemished character. He promised to see that the emperor 'in future, even in his private utterances, observed that discretion which is indispensable both in the interests of a uniform policy and to the authority of the Crown'. William signed an undertaking reaffirming the responsibility laid down for him in the Constitution and assured Bülow of his full confidence. He had a nervous breakdown and even thought of abdication.

The 'Daily Telegraph Affair' almost equals the decisive year 1897 as the most significant turning-point in the reign of William up to 1914. The emperor's self-confidence was shattered and he abandoned his leaning towards 'personal rule'. The Reichstag had shown its power and had reprimanded him sharply. The Imperial Chancellor appeared to have come off very lightly. But if he had repeatedly shown himself to be astute, he had also been morally small-minded; and despite their apparent reconciliation he had lost his sovereign's confidence. He was dismissed in the summer of 1909, when the Reichstag rejected the introduction of the first direct imperial tax, the Death Duty. The Conservatives, the Centre and smaller groups voted against it. It was almost a case of parliament bringing about the fall of a Chancellor. The 'Daily Telegraph Affair' and Bülow's departure mark the beginning of an evolution towards parliamentary authority in the Imperial Constitution, which was an unsettling factor in the years before the war and which was eventually completed only under the stress of war in 1917–18.

Bülow's successor was von Bethmann Hollweg, Secretary of State and Prussian Minister of the Interior. He was an outstanding administrator with the widest interests. His insight into Germany's foreign and domestic problems was more profound than that of most representatives of the 'bureaucracy' of the day. But he was too diffident and not vigorous enough to assert himself either in the worsening situation in domestic politics before the war or, later, during the war itself. All he was able to attempt was to hold the balance between opposing forces. It was with outward splendour and mounting prosperity but with many of its internal problems yet unsolved that the empire moved on towards the great world war—a war which the imperial administration had neither desired nor prepared for, but which many Germans, sharing the general assumptions of the Europe of that day, regarded as inevitable.

CHAPTER XI

THE FRENCH REPUBLIC

I T is impossible to understand the following pages[1] if it is not first realised that the French in 1871 were dominated by memories of the peculiarly eventful three-quarters of a century since 1789. The peasants, who remained by far the largest social group, only slowly absorbed new ideas. They still feared the re-establishment of an aristocratic and clerical regime that would reimpose feudal dues and tithes on them; conversely, they had acquired a very acute sense of their property rights and, particularly since 1848, it had become easy to rouse in them an irrational fear of 'the Reds' or the *partageux* (redistributionists), by whom they meant the politically more advanced town-dwellers who would come and take away their land or at least their savings (kept in the famous woollen stockings). Undoubtedly the landed nobility, still very important in certain regions, and the upper middle class did not dream of challenging, yet again, either the freedoms proclaimed in 1789 or even the civil equality consecrated by the Code Napoléon; but they remembered with dread the Terror of 1793-4, the rising which brought in the July Monarchy, the February Revolution of 1848 and the rising of June 1848. They consequently refused all compromise with the new ideas and the popular aspirations of the *nouvelles couches*, in which they were incapable of seeing anything other than purely destructive forces. As for the convinced republicans (industrial workers, artisans, and many in commerce and the liberal professions), their ideal was 1793: the Constitution of the Year One, which had provided for a very liberal, very democratic, very decentralised regime, but also the supremacy of the convention and the great committees; in other words an all-powerful assembly acknowledging no limit to its power. On every occasion it was to 1793 that they turned for precedent and example.

The class-struggle between the workers and the bourgeoisie did not directly affect a very large part of a country where heavy industry was not far developed, but it did awaken a considerable sentimental response. The workers had not forgiven the bourgeoisie, even the republican bourgeoisie, for the repression of the June risings in 1848, and another

---

[1] It is not much of an exaggeration to say that the history of the Third Republic has not yet been written, even in part. The numerous books dealing with it have been, until recently, more often inspired by political preconceptions or the need to provide a general outline than based on methodical research. In the last few years, however, many research theses have been projected; obviously, when they are published many questions will be revived. The present chapter, then, has a provisional character; it is largely based on a personal study of the sources, for the Boulangist period at least.

event now roused the old antagonism to its highest pitch: the Paris Commune.

This last episode is still passionately debated and this is no place to decide between the opposed theories. The circumstances may be briefly recalled. Paris had just surrendered to the Germans after a siege during which her inhabitants had suffered cruelly in body and in mind; the rest of France had just elected, as will shortly be described, an assembly with a royalist majority. After fortuitous incidents that it would take too long to recapitulate, a popular revolt broke out on 18 March 1871 and the government of M. Thiers, retreating to Versailles, abandoned Paris to the rebels. For two months the capital was in the hands of its own elected assembly, which called itself 'the Commune'. It is difficult to define the relative importance in this popular movement of wounded patriotism, republican anxiety for a threatened ideal, the irritation of the capital against the provinces which it had long been accustomed to dominate but which this time imposed their will on it, and, finally, of the misery of the poorer classes. The socialists, properly so-called, had notable roles in the Commune but they were only a minority. Nevertheless, it can be said that when the army under Thiers' orders reconquered Paris it was the working-quarters in the east which offered the most stubborn resistance. The reconquest—the Bloody Week of May 1871—had a particularly savage character and left an enduring bitterness between he two adversaries. The partisans of order—the *Versaillais*—long denounced the Commune for its execution of hostages and the burning of so many of the monuments in central Paris; they labelled as *communards* all champions of social reform. On their side the workers did not forgive the bourgeoisie for the executions and mass-deportations, and the socialists later adopted the custom of going on a pilgrimage each year to the cemetery of Père Lachaise, where the last defenders of the Commune had fallen.

In the rest of France, meanwhile, much was happening. Bismarck had begun *pourparlers* with the provisional government which was set up on 4 September 1870. But he would only conclude a peace with a representative and undisputed government which France would be unable to disavow. Hence it was necessary, in a country to a large extent occupied by the enemy, to hold hasty elections. These took place on 8 February 1871. They returned 150 republicans, 80 liberals, 400 royalists, 20 bonapartists. Given these figures, how was it possible for a republic to be established within a few years? This apparently paradoxical fact must now be explained.

To begin with, the elections were essentially fought on the question of peace or war. Gambetta, the best-known of the republican leaders, was the embodiment of last-ditch resistance. Those on republican lists very often made use of his name and his ideas. The conservatives, on the other hand, proclaimed themselves the party of peace and took shelter under Thiers' prestige. The vast majority of the voters, above all those in the countryside, being convinced that the war was hopelessly lost, wanted peace before anything else. Almost nowhere, moreover, had there been the time or the opportunity to conduct a real election campaign. The citizens voted for the only candidates they knew, those of the local notables who were not excluded by the discredit that had fallen on them for having served the Second Empire; in other words, largely for the great landowners and lawyers, who were usually conservatives. But as soon as the Treaty of Frankfurt was signed and the question arose of re-establishing the monarchy, the peasants began to fear that the experiment might lead to the return of the Old Regime. From that moment republicans generally won in by-elections.

In the assembly itself the royalist majority was chiefly composed (apart from fifty to eighty deputies on the extreme right) of liberal conservatives. They not only did not attack the social achievements of the Revolution, but were sincerely attached to representative institutions and naturally drawn to a parliamentary regime. But the legitimist pretender to the throne, the Comte de Chambord, was a man of the Old Regime. He claimed power on the grounds of his divine right and not by delegation from the sovereign people. In fact he would probably have left the new institutions of post-revolutionary society alone, but he would not accept that society's principles, and in France at that moment principles played an essential part. The clash was symbolised in his wish to bring back the white banner of Henry IV as the national flag in place of the revolutionary tricolour. Twice, in July 1871 and in October–November 1873, the assembly was obliged to abandon the attempt to set him on the throne because it could not obtain from him essential concessions to the spirit of the times. The royalist majority was reduced to playing for time: for on the death of the Comte de Chambord his rights and pretensions would devolve on the Comte de Paris, representative of the Orleans family, heir of Louis-Philippe and therefore of the Revolution. It was for this reason that the assembly fixed the duration of Marshal MacMahon's tenure of power at seven years, he being a royalist officer who had replaced Thiers as President in May 1873, and undertook the construction of a constitution which could be adapted to a monarchy in due course.

But it was well aware that it was losing its hold on the country; and, haunted by historical memories, it considered that its first duty was to strike at subversive doctrines. As was officially reported to it by Batbie, one of its most authoritative representatives: 'There exists in our unhappy country an army of chaos that is larger and more powerful than in other countries....In 1848 the soldiers of this army called themselves socialists, in 1871 *communards*, and today they are usually known as radicals, a name which, in these latter days, has been adopted to denote the League for our Destruction.'[1] It was for having refused to join battle with 'radicalism' that Thiers was voted down and replaced by Mac-Mahon, in whose name, from May 1873 to May 1874, the Duc de Broglie presided over the Ministry of Moral Order. This name was exactly descriptive: the ministry set about defending not merely the interests of the ruling classes but an entire complex of religious, social and domestic values that it decided were in danger. But the government had nothing at its disposal in the struggle against the republican opposition except an arsenal of bureaucratic vexations that were without serious effect. It did not offer the nation what was most desired: a road away from provisional government. It only managed to identify the Catholic religion with political and social reaction more completely than ever, and to accentuate the latent divisions in the conservative majority.

It was because of these divisions that the constitutional statutes of 1875 finally established a regime to which the republicans were easily able to reconcile themselves. The Duc de Broglie, leader of the Orleanists, had envisaged a Great Council as a guarantee of conservative interests, a sort of House of Lords or *Chambre des Pairs*. It was to be composed of some members in their own right and others nominated by the President, and would serve as a counterbalance to a chamber elected by universal suffrage, which no one thought of abolishing. This conception was not retained. The Senate became merely an emanation of the general councils and the municipal councils. But it remained approximately equal to the Chamber in power and dignity, and a President of the Republic was set up who could easily be changed into a king and who had far larger powers than the monarch had in England at that time. The President of the Republic had initiative in introducing laws; he could exact from either house a second deliberation if a measure displeased him; he could dissolve the Chamber on the advice of the Senate. He chose the ministers; these were, it is true, responsible to the houses, but it was not made clear whether their responsibility was individual or collective; no Prime Minister was foreseen. All in all, nothing forbids the supposition that the Constitution of 1875 could have evolved towards a Presidential system like the American, and it is to be noticed that progress towards such a system had already been made when, from 1871 to 1873, Thiers was in power.

But events decided otherwise. The Chamber of Deputies elected in March 1876 when the conservatives were in confusion, had a republican majority; President MacMahon and the Senate remained conservative. The work of the ministers became gradually impossible in these conditions; on 16 May 1877 MacMahon dismissed them and, on the Senate's

---

[1] French text: 'Il existe dans notre malheureux pays une armée du désordre plus nombreuse et plus puissante qu'ailleurs....En 1848, les soldats de cette armée s'appelaient socialistes, en 1871, Communeux, et aujourd'hui on les nomme plus ordinairement radicaux, nom qui, dans ces derniers temps, a été adopté pour désigner la ligue de la destruction.'

advice, appealed to the country by dissolving the Chamber. The *Seize mai* was not, as was alleged in the heat of battle, a *coup d'état*: the President had not exceeded his constitutional powers. But in the circumstances his action looked like a defiance of the universal suffrage. The elections, in spite of government pressure, confirmed the republican majority. Mac-Mahon, when receiving a ministry acceptable to the new Chamber, was obliged to declare in a message: 'The Constitution of 1875 founded a parliamentary Republic when it established my irresponsibility at the same time as it instituted the collective and individual responsibility of ministers.'[1] It was this interpretative text that really established the parliamentary system.

In January 1879 a partial renewal gave the Senate a republican majority and MacMahon resigned and was replaced in the Presidency by the republican Jules Grévy. The convinced republicans, 'republicans by birth', were thenceforward masters of the Republic. The vital task to which they set themselves without delay was that of 'laicising' public authorities. This is a notion whose meaning is difficult to grasp unless it is borne in mind that the greater part of the country was Catholic. It must be remembered that the Roman Church is a very hierarchical organisation based on the principle of authority, and charged with the upholding of immutable dogmas. In 1864 Pope Pius IX had published the Syllabus, a catalogue of errors condemned by the Church, and this publication had been interpreted by many as Catholicism's declaration of war on modern thought, on the scientific spirit, on democratic freedoms, on the principle of popular sovereignty. Whether this interpretation was well-founded is debatable; but it was adopted by most of the republicans, who were thus led to see in the Catholics their natural opponents. Besides, many of these republicans were without any religious belief, and aspired to build a new world in which Science would replace Faith. To attain that end it was first necessary to remove education from the control of the Church.

In France primary education was one of the responsibilities of the communes; and very often it was given by members of the religious 'congregations', monks or nuns. For boys' secondary education Napoleon I had created state *lycées*, besides which there were religious colleges run, among others, by the Jesuits; but girls for whom more than an elementary education was wanted were brought up in convents. Only higher education was entirely the affair of state faculties. At first an attempt was made to forbid members of unauthorised congregations to teach; then, this measure having been rejected by the Senate, they were expelled, the Jesuits being conspicuous among them. Secondary education for girls was begun in the form of state *lycées* analogous to those for boys. Finally,

[1] French text: 'La Constitution de 1875 a fondé une république parlementaire en établissant mon irresponsabilité, tandis qu'elle a institué la responsabilité solidaire et individuelle des ministres.'

in 1882, state education was proclaimed to be 'laic', that is, not merely neutral but divorced from all religious ideas; religious teaching might be given by ministers of the various sects, but outside school hours and without relation to the rest of the teaching. Jules Ferry gave his name to most of these reforms, but he was supported in putting them through by many earnest collaborators, and was energetically backed by almost all the republicans. Nor were the school laws presented as an *œuvre de combat* only. To make primary education free and compulsory was thought of as a patriotic action which would enable the French to rival 'the Prussians' (it was said that Prussia had conquered France thanks to her schoolmasters). It was thought too that here was realised a social reform *par excellence*, one that would assure to all citizens equality of opportunity. Nevertheless, the 'laic' laws were perhaps most important in their political consequences. They deepened the gulf between the 'two Frances' so that in many villages the republican party was thenceforward 'the schoolmaster's party' as opposed to 'the priest's party'. And the new primary education played a very large part in determining the ideological and political alignments of the Third Republic. At the same time the government lavishly dealt out fundamental freedoms: freedom of the press (for the future, breaches of such regulations as remained were to be tried by jury) and liberty of assembly. Only freedom of association, though recognised in practice, was not yet allowed in law, for it raised the problem of what to do about the 'congregations'. A law was passed conferring the nomination of mayors on municipal councils, though it is true that central supervision was retained.

But even while this considerable work was being done a deep split appeared among the republicans that was to dominate political life until the end of the century; the 'Opportunists'—whose various leaders held office until 1885—were opposed by the 'Radicals'. At first it was a tactical conflict. Many republicans, reckoning up the difficulties the Republic had had to overcome to establish itself, thought it necessary not to disturb a still largely uncommitted public opinion, above all in the countryside: their formula was, 'Nothing must be put in the republican programme that the majority of the nation cannot be induced to accept immediately'. To this the Radicals or 'Intransigents' replied by another: 'The complete application of republican doctrine must be demanded, and no point of the programme must be renounced until proof has been given that the nation does not want it.'

This tactical disagreement corresponded, to a certain extent, with the conflict of generations. The Radicals, men of principle, often sentimentalists, were the heirs of the 'Republicans of 1848' (it was one of the latter, Louis Blanc, who founded their first parliamentary group); they found recruits among veterans and among the young men who naturally went to extremes. The Opportunists often belonged to the intervening generation which had been moulded in the struggle against the Second Empire by the process of exploiting to the utmost the half-freedoms that were all that then remained. This was a more positive, more realistic generation, living more in the present and considerably less upon the memories of 1793. Above all there was a difference of temperament and mental habit. For the Opportunists, to govern was to do the nation's business, to deal with problems as they arose: they were empiricists. For the Radicals, to govern was to reform. Both were anti-clericals and believers in science, but the Radicals commonly hoped that science would give laws to human society like those which governed the universe, while the Opportunists borrowed from the methods of scientific research those of 'experimental politics'. Matters were, of course, made more confused by individuals. The first of the great Opportunists, Léon Gambetta, was leader of the Radicals until 16 May 1877: his supple Mediterranean intelligence and heated eloquence, his ample endowment with what the French call *sens de l'État*, enabled him to excel in disguising the most moderate and practical of proposals in the cant of the most extreme republicanism. He, perhaps, could have made straight the highway which the republicans had to travel from their past in opposition to their present as the party of government; but the very force of his personality gave his enemies opportunities to accuse him of 'caesarism': and he died prematurely in December 1882. His political heir, Jules Ferry, was a quite different character: an Easterner, cold, reserved and frequently abrupt in manner, he made the mistake of making all too clear what he would have done better to have left obscured: once, for example, when he was denouncing the unrest and excesses of the Radicals, he used a phrase that was immediately taken up as 'the danger is on the left', which was at the time, for many republicans, inconceivable, almost monstrous. It should be added that the impetuosity and entire character of the Radical chief, Clemenceau, who was called, with some exaggeration, 'the destroyer of ministries', did not make for calm either.

The attack on Gambetta's dictatorial bent and the hatred felt for Ferry were basically expressions of the contempt felt by many for those who had abandoned a large part of the original republican programme, that on which Gambetta himself had been elected in 1869 at Belleville (the Parisian equivalent of Whitechapel). It is in fact true that although the Opportunists put through many far-reaching reforms they dropped many others.

Many republicans held that, power having been secured, it was necessary to destroy the monarchical Constitution of 1875 and the system of administration which had hardly changed since the First Empire; the Belleville Programme had even included a proposal that all public functionaries should be elected. Extreme republican hostility was vented above all on the Senate, the Prefects, and the Council of State. The Opportunists, however, made a very limited revision of the Constitution in 1884 and were thereafter its determined defenders; in particular they regarded the Senate as a useful institution, as a brake on the occasionally thoughtless impulses of the Chamber and as a faithful picture of those country voters whom they were especially afraid of alarming and alienating from the Republic. The Napoleonic centralisation also had its good points in the republicans' eyes as soon as they controlled it: if they destroyed it they would leave the monarchists free to make themselves masters once more in a whole series of departments, where the application of 'laic' laws in particular would become impossible. The election of judges, the only measure in this direction which they ever seriously contemplated, was also abandoned in the end—in July 1882. Thus, little by little, a regime was consolidated which was very unlike that of which the most enthusiastic republicans had dreamed.

Understandably enough the Opportunists attached great importance to material interests and to economic prosperity. But they had a great stroke of historical bad luck in that it was precisely during their period of power that there occurred one of the worst and longest crises that the French economic system has ever had to endure. This crisis was linked with the depression that affected many countries, especially in Europe, from 1873 to 1896, but it had its individual characteristics. For one thing, the international crash in 1873 only slightly affected the French economy: in France the prosperity of the Second Empire lasted until 1882. But that year did not merely introduce a procession of difficult years; stagnation, and in many areas regression, began which lasted until 1895 at least. This was a handicap compared to other leading nations which some would say that France did not overcome until recent years. To give only one example, France was alone among the great industrial countries in having fewer exports in 1895 than in 1875 and 1883.

The first cause of the crisis was agricultural. Agriculture, easily the country's principal economic activity, suffered acutely from the competition of new producers, those of wheat especially, the price of which shrank by half between 1871 and 1895. At the same time France's other great crop, the grape, suffered a real disaster, the phylloxera invasion which ruined one region after another. As a natural consequence the ruined farmers bought less from industry.

But French industry was hit in other ways as well. Its most important branches had derived their reputation and their prosperity from producing luxury and quality goods; in many cases the principal advantage over competitors lay in the 'know-how' and good taste with which workers who were essentially craftsmen carried out their work. They served, especially the export industries, an aristocratic clientele. But as the century drew towards its end the world grew more democratised; luxury declined, especially in the years of the depression. Expensive articles of high quality were abandoned in favour of mediocre articles costing less, made with less skill, and more and more often by machines. These consumer goods of mediocre quality were the very ones which the newly industrialised countries, particularly those of central Europe, set out to produce. The fabrics of pure silk or pure wool, the pride of French industry, were rivalled by fabrics made of mixtures—silk and wool, wool and cotton, silk and cotton. The leather industry abandoned strong hides for lighter ones, and furthermore the great cattle-raising countries of the Americas increasingly took to working their leather themselves. France was ill-adapted to this development because of her traditions, because of those very high qualities (and, in certain cases, the consequent relatively high wages) which distinguished her craftsmanship. Many manufacturers thought it degrading to fall in with fashions which they believed to be transient and which they denounced for being in abominable taste.

But, above all, France was ill-equipped for mechanical production, which needed a great deal of plant, metals, and power. At the end of the nineteenth century the dominance of coal was at its height, and France had very little of it. What was perhaps even more serious, the price of mining even such coal as there was was prohibitive: in the most important French field, that of the *Nord* and of the Pas-de-Calais, exploitation was much more difficult because of the depth and geological faults of the strata; the fields of the Massif Central were far from the chief centres of consumption and, there being no navigable waterways in the area, the railways had to be used, at a far higher cost. As a result France was the only leading industrial power whose production of coal was permanently and markedly inferior to her consumption of it, however low the latter was. The consequence was that her metallurgical production scarcely increased at all before 1895, while that of Germany tripled and that of the United States quadrupled. As to British metallurgy, it remained four times as important as the French throughout the period. Since the Second Empire France had been the second financial power in the world, the second creditor country; but as time went on it became increasingly clear that she lacked the material foundations of power because of her poverty in minerals.

There was another fundamental cause of French economic stagnation. Since about 1825 population growth in France had steadily decreased. The annual excess of births over deaths for 10,000 inhabitants fell from sixty-seven in the period 1821–5 to twenty-seven in the period 1881–5. This phenomenon was different in kind from that which became observable in the most economically advanced countries after 1920, notably Great Britain; for in France the collapse of the birth-rate came well before the triumph of material well-being and the modern way of life, instead of following it. The causes of this considerable anomaly have not so far been explained satisfactorily. Its repercussions, on the other hand, are perfectly clear: France was deprived of the stimulus given by the emergence of new consumers who quickly became new producers as well. The great economic crisis in its turn gave a sharp setback to demographic recovery: the annual excess of births over deaths for every 10,000 inhabitants fell from twenty-seven in the period 1881–5 to twelve in the period 1886–90, then to three from 1891–5, and rose only to sixteen from 1896–1900. France was caught in a descending spiral, so that population, markets and production all shrank. It is not too much to see in this period the beginning of an enduring decline rather than a transient crisis.

The effects of the great economic depression were persistent and of great importance in many fields. In agriculture it was at first the great landowners who were chiefly hit. They were affected simultaneously by the collapse of land-values and the fall in rents; the political decline of the 'Notables' was thus accentuated by their economic decline. At the same time the exodus to the towns of landless peasants, 'journaliers' (day-labourers) and 'domestiques de ferme' (farm-servants) increased. The number of peasant proprietors cultivating their own land rose steadily, but this development, joyously hailed as a token of social and political stability, was not always a sign of economic progress. On the contrary, the solvency of the peasant smallholding proved not that it was in a better condition to stand up to competition, but that the peasant family was living off its farm, producing a little of everything for its needs, only buying and selling the minimum. As for the industrial workers, if their wages on the whole remained stable or even increased, many of them suffered prolonged unemployment; and, in spite of the shortage of statistical evidence, it seems nevertheless that in several of the most important branches of industry the number of workers in effective employment declined to a lasting extent. Commercial professions, however, were inflated by those who abandoned agriculture and industry for these havens. It is still true today that the excessive importance of the trading sector, and the high prices that are the result, constitute one of the heaviest burdens which the French economy has to carry.

The length and the gravity of the crisis contributed also to the discouragement of any enterprising spirit in France. The country shrank back into its shell. The most obvious indication of this state of mind was the triumph of Protectionism. Already in 1885 and 1887 tariffs on cereals and cattle had been raised. In 1892 a new, general, tariff was adopted, the Méline Tariff, which not only increased the customs dues on a large number of products, but severely restricted a government's freedom of action in the negotiation of commercial treaties.

The political consequences of the economic crisis were no less important. They first made themselves apparent in the 1885 elections. In these the conservative vote, which had shrunk considerably in 1881, rose again almost to the 1877 level. It was swollen not only because of Catholic resentment at the 'laic' laws, but because the peasants had been successfully persuaded that the farmers' woes were the doing of the republican governments, whose financial management was especially under fire. On their side the Radicals more than tripled their number of seats, largely by exploiting the workers' sufferings and the difficulties of the small tradesmen in the big cities. It is also true to say that both of these forces drew strength from the mistakes, real and rumoured, of the Tongking expedition; but colonial policy did not produce any political re-grouping: those who attacked it were already opponents of the Opportunist governments over questions of home politics.

The practical result was that the Chamber elected in 1885 was without a majority: three opposing tendencies, Opportunist, Radical, Conservative, commanded almost equal forces. The resulting impotence soon provoked a strong anti-parliamentary trend, and this was one of the leading factors in the Boulangist movement.

Nothing could be more mistaken than to see in Boulangism an attempt at a military *pronunciamiento*; nor was it, in origin at least, to any greater extent a plot of the right to overthrow the regime. As for the interpretation which makes it the expression of a nationalist and 'revanche' state of mind, one thing must be made clear. The hope of military revenge for the defeat of 1870 was from an early date the hope of a small minority only, the great majority of Frenchmen having judged that Germany was much too strong for an isolated France. Many, however, believed—wrongly— that Germany was only waiting for an excuse to complete her victory of 1870 and dismember France. Thus nationalism was no more than a defensive reflex, which changed easily enough, nevertheless, into the hysteria of the besieged. This was exactly what happened in 1887, when Bismarck saw fit to rattle the sabre in order to obtain a complaisant Reichstag that would vote his septennial military law. When, following on this, there were several frontier incidents, above all the Schnaebelé affair, Boulangism was naturally strengthened.

But Boulangism was first and foremost a popular movement of the extreme left; it even had a socialist side. The political career of General Boulanger began with the attempts of advanced republicans to democratise the army. The army of the Second Empire was founded on the long-term service of a certain number of conscripts chosen by lot; the republicans, at that time in opposition, demanded the suppression of the regular army, the chief support of personal power, and its replacement by a militia. The war of 1870 put off this plan by making them take into account the necessities of national defence; but they did at least demand short-term conscription, the same for everyone, which would make it impossible to use soldiers against other citizens. The military law of 1872 only partly satisfied them: universal conscription was introduced, but while it remained fixed at five years' duration for the greater number of men, a much shorter time was laid down for those privileged by the selection system, by wealth and by education; and those who were to be teachers or—far worse!—were to go into the Church were wholly exempt. Republicans set out to bring the law into harmony with their principles.

Besides, the army was increasingly becoming the refuge of the sons of the great royalist and Bonapartist families, effectively excluded from many administrative careers since 1879. True, these officers did not dream of using their commands to re-establish monarchy by force, but they rebelled against the Republic in jeers, and quite often republican or non-Catholic officers were discriminated against or sent to Coventry. This situation, too, needed reform.

It was in order to perform this double task that in January 1886 Boulanger was imposed on the government as Minister of War by the Radicals. While holding that office he busied himself with the well-being of the common soldier, which earned him great affection on the part of the masses. Many of the professional officers, on the contrary, disliked him immensely, forgiving him neither his careerist thirst for publicity nor the way in which he disciplined some Conservative officers who gave way to untimely displays of feeling. On their side the Opportunists were angered by his flaunting of his Radical alliance, and from the summer of 1886 onwards Jules Ferry was at war with him. In the spring of 1887 Opportunists and Conservatives, exploiting the indiscretions into which, during the period of Franco-German tension, Boulanger's impulsive temperament had led him, formed a coalition to drive him from power. Many Radicals thought that this manœuvre was directed against them. They violently attacked ministers among whom General Boulanger was no longer numbered, and who could only survive by grace and favour of the right. Boulanger, moreover, did not resign himself to a disappearance into obscurity. New outbursts on his part got him dismissed from the army. At that moment he was put up as a candidate in several by-elections as a form of protest against Opportunist politics; and a large part of the right worked in support of him, more or less behind the scenes, in order to make republican confusion worse. Thanks to the backing of the right and of the extreme left Boulanger won sensational election victories. Most notably, he was twice elected in the Nord department (April and August 1888) and once in the Seine (January 1889): in other words, he built up a majority in the two largest departments in France that were also the most industrialised. In broad outline his programme was of a piece with the old Radical demands: he wanted the revision of the Constitution by a Constituent Assembly, and his followers, veteran Radicals, explained to the workers that the suppression of the Senate would remove the chief obstacle to social reforms that would put an end to all their distresses. As for the alliance with the royalists, who were supplying the money to pay for the Boulangist propaganda, it was of course kept secret.

The Radicals, in deep disagreement and confusion, were in no condition to fight Boulangism effectively. It was an Opportunist government which took on the job. It frightened the ex-general into inglorious flight to Belgium and then to England; and it arraigned him, along with his chief supporters, before the Senate constituted as a Supreme Court of Justice. In the elections of 1889 only a few dozen Boulangists were elected (chiefly in Paris, which had been previously a Radical stronghold) and the republicans kept their majority. The regime emerged strengthened from this adventure, which did, however, have important consequences. The Radicals had been severely shaken: their chief proposal, constitutional revision, was discredited because of the use to which the Boulangists had put it. The Conservatives, by allying with Boulanger, had sacrificed their principles, and their shady collaboration had, in the end, been exposed; furthermore, they no longer had any reasonable chance of overturning the Republic, and the young who had followed them up to this time now risked travelling down a road with a dead end. As a final consequence many workers suddenly abandoned the traditional republican parties: this was an ominous indication of the future.

But for the time being the Opportunists, reinvigorated by their victory over Boulanger, continued to hold power almost uninterruptedly from 1889 to 1898. By French standards this was a period of governmental stability: two ministries of this period had lives of two years each. It was also a period rich in achievements. After long negotiations the Franco-Russian Alliance was brought into being, so that French isolation was at an end and the Republic had achieved some sort of definitive recognition from the European monarchies. The policy of colonial expansion also triumphed, after so much previous disputation. It was also at this time that a large part of the edifice of French social legislation was erected. Although previously no four years' legislature had produced more than five new social laws, fifteen were passed between 1889 and 1893, and seventeen between 1893 and 1898. This point, seldom made, deserves attention.

The workers—those, at least, who lived in the large towns—had always been among the firmest supporters of the republican party. When newly returned to power, the party naturally had a marked sympathy with their problems and was prepared to give them what they wanted; besides, it was preoccupied with the manifest contrast between political equality, one of its fundamental principles, and economic inequality. In this respect there was no very profound difference between Radicals and Opportunists. The latter often let themselves be guided by ex-working men who had grown into political moderates, but who nevertheless remembered their experiences and problems as workers: Martin Nadaud, the mason, who became a deputy and one of Gambetta's advisers; Tolain, the bronze-founder, who had played a very important role in 1864 in the beginnings of the autonomous Workers' Movement and had now become a senator and one of the Opportunist leaders in the Seine department. Conversely, some Radicals, like Yves Guyot, figured among the most determined champions of *laissez-faire* economics and in their name fought against any state intervention in working conditions.

But the French republicans lived in a country where the growth of heavy industry was particularly slow, and only slowly did they become aware of the new problems such growth creates. Children of a world of peasants and artisans, they were all too ready to suppose that universal education and the setting-up of free workers' associations, which were to become, little by little, substitutes for employers, were the real answers to the social problem. They had plainly been influenced by the great French socialist thinker Proudhon. In order to put his ideas into practice they had made primary education compulsory and, in 1884, given legal recognition to trade unions. To grasp the importance of this last action, it must be remembered that the Republic had not established freedom of association because of the governing party's fear that it would protect the religious congregations; and, according to the penal code, all associations consisting of more than twenty people had to be submitted to governmental approval. The trade unions, therefore, were now in a privileged position.

Many other social proposals were discussed between 1880 and 1885, and were even passed by the Chamber. But they were thrown out by the Senate, representing the rural voters; these either had no idea of the needs of the new urban and industrial society or even rebelled against the notion of giving privileges to townsfolk from which they would not profit themselves.

The years from 1885 to 1889 were, in this field as in others, almost barren, but it was probably during this period that the movement of opinion quickened and that many problems grew acute. To begin with, the trade-unions law of 1884 did not have all the expected results. In many places the setting-up of unions was met by the steady opposition of the employers; the 'associations ouvrières de production' remained more of a dream than a reality; the repercussions of the economic crisis made the workers more impatient and reform more urgent; and in the eyes of the politicians the Boulangist bid underlined the reality of the danger.

Consequently, the Opportunists, in power again from 1889 onwards, threw their weight behind the reforming movement and forced their will on the Senate which, being of their own political persuasion, had neither right nor reason to distrust or obstruct them. As early as 1890 the *livret ouvrier* (worker's pass), a survival of the Empire's policing methods, was abolished, and a law was voted which provided for workers' delegates whose business would be to ensure that rules for hygiene and safety in the mines were observed. This law was extended in 1893 to all industries; in 1891 the working-time of women and children was shortened by law.

1898 at last saw the passing of a law on accidents at work; it had required long gestation for it was necessary to abandon the principle of civil responsibility in common law and create the notion of professional risk. Finally, in 1891 Freycinet's Opportunist government launched a project of workers' pensions that was only completed twenty years later.

While the Opportunists thus ensured that, in spite of many surface incidents, government should really be stable, the bases of French political life were being profoundly changed. Up to that time France was sharply divided into two camps: on the one side the republicans, who, whatever their disagreements about particular issues, were all believers in the same fundamental principles: in political freedom; in loyalty to the democratic system as something capable of solving all problems and something that made any new revolutionary violence illegitimate; in 'laicism' which really meant 'anti-clericalism'. All the republicans were ready to forget their quarrels and unite whenever it seemed that the Republic was in danger. Opposing them was the irreconcilable right, whose political and social conceptions were undoubtedly far from harmonious, but whose principal bond was the defence of all that was Catholic. But from this time efforts were to be made to obliterate the great division between Frenchmen by the *Ralliement* (rally) of the Catholics to the Republic. And on the other hand a political factor appeared that became steadily more important, a socialist party which, in theory at least, repudiated the 'Bourgeois Republic' and worked for the new Revolution, the Social Revolution.

The Catholic 'Rally' to the Republic was the result of several factors. There was, first, the natural weakening of the conservatives as the future was closed to them: the more time passed the slighter grew their chance of regaining power, and the failure of Boulangism was the last straw. Already after the elections of 1885, and again after those of 1889, tentative efforts had been made to create a 'constitutional' right which accepted the existing institutions; but they were as yet too timid, and did not get many supporters.

The decisive role was played by Pope Leo XIII, a man remarkable for his flexible mind and clear-sighted political ability. Reacting against the common interpretation of the Syllabus he declared, in the Encyclical *Libertas* in 1888: 'It is a vain and baseless calumny to allege that the Church looks unfavourably on most modern political systems and rejects all the discoveries of contemporary genius together.' In consequence the French Republic was not in principle more unacceptable to him than any other regime. Besides, he was well enough informed of the situation in France to decide that the Republic had a long life ahead of it, and that by persisting in an intransigent opposition the Catholics would hurt nobody but themselves. In February 1884 Leo XIII published the Encyclical *Nobilissima Gallorum Gens* in which he insisted on the necessity of preserving the Concordat of 1802. Little by little circumstances began to favour him. After the last of the great 'laic' laws had been passed in 1886, anti-clericalism no longer had a definite object with which to rally the republicans: for the further step of the separation of Church and state, in other words the denunciation of the Concordat, though always demanded by the Radicals, was rejected by the Opportunists. Meanwhile the eclipse of Boulangism must have convinced royalists of the vanity of their hopes.

Leo XIII, then, was seeing how the land lay. In this spirit Cardinal Lavigerie, Primate of Africa, when receiving some naval officers in 1890, proposed a toast to the Republic. This initiative provoked violent reactions. Not only were the royalists indignant, but the Catholics, and above all the bishops, attacked the Republic as the persecutor of the Church. However, after some time had passed, Leo XIII returned to the charge. In February 1892 he published, in French, the Encyclical *Au milieu des sollicitudes* in which he declared that all the established governments were legitimate; Catholics must devote themselves to modifying legislation. At the same time the pope let it be understood that he did not want the formation of a Catholic party which would again involve the Church in French political struggles, but a big government party with no confessional character, which Catholics could enter and which would drive the doctrinaire anti-clericals back into opposition. The royalist deputies of the right replied in June 1892 with a resounding *non placet*: they declared that though, as Catholics, they owed obedience to the pope in all matters of faith, as citizens they needed to take nobody else's advice as to their political conduct. Nevertheless, a certain number of them did retire from political life. The result of all this was a deep split in the right. In the 1893 elections only thirty-five of the 'Catholic Rally' candidates were elected. It is not therefore true to say that Leo XIII's policy had broken down. In fact, during the sessions from 1893 to 1898 the moderate republicans responded to the advances of the Rally by advocating the ending of religious struggles. A long time, however, was necessary before that became possible, and in the years that concern us the least incident revived quarrels between clericals and anti-clericals as violent as the pretexts for them were slight.

The elections of 1893 also sent to the Chamber for the first time forty to fifty 'socialist' deputies. Where did they come from? There is no more complicated history than that of the French socialist movement. Before 1870 France had produced a fairly large number of thinkers and authors of socialist systems, of whom the latest, Proudhon, undoubtedly had the greatest influence. But the repression of the Commune entailed the complete eclipse of the movement. The few unions which survived, or which were formed, occupied themselves with the problems of their trades alone.

When, in 1877, the republicans came to power, socialist propaganda had a chance to be heard once more. New ideas were put out, no longer in the French tradition but inspired by Karl Marx. The principal architect of this change was Jules Guesde. In 1879 he founded a 'Workers' Party' (*Parti Ouvrier Français*), which, following the example of the German Social Democrats, was Marxist and composed both of political groups and of trade unions, these last being subordinated to the party. But it remained small in numbers and in 1882 it split: Jules Guesde, thought to be too doctrinaire, was voted down by those known as 'possibilists', who were mostly workers, more anxious than the 'intellectuals' to obtain immediate results, and who, under the leadership of Paul Brousse formed the *Fédération des Travailleurs Socialistes de France*. Meanwhile, in 1880, the 'Central Revolutionary Committee' (*Parti Socialiste Révolutionnaire*) was formed, which took Auguste Blanqui for its prophet. Organised somewhat after the fashion of a secret society, this committee did not include any unions; neither did it adhere to Marxist doctrine, but held itself ready to profit by any circumstances to launch a *coup de force*. Let it be added that many Radicals freely called themselves 'socialists', wishing only to indicate that they were particularly concerned with the condition of the working classes.

Obviously the great economic crisis could not but cause repercussions and distress among the working masses. But the little socialist factions, which passed most of their time in quarrelling among themselves, were not immediately able to profit by it. On the contrary, in 1886 efforts were made to constitute a *Centrale Syndicale* which should at the same time adhere to revolutionary principles and be independent of all political organisations: this conception, which was to be characteristic of the French working-class movement, was originally due to the wish to protect union action from the quarrels of the political factions, which were paralysing it. Thereafter the movement towards an independent syndicalism (trade union movement) was supported and reinforced both by those who were opposed on principle to all political action—the anarchists—and by the militants of the factions, who were at a disadvantage in political warfare.

It was the Boulangist movement that profited most from the workers' discontent, detaching a large part of them from the Radicals for whom they had previously voted. Faced with Boulangism, the various socialist groups did anything but take up a common position: the Possibilists fought it with all their energy, the Blanquists were to a large extent in favour of it. The episode provoked new schisms in both parties, to such an extent that the Guesdists, who had known better than to become deeply involved, and thus preserved their unity, became the most influential group. In consequence, while developing a more and more lively interest in electoral action, and while seeking a practical programme for immediate fulfilment, they came, during several years, to dominate the unions.

Inside the unions a change was taking place under pressure not only from the anarchists, but from many Possibilists also. By that time the militant workers, even the most determined of them, had for all practical purposes abandoned the idea of an armed insurrection. Since the parliamentary and electoral activity of the Guesdists was also repudiated, and 'gradualism' in the fashion of the British trade unions was disliked, some new way had to be found. It was thus that the idea of the General Strike materialised, the idea, that is, of a revolution to be achieved solely by economic weapons and by corporate action. And so, while the final objective remained revolutionary, the unions applied themselves, under the leadership of Fernand Pelloutier, to the practical tasks which had often, in the past, been disdained. The vital instrument of this work in France at that time was not the big federation of a trade or an industry but the Bourse de Travail, which united all the unions in a town, of the widest variety of trades, and which provided a labour exchange, unemployment benefits, general and technical education and economic studies.

But already the unions and the various socialist groups joined each year in the great May Day demonstrations in favour of the eight-hour day, which exhibited the power that a united working-class action could have. And from the other side a certain number of Radical deputies, who were no longer satisfied with the traditional attitudes of their party, were trying to devise a socialism free of doctrinaire sterilities and factious quarrels, which should be the creed of the many who called themselves socialists without going so far as to be 'Guesdists' or partisans of any of the groups already in existence. Millerand and an ex-deputy, the *républicain sans épithète* (short-and-sweet republican), Jaurès, were the inspirers of this regrouping, which helped the old socialist factions just as much by creating a sympathetic atmosphere around them, and which on the other hand drew a fair number of ex-Boulangists to itself.

This, then, was the background of the socialist successes in the elections of 1893. The question must be asked—though it cannot, of course, be answered—whether these successes were not made easier by an incident which thoroughly shook up the political *personnel* of the period, the Panama Affair. Shortly after the failure of the French company which had undertaken the cutting of the isthmus of Panama certain important political personages, and a large number of less well-known deputies, were accused of having accepted money for favouring this company, and above all for authorising the issue of shares in a lottery (the failure of this issue, by the way, gave the signal for the final collapse of the enterprise). There was no decisive proof against most of the individuals accused. But the affair was exploited to the utmost to discredit the republicans, above all by the ex-Boulangists and the conservatives; for their part, the socialists could not miss this opportunity to denounce capitalist corruption. The idea took hold on the public that all politicians, or almost all, were '*pourris*' (rotten to the core) and thought of nothing except using their positions to enrich themselves. It is by no means certain that the standard of public morality was lower at that time in France than in any other country. But it should be observed that, particularly in Paris, the number of political daily newspapers was at that time very large (more than ten times what it is today); each individual deputy had to have his own organ to express his own particular shade of opinion (and French political thought is extremely rich in such infinitely subtle shades) and to affirm his own particular position. Naturally, most of these newspapers could not live on their declared resources: their circulation was very limited; regular publicity and advertising hardly existed. They had to secure the backing of financial and business interests, either by making propaganda for them or by threatening them with unpleasant revelations; naturally the most adventurous enterprises were those most often laid under contribution, and that of Panama more than any other. Many politicians thus made alliances with shady businessmen not in order to obtain the wherewithal to indulge their private vices, but in order to supply the financial requirements they incurred politically, and especially to cover their papers' deficits. It is plain that the Panama Affair did much to change the way in which the press was exploited; and the dramatis personae of political life were to some extent replaced. But the balance of parties in parliament was scarcely affected, except for the socialist rise.

The royalist right being reduced to impotence and doomed to decomposition, and the *républicains de gouvernement* (constitutional republicans) being firmly in power, it might seem that France was about to enter an 'era of goodwill' in which political struggles would lose much of their importance. But the truth is that in France such situations come about only with great difficulty. The years 1893 and 1894 were exceptionally disturbed because of a series of anarchist outrages, which culminated in the murder of Sadi Carnot, President of the Republic. Several explanations have been put forward to explain the occurrence of these outrages at exactly this moment—there being hardly any before or afterwards—but none of them is completely satisfactory. The outrages, though they provoked a great outcry at the time, had in the end no very important consequences. Nevertheless, various governments passed repressive measures against them which provoked much lively opposition from the socialists and the extreme Radicals: they called them 'les lois scélérates' (miscreant laws).

Much more important was the political regrouping that was beginning. While the Opportunists were gradually coming to benefit from the support of a section of the old right, the Radicals were trying to discover a new doctrine and a new programme. Constitutional revision having been dropped, the Radicals pressed on with their anti-clerical campaign and rejected all the Catholic Rally's gestures with contempt. But this was hardly enough. Their real problem was to decide on their attitude to the socialists, whose ideas they could not accept, as being too incompatible with their own individualist philosophy, but whom they could no longer restrict themselves to attacking, as this would tend to 'throw them back on the right'. So they tried, without much success, to evolve a new social doctrine which should reconcile liberalism and state intervention: the 'solidarism' of Léon Bourgeois. They had much better success in concluding a *de facto* alliance with the socialists. These were, moreover, making a *rapprochement* easy; unprotesting, they allowed one of their leaders, Millerand, to describe, in the 'discours de Saint-Mandé' of May 1896, a much-moderated socialism which employed parliamentary, non-violent, methods, which no longer threatened small properties, and which cast no doubts on patriotism. And previously the socialist deputies had voted for an all-Radical ministry, led by Léon Bourgeois, which made great efforts to introduce what had become the essential point in the Radical programme: income tax.

The French fiscal system, very little changed since the Revolution, had for a long time been denounced as unjust and anti-democratic. The direct taxes were based on arbitrary assessments—like the tax on movables—or on thoroughly out-of-date evaluations—like the land-tax. The greater part of public income came from indirect taxes on items of current consumption. These weighed more heavily on the poor than on the rich, though it is true that one of the principal taxes of this kind was that on alcohol, against which the arguments of social justice were not entirely convincing. For a long time financial reforms had been proposed on several sides. But Léon Bourgeois' ministry was the first to stake its existence on a scheme of general taxation, to be levied on the entire income, carefully ascertained, of each taxpayer. The system was irreproachable in theory. But it came to grief because of great practical and psychological difficulties. France is characterised by her multitude of small concerns—in trade, the crafts and agriculture—which operate without a careful accountancy, and whose real financial position is very difficult to discover. Besides, the French cannot tolerate the idea that their neighbours, or the state, should know how their affairs stand. Only someone who has lived in the French countryside can fully appreciate this intense mistrustfulness. The universal income tax, if it was not to be farcical, would have had to put an end to the traditional secretiveness; already 'this financial inquisition' had been attacked. The Senate, representing ruraldom, forced the Bourgeois ministry to climb down by systematic obstruction. Income tax, after long and violent discussions, was in the end adopted, but only on the eve of the 1914 war; and agricultural incomes have not been properly brought under control to this day.

After the fall of the Bourgeois ministry the long-lived moderate ministry of Méline came to power under the banner of political 'appeasement'. This was, it may be said, the calm before the storm, for it was under this ministry that the Dreyfus affair exploded, the Affair which by completely overturning both the political and the moral situations unmistakably put an end to a period.

The Dreyfus affair can first of all be regarded as one of the best detective mysteries in history, one of the most complicated and most baffling. It has never been entirely cleared up, in spite of the many volumes which have been devoted to it; many hypotheses have been put forward, of which none is entirely convincing. In 1894 Captain Alfred Dreyfus was found guilty of espionage, as he was thought to be the author of a *bordereau* (memorandum) announcing the dispatch of certain confidential pieces of information, which, it was said, had been found in the German embassy (but even this detail has been challenged). The author of the *bordereau* was really another officer, of foreign extraction, Commandant Esterhazy. But during years of discussion and intrigue, a retrial was steadily refused. This resistance to the recognition of the truth was to a very large extent due to the machinations of Commandant Henry of the Intelligence Bureau who, as part of his job, was involved in the affair from the start. Henry did not scruple to forge documents in order to prove Dreyfus' guilt and to compromise the man who discovered that of Esterhazy, Colonel Picquart. If Henry's motives were known, there would be no more mystery: unfortunately, when his forgeries were detected he committed suicide (or was deliberately silenced) and took his secrets to his grave. But what really mattered was the upsetting of political ideas and positions of which the affair was the occasion or the pretext.

The following period, up to 1914, was to be characterised, first, by the triumph of the Radicals, who had been all at sea since 1889, but were from this time almost continuously in power, often with the help of the rapidly rising socialists; second, by a vigorous resurgence of the anti-clerical campaign, which had appeared to be on its way out after 1892; and third, by the fact that the most ardently patriotic or nationalistic feelings, which previously were to be met with in all shades of opinion, but above all on the left and conspicuously among the Radicals, appeared from this time as the prerogative of the right.

These very important phenomena have not lacked commentators; notably, the essayist Ch. Péguy has asked 'comment la mystique s'était degradée en politique'. But we do not yet have the indispensable scientific studies of this subject, and all that one can write on it today is therefore largely conjectural. In particular, it is not clear that the future destiny of the parties was directly linked to their attitude in the Dreyfus affair. If the affair was the question of the day in Paris, it was often but poorly understood in the greater part of the country. The first Dreyfusards, and the most active, were isolated adherents of the most diverse tendencies; their principal supports were a journal of the right, *Figaro*, and a journal of the left, *L'Aurore*. Among the Radicals, their ex-leader Clemenceau was one of the champions of a review of the Dreyfus case, while their current chief, Cavaignac, fought revision with all his might. The Opportunists, who were to be shattered politically by the affair, supplied 'revisionists' of mark—Scheurer-Kestner, Joseph Reinach, Waldeck-Rousseau, and the rising hopes of the party, Poincaré and Barthou—but on the other hand the Prime Minister, Méline, tried to prevent the investigation of an affair which was extremely embarrassing for his government.

Many Catholics, on the other hand, showed themselves violently and noisily anti-Dreyfusard, particularly the newspaper *La Croix*. And perhaps the relentlessness of a good number of them can be explained as expressing their resentment at the policy of the Rally that had been imposed on them against their wish; in any case Leo XIII, personally convinced of Dreyfus' innocence, was never able to moderate their campaign. Military circles were all anti-Dreyfusard, so much so that the Dreyfusard campaign, on its side, often took on an anti-militarist character. But here again all generalisation is imprudent. In the following period many of the most active Dreyfusards were to show themselves to be intransigent patriots and energetic defenders of the army: such men as the Opportunist Joseph Reinach, the ex-socialist Charles Péguy and, the most celebrated of them all, the Radical Georges Clemenceau.

It is certainly true that the violence of anti-Dreyfusard passions can to a great extent be explained by the anti-semitic tendency which appeared in France—and even more strongly in other European countries—at this time. But this tendency itself appeared with a fundamental ambiguity. It had been developing for a number of years, notably in two very different sectors of opinion. For the average Catholic aversion to the Jews went a very long way back, and thus may be said to have become part of the religion. For the extreme, socialist, left, the Jew was a useful personification of that international high finance to which were charged all the ills of the age. Lastly, there existed from 1892 onwards a specifically anti-semitic movement, inspired by Édouard Drumont and feared by many politicians for its noisy campaigns. The first attempts to secure a revision of the Dreyfus trial were denounced as a 'Jewish conspiracy', and at first many socialists accepted this explanation. Jaurès, on the other hand, was one of the most ardent Dreyfusards, and his actions then were one of the reasons for the battle in which, from this time until 1905, the two great socialist factions, the 'Jaurèsists' and the 'Guesdists', opposed each other.

But the history of the political regroupings that were effected in the course of the Dreyfus affair can scarcely be separated from that of the period which followed it. We must therefore finish our account here, leaving the years 1898 to 1902 a sort of historian's 'no man's land', a huge field of investigation for new researchers, now that the savage passions of those dramatic years have subsided.

It is unnecessary to include in this chapter any account of the intellectual life, literary and artistic, of the time, which has been dealt with elsewhere.

This does not involve the omission here of any essential element. Not that one could not supply, for this period as for others, a catalogue, more or less detailed as one wished, of artists and of their works. But what strikes the historian is the profound gulf which during this period divided intellectual life from the life of the rest of the nation. When Victor Hugo died in 1885 an entire nation went to his funeral; his works could be found in many humble homes, where they were known by heart. This popularity—comparable or even superior to that of Lamartine in 1848—belonged to a vanished age. The writers of the Third Republic had no such huge audience and no such influence on their times; often indeed they disdained or shunned it. Undoubtedly Émile Zola tried to make a huge picture of the society of his day, of which he shared and tried to express certain ideas and certain aspirations. But a Stéphane Mallarmé, or the Maurice Barrès of the *Culte du Moi*, only wished to speak to the subtlest intellects. Anatole France, although more accessible, was too fond of the well-turned phrase, and too sceptical, to move his public deeply. In the plastic arts it was the age of the official academicians' triumph, against which the Impressionist painters, for example, were not able to make much headway. In no field has the 'style 1900' left a great memory behind it. Only in music did the French school, after the death of Wagner, acquire a sort of primacy, with Bizet, Chabrier, César Franck, and then with Fauré and Debussy; but in France music was merely the idol of a little group of the faithful.

We have indeed seen how the republican regime was linked, in its origins, to a philosophy which placed science in the first place. But this official philosophy was not taken up by any great thinker. True, Taine and Renan had exalted science; but their liberal-conservative beliefs left them isolated in the age of triumphant democracy. And neither the profound Lachelier nor even the dazzling Bergson managed to shake the rather naïve confidence of their contemporaries in a science of which they so simplified the image that their belief has been called 'scientism'.

Truth to tell, more ignoble manifestations of intellectual life dominated conversation, and still more the columns of newspapers. The last play performed 'sur les Boulevards' was always 'un événement bien parisien'. Paris always offered the same seductions to the foreigners that she attracted. But it must be underlined that the brilliant life of the capital was now superficial, that he who judged France by his stay in Paris—many do it today—made a mistake. From 1789 to 1870 Paris really did dominate France, imposing on the country without resistance her tastes and passions and a succession of political regimes. But after the triumph of universal suffrage Paris constituted no more than a fraction of the nation; and after the commune, Paris was in opposition. The capital upheld Boulanger, then anti-Dreyfusard nationalism, while the great majority of Frenchmen showed themselves to be definitely hostile to these movements. The Third Republic was, *par excellence*, the provinces' regime.

CHAPTER XII

AUSTRIA-HUNGARY, TURKEY AND THE BALKANS

AFTER the final triumph of Italian and German nationalism in 1870 the Danubian lands and the Balkan Peninsula remained the one considerable area of unsatisfied nationalist aspirations in Europe. These aspirations provided the most considerable threat to the multi-national empires of Austria-Hungary and Turkey. Yet in both cases the dynasty, in spite of recent challenges, was still sustained by a tradition of inevitability; both had existed for so long, and in spite of the declining glamour of the imperial or any other embracing role each could still ask with some plausibility what was to be put in its place. The question in the international field found a ready answer from the new Germany, which was soon to tell Russia that Austria-Hungary was a European necessity, and from Great Britain, which was still making the same extravagant claim for Turkey; and if Russian views were divided they were not pressed to the limit. At home, many could still not conceive of life without emperor or sultan. Echoing Palacký, Prince Charles Schwarzenberg asked the Young Czech extremists in 1891, 'what will you do with your country, which is too small to stand alone?' and in 1897 the Young Turk exile Murat Bey said that the ruling dynasty must remain at the head of the empire, for without it Turkish power had no existence. Nevertheless, the chance of survival for both Habsburg and Ottoman came to depend less and less on past glory or present convenience and more and more on two conditions: the international stalemate after 1878 and the hostilities which divided the national minorities and which postponed and confused their challenge to the state. After humiliating external defeats at the beginning of this period, both were able to restore and in some measure strengthen the central authority, and to survive into the twentieth century. But the respite was temporary. Although at the turn of the century the Habsburg monarchy seemed to have made a more distinguished contribution than the Ottoman to the problem of survival, in fact both dynasties were near their end.

The more favourable picture of Austria-Hungary was due in part to the dramatic qualities of 'Abd al-Hamīd's sins and the excesses of his bizarre regime; partly to the prestige of the Austro-German Alliance, the aura of liberal respectability which accompanied the Magyars into the twentieth century, the vast superiority of the Austro-Hungarian to the Ottoman bureaucracy, and the obscurity and complexity (to the eyes of foreign observers) of the nationalist struggle inside the monarchy. The two empires and the Ottoman succession states in the Balkans were nevertheless (if only because of geographical proximity) closely interlocked, and there was in their relations something of the confusion of working bargains between antipathetic partners which also distinguished the purely internal affairs of each empire. At many points it was to the interest of Constantinople and Vienna to look to each other for support against the rising tide of Slav nationalism in the Balkans, and they and the small Balkan states had all learned to look with some suspicion on Russian designs, although the Russian government could claim a qualified interest in the political survival of all of them.

In the early 1870's the Ottoman government still retained, despite the misgivings of the better informed, numerous friends and a fair reputation in western Europe. The reform programme promised or foreshadowed in the *Hatti-Humayoun* of 1856 had not been entirely a failure. There seemed to be sufficient vitality and determination in the Turkish army and administration, and perhaps a sufficient measure of loyalty or fatalism among the masses of the population, to enable the Sublime Porte (the Turkish central government) to struggle along, to turn the more difficult corners, even to score some successes. The international situation was not unfavourable; none of the great powers wanted a Near Eastern crisis. The effect on Europe of a prolonged or general Christian revolt was incalculable; but for the time being the subject populations were quiescent.

For nearly a hundred years, since the days of Selīm III (1789–1807), the initiative in reform had come from the sultanate; and the accession of 'Abd al-Azīz (1861–76) had aroused hopes of a fresh impetus. The westernised and well-meaning Tanzimatists in Constantinople, and in particular the two Grand Vezirs, Mehmed Kecheji-zāde Fu'ād Pasha and Mehmed Emīn 'Alī Pasha, made a fairly good impression. When the British, French, Austrian and Russian governments in 1867 undertook an examination of the progress of the reforms, their conclusions, while recognising inefficiency and misrule, had not been wholly pessimistic. The Turkish government (which had itself presented a report) could claim credit for a scrupulous regard for the traditional rights, civil and religious, of the Christian millets; it could argue that, if Article 9 of the *Hatt*, which threw open the civil and political institutions of the empire to all citizens, had been generally ignored, the fault was not entirely that of the Turkish authorities, for the Christian *ra'iyeh* had clearly no liking for military service and were usually too servile to assert themselves in office. Nor were they very willing to accept reforms in their own millets. The new *vilayet* system, which was closely modelled on French administrative legislation, was considered to have been a marked success in the Danubian province under Midhat Pasha from 1864 to 1867 and was extended (1867–8) to other provinces except 'Irāq and the Yaman. A Council of

State with Midhat as President was appointed at the beginning of 1868; it included both Christian and Muslim members, and was charged with the elaboration of further reforms and the preparation of the budget, among other duties. While the French saw in these developments a vindication of their centralising programme, 'Alī Pasha could commend them as a popular check on administrative absolutism. But the advance was small; the façade of progressive intent proved increasingly hard to maintain. 'Alī and Fu'ād never had more than a precarious hold on office, and the sultan, who was said to have offered the office of Grand Vezir to an elderly dancing dervish in 1863, finally became the chief saboteur of his ministers' programme.

Reform to the western powers meant primarily the strengthening of the Turkish armed forces, the achievement of national solvency, and administrative changes which would reconcile the sultan's provincial subjects to the government. The three problems were closely related, for a strong and loyal army was important for policing as well as for defence, and cost money; while the threat of bankruptcy would be bound to aggravate the most potent cause of provincial unrest, the exactions of the tax-gatherer. The French looked for a Turkish state organised to respond to the direction of an enlightened, efficient, and of course solvent, central government, which by a more and more sincere application of the principles of administrative uniformity and of civil and political equality would achieve a fusion of the races of the empire. Reformers of the Reshīd–Fu'ād–'Alī school may have been sincerely prepared to accept this kind of Turkish state, although there is nothing in their very superficial and limited concessions to the Christians to suggest that they had any real conception of the tremendous revolution in outlook and policy which such a welding of Christian and Muslim would imply. What is quite clear, as the French rightly assumed, is that the near miracle of fusion could have been achieved only by sustained pressure from the centre, where the abilities of Fu'ād and 'Alī and the handful of competent and progressive officials whom they had fostered were at the mercy of the sultan's fitful moods.

Yet the forms of Ottoman reaction involved in the yearnings of 'Abd al-Azīz and his entourage for the old autocratic grandeur did not find any genuine response in the conservatism of the devout and orthodox Muslims, and they did something to foster the stirrings of Turkish nationalism among the Turkish intelligentsia. The latter first became marked in the 1860's among some Turkish writers, who were becoming aware of western, and particularly French, literature, and were beginning to use the phraseology of western nationalist liberalism. Talk about the fatherland and parliamentary government soon led to more specific criticisms of the despotism of the sultanate and to the assertion of the need for western institutions as the basis of a strong state. Like most revolutionary liberals they were prepared to tolerate the minorities but not to accept them as partners. This was the Young Turk (or New Ottoman) movement in its first phase. The movement appears to have had little political importance at this time. The leading figures found it expedient to live abroad, although their writings were known to a restricted circle of readers at home. Rifat Bey edited the first Young Turk journal, *Hurriet* (Liberty), which was founded in London in 1864. Nāmik Kemal's patriotic drama, *Vātān, yahud Silistere* (Fatherland or Silistria) was first produced in 1873. These and other writers, including Zīyā Bey, Shināsi Efendi, Nuri Bey, and 'Alī Su'āvī, were able by their writings to familiarise a limited but growing circle with the picture of a constitutional nationalist state. They were to play some part in the revolutions of 1876.

Neither they nor the reforming vezirs nor 'Abd al-Hamīd after 1877 seemed able to understand the need for a modernised economy to support and sustain the reforms. The western powers were shocked at the prospect of the bankruptcy of the state, but they too thought of its salvation too exclusively in terms of financial reform. Yet there was little doubt that the root cause of Turkey's peculiar difficulties went back to the attempts of Mahmūd II to save the state at heavy cost by the creation of professional fighting forces on the European model without a corresponding revolution in economic life. In Egypt in similar circumstances Mehmed 'Alī had shown greater awareness of the need for economic advance, although with no greater ultimate success. The state of the Turkish armed forces was in many ways impressive by the early 1870's and certainly formed the most solid achievement of the reform period. The navy, administered by the retired English Rear-Admiral, Hobart Pasha, with good sailors and a total of twenty-one armour-clad vessels, was counted the third strongest in Europe, in spite of its lack of sea training and the doubtful quality of the officers. Early in 1877 Colonel James Baker, while recognising that 'a paper army in Turkey is even more unreal in point of numbers than it is in other countries', put the total army strength at 416,530 men, with a further 250,000 from the *levée en masse* which might be used to replace casualties. He thought the army 'superlatively good as regards the men' and was impressed by the quality of much of the equipment. The heavy expenditure on the army had not yet succeeded in solving the problem of an adequate and efficient force of officers, but the latest phase of the army reforms, which owed much to Husain Awnī Pasha after 1869, showed that the problem of education was at least understood. Students were drawn from eight military preparatory schools at the age of 16 to a number of good military schools; the Imperial Military College, founded by Mahmūd II, produced after a five-year course officers who went straight into the army with the rank of captain, while the College of Artillery and Engineering produced sub-lieutenants after a four-year course. Elementary schools to supply the preparatory schools were established in 1875. There was a Military College of Medicine at Constantinople.

But this ambitious effort, which had brought notable rewards in the Crimea, and which was to justify itself again at Plevna, would lose much of its political value if Turkey failed to retain the military support of the western powers. And this would be a likely result of the collapse of her antiquated economy under the armament burden, accelerated by the lush wastefulness of the palace. The military effort was in any case incomplete. There seemed so far little to show for the work and expense of the military colleges. Irregular pay and poor prospects of promotion (with the higher grades often filled by favouritism without regard to military ability) no doubt depressed and discouraged the trained young officer; he would be further depressed by the frequent promotion from the ranks of officers who had received very little training of any sort. There is nothing surprising in the process whereby the products of the military schools came in time to reinforce the Young Turk advocates of political reform. Conscription, which fell heavily on certain areas, was also a contributory factor in the impoverishment of the state. Baker estimated that about one in 450 of the Muslim population was called to the army annually, and as the recruiting for each corps was confined to the military districts, some with a large Christian majority, the drain on the Muslim population in many cases was severe. Yet there could be no relaxation; without Christian recruits the source of supply, considering the extent of the empire, was extremely small for an army which might have at any time to fight a first-rate European power in a lengthy campaign.

There was thus an unsolved problem of survival for Turkey and the sultan's personal interventions made him merely the most obvious and grotesque symptom of the deeper maladies of the state. His unproductive expenditure included battleships, but it also included marble palaces. His personal oddities—a growing taste for fulsome speech and obsequious ceremonial, for bonfires and red ink—might have been accepted as no more than the whims of an unbalanced man if somehow a reasonable conduct of public business had been maintained. But as it happened his interferences with the central government became so open and absurd after 'Ali's death in 1871 that the reformers were bound to make him the scapegoat for the disasters of 1875-6. On the one hand there was the vast expenditure on new palace building, the harem, personal favourites, and personal indulgence on a scale which seriously depleted the state revenue; on the other, an obvious intention to appoint servants who would satisfy his demands, financial and otherwise. The office of Grand Vezir changed hands six times between September 1871 and February 1874. During this period the Porte continued to announce additions to the reform programme, although they seemed a more and more unconvincing façade to the depressing reality of government policy. By 1874 the ministers had long since abandoned any hope of making the palace understand the gravity of the financial crisis. In August 1875 the palace had exhausted its account at the Imperial Ottoman Bank, which refused further supplies: but when the British ambassador asked what the sultan's reaction would be the Foreign Minister replied that he doubted whether the sultan would ever hear the news.

Turkey was now on the verge of national bankruptcy. In the absence of sufficient economic progress to augment the national revenue the Porte had been led to meet increased expenditure by foreign loans, an easy but fatal expedient in the absence of either a regular surplus or even an efficient system of tax collection. Tax farming was declared abolished in the reform programmes in 1839 and 1856, and again in 1875; on each occasion it had to be restored, owing to the immediate need for revenue which the attempted modernisation of the financial structure seemed unable to supply. The first loan, of £3,000,000, was issued in 1854 to meet the expenses of the Crimean War, with an issue price of 80, and interest at 6 per cent; it was contracted by Messrs Dent, Palmer, of London on the security of the Egyptian tribute. By 1875 there had been thirteen further loans, with a nominal capital of £184,981,783; the last, for £40,000,000 in 1874, had interest of 5 per cent and an issue price of only 43½, and it followed the disastrous failure of the attempt to raise £28,000,000 at 58½ in 1873. The creditors were mainly British and French. In the process more and more sources of revenue were assigned as security: the remainder of the Egyptian tribute, Syrian customs duties, customs duties and octrois of Constantinople, tobacco, salt, stamp, and licence duties, the sheep tax of Roumelia and the Archipelagos and the produce of the mines of Tokat, and 'the general revenues, present and future, of Turkey'. National bankruptcy, in the form of either a repudiation of part or the whole of the debt or a partial, temporary, or permanent suspension of interest payments, might mean the death of the Sick Man through the paralysis of the central government and of the use of its armed forces against domestic or foreign foes; and it would mean the collapse of Turkey's carefully fostered reputation for progress in the west. It would be a dismal commentary on the French faith in enlightened centralisation. It is not surprising that the Russian ambassador was believed to have inspired the partial suspension of interest payments announced in October 1875.

Meanwhile the provincial administration had survived a number of crises under 'Abd al-Azīz; in the end it was in Bosnia alone that the combination of circumstances made a continued insurrection possible. It is unlikely that even the attainment of the standard of equitable tax collecting, equality before the law, maintenance of traditional ecclesiastical privileges, and honest policing promised by the *Hatt* would have been sufficient to revive the old loyalty to the sultan, to reconcile Christian and Muslim, and to reverse the rise of nationalism in the Balkans. In spite of the success of Mahmūd II in arresting the process of disintegration in the Muslim areas of the empire (other than Egypt) the peripheral Christian communities in Serbia, Montenegro, Greece, and the Principalities had attained virtual or complete independence by the middle of the century. The survival of the Porte's authority elsewhere came to depend far more on the vigilant suppression of embryonic revolutionary violence, and the damping down of innumerable local discontents before they reached a violent or widespread form. In this essentially hand-to-mouth process, however, the Turkish authorities always had a considerable asset in the confusion of interests and animosities, social, religious, racial, economic perhaps, among the mixed-up groups of the sultan's subjects, Muslim and Christian, so that anything like a general or concerted rising would be difficult to sustain.

The Bulgarian areas show the Turks always able to maintain their authority, in spite of clashes that advertised the sources of discontent. Although the Bulgarian peasantry formed a more or less homogeneous mass between the Danube and the Balkan Mountains they were interspersed even here with some Muslim communities, and elsewhere, south of the Balkans and in Macedonia, with larger Turk, Greek, Serb, or Albanian groups; the bulk of them were too poorly armed and too accessible to the main centres of Turkish military strength to be able to revolt successfully. They had always the age-long instinctive grudge against the Turk as an infidel, a tax-gatherer, and a conqueror; Turkish patronage of the Greek church, while diverting some animosity, did not remove the ultimate barrier. But the setting-up of the Bulgarian exarchate in 1870 effectively destroyed for over forty years the chance of a united Christian opposition. Since 1864 the planting of colonies of Circassians, refugees from Russian heavy-handedness, among the Bulgarians had been an additional grievance. On the other hand the peasantry, particularly since Midhat's administration of the Danubian *vilayet*, were relatively prosperous. The *chorbadjis*, the small better-off middle class and trading community, wanted only peaceful advance, and were disposed to await the inevitability of Ottoman gradualness, or at least the arrival of Russian armies, meanwhile looking with favour on plans for a dualist Turco-Bulgar solution. The genuine small extremist groups, the active revolutionaries plotting their impracticable uprisings, were often suspicious of the Russian government, which was equally suspicious of them. The Russian government, which had left the Bulgarian insurgents to their fate in 1829 and 1853, and was not ready for a widespread crisis in the Balkans in the decade before 1875, saw an unpleasant similarity between the young Bulgarian extremists and its own Nihilist revolutionaries. This did not prevent Ignatyev, the Russian ambassador, from dabbling in some of the Bulgarian plots, particularly through Naiden Gerov, a Bulgarian leader who was also Russian Vice-Consul at Philippopolis. The small risings in 1867 and 1868, for example, were partly financed from this source. But the striking fact is that these risings, and those in 1872 and at

Stara Zagora in September 1875, all failed ignominiously; there was no general support for the revolutionaries, and the Turks, who were kept well informed, took prompt and not excessive counter-measures.

The Bosnian problem was, however, a vastly more complex affair because of the existence of a dominant Muslim minority and of a tri-angular international competition. The Turks were unwilling to repress their Muslim subjects unduly; on the other hand either the Austro-Hungarian empire or the smaller Slav states of Serbia and Montenegro would be the residuary legatees if the insurgence of the Christian inhabi-tants made the continuance of Turkish rule impossible. The Turkish conquest of 1463 had been followed by the conversion to Islam of the bulk of the landowners; by the nineteenth century these *begs*, numbering with their semi-feudal retainers probably a good third of the total population, were among the most fiercely conservative, politically loyal, and effectively autonomous of the sultan's vassals, and repressive in the extreme towards the unarmed, much-exploited Christian peasantry. A long struggle, initi-ated by Mahmūd II, had led to Omer Pasha's success between 1850 and 1852 in destroying the virtually independent feudal powers of the *begs*; in theory Bosnia now came under the control of Ottoman officials, respon-sible to the central government, and a suitable field for Tanzimatist reformers. In practice, grievances remained. Although the reforms had included improvements in the legal status of the *ra'iyeh* the Ottoman authorities could never risk the complete alienation of the *begs*, and acquiesced more or less willingly in their retention of the realities of Muslim predominance. In the new councils or *medjliss* in European Turkey there was usually a Christian representative and Christian testi-mony was on an equal footing with Muslim; in practice there were invariably Muslim majorities, and in Bosnia they seem to have been remarkably capricious in their bigotry. In the field of taxation it is probably correct to say that the new system, which brought in the Otto-man tax-farmer with heavy-handed police support while preserving the landlord's right to one-third of the peasant's crops, had less studied brutality but more systematic extortion than the old; and while the *begs* were feeling the pinch and increasing their demands, the imperial finances were in too parlous a state to allow any remission of state taxation, let alone an abolition of tax-farming itself. The conditions produced periodic and more or less serious risings, repressions, and emigrations; finally, the bad harvest of 1874 and continued pressure of the tax-gatherers led to a number of more or less simultaneous clashes, of which that between Orthodox and Muslims at Nevesinje in the Hercegovina in June 1875 is usually regarded as the immediate cause of the great Bosnian revolt.

A collapse of Turkish rule in Bosnia was bound to shake profoundly the uneasy equilibrium of political forces in Austria-Hungary. The stultifying factor in the monarchy was the internal political deadlock which, while preventing any fundamental challenge to the imperial government, also prevented the growth of any overriding loyalty to the state or of any great satisfying lines of domestic or foreign policy. There is an obvious truth in the assertion that Austria-Hungary, having been turned out of Italy and Germany, found her main opportunity henceforth in the Near East. Yet it is also true that her changed domestic and diplomatic circumstances after 1866 severely limited the extent to which she could exploit even this opportunity.

The working alliance between Francis Joseph and the Magyars, foreshadowed in the creation of the Dual Monarchy in 1867 and established in 1871, dominated both the foreign and the domestic affairs of Austria-Hungary to the end, and did much to bring it to its end: it was an alliance of convenience, and not of regard, between the only two genuinely conservative forces in the empire. The emperor, whose meticulous, reticent, bureaucratic handling of the business of state expressed at once his authoritarian outlook, his will to survive, and his lack of creative political imagination, was by the 1870's an experienced and somewhat disillusioned opportunist who could see the dangers of Magyar inflexibility. He could also see, however, frustration in an exclusive reliance on the German liberals. Without any very clear idea as to where he was going he had embarked on a long series of constitutional innovations in 1866 whose starting point was the desire to avenge Sadowa, but whose ultimate justification was the failure of the supranational system which the defeats of 1866 and 1859 were thought to have underlined. The original purpose had seemed clear in such moves as the programme of army reform and the appointment of the Saxon Prime Minister, Count Beust, as Foreign Minister; but revenge could not be carried out immediately, and Bismarck speedily frustrated the more promising of Austrian (and French) counter-moves among the south German states. Imperceptibly the anti-Prussian purpose became a policy of wait-and-see, as the consequential adjustments to the new course became problems in themselves; and while this transition had its vindication in the French defeat in 1870 its explanation is to be found as much in the domestic situation as the foreign.

In the 'Compromise' or *Ausgleich* of 1867 the Magyars secured complete internal self-government for Hungary, which was placed constitutionally and practically on an equality with the larger and richer 'other half', now usually called Austria, and sometimes Cis-leithania. There was still a 'common monarchy' for the whole empire, with three ministers—of War, Foreign Affairs, and Finance—to deal with its affairs. The delegations (bodies consisting of sixty representatives of each half of the monarchy) met alternately in Vienna and Budapest to debate the common affairs of the empire; Austria contributed 70 per cent and Hungary 30 per cent to meet the common expenditure; and there was a customs union between the two parts which could be renewed every ten years. The Austrian Germans, who had hitherto been the agents and essential supporters of the idea of the *Einheitsstaat*, were the most obvious sufferers from these arrangements, for with the *Ausgleich* there disappeared not only the idea of a supranational empire but also the unchallenged predominance of the German elements in their own lands. This was partly because Francis Joseph, while willing for the time being to entrust office to the German liberals, was more irritated by their pretensions than he was by those of the Magyars; partly because it was inherent in the new policy that concessions must be made to other national groups outside Hungary. To the emperor and the imperial bureaucracy the 'other half' remained a group of historic political units and not the residuary legatee of the Habsburg monarchy: although they were willing to grant extensive local rights of self-government to the more vociferous and aggressive nationalities they were more than ever conscious of the need to maintain the ultimate authority of the central power. Only in one case was a satisfactory bargain on these lines achieved. A special Austrian ministry for Galician affairs was established in 1871; Polish was recognised as the language of administration and secondary education, financial arrangements were favourable, and the government thus secured the support of the Polish vote in the imperial parliament and confirmed the position of the Poles as the dominant element in Galicia. The Poles were henceforth accommodating and loyal, subject only to an ultimate and overriding loyalty to an independent Poland. There remained in Galicia a subordinated, but at first rather inarticulate, Ruthenian peasantry to brood on the alternative possibilities of becoming Great Russians or independent Ukrainians, and to remind the Polish aristocracy that the imperial government had the Ruthenian card in reserve.

No such expedient bargain could be achieved elsewhere. The Czechs had also been asking since 1868 for a status similar to that of Hungary, and they appeared to be in sight of it with the proposals of the Hohenwart ministry in 1871. The final form of the Czech demands, formulated after the Bohemian Diet in September 1871 had received the emperor's rescript promising to recognise the rights of the Bohemian kingdom and to confirm this recognition by a coronation oath, were set out in eighteen 'fundamental articles' negotiated by the ministry with the Czech leaders. They did not go quite so far as to propose the setting up of a triune Austro-Hungarian-Bohemian kingdom; they recognised the dual system and proposed that the Austrian representatives in the delegations should be directly elected by the Bohemian and other provincial Diets. They wished, nevertheless, that the Bohmeian Diet should take over almost all the functions of the Austrian *Reichsrat*, which would become a mere congress of delegates in a federal Austrian state. The Austrian Germans were thus faced with the loss of their influence and importance in the official, business, and perhaps intellectual life of both the empire and Cis-leithania and also with the loss of their political control in Moravia and Silesia. The Magyars foresaw both the future interference of the aggrandised Czechs with the Slav minorities of Hungary and a possible weakening of Magyar influence through the alliance of the discontented Austrian Germans with the new German empire. No doubt the Czechs could have secured useful and indeed extensive concessions if they had asked for less; but, while the resolution of Francis Joseph was weakening, the Czechs, under the leadership of Ladislaus Rieger, were kept from any compromise by the intransigence of Count Henry Clam-Martinič, their ally and the leader of the Bohemian landed aristocracy. The essential point, nevertheless, was the open challenge of the Germans, voiced after some hesitations by Beust, and the root and branch opposition of the Magyars, voiced by Andrássy. Hohenwart was dismissed, Andrássy replaced Beust, and the Habsburg-Magyar marriage of convenience was consummated.

In all essentials it was to remain, with a slightly contemptuous utilisation of German loyalty, the permanent basis of Francis Joseph's rule. A German liberal ministry under Prince Adolph Auersperg succeeded that of Hohenwart; its members were somewhat doctrinaire and politically rather inexperienced Austro-Germans whose theories were quite compatible with repression of the national minorities; General Kollar, as Military Governor of Prague, carried out this policy with severity, muzzling the press, prosecuting Czech journalists before German juries, severely restricting public meetings. The Czechs sulked, refused to give in, and boycotted not only the *Reichsrat* but also the Diets of Brno and Prague. On top of this there came the financial crash of 1873 with distress and parliamentary scandals which did nothing to strengthen the regime.

In these circumstances neither the German nor the Magyar political leaders could look with any enthusiasm on an increase in the Slav population of the monarchy, although equally they could not welcome the annexation of Bosnia by Serbia or Montenegro to form a great southern Slav state. All things considered, and in spite of expansionist ambitions in the Hofburg itself, the simplest course was to maintain Turkish authority as long as possible. This was recognised, however, as merely the postponement of an issue which would probably have to be faced sooner or later, and there were not wanting arguments in favour of a forward move by Austria-Hungary at a time of her own choosing.

The Serbian regency had indeed been sounded in 1870 on a plan to divide Bosnia; this would have given the north-western triangle, predominantly Catholic-Croat, to Austria-Hungary, while the remainder went to Serbia. Andrássy, influenced by Benjamin Kallay, the somewhat Serbophile consul in Belgrade, was at first favourable: apart from satisfying the military by providing a hinterland for Austrian Dalmatia, the plan might bring Serbia into friendship with and dependence on Austria-

Hungary, while providing a bone of future contention between Croats and Serbs. However, the Serbian government, which, as Andrássy rightly suspected, hoped in due course to acquire the whole of Bosnia, turned down the proposals, and with the pro-Russian turn in the policy of the Serb regency which followed he began to speak with irritation of the Pan-Serb pretensions. The incident had nevertheless focused attention on some unattractive alternatives.

The Croats had not (at least in Magyar eyes) very much to complain of. They had been left in 1867 to settle with Hungary as best they could and had made their own compromise with the Magyars. They had secured from Deak and Eötvös a separate existence within the kingdom of Hungary for the united state of Croatia-Slavonia with a considerable measure of self-government, although finance remained strictly, but not inequitably, under the control of the Hungarian parliament. Their share in the transaction of the common affairs of the monarchy was recognised by representation in the delegations and in the Hungarian parliament, and they could speak Croat wherever they liked. Nevertheless, there was the usual fierce haggling over political rights and even a minor insurrection. Some fiscal and educational concessions and the appointment of a popular poet of peasant stock, Ivan Mažuranić, as Ban in 1873 eased tension and appeased moderate opinion. But the Croats still resented the Magyar rule and the Habsburg desertion, and were beginning to find solace in the allurements of the Yugoslav idea. In the form both of Gaj's 'Illyrianism' in the 1840's and the southern Slav cultural propaganda of Bishop Strossmayer and his associates in the 1860's and 1870's this movement contained a challenge to Habsburg-Magyar authority on the one hand and Serbian aspirations on the other; it was for this reason that Andrássy had grasped at the hope of a perpetuation of Serb-Croat rivalry which could at least be expected to lessen the self-assurance of the Croats in their dissatisfaction with the Hungarian government.

Beyond this point it was difficult to plan with any assurance. Strossmayer's ardent and generous programme, which gave particular encouragement to Croatian scholars but extended its patronage to cultural societies and activities among all the southern Slavs, was accompanied by political aspirations which looked to the reconciliation of Orthodox and Catholic Slavs in a unified state. One party in Croatia dreamt of the union under one crown of all the southern slavs, with Agram (Zagreb) as the headquarters of a state of some 6,000,000 persons which would include the triune kingdom (Croatia–Slavonia–Dalmatia), Bosnia, the Hercegovina, Montenegro, Serbia, and Old Serbia; others in Croatia would have been content more modestly with the triune kingdom alone. Serbian aspirations were confined to the uniting of the Slav populations on the right bank of the Save; the Croats and their Catholic propaganda were looked on with suspicion, and in any case Pan-Serb expansionists could not think seriously of trying to detach the lands of the Austro-Hungarian Slavs from the Dual Monarchy. The greater Serbia, expanded at Turkey's expense, would nevertheless include Old Serbia and Bosnia-Hercegovina, as well as Montenegro. There was no lack of even wider visions. Among Hungary's Serb population in the *Voivodina* there were dreams of a southern Slav federation which would include the Bulgars; some even proposed to include Roumania and the Bukovina. Svetozar Miletić, the leading figure among the Hungarian Serbs, had the usual weakness for all-embracing schemes of Slav unity, combined with a tendency to quarrel with most of his neighbours. He deplored the handing over to the control of the Hungarian government of the areas hitherto known as the military frontiers. The inhabitants of these areas were villagers of Croat and Serb stock, brought up in a tradition of dynastic loyalty to the Habsburgs, who for several centuries had formed the spearhead of Austrian attack and the first line of defence against the Turks; hitherto they had been governed by the Minister of War in Vienna. Miletić was also on bad terms with the Serbian regency and the Orthodox clergy, and found much to criticise in Russian Pan-Slavism.

But on balance it must have appeared to Andrássy that while an occupation of Bosnia might drive a wedge between the Croats and Serbia it was likely to make the Hungarian Serbs more obstreperous than ever. Against this had to be set the apprehension, difficult to evaluate, as to Russian aims. Everyone knew that Russia spoke with two voices; but the voices themselves were equivocal. If the Russian foreign office frowned on the revolutionary radicalism of Serbian and Bulgarian youth it encouraged the aspirations of Prince Nicholas of Montenegro and maintained numerous consulates and vice-consulates in Bosnia and Macedonia, where there was little orthodox business for them; and if Ignatyev and the consuls professed to be seeking no more than the welfare of the Christians under Turkish rule there were individuals among them who did little to conceal their revolutionary zeal and animosities, which were often more anti-Austrian than anti-Turk. In the circumstances the tendency was to exaggerate the extent of Russian influence. It made no impression on the Croats. Among the Serbs the *Omladina*, a secret society in which Miletić had played an active part since its foundation in 1866, had somewhat strained relations with the Serbian government and was naturally regarded in many official circles in Vienna and Budapest as the agent of Russian Pan-Slavism, although it seems to have had no such function.

The case for an Austrian forward policy was one of prestige, strategy, and commercial advantage. Some striking and not too difficult foreign success would balance the losses of 1859 and 1866. The soldiers wanted a part or the whole of Bosnia to provide a hinterland to Austria's narrow Dalmatian territory. The handing over of the military frontiers was considered to have increased the need (or strengthened the case) for this advance. Andrássy, in spite of his increasing caution after 1871, was susceptible to the prestige argument, both from the general European angle and as a gesture to the emperor. He was equally or perhaps more strongly influenced by the conviction that Austria-Hungary must assert herself as the natural protector of the west Balkan peoples and that her natural role was that of a powerful good neighbour in ensuring their equitable treatment by the Turks. The commercial argument was also based on both defensive and expansive interests. Austria-Hungary had dominated the external trade of European Turkey before the Crimean War and had lost much of her position to the British after it, a process which had been helped by the opening up of railway lines from Salonika to Mitrovica and from Constantinople to Adrianople and Philippopolis, with branches to Dedeagach and Yamboli. North of Mitrovica and the Balkan Mountains there were, in Turkish territory, only two lines from the Danube to the Black Sea and a shorter one still from the Austrian frontier to Banjaluka in northern Bosnia. The Austrian business world in the 1870's was awakening to the need and possibility of the opening up of adequate trade-routes from the north, and these were to be given definite shape during the eastern crisis of 1875–9 by the influential director of the commercial section of the Austrian foreign office, Baron Schwegel. The main aim was to complete the great Orient railway from Vienna to Constantinople, linking up with the Turkish section at Nish, and with the Salonika–Mitrovica line; occupation of Bosnia would facilitate an exercise of Austria's political influence that would keep Serbia in her commercial orbit and ensure the safety of her trade-route through Scutari. This in turn pointed to friendship with the north Albanian tribes and control of the sanjak of Novipazar; it suggested an economic reason for restraining the territorial ambitions of Montenegro.

For all its immediate success, Andrássy's tenure of the foreign ministry (1871–9) merely perpetuated in the field of Austrian foreign policy the deadlock which had descended on domestic affairs. He showed some satisfaction with his own diplomatic skill when Bosnia-Hercegovina fell into the lap of the monarchy in 1878 as a result of Russia's exertions; in general, however, the course of the Near Eastern crisis from 1875 to 1879 amply confirmed the view that any change in Austria's foreign relations had its counter-balancing disadvantages, and that, politically and strategically, the best of all possible policies would be to avoid change altogether. What Andrássy secured at the Congress of Berlin was a balance of power in the peninsula which sharpened all the political and strategical issues: the Russians back on the Danube in Bessarabia, a small autonomous Bulgarian state which carried Russian influence down to the Balkan mountain chain, a Macedonia still Turkish but threatened by Bulgarian, Greek, Serbian, and even Albanian nationalism, an Austro-Hungarian occupation of Bosnia-Hercegovina, and a sulky and discredited Serbia, cast-off by Russia and viewing distastefully the need for accommodation with the monarchy.

The new position was viewed uneasily by many elements inside the monarchy, and Andrássy had to face difficulties over the Bosnian occupation which had nothing directly to do with the longer-term foreign problem. The occupation was unsatisfying both to those who wanted more of Turkish territory and to those who feared even this degree of disturbance of the internal racial and political balance. Partisanship was open, violent, and contradictory. Croats in Agram and Slovenes in Laibach had demonstrated in favour of Balkan Slav aspirations; Czechs and southern Slavs extolled the tsar and the Russian armies, and Rieger exclaimed to the Russian Pan-Slavist, Ivan Aksakov, that Slavdom could achieve great things for mankind, if its strength were not lamed by disunion. But in Budapest after the Turkish defeat in 1877 a mass meeting called for war with Russia, and sympathy for Turkey was widespread. While Budapest citizens presented a sword of honour to 'Abd al-Kerim, the conqueror of the Serbs in 1876, Czechs presented a sword of honour to Chernyaev, the Serbs' defeated commander. The expansionists included the emperor himself and were strongly represented among the army leaders; to them it seemed that Andrássy was throwing away a heaven-sent opportunity not only to annex Bosnia-Hercegovina outright, but to dominate, and evenly possibly annex, the western Balkans as far as Salonika. Francis Joseph's clear approval of the forward policy helped Andrássy up to a point; in both Austria and Hungary the emperor's wishes helped to secure the ratification of the Treaty of Berlin, but only after major political crises.

The grounds for attack had certain points in common in each country. In Austria, led without much discretion by Edward Herbst and other German liberal leaders and backed by the *Neue Freie Presse*, it did not represent any particular concern for the feelings of the Turks. But it did express violent alarm at the danger to the precarious Austrian-German position of an influx of 2,000,000 Slavs into the monarchy, and was also an outlet for gathering resentment at the party's virtual exclusion from a voice in foreign policy. In Hungary there was also a basic fear of the influx of Slavs, but it came from conservative quarters and the Independent party and was influenced by some spontaneous friendliness for the Turks. There was also great concern at any change in the political *status quo* which would reduce the relative strength of Hungary in imperial affairs. The result was that both Francis Joseph and Andrássy felt that they had no more use for the German liberals, whose main virtue had consisted in acquiescence: deprived of the imperial influence, Prince Adolph Auersperg resigned and the party was defeated at the general election in June 1879. In Hungary, on the other hand, where the premier, Koloman Tisza, leader of the Liberal party and the Magyar protagonist of dualism since 1875, had lost ground heavily through his support of the Bosnian occupation, the ultimate effect of the crisis was to consolidate his position in the emperor's regard.

The result was to increase inside the Dual Monarchy the deadlock that was inherent in dualism, and to perpetuate in the Balkans the deadlock which had followed the Russian and Austrian advances in 1878. But the immediate consequences to Austria-Hungary were favourable: in domestic politics a period of relative tranquillity, and in the Balkans a successful bolstering of the Turkish state which the monarchy had now no desire to disturb.

In Count Eduard Taaffe, the Austrian premier from 1879 to 1893, Francis Joseph had a loyal and accommodating servant who could make the most of this temporarily favourable situation. The strengthening of the empire abroad and the weakening of dissident elements at home enabled him throughout the 1880's to keep together a bloc of supporters ('the iron ring') and to increase the emperor's influence and authority. The basis of his success was the collapse of Czech intransigence. The boycott of the *Reichsrat* since 1868 had brought Rieger and his followers no profit, and in 1878 he had been compelled to satisfy those of his countrymen who were prepared to see what could be gained by co-operation. Taaffe was thus able to bring the Czech deputies to the support of his ministry. The Poles, ready, on conditions, to respond to the emperor's call on their loyalty, and the Catholic Centre were the other two elements that gave him his majority over the German liberals and progressives. The three groups were of approximately equal size and Taaffe, while evading fundamental changes, could offer a certain range of immediate concessions together with the hope of an ultimate settlement of the nationalist claims. The Czechs, unsatisfied but not unhopeful, secured various rewards, mainly linguistic and cultural; their language was given equality with German in the public affairs of Bohemia and Moravia, a national Czech university was founded in Prague in 1881, some Czech secondary schools were established, some posts made available to Czechs in the state administration. The Poles and the conservatives also had their rewards. In the meantime the Austrian state finances were slowly put into good order; control of the railways by the state was resumed, and the 'Austrian idea', which could no longer command general political acceptance, was vindicated administratively by a competent and omnipresent bureaucracy. But all the empire's fundamental problems remained, and Taaffe was merely the pleasantest and most adroit of the instruments whereby Francis Joseph postponed their solution.

If the empire was to survive it must win the tolerance of the nationalities, but the nationalities had no tolerance towards one another. The Austrian Germans were no more ready to concede the demands of the Czechs than the Magyars were to concede those of the Croats. Their refusal to compromise was not due to any desire to destroy the empire; on the contrary, the pushing of irreconcilable nationalistic claims to their logical extreme presupposed an unshakable imperial framework within which an eternal struggle for concessions could proceed. As the limits of Taaffe's concessions came in sight in the late 1880's, Rieger and his 'Old Czech' followers rapidly lost ground before the rising Young Czech party, which in turn was kept on its toes by the Czech Radicals and Agrarians. The Young Czechs gained control of the Diet of Bohemia as a result of the elections of 1889. They were faced by a correspondingly uncompromising German opposition. The Linz Programme of the German Nationalists in 1882 was an attempt to restore German supremacy in Austria; it looked to Bismarck, who had no desire to help, and emphasised its own exclusiveness by a growing anti-semitism, which was one means whereby the demagogic violence of one of its leaders, Schönerer, came to dominate the movement. In Bohemia the battle was waged furiously throughout the 1880's. The Germans loudly denounced the dangers of Pan-Slavism and fought any concessions to the Czechs in matters of language, education, and administration; the Czechs were equally inflexible in fighting for every concession that they could secure. In an attempt at a solution Taaffe initiated discussions in January 1890 which led to a plan whereby each nationality would be administratively supreme in its own area. This meant in effect the administrative division of Bohemia between Germans and Czechs; and the Old Czechs were agreeable. The Young Czechs on the other hand were not prepared to renounce their claim to the whole. Nor were the Germans, although a minority, prepared to accept minority status. Taaffe had come to the end of his compromises. In 1893, after a proposal for almost universal suffrage had shocked nearly all his followers, he was dismissed. His view was that the enfranchising of the masses would sweep away the narrow issues which made up the political life of the existing party groups. The emperor was not ready for the leap: he thought that it would land him in more problems than those from which he escaped, and certainly threaten his own authority by forcing him to accept representative governments. The unrepresentative groups of politicians who were called on to form governments for the next few years were agreed on nothing except their dislike of the universal franchise, and could find no solution of the German-Czech issues.

Hungary had its own form of deadlock, but here the nationalist problem was that of a group all too firmly in power. The Magyars, a bare 50 per cent of the population, kept the other groups firmly in check. In Austria, Germanisation was on the defensive; in Hungary, Magyarisation was still being pushed to the limit. In the Linz Programme the Germans had been only too willing to propose the transfer to purely Hungarian rule of Dalmatia, Bosnia, Galicia, and the Bukovina, a device which would have increased the relative strength of the Germans in Austria while placing the Magyars in a decisive minority, and was significant mainly as a further confession of failure to solve the empire's basic problem. Bosnia remained under dual control, although it was the Hungarian, Benjamin Kallay, who was entrusted as Minister of Finance with its administration in 1882. Koloman Tisza, Hungarian premier from 1875 to 1890, relied mainly on the support of the gentry and led a liberal ministry of faithful but exigent followers. The denunciation of Pan-Slavism and a thoroughly repressive policy towards the nationalities was a convenient way of demonstrating that while serving the emperor Tisza and his followers remained true Magyars. The limited franchise was maintained on a severe linguistic basis which effectively preserved the Magyar monopoly even in non-Magyar constituencies. It also, as in Austria, kept the vote from the working man. The literary or religious aspirations of Roumans, Slovaks, Croats, and Serbs were resisted; weaker groups, such as the Saxons of Transylvania, lost their local privileges. The main problem, however, was that of the Croats, whose dream of a southern Slav state in a triune kingdom had been strengthened by the Bosnian occupation. They were able to put up a better resistance than the other minorities to some of the Magyar encroachments, and after some serious clashes the Hungarian-Croatian compromise was renewed in 1879 and again in 1889. Meanwhile the Hungarian magnates found a policy of their own in attacking Dualism itself; this proved a useful politicians' device for undermining Tisza, who remained loyal to the *Ausgleich* and the emperor. Nevertheless, the royal title was amended to 'imperial and royal' in 1889, and this led on to demands for the removal of other symbols of the connection, such as the common army.

By the end of the 1890's the collapse of constitutional government in Austria and the unyielding nationalism of Hungary meant that Austria-Hungary was ceasing to be a viable state: but she was still sustained by the conviction of most of her politicians that there was nothing to take her place.

In the crises of 1875–8 the sultanate had been faced with the possibility of the complete loss of its European possessions through insurrection and foreign attack. The process was arrested through a variety of causes: the intervention of the great powers, unable either in 1876 or 1878 or 1880 to agree on the limits of coercion; the continued rivalries between the Christian minorities, and the continued acceptance of the Hamidian regime by the majority of Muslims; above all, perhaps, the tenacious, unsleeping defence of his authority by the sultan 'Abd al-Hamīd in the 1880's and 1890's. This does not, however, quite solve the mystery of the Sick Man's continued survival. In European Turkey as in Austria an imperial system was making its last stand; but 'Abd al-Hamīd, unlike the Habsburgs, could offer neither prosperity nor good administration nor the comfort of great power status to satisfy the Christian and Muslim communities in the peninsula.

One reason for the real, if limited, recovery after 1880 was that the revolutionary movement of 1875–6 had at least meant the removal of some of the grosser abuses inherent in the reform programme. There would be no repetition of 'Abd al-Azīz's whims and extravagance. He had been forced to abdicate on 29 May 1876, and was found dead six days later; his successor Murād V had apparently collapsed mentally under the strain of the crisis and was deposed on 31 August. 'Abd al-Hamīd II who followed was by nature parsimonious; but in any case the national bankruptcy made austerity inevitable. For some years the contrast was striking: all outward display was abandoned at court, even on formal occasions the sultan wore only a simple military great-coat without decorations, his servants were poorly dressed and even slovenly, and the high officials were careful to avoid any show of prosperity and self-importance, many of them being genuinely in straitened circumstances. This mean show took the edge off the revolutionary discontent in the capital itself: those who found little glory in the regime had to recognise its limited resources, and 'Abd al-Hamīd in the early days could parade and at the same time postpone reformist plans with some plausibility.

Indeed, he convinced many close observers of his zeal. For a time he convinced Midhat Pasha, who interviewed him in August 1876 on the eve of Murād's deposition; he not only accepted the condition that he should promulgate a new constitution and take the Young Turks Zīyā Bey and Kemāl Bey as his private secretaries, but spoke yearningly of the more advanced reforms that he proposed to introduce. He half convinced Sir Austin Henry Layard, the British ambassador, in many cosy chats in which he talked sadly and apparently sincerely of his hopes and difficulties. He was morbidly afraid—as well he might be—for his own safety; this was a legacy of the events of 1876 and the ease with which his two predecessors had been deposed. After the killing of the Young Turk, 'Alī Su'āvī, who was shot on 24 May 1878 in an attempt to seize the Cheragan Palace and restore Murād, 'Abd al-Hamīd was on the verge of a nervous breakdown for some days, and made panic-stricken appeals to the British and German ambassadors to protect him and arrange for his escape to England. After this affair he scarcely ever went outside the palace and its garden except to attend a mosque on Fridays at one of the gates. It was possible for some time to believe that the exiling of Midhat in February 1877 and of other reformers and Young Turks might be due to these personal fears and not to an aversion for reforms in general. Having disposed of Midhat he summoned the promised parliament, which endorsed the war with Russia in April and was not dissolved until July 1877; after the Congress of Berlin he agreed in October 1878 to the British proposals for reform in Asia Minor, and the unexpected appointment of the burly Tunisian minister, Khair al-Dīn Pasha, the author of a brochure reconciling western civilisation with Islamic law, seemed a further guarantee of liberal intentions. The constitution remained in being, even if parliamentary government was suspended, and he continued to protest that he ruled only through his ministers. It is not necessary to assume that 'Abd al-Hamīd, a hard-headed, narrow man with a practical turn of mind, an excellent revolver shot and the competent manager of a small estate before his accession, had any difficulty in understanding the material advantages that would come from a stable and contented community. His sorrowful talks to Layard about the lamentable lack of capable men and the desire of everyone for luxury and sensual enjoyment were interspersed with more and more shrill pleas for money, and show a progressive sense of frustration. One clue to his policy throughout is a fear of domestic enemies so morbid as to prevent his entrusting real authority to anyone for long. The other is a genuine lack of resources which was most strongly marked in the field of finance. With this went a growing understanding of the unwillingness of the powers to involve themselves in further crises in the Near East. By 1881 he had taken the measure of his domestic and foreign opponents; he had assessed remarkably well the limits of concession and defiance, and could remain, without progress and without disaster, the master of his own house for the next twenty years.

The first problem was to salvage as much as possible from the wreck of 1878. Although the Treaty of Berlin had provided for cessions of Turkish territory to Austria-Hungary (Bosnia), Russia (Bessarabia), and all the Balkan states, the new frontiers had in many cases been sketched in only general terms on partly deficient maps, and there were opportunities for a good deal of haggling in the boundary commissions. Where the sultan retained his titular sovereignty, as in Bosnia and Bulgaria, there were struggles to retain some vestiges of authority, although it was soon evident that it was only against the Austrians that he intended to make any real fight. It was not until 21 April 1879, after much stubbornness on both sides, that an Austro-Turkish convention regulating the conditions of occupation of Bosnia, Hercegovina, and the sanjak of Novipazar was signed; there was a desperate last-minute effort on the part of the Porte to persuade Andrássy to renounce Austrian rights of garrison in the sanjak. The convention contained a secret clause providing for joint Austro-Turkish resistance to an attack on the garrisons of either power in the sanjak, but immediately after the signature the sultan pressed for its cancellation, on the ground that it might involve him in operations against Muslims who had been driven to revolt by Austrian cruelty and oppression. The clause had aroused the hostility of Osman Pasha; Russia was known to have denounced it to the Porte. Andrássy agreed to the cancellation on 20 May. 'Abd al-Hamīd's scruples were probably genuine. He was, nevertheless, well aware that there were three widely dispersed areas of Muslim resistance to the Berlin settlement and that his Muslim subjects would have to be handled carefully.

Of the three, the Bosnian rising was on a formidable scale: 90,000 rebels, mainly Muslim and Orthodox, stiffened with some regular Turkish soldiery and Albanian volunteers, resisted the entry of the Habsburg troops, and only the Roman Catholic population welcomed them with any enthusiasm. The Orthodox wanted union with Serbia or Montenegro. What the Muslims wanted was not so clear; many of them had had their grievances against the Turkish government in 1875. What they did not want was Habsburg rule. A Croat general led the occupying armies, and after several weeks of serious fighting the rising was crushed, with sufficient publicity to discredit the government in Vienna and Budapest, and sufficient brutality to discredit it in the two provinces. The sultan kept aloof, but secured in the April convention the acknowledgement of his sovereignty and of his rights as head of the Muslim community; as it turned out neither of these provisions meant very much, and after the rising the administration was thoroughly assimilated to the Austro-Hungarian imperial system, mainly by Croat officials. There was a further rising in 1882.

Nor could the sultan or the Porte give any help to the most obscure, most tragic, and, because of their proximity to the capital, most vulnerable group of Muslim insurgents, the Pomaks. The so-called Rhodope rising went on intermittently from April to October 1878, the leader being an adventurer of British stock. In the mountain region south of the Maritza the insurgents had done their best to resist the Russian forces and to shelter the columns of Muslim refugees escaping from the war areas and from the hostility of the Bulgarians. At one time there were some 50,000 men under arms, and a 'provisional Pomak government' issued manifestos and was believed to have agents in Constantinople. The back of the rising was broken by some large-scale brutalities on the part of the Russian troops and Bulgarian militia. There are signs that the Turkish authorities both encouraged and feared a movement which, while defending Turkish territory, was taking its affairs into its own hands.

There was a similar problem, on a bigger and more dramatic scale, in Albania. Here there was the beginning of a genuine national movement, in spite of Bismarck's denial. Before 1878 Albanian risings had not been infrequent, although they were due to taxation, conscription, and the tenacious resistance of wild mountain people to centralising pressure rather than to any concerted political programme. The Treaty of San Stefano, which had proposed to include Albanian-inhabited territory in the new frontiers of Montenegro, Serbia, and even Bulgaria, brought the leaders of various Albanian districts to agree at Prizren early in June 1878 to set up an 'Albanian League for the Defence of the Rights of the

Albanian Nation' and they presented a resolution in defence of Albanian rights to the Congress of Berlin on 15 June 1878. The subsequent struggle to vindicate Albanian claims had three important features.

The first was the high nuisance value of Albanian armed resistance. The Berlin settlement had maintained peace between the great powers by complicated and awkward compromises which might again develop into divergences unless the new boundaries were accepted without too much delay. Serbia occupied the Albanian districts assigned to her without challenge, but in September 1878 Albanian tribesmen fought a considerable battle to prevent Montenegrin troops occupying Gusinje and Plava, and subsequent attempts by the powers during the next two years to redraw the frontier line all failed in face of Albanian hostility. A southern branch of the League, with Abdul Frashëri as its leader, had 30,000 tribesmen under arms in an equally determined effort to resist the Greek claims in Epirus. The lesson, significant for the future, was of the disproportionate political importance of a determined Balkan minority when the powers were deadlocked.

This pointed to a second significant feature: the inability of the Turkish government to exploit this predominantly Muslim movement to its own advantage. It is true that for a time the Porte welcomed Albanian intransigence as a means of postponing inevitable concessions; it was widely assumed abroad that the League was a put-up job on the part of the Porte. But as the struggle developed during 1880 it became clear that concessions were in fact inevitable—the Montenegrins would get in the end the substance of what had been promised them—and that the League might not only prolong the struggle dangerously but develop a national self-consciousness which would challenge the authority of the sultan himself. On the other hand the sultan did not wish to lose Muslim-Albanian support. This dilemma was increased by differences of opinion in Constantinople, where the officials of the Porte appear to have been more ready than the sultan's secretariat at the palace to suppress the Albanian League. After the British threat to seize Smyrna in October 1880 the sultan at last agreed to decisive action, and Albanian resistance was crushed, not without serious fighting, by a strong force of Turkish regulars under Dervish Dorgut Pasha.

The third feature of the Albanian issue was that, like almost all the post-Congress developments, it facilitated the strengthening of Austrian influence, economic and diplomatic, in the peninsula. Having consolidated its hold on Bosnia the monarchy was determined to restrict the expansion of Montenegro and Serbia, and to keep open the trade routes from Bosnia and the sanjak through Macedonia to Salonika and through Shkodra (Scutari) to the Adriatic. Britain and Austria had destroyed the big Bulgaria of San Stefano which had included Albanian regions in the province of Korça (Koritza), but after Gladstone's leadership of the pro-

Montenegrin naval demonstration of the powers in September 1880 Great Britain could scarcely be regarded as a friend, although Gladstone thought seriously for a time of supporting Albanian moves for autonomy. With Russia openly opposing Albania as being a centre of anti-Slav influence, with the Porte increasingly suspicious of Albanian demands for local schools, officials, representative institutions, and tax relief, there was little to counter the Austrian domination of the western Balkans for the next twenty years. In the negotiations for the Three Emperors Alliance of 18 June 1881 Austria felt strong enough to abandon her co-operation with England and to rely on Bismarck to keep Russia quiet; and in spite of her complaints of Russian hostility and of the machinations of Russian agents it soon became evident that it was Russian political and economic influence that was on the defensive during the succeeding years.

Meanwhile the sultan had again shown, in the settlement with his European creditors by the Decree of Mouharrem (20 December 1881), a good sense as to how far he should yield to necessity. His most pressing financial need after the Congress had been a temporary arrangement with the local Constantinople banks, which had financed the war with Russia mainly by arranging short loans on somewhat questionable security and by negotiating a Defence Loan in which the London house of Glyn Mills, Currie and Company had taken part. After the Congress foreign aid was for the time being unprocurable; the attitude of the House of Commons in December 1878 frustrated all hope of an English loan, and a French attempt through the Comte de Tocqueville had failed by March 1879. The sultan had no credit, at home or abroad. 'Patience and bankruptcy will set him quite straight', had been Salisbury's unhelpful comment. 'It is true he will have no credit: but an absolute sovereign is better without credit. He only uses it to build palaces and ironclads.' However, something had to be done. The first step was a *modus vivendi* with the local banks, whose claims were met by an agreement on 10 November 1879 granting them the yield from certain sources of revenue. The Porte had, however, reserved the right to merge the agreement in a wider one, and appears to have abandoned during 1880 any hope of avoiding concessions. It made comprehensive proposals for a financial settlement in its note of 3 October 1880, at the height of the Montenegrin crisis, although this coincidence seems to have led the powers, highly suspicious of Turkish promises, to underrate their significance. But on the Porte's invitation the various national groups of foreign bond-holders appointed representatives who began discussions in Constantinople in September 1881. The final result was a compromise between the desire of the bond-holders for full indemnity, and the Turkish determination to avoid any such crippling obligation and any guarantees of payment which would vitally impair Turkish sovereignty. While the total indebtedness was scaled down from £191 million to £106 million, the government ceded a wide range of revenues 'absolutely and irrevocably' until the debts were discharged. These included the revenues allocated under the agreement of 10 November 1879, together with certain direct taxes and the yield of the Bulgarian tribute, revenues from Cyprus and eastern Roumelia, and any income accruing to the imperial government under the provisions of the Treaty of Berlin from the succession states.

It is significant that this far-reaching settlement was delayed until the completion of the outstanding negotiations over the Berlin Treaty; the stubbornness of the sultan's resistance to the powers had been a warning to his creditors that Turkey was not going the way of Egypt under cover of an international financial administration. There was no international commission, such as had been visualised in Protocol XVIII of the Treaty of Berlin, to control Turkish finance, but only a council of administration consisting of representatives of the various national groups of bondholders, including the Turkish. On the other hand the commission had wide powers and guarantees, and the fear that it would be as ineffective as its predecessors was not justified. The decree set up an executive committee of the administration with its seat at Constantinople and authority to collect and administer the ceded revenues, the total yield, after paying administrative charges, being applied under its direction to redemption and interest payments of the debt. Officials of the imperial government had a consultative voice in the proceedings of the council, but it was expressly stated that 'under no conditions will they be able to interfere with the administration', and on the other hand the council could appoint, employ, and dismiss government officials for its purpose as it saw fit. On this basis the administration continued to the satisfaction of the bondholders and without interference or obstruction from the government for the next twenty years.

But after salvaging at a cost the remnants of his European possessions, 'Abd al-Hamīd settled down to a tenacious defence of his life and authority of too hand-to-mouth a character to provide any hope of the permanent survival of his empire. The imbecile ostentation and showy petulance of 'Abd al-'Azīz and the half-sincere and half-baked reformism of the 1850's and 1860's were replaced by a police regime whose sole claim to statesmanship lay in its circumspection. The sultan gauged successfully the disunity of the powers and the limits of necessary concession to them. The main lesson of the 1870's was that, of all the powers, Russia alone did not possess inexhaustible patience. Accordingly, her essential demands were met, and the sultan soon made the discovery that she was then prepared to leave him alone. But this meant in turn that he had to leave many of his own discontented subjects alone, and increased the negative character of his internal policy. When Russian troops evacuated the Balkan peninsula in the summer of 1879 the sultan threw away the main advantage that he had gained under the Berlin Treaty by failing to send his own troops forward to garrison the Balkan Mountains. This was a recognition of the futility of any challenge to Bulgarian nationalism, which it was assumed that Russia would resent; and although eastern Roumelia remained under Turkish rule until 1885 there was no serious attempt to consolidate the Turkish position there. When after a bloodless revolution at Philippopolis in September 1885 the two Bulgarias declared themselves united the sultan did not intervene, although the tsar, incensed by the effrontery of the Bulgarians in deciding something for themselves, rallied the Three Emperors League to the support of the *status quo*. The most striking fact about the subsequent Bulgarian crisis, which complicated international relations for the next three years, was the passive role of the Porte throughout. One of its few positive acts was an attempt to prevent the appointment of the russophobe Sir William White as British ambassador to Constantinople in September 1886.

Eight years later the Armenian problem produced an international crisis which in some respects followed the Bulgarian pattern. As in Bulgaria in 1876, an ill-advised rising in the Sassun region by Armenian mountaineers in 1894 was crushed by Hamidian troops, and some organised massacres followed. The powers went so far in May 1895 as to present a reform scheme which the sultan accepted in October; but he showed his lack of concern for these international interferences by simultaneously giving authority for massacres in which 80,000 Armenians are believed to have perished. On a smaller but equally publicised plane were the Constantinople killings in August 1896; after an Armenian attack on the Ottoman bank the Turkish mob murdered some 6000 Armenians in the capital. The revolutionary leaders made the tragic mistake of assuming that by courting reprisals they would secure foreign intervention. Russia's opposition, however, made this impossible. The Armenians, to a greater extent even than the 'ungrateful' Bulgarians, had links with revolutionary groups in Russia, and the tsar saw no reason to interfere with the Turkish repression of a movement which made no appeal to Pan-Slav or Orthodox sentiment, and which might if successful lead to the weakening of the useful Turkish buffer against the West. The British were more actively hostile to the Turk and also, ultimately, less to be feared. Naval demonstrations in October 1879 and September 1880 to enforce boundary settlements and Asiatic reforms were, the sultan decided, alarming only if they were supported by other powers, and he asked in August 1880, and with more assurance as British indignation mounted during the Armenian crisis in 1895, whether the Royal Navy had any ships that could ascend mountains. This progressive emancipation from British tutelage was at the cost of his last chance of holding Egypt; he hesitated until too late to intervene there in 1882, and he rejected a conditional offer of British withdrawal in 1887. The chance did not recur. But Germany, whose support he had been courting since 1880, was demonstratively friendly under the Emperor Wilhelm II from 1889 onwards, and the French were more interested in frustrating the British than in harrying the Porte, although they co-operated with other naval powers in April 1898 to set up an international administration in Crete after the Christian islanders had revolted against Turkish rule in 1897.

Nevertheless, Austria was alone among the great powers in being in a position to exploit the disintegrating position of Turkey in the Balkans. She was able with the help of King Milan to dominate the economic and political life of Serbia; Greece made approaches for an alliance in the early 1880's, and Roumania was drawn into a secret anti-Russian alliance in 1883; even in Bulgaria the Russians were on the defensive both economically and politically after 1881. Bosnia joined the Austro-Hungarian customs union in 1880. The link in the main Balkan railway line through Serbia and Bulgaria was completed by August 1888, and this helped to further Austria's commercial penetration of the peninsula. The British, whose favourable commercial position had depended largely on the low cost of sea freights and access to the Aegean ports, were steadily losing ground to Austrian salesmen of manufactured goods in Bosnia, Serbia, northern Macedonia, and Bulgaria throughout the 1880's and 1890's, a process which was helped by the fact that Austrian goods, though often of poorer quality, were usually cheaper, and presented with a better sales technique and easier credit facilities. In Macedonia, the last substantial area of Turkish rule and misrule in the Balkans and the obvious field for a further crisis in the not too distant future, Austria was also the dominant influence. It was considered to be axiomatic among the smaller states that Macedonia would fall in due course to one or other of them; but they could not agree on any plan of division, and in the meantime each sought to strengthen its claims on economic, cultural, and historical grounds. Austria had no intention of furthering these ambitions. She took care in the Three Emperors Alliance negotiations in 1881 to insist on Russia's repudiation of propagandist activities in Macedonia, and she was prepared for a time to encourage King Milan with hopes of territory in northern Macedonia, but not to an extent which would jeopardise her own strategical plans. These clearly pointed towards Salonika, where her interest remained in spite of the fact that southern Macedonia never provided a profitable field for Austrian commerce. A general Macedonian revolt against Turkish authority finally broke out in August 1903; Austria and Russia had anticipated it by proposals for reform in the previous winter.

Of the immunity which he had secured from foreign interference in the domestic affairs of the empire 'Abd al-Hamīd could make little effective use, for he was not prepared either to devolve authority or to lay out his restricted financial resources in long-term constructive programmes. Turkey became a police state not only in its vigorous hunting down of real and imaginary plotters against the sultan, but in the meticulous supervision which the sultan himself gave to all the affairs of state, particularly the more petty. This jealous preoccupation with details of administration—road-making, bridge-building, minor diplomatic appointments, police reports on the private lives of innumerable unimportant citizens and the like—took up a great deal too much of the despot's time and affairs of greater importance stagnated. The censorship was pervasive and severe, and suspicion of the higher officials more marked than ever. The familiar extravagances and corresponding parsimonies remained in some cases. Favoured officials continued to enjoy heavy emoluments; soldiers remained unpaid. On the whole, however, the sultan trusted no one very far. The constant changes of ministry and exiling of suspects were a further obstacle to the rapid transaction of business. These were not, of course, new features of the Turkish administration. Nor was the duel between the palace and the Porte, although 'Abd al-Hamīd gave this futile proceeding a new twist in his determination to control every detail of public life and policy. Government by the *Mabeyn*, the imperial secretariat, would have been no better or worse than that of the Porte (which was no model of efficiency) but for the inevitable congestion of business as reports accumulated (even after preliminary sifting and classification by the secretaries) on the sultan's desk. The chief secretary in the later stages of 'Abd al-Hamīd's reign was Tahsīn Pasha, who had a busy time struggling to keep all the sultan's business in his own hands and his rival Izzet Pasha el-Abid, the second secretary, at bay. There were other and usually more transitory officials of the *Mabeyn* who served and flattered and rose or fell in the sultan's favour, providing him with spies in his own ministries and a constant flow of reassuring or disturbing gossip about the machinations of his alleged enemies, and leading to a further waste of everyone's time.

In these circumstances it is impossible to deny the sultan considerable success in re-establishing the central authority, although there was little statesmanship in his policy beyond a stubborn resistance to pressure, domestic or foreign. The policy succeeded for a time because the great powers were divided, not because 'Abd al-Hamīd had divided them; in the same way there was as yet no effective opposition at home to which his domestic critics could appeal. It is equally the case that he failed during the breathing space that had been given him in the 1880's and early 1890's to create much positive loyalty to the regime.

The great efforts that were made from the beginning of the reign to capitalise the sultan's position as caliph, with claims to spiritual authority over the Muslim world which were no better founded that the tsar's claim to protect the sultan's Orthodox subjects, had some measure of success. Their real purpose, however, was to embarrass foreign powers, particularly Great Britain, which might hesitate to quarrel with a Turkey emotionally supported by Muslims in India or elsewhere. There was indeed no other purpose than this defensive one that the policy could serve, for the sultan can scarcely have aspired to political control over the Indians, Malays, Central Asian Turkis, Persians, and Pathans who were included in the propaganda. One of the criticisms of the Young Turks in the 1890's was that he had failed to make sufficient use of the caliphate. Within his own dominions there was more solid provision for the Muslim population than he is usually given credit for, including the setting up of numerous elementary schools in Anatolia; later (after 1900) came the Hejaz railway. The Muslim workers of Constantinople, who so often felt themselves outsmarted by their Jewish, Armenian, and Greek rivals, seem to have been ready enough to regard the sultan as their protector; the porters' guild was largely responsible for the massacre of Armenians in the capital in 1896. For the most part, however, the sultan's Muslim subjects, when their mood was other than that of a traditional and somewhat fatalistic loyalty, were developing grievances, and it was at the hands of his own Muslim subjects that 'Abd al-Hamīd, like his two predecessors, lost his throne.

Up to the turn of the century, however, he kept his enemies, who clearly did not exist only in his imagination, in their place. 'Alī Su'āvī's attempt to rescue Murād V in 1878 was no more than a final and isolated gesture of the New Ottomans, and it was not until the end of the 1880's that signs of a new revolutionary movement begin to appear. A revolutionary society for the overthrow of the sultan was growing in Constantinople between 1889 and 1897; it had close links with Young Turk exiles abroad, mainly Paris. 'Abd al-Hamīd emerged successfully from his first trial of strength with both groups. The Constantinople society probably had its origin in 1889 among the students of the military medical school in the capital. Its first leader, Ibrahim Temo, an Albanian, had talked to Freemasons in Italy and sought to model the society on the Carbonari. Membership was quickly extended to students of the military and naval academies and other government schools. The society soon became known to the authorities, and there were some arrests which did nothing to check its growth; more prominent men joined it and it began to recruit members outside the schools; finally, it became over-confident, planned a *coup d'état* for August 1896, and was astonished when all the participants were arrested just before the decisive hour. This was a tribute to the efficiency of the sultan's agents, but also a sad revelation of the incompetence of the conspirators. In the following year he achieved a greater success. This was none other than the overthrow of the Young Turk movement abroad, a result aided but not created by disruptive tendencies within the movement itself. The two most prominent figures at this period, Ahmet Riza and Murat Bey, did not differ greatly in their rather unimaginative political programmes; they saw nothing fundamentally wrong with the empire apart from 'Abd al-Hamīd. Get rid of him, restore

Midhat's constitution, reform the governmental organism so that it can protect the laws against the encroachments of the palace, and 'Oriental flexibility may work wonders', wrote Murat in 1897; 'the population is young, vigorous, temperate, devout; their crime is their blind obedience to the infamous authorities'. Murat accepted the sultanate as indispensable; 'without it Turkish power has no existence'. He was a Pan-Islamist whereas Ahmet Riza was a devoted Comtist, whose Positivist convictions set him resolutely against violence. It was however Murat, the protagonist of revolutionary violence and the recognised leader of the movement against Ahmet Riza's evolutionism, who suddenly gave up the struggle along with nearly all of the Young Turks abroad.

The collapse owed much to the assiduity of Ahmet Jelaleddin Pasha, one of the most trusted of 'Abd al-Hamīd's agents, who discovered Murat's secret yearning for reconciliation and return; whatever the reason, the bulk of the exiles agreed to abandon their propaganda in return for empty promises of reform and a gradual amnesty, and many, including Murat himself, went back to Constantinople. The arrangement was described as a truce, and Murat was described as a hostage; but he became a pensioner of the sultan, and Ahmet Riza, austere, uncompromising, and ineffective, was left with a few associates to carry on his propaganda almost alone.

It was in this rather extraordinary way that the Ottoman empire survived into the twentieth century, execrated in many foreign capitals, but tolerated in all. In spite of the collapse of the very considerable regard which 'Abd al-Hamīd had built up abroad in the 1880's he could still look back on the 1890's as a vindication of his skill in immunising himself from the malice of foreign and domestic foes. It was not until the almost chance fusion of revived Turkish nationalist groups in 1907 that the Hamidian despotism was at last seriously threatened.

CHAPTER XIII

RUSSIA

O F all the European powers, Russia made the least concessions to the liberal spirit of the late nineteenth century. Until 1906 the tsar remained an all-powerful autocrat; he could make and un-make laws without the consent of his ministers, who were responsible to him alone. Efforts at constitutional reform met with stubborn opposition from conservative elements amongst the bureaucracy and landowning gentry, the two main bulwarks of absolutism. The survival of the regime depended ultimately upon the political inertia of the peasants who formed the overwhelming majority of the population. Modern ideas were slow to penetrate into the Russian village. To millions the tsar was still an almost superhuman being who had their interests at heart and whose rule, they long believed, brought them solid advantages.

An immense social and cultural gulf separated the masses from the tiny educated minority. The position of this élite looked impregnable, so great was its power and prestige. In reality it was poised over an abyss. A land of extremes, Russia lacked a strong middle class. The most important inter-mediate group, the intelligentsia, who provided the leadership of the opposition movements, did not succeed in acquiring a mass following and forcing the government to grant concessions until the turn of the century. But the long and bitter struggle between the autocracy and its enemies began in earnest soon after the accession of Alexander II.

Alexander's reign (1855–81) opened auspiciously with the inauguration of a broad programme of social, cultural and administrative reforms; it ended with an unprofitable war and a wave of revolutionary violence, of which the tsar himself was the most prominent victim. In part, this tragic outcome could be attributed to Alexander's own inconsistencies. He was a reformer by circumstance rather than conviction. Well-intentioned but weak-willed, he succumbed all too readily to pressure from small but influ-ential reactionary groups concerned only to maintain their own privileges. After the Polish insurrection of 1863, and an attempt on his life three years later, he was still less willing to take risks; the reforms, although not entirely suspended, were introduced with much modification and delay. The tsar rapidly forfeited the public confidence which he had initially enjoyed; and the new nationalism, to which he was half-inclined to look for support, proved more of a liability than an asset.

After the Crimean War it had become clear that if Russia were to progress, or even maintain her status as a great power, the first essential was to liberate the $22\frac{1}{2}$ million serfs who still languished in complete dependence upon private landowners. The emancipation edicts of 19 February 1861[1] constituted a major turning-point in Russian history. Serfdom was finally abolished. But the great reform was motivated by *raison d'état* rather than disinterested concern for peasant welfare. It was the product of a compromise between relatively enlightened bureaucrats, who sought to ensure that the liberated serfs should at least be able to meet their obligations to the state, and reactionary elements amongst the gentry, who tried to make them pay for their liberty as dearly as possible. The 22 million state and 2 million court peasants, who were the object of separate legislation, generally obtained better terms. In their case the reformers had not the gentry's interests to consider.

For the ex-serfs the provisions of the emancipation settlement were most unsatisfactory. They were to conclude agreements with their masters whereby they received allotments of land varying in size from area to area. These were generally smaller than the plots which they had cultivated for their own use under bondage. The average size was less than 3 *dessyatines*,[2] and still lower in the overcrowded central black-earth zone. They consisted mainly of arable, since the proprietors reserved for themselves a disproportionately large share of the pastures, meadows and forests. These allotments had to be redeemed at grossly inflated prices, based upon the rent previously paid, which bore no relation either to the market value of the land or its potential yield. Redemption payments were made in instalments through the village commune (*mir*), which was to hold the land corporately until the debt had been paid. As many as forty-nine years might elapse before the peasant could call his land his own. Pending conclusion of an agreement, he was still obliged to pay rent or perform labour-services for the landowner as before. Many hesitated to conclude agreements on such burdensome terms, and as late as 1881 15 per cent of former privately owned peasants were still serfs in all but name.

The commune was retained partly as a convenient fiscal and administrative organisation and partly in the belief that it would prevent the formation of a depressed landless proletariat. But its advocates failed to appreciate sufficiently that, whatever its possible social merits, it was economically retrogressive. It perpetuated the ancient three-field system of farming, whereby each household possessed scattered strips in several fields, which (in Great Russia, at least) were periodically redistributed to ensure some rough correlation between the resources of each household and its obligations. The more enterprising members thus had no incentive to improve land which they might lose at any time. The peasants' natural individualistic instincts were crushed or diverted into unhealthy speculative channels. The communal authorities punished severely those who defaulted on their taxes or dues, or otherwise infringed the law, and issued the passports without which travel beyond the village was forbidden.

---

[1] Dates are old style.   [2] 1 *dessyatine* = 2·7 acres.

A myriad obstacles prevented peasants selling their allotments and withdrawing from their communities. Above the commune stood the cantonal (*volost*) authorities which were conceived as organs of peasant self-government but which in practice degenerated into obedient instruments of the large army of officials, most of whom were appointed from the landowning gentry who held supreme power in the countryside. The peasantry still formed a separate 'estate of the realm', subject to discriminatory legislation. Though no longer serfs, they had not become citizens.

The onerous terms on which the peasantry were emancipated intensified the crisis which was developing from the rapid increase of the rural population—from some 50 million in the early 1860's to 82 million in 1897, in European Russia alone—without any corresponding increase either in agricultural productivity or in opportunities for alternative employment. Signs of impending trouble were the steadily mounting sums owed in tax arrears and the famine which struck the rich grain-growing area of Samara in 1873. The peasants felt instinctively that they could best improve their lot by seizing the landowners' estates and parcelling them out amongst the needy. Rumours circulated of a supposed 'golden charter' in which the tsar permitted them to take by force what was theirs by right. For the present there were no revolts, but violence was never far below the outwardly calm surface of the Russian countryside.

The landowners, too, had their grievances against the emancipation. Of the sums due to them through the redemption operation, half was retained by the state in payment of old debts, whilst the market-value of the bonds they received depreciated sharply. Some squandered their funds; many withdrew from farming; few had the skill and determination, and the necessary capital, to revolutionise the management of their estates. With labour plentiful, it was tempting to try to maintain at least the façade of bygone grandeur. The landowning gentry was a class in decline. Only in the southern Ukraine did relatively prosperous new latifundia develop, growing grain for western European markets. Within twenty years exports quintupled, but yields remained low by international standards. From the mid-1870's North American competition brought about a depression in Russian agriculture which hit landowner and peasant alike.

Russia was caught in a vicious circle: rural poverty hindered the development of industry by restricting the domestic market; lack of industry prevented the absorption of surplus agricultural population, the chief cause of poverty. Despite energetic efforts by the government, industrial progress during the quarter-century that followed the emancipation remained unimpressive, particularly when compared with the expansion taking place in western Europe. The principal centre for mining and metallurgy was still the Urals, with its notoriously outdated technique. By 1880 Russia's output of coal and pig-iron had reached only 4 million and $\frac{1}{2}$ million tons respectively. The industrial labour force numbered less than half a million and was almost wholly unskilled; many workers still owned land and returned to their villages annually for the harvest. Employers sought to compensate for low productivity by the intensive exploitation common to most countries in the early stages of industrialisation. Wages were low and tended to fall; hours were long and factory conditions generally appalling. The state did not as yet intervene in such matters, but the police were quick to suppress any signs of labour unrest.

The most encouraging development in the economic sphere was the ambitious programme of railway construction now undertaken, for the lack of communications in a country so vast as Russia had hitherto constituted a major obstacle to progress. The total track length, less than 1000 miles in 1861, exceeded 13,000 miles twenty years later. A network of lines now linked the chief grain-growing areas with both capitals and the Baltic and Black Sea ports. But the price paid for this achievement was high. The Minister of Finance, M. von Reutern, concerned to restrict government spending, favoured construction and ownership by private companies raising their capital abroad. The Treasury sought to attract promoters by offering them a generous guaranteed rate of interest or other exceptionally advantageous concessions, and owing to the laxity of the authorities speculation and corruption flourished.

Reutern's *laissez-faire* policy had vocal critics in official circles, but he justified his methods on financial grounds. The loans floated abroad brought in foreign capital and helped to overcome the prevailing acute shortage of money. Hitherto, free capital accumulation had been impeded by the heavy demands of the state; Reutern now proclaimed it his aim 'to infuse new blood into the dried-up arteries of commerce'. An extensive network of private banks was brought into being. The national accounts were made public, and the Treasury endeavoured to prevent wasteful expenditure by maintaining stricter control over other government departments. A reserve fund was gradually built up to prepare for conversion from paper to metallic currency—a first necessity in order to attract foreign investors. But the war of 1877–8 with Turkey, which Reutern vehemently opposed, postponed hopes of achieving stability for a generation. Russia emerged from the war with a greatly increased national debt and a series of deficits on her annual budget.

The most serious aspect of the financial situation was the constant uncertainty about revenue. The taxation system remained basically unreformed, the heaviest burdens continuing to fall upon those least able to bear them. The archaic poll tax, to which peasants alone were liable, was still the principal source of direct taxation, the idea of a graduated income-tax being dismissed as dangerously revolutionary. The greater part of the revenue was derived from indirect taxes, levied chiefly upon articles of mass consumption. Thus Russia remained a land of sharp contrasts in wealth, in which those responsible for economic policy all too frequently identified national interests with those of the privileged élite. Hopes that Alexander's 'great reforms' would lead to striking progress towards general prosperity were disappointed.

The same story of unfulfilled promise can be told of Alexander's other reforms. Despite their limitations and inconsistencies, they helped to spread respect for law and individual dignity in a land where, traditionally, 'might was right', and they helped to reduce social tensions by developing feelings of common citizenship. On the other hand, though more far-reaching than anything undertaken since the days of Peter the Great, they left the bureaucratic structure still intact as they made no change in the organisation of the central government. Moreover, the momentum of reform was not maintained.

The most important changes concerned the judiciary and local government. Russian justice was notorious for its arbitrary character, and few doubted the need for radical reform, particularly after the emancipation had given legal rights to millions of serfs who had hitherto been almost completely under their masters' jurisdiction. The statutes of 1864 were encouragingly comprehensive and enlightened: the relationship between the various courts was regularised and simplified; cases were to be heard in public according to modern litigatory procedure, the guilt of the accused being determined by jury; judges, formerly often ignorant and corrupt, were to be chosen from amongst the best minds in the legal profession and appointed for life to ensure their independence; measures were taken to prevent abuses by the police when investigating suspects; and— last but not least—barristers were allowed to practice and to maintain their own autonomous organisation on western lines.

This promised a veritable revolution in the administration of justice. But the reform was introduced slowly, and in some remote or politically sensitive regions was never fully applied; moreover, there were still several important loopholes or omissions. The 'justices of the peace', elected from amongst the local gentry to hear minor cases in rural districts, were not fully integrated into the new system: they decided cases according to the vagaries of local custom and there was no appeal against their verdicts. Secondly, the reformers did not effect a thorough revision of the outdated penal code but contented themselves with mitigating the severity of some penalties. The worst forms of corporal punishment were abolished, but peasants could still be beaten with rods by court order. Thirdly, there remained spheres beyond the reach of the new system. Officials only appeared in court if their superiors consented. The senate, supposedly the citizen's main shield against administrative abuses, remained unreformed: its elderly members, who were political appointees, in practice cared more for state interests than individual rights. More important still, political suspects could be detained for long periods without trial and exiled by 'administrative order' without reference to the courts. The *gendarmerie*, or security police, exercised considerable authority, and offenders sentenced to forced labour in Siberia endured conditions of extreme harshness and brutality. It was in the mines of Sakhalin or the dungeons of Schlüsselburg that the regime showed its darkest side: here the petty official was supreme, and of legality there was little trace.

In a state where the bureaucracy wielded such power, an independent judiciary was something of an anomaly, and conflicts between the courts and the administration soon developed. In 1867 D. N. Zamyatin, who as Minister of Justice had been closely identified with the reforms, was dismissed and replaced by the arch-conservative K. I. Pahlen. The reactionary press continually attacked the lawyers as a potentially subversive element and the jury as an inappropriate importation from the west. The judiciary was soon forced on to the defensive, but the legal profession offered stout resistance to efforts by officialdom to undermine or circumvent the law. The reforms, once granted, could not easily be revoked.

The local government statute of 1864 was an equally important step forward. It provided for the establishment in each province and district of European Russia (except the border territories) of a rural council, or *zemstvo*. This consisted of a permanent executive board appointed by an annual assembly of deputies; the deputies were elected by landowners, peasants and townsmen, meeting separately. Broadly similar in purpose and structure were the municipal representative institutions introduced in most towns in 1870, but owing to the relatively small size of the urban population these were less important than the rural *zemstva*. Their significance was twofold: first, they provided a tenuous bridge across the great chasm dividing Russian society by giving former serfs and former serf-owners an opportunity to collaborate; secondly, they encouraged people who had hitherto been accustomed to expect the initiative in all matters to be taken by some distant omnicompetent authority to think and act for themselves, at least on local issues. The *zemstva* stimulated wider political ambitions and were regarded by most liberals as the first step towards a constitutional regime. The government, aware of these implications, took care to limit their competence very precisely to such matters as education, health, road-building and famine relief, and to subject their activities to close bureaucratic control. Members of different *zemstva* were prohibited from meeting to co-ordinate policy, even on questions of a purely technical nature. They had to obtain their revenue almost entirely by taxing the already over-burdened peasantry. The conservative-minded gentry who set the tone in most councils, oblivious of the many pressing social problems which confronted them, were in any case inclined to cut down expenditure. But many *zemstvo* leaders devoted themselves with exemplary idealism to the advancement of popular well-being and felt frustrated when, with increasing frequency, their work was hampered by official interference and obstruction.

Despite these formidable obstacles the practical achievements of the *zemstva* were far from negligible. Wisely, they concentrated upon the task of combating the almost total illiteracy that prevailed in the countryside. By 1881 they had brought into being some ten thousand elementary schools. This was at least a beginning, although the quality of these schools was not high and the main burden of supporting them fell upon the *volost* and village authorities. However eager for enlightenment some peasant communities might be, none could afford to spend much. The educational coverage varied widely, and it was generally the poorest areas that had the fewest schools. This was only one of many ways in which the work of the *zemstva* suffered from lack of central co-ordination.

In this vital activity they met with more hindrance than encouragement from the administration. D. A. Tolstoy, who replaced the liberal A. V. Golovnin as Minister of Education in 1866, was a narrow-minded and self-willed official, contemptuous of anyone who dared oppose his policies, and less concerned with promoting the spread of knowledge than with stamping out revolutionary ideas. He established a strong corps of inspectors who acted as his agents in the provinces. The local school boards, elected by the *zemstva*, were reformed and placed under the supervision of a representative of the gentry.

The reaction was felt still more severely in the secondary schools which, being generally run by the ministry, were more easily controlled. The most controversial measure was the revision of the syllabus, whereby the time spent in the study of classical subjects was considerably augmented. Although opposed by many prominent officials as well as by the general public, Tolstoy's proposals enjoyed the tsar's support and not even a decisive defeat in the state council could prevent them from becoming law. The classics were taught in a particularly pedantic manner, almost as though the authorities hoped that constant conjugation of Latin verbs might divert the pupils' attention from the natural sciences, with their awkward Darwinian implications. The result, naturally enough, was to accelerate the drift to materialism among Russian youth. Tolstoy was not opposed on principle to the teaching of science, which indeed he promoted with some effect. His aim was primarily social and political: by drawing a sharp distinction between the classical *gymnasia* and non-classical *realschulen*, and by ordaining that only pupils from the former should be admitted to university, he hoped to make the student body more select and more reliable.

In fact, it was in the universities that Tolstoy suffered his sharpest defeats. Student disturbances, originating with local grievances, soon acquired a political flavour and brought a steady stream of recruits into the radical camp. The government, after an initial attempt at repression, had tried to solve the problem by granting the universities full internal autonomy (1863). But the mood of rebelliousness persisted, and the fact that it was a student, D. V. Karakozov, who made a single-handed attempt on Alexander's life (April 1866) led the government to adopt the more repressive policy of Tolstoy, who set up several official commissions to devise stricter measures of control. But their labours were frustrated by the university authorities, who clung doggedly to the rights granted them in 1863. Tolstoy's projected revision of this statute had yet to be approved when, as a gesture to public opinion, he was obliged to resign (April 1880).

The means at his disposal had been inadequate to deal with a complex sociological problem common to all countries at a certain stage of evolution: the problem of an emergent intelligentsia. The composition of the student body was changing: sons of landowners and officials were being joined by men whose fathers were priests, merchants, artisans or (very infrequently) peasants. By 1880 these so-called *raznochintsy* (literally, 'men of various rank') constituted over half the total number of students. The heirs to a long tradition of abstract philosophical and political speculation, they were the sharpest critics of existing conditions. The circulation of ideas was also greatly facilitated by the expansion of the periodical press—ten times as many papers and journals appeared between 1856 and 1865 as in the previous decade—and the relaxation of the censorship. By the regulations of 1865 the government retained the power to suspend any periodical, but it no longer questioned the right of public opinion to exist, and writers were adept at circumventing the law.

Most intellectuals now rejected as too moderate the views of A. I. Herzen, whose *émigré* newspaper *The Bell* (*Kolokol*) had exercised such phenomenal influence in Russia during the first few years of Alexander's reign. They preferred to follow the lead of writers connected with the journal *The Contemporary* (*Sovremennik*) of whom the most important was the socialist N. G. Chernyshevsky. His political philosophy combined elements of Utopian idealism and economic determinism. With a wealth of economic and sociological argument, he developed Herzen's thesis that the Russian peasants could set an example to the proletarians of western Europe by finding their own way to a better social order based upon collective ownership of land. More extreme were the views of D. I. Pisarev whose cult of the individual ego and rejection of accepted social and moral restraints earned the radicals the name of 'nihilists'. Another prominent figure whose colourful personality endeared him to young Russian intellectuals was M. A. Bakunin, the fiery prophet of anarchism.

Their attempts to pass from words to deeds were not markedly successful. In 1861 the clandestine organisation 'Land and Liberty' was broken up by the police before its members could establish contact with the peasantry. Chernyshevsky and Pisarev were arrested in the following year. With the loss of its leaders, and the suspension of the two main radical journals in 1866, the revolutionary movement was temporarily reduced to ineffectiveness.

Another reason for this was the changed intellectual climate in Russia after the Polish insurrection of 1863. The nationalistic notes sounded in Warsaw called forth a louder echo in St Petersburg and Moscow. Most Russians agreed in dismissing the Poles' struggle for liberty and independence as an oligarchic conspiracy against the integrity of the empire. Support rallied to the government. Liberals who had been toying with parliamentary ideas decided that such thoughts were premature; some buried themselves in practical work on the new *zemstva*, others added their voices to the patriotic chorus. M. N. Katkov, a leading Moscow publicist who had warmly welcomed the reforms, emerged as the most vocal spokesman for the new nationalism. In the writings of I. S. Aksakov the doctrines of the early Slavophiles underwent a subtle change, exalted religious idealism yielding to the cruder motif of national self-assertion. The journalists of Moscow inveighed against the bureaucrats of St Petersburg, allegedly infected with the dangerous germ of western liberalism. The government, they declared, must remain strong, and in particular consolidate its hold upon the borderlands. Only thus could Russia fulfil her historic mission, expanding her territory in Asia and helping to liberate the Balkan Slavs from alien rule.

The Pan-Slav aspect of the nationalist creed was emphasised most strongly by such writers as N. Ya. Danilevsky, who gave it a fashionable pseudo-scientific *cachet* by applying to international relations the Darwinian concept of a struggle for existence. But the name 'Pan-Slavism', as conventionally applied, hardly suffices to cover a complex movement concerned with much else besides Balkan policy. The Moscow nationalists had many sympathisers in the army and the diplomatic service, and at court. Even Alexander was at times inclined to look upon them with favour. This influence, which could prove decisive in a crisis, compensated for their failure to attract any significant mass support, either in Russia or amongst the other Slav peoples.

The main obstacle to Slav unity was the Polish question. The ruthless suppression of the insurrection was followed by a radical land reform designed to weaken the politically unreliable gentry and win peasant support. Religious and educational policy was also framed with the object of eliminating Polish national sentiment. In the western provinces of Russia itself, where there had been considerable sympathy for the rebels, similar measures were carried out. At the same time latent national antagonisms developed in the Baltic provinces and the Ukraine.

The Pan-Slav cause suffered a still more serious setback when the Eastern Question was reopened by the Balkan revolts of 1875. The Russian government vacillated, collaborating half-heartedly in international efforts to obtain a peaceful settlement, but at the same time allowing itself to be carried forward by an upsurge of nationalist sentiment into a lone struggle against Turkey (April 1877–March 1878). By this date Russia's military reputation, so severely shaken by her defeat in the Crimea, had been greatly restored by several important reforms carried out by Alexander's energetic and liberally minded War Minister, D. A. Milyutin—in particular the introduction of conscription (1874), whereby the officer corps ceased to be an aristocratic preserve and service obligations were distributed fairly amongst all social classes. The new Russian army, a small permanent force backed by a large trained reserve, had the makings of a formidable military instrument. But the call to arms sounded before these reforms had taken full effect, in circumstances of which Milyutin himself strongly disapproved. The advantage of surprise had been lost; the easy victory confidently expected by the high command failed to materialise. The army still suffered from its traditional weaknesses of muddled leadership and inefficient supply services. Not until December 1877 was the vital key-point of Plevna taken, and the road opened to Constantinople.

Carried away by this success, the high command imposed upon the Turks the crushing peace of San Stefano. But this settlement aroused fierce opposition from Austria and Great Britain, and for some weeks war with the latter power seemed imminent. Anxious as he was to reinforce his victory with a diplomatic triumph, Alexander had reluctantly to accept the convening of a conference in Berlin to refashion the San Stefano treaty. From the settlement that resulted (July 1878) Russia gained little: Batum and Kars in Asia, and in Europe the return of the Bessarabian districts lost in 1856. Nor could she salvage much for her Balkan protégés: Bulgaria was reduced to one-third of its proposed size (although ample opportunities remained for Russian penetration); Serbia and Montenegro gained some territory, but no common frontier; and Bosnia and Hercegovina came under Austrian occupation.

The Berlin Treaty aroused bitter resentment in Russia. Nationalists denounced the government for yielding to Western pressure. But the real cause of Russia's diplomatic defeat—the fact that Bismarck's Europe was too small for successful expansion by a single power, least of all by Russia, whose social and economic backwardness made her more dependent than ever upon the goodwill of the Germanic empires—was not lost upon Alexander. After a few months of fruitless isolation he set about repairing the *Dreikaiserbund* of Russia, Germany and Austria-Hungary, the linchpin of his foreign policy, which had been disrupted by the Balkan crisis. In September 1879 he met William I at Alexandrovo; two years later the alliance was ceremoniously re-established by his successor. From the Russian standpoint, it now served principally to provide protection against Great Britain: Germany and Austria undertook to help prevent the Turks from allowing British warships to pass the Straits and threaten her almost undefended Black Sea coast.

At home the results of the war were equally alarming for the government, since the suffering and dislocation which it caused gave added strength to the opposition. Already in the early 1870's revolutionary ideas had gained much ground amongst the intelligentsia. Some radicals were attracted by the 'populist' (*narodnik*) socialism of P. L. Lavrov and N. K. Mikhailovsky, others preferred the more intoxicating teachings of Bakunin; but all agreed upon the desirability of propaganda and agitation amongst the peasantry. In the summer of 1874 hundreds of young intellectuals 'went to the people' with this aim in view, only to find themselves speedily arrested by the police, sometimes with the co-operation of those whom they had come to liberate. Lacking mass support, the revolutionaries were not a serious threat to the regime, but the *gendarmerie*, for reasons of its own, exaggerated the danger and kept the tsar and his ministers in a perpetual state of alarm. But mass arrests and trials served only to earn for the revolutionaries the sympathy of the general public, and this was increased by exasperation at the conduct of the war. The populists for their part were driven to retaliate by acts of terror. In January 1878 a young woman of noble birth, V. I. Zasulich, avenged an imprisoned fellow-revolutionary by shooting a senior police officer. Her *coup* was followed by a number of other attempts, some of them successful, upon the lives of prominent officials. Not all populists approved of these tactics, and their party, 'Land and Liberty', which had been re-established in 1876, collapsed in a welter of argument. Led by A. I. Zhelyabov, those who did approve formed a new organisation, 'The People's Will' (*Narodnaya Volya*), which placed the assassination of the tsar in the forefront of its programme.

In response to the government's appeals for public support, some liberals cautiously petitioned for civil and political liberties: why should the tsar refuse his own people the constitution he had granted the Bulgarians? Alexander, alarmed by a narrow escape from death in an explosion engineered by *Narodnaya Volya* in the Winter Palace (February 1880), realised the advantages to be gained by driving a wedge between the terrorists and their moderate sympathisers. A Supreme Executive Commission was established and its head, M. T. Loris-Melikov, invested with almost dictatorial powers. While security measures against revolutionary violence were tightened, the press, *zemstva* and schools benefited from a relaxation of administrative pressure. The success of this policy allowed Loris-Melikov first to disband the commission, reserving for himself the key office of Minister of the Interior, and then to take a further step forward by drawing up a complex scheme for associating elected representatives in the drafting of certain laws (December 1880). But these proposals, which characteristically were worked out in secret, did not go far enough to satisfy the moderate opposition, let alone appease the revolutionaries. On 1 March 1881, returning to his palace after giving final approval to this scheme, Alexander was fatally wounded by a terrorist's bomb.

The leaders of *Narodnaya Volya* had hoped that the assassination of the tsar would at the least shock the government into granting the nation constitutional liberties, even if it did not trigger off a peasant rising. Neither of these expectations was realised. The assassination only hindered the cause which the populists had at heart. The new tsar, Alexander III (1881–94), was a stern and autocratic figure, respected for his sincerity and conscientious devotion to duty but lacking in imagination and intellectual ability. His natural conservatism was enhanced by the circumstances of his father's death, which he attributed to the weakness and inconsistency of government policy in the preceding reign. He set out to eliminate the threat of revolution by asserting his imperial prerogative, consolidating authority at every level in society and bolstering up the position of the landowning gentry. This experiment in reaction was foredoomed to failure: Russian society could not for long be forced back into the strait-jacket from which it had so painfully emerged. Ultimately the security of the autocracy depended upon the adoption of energetic measures to solve the pressing problems raised by agrarian impoverishment and nascent industrialism—a sphere in which the government's actions were tardy and inadequate.

The new tsar's ideas were in large measure those of his ex-tutor and close confidant K. P. Pobedonostsev, the Chief Procurator of the Holy Synod. An archaic figure, Pobedonostsev was ill-equipped for the role of a Russian Bismarck. He nourished a deep aversion for modern civilisation and dreamed of resurrecting in Russia an inert theocratic society, rigorously safeguarded from corruption by such alien western ideas as constitutional government or the rule of law. In practical terms his programme resolved itself into an effort to stamp out dissent by police measures, the promotion of Orthodox religious education and the russification of the borderlands. At first Alexander III briefly toyed with the idea of implementing Loris-Melikov's proposed reform. But Pobedonostsev, skilfully exploiting his fears and suspicions, succeeded in persuading him to issue an imperial manifesto proclaiming his 'trust in the strength and truth of autocratic power' and hinting ominously that he would 'introduce order and justice' into the institutions established by his father (29 April 1881).

This was a direct challenge to the liberal ministers, who resigned or were dismissed. But Loris-Melikov's successor, N. P. Ignatyev, had Slavophile sympathies and did not enjoy Pobedonostsev's confidence. Desiring to strengthen the autocracy by encouraging direct contact between tsar and people, he rashly endorsed a fanciful project to summon a consultative assembly of estates of the realm modelled on the medieval *zemsky sobor*. Pobedonostsev used the incident to engineer his dismissal and replacement by a more orthodox conservative, D. A. Tolstoy, whose educational policies had so aroused public opinion during the previous reign. With the submissive I. D. Delyanov in the Ministry of Education, Pobedonostsev appeared to be the complete master of Russia, interfering at will in departments other than his own, although he had many enemies in high places who contrived to obstruct and delay ultra-reactionary measures of which they disapproved.

The new government succeeded with comparative ease in restoring calm to the surface of Russian politics. The terrorist leaders were rounded up; Zhelyabov and four colleagues were hanged, despite appeals for clemency, and others were sentenced to long terms of imprisonment and exile. Those who managed to emigrate surrendered themselves to barren theoretical disputation, and efforts to resume terrorist activity met with no success. The heroic age was now past. Most young intellectuals with *narodnik* sympathies decided that they could best aid the popular cause by quietly pursuing their professional careers and undertaking such social and phil-anthropic work as the law allowed. The collapse of the revolutionary movement also put a speedy end to the liberal agitation in *zemstvo* circles. It was a peculiar feature of Russian liberalism that it lacked a firm social basis, but was primarily an intellectual trend, fluctuating according to the ebb and flow of the revolutionary tide. With the tightening of the censor-ship regulations, most newspapers and journals critical of the government closed down. The authorities made the most of the revulsion felt by many moderates at tsaricide, and the *zemstva*, dutifully conforming to instruc-tions, relapsed into their previous silence on national issues.

These cherished institutions were now very much on the defensive and could only expand their activities on a modest scale. Tolstoy set out to integrate them into the bureaucratic hierarchy, but was obliged to take account of hostile criticism and modify his plans. The law of June 1890 gave provincial governors and other officials increased powers, in particu-lar to confirm elections and appointments and to suspend implementation of decisions deemed harmful to state interests. The electoral system was arbitrarily manipulated to reduce the franchise and increase still further the representation of the gentry. Similar measures were taken in 1892 in relation to the municipalities.

Tolstoy's policy reached its climax with the introduction, in July 1889, of the 'land captains' (*zemskiye nachalniki*). These officials, chosen by the governor from amongst local landowners and responsible to the central government, became the veritable seigneurs of the Russian countryside. They could veto decisions of *volost* or communal assemblies and punish elected peasant authorities after summary proceedings. The justices of the peace, who had earned a good reputation for fair dealing, were now abolished and their functions transferred to the land captains. This opened the way to arbitrary action and was a deliberate blow against the integrity of the judicial system, already threatened by the undermining of judges' independence, restriction of jury trials and other measures. But none of these reforms produced the desired effect. It was fruitless to entrust the gentry with greater political power at a time when their economic strength was being steadily and inexorably whittled away. Despite generous concealed subsidies from the Nobles' Land Bank, established in 1885 with the express object of helping them to maintain their estates, their holdings shrank by over one-third between 1877 and 1905—from 73 million to 46 million *dessyatines*.

The government's educational policy similarly accentuated the tendencies characteristic of the preceding epoch. An expansion of facilities occurred, but the credit for this is due rather to the *zemstva* and other public bodies than to the state. In the elementary schools Pobedonostsev ensured that emphasis was laid upon religious instruction, with the object of inculcating a spirit of submissiveness to all authority, whether ecclesiastical or secular. Though the Synod did not acquire control of the entire primary-school network, as had originally been intended, it established an educational administration of its own, thus creating a rivalry which could not fail to affect adversely the development of education as a whole. Qualitatively the parochial schools were greatly inferior to those run by secular authorities.

Secondary and higher education Pobedonostsev wished to make the preserve of the élite. Social segregation could hardly be introduced by decree, but the government attempted to achieve this indirectly by ordering an increase in fees. The universities finally lost their autonomy (1884) and acquired a barrack-like atmosphere which helped to foster sentiments of opposition. The students generally managed to evade the ban on any form of organisation and remained 'the barometer of society', ever ready to respond to fluctuations in the political climate. Pobedonostsev could deny educated Russians freedom of expression but could not win them over to positive acceptance of his ideals.

He met with still greater disappointment in his efforts to secure the intellectual allegiance of the non-Russian and non-Orthodox inhabitants of the empire. Pobedonostsev had no respect for the principle of religious toleration, and sought by every means to enhance the position of the established Church. Orthodox missionary work was actively encouraged; proselytism by adherents of other faiths was forbidden by law. He harassed and persecuted the evangelical sects, particularly those whose doctrines were tainted by social or political radicalism. Since his religious policy was motivated chiefly by considerations of state security, its effects were felt most severely in the borderlands, where religious dissent was often closely allied to national sentiment.

The worst afflictions befell the six million Jews confined within the permitted zone of residence, or 'Pale of Settlement'. Both Alexander III and his successor, as well as many persons prominent in official circles, held pronounced anti-Semitic views. The relatively enlightened assimilationist policy pursued in the previous reign was now abandoned. In 1882 Jews were prohibited from settling in rural districts even within the Pale, thus increasing still further the overcrowding and impoverishment in the towns. A *numerus clausus* fixed the proportion of Jews allowed to receive secondary or higher education. The few privileged Jews who were still permitted to live in cities outside the Pale suffered from various measures of discrimination.

In Poland, as well as in the western and Baltic provinces, the schools and the Orthodox Church became the principal instruments of russification. The situation was particularly complex in the Baltic area. Russian officials there competed with the German-speaking aristocracy for the allegiance of the Letts, Lithuanians and Estonians, who were rapidly developing political aspirations of their own. Alexander III cared little for the ancient connection between the dynasty and the Baltic German nobles. Although local government was left in their hands, the police and judiciary were remodelled on the Russian pattern, and the educational system was placed under centralised control. This led to the collapse of the efficient Lutheran schools, which had a long history of distinguished achievement, and to an actual decline in the rate of literacy. Serious conflict also developed over the status of thousands who hesitated between the rival religious confessions. But Pobedonostsev's drive for integration failed. His methods were totally inadequate to combat the powerful upsurge of nationalism now spreading through eastern Europe, and not least within the Russian empire. The government's repressive measures, though not the direct cause of opposition to Russian rule by the national minorities, as contemporaries often assumed, only fomented the centrifugal tendencies they were designed to forestall.

An additional reason for the failure of Pobedonostsev's Baltic policy was that Russia could not afford to allow this relatively minor issue to disturb the good relations with Germany which she was now more concerned than ever to uphold. It was ironical that Alexander III, who sought to pursue a thoroughly traditionalist foreign policy, should end by sanctioning a radical change of alignment. By 1887 Russia had become estranged from Austria as a result of her involvement in Bulgaria and from Germany as a result of Bismarck's bellicose moves against France and apparently successful *rapprochement* with Great Britain, Russia's principal adversary. The *Dreikaiserbund* lapsed; and the 'Reinsurance Treaty' with Germany which replaced it, an engagement of much less value to Russia, lasted only three years before being repudiated by Bismarck's successor.

Russia showed no eagerness to overcome her consequent isolation by concluding an alliance with republican France. Although a loose understanding was arrived at in August 1891, it was not until December 1893 that Russia reluctantly undertook to support France in the event of a German attack. On the diplomatic plane, moreover, the new alliance proved no obstacle to the maintenance of good relations with Berlin and Vienna. Indeed, Russia now embarked upon several years of harmonious co-operation with Austria in Balkan affairs and with Germany. But viewed in wider perspective the change of alignment was a milestone in the decline of imperial Russia. Instead of being allied to empires whose political and social order corresponded to her own, Russia became increasingly dependent on the friendship and credit of France. The financial aspect of Franco-Russian relations rapidly gained in importance until, by 1905, the alliance had become a vice of steel from which Russia could escape only at the price of revolution. She did not, of course, suffer any actual loss of sovereignty; but the frustration in 1905 of the Russo-German Björkö agreement showed the extent to which she had surrendered her freedom of action. She could not afford to alienate the ally whose financial aid assured the continued existence of the regime.

Reliance upon foreign credit was inevitable: Russia's domestic resources could not provide the capital necessary for development. The government, though not directly responsible for the country's economic backwardness, for many years did far too little to overcome it. Alexander III's first Minister of Finance, N. Kh. Bunge, although not a statesman of vision, realised the importance of fiscal reform. In 1882, shortly after the last ex-serfs had been compulsorily transferred to a redemption basis, the amount of these dues was reduced; and in 1885 the inequitable poll-tax was belatedly abolished. The Treasury offset its losses by almost doubling the rent paid by peasants on state-owned land and by further increases in indirect taxation. Despite their modest scope, Bunge's reformist measures aroused strong criticism from his ministerial colleagues, who forced him to resign (January 1887). His successor, I. A. Vyshnegradsky, was an experienced financier whose attention was chiefly focused upon the international money market. The long-suffering peasantry were entrusted to the ministrations of Tolstoy and his successor P. N. Durnovo, who both saw the agrarian problem purely from a security point of view. The peasants were expected to submit unquestioningly to the land captains and other representatives of authority. A decree of 1886, ineffective in practice, required official approval for dissolutions of large peasant families of the traditional patriarchal type, which were succumbing to the inexorable pressure of individualism. The government also took the rural commune under its wing: even after they had redeemed their allotments, peasants were not to be free to withdraw from the *mir* and exercise full rights of ownership over their land unless their fellow-villagers consented. The inadequacy of this approach was clearly demonstrated by the catastrophic famine of 1891–2 which, with the accompanying cholera epidemic, cost some half a million lives. In the absence of sufficient reserves of grain even a modest crop failure brought widespread starvation. More fundamental action to raise mass living-standards was obviously essential.

The Ministry of Finance was now entrusted to S. Yu. Witte, the most capable servant of the imperial regime in its declining years. An experienced administrator who mixed easily in business circles, he realised that Russia's role as a world power depended upon the rapid development of her rich natural resources. Industrialisation, he believed, was fully compatible with the maintenance of tsarist autocracy; indeed, only by undertaking an ambitious programme of guided economic development could the absolutist regime hope to survive. If the state took the initiative, he argued, it would obtain the willing co-operation of private enterprise and the esteem of the general public. Witte's forceful and somewhat contradictory character, coupled with his extreme vanity, earned him many powerful enemies, but for ten years he was virtually an economic dictator.

The means he employed to foster industrial progress did not differ in principle from those of his predecessors, but they were better co-ordinated and applied with greater sense of purpose. In the 1890's, after a decade of consolidation and financial regularisation, Russia embarked upon a new spell of railway construction, financed mainly by the state. By far the most important project, both economically and strategically, was the Trans-Siberian line, commenced in 1891 and completed within the short span of fourteen years. By 1905 the total length of railway track had reached approximately 37,500 miles, of which some two-thirds were state-owned.

Domestic industry could now supply much of the rails and other metal equipment required. In the 1880's a new mining and metallurgical centre sprang up in the Donetz basin. By 1900 this supplied half of Russia's output of pig-iron, which stood at 3 million tons; by this date coal production had reached 15 million tons. This was only a small fraction of world output, but in the production of one increasingly important commodity, oil, Russia at this time took first place as a result of rich discoveries in Transcaucasia. The textile industry, centred in the Moscow region and in Poland, made rapid strides, assisted by the development of cotton planting in central Asia. In the last fifteen years of the century total industrial output nearly trebled, progress being particularly marked in the late 1890's. By 1900 some two and a half to three million workers were employed in industry and transport.

This industrial expansion owed much to the government's tariff policy, which inclined increasingly towards protection. Dues on imported industrial products and raw materials were continually raised during the 1880's, and two large general increases followed in 1890 and 1891. This led to trouble with Germany, now gradually replacing Britain as Russia's chief trading partner. An even more important characteristic of her incipient industrial revolution was the reliance upon foreign investment, which by 1900, after an eightfold increase in twenty years, comprised almost one-third of the total capital in private Russian industry. Foreign capital also found its way into Russia in the form of direct loans to the government. It was above all the desire to attract foreign investment and reduce heavy interest charges which led Russia to adopt the gold standard (1897), a step which greatly strengthened her financial position.

But the price of this aid, whether direct or indirect, was reflected in the constantly mounting figures of Russia's indebtedness. During the years 1894–1903, it has been estimated, annual payments to foreign creditors averaged some 300–400 million roubles. By 1904 the state debt alone exceeded $6\frac{1}{2}$ milliard roubles, of which almost half was owed abroad. Since it was only through foreign loans that the budget was balanced at all, the need for credit continually increased and the prospects of regaining solvency seemed ever more remote.

Witte's right-wing critics feared that excessive dependence upon foreign bankers endangered Russia's sovereign status, whilst the left urged priority for agrarian reforms that would raise the peasants' revenue-yielding capacity. Witte could reply that, without the aid of foreign capital, industrialisation would impose far greater hardships upon the peasantry (an argument borne out by later experience in the Soviet Union); that industrialisation offered the only long-term hope of solving the agrarian question and breaking out of the vicious circle which hindered economic progress; and that therefore a certain strain in the economy must be accepted as inevitable. The faster Russia industrialised, the less painful the transition process would be.

But it was equally true that the peasant taxpayer could ill afford increased burdens, even in the worthy cause of industrial progress and ultimate general prosperity. During Witte's tenure of office state revenue doubled. By 1903 one-quarter of total receipts were provided by the government spirits monopoly, established in 1894. This in effect gave the Treasury a vested interest in perpetuating drunkenness, the acknowledged bane of peasant life. Another of Witte's dubious revenue-producing measures, state control of sugar-beet production (1895), kept prices artificially high and made sugar more of a luxury than ever at the peasant's table.

By the turn of the century the growing misery in the villages was revealed by official data. Investigators in Tula province (1902) found peasant families living in insanitary huts with leaking roofs, using manure for fuel, and subsisting on a thin diet of bread, *kvass* and potatoes. In the late 1890's one-fifth of all army recruits were rejected as physically unfit. At 35 per thousand, Russia's mortality rate was the highest in Europe; characteristically, it was higher in the countryside than in the towns. From the government's point of view, perhaps the most ominous sign was the ever-increasing sum owed in tax arrears, which in 1896–1900, despite local cancellations and deferments, exceeded by one-fifth the average annual assessment.

How could the peasant hope to meet his obligations to the state and still provide for himself and his dependents? Purchase of additional land was rendered difficult by lack of adequate credit facilities. The operations of the Peasant Land Bank, founded by Bunge in 1882, were restricted by pressure from powerful landowning interests. Between 1861 and 1905, it has been estimated, some 16 million *dessyatines* had been bought by peasants actually engaged in farming, over half of this through the Bank. Much of this land was bought, either by peasant communities and associations or by individual peasants, directly or indirectly, from the gentry, whose landholdings decreased by 27 million *dessyatines* (from 73 million to 46 million) between 1877 and 1905. It was simpler to lease land, where it was available; but the heavy demand in areas of acute shortage caused rents to soar, especially for the short-term leases concluded by the poorest peasants, who, driven by sheer need, tended to exhaust the soil. Nor did leasing land encourage technical improvements. From the early 1890's the government belatedly began to facilitate migration to the spacious untilled lands of Asiatic Russia, and by 1904 nearly one million prospective settlers had crossed the Urals. But many who left without adequate preparation, disregarding official advice, returned in disillusionment. Migration could in any case absorb only a fraction of the natural growth of population in European Russia. Statistics show that, however great the land shortage, peasants preferred to seek employment nearer home—either on the large estates in the southern Ukraine, which attracted a million seasonal labourers annually from the over-populated central districts, or in the cities and industrial settlements.

Here the peasant was suddenly plunged into a totally unfamiliar civilisation, where the rapid tempo of life stood in sharp contrast to the slow rhythm of the countryside. This sense of estrangement intensified his natural aversion to industrial conditions, still almost as harsh as ever. Bunge regulated the working hours of women and juveniles (1882) but pressure from certain industrial interests prevented the law from being generally enforced. It was not until 1897 that the working day for men was limited to $11\frac{1}{2}$ hours. The new factory inspectors were soon intimidated into subservience to the authorities. Wages, though now paid regularly in cash, were kept low by the influx of rural unemployed. Strikes and any form of labour organisation were strictly outlawed. The industrial workers, concentrated for the most part in large enterprises, formed a natural reservoir of revolutionary sentiment, abundantly fed by the swelling flood of peasant discontent. In the cities there was open turbulence, rendered still more ominous by the mood of sullen resentment in the villages. By the turn of the century absolutist Russia, despite a superficial appearance of stability, was heading for revolution.

For the more organised character which this mass opposition acquired it was primarily indebted to the intelligentsia. The famine of 1891 shocked

Russian society from the enforced passivity of the preceding decade. As the activities of the *zemstva* again expanded so also did the numbers and self-confidence of their employees (teachers, doctors, statisticians, etc.), who made their influence felt in professional and other bodies. The revival also affected the elected *zemstvo* deputies, many of them members of the gentry whose public spirit proved much stronger than the class egoism upon which Tolstoy had reckoned. It was not, however, the comparatively feeble voice of Russian liberalism which set the tone of public opinion. In intellectual circles the debate on the perennial question of Russia's future was dominated by the partisans of populism and Marxism. The former laid the blame for the peasants' misery upon capitalism, which they saw as something alien, artificially superimposed upon Russia's pristine agrarian economy by deliberate state action. For the Marxists capitalism was a natural organic growth, an inevitable stage in social development, which held out the prospect of great material progress as well as of a revolution led by the industrial proletariat. They condemned the populists as Utopian and reactionary; their opponents charged them with sharing Witte's callous indifference to the people's immediate welfare. In this dispute between the head and the heart of the Russian intelligentsia, victory lay with the head: in a scientific age, the ethical idealism of the populists had less appeal than the cold logic and apparent certainties of Marxist doctrine.

Intellectuals with Marxist convictions sought to translate their theories into practice by obtaining leadership of the incipient labour movement and diverting the workers' attention from industrial to political objectives. They achieved some success when a major strike broke out in the St Petersburg textile mills (1896) and a local labour union was formed which found emulators in other cities. But these clandestine organisations were soon broken up by arrests and during the next few years the number of political strikes remained low. In 1898 a Social-Democratic party was formed but it did not command any significant mass support.

The labour movement was a more powerful force in the border regions, where nationalism and socialism were curiously interrelated, part allies yet part rivals. The Ukrainian opposition was predominantly socialist and integrationist, but nationalist groups emerged after 1900. In Poland conciliatory tendencies prevailed for twenty-five years after the defeat of the 1863 insurrection, but then yielded to an upsurge of political activity. The strongest group was the Polish Socialist party, which placed independence in the forefront of its programme. To the right stood the National Democrats, to the left the ultra-orthodox Marxists, who were both more internationally minded. Russia's strongest revolutionary organisation was the Jewish social-democratic *Bund* which, however, was prevented by friction from collaborating closely with non-Jewish opposition groups. Many Jews were attracted by the more nationalistic current represented by Zionism. Farther north, the Baltic provinces now became the scene of intense political activity, with social-democracy prevailing in Latvia and moderate nationalism in Estonia. Two new recruits were added to the army of discontented nationalities: the Finns and the Armenians. In 1899 the imperial government, bent on integration, virtually abrogated Finland's ancient constitutional rights, and the entire nation rallied under liberal leadership in an impressive campaign of passive resistance. In Armenia, where opposition arose over the government's tacit support for Turkey during the massacres of 1896, nationalism proved a much stronger force than socialism, as was also the case in Georgia.

The acute tensions which had by now developed in Russian society posed a formidable threat to the absolutist regime. It could overcome them only by showing extreme foresight and flexibility. But the throne was next occupied by a monarch conspicuously deficient in such qualities. Nicholas II (1894–1917), last of the tsars, inherited his father's faults without his modest virtues. Though a stubborn advocate of firm government, he was weak in character and in intellect. He mistrusted ministers whose abilities surpassed his own, preferring to rely on backstairs advisers, often of unsavoury reputation. There was thus ample scope for intrigue and jostling for power within the ruling group, the effects of which were felt throughout the bureaucracy. In particular, a rivalry developed between the Ministries of Finance and the Interior which to some extent reflected fundamental differences on policy. Nicholas had no sympathy for the dynamic absolutism contemplated by Witte; he was a traditionalist, with a most naïve view of his functions as autocrat. By his own actions he helped to isolate the monarchy from the whole of Russian society, not excluding even the most moderate elements who were its natural allies against revolution.

Shortly after his accession Nicholas crudely dismissed as 'senseless dreams' the *zemstvo* leaders' aspirations for constitutional government. This declaration was intended to reproduce the effect of Alexander III's inaugural manifesto, but it stimulated sentiments of opposition. Led by D. N. Shipov, a nobleman of impeccably conservative views, the chairmen of many *zemstvo* executives met and established a 'Bureau' to co-ordinate their activities. I. L. Goremykin, the vacillating Minister of the Interior, became alarmed and ordered it to be dissolved. But his inconsistencies led his enemies, amongst them Witte, to plot his downfall (1899). His successor, D. S. Sipyagin, pursued a straightforward policy of obstruction which widened the breach between the government and society. At this time of widespread distress, the contrast between the *zemstva's* achievements and the ineptitude of the bureaucracy was particularly striking. Yet Witte had compiled a confidential memorandum warning the tsar that the *zemstva* were fundamentally incompatible with the maintenance of autocracy and, although he carefully refrained from recommending their dissolution, it was widely feared that the government had such a step in mind. Efforts to form a national organisation were resumed with greater determination. The initiative was taken by a group of radical intellectuals led by P. B. Struve, a convert from Marxism to liberal democracy. In June 1902 he began publication of an illegal newspaper, *Liberation* (*Osvobozhdeniye*), which played an important part in shaping moderate opinion.

A few months previously peasant resentments had flared into revolt in two Ukrainian provinces. The rioters were indiscriminately whipped into submission, whilst the fundamental causes of agrarian unrest were examined by a 'Special Conference' established by Witte. This body, unlike numerous predecessors, was conceived on a grandiose scale, with hundreds of local committees which *zemstvo* leaders were in many cases invited to join. Despite official restrictions the latter were often able to widen the scope of the discussions and advance demands for social and political reform. The liberals thus obtained a valuable opportunity to rally around a common practical programme.

In the meantime the peasant disturbances had given great encouragement to the populists, now reborn as 'Socialist Revolutionaries', who undertook extensive propaganda in the countryside. More spectacular, though ultimately perhaps less significant, was their terrorist campaign, which claimed amongst its first victims the Minister of the Interior (April 1902).

His successor was V. K. Plehve, a former police chief who had his own characteristic methods of dealing with the crisis. Seeking to reduce the *zemstva* to acquiescence, he gave private assurances that he favoured conciliation. But in practice the *zemstva* continued to be harassed, and the multifarious concessions granted by an imperial manifesto of 26 February 1903 were discouragingly vague and trivial. The liberals soon dismissed Plehve's overtures as insincere. In July 1903 they took the decisive step of forming a clandestine organisation, 'The Liberation League', which when formally constituted six months later adopted a radical programme calling for a constituent assembly elected by universal suffrage, extensive social reforms, and national self-determination.

Plehve met with greater initial success in his efforts to gain control of the labour movement by forming unions managed by police agents. The industrial workers, although increasingly responsive to social-democratic agitation, were not firmly committed ideologically. A group of *émigré* Marxist intellectuals, prominent amongst whom was V. I. Lenin, attempted to reconstitute the party by recruiting support for their newspaper, *The Spark* (*Iskra*). But at a congress called in 1903 personal and doctrinal differences among the leaders of the infant party split it into two warring factions, Bolsheviks and Mensheviks, each claiming the mantle of Marxist orthodoxy. This fluid situation gave Plehve his chance.

Workers in Moscow, eagerly grasping at any opportunity to organise, flocked to join unions established by the local security chief, S. V. Zubatov. But the police, to avoid losing control, were obliged to endorse limited strike action, which led to complaints by employers and recriminations within the government. A similar endeavour to weaken the *Bund* by forming an ostensibly 'independent' Jewish labour party accidentally ignited a general strike throughout the Ukraine (July 1903). The outcome of Zubatov's activities was the reverse of that intended: a growth in revolutionary sentiment amongst the workers.

Plehve did not shrink from more vicious methods: in April 1903 he connived at a serious *pogrom* at Kishinyov, Bessarabia, in which many Jews lost their lives. In Finland and Armenia measures of russification were ruthlessly pressed forward. But the tide of revolution still mounted. Plehve saw one hitherto untried means of diverting it: 'a victorious little war'. Towards such a catastrophe Russia was now being irresistibly led by her rulers' eagerness for profit and glory in the Far East.

For thirty years after the Treaty of Peking (1860) Russia had been content to consolidate her position on the Pacific seaboard. But the disintegration of China awakened her latent expansionist ambitions. Witte, anxious to avoid war in Russia's present state of weakness, favoured a policy of limited military commitments and gradual economic penetration, to be carried out as far as possible in collaboration with the Chinese. But the generals and diplomats for the most part preferred a less subtle policy of outright territorial annexations. At first Witte prevailed, but after 1898, when Russia acquired the Port Arthur enclave, her influence rapidly spread through the whole of Manchuria, and aroused determined opposition not only from China but also from Japan and Great Britain.

Russia could have bought off Japan by conceding her rights in Korea equivalent to those she reserved for herself in Manchuria, but on several occasions she let slip opportunities to negotiate a bargain on such lines. After 1901 Nicholas fell increasingly under the influence of a group of unscrupulous adventurers, who eventually obtained the support of Plehve and secured Witte's dismissal (August 1903). Power now finally passed from the regular administration to this irresponsible clique. Arrogantly contemptuous of the Japanese, Nicholas and his advisers failed to prepare for the conflict which their aggressive actions rendered inevitable, and the war, which broke out unexpectedly in January 1904, was an unrelieved series of military and naval disasters. After the final catastrophe of Tsushima (14 May 1905), Russia was obliged to sue for peace. By the Treaty of Portsmouth in August Japan gained southern Sakhalin and Port Arthur, and recognition of her rights in Korea, but in northern Manchuria Russia retained her mastery. It was an extremely modest price to pay for a peace which she so desperately needed.

For by this time the domestic situation had been transformed beyond all recognition. From the start public opinion had generally condemned the war as transparently against the national interest. The responsibility for its outbreak and inefficient conduct fell foursquare upon the government. The war acted as a catalyst, focusing the separate currents of opposition into a single surge of indignation, which rose ever higher with the news of each successive defeat. By its own actions the absolutist regime provided a powerful argument in favour of responsible government. Demands which had hitherto appealed mainly to the educated few—for civil rights, political liberties, and constitutional reform on democratic lines—rapidly commanded mass support. The common opposition to autocracy gave a deceptive appearance of solidarity to a movement which in reality was composed of many diverse elements, each with its own motivations and objectives.

The crisis exposed mercilessly Nicholas' lack of statesmanlike qualities. Haughtily scornful of the opposition, whose strength he greatly underestimated, he played for time, turning helplessly from one desperate expedient to another, consistent only in his determination to yield none of his power. After Plehve's assassination (15 July 1904) he hesitated for a month before naming as his successor the honest and intelligent P. D. Svyatopolk-Mirsky, who set out to re-establish mutual confidence between the government and the public. Inexperienced in politics, Mirsky was soon forced to go farther along the road of concession than he wished. Not realising the implications of his action, he authorised *zemstvo* leaders to hold a national congress at which they intended to discuss constitutional questions. Once granted, permission could not easily be withdrawn without prejudicing the success of his policy. The congress justified the government's worst fears by enthusiastically endorsing a comprehensive reform programme culminating in a demand for a national assembly, which two-thirds of those present wished to endow with legislative power. They concluded by appealing to the tsar to summon such an assembly immediately (9 November 1904).

Mirsky now devised a compromise plan for the admission of elected *zemstvo* representatives into the state council, to which Nicholas first reluctantly consented; but then, warned by Witte that it was the first step towards a constitution, he changed his mind. A decree of 12 December promised reform on various matters, including some raised by the *zemstvo* congress; but these measures were to be elaborated by the usual bureaucratic procedure, without consulting any elected representatives; and the Fundamental Laws of the Empire, it was declared, would be 'unshakably maintained'. A peaceful compromise with moderate opinion was thus ruled out. Instead, Russia had to win its constitution as an indirect result of revolutionary action.

Within less than a month the people of the capital had put forward their own demands. Here Zubatov had established a labour union which, like its predecessors, emancipated itself from police control. Its leaders, prominent amongst them a priest of uncertain loyalties, G. A. Gapon, adapting themselves to the mood of their followers, endorsed a plan to hold a giant demonstration before the Winter Palace, during which the tsar was to be presented with a petition calling attention to their economic grievances and demanding fundamental political reforms. The authorities were warned of the plan but took no effective counter-measures. Early on 9 January 1905 the marchers, unarmed and some bearing icons and portraits of the tsar, were cold-bloodedly shot down. About one hundred were killed, hundreds more injured. The massacre dispelled the last shreds of popular trust in the autocracy, which henceforward became a symbol of oppression capable of evoking violent passions.

A wave of industrial unrest spread spontaneously throughout the country. In Warsaw and Riga there were clashes with troops and further loss of life. In Transcaucasia rioting broke out between Armenians and Tartars. The peasants, too, were thoroughly aroused. Their action took the form of illicit pasturing of cattle and cutting of timber, refusal to work or pay rent, and sometimes even pillaging of estates and seizure of land. By the summer one-sixth, and by the autumn one-half, of the districts of European Russia had been affected by disturbances. In the Baltic provinces and in Georgia events took a particularly severe turn, with the peasants expelling landowners and officials and establishing their own *ad hoc* revolutionary committees. Even more serious were the mutinies which broke out in the navy, where discipline had been shattered by defeat. The army was slower to follow the navy's example but morale was low and many units were politically unreliable.

This upheaval was an elemental, and often anarchic, movement, which owed relatively little to the exertions of the small organised opposition groups. All of these now swung sharply to the left in an effort to catch up with the rapid march of events. In all the border regions nationalist parties yielded ground to their socialist rivals. The populists helped to create an All-Russian Peasant Union, which, however, had insufficient opportunity to gain support on a nation-wide scale. The Social-Democrats discarded their doctrinal scruples and endorsed direct action by the peasants. The Bolsheviks especially were keen to win rural support, but had negligible success. Their strident propaganda for armed insurrection found favour only with a comparatively small ultra-militant element in the cities. The more prosaic and orthodox Mensheviks sought to encourage the formation of trade unions and to capture other rights and liberties by taking advantage of the breakdown in governmental authority. Their tactics had much in common with those of the Liberation League, which succeeded in establishing a number of professional organisations, soon loosely co-ordinated into a League of Unions.

It was this body, led by P. N. Milyukov, which was largely instrumental in pressing the *zemstvo* liberals still farther to the left. In April 1905 they held a second congress, on a more representative basis, which endorsed by a large majority the demand for a constituent assembly elected by universal suffrage, as well as a radical programme of social reform, including even the expropriation of some private estates against limited compensation. One month later, meeting under the impact of Tsushima, delegates of *zemstva* and municipalities approached the tsar personally with another appeal for the immediate convocation of a national assembly. Nicholas' reply was as usual contradictory, and in July they met again to declare their intention of seizing liberty by 'entering into the closest contact with the broad popular masses'. This appeared to promise the absorption of the liberals into the general revolutionary torrent. But the rising tide of peasant violence caused a more cautious note to be sounded. A small minority rallied to Shipov, who was prepared to accept a purely consultative assembly, elected by restricted and indirect franchise. But even Shipov could not accept a puppet assembly such as the government now proposed. The plan for a 'State Duma' prepared by A. S. Bulygin, the ineffectual new Minister of the Interior, evoked a storm of protest.

The fate of Bulygin's proposal was determined, not by the liberal opposition, but by those he planned to disfranchise. Early in October a railway strike broke out in the Moscow area. It spread like wildfire to other regions and industries until the whole country unexpectedly found itself gripped by a general strike. The cities were paralysed; even schools and government offices closed down. The government was understandably panic-stricken at this startlingly effective demonstration of national opposition. Nicholas summoned Witte, who with his usual realism pointed out that, unless he were prepared to institute a military dictatorship, the tsar must grant a constitution. Nicholas had no real choice. On 17 October an imperial manifesto promised full civil liberties and a Duma with legislative powers, elected on an extended franchise. Witte was elevated to the status of Prime Minister and charged with forming a new government.

A new era in Russian history had begun. But the promises of the 'October Manifesto' had yet to become reality. Witte faced the superhuman task of consolidating the new order against powerful opposition from left and right. The manifesto did nothing to appease the revolutionary spirit in the country at large. On the contrary, peasant disturbances now reached their zenith, whilst the industrial workers, emboldened by their success, were eager to continue the struggle until absolutism had been irrevocably overthrown and a constituent assembly called to plan a new democratic future. Such views were energetically promoted by the socialist parties, and in particular by L. D. Trotsky, a dissident Menshevik, who became the most prominent figure in the St Petersburg *Soviet*. This was an organisation of factory representatives, formed for liaison purposes during the strike, which now consolidated its authority in the capital, established contact with other centres and became virtually a rival government. The same radical demands were voiced by the liberals, now emerging as the Constitutional-Democratic ('Kadet') party. Suspecting that Witte neither would nor could implement consistently the principles of the October Manifesto, they rejected his invitations to join a coalition government and offered him only conditional support. Even Shipov's moderates, now known as 'Octobrists', refused to participate in a government which contained the discredited P. N. Durnovo as Minister of the Interior.

In his desperate efforts to restore order Witte wavered between conciliation and repression, with increasing emphasis upon the latter as it became practicable. The Soviet soon alienated its middle-class sympathisers by its extremism. Its leaders developed an exaggerated idea of their power, and impetuously challenged the government before making sure of support from the peasants or armed forces. Durnovo, seizing his chance, provoked a conflict by arresting the Soviet's president (26 November); a week later the entire membership followed him into imprisonment. A final call for another general strike evoked little response in St Petersburg, but in Moscow led to a struggle between several hundred partisans, with some popular support, and loyal troops. By the end of 1905 the government's position was greatly strengthened. Punitive expeditions toured the country wreaking vengeance upon those suspected of revolutionary activity.

But every success in the struggle against revolution weakened Witte's own position *vis-à-vis* the extremists of the right. Amongst his numerous enemies at court none was more dangerous than the tsar himself. Nicholas blamed Witte for the October Manifesto, which he now deeply regretted and sought to retract. To counterbalance Witte's influence he leaned for support upon various reactionary groups, amongst them the notorious ultra-nationalistic 'Russian People's League', which organised acts of violence against opponents of autocracy. By a tragic paradox, the constitutional era dawned amidst widespread *pogroms*, in which highly placed persons were sometimes directly implicated. Nicholas willingly overlooked such unlawful acts, which had his personal sympathy.

In these circumstances Witte felt obliged to make concessions to the right. Whilst the elections to the Duma were allowed to proceed without interference, several edicts were issued restricting the assembly's powers. The assent of the state council, now expanded to include an elective element, and of the Sovereign were necessary for its proposals to become law, and its rights of budgetary control and legislative initiative were minimal. Shortly before the Duma met, new Fundamental (that is, constitutional) Laws were promulgated which, in conflict with the spirit if not the letter of the October Manifesto, stated that the tsar still exercised the prerogatives of an autocratic ruler. On the same day (23 April 1906) came Witte's dismissal, which ended his public career. Having set out to establish the conditions for a constitutional regime, he had merely succeeded in facilitating a restoration of absolutism, disguised by a mock legislature. His last act as Premier had been to assist in negotiating the largest loan to date in the history of international finance, which enabled the government to face the Duma from a position of strength.

This augured ill for the future of Russia's parliamentary experiment. The first Duma (27 April–9 July 1906) expressed faithfully the popular mood of frustrated indignation. Nearly half the deputies were peasants, for the government, in drafting the electoral law, had provided for their generous representation in the belief that they would constitute a moderating force. In the event most of them followed, or stood to the left of, the Kadets, the strongest and most influential party. The Kadets sought to realise through the Duma the objectives which revolutionary violence had failed to achieve. The government, on the other hand, envisaged the Duma as a subservient consultative body. The inevitable clash came on 13 May when Goremykin, the new Premier, rejected the Duma's statement of its legislative intentions, in particular the idea of compulsory expropriation of private estates where necessary to assuage land-hunger. Subsequently the deputies occupied themselves with drafting laws which stood little chance of acceptance, and debating the agrarian question, hoping that their deliberations, backed by a new wave of peasant disturbances, would force the administration to yield. Some members of the government were sufficiently alarmed by the situation in the country to favour conceding the Duma's demand for a responsible ministry. Exploratory talks were held privately with Kadet leaders, but were rendered nugatory by Nicholas' refusal to countenance any surrender of his autocratic power. He sympathised with those ministers who feared the Duma as a source of dangerous agitation. The assembly was provoked into exceeding its lawful rights, and dissolution speedily followed. The opposition leaders met in Vyborg, Finland, and called for a national campaign of passive resistance. But their appeal went unheeded: such scattered outbreaks as occurred showed that the peasants and workers had little zeal left for revolution, and were in any case not disposed to rebel over a constitutional issue they barely comprehended.

The government was now led by P. A. Stolypin, an energetic and strong-willed ex-governor, who set out to pacify the country by ruthless repression coupled with measures of agrarian reform. In August 1906 he established field courts-martial which within eight months had claimed over 1700 victims. For Stolypin the interests of the state took precedence over legal proprieties. During this crucial period he ruled Russia by decree without due constitutional authority. Though not averse to collaborating with the Duma, he considered it justifiable to exert pressure during the elections in an effort to manufacture an assembly of acceptable political colouring.

These dubious methods, however, only resulted in the second Duma (20 February–3 June 1907) proving even more intractable than the first. It contained a strong left wing, with no less than sixty-five social-democratic deputies, as well as a small but vocal group of right-wing extremists. The Kadets, though much reduced in strength, tried desperately to avoid another dissolution by keeping strictly within the law, but their caution merely infuriated the left, which adhered unrealistically to revolutionary slogans rendered obsolete by the course of events. Stolypin skilfully exploited this mutual bickering, but was unable to persuade the Duma to endorse his legislative programme, and in particular his agrarian policy. Nor would the deputies make the unequivocal repudiation of terrorism which he required in order to counter pressure by reactionary groups for dissolution. Once convinced that collaboration with the assembly was impossible, Stolypin presented it with evidence implicating the social-democratic members in subversive activity, and demanded their surrender to stand trial. When the Duma temporised, the order was issued for dissolution (3 June 1907). It was accompanied by a new electoral law radically altering the franchise in favour of the propertied classes. With this virtual *coup d'état* the first Russian revolution was brought to an end.

To all external appearances, autocracy had triumphed. Active resistance had been crushed, and the instruments of coercion were again firmly in the government's hands. But the real criterion of its success was the degree to which it could relieve the acute social and political tensions from which the revolution had sprung.

In the social sphere the position varied significantly in town and country. The urban workers gained little from the revolution except a taste for the heady wine of power. For some groups the 1900's brought higher wages, but the improvement in living-standards was nowhere very marked. Although trade unions were now legally permissible, most of the numerous organisations that had mushroomed into existence during the revolution were suppressed as subversive. Russia could not develop a stable mass labour movement on the western European pattern. The rapidly expanding urban proletariat now relapsed into sullen passivity, but remained a highly volatile force, easily agitated in time of crisis.

But in the villages a serious effort was at last made to grapple with the agrarian problem. The revolution had shattered the myth of the supposedly conservative influence exerted by the commune. Stolypin's decree of 9 November 1906 allowed peasants to leave the commune and consolidate their holdings as individual property. Siberian migration was promoted more energetically, and much crown and state land was transferred to the Peasant Land Bank for sale to its clients. Stolypin sought to mitigate land-hunger by all means short of sanctioning expropriation of the gentry's estates, and to create the class of individualistic peasant proprietors, with a firm stake in the existing social order, which Russia had hitherto so conspicuously lacked. It is no exaggeration to say that Russia's whole future depended upon the extent to which his policy would succeed in assuaging peasant grievances before the next revolutionary crisis broke.

Little progress was made in relieving tensions in the political sphere. One decreasingly important source of discontent was eased by the greater degree of religious toleration granted in April 1905. Some of the national minorities improved their position. In Finland, where events had followed much the same pattern as elsewhere in Russia, repressive legislation had been revoked, and civil liberties and a democratic constitution granted. But the new parliament, in which the Social Democrats formed the largest party, was naturally regarded with suspicion by the imperial government, which did not consider itself bound by the concessions it had made. In Transcaucasia a more liberal line was pursued. But the Letts and the Poles, who had been the most active in the revolutionary struggle, won no concessions. Everywhere the crisis stimulated nationalist sentiment—not least among the Russians themselves. Stolypin's new electoral law, which decreased the minorities' representation in the Duma, was a harbinger of renewed efforts at russification.

Still more important was the continued tension arising from the lack of assured civil and political rights. The scope of such liberties as existed on paper was determined in practice by the whims of officialdom. Although Stolypin's regime was not the unrelieved tyranny it was often made out to be by contemporary critics, conditions were oppressive enough to keep most educated people in opposition to the government. For liberal public opinion the Duma, even in truncated form, remained the symbol of their aspirations. It constituted, they believed, a breach in the fortress of autocracy which could subsequently be widened further until Russia became a modern democratic state.

It is clear in retrospect that these hopes of progress along Western lines were exaggerated. In reality the semi- or quasi-constitutional regime which emerged in 1906 rested upon a very insecure basis. There was an underlying contradiction in the fact that the Duma and the other rights cherished by the liberals had not been won through their own efforts, but through pressure exerted by millions to whom these gains meant very little. The peasants valued the Duma chiefly as an instrument for obtaining the land which they coveted. The workers, who spoke so freely of democracy, interpreted it in the sense of economic levelling. Relatively few outside the educated minority had any strong abiding interest in political liberty or individual rights as such. The mass movement, to which Russian liberalism was indebted for its successes, also contained a distinctly illiberal streak.

When put to the test, it might be said, most Russians were prepared to subordinate liberty to the aim of social and economic progress. Witte was right in seeing that a dynamic progressive authoritarian regime would be appropriate to Russian conditions, but wrong in thinking that the initiative in this direction might be taken by the monarchy. The imperial dynasty was too firmly wedded to the interests of the social élite to be able to effect a radical transformation of the structure of power. Had Nicholas II been another Peter the Great it is perhaps conceivable that Witte's ideas might have borne more fruit—but here one enters the realm of hypothesis. The Russian right wing, hamstrung by class-consciousness and loyalty to the traditional conception of autocracy, showed itself deficient in original thought. Instead, Witte's design was to be realised from the left, in a manner and on a scale which would have far surpassed his imagination. The revolution of 1905 proved to be merely the prelude to a still greater cataclysm which was to sweep away the heritage of nineteenth-century Russia and open up new perspectives of intoxicating and intimidating grandeur.

CHAPTER XIV

GREAT BRITAIN
AND THE BRITISH EMPIRE

A T the half-way mark of the Victorian era Britain held an undisputed position as the greatest power in the world. Her economic, political and social institutions rested on firm foundations, and served as models for old and new states both in Europe and overseas. The empire controlled by Britain included large areas in Africa, America, Asia, and Australasia; British sea-power dominated the oceans; British trade spanned the globe; and Britain had long been recognised as the financial and industrial centre of the world. While in some particulars this picture changed before the end of Queen Victoria's reign, British influence and power were still immense, and the British empire of 1901 was vastly larger and richer than that of 1870.

Throughout the eventful closing decades of the nineteenth century Britain played a leading part in all aspects of world affairs. She pioneered in fields of science and technology; she promoted the development of communications by land and sea and furthered the Europeanisation of Africa, Asia, and Oceania; her capital and entrepreneurial and technical skills helped to unlock the resources of far-away lands; her cultural, economic, political and social institutions were planted in regions throughout the world. The period witnessed a large *diaspora* of British peoples and the unpremeditated role of Britain as a builder of nations.

In 1870 the leading British statesmen believed that Britain was sated territorially. But in the next thirty years Benjamin Disraeli and Joseph Chamberlain urged expansion of the empire. Both were converts to this cause. In the 1860's Disraeli had advised abandoning British outposts in West Africa; in the early 1880's Chamberlain had fought imperialism. That many other Britons changed their views may be seen by comparing the results of the general elections of 1880 and 1900. In the former an overwhelming majority repudiated the romantic imperialism of Lord Beaconsfield; twenty years later they endorsed the aggressive imperialism of Chamberlain even though his policy had provoked a costly and disillusioning war in South Africa.

Fast-changing world conditions wrought this revolution in the British attitude toward the overseas empire. After 1870 the population of most European countries grew rapidly, and so did their industrialisation. Living-standards rose; the demand for exotic products waxed; improved communications made those products more readily available; international trade expanded; and a relatively long period of settled internal conditions turned the attention of European powers to the acquisition and exploitation of African and Asian lands. Russia relentlessly pushed forward her imperial frontiers; France nervously sought to recover by overseas ventures the prestige and self-confidence lost by her war of 1870-1; Germany and Italy energetically entered the competition for colonies and for an increased share of international trade.

Aware of economic opportunities in Africa and Asia and aroused by the appearance of foreign rivals, British industrialists and traders clamoured for a resolute imperial policy. In the 1870's British investors lost heavily when Egypt, Turkey and several Central and South American states defaulted. They then wanted new fields for investment, and demanded that their government should widen the imperial orbit. Finding both Conservative and Liberal governments reluctant to move frontier posts forward, private empire-builders resurrected an old device for overseas enterprise—the chartered company. In the 1880's four such companies were authorised to operate in Borneo and Africa. Though theoretically under close government supervision these companies actually had a free hand in dealing with native rulers. When their activities clashed with those of other Europeans, the British government was forced to step in since powerful economic interests as well as strong humanitarian sentiment were readily mobilised in support of claims by British subjects.

In Africa especially, God and Mammon co-operated closely in the expansion of British imperial responsibilities. Early in the nineteenth century, when Britain brought to an end first the Atlantic slave trade and then slavery within her empire, abolitionists headed by Sir Thomas Fowell Buxton sponsored a movement to uproot the slave trade and slavery within Africa by developing trade in material instead of human resources of the continent. This plan received immediate support from the missionary societies. The greatest friend of the African natives, Dr David Livingstone, upon seeing the horrible results of the ravages of Arab slave traders, declared that the cure for the ills of Africa was to be found in 'Christianity and commerce'. The prescription of this sincere servant of the 'Man from Galilee' was accepted wholeheartedly by both Christian humanitarians and business promoters.

During the last quarter of the nineteenth century British missionary organisations worked zealously among African natives. They were especially active in East Africa where successes in Uganda encouraged the belief that here was a vast field ready for harvest. The Arab slave-hunters were, of course, implacably hostile to the Christian missionaries who sought alliance with European and especially British traders. Aid was finally obtained from the British government. With the occupation of Zanzibar the depredations of the Arabs were checked. Although profit was the primary objective of the British trading companies, the most active of their agents, Sir Harry Johnston and Frederick, Lord Lugard, were ardent humanitarians. The termination of the slave trade brought sorely needed relief to suffering Africans.

In Oceania also British humanitarianism was a potent factor in shaping British policy. As cotton and sugar plantations were established in Fiji and Queensland, labour shortages were relieved by recruiting Polynesians under an indenture system. Unscrupulous European, American, and Australasian traders often kidnapped natives whose status on the plantations became little different from that of slaves. After some hesitation the British parliament passed the Pacific Islander Protection Act, annexed the Fiji Islands, and created the office of High Commissioner for the Western Pacific. With the increase of German trading activities in this region the Australasian colonies persistently urged further British annexations, but not until Germany had seized north-eastern New Guinea and adjoining islands did Britain occupy south-eastern New Guinea.

While colonial pressure for new British annexations was frequently ignored, the need to safeguard trade routes and existing imperial boundaries often brought aggressive action. This was especially true after the Suez Canal had proved to be an important high road for British trade with the East. Soon Britain became deeply involved in the eastern Mediterranean, in Egypt and eastern Africa, and in the Red Sea region. Concern for the safety of India resulted in the annexation of Baluchistan and the remainder of Burma, and the extension of British influence in Persian Gulf lands and Malaya.

In the international scramble for African possessions, Britain carried off many valuable prizes. Here the Imperial East Africa Company, the Royal Niger Company, and the South Africa Chartered Company were the chief instruments for expansion. Though conferences and bilateral agreements between interested powers accomplished the partition of Africa without international conflict, in some areas natives offered stout resistance—the Ashantees on the Gold Coast, the Kaffirs, Matabele and Zulu in South Africa, and the fanatical Mohammedan dervishes in the Sudan. But it was the European republics in South Africa which most resolutely resisted British annexation. Gold discoveries within the Transvaal brought British adventurers and capital into this country whose western boundary abutted on the relatively narrow strip of habitable land connecting the Cape Colony with Rhodesia. Friction between the foreigners and the burghers in the Transvaal, British fear for the safety of the Missionary Road to the interior and of a coalition between the Transvaal and Germany, and the unwillingness of Transvaalers to treat the Britons as equals resulted in the greatest British colonial war since the American Revolution. The heroic Boers repeatedly defeated superior British forces. Though their land was annexed in 1900, not until 31 May 1902 did the uneven conflict come to an end with the surrender of the last Boer forces in the field.

As the long reign of Queen Victoria closed in January 1901 there was much activity on the periphery of her empire. In South Africa the war was still on; in Malaya and in Nigeria British rule was gradually being established and consolidated; in the Anglo-Egyptian Sudan British officials were bringing order and security to a much plundered country; in India a masterful viceroy, Lord Curzon, endeavoured to improve the condition of her vast population and to make her safe against foreign attacks; in the Far East British emissaries cast about for means to protect valuable British economic interests. At home Joseph Chamberlain strove to rescue the West Indian colonies from ruin, and to promote economic development and welfare in British dependencies.

The dynamics of imperial expansion were matched by shrewd steadiness of management and constant readaptation in new as well as old units of the overseas empire. The chief objectives of the British government were to establish the framework of an ordered society wherein cannibalism, human sacrifice, and slavery would cease, to provide security for life and property, and to ensure essential conditions for private enterprise, profit for investors, and employment for the native population. The system of indirect rule prevailing in the princely states of India was extended to the Fiji Islands, to Malaya, and to large sections of Africa. Under this system native chiefs continued to enjoy their former prestige and privileges while, except for laws relating to crime, native customs were undisturbed. Many of the areas so controlled were labelled protectorates or protected states, and their inhabitants were not British subjects. In Egypt Britain ruled (subject to many international restrictions) through an agent and consul-general at Cairo. From 1883 until 1907 the able and energetic Evelyn Baring, Earl of Cromer, held this dual post. Theoretically the Anglo-Egyptian Sudan was governed by Britain and Egypt under an arrangement called a condominium—actually Britain was the dominant partner.

Since the middle of the nineteenth century the British colonies of North America and Australasia had enjoyed self-government. Later this boon was extended to the South African colonies of the Cape of Good Hope and Natal. Efforts to unite colonies into regional federations were vigorously supported by the imperial authorities; they met with success in North America and Australia but failed in South Africa and the West Indies. As no definite limits of autonomy had been prescribed for self-governing colonies, they won by degrees the attributes of sovereign states. The imperial government scrupulously refrained from meddling in their internal affairs, even in cases where actions were deemed unwise, as in New Zealand's confiscation of Maori land in 1880-1 and Newfoundland's sale of public utilities to a private firm in 1897. Colonial immigration Acts which discriminated against non-European British subjects and citizens of friendly Asian countries evoked protests from Downing Street, but in the end the colonies had their way. British economic interests resented colonial protective customs duties but to no avail. Before the century closed colonial fiscal autonomy was an established fact; self-governing colonies could not, without their consent, be bound by British commercial treaties, and in 1893 Canada created a precedent by negotiating commercial agreements directly with France.

While the colonies, free to pursue their own interests, neither paid tribute to Britain nor had any other obligations to the imperial centre, they profited by their membership in the British empire. They were protected against foreign foes; they were served by the British consular and diplomatic representatives; they were a favoured field for British investments; and they could borrow on advantageous terms in the London money market.

In general, Britain conducted intra-imperial relations on the basis of 'freedom and voluntaryism'. Not until 1895, when Joseph Chamberlain became Colonial Secretary, was *laissez-faire* replaced by a purposeful, constructive imperial policy at government level. A resourceful administrator, Chamberlain looked upon the overseas empire as an underdeveloped estate. He recognised that Britain had definite obligations toward her dependencies and that therefore—as John Morley wrote of him—she should justify her rule 'by bringing security, peace, and comparative prosperity to lands that never knew them before'. His development and welfare programme was tied in with efforts to bind the colonies more closely to Britain and to extend imperial boundaries. These efforts failed, as did all the efforts of imperial enthusiasts to federate the empire, because conflicting economic and political interests of Great and Greater Britain could not be reconciled. But if consolidation was rejected by the self-governing colonies, a common allegiance to the Crown and periodic consultative colonial conferences still linked Great and Greater Britain. Although the leading colonies had legislative autonomy, their laws were not permitted to conflict with British laws, and the Judicial Committee of the British Privy Council was the supreme court for all overseas sections of the British empire.

The British political scene was dominated by two giants, Benjamin Disraeli (later Earl of Beaconsfield) and W. E. Gladstone. As in the case of Pitt and Fox the leaders aroused either devoted attachment or bitter hostility. Interest in politics was keen; parliament enjoyed immense prestige; the House of Commons attracted men of ability and character; reports of debates were widely read; and the dramatic duel between Gladstone and Disraeli lent an heroic quality to party warfare. Although diametrically opposite in outlook and temperament the two leaders were well matched. Gladstone, Prime Minister since 1868, was at the height of his power as administrator and parliamentarian. A brilliant orator, he was also an eager crusader for moral causes. He was intent upon righting the wrongs of Ireland and liberalising British institutions. His government inaugurated a tax-supported elementary school system, opened the civil service to men of talent, ended the purchase of army commissions, provided protection for trade union funds, reorganised the English judiciary system and extended government control to the relations between Irish landlords and tenants. As the head of a strong government, supported by a large Liberal majority in the House of Commons, Gladstone made the period of his first ministry, 1868–74, extremely important in the annals of reform legislation.

Facing Gladstone was Benjamin Disraeli, undisputed chief of the Conservatives. Cool, detached, sceptical, an effective debater, he was extraordinarily adroit both as strategist and tactician. He had overcome tremendous obstacles, and had educated his party to accept reforms. Although admired by many he was trusted by few—among the latter was the Queen whom he completely captivated. More than any other of her Prime Ministers Disraeli appreciated the need for social reform, and as Prime Minister, 1874–80, he supported legislation dealing with labour conditions and trade unions, housing, the enclosure of commons, and merchant shipping. But imaginative and romantic, fascinated by the glitter and pomp of monarchy, Disraeli stressed imperial issues above all others. He had the Queen proclaimed Empress of India, purchased nine-twentieths of the shares of the Suez Canal Company, sanctioned imperial expansion in Africa and Asia, and held the centre of the stage at the Congress of Berlin, 1878.

On the domestic political scene, Irish problems aroused fierce and prolonged conflict. Gladstone sought to pacify Ireland by disestablishing and disendowing the Anglican Church in the island, by improving the lot of the Irish peasants, and finally, in his third administration, 1886, by giving Ireland a separate parliament. This programme threatened privileges warmly defended by the Conservatives, but not until Gladstone proposed Irish Home Rule were the British voters really aroused. By representing home rule as a measure which would imperil the United Kingdom and establish 'Rome rule' in Ireland, opponents revived English antagonisms and fears. In vain Gladstone pleaded that the self-determination which Britain had advocated for European national entities and conceded to her own overseas colonies should be granted to Ireland as a right and a means for bringing peace to the island and a union of hearts in the British Isles. The issue split his own party, old friends and associates deserted him, and he was reviled in unmeasured terms. In addition to causing a deep cleavage in British politics and society the Irish Home Rule question impeded the progress of economic and social reform. It damaged Britain's relations with Australia, Canada, and especially with the United States where Irish immigrants nourished in their hearts bitter hostility to England, implanted it in their children, and injected it into American politics.

With the death of Lord Beaconsfield in 1881 and the retirement of Gladstone thirteen years later, the political stage lost its greatest performers. Lord Salisbury, leader of the Conservatives at the close of the century, had the support of a large parliamentary majority and enjoyed the confidence of the Queen. But Salisbury, competent in handling foreign relations, neglected pressing social problems. The decade of the 1880's saw the meteoric rise and catastrophic fall of the brilliant Lord Randolph Churchill, and the remarkable success and final ruin of the skilful but ruthless Irish leader, Charles Stewart Parnell. In the 1870's Joseph Chamberlain won national recognition as a champion of social reform; in the latter half of the 1880's he stood forth as the implacable foe of Irish Home Rule; after 1895 he emerged as the outstanding member of the Salisbury government and as the most ardent and resolute of British imperialists.

In the overseas countries statesmen operated in the restricted field of small democratic societies. Here the transplanted British institutions had to be adjusted to frontier conditions. Though rich in natural resources, all colonies suffered from shortages of capital and manpower, and their leaders faced problems fundamentally different from those in the United Kingdom. The largest among the budding nations of Greater Britain was the Dominion of Canada whose constitutional framework was modelled in part after that of the United States, but whose operating institutions—the monarchy, parliamentary government, and law courts—had come from Britain. Here the Conservative Sir John A. Macdonald successfully guided a vast and thinly populated country through its difficult formative period. It was his political opponent, the Liberal Sir Wilfrid Laurier, who at the close of the century became Macdonald's successor as a Canadian nation builder. Laurier was proud of his French blood, but like Macdonald he was loyal to Canada's British connection and dedicated to her upbuilding as a British nation. His advent to the premiership in 1896 marked the beginning of a long period of unparalleled progress; Laurier optimistically proclaimed that the twentieth would be Canada's century.

Among the other self-governing British colonies only New Zealand produced leaders whose achievements entitle them to be listed with Macdonald and Laurier as nation builders. In the 1870's Julius (later Sir Julius) Vogel, an immigrant of German-Jewish origin, led New Zealand out of the deep depression which had followed a series of native wars. He promoted public works, attracted capital and immigrants, and changed the colony from a loose federation of provinces into a well-knit unitary state. Twenty years later New Zealand-born William Pember Reeves spearheaded a series of reforms which focused world attention on the tiny democracy in the South Sea as a laboratory for economic and social experiments. Basic factors in New Zealand's progress were the protection and the capital, manpower, and technical skills which the mother-country provided.

Common to Great and Greater Britain in the latter part of the Victorian era was a steady advance toward political democracy. At home the traditional outline of the national government remained unaltered, but details of its organisation were materially changed. The reform bill of 1867 gave the vote to labourers in the towns, that of 1884 extended the same boon to rural areas. Moreover, the redistribution of seats in the House of Commons which accompanied these measures put representation more squarely on a population basis. The Ballot Act of 1872 reduced the opportunities to intimidate voters while a later corrupt practices Act diminished the influence of money power in general elections.

But in the advance toward political democracy Britain trailed behind the self-governing colonies. Led by Australia (South Australia in 1855; Victoria in 1857; New South Wales in 1858) they had early adopted universal manhood suffrage, and by 1901 New Zealand and South Australia had granted the vote to women also. Furthermore, 'one man one vote' was the general rule in the colonies. In Britain, on the other hand, the Reform Act of 1884 still denied the vote to sons living at home and to servants—that is to approximately 15–20 per cent of the adult male population—while men in business or with residences in several districts might meet the electoral requirements in each place and thus have several votes. The possibility for plural voting was increased by the fact that not all constituencies were polled on the same day. While the number of plural voters was relatively small they sometimes decided the outcome in close contests, and since they generally belonged to the upper classes, the arrangement favoured the Conservative party. The custom of not paying members of the British House of Commons had a similar effect. The more democratic colonial societies paid salaries to their legislators. However, the chief difference between the legislative machinery of Great and Greater Britain was in the second chamber. At home the House of Lords with its majority of hereditary peers continued to wield much power. Proposals to 'mend or end' that house aroused little public interest even though the Conservatives held such an overwhelming majority that it had become almost a one-party chamber. Overseas the members of the second chambers were either appointed or elected. Both in Great Britain and in the colonies, however, changes in legislative practice or in the method of selection weakened their power and compelled them to heed public opinion.

A series of reforms advanced democracy in Britain on the local level. School boards set up by the Education Act of 1870 were chosen by elections in which women could vote. In 1888 the Conservatives under Lord Salisbury ended the old system of county government by justices of the peace in quarter-sessions, replacing it with elective councils. Six years later this democratisation was continued by the Liberals with the introduction of elected parish and district councils. But reforms in Ireland lagged behind those for Great Britain, and not until 1898 was the elective principle introduced in the local government of 'John Bull's other island'.

The English system of county government had not been transplanted to the principal overseas colonies. Australasia, Canada and South Africa handled local affairs in various ways with the general pattern following distinctly democratic lines.

Robert Lowe, the famous opponent of electoral reform in Britain, is quoted as saying after the passage of the 1867 Reform Act, 'Now we must educate our masters'. This sentiment furthered the adoption of free, compulsory elementary education in Great Britain, and a type of political education for adults spread rapidly after the labouring classes had been enfranchised. Because the aristocratic political clubs in London could not hope to manipulate the votes of the masses, new devices were invented by both parties. Starting with small local units and ending with powerful national organisations they gave the voters the opportunity to choose party managers who directed political strategy. Joseph Chamberlain 'insisted', to quote Morley again, that 'democracy to be strong must be concentrated; its force would be wasted unless units organised themselves for electoral purposes in free, open, representative, local associations with freely chosen and recognised leaders'. Gladstone blessed the change at the outset but Lord Randolph Churchill, who sponsored it among the Conservatives, had difficulty in gaining Salisbury's consent. The interest of the masses was aroused, and the borders of the political community were widened by the new type of party organisation. The increase of party cohesion and discipline made the whip more important than formerly, and the road was cleared for the subsequent appearance of the party boss. Charles Stewart Parnell had already achieved that position when for several years up to 1890 he held absolute control over the Irish Nationalist party.

Although British women were denied the right to vote in national elections, they were enlisted as unpaid party workers after the Corrupt Practices Act of 1883 had outlawed the employment of paid canvassers. The Primrose League served the Conservative party without reward, but the Women's Liberal Federation demanded that candidates whom they helped should support women's suffrage. They had little success. The women of New Zealand and South Australia obtained the franchise a quarter of a century earlier than their British sisters.

Mass political education took a long step forward in November 1879, when Gladstone opened his famous campaign in the Midlothian county of Scotland. In a series of great speeches to huge audiences he analysed contemporary issues and charged the Conservative government with moral laxity in domestic and foreign affairs. Masterfully he exposed its mistakes, fervently he appealed to the voters' sense of justice and fair play.

That a former first minister of the Crown should discuss matters of high politics at mass meetings scandalised the Queen; Beaconsfield sneered at his rival's 'drenching rhetoric'; but voters liked to be addressed as people endowed with reason. They returned Gladstone to office and power; henceforth his method of popular appeal became common practice in British political campaigns—a practice which had been applied in the colonies long before Gladstone started his Midlothian crusade.

Accustomed to guidance by their 'betters' the British labouring classes were slow to use for their own advantage the powers conferred upon them by the reform bills. Despite the fact that many captains of industry and merchant princes supported the Liberals, and Gladstone himself was a staunch individualist, the masses had faith in him and his party. To them the Liberals represented progress and Gladstone stood for righteousness. He became 'the People's William'; his efforts to increase social opportunities and his ethical standards had powerful appeal to Bible-reading labourers. Disraeli, who saw the need for attracting the labour vote, coined the slogan 'the Monarchy and the Multitude'—the government should be paternalistic. His Home Secretary, 1874–80, R. A. (later Lord) Cross, with the assistance of the Prime Minister, passed several social reform measures. After the death of Beaconsfield Tory Democracy was upheld by Lord Randolph Churchill. But the rank and file of labour suspected the Conservative party, where 'the solid phalanx of the great families' remained influential and solicitude for the privileges of the landed interests and the Church continued strong. Because the two-party tradition dominated politics, labour leaders gained benefits for their class by boring from within.

In the 1880's two new remedies for economic ills were offered to the British public—Marxian socialism and Henry George's single tax. While some middle-class intellectuals accepted Marxism, labour at home and overseas distrusted both nostrums. But in the late 1890's they were attracted by proposals for independent political action. Times had been hard. Workers refused to believe that they were 'born only to endure'. They still found consolation in religion and might troop to labour meetings in Methodist chapels singing

> O God our help in ages past,
> Our hope for years to come,

but heavenly support seemed to take an unconscionable time in arriving. In 1894 'the People's William' retired from politics. A year later Joseph Chamberlain shelved the cause of social betterment for that of imperialism. Salisbury's detached inactivity held no hope for the underprivileged. In Australia a young Labour party was gaining strength. Reluctantly the British Trades Union Congress endorsed a move toward independent political action. As the century closed British labour took the first step toward the organisation of a national labour party.

In politics as in the system of government the colonies followed British models. But in the wilderness the precedents of an old society sometimes hindered rather than helped. Colonial society was democratic while that of Britain was still mainly aristocratic in structure. Since the colonies were not yet sovereign states the development of their natural resources rather than foreign relations shaped party politics. Only in South Africa was the problem of foreign relations a serious one, and only there was the existence of a non-European population a further serious complication.

Canada borrowed her party labels from Britain. Macdonald, the Conservative, studied the political ideas of Disraeli; Laurier, the Liberal, drew inspiration from Gladstone. But the party alignments in the new federation came closer to American than British models. Issues such as protective tariff and provincial rights had counterparts south of the international boundary, not in the United Kingdom. In Australia, too, the tariff was much discussed and that question delayed federation. In one form or another, land and labour were perennial themes for political platforms overseas. Canada adopted the American plan of free land grants of moderate size to bona fide settlers, but in Australasia immense areas of the public land had passed into the hands of individual owners or occupiers early in the period of settlement so that repossession by the Crown or the breaking up of the large holdings were live political campaign topics. All self-governing colonies needed labourers but this need varied according to the ebb and flow of economic prosperity—therefore subsidising immigration occasioned endless debate. Then there was the question of who should be admitted. Railway builders in western Canada and in East Africa brought in coolies from China and India; plantation owners in Fiji, Natal, Queensland, and the West Indies recruited under indenture labourers from India and Polynesia. In self-governing colonies these practices caused stormy debates, for resident labourers feared that an influx of Asians would depress living-standards. In British Columbia and in Australasia the exclusion of Asians and of Polynesians aroused intense feeling. No sooner was the Commonwealth of Australia formed than federal legislation was passed to ensure a white Australia.

The debate about the exclusion of Asians helped to bring labour into politics and encouraged the Australian colonies to federate. Uniform legislation was needed to keep Australia a white-man's continent. It was not a sense of racial superiority but the desire to protect their jobs which made Australian labourers take a resolute stand on the immigration issue. In the depressed 1890's labour in New South Wales entered politics as an independent political party, while in New Zealand labour formed a Liberal-Labour (Lib-Lab) alliance to promote pro-labour legislation.

Despite these differences of circumstances the colonies generally accepted British political concepts and methods. French-speaking Canadians and Afrikaans-speaking South Africans skilfully used instruments for government that had been made in Britain. Before the nineteenth century closed a nationalist movement arose in India; and the goal of the Indian National Congress, founded in 1885, was to secure for the ancient races of the Asian sub-continent self-government on the British model. On 26 January 1901 *The Economist*, a leading British journal, observed that 'as a nation we are not greatly loved by the world at large; but it is clear that our sources of political strength are appreciated'. Proof cited was the fact that the British system of government had been widely adopted throughout the world. Of Queen Victoria, recently demised, this journal said that she was 'the only one whom, for the last thirty years of her life, her millions of subjects, the conquerors and the conquered alike, would have chosen by plebiscite to occupy the throne'. Neither the leader-writer nor the public knew that the Queen had vehemently declared in 1880 that a ruler of a democratic country she would not be. That secret had been well kept. The country had steadily grown more democratic but she had not abdicated. Republican voices speaking softly in England in 1871 and raucously in Australia twenty years later were mute in 1901.

Improvements in communication exerted a profound influence on the course of events in Britain and the empire. Iron and steel replaced wood in shipbuilding, the new compound steam-engine was vastly more efficient than its predecessors, and by the end of the century the internal combustion engine promised to revolutionise mechanical propulsion on land and sea. Britain was the world's greatest shipbuilder, shipowner, and supplier of bunker coal. Her position on the sea remained dominant; her merchant marine aided mightily in the spread of British influence and trade and in maintaining close contacts between the imperial centre and its far-flung dependencies. Income from freight, brokerage, insurance, shipping and other services reached large proportions, and the introduction of refrigerator-ships gave a tremendous boost to Australasian dairy farming.

The great era of railway building was already over in Britain by 1870 but she was an important producer of railway supplies; her engineers and technicians enjoyed an excellent reputation; and she had capital available for railway construction both within and outside her empire. In the years 1870–1901 British enterprise and money united countries with bands of steel and opened up for exploitation agricultural and mineral resources in Africa, America, Asia and Australasia. Much of the British capital exported was in the form of goods needed for building and equipping railways. The clank of the train rang in the dawn of better days for the dwellers on the Canadian prairie and in the Australian bush. Only by improved communications could their toilsome life be made easier and hope blossom for reward. But with the lowering of transportation costs the production and marketing of goods became highly competitive. What was a boon for cattle raisers, dairymen and wheat farmers abroad spelled ruin for their counterparts in Britain.

The opening of the Suez Canal in 1869 was an event of tremendous economic and political significance for the British empire. In Britain the local canals lost out in the competition with the railways; the only considerable new canal-building venture was the Manchester Ship Canal which transformed that inland city into a seaport. It was otherwise in Canada where canals continued to furnish the cheapest transport for wheat and other bulky products of the interior. Here the waterway from Montreal to Lake Superior was much improved in the years 1885–1900. The bicycle and electric tram-car changed conditions for work and play. But Britain lagged behind continental Europe and the United States in developing the internal combustion engine. British regulations, which limited to four miles an hour the speed of mechanically driven vehicles, delayed the introduction of the motor-car.

It was otherwise with the electric telegraph. State-owned in Britain, this device revolutionised news service and gave London direct contact with distant places. Important for business, the telegraph was also significant culturally and politically for the British empire. Expatriated Britons could get news daily and speedily from home. No longer did the imperial government have to wait for weeks and even months—as in the case of the Indian Mutiny—for information about events at remote outposts. Necessary aid and directives could be dispatched promptly. Instead of being the man on the spot with much latitude in handling his problems, the colonial governor became an official at the end of the wire, receiving his orders from Downing Street. Though to obey instructions ceased to be 'an eccentric quality in a governor', the British empire was not entirely without strong-minded proconsuls, among whom Lord Curzon, viceroy of India from 1898 to 1905, was the outstanding example.

The improvements in communications brought trade expansion; new areas were reached and additional resources tapped. The growth of population and the rise in living-standards stimulated the demand for goods. Ships, bunker coal for foreign vessels, and capital goods, especially machinery, ranked high among items of British export. The entrepôt trade remained important. British merchants continued to be middlemen for colonial as well as for a multitude of continental European consumers. However, many factors worried British industrialists and traders. Although there were fluctuations, price levels dropped after 1873, reaching a record low level about 1894–5. The 1886 report of the investigations of a Royal Commission on the Depression of Trade disclosed that Britain had powerful rivals among whom Germany and the United States were the most formidable. New as industrialists and international traders, the nationals of both these countries were unhampered by old traditions. Energetic and ingenious, they had no hesitancy in adopting the latest methods in the making and selling of goods. Unlike British manufacturers, who found it necessary to weigh the advantages of new plants over old, they had no such handicap. More adaptable than the British, American and German salesmen were eager to please customers, and the Germans were especially aided by flexible credit systems. Both Germany and the United States, which had extensive natural resources and large domestic markets, protected new industries with customs tariffs. The dream of Richard Cobden, that the world generally would adopt free trade, failed to materialise. Except for New South Wales and the Cape the self-governing British colonies refused to become free traders. To Canadians a 'National Policy' meant protection for their own industries. Even tiny Victoria sought to industrialise by means of high import-duties. India alone among British dependencies had a tax structure arranged for the benefit of British manufacturers. Though Britain gave no tariff preference to goods from empire countries, in 1896 Canada began to grant preferential treatment to some articles of British manufacture.

British industrialists continued to support free trade until the end of the nineteenth century. A feeble fair-trade movement of the 1880's failed miserably. Britain, in order to sell, had to buy goods from abroad. Because cheap food suited the interests of industrial employers and employees alike, West Indian planters and British farmers received no aid in facing pitiless foreign competition. Political changes and the dominant economic theories were unfavourable to the interests of British and West Indian agriculture.

A change in favour of the West Indies finally occurred after Chamberlain became Colonial Secretary. Realising that British colonial sugar-producers faced unfair competition from the bounty-supported beet sugar of continental Europe, he took action with characteristic vigour. By threatening to impose countervailing duties on bounty-fed sugar he obtained some relief for the depressed West Indies. But later when he took up tariff reform in earnest, Chamberlain offered no help to British farmers.

By the closing decades of the nineteenth century the British landed interests had lost their once-dominant influence in government, and British agriculture no longer led the world in the production of low-cost high-grade produce. New types of wheat from the American fields were superior in milling quality to the British wheat. Year after year the virgin soil of the American prairie produced crops without the use of fertiliser. In England the land had to support three distinct classes—the landowner, the farmer, and the agricultural labourer. Only about 10–15 per cent of the land of England and Wales was farmed by owner-occupier. The typical American wheat farmer had either secured his land free or at a low cost from government or railway companies. He worked in the fields with his hired hands, generally newly arrived immigrants from Europe who toiled long hours at low wages. They were hired only for the busy season; during the rest of the year they might go to the pineries or do the farmer's chores for room and board alone. Knowing that they too could soon become freehold farmers American field hands worked at a tempo unknown in the old world. Moreover, modern machinery drastically reduced production costs of American and Canadian wheat. Improved ways of handling the grain in bulk, and low freight rates, meant cheap food for the British consumer but disaster for the British wheat farmer.

In the 1880's refrigerated cargo vessels began to transport perishable goods over long distances. Thenceforth dairy products and chilled or frozen meat from America and Australasia appeared in increased quantities at reasonable prices in English markets. In the year 1900 New Zealand alone sent four million frozen lamb and sheep carcasses to England. Australasian dairy farmers presently vied with those of Denmark for control of the English market.

Inventions and scientific discoveries benefited the dairy farmer as they had the wheat grower. Stock was improved by careful breeding, fodder and pastures were enriched by suitable fertilisers and grasses, the cream separator and the milk tester revolutionised milk handling, and butter and cheese factories were established. The average farmer of the Antipodes was more progressive than his British confrère who failed to capitalise on his nearness to the world's best dairy market.

In the 1870's nature combined with economic factors to add to the woes of the British farmer. A series of wet seasons damaged crops while a successful labour union movement secured an increase in wages. The steady fall in prices was ruinous to British agriculture. Wheat prices, 1894–5, dropped to the lowest level in 150 years. An easing of the local tax burden and small rent reductions failed to save the situation for the farmers of England and Wales. Between 1870 and 1901 two and a half million acres changed from arable to grass, and the number of farm labourers dropped by about 300,000. While the situation in Scotland approximated to that of England, in Ireland improvements took place toward the end of the century. Chiefly for political reasons, the Irish land problem received much attention. New laws improved the lot of tenant farmers, and large sums of money on easy credit were made available for those who wished to become freeholders. A vigorous Irish agricultural reform movement headed by Sir Horace Plunkett stressed the need for agricultural education, for dairying, and for co-operatives on the Danish model. Danish experts were brought in, and by 1900 the outlook was very promising.

English interest in scientific farming revived late in the century. A board of agriculture was established, a minister of agriculture was appointed, agricultural education was emphasised, the English Agricultural Society was founded, and research was subsidised by the government. But because the average English farmer was intolerant of new ideas results were much delayed. Since imported foodstuffs enabled the importing countries to pay for the purchase of British manufactured goods Britons saw little need for increased agricultural production.

It was otherwise in the colonies, especially in Australasia, where the products of the land had to pay for railway supplies, heavy machinery, and other capital goods. Wool continued to be the mainstay of the economy, but in some colonies, notably New Zealand, meat production and dairying were coming up fast. The North Island of New Zealand, with its equitable climate and adequate rainfall, had many natural advantages for dairy farming. These were intelligently exploited by alert agriculturists who availed themselves of the latest discoveries, established butter and cheese factories, and took full advantage of lessons learned from Danish pioneering in agricultural co-operation. After 1891 the New Zealand government put more farmers on the land, made arrangements for easy rural credit, and assisted in the grading of dairy produce. The dynamic force behind this movement was practical experience rather than abstract theory.

In contrast with the policy at home, the British government actively sought ways to increase production of primary goods in the dependencies. For the benefit of the native population as well as that of the imperial power, special efforts were made to improve economic conditions. Mining was left to private enterprise but the products of the soil were fostered by the government. Support was given to cocoa, coffee, cotton, ground-nuts, sisal, and tea production. The Royal Botanic Gardens at Kew served as headquarters for the entire empire, sending out seeds and seedlings, giving expert advice, and maintaining contacts with botanical institutions in Ceylon, the Straits Settlements, and the West Indies. Experimental stations were established to help both planters and peasants. Hope of profit attracted private capital to the colonies. In Ceylon and Malaya tea and rubber plantations sprang up, communications were improved, and trade furthered. Although some of the newer biological sciences such as genetics and plant pathology were still in their infancy, the British government tried to extend all known scientific benefits to the dependencies.

In the great manufacturing industries—iron, steel, and textiles—Britain had long dominated. But as she spread the industrial revolution by improving communications and exporting capital, machines, scientific ideas, and technological skill her pre-eminence waned and rivals challenged her leadership. This was particularly true in the iron and steel industries. In 1880 the British export was twice that of France, Germany and the United States combined. But during the following decade British iron and steel production stagnated. In Germany and the United States ironmasters applied British inventions and discoveries—which had been ignored by conservative British industrial magnates—and output mounted. British ironmasters, loath to scrap old machines and plants, lost out in competition with foreign rivals who started from scratch. Moreover, Germany and the United States had immense deposits of coal and rich iron ore, and their domestic markets were protected by tariffs. Consequently, before 1900 both the United States and Germany had forged ahead of the United Kingdom in steel production.

Despite sharp competition, the British textile manufacturers held their own. Most of the raw cotton still came from the United States; Australasia supplied vast quantities of excellent wool. Lancashire, centre of British cotton industry, had much political influence, and when a growing cotton industry in India threatened that very important market the cotton manufacturers of Lancashire became ardent crusaders for humanitarian Indian factory laws; they also succeeded in having an excise duty imposed on Indian cotton manufactures which matched the revenue duty levied on imported cotton goods.

The conservatism which had deterred British ironmasters from capitalising on new British ideas in steelmaking also hindered the growth of British chemical industries. The British discovery that dyes could be produced from coal-tar was not appreciated in Britain as quickly as in Germany. A powerful German industry sprang up whose aniline dyes soon drove vegetable dyes from the world market. Since some of the latter were products of the West Indian logwood, the new industry added to the troubles of the distressed British West Indies.

While some British industries had suffered setbacks by 1901, in finance as in shipping Britain continued to hold undisputed first place. The pound sterling based on gold remained the most stable of world currencies, and the Bank of England, 'the Gibraltar' of the financial world, acted as the reserve bank for the British empire. By amalgamation and the growth of branch banking, five English joint-stock banks acquired tremendous power. Although jolted by the failure of the City of Glasgow Bank in 1879 and the collapse of the Barings eleven years later, the British banking system survived strains which caused ruin in other countries; it provided the security necessary for healthy financial operations. Conscious of their responsibility to depositors and investors, the English joint-stock banks were cautious in granting credit and hesitant to operate outside England— of the five only Barclays Bank had overseas subsidiaries. With self-government, imperial control over colonial banks vanished. They welcomed deposits but resented supervision from London where the leading colonial banks still kept reserves. Some banks chartered overseas and established with British capital had their headquarters in London, the centre of commercial, insurance, mining, shipping and other companies whose operations were world-wide. In fact, 'the City' was the capital of a financial domain far more extensive than the British empire.

Chancellors of the Exchequer, Conservative as well as Liberal, followed the principles laid down by Sir Robert Peel and W. E. Gladstone—they were 'trusted and confidential' stewards of the people 'under a sacred obligation' with regard to public expenditures. As a result taxation was light, the national debt declined from £747 millions in 1870 to £635 millions in 1899, and the interest rate was reduced from 3 to 2½ per cent. Thus more money for business ventures became available, and much of it went to the empire. Despite some heavy losses, long-term British foreign investments rose from one to 2½ billion pounds in the period 1870–1900, about one-half of which was invested within the British empire. The profit from these investments, added to the earnings for banking, insurance and shipping services, helped to balance Britain's foreign trade account and contributed materially to the national income.

Financially all dependencies were debtors and all reaped great benefits from their British connections. Colonial loans Acts supplied funds at very low interest rates for public works and relief in African and West Indian dependencies. Since British political control provided assurance of stability the Indian and colonial governments could borrow cheaply in London for harbour and irrigation works, railways, telegraph and telephone construction. In this connection the Colonial Stocks Act, 1900, which made it possible to invest trust funds in colonial securities, conferred substantial benefits on borrowers. Moreover, political security encouraged British investors and business promoters to start industrial developments in many parts of the empire, including India.

The capital outflow generally took the form of sale of capital goods, investment in overseas enterprise, government or private loans, and bank deposits. Irrigation works in India, railways in India and elsewhere, docks, harbours, and public utilities were made possible because money could be obtained cheaply in London; Chamberlain's Colonial Stocks Act was particularly helpful in this respect. Private venture capital went into the chartered companies already mentioned, the establishment of colonial plantations, the exploitation of forests, the opening of mines and other enterprises which promised profit. At the close of the 1880's a good deal of British money was deposited in Australian banks. This proved unfortunate, for the large deposits encouraged speculation and, when the failure of the Barings tightened the London money market, Australian banks discovered the folly of lending long and borrowing short. Deposits were withdrawn and banks were forced to close.

In the financial crises of the early 1890's governments within the British empire pursued varying policies. The Bank of England, aided by the joint-stock banks but with no government help, averted a panic in the Baring crisis. The government of Victoria failed to act and there the banks closed. In New South Wales and New Zealand prompt governmental action saved the situation. Newfoundland, the oldest colony of England and the poorest with self-government, was so hard hit that the local banks closed permanently. In 1894 a Canadian bank, the Bank of Montreal, upon invitation, established a branch in the island. Some Canadian banking institutions, notably the Bank of Montreal and the Bank of Nova Scotia, had become powerful enough to operate outside the Dominion. Scottish influence was strong in Canadian banking. Canada chartered only a few banks which established branches as settlements expanded and need for more banks arose.

Much of the new capital formation in the colonies took place in what has since been labelled the 'public sector'. Australasian and Indian railways were built by the various governments because sorely needed lines held out so little hope of profit that private companies could not be induced to undertake their construction. Newfoundland built a short railway line which with other public utilities were later handed over to a Canadian capitalist almost as a free gift. At the time of the confederation in 1867 the Canadian railways were privately owned. But the Intercolonial Railway linking Halifax with Quebec was constructed and operated by the government, and the Canadian Pacific was built by a company which received extensive aid from the Dominion government. Practical needs rather than theories concerning government ownership shaped the railway policies of Greater Britain.

The trend in currency policies, which ultimately placed all the leading trading nations on a gold basis, led to a decline in commodity prices which by the 'nineties threatened disaster. In the nick of time gold discoveries in Africa, America, and Australia saved the situation. Many of these discoveries were in British lands—all of them stimulated action in the financial world. The resultant up-swing in price levels benefited the economy throughout the British empire.

In addition to capital Britain supplied manpower to the young countries beyond the seas. Between 1870 and 1901 more than six million persons emigrated. This mass migration which relieved unemployment at home provided an immense contribution of young and vigorous producers of wealth to the new lands. Though about 65 per cent of the migrants went to the United States, the hundreds of thousands who chose to remain British subjects settled empty areas and developed the natural resources of Greater Britain. New Zealand's population trebled, Australia's substantially increased, and in Canada the influx of British immigrants offset emigration to the United States.

Migrations of a different type altered the demographic picture in several sections of the empire. Coolies recruited in China helped to build the Canadian Pacific Railway; India provided labourers for railway building in East Africa. The Fiji Islands, like Natal and the West Indies, obtained Indian workers for plantations. The attempt of Queensland planters to bring in Polynesians was thwarted by the combined efforts of Australian labour and British humanitarians. Ultimately the self-governing colonies devised methods to bar orientals. Canada was more hospitable to immigrants from continental Europe than was Australia. Before the end of the century the province of Manitoba had polyglot communities of Germans, Icelanders, Russians, and Ukrainians, but the Australasians maintained their marked preference for English and Scottish immigrants.

Within the British Isles shifts of population intensified old troubles and created new ones. Large movements of peoples from rural to urban areas and from Ireland and Scotland into England brought about serious housing and sanitation problems. An influx of Jewish refugees from Poland and Russia boosted the number of slum dwellers and furthered the growth of sweated industries. Sweating was, however, not confined to English cities. In the early 1890's its prevalence in Melbourne worried Victorian social workers.

The cause of the British farmer's plight was a boon to the industrial labourer. When food prices declined real wages rose. Still, millions lived in squalor and suffered want. A study sponsored by Charles Booth, an English shipowner, of *Life and Labour in London* revealed that in the richest city in the world hundreds of thousands were undernourished and dwelt in quarters unfit for human habitation. Other British cities, especially Glasgow and Liverpool, also had extensive areas where people lived meanly. Nor were the crowded and insanitary housing conditions confined to the cities. Cottars and crofters in Scotland and peasants in Ireland lived in hovels little better than cattle byres. Housing legislation, sponsored principally by the Conservatives, failed to correct the situation. Better results were achieved in the 1890's by the newly established London City Council.

Meanwhile the social conscience of the British people was aroused by efforts inspired by Christian as well as secular humanitarianism. William Booth, founder of the Salvation Army, painted in his *Darkest England* a grim picture of the misery in the great cities and earnestly appealed for relief funds. Both the Salvation Army and Dr Barnardo (who devoted his life to improving the lot of East London waifs) tried to give the destitute, friendless, and homeless children and adults a start in life by helping them to emigrate. An Oxford don, Arnold Toynbee, aroused so much interest in the suffering of the under-privileged that after his death a settlement house bearing his name was founded in East London. The clergy of the Established Church took a more active interest in social problems than they had hitherto done. Missionary societies expanded their activities both within and outside the empire, and shifted from mere denunciation of the evils of idol worship to efforts to improve the mundane existence of the Africans, Asians and South Sea Islanders. The Grenfell medical mission in Labrador showed the need to improve the life of English-speaking inhabitants of that neglected segment of the empire.

Proof of the quickened sympathy for the lot of toilers was evidenced by the public support for match girls and dock labourers in their strikes for higher pay and improved working conditions. The dockers were ably led by John Burns, Tom Mann, and Ben Tillett; they received valuable assistance from Cardinal Manning and substantial material aid from Australian labour. Their strike succeeded, and their leaders then compelled the conservative Trades Union Congress to admit representatives of unskilled workers to its deliberations. Thus the New Unionism came into existence and the tempo of labour agitation was noticeably quickened.

By legislation of the 1870's the status of the British trade unions was much improved and factory laws were consolidated and extended. Conservatives and Liberals alike courted the labour vote; the eradication of illiteracy and the appearance of cheap, popular newspapers opened new ways to reach the common people. This was appreciated by middle-class intellectuals who were impressed with the gospel of Karl Marx. A coterie of the most gifted among them founded the Fabian Society which hoped to reconstruct society 'in accordance with the highest moral possibilities' by a process of 'gradualness'. For this purpose the Society published a large number of tracts which discussed pressing economic and social questions. The Social Democratic Federation and the Independent Labour party were more definitely Marxist in outlook. But none of these organisations attracted a large following among the masses whose real leaders cherished social ideologies based on Christian traditions. The governing classes took cognisance of the spread of socialistic doctrines and the growth of socialism on the Continent; they were also disturbed by the flight of labour from the land and the complete dependence of workers on daily wages. To remedy this situation it was proposed to obtain—with public assistance—allotments or smallholdings for labourers. Laws were passed to further these aims, but they failed to achieve much influence on British economic and social conditions.

Although in social legislation Britain lagged behind Germany and Australasia, ideas for alleviating social ills and ending wasteful economic warfare were not wanting. Political theorists stressed consideration for human dignity and self-respect; practical statesmen advocated old-age pensions and government arbitration in labour disputes. But the passions aroused over Irish home rule and the renewed attention to imperial expansion diverted men's minds from 'the condition of England question'. Young overseas communities, unhampered by the restraining influences of an old society, could devote themselves more wholeheartedly to making 'the gift of life more valuable and the men more worthy of the gift'. In the language of one of their leaders, William Pember Reeves, in his book on *State Experiments in Australia and New Zealand* (1902), the peoples of Australasia looked 'upon their colonies as co-operative societies of which they, men and women, are shareholders, while the governments are elective boards of directors'. Though they borrowed many ideas from

Britain and some from America 'their needs, their aims, their methods and their reasoning were chiefly the result of their environment and local experiences'. Breathing 'the free air of a virgin country' but trained to respect order, the Australasians, with Britain as their banker and defender, could concentrate on local problems. They passed comprehensive factory laws limiting the hours of labour and fixing a standard minimum wage; they eliminated sweating; established wages boards and compulsory arbitration in labour disputes; and inaugurated old-age pensions. They broke up large landed properties thus providing land seekers with farms, arranged easy rural credit, and promoted co-operatives. The rise in price levels after 1895 and the easier credit conditions facilitated experiments and attracted more and more immigrants.

Social legislation had been entrusted in Canada to the provinces, but they lagged behind Australia in tackling social problems. The subsistence farming in Quebec, the Canadian homestead Act, the opportunities for employment in lumber camps and railway construction, the nearness to the United States which drew job-hunters, the lag in industrial development and an aversion to government interference, all combined to create a Canadian climate of opinion on social and economic issues far different from that which prevailed in Australasia. In South Africa and the West Indies the colonists had problems aplenty but neither the means nor the will to face them. This was also true of India where suffering millions had been taught to endure patiently all earthly misery and to hope for better things through rebirth.

In the field of education the changes were many and the progress uneven. Nationalistic aspirations, racial and religious diversities, lack of financial support, and disagreements over aims and methods hindered advance in man's search for knowledge. As might be expected, educational opportunities multiplied most rapidly in Britain and in the self-governing colonies of Australasia and North America. Elementary education was made compulsory and free, though only in Australasia was it wholly secularised. Tax-supported secondary schools, universities and university colleges were founded both in Britain and overseas. In Africa and India Christian missions continued to play an important role in education on every level. Among the crown colonies only Ceylon made serious efforts to organise compulsory education for all children. While Oxford and Cambridge provided curricula patterns and often teaching staffs for the new universities, administration frequently followed the federal model of the University of London.

In both Great and Greater Britain warfare raged between the secularists and the advocates of religion as the basis for all education. The success of German education in which natural science was emphasised brought conflict between proponents of the traditional classical studies and reformers who urged adoption of the German system. Whether free education for all should end at the elementary school level and whether women should be admitted to the universities supplied further topics for hair-splitting academic disputes, with the traditionalists steadily losing ground, especially in the colonies.

With the passing of time democratic ideas concerning equality of educational opportunity won wider acceptance. Joseph Chamberlain, who on so many topics voiced the opinion of true progressives, favoured a Jacob's ladder in education enabling 'the poorest amongst us, if he has but the ability,...to rise to the greatest height of culture'. The leading traditionalist, Benjamin Jowett, Master of Balliol, distrusted new philosophical systems, enthusiasm, and the emotional approach. He warned tutors 'to refrain from *any* kind of proselytism', but in harmony with modern views he welcomed the reduction of 'the estrangement of class from class'. To Jowett the main purpose of education was to develop in the student 'the sense of power which comes from steady working'. He scorned the aristocratic idlers who sauntered through Eton and Oxford and imagined themselves superior beings. His motto was a challenging, 'Cease to drift', and under him 'Balliol became the nursery of Bishops, Viceroys, and Cabinet Ministers'.

Jowett's influence extended to the universities of the empire though his admonition 'Cease to drift' was more applicable to students at Oxford than to colonials who faced in life a constant challenge to modify what had been transplanted and to build anew in recently founded communities. English and Scottish influence was strong in the universities of Greater Britain, but before the end of the century some followed the German lead in curricula construction, and those of Canada could not escape 'contamination' from south of the border. However, the province of Quebec formed a notable exception; there French-speaking Canadians moulded their educational system on that of France, the homeland which had long ignored them.

Despite the growing materialistic and secular approach of intellectuals, the average man in the new democratic age continued to be a religious as well as a political being. Issues rooted in religious differences frequently aroused angry discussion in press and legislative halls at home and overseas. Religious tests for university degrees were abolished (except, of course, in theology); religious equality became general; the Church of England was disestablished in Ireland and in nearly all of the West Indian islands; in the early 1890's a demand arose for its disestablishment in Wales. Efforts to secularise English elementary education failed; in some of the Canadian provinces denominational control over education had constitutional safeguards; the abolition of denominational schools in Manitoba aroused sharp political controversy. Denominational colleges sprang up in Australian and Canadian universities. While these colleges did not acquire the academic status of those at Oxford and Cambridge, they clearly indicated religious cleavages within the university community. In Britain debates over Irish home rule were coloured by religious bias. In the provinces of Ontario and Quebec and in Australian Victoria religion was a live political issue. In England attendance at church and chapel might be declining, but long after the retirement of Gladstone the non-conformists formed a distinct political force. Interest in religion continued strong: vast contributions were made to Christian missions in distant lands, Londoners by the thousand flocked to hear the Baptist preacher C. H. Spurgeon, the Bible was *the* best seller among books, and the Sermon on the Mount was more potent than the Communist Manifesto in determining the social attitudes of British labourers.

With the growing literacy the newspaper-reading public vastly increased. A special type of cheap paper which appealed, as Lord Bryce put it in his *Modern Democracies*, to the 'uninstructed, uncritical, and unfastidious mass of readers' gained vogue. *The Times*, under its great editor John Thaddeus Delane, had shunned vulgar commercial methods, avoided party bias, and sought to instruct and elevate public opinion. Delane's successors departed from some of his most salutary ideals. With the issue of Irish home rule *The Times* became morbidly partisan, and when it was disclosed that documents discrediting Irish leaders and printed in *The Times* were forgeries the paper lost its commanding position in British journalism. Even before that catastrophe *The Times* had ceased to appeal to those who liked spicy news, brightly and cleverly presented. Some of the new type of journalists, notably W. T. Stead, used their talents to arouse public sentiment for much-needed social reforms; others, and they were the successful ones, were mainly interested in profit. Chief among the latter was Alfred Harmsworth (later Lord Northcliffe) whose achievement is one of the amazing success stories of the 1890's. He and the journalists of his school appealed to emotion rather than reason; they magnified trivialities, gloated over scandals, played up gossip and treated rumours as facts. The growing tension among the powers provided material for sensational headlines; the cloak of patriotism concealed vulgar commercialism and hatred was fostered in the minds of millions. Lord Salisbury might sneer that Harmsworth's *Daily Mail* was written by 'office boys for office boys', but by 1901 its daily circulation reached a million copies and it had become an important moulder of public opinion.

Among the leading overseas newspapers were the Toronto *Globe* and the Melbourne *Age*, both strongly partisan in politics. Although on the editorial page they stressed the special interests of their local areas, news from Great Britain was featured prominently in their columns, thereby keeping green the memories of the old homeland.

The growing interest in outdoor sport had both social and imperial importance. Cricket and football were inexpensive and gave young men a chance to win distinction without regard to race or social class. Between 1870 and 1901 these games became very popular, and regional and intra-imperial contests brought about friendly contacts between scattered units of the realm. British standards of sportsmanship spread even to remote corners of the empire.

Many of the colonial political leaders of the nineteenth century were born in Britain. Prominent among them were Sir Henry Parkes of New South Wales and Richard John Seddon of New Zealand. Because they as well as several of their colleagues had risen from the ranks of labour, their British origin was probably more of a hindrance than a help to good understanding between the colonies and Britain. In colonial as in American politics a humble social background rated as an asset whereas in England those who had been educated at the famous public schools and national universities had an advantage even in working-class constituencies. The condescending attitude of British society toward visiting colonials was a serious obstacle to a union of hearts between Great and Greater Britain.

Although the progress of political and social reform in Britain and the growth in the colonies of social amenities and wealth narrowed the gap between the two societies, the divergencies were still wide and very real. Adventurous, aggressive men and women had broken home ties and founded new communities in far-off regions. They rejected Whitehall dominance over their government and economic life; they defeated efforts to saddle them with an established church; basically egalitarian, they resented aristocratic pretensions. British sojourners in the colonies were as aghast at colonial society as were Charles Dickens and Mrs Trollope at American social life. It was Robert Lowe's eleven years in Australia which made him a bitter opponent of political reform in Britain, and Governor Sir Arthur Gordon's experience with colonial assemblies in New Brunswick and New Zealand convinced him that colonial self-government was a mistake. In 1872 Disraeli lamented that in granting autonomy to the colonies Britain had not retained control over crown land and customs tariff nor imposed the stipulation that in a war the colonies should be obligated to aid the mother-country. The true spirit of overseas Britain was appreciated more fully by his rival, Gladstone, who, as a follower of Edmund Burke, insisted that 'freedom and voluntaryism' should govern the relations between Britain and her colonies, and who proclaimed his firm belief that if given freedom they would of their own volition aid Britain generously in times of trial. This faith was splendidly vindicated during the Anglo-Boer War when thousands of volunteers from Canada and Australasia fought for Britain.

Colonial self-government advanced and became more meaningful between 1870–1901. At the close of this period the Commonwealth of Australia stood ready to assume its place side by side with the Dominion of Canada as a federal state with immense future possibilities. Politically the overseas communities progressed rapidly toward a sovereign status, but culturally and economically they remained dependencies. In art, education, and literature British patterns dominated. The self-confidence colonists displayed in subduing the wilderness was not matched in cultural fields. Their society was too new for that, and aspiring writers such as Katherine Mansfield had to seek careers in Britain. The United States attracted talented Canadians. Only one colonial novel, *The Story of an African Farm*, won recognition outside its region of origin, and its author, Olive Schreiner, was the daughter of a German Lutheran missionary to Bechuanaland.

In March 1894, upon retiring as British Prime Minister, Gladstone deplored the fact that 'the world of today is not the world in which I was bred and trained, and have principally lived'. He was quite right, though in many fields his own reforms—the 'opening of windows' of which he was so proud—combined with those supported by Disraeli had produced the changes. Rapidly shifting economic and social conditions and the growth of political democracy compelled both Liberal and Conservative governments to depart from John Stuart Mill's theory of individualism and to sanction interference with vested interests. The owners of factories, farms, and ships had to accept government supervision; parents were required to send their children to school; householders were forced to observe sanitary regulations. The national government owned the telegraph and telephone systems and municipalities operated public utilities. The good life for which people yearned could materialise only if the power of the state was enlisted to remove abuses and protect the weak against the strong.

In 1901 the principle that government should be *by* the people and function *for* the people was more widely recognised overseas than in Britain. Antipodean colonies accepted the creed, to quote Lord Bryce's book again, that 'Wealth produced by the toil of the Many must not be allowed to accumulate in the hands of the Few'. At home Stanley Jevons, T. H. Green, and other theorists of the 1880's turned the tables on Mill by emphasising that the promotion of 'human development in its richest diversity' could succeed only if the state provided the individual with opportunities for such development. The principle here enunciated had by the end of the nineteenth century been applied more extensively in the Australasian colonies than in Britain for the simple reason that the people who controlled their governments desired to improve economic and social conditions. As individuals they wanted the good life which could be obtained only with government assistance. These small societies became laboratories for legislative experiments which were keenly watched by the outside world. Thus did Britain's daughter-nations alter age-old conceptions of the functions of the state.

The wide acceptance of Darwin's theory of evolution created a climate of opinion in intellectual circles far different from that in which Gladstone 'was bred and trained'. Bravely the old statesman sought to stem the swelling tide of materialism and scepticism by affirming his unshakable faith in 'The Impregnable Rock of Holy Scripture'. Support came from an unusually able political opponent, Arthur James Balfour, who in 1895 published a clever polemical essay, *The Foundations of Belief*. But the virus of unbelief was spreading. As British labourers deserted the chapel for the labour temple they became more and more impregnated with the tenets of materialism.

Britain had advanced towards political democracy and, with the great increase of educational opportunity, the foundations had been laid for a social democracy of the type found in the colonies. But few outward signs of the latter process were discernible by 1901. Britain's old social structure was being constantly undermined, but social pageantry was still unchanged; the stately city mansions and country palaces of the aristocrats were well staffed; peers of recent creation were eager to adopt the standards established by those of ancient lineage; the lower classes were politely deferential; glitter and gold abounded. Despite this, a few statesmen were uneasy. Foreign competition grew keener, and the perils of diplomatic isolation could not be ignored. Among those who espied breakers ahead was Joseph Chamberlain. He was so disturbed that he considered the possibility of a new tariff policy, and he advocated a triple alliance—Britain, Germany and the United States. But neither his own countrymen nor the prospective allies fell in with the alliance proposal.

Both Great and Greater Britain were affected by the currents of nationalism which grew steadily stronger toward the close of the nineteenth century. A Secretary for Scotland was appointed, Wales obtained a national university, and the Irish national movement broadened to include culture and language. Signs of an Indian renaissance multiplied, and the ancient races of the vast Asian sub-continent grew politically restive. Although Australasians had not yet developed a genuine 'at homeness', they became more self-assertive. The debtor-creditor relationship between them and Britain created friction. In common with Canada they might delight in the privileges of being daughters in their 'mother's house' but they were also insistent upon recognition as complete mistresses of their own.

In Canada the growth of nationalism was hindered by sharp division between French-speaking and English-speaking Canadians. The former held that as the first settlers in the land they and they alone were the true Canadians. They cherished their language and their Roman Catholic religion. The latter was a barrier between them and the people of Ontario where the powerful Association of Orangemen kept alive religious animosities imported from Ireland. However, *habitans* of Quebec, Orangemen of Ontario, and descendants of the loyalists who had abandoned homes in the United States to remain British subjects were united in a determination not to have their country swallowed up by its powerful neighbour. They wanted to be Canadians and to prove that cultural differences would not prevent the development of a Canadian national state. Their Prime Minister, Sir Wilfrid Laurier, might speak eloquently to British audiences of his pride in being a British subject, but he showed time and again that first and foremost he was a Canadian, a true son of the land to which in 1665 his ancestors had come.

In 1901 white South Africa was politically united by the British annexation the previous year of the two Boer republics, the Transvaal and the Orange Free State. It was hoped that this annexation would result in the establishment on the African sub-continent of a new nation resembling the Dominion of Canada. But even before Briton and Boer were locked in the mortal combat of the South African War signs had appeared heralding the rise of a new national movement rooted in the soil of South Africa, a movement centred about the memory of forbears who had settled the land, migrated to the interior to found their own states, defeated fierce tribes, and steadfastly refused to become Anglicised. Unlike the French-speaking Canadians, the Afrikaaners of South Africa were anxious to cut cultural bonds with the homeland, the Netherlands, and to elevate the status of their spoken language, Afrikaans. They hoped that this language and the traditions built up through generations of conflict and toil would form the bases for a European South African nation.

Meanwhile the sands in the hour-glass were running out for the old Queen. Her reign had lasted longer and been filled with more changes than any other in British history. She had been out of sympathy with the democratic ideals which won wide acceptance during her era. She had never visited any of her dominions overseas. In most respects the spirit animating their peoples was not only foreign but was actually repugnant to her. Still, she had been an inspiration to her subjects; she was the outward symbol of the unity of a far-flung empire. Her unflinching courage, stern devotion to duty, and great strength of character had set a pattern of conduct and provided encouragement and hope in times of trial. When black tidings came thick and fast from South Africa, word went out that the Queen was not discouraged. This well publicised message had a bracing effect all around. Since her accession to the throne the British empire had grown immensely. The Queen had welcomed territorial annexations and resented the abandonment of outposts whether in Africa or in Asia. The idea of home rule for Ireland she absolutely detested. But by approving the grant of self-government to overseas colonies Queen Victoria furthered the service of Britain as a founder of nations. Her place in history is comparable to that of England's Gloriana, Queen Elizabeth I.

CHAPTER XV

INDIA, 1840–1905

IN tracing Indian developments in the second half of the nineteenth century it is important to balance carefully the Indian and British sides of the scales. And the British side was not British only, but European and western as well, for in much of their activity the British were har- bingers of general western culture rather than the purveyors of Anglo- Saxondom. In the past there has been a tendency to regard the significant features of Victorian India as the completion of the British dominion, and the gradual spread of British administrative techniques and public works, of western cultural ideas and western humane values. The groups who secured the decision to introduce western institutions into India believed that Indian institutions were effete and Indian traditional ideas inferior if not positively harmful. They looked to a gradual replacement of things Indian by things European, though they did not all clothe their expecta- tion in the vivid imagery of Macaulay. The first school of writers on British India were fascinated by the spectacle of the rise of British power, the most striking and lasting, as they believed, in the long procession of Indian empire. There followed, with James Mill's *History* as a bridge, those who thought that the true significance of British Indian history consisted in the introduction of western institutions. Both schools were absorbed in the British *raj*; while the first emphasised the *raj*, the second emphasised the British. Neither, along with most contemporary admini- strators, thought that India herself had much to offer towards her own future. When Indians seemed slow in accepting things western it was put down to darkness of mind or obstinacy and the men of the Panjab school developed an administrative puritanism which toiled without hope of reward (from India), determined to do India good in spite of herself.

With the rise of the nationalist movement in the twentieth century this perspective radically changed. It was realised not only that India had a great deal to do with her future but that the forces moulding Indian opinion were by no means wholly western. Indian ideas, discounted by all but a few in Victorian times, were as important as western ones, and Indian opinion as the views of Whitehall or Simla. The study of the development of Indian opinion and society, virtually 'put on ice' at the end of the eighteenth century, was resumed and seen to be as significant as that of British political or administrative measures. Indian history was seen to be Indian once more. Its significance lay not only in what the British did in India but in how the Indians reacted. This process has yet far to go, at the hands of both British and Indian historians, before a true balance is achieved, but it is from this point of view that this brief survey is attempted. We first see a flowing tide of western influence stirring the apparently stagnant waters of traditional India; we then witness those waters stirring in their turn to form in the twentieth century a composite current of unanalysable proportions flowing towards an unknown destination. It is the study of what the Englishman did and what the Indian thought about it.

It was only when inter-Indian wars deepened into anarchy at the end of the eighteenth century and the French menace reappeared with Napoleon that both Company and British government agreed that hegemony was the necessary condition of continued trade. The final decision was taken in 1815 and supremacy achieved in 1818. Thus far British rule in India, despite parliament's insistence that it should be a just rule, was a rule for trade. Neither glory nor welfare was a primary object.

Coincidentally with the final establishment of supremacy the Company felt the force of the free trade and humanitarian winds then ranging Britain. It thus came about that just before hegemony was completed private traders and missionaries were admitted to India. There was to be free trade in both goods and ideas. This political decision to control India and this ending of monopoly set up a ferment of ideas and opinions, which in turn involved further decisions. It was necessary to exclude rivals from the north-west as well as from overseas. Beyond Afghanistan lay Persia and beyond Persia Russia. From these considerations sprang the north-west policy of successive Indian and British governments. Within India itself it was necessary to organise an administration on a stable basis. This involved a recasting of the revenue system and an intensive study of old land systems upon which the revenue mainly depended. It involved regularising relations with the Indian princes who still controlled more than half the area of India and a third of its population. And along with the administration of the people, it involved the question of the policy to be pursued towards the ideas and traditions of the people.

In the decade 1820–30 the second great decision of nineteenth-century British Indian policy was worked out. The pressure groups concerned with it in Britain were the Utilitarians and the Evangelicals; they were supported by the first sign of articulate public opinion in India in the form of Ram Mohan Roy and his friends in Calcutta. The decision to introduce British institutions and western knowledge into India (the latter through the medium of the English language) meant that the East India Company's dominion was no longer to be old Mughal empire writ large, the concept of Warren Hastings and the old school of Anglo-Indians. It meant the inauguration of a cultural revolution and its purpose was the eventual westernisation of India. The means were characteristically moderate and British. Indian institutions, with few exceptions, were not to be openly attacked or brushed aside. They were to be matched by British counterparts as it were and the people left free to opt between them. The decision was implemented by the Whig government of the reform era in Britain and by Lord William Bentinck in India.

A third decision dates from this period, though it will not be found in any enactment or statement of policy. It was taken for granted rather than argued about. It was the economic subordination of India to Britain. In the days of the Company there was no thought of putting obstacles in the way of British trade in the possible interests of India. To this general attitude two factors must be added. Free-trade theories were spreading their influence, making it possible to argue that the non-regulation of trade in India conformed with economic doctrine and so was in the best interests of India herself. Secondly, the industrial revolution had developed to a point where cotton technology, taking its raw product from America, could sell the finished article more cheaply in India than the India hand-weaver using his own raw materials. India became a market for British industry in a way it had not been before. Both theory and interest dictated that non-interference should continue; and technology ruled that the age-old Indian weaving industry should be undermined.

It is the effects of these decisions and developments which we see being worked out in the years succeeding 1840. On the political side a new all-India government had been developed, bearing a recognisable resemblance to its Mughal predecessor. Slowly and diffidently western ideas were introduced, caution ruling that the changes should be peripheral rather than fundamental. Internationally India had again become a single entity and one of the Asian powers. Her government was foreign, as in the sixteenth century, but whereas in the sixteenth century foreign influence came from the north-west, in the nineteenth it came from overseas. Both powers were expansionist but in opposite directions, the Mughal empire extending steadily from north-west to south-east, the British from south-east to north-west. But the foreign policy of the new Indian state was affected by factors external to itself in a way in which that of the Mughal empire never was. Frontier and foreign policies were influenced by the power-politics of Europe; Russian moves in the Balkans or eastern Europe as well as in central Asia could modify the action of the Indian government.

The second major result was a social and cultural revolution. By a series of measures, not specifically designed for the purpose, the old dominant classes were undermined, and the rise of a new class, whose interests were intertwined with the new regime, was promoted. At the same time a cultural revolution was launched by means of the new westernising educational policy. The two revolutions were interlinked, for the social changes pushed into the background the old classes who clung to the old culture and provided at the same time in the new class a social soil in which western culture could take root. By these measures the seed-bed and the seed of modern India were produced.

The third result was a period of economic colonialism when India was regarded as a source of raw materials for the industries of Britain and a market for British goods. Whereas the second result was the cause of most of the goodwill and influence which Britain has enjoyed in modern India, this third caused much of the criticism and resentment felt by the politically minded classes in the twentieth century.

The period may be divided into three phases. The first, to 1858, covers the completion of the Company's dominion and includes the Mutiny and its suppression. The second, which may be called the heyday of imperialism in the sense that there was no practical or theoretical rival to British rule, lasts to 1880. The third, from 1880 to 1905, a period during which the British power in India apparently reached its zenith, is more significant for the development of forces which were eventually to replace it. In dealing with the first period it will be convenient to recall the political background against which the various developments are set. The Indian government was far from being a mere puppet manipulated on cabinet strings, but it was nevertheless a subordinate agency. A Governor-General could annex a province and inform Whitehall afterwards but he could also be and was in fact on occasion recalled. Local discretion was large, but in the main Indian policy was London's policy. The period opens with the reforming Whig administration of Lord Melbourne in its last stage of decrepitude. Its nominee Lord Auckland reflected, by comparison with his predecessor Lord William Bentinck, the declining Whig energy. Intending to be a reforming Governor-General he had become entangled in Afghan affairs at the joint behest of his political advisers and Lord Palmerston. His retirement synchronised with the advent of Sir Robert Peel's Conservative government, and his successor was Wellington's President of the Board of Control, Lord Ellenborough. Ellenborough found himself confronted with the Afghan disaster of 1841–2 from which, after some hesitation, he extricated the Company with skill. But his exuberant imagination led him to the annexation of Sind in very doubtful circumstances while his autocratic temper aroused so much opposition that the Directors exercised their power of recall for the last time after he had ruled India for little more than two years. Peel's cabinet softened the blow by appointing as his successor his brother-in-law, the first Lord Hardinge. He was a Waterloo veteran, a cautious soldier-statesman who had been Secretary-at-War and Chief Secretary of Ireland, and was chosen partly in view of the threatening Sikh situation. He carried through the first Sikh war and retired when the Whigs were again in office under Lord John Russell. Though it was his military achievement which clung to his name, in fact he carried on the internal policy of his predecessors. The new conservatism of Peel derived from liberal Tories like Canning and Huskisson in the 'twenties rather than from Wellington or Eldon. There was no serious party cleavage on Indian internal affairs and that which existed on its external policy was linked with the debate on British foreign policy in general. So the suppression of suttee—the burning of widows on the funeral pyres of their husbands—and of infanticide in Indian states was promoted, the educational developments continued unchecked. In addition the great irrigation system of the Ganges was commenced and the first plans made for an Indian railway system.

Hardinge's successor was the Earl of Dalhousie, a Peelite who had made his name as Vice-President of the Board of Trade under Gladstone in Peel's cabinet, where he wrestled strenuously to control the railway boom of the 1840's. Only thirty-six years old, he was endowed with great energy and will-power, and he dominated India for the next eight years. He combined an imperious temper with his enthusiasm, but did not add much human sympathy to his imagination. Such a man, who wore himself out with his labours, and possessed an artist's sensibility to any check or criticism, might easily have clashed with the Home authorities. That this did not happen was due to two factors. One was that his outlook accorded with the general spirit of early Victorian England. He embodied its restless energy, its belief in material progress and in the superiority of western civilisation. The other was the confused political situation in Britain at the time. The break-up of the Conservative party in 1846 left Britain virtually in the hands of a central corps of Whigs and Peelites with Radicals and Protectionists skirmishing on the wings. Four ministries were in office during Dalhousie's tenure and all were inclined to leave their capable lieutenant in India to his own devices. Might he not reorganise *them* if he came back too full of energy? Dalhousie went to India in 1848 as an apostle of western progress which he hoped to intensify. The rebellion of Mul Raj in the Panjab diverted his attention and led to its annexation, but he was not in intention an annexationist. He was led into this course by his very belief in western progress. Western administration, he believed, was immeasurably better for the people than Indian, and therefore the more Indian states that could be absorbed the better. This belief in westernism explains the other activities of his government which are so often overlooked in criticism of his imperialism and arguments about the doctrine of lapse. (The doctrine of lapse claimed that paramountcy involved British recognition of heirs of princely states. In the absence of direct natural heirs Hindu law allowed adoption. The doctrine of lapse insisted that adoption must be recognised by the supreme government; otherwise the state would pass by 'lapse' to the Company.) It was he who planned the railway system of India and introduced the telegraph; who with Sir Charles Wood planned the first Indian universities; who proposed to place Indians on the new Legislative Council. It has been said that his administrative monument was the Panjab and the Panjab school and his political legacy the mutiny; more important than either were the foundations he laid for twentieth-century India.

Against this background of solid support in Britain and naïve belief in western moral superiority, in material progress and the virtues of commercial enterprise we can set the events of these eighteen years. In the realm of power the policy was one of security. At no time was the government of India consciously aggressive. That is, it never desired more than the security of the natural Indian frontiers. But it periodically suffered from nerves about possible dangers, and tended to over-insure against exaggerated perils. This mentality was later described by the great Lord Salisbury as the proposal to occupy the moon in order to guard against an attack from Mars. The first Afghan entanglement of 1838–42 was partly created by this neurosis as well as by the exigencies of Lord Palmerston's Russian policy and by downright bad judgement. The second Afghan war, the third Burman war (1885–6) and Curzon's invasion of Tibet were all cases of aggressions by the over-fearful. In Burma the bogey was the French, elsewhere the Russians. In the case of the second Burman war (1852) and the Tibetan campaign we see another basic motive at work as well—the desire for markets which it was believed benighted regimes were denying to honest traders.

The result of the Afghan adventure convinced the authorities that India had not the resources to dominate the Iranian plateau. For the next generation the policy was to rely on the weakness of the powers in that area and to use a friendly Afghanistan as a buffer state. It was only when nervousness again overcame common sense in the 1870's that this policy was reversed. In historical geopolitics the security of India has depended primarily on the existence of a strong north Indian power which could effectively dominate the sub-continent. It has been when this condition was lacking that the major successful incursions into India have occurred, like those of the Kushans, the Huns and the Turks, of Taimur, of Babur and the British. Even Chinghiz Khan knocked in vain at the door of the determined Tughluq Delhi sultanate. This condition satisfied, security next required a friendly or controlled Indonesia to the east and Iranian plateau to the north-west. Historically Indonesia never proved threatening. On the north-western plateau has existed historic Iran with the central Asian regions beyond, from which came periodical incursions of Turks and Mongols. Central Asia may be compared to a reservoir fed from hidden springs which periodically and unpredictably overflowed to flood the adjacent regions. Since India could not dominate the Iranian plateau, her interest lay in the existence of a strong Iranian power, which would provide an adequate political dam against the flooding of the central Asian reservoir. The natural balance of power, which the Company vainly sought within India in the late eighteenth century, was in fact to be found outside. It lay between a north Indian and an Iranian power centre, whose understood balance would enable them to withstand pressure from the west, north and east. This condition had been satisfied in the sixteenth and seventeenth centuries, when the Mughal Indian empire had been balanced by the Safavid dynasty of Persia. In the eighteenth century both powers collapsed. The Company provided a revival of the Indian power in the nineteenth century, and its position was strengthened in the east by the virtual British control through sea-power of the Dutch rulers of the East Indies. In the north-west, however, Iran remained weak and the first Afghan war showed the perils of attempting to control the plateau from India. Beyond Iran the Khanates of Turkestan were in obvious decay. But as their strength drained away, Russia began to take their place as the replenishing force of the reservoir. Indian policy in the north-west, apart from European considerations, depended upon current readings of the gauge in this central Asian reservoir.

Within India itself power-politics took the form of completion of dominion. The motives of security, of commerce and even of humanism can be noticed, but the dominant one was that of security. The Afghan war involved the use of independent Sind as an avenue of approach, since it was not desired to depend wholly on the Panjab route in the unsettled conditions following the death of its ruler Ranjit Singh in 1839. The Amirs of Sind were divided, incompetent and obscurantist. They formed a splinter of the former Afghan Durrani monarchy and had themselves no great claim to legality. Their country invited development. The temptation to secure a good frontier was strong. The territory was annexed in 1843, the shabby glories of Miani providing Ellenborough with some compensation for his withdrawal from Afghanistan. Thereafter it was ruled with rude vigour for some years by Sir Charles Napier, its conqueror. It became a part of the Presidency of Bombay and the newly acquired Karachi the port for the Panjab and a model city. The Panjab was acquired as the result of two wars in 1845–6 and 1848–9. The first campaign was precipitated by the anarchy which supervened on the death of Ranjit Singh in 1839. The fine Sikh army dissolved into committee-run factions manipulated by ruthless and ambitious chiefs. There were four rulers in six years and the army was eventually encouraged by the Regency Council to cross the Sutlej in the hope that the British would draw its sting. In the first settlement the method of a protected state was tried with a reduced army and a Regency Council headed by Henry Lawrence. In 1848 a revolt in Multan was allowed to gather strength throughout the hot weather and was then crushed in a series of bloody battles. The British had little more generalship than the Sikhs, but they had reinforcements. On this occasion Dalhousie decided on annexation, which he carried out before referring to London. His reasons were the apparent irreconcilability of the Sikh *sardars*—the word widely used in northern

India, especially by Sikhs, to mean nobles, leaders, gentry—and the necessity of safeguarding the frontier on the north-west. The fact that the Sikhs had been an unloved ruling minority reduced the danger of conspiracy within, a danger which was further reduced by John Lawrence's policy of encouraging the peasant at the expense of the *sardar* and promoting material improvement. Irrigation washed away revenge. The Panjab was won by the sword and retained by the spade. At the mutiny crisis the Muslims could be relied upon to check any Sikh attempt at revolt, and the Sikhs enjoyed frustrating the Mughal revival in Delhi. It may be said that the British did everything with the Panjab except integrate its people. The third measure of completion was the annexation of Burma. Lower Burma with Rangoon was annexed by Dalhousie in 1852 after a model campaign in a war provoked in about equal proportions by Burman obtuseness and British commercial brashness. This was the real beginning of British Burma for here were the Burman people as distinct from the hill tribes of Arakan and Tenasserim and here were the rice areas which were to give modern Burma its wealth and its problems. Upper Burma was annexed in 1886 from the crazy King Theebaw. The motive for this final act was fear of French influence and a desire to counterbalance their threatened intervention in Siam. The Burmans differed both by race and culture from the Indian peoples and were never assimilated. The Indian administrative system, applied with such care by Dalhousie's Chief Commissioner Phayre, proved a major misfit.

Within India itself the government had to deal with the remnants of earlier authorities. Their military power had been effectually curbed by the rise of British control, but many of them retained a traditional or tribal appeal. First among them was the Mughal emperor himself at Delhi: Wellesley, while providing the blind Shah Alam with comfort and honour in 1803, had carefully avoided committing himself either to allegiance or repudiation. Later official generations gradually, in Charles Metcalfe's words, 'renounced their former allegiance to the House of Taimur'. The Mughal became an expensive nuisance. The sovereignty of the Crown in India was declared in the Charter Act of 1833; the recognition of the Mughal imperial status was gradually whittled away until in 1856 the heir was induced to agree to vacate the palace and renounce the imperial title on his father's death. The case of the princes was somewhat different, for they still controlled nearly half of the country and one-third of the people. The paramountcy of the Company was assumed rather than proclaimed. But the princes were not integrated in the new system. They were placed in 'subordinate isolation', secluded estates as it were, where the old life could continue behind diplomatic walls untouched by the rush of western progress without. The difficulty of this policy lay in the fact that the new world and Europeans could not in fact be kept out, while the princes, shorn of ambition by British restraint and of fear for themselves by British support, ceased to interest themselves in government. This created a contrast between British and princely standards which posed a moral dilemma to the ruling power. How could non-interference be reconciled with princely behaviour and British public standards, or interference with British obligations? The first attempt to resolve this dilemma was made by Dalhousie with his annexation policy. Dalhousie believed that British administration was immensely better than Indian and that annexation was desirable whenever possible. While blind neither to ancient rights nor to modern dangers, he shared to the full the self-confidence of his generation. One side of his policy was the doctrine of lapse, which enabled him to take over several Hindu states including extensive Nagpur and influential Satara in the absence of direct heirs. Another was the belief that misgovernment justified acquisition, which secured the Panjab by conquest, Berar by negotiation and Oudh by annexation. In eight years princely India was reduced by a quarter in area and population; then the process was abruptly halted by the Mutiny.

The government itself attained its highest degree of centralisation at this time. The Charter Act of 1833 created a Governor-General of India in place of Fort William in Bengal. Legislative power was concentrated in Calcutta, its sole distinction from the executive being the presence of an additional Member of Council for legislative purposes. (The first 'Law member' was Thomas Babington Macaulay.) In practice the other presidencies became local agencies; though they retained their own forces these were overshadowed by the size and prestige of the Bengal army. The Civil Service was similarly divided, with Bengal enjoying a corresponding eminence. In 1853 this service was thrown open to competition, with a resulting rise in general standards though not in exceptional talent. The most interesting development was the institution of a separate legislative council in 1853 which, though official and judicial in composition, had some representative character and quickly claimed a freedom of speech which won it the name of the Little Parliament.

The third theme of this period is that of western influence. The movement given official recognition by Lord William Bentinck and his advisers went steadily forward. It had three main aspects. The first, largely unintentional in its results, but an essential part of the whole process, was the breaking down of the old governing and privileged classes. The second was the policy of introducing western education and ideas, with institutions allied to them, and the third a policy of public works which involved western techniques and a western-trained class for their maintenance. The first set of measures displaced and rendered powerless the classes who clung to the old order, political and cultural; the second and third both injected western ideas into the country and created conditions for a class imbibing them. The rise of modern India has depended not only upon the entry of western ideas into India but upon their absorption by a specially created class.

The social revolution, too little regarded but fundamental for an understanding of modern India, began in the time of Cornwallis in the late eighteenth century. An outward sign was the exclusion of Indians from higher government service. The Charter Act of 1793 reserved all administrative posts worth more than £500 a year to covenanted servants of the presidency concerned; no Indians were covenanted servants. The repositories of Indian political tradition were thus thrown back upon themselves or into Indian state service. Still more important was the series of land settlements, beginning with the Permanent Settlement and continuing beyond the Mutiny. This work grew increasingly accurate and mindful of local conditions. It was informed by a desire to define and delimit, to do justice to peasant and landlord and to preserve if possible the village communities. But the improving spirit of the age would creep in, giving a twist which ruined the old landed aristocracy and extinguished the village communities. There was at first a general tendency, through ignorance, to over-assess. The penalty of unpunctual or incomplete payment was the un-Indian one of dispossession, legalised in the hated Sales law. By these means the character of the whole landed class in Bengal and Behar was changed and much land changed hands elsewhere. This process was reinforced by the widespread resumption of rent-free tenures, extensively practised in northern and western India up to the Mutiny. R. M. Bird and J. Thomason carried this on in the North-Western provinces, and the Inam Commission in Bombay. These lands were granted for services rendered, for educational and religious purposes; while in many cases the grants had been forgotten or their purpose abused, the result of wholesale confiscation was to ruin an influential class which supported the old culture and religion. By deprivation of office, by loss of land and public esteem, this class was driven into a back-water of the national life, there to stagnate amidst memories of past glories.

Their place was to be supplied by a new class filled with new thoughts. But first the thoughts had to be made available. The policy of imparting western knowledge through the medium of English was launched by Bentinck and Macaulay in 1835. During the next twenty years a network of schools spread over the country. In 1853 Sir Charles Wood's dispatch led to the establishment of a grant-in-aid system which enabled private schools and colleges to be established, gave the educational system form and crowned it with the first three universities, opened in 1857. Alongside government activity in this direction must be noticed that of Christian missionaries, whose outstanding leader was Alexander Duff of Calcutta and greatest monument the Madras Christian College. Along with western education went western law. In 1861 the new penal code, based on English law, finally came into force. Perhaps even more important was the introduction of English procedure and legal assumptions in the Company's courts. Western concepts were absorbed by the new lawyers as it were *ambulando*. Hindu and Muslim private laws were preserved, but doubtful cases, of which there were many, were decided on the principles of English equity. Much of the western influence in the courts was subliminal, and perhaps all the more effective for that. The tale of governmental western influence was completed by the replacement of Persian by English as the language of the courts and official business. This provided an urgent reason for learning English, and learning English meant attending the new colleges and absorbing western ideas. Government servants, lawyers, merchants and professional men all over India needed English for their work and you could not learn English, any more than you could learn Persian or French, without tasting, however slightly, the flavour of its culture. The process was helped on by professional education establishments such as the Medical College in Calcutta, where dissection involved the breaking of high-caste rules, and Dalhousie's engineering college at Roorkee. Apart from direct evangelism, perhaps more a hindrance than a help, mission activity in promoting schools, hospitals and orphanages furthered the process in the countryside.

The remaining aspect of western influence was the policy of public works. Here was something which could be pursued without regard to vexing questions of caste and culture, of ethics and local custom. The moral reformer and the upholder of tradition, the innovator and the nervous realist, could compromise on bricks and mortar. This development is specially associated with Dalhousie. The first activity was that of communications. Road-building began systematically after 1818. The seal was set on it, as it were, by Dalhousie's completion of the Grand Trunk Road to Peshawar, in which he took an almost lyrical pleasure, and the cutting of the Simla hill-road to the Tibetan border. For several months in 1850 he governed India from the mountain fastness of Chini, 200 miles from the plains. Roads were the prelude to railways. The first steps towards their introduction were taken by Lord Hardinge, but their planning as a system was the work of Dalhousie. Equipped with the experience of grappling with the English railway boom of the 1840's, he set about planning on a comprehensive scale. With the support of Sir Charles Wood in London his Railway minute of 1853 became the basis of an integrated system of rail communication which was to have incalculable consequences for the country. In the absence of good rivers outside Bengal and the northern plain, railways provided a system of social and economic arteries through which the life-blood of the new India could pour. The third form of public works was irrigation. The first step in this direction was the restoration of the Mughal and Tughluq Canal from the upper Jumna to Delhi in 1820. Major early works were the Grand Anicut two miles across the river Cauvery in the south (1835–6) and the Ganges

Canal, completed by Dalhousie in 1854. These measures between them began to knit India together into a physical unity unknown before and to make the first serious inroads on the tyranny of nature, with its periodical flail of famine, over the Indian peasant.

The Indian response to these influences was significant. Philanthropists' hopes of an early collapse of the Indian social and religious systems were disappointed. But the small group which gathered round the remarkable figure of Ram Mohan Roy, who died in 1833 while on a visit to England, in Bengal welcomed western thought as well as western works. The *Brahmo Samaj*, founded by him in 1828, and supported by the Tagore family, began the process of assimilation on the religious and social plane. Bodies like the Landholders Association and the British India Association pushed the work into the political sphere. The ideas of this group were to percolate, by means of the new press, personal contacts, the new means of communication, and the Bengali migration to the north in government service, all through the growing class of people attached to the new activities of the government.

The developments here mentioned acquired a faster tempo, a greater sense of urgency, as it were, in the time of Dalhousie. He was an embodiment of the improving Victorian, too anxious to drive forward to notice the jolts given to the car of progress by the stones of custom and prejudice. His record was one of ceaseless activity: in politics, annexations; in material matters, public works—the Public Works Department was created by him in 1853—and irrigation; in the world of ideas, western education. There was a general feeling of confidence and security.

Upon this decorously improving world burst the mutiny of the Bengal army, which is generally dated from the Meerut outbreak of 10 May, or the seizure of Delhi on 11 May 1857. Originating from a caste grievance provoked by administrative bungling, it developed into a general rising of the Bengal army backed by agrarian and religious movements in a number of districts. Both Mughal and Maratha sentiment was stirred with a cross-current of Muslim as distinct from imperial sentiment. In a military sense the situation was saved by the defence of Lucknow, the investment of Delhi against greatly superior forces and the firmness of John Lawrence in the Panjab. Politically the government owed much to the loyalty of the Sikhs and the princes. Notable features were the shock caused by the outbreak and the intensity of the feelings aroused on both sides with their respective legacies of memory and bitterness. When we come to analyse the forces at work, it is clear that the soldiers were not moved to such lengths by an isolated caste grievance. The soldier and, to some extent, the country as a whole were suffering from a divided soul, and the extremity of their behaviour was in proportion to the degree of tension from which they suffered. To the soldier the choice seemed to be loyalty and loss of caste and self-respect—but the word self-respect does not express the full depth of meaning involved, which is expressed in the untranslatable word *'izzat* (عزت)—or mutiny and almost certain death in view of the quickly ascertained implacability of the British. Only in some such way can the sudden mutinies following professions of loyalty be accounted for. The suspicions of the soldier had a general background; specific sources of discontent, like the General Service Enlistment Act and the annexation of Oudh, do not in themselves explain the nature of the outbreak any more than does the greased cartridges incident, which was merely the spark to the powder train. In other circumstances the incident would have been explained and forgotten but, as it was, the more the authorities tried to explain and redress, the deeper grew the soldier's conviction of ill-intent. The general feeling of the country, which the soldier sensed through his family connections, arose from the impact of the new measures on traditional society. Both the new measures and the new thought challenged traditional habits and their underlying assumptions. In various ways caste taboos were threatened—by the abolition of suttee; allowing Christians to inherit their share of the family property; the caste-defying attitude of the advanced class in Calcutta—while the new ideas of equality and moral obligation—spread through the law as well as the colleges—ran quite contrary to the inequality and privilege of Brahminism. Orthodox society, still under Brahmin influence, was affronted, and found a convenient scapegoat in the activities of some Christian missionaries. Political Hindu India had given up the struggle and accepted the Company as a new irresistible Mughal; it was orthodox India that felt itself threatened. So Hindu India was disturbed in its most vital part, that of religion and custom. The Sepoy revolt arose out of this unrest, bringing it to a focus. The mutiny as a whole was essentially a convulsive effort by Indian conservatism to put the clock back before it was too late. It is noticeable that wherever there was a rebel success, there was a harking back to traditional models, Mughal or Maratha. The new westernised class, the ancestors of the modern nationalists, were everywhere on the side of the British; to the rebels they were enemies of the old order.

The Muslims, who were eventually blamed for the outbreak more than the Hindus, had their own grievances. Here, too, the politicians had given up. But orthodox Islam had long taken exception to the British occupation, and expressed itself in the militant *Wahabi* movement. Orthodox sentiment objected to much in the western innovations. The objection was more on moral and customary than on doctrinal grounds, for while on fundamental ideas Islam was nearer to the Christian west than Hinduism, its horror of innovation and change was greater. The *maulvis*, unlike the more subtle Brahmins, kept themselves unspotted from any taint of western thought and dwelt in a medieval world of scholasticism and textual disputation. India, for them, was a *Dar-ul-harb*, or house of war, where revolt was morally justifiable. Thus, while they did not originate the rising, they took greater advantage of it than the Hindu pundits—men like the Maulvi of Fyzabad—and so incurred the odium of the chief responsibility for the revolt. In addition to this there was nostalgia for the empire in which both the British and the Marathas had supplanted them. Delhi with its Mughal pensionary was its natural centre and that is why its seizure proved so important a rebel success.

The violence of the British reaction had important consequences and demands explanation. The cases of Neill in the Ganges valley and Cooper in the Panjab are only the extreme examples of the incidents which fill the other side of the medal of mutiny horrors. This spirit was compounded of shock at such violence from so unexpected a quarter, which induced a feeling of total insecurity, and fear bred by the sudden awareness of isolation amidst an immense and hostile population. The result of these deeds on both sides was a scar in Indo-British relations which it needed two generations to heal.

To sum up, the Mutiny was not inevitable, but it was made possible as the result of the impact of the west upon traditional India. More caution might have prevented an explosion until the emotional danger-point had passed, but nothing could have prevented tension when forces so powerful and dissimilar met. Conservative India made its protest and then settled down to come to terms with the new world; in the process a degree of passion was generated which for many years hindered the growth of understanding on both sides.

The next twenty years may be described as the heyday of imperialism. The British government was not only all-powerful but was seen to be so. It not only possessed the initiative in the world of ideas, but was acknowledged to have it. There seemed to be some justification for the confidence expressed by Sir W. W. Hunter in the book *India of the Queen* which he wrote at the end of this period.

The first points to be noticed are the external effects of the Mutiny. At first there was a cry of vengeance, taking such forms as the expulsion of the inhabitants of Delhi from their city and a proposal to demolish the great mosque of Shah Jahan. When this had been stifled by Canning and John Lawrence in India backed by the authorities in Britain, the dominant feeling was 'never again'. A balanced judgement gradually recovered its sway. The theme of physical precautions gave place to the theme of amendment and reform. The lost touch with the people must be restored. Evidence of the two trends can be seen in most of the early post-mutiny measures. The Company was abolished and the Crown became suzerain in India. The army was reorganised, Panjabis, Sikhs, Pathans and Gurkhas being brought in to replace the Brahmins of the Ganges valley. The artillery arm was abolished except for some mountain batteries. At the same time the relationship of the British officers with their men was drawn so close that an *esprit de corps* was established which was carried over into independence. The proportion of British troops was increased. Communications were improved and in particular the construction of the railway network was expedited.

The next series of measures showed more clearly the desire to avoid the mistakes of the past, and the belief that these arose mainly from too great a disregard of Indian tradition and too little knowledge of the public mind. The princes had been regarded by Dalhousie as corrupt survivors of an obsolete age. Their general loyalty during the Mutiny caused Canning to call them 'breakwaters in the storm'. Their attitude, in fact, prolonged their existence for nearly a century. The doctrine of lapse was given up; states were guaranteed their integrity and given *sanads* or deeds of recognition. The policy of 'subordinate isolation' under the Company's rule became that of subordinate partnership under the Crown. This policy was steadily pursued and unfolded in obedience to its logic until 1914, when the outburst of princely loyalty on the outbreak of the first World War proclaimed its triumphant success. Its essential problem was to reconcile princely and British-Indian standards of administration. What had been desirable in subordinates became essential in partners. The solution was to find a common basic policy and to educate the princes to that end. The common basis was enlightened despotism. To liberal minds the difficult word was despotism but for the princes the important one was enlightenment. They were brought from sixteenth-century India to eighteenth-century Europe, and the method was encouragement and western education. They were treated with a new deference and sympathy. Lord Mayo started the first of the Chiefs' colleges—Mayo College, Ajmer, in 1869, and Aitcheson College, Lahore. Lord Ripon restored Mysore to the old ruling family in 1881. Lord Lytton projected an Indian peerage. Lord Dufferin created the Imperial Service Corps in which princely cadets received up-to-date military training. The results were substantial. While for some princes western culture led to Parisian nights, others, and these some of the most important, took their ruling duties seriously. By 1905 Maratha Gwalior and Baroda, Rajput Bikanir, with Mysore and Travancore in the south, could all claim comparison with British Indian standards and in some respects had gone beyond them.

The doctrine of religious neutrality was underlined in the Queen's Proclamation on taking over the government of India in 1858. It had in fact never been abandoned but now all appearance of encroachment was eschewed. Officials kept carefully apart from evangelistic Christian activity. The most important effect was a reluctance to interfere in social matters which continued even when a demand for interference had grown up in the dynamic westernised class.

The last measure of reform was an attempt to secure closer touch with Indian opinion. The best official opinion agreed with the most authoritative Indian voice, that of Sayyid Ahmad Khan, in considering the aloofness of officials from the people and officers from their men as a major cause of the catastrophe. From this arose the dual policy of Indianisation of the services and consultation. The first major steps in Indianisation had been taken by Lord William Bentinck when two grades of judges were thrown open to Indians. From 1853 Indians were eligible to compete in the Civil Service examination, though the first Indian entrant, Satyendra Nath Tagore, did not join till 1863 and conditions prevented more than a trickle entering by this means. But the judicial services up to High Court level were opened to Indians and the provincial civil services, from which one-sixth of the all-India Civil Service came to be recruited, were almost entirely indianised. The underskin of an indigenous administration thus began to take shape while the outer sheath remained almost entirely British. Consultation took the form of the development of legislative councils. The all-British Legislative Council of 1853 was reformed in 1861 to admit Indians under the guise of non-officials; there were three on the first Council. Councils were established in Madras and Bombay and thereafter extended to the other major provinces. These councils had been described as 'committees by means of which the executive government obtained advice and help in legislation'. They were, in fact, expressions of the *durbar* principle of Indian tradition, where the ruler hears the opinions of his counsellors and then takes his decision. But it was a *durbar* in western dress, and this made it easier to insert later within it the western body of representation and responsibility. The *durbar* principle received its final expression in the Morley–Minto reforms of 1909. Before then, however, the principle of representation had been smuggled in, as it were, by the Indian Councils Act of 1892 under the guise of 'recommendation for nomination'—a procedure by which various public bodies recommended individuals for nomination by the government to the several Legislative Councils, and the nomination followed immediately.

The Mutiny gave a shock to the whole texture of Anglo-Indian relations. Not only was there the inevitable *post-mortem* about its causes, there was a searching discussion of the ends and means of the British government in India. British confidence in the superiority of western civilisation and the inevitability of progress was greater than ever. The inferences of the new knowledge of Indian art and philosophy and Sanskrit literature had hardly yet impinged on the general intellectual consciousness. The moral urge which, together with this confidence, secured the westernising policy in the 1830's was no less strong. But there was greater caution in the implementation of the policy and less optimism about its reception. Whereas the early reformers thought of the Indians as bound by superstition, tradition and priestcraft, only awaiting the light of reason to emerge from darkness, the new generation was inclined to consider them unresponsive or incorrigible. Only a few could perceive the ferment already working within Indian life. A sign of this change of attitude was the substitution of the *durbar* method of consultation for the western system of self-government (proclaimed by Macaulay in 1833 and still accepted by Dalhousie) as the principle of political development.

The tension between the determination to advance on western lines and pessimism about the Indian response produced the peculiar features of the Panjab school of administrators. Dalhousie was its founder and Henry Lawrence its high priest, but it was John Lawrence who gave it its permanent form. The gospel of hard work and hard living, the devotion to duty, the fierce zeal for public works had behind them the assumption that the Indian must be improved even if he would not improve himself. There was a Loyolan ring about the early Panjab officers—'to toil and not to seek for rest, to labour and not to ask for any reward...'. Since the Indian mind seemed so largely closed, attention was diverted to the material aspects of the west in the form of public works. Education formed a bridge between matter and spirit, since self-interest could be used as a motive for attending schools of western knowledge. This general attitude was widespread in India. The formula was: ignore Indian apathy, avoid open clashes with tradition, press on with public works and education. The general attitude was that of trustees of an estate who considered themselves likely to be in charge for the foreseeable future. Many indeed doubted if the ward would ever be able to take over. It was this attitude, so different from that of Elphinstone, Bentinck and the 1830 reformers, which the rising class of Indian nationalist politicians found in control of the administration in the 1880's and which raised suspicions in their minds that were not finally exorcised until 1947.

It is true that the Indian government continued to look for Indian collaborators with more or less zeal. But they continued to lament that they could not be found. This was because the government persisted in looking in the wrong direction. In princely India the education of the princes had been begun and results began to show. In British India it was hoped that the same class would come forward. This its members would not do because they had no entry to the only type of service they were willing to undertake. They were denied commissions in the army, were unqualified to sit for the I.C.S. examination in London and had hardly any opportunities of sitting on public bodies. They were wedded to the old culture; if western education could not provide at least a utilitarian appeal they would have none of it. Lord Lytton endeavoured to meet this situation in 1879 with his Statutory Civil Service to which admission was by nomination and from which one-sixth of the I.C.S. was to be recruited. But this, like so many of Lytton's measures, was imaginative but unsuccessful.

The conception of India as an estate to be improved had various aspects. If it was short-sighted it was honest; if it was matter-of-fact it was comprehensive. It embraced both the tenants, as it were, or Indians, and the landlords or British. In the former case there was the reform of the finances, carried out by James Wilson and Samuel Laing between 1858 and 1862. India was given a modern financial structure with annual budgets, income tax and a tariff system. This was followed up in the 1860's by permission to borrow for public works. Public works was the religion of the mid-Victorian Indian administrator. The two most notable achievements were railways and irrigation. In 1857 there were 200 miles of track open to traffic; by 1880 India possessed an integrated railway system, the first in Asia; by 1905 the railway mileage was 33,000. Irrigation was well under way before the Mutiny. It was pushed ahead steadily to the culminating achievement of the Sukkur barrage in Sind. By the close of the British period one-fifth of the cultivable area was irrigated land—32·5 million acres in 1940. A third achievement was the conquest of famine, whose periodical devastations had been virtually irremediable for lack of food surpluses and transport facilities. The Orissa famine of 1866 carried off nearly a million lives because the Bengal authorities failed to act in time. The great famine of 1876–8 was attacked energetically and gave rise to the Famine Commission of 1880 and the Famine Code of 1883. Thenceforth, until 1943, by the use of railways, sea transport, and a considered pattern of procedure, famines of food became famines of work. Famine no longer caused starvation but only loss of agricultural work, food being provided by government agency. Alongside these public works, for the reason already mentioned, may be placed education. The landmarks were the Hunter Commission of 1882 and Curzon's reform of Calcutta University. Education was heavily over-weighted at the college and high-school level at the expense of primary education, but by the end of the century the country was covered with a network of schools and universities which were the nurseries of the rising westernised class.

While these measures may be said to have benefited the Indian 'tenants', the British 'landlords' were not forgotten. When the Indian trade was thrown open in 1813 it was expected that private enterprise would develop the potential Indian market without government assistance. But it soon became apparent that there were formidable practical obstacles to such a process in the size of the country and the lack of good communications. Neither markets nor raw materials could be easily tapped. British capital available from 1815 onwards found better prospects in Europe and in the Americas than in India. The Indian trade was left largely to those already engaged in it, whose capital was the savings of government servants and their own profits. Not until a series of enabling measures had dealt with the transport difficulty was there a large-scale development. The most important of these was railways, which have already been dealt with. After the Mutiny security combined with the profit motive to promote their construction and at the same time secured capital in England.

Between 1855 and 1870 half the total investment of £150 millions of British capital in India was spent on railways. While the government kept the planning and ownership of railways in its own hands, it brought in private promoters for construction and operation. The close-up view of Indian conditions gained by these people encouraged a realisation of the possibilities opened up by railways. Railway building was the turning-point of modern Indian economic development. Upon the hinge of railway reconstruction turned the door of modern Indian industrialism. Railways attracted capital in the first place and capital then took advantage of the new conditions they created.

The most important industry to be affected was cotton. Cotton goods from Lancashire (using American cotton) had already ruined the old highly skilled hand-weaving cotton industry. Railways completed this process by enabling Lancashire goods to penetrate farther inland. But they also made possible a local mill industry which took shape in western India; its centres were in Bombay and Ahmadabad and the initiative came from enterprising Parsis and Hindus. The value of railways here was in transporting raw cotton from the Deccan to the mills and in distributing the finished product. The first successful mill was opened in Bombay in 1853; major developments followed the opening of the Empress Mill in Nagpur in 1887 by J. N. Tata. Some of the cotton profits were in turn used by Tata in developing the iron industry. His sons founded the Tata Iron and Steel Company in Behar in 1907, producing the first iron in 1911 and steel in 1914. Long before this railways had made possible the large-scale development of the coal industry. There was prospecting in the time of Warren Hastings and from 1814 operations were carried on with success; the output in 1846 was 91,000 tons. Railways made distribution possible and themselves took one-third of the output. Production reached six million tons in 1900 and 38 millions in 1938, making India self-supporting in one of the vital components of heavy industry. Jute was first exported to Dundee in Scotland in 1838. The loss of Russian supplies during the Crimean War created a boom which led to the establishment of the Indian jute industry around Calcutta about 1859. In addition to these there were the plantation industries, the most important of which were tea and coffee. At first the Assam tea plant was regarded as a weed and it was only the difficulty of ousting the Indian plant for the Chinese which led to the former's cultivation. From 1850 the industry expanded rapidly. The 10 million pounds of Indian tea imported by Britain in 1869 against ten times the amount of Chinese tea had grown to 137 million pounds in 1900 against 24 million pounds from China. The career of coffee in the south was more chequered but nevertheless substantial.

All these activities provided an outlet for British enterprise in various ways. The cotton and later the iron industry was built up mainly with Indian capital, but it relied extensively on British managers and technicians. The coal and plantation industries were entirely British in capital and management, while in the case of jute the ownership was about half and half. The gap between the provision of capital in Britain and the sale of the article in India was supplied by the 'managing agency', organisations which 'undertook' for financiers and producers by providing the necessary local knowledge and facilities. They may be described as local financial transformers. These again were British.

The scale as well as the nature of these operations was bound to provoke a reaction in the Indian mind. The widespread assumption that Indians were looking on in apathy so long as their religious feelings were not touched was erroneous from the start. None of the activities described, from teaching English in a college to building bridges or operating coal mines, could be carried on without skilled Indian assistance. By 1860 there was a significant segment of the population committed to the new era by skill and by employment. Non-involvement was a luxury for the rich, with the penalty of idleness. The first response came from the quarter one would naturally expect in India. There was a traditional instinctive reaction of dislike of the new, which the orthodox always found was upsetting to caste because it tended to disturb the intricate network of relationships which the caste system involves. This conservative reaction found vent in the explosion of the Mutiny. Thereafter Indian society as a whole realised that in some way it must come to terms with the new world. The question was, how? There was the group of Bengali intellectuals, inspired by Derozio and encouraged by the nationalist Hare and the missionary Duff, who advocated a complete break with the past, to the point, in some cases, of taking the religion of the west along with its learning and its science. This died away in the 1840's but there followed a series of movements which all aimed, in various ways, at meeting the western cultural challenge. The *Brahmo Samaj*, founded in 1828 by Ram Mohan Roy, combined a traditional theism with a tincture of Christian ethics; the *Arya Samaj*, founded in the Panjab in 1875, was a militant body which looked back in Protestant fashion to the primitive faith of the Vedas. Ramkrishna and Vivekananda (whose appearance at the World Congress of Faiths at Chicago in 1893 was the first overt sign of the vitality of Indian religious thought) combined the Indian doctrine of realisation with missionary methods of good works. Amongst the Muslims there were the *Wahabis* and other groups who sought renewal through a return to primitive Islam.

All these groups had a measure of success but none of them captured the country as a whole. In particular they failed to appeal to more than a section of the rising westernised class, attached to the new era by training, occupation and conviction. The reason was that all these movements, except perhaps the first, looked on things western with a degree of disapproval. They could not therefore meet the inner need of the new class, for whom some acceptance of the west was a postulate. Their need was for a reconciliation of old and new, not by excusing the new, but by excusing the old. This reconciliation was provided by the ideas of the Bengali thinker Ram Mohan Roy (*c.* 1770–1833) for the Hindus and by Sir Sayyid Ahmad Khan (1816–98), founder of the Aligarh College in 1875, for the Muslims. Both found a connecting link between the respective old and new systems in the principle of reason which provided a criterion both for the rejection of old abuses and for the acceptance of new truth. In this way the new classes could accept the present while avoiding a painful sense of treason to the past.

One thing they lacked in the new circumstances: a sense of religious devotion. This came from an unexpected quarter: in the religion of the secular west—nationalism. Similar emotional needs in different continents bred similar results. As no Indian nation existed in fact, these classes proceeded to create one. The genius of men like Bankim Chandra Chatterji conceived of India as a personality in a way quite different from the past. A literary figment became a political myth; the myth in turn generated a purpose and political programme. This compromise was not permanent, but it sufficed for the needs of the moment. The new classes lived in two worlds, traditional patterns prevailing in the private sphere and western concepts in public life. Sooner or later the one had to impinge on the other, but the time was not yet. This duality produced many strange results evoking jibes and sneers from unsympathetic observers. But it was the embarrassment, not of the man with clothes that won't fit, but of the animal in the process of changing its skin. Unknown to the home authorities, and unperceived by the olympian official class in India itself, the subordinates who amused them were forming themselves into a dynamic minority able to take over the country at three generations' remove.

The last twenty-five years of the period saw the British empire in India attain the height of its power and prestige. What may be called the period of imperial India was ushered in by the pageantry of Lytton's Durbar of 1876, when the Queen was proclaimed Empress, and closed by that of Lord Curzon in 1902. It had the outward splendour of a late summer's afternoon, but to the discerning the shadows were perceptibly lengthening beyond the glare of the imperial sun. The benevolent despotism of post-Mutiny India had impressive results to show, but it was beginning to be challenged. As a system and as a political concept it had reached a dead end; from creative activity men were increasingly turning to self-admiration. The future lay elsewhere.

At this time India became a centre of party controversy in Britain as it had not been since the time of Warren Hastings. The issues were foreign policy, where India was involved in the Russian policy of Disraeli, and democratic self-government, which Gladstone accepted as the ultimate goal of Indian development during his second ministry. The former for a time made Indian policy a matter of party passion involving the resignation of two viceroys; the latter made Lord Ripon's government (1880–4) the most controversial between Bentinck's (1828–35) and Lord Irwin's (later Halifax) in 1926–31. Both these issues were removed by the mid-1880's, the one because the parties in Britain reached tacit agreement on foreign policy, and the other because the Irish Home Rule split in 1886 and the growth of Liberal imperialism rendered the radical wing of the Liberal party almost powerless. Ripon was liberal-minded but indecisive; Dufferin was impressive but apathetic; while Elgin, the last Liberal appointment of the century, might have belonged to either party or none. The imperial caravan moved on with its economic and educational development, its ripening administration, its British-manned higher services, its conviction of paternal superiority and of indefinite Indian tutelage. But the first impression had been made on its stately order and by its side appeared the first signs of an alternative team of drivers.

Through the mid-century, when faith in an Indian response to western influence was declining, the ideal of the 1830's had been kept alive by radicals and humanitarians like Cobden, Bright and Joseph Hume. But it was not until Gladstone had entered his more advanced phase that any attempt was made to realise it. In 1880, at the outset of his second ministry, two decisions of the greatest import for the future were taken. One was to commence the development of representative institutions in India and the other to adopt western models for the purpose. By these decisions the 'durbar' plan of Indian constitutional development was virtually ruled out. Morley in 1906 and after found that any extension of the representative principle would have to take a western form because of the measures already in force. The same decision involved the handing of the future to the new westernised class because they were the only people who wanted these forms or in any way understood them. Their imperfect working of them arose from their imperfect understanding, and their friction with the government from the contrast between representation and some degree of democracy below and authoritarianism above. Officials as a class contrasted the manners and tact of the old classes with the gaucheries of the new; they still looked in the main for self-government from above and resented that which began to be forced on them from below.

Before 1880 there was little municipal self-government except in Bombay. Ripon's constructive achievement was the creation of local representative institutions in the form of municipal committees and district boards. A half to two-thirds of their numbers were elected by local taxpayers. They were endowed with considerable powers in the fields of education, sanitation, public works and health; they had power to levy octroi, terminal, property and other duties; they could elect non-official chairmen. His successor Dufferin followed this up by proposing the extension of the elective principle to the provincial and all-India legislative councils. This was achieved in 1892 (after five years of discussion) by the Indian Councils Act, under the pseudonym of 'recommendation for nomination'. This Act, though microscopic in its immediate effects, was important in that it enabled a small group of able new Indians to enter the national public arena. Once there they formed a focus for Indian attention and a rallying point for the new Indian public opinion. Once there, they began by personal contact the conversion of British officials from the general belief in Ripon's time that 'no one but an Englishman can do anything'. The most distinguished of their number was the Poona Brahmin Gokhale, who in this way became a national figure.

These measures would have had little effect if there had not been a class of Indians ready to take advantage of them. In parts of India British administration had now existed for upwards of a century. Western education through the English medium had been developing for nearly fifty years. Governmental activities had steadily expanded, calling for large numbers of Indians with some acquaintance with western knowledge and techniques. The railways, the telegraphs, the public works, the schools and colleges, the law courts are examples of these. Most of the posts available were subordinate. But some carried real responsibility, and the professions like law, teaching and medicine offered independent careers for qualified persons. There was also a westernised class of monied men such as the Parsis of Bombay and some of the *zamindars* of Bengal. These people, through the fact of a common ideological background and a common connection with an exotic administration, were developing an all-India consciousness which found expression in attachment to a still largely notional Indian nation. Nationalism existed in their minds so it was necessary to create an Indian nation. The first stage was a demand for representation which came from the organised groups of Bengal landholders. The British India Association put forward the first Indian plan for a constitution in 1852.

The movement gathered force under the joint stimuli of encouragement and irritation. Under the first heading came the European discovery of Sanskrit literature and philosophy, beginning with Sir William Jones' discovery of the kinship of Sanskrit with other Aryan languages. A long succession of scholars like Prinsep, Mill, H. H. Wilson, Deussen and Max Müller made thinking Europeans aware of Sanskrit literature and impressed them with its range and depth. There followed a rediscovery of Buddhism, of the achievements of the Mauryas and the Guptas, and a romantic portrayal of the Rajputs by James Tod. Thus Hindu India found favour in European learned circles just at the moment when the westernised Indian was looking for a past to be proud of. This appreciation of things Hindu spread, with the work of men like James Fergusson and Alexander Cunningham, to architecture and later to the arts of sculpture and painting. While scholars encouraged the new Indian to be proud of his past, a group of liberal-minded Englishmen encouraged them to be confident in their future. Men like Sir Evan Cotton, Sir William Wedderburn, A. S. Hume and Sir David Yule—the first three of whom were Presidents of Congress between 1885 and 1900—encouraged the leaders of the new class to think in terms of eventual self-government on western lines. The achievements of their ancestors were a guarantee of the potentialities of their descendants.

Then there was the stimulus of irritation. One source of this was race feeling and discrimination which tended to grow as the British lost touch with the aristocrats, whom they had formerly treated as equals, and as the commercial element among them increased with the growth of British enterprise. The Mutiny encouraged a process which was already in progress by adding the emotions of fear and resentment to the predisposing causes. This feeling was more pronounced with the half-educated westerners, but it was these who had most personal touch with the new Indians and whose rudeness was the more galling. Too many Europeans were still looking to the old landed classes for possible colleagues and resenting the presence of the new educated as an intrusion of upstarts. The effect of this prejudice on a sensitive people was profound though difficult to define. It created a climate of opinion in which suspicions and resentments could easily grow. Its blending with the pre-existing admiration for things western held by this class created that divided mind which so puzzled so many western observers in the next fifty years.

It was in this mental atmosphere that more specific grievances acquired a sharper form than might otherwise have been the case. There was the virtual exclusion of Indians from high executive office, owing to the difficulty of sitting for the I.C.S. examination in London. The lowering of the age-limit in 1879 was interpreted as a deliberate step to make things more difficult. In the economic field there was a belief in discrimination in favour of Lancashire, created by the abolition of the cotton tariff in 1879 and confirmed by the cotton excise of 1895. In the political field there was resentment at the press restrictions imposed by the Vernacular Press Act of 1879 and the use of Indian troops (at Indian expense) in such adventures as the second Afghan war and their dispatch to Cyprus in 1878. The final goad was the Ilbert Bill of 1883, which proposed to make Europeans amenable to certain courts presided over by Indian judges. The outcry of non-official Europeans, who went to the length of proposing to kidnap the Viceroy and who were supported covertly by many officials, led the indecisive Ripon to agree to a compromise which satisfied neither side. The new Indians felt themselves challenged in the one field of the law where they had made a considerable advance. It was in these circumstances that, with liberal European support, the Indian National Congress came to birth in 1885.

During the first few years of its existence the Congress was cautious and moderate. It was aware of the smallness of its constituency: Lord Dufferin described its supporters as a 'microscopic minority', unaware that they were, in fact, the creative minority who were to lead the whole people of India. Nevertheless, it provided an all-India forum for political discussion, it evolved a representative and democratic machinery, and it gradually captured the attention of the country. Its annual sessions became the principal non-official event. In Surendranath Bunnerjea, G. K. Gokhale and B. G. Tilak it threw up leaders of eminence and, in the latter, one who was not bound by ties of imitative Gladstonian liberalism. He experimented with appeals to orthodox sentiment and local Maratha sentiment on the one hand and with direct action methods on the other. For a time the Congress supported, if rather gingerly, the reforms of Curzon, but it was his partition of Bengal in 1905 against popular remonstrance which turned a middle-class movement into a semi-popular party. Here was an issue which appealed to every Bengali, which could bring westernised Indian and Hindu Bengali into passionate understanding. The public meetings and demonstrations, the boycott of foreign cloth and the *swadeshi* movement—which promoted the use of home-made and the exclusion of foreign goods—and the outer fringe of terrorist activity under religious sanction made the national movement a popular one in Bengal. Gandhi was to complete the process for India at large.

While the underskin of the new India was thus developing, the outer skin of empire was apparently more glossy than ever. Matters of politics and administration absorbed the civil servants who bemused with their glitter the historians of the day. Frontier policy, with its Forward school, led to the delimitation of the Durand Line in 1893 and the tribal campaigns of the end of the century. Famine policy was codified and developed; the rupee was devalued and education extended. Kipling sang his Te Deum to the imperial Atlas. This phase of Indian history was fittingly summed up in the viceroyalty of Lord Curzon from 1898 to 1905. He had integrity, vigour, imagination and a sense of history. He was proud of his country as of himself, he served India in his own manner with unremitting toil. In everything administrative he excelled; in everything requiring any understanding he lacked and failed. He could relieve famine and extend irrigation, build railways and encourage commerce, reorganise the frontier and overhaul the educational machine, exhort princes and uphold racial justice. He could preach the gospel of imperial service and match precept with practice. But he could not understand the working of the new Indian mind, appreciate its feelings or sympathise with its aspirations. He was unaware that his moral lectures struck Indians as odious, his dealings with Calcutta University as an attempt to restrict autonomy in the one sphere in which Indians enjoyed it in some measure, and his administratively justified partition of Bengal as an outrage against the Bengali people and educated India in general. In his insensitiveness as in his zeal and vigour he was an epitome of the dilemma in which the British now found themselves. The class which they themselves had created and then failed to recognise in its real nature was knocking on the door of power. Seventy years before a fair prospect of this door had been given: now that Indians came near it was found to be cumbered with the bars of imperialism, superiority and vested interest.

CHAPTER XVI

CHINA

THE summer of the year 1870 in China saw two events which taken together have been recognised as marking the failure of the movement known to Chinese historians as the T'ung Chih Restoration, the rally of the dynasty which followed the successful suppression of the great T'ai P'ing Rebellion (1850–64). On 7 July 1870 the British Under-Secretary for Foreign Affairs announced in the House of Commons that the government had decided not to ratify the Alcock Convention, an instrument which the British Minister to China, Sir Rutherford Alcock, and the Chinese plenipotentiaries had signed in Peking on 23 October of the previous year. On 21 June there had occurred in the treaty port of Tientsin a violent anti-foreign outbreak, in which several lives were lost, known as the 'Tientsin Massacre'. The rejection of the Alcock Convention marked the failure of the foreign policy associated with the T'ung Chih Restoration; the Tientsin massacre equally emphasised the triumph of reactionary forces opposed to the cautious programme of modernisation which the Restoration statesmen had pursued. Both events were the product of popular ill-informed chauvinism, in the one case inspired by the pretensions and greed of the European merchant community in China, in the other by the ignorance, pride and xenophobia of the Chinese people.

The British government had yielded against their better judgement to the clamour raised by the merchants of Shanghai and other ports in China, an agitation directed not merely against the fact that the stillborn Alcock Convention made some modest changes in the treaty relations between the two countries in favour of China, but even more against the policy which inspired the author of this diplomatic initiative. Alcock believed that the modernisation of China must be gradual, that the sweeping reforms which the merchants demanded could not be expected, and would not be in fact beneficial immediately, and that the Chinese government was entitled to be treated as an equal in diplomatic negotiations. The abortive Convention which bears his name has been rightly described as 'a genuine attempt at treaty revision based on bilateral concessions'. This was the first and for many years the last occasion on which the Chinese government had freely negotiated an agreement with a western power on a basis of equality, without being under threat of force or acting in an atmosphere of crisis.

The Chinese government, for its part, had no hand in the Tientsin massacre, a tragedy in which the fury of the Tientsin mob had been exacerbated and provoked by the arrogance and folly of the French consul. A government which had in reality made a very real and genuine attempt to regulate and safeguard the activities of Christian missionaries, was on the one hand attacked by its own subjects for yielding to the insensate demands of foreigners, on the other accused of fomenting mob violence and conniving at cruel atrocities. Those statesmen who on both sides had sought to build a saner relationship between the two countries were discouraged and neglected; those who were more prepared to follow or accept popular prejudices remained in power. The foreign powers reverted to policies based on coercion, to 'gun-boat diplomacy', the Chinese government fell into the hands of men who distrusted the western world and all its works. The promise of the T'ung Chih Restoration was never fulfilled, and China entered upon a road which led to the distant, but henceforth almost inevitable, revolution. Rightly or wrongly it is the conviction of modern Chinese historians that the period 1860–80 was the last in which China had the opportunity to make those changes and adjustments which would have led to the modernisation of the country under the established leadership and avoided the calamities of revolution, civil war and foreign invasion.

When he died in 1861 the seventh emperor of the Ch'ing, or Manchu dynasty, I Chu (reign title Hsien Feng) left two principal consorts, the Empress Tz'u An, who had given birth to no children, and the mother of his son, Tz'u Hsi, born Yehonala, and later the famous Empress Dowager. The two empresses were entrusted with certain powers at the emperor's death, and retained seals without which no decree was valid. No sooner was the emperor dead than a dangerous conflict began between the two empress dowagers and the eight co-regents. In conjunction with I Hsin Prince Kung, who then controlled the city, the empresses arrested the co-regents, and, after convicting them of conspiracy to seize power, had them promptly executed. In this way the young empress dowager, Tz'u Hsi, then twenty-six, assisted by her retiring and much weaker colleague Tz'u An, obtained the regency and henceforward for more than forty years never really relinquished power.

In the period of eleven years covered by the First Regency of the two empress dowagers, much of the imperial authority was exercised by I Hsin Prince Kung. Although limited by the narrow background of his education and the conservatism of the court, Prince Kung had come to appreciate the need for reforms and cautious modernisation. Thus the movement known as the Restoration was furthered by the support of the most powerful member of the imperial family, who in these years guided and controlled the regency. Nevertheless, neither Prince Kung nor the great ministers who had risen during the T'ai P'ing rebellion and who were with few exceptions Chinese, not Manchus, were in any real sense progressives or modernisers. Their object was to restore the Confucian state, bring back to the distracted empire the calm assured rule of the traditional autocracy working through a hierarchy of classically educated officials who should be primarily scholars, and not experts in any branch of administration. Consequently these men looked upon western learning and technical achievements with caution and doubt. Some of these things were useful, but the western culture as a whole (in so far as they were aware that it existed) was incompatible with the Confucian philosophy and the state system built upon it. It must therefore be kept at arm's length.

The experiences of a long war had indeed convinced them that some changes were essential. Modern firearms were, to them, the most useful and characteristic product of western civilisation. At a very early date in the Restoration arsenals and shipyards were opened at Shanghai, Nanking and Foochow. Having campaigned for years up and down the Yangtse the great provincial viceroys saw the utility of steamships, but opposed all suggestions for the building of railways, which they thought would aid foreign aggressors to penetrate deeply into the country. Foreign commerce they accepted as a necessary evil, but resisted the reiterated desire of the foreign merchants to trade and travel freely in any part of China. Trade must be confined to Treaty Ports, and the Chinese government never at this period willingly increased the number of these. Such western diplomats as Sir Rutherford Alcock, who had come to know the country well, often agreed with the Chinese view of these matters rather than with that of the merchants. Alcock repeatedly expressed great doubt whether the 'opening up of the interior', to use the contemporary phrase, would result in any benefit to trade, while he showed good reasons for fearing that it would lead to riots, murders and incidents, which he, as much as the Chinese authorities, wished to avoid.

For, contrary to the belief then current among the foreign community, the persistent and widespread xenophobia of the Chinese people was not encouraged by the senior imperial officials, although it was shared by the powerful class of provincial gentry. The main irritant to the mass of the people was the presence of foreign missionaries and the activities of Chinese Christian converts. The causes of complaint were both general and practical. To a people with a very strong sense of social solidarity welded by centuries of relative isolation and a pervasive and remarkably comprehensive culture, the preaching of new religion, associated with an alien culture contradicting many ancient social practices and repudiating beliefs universally held, was in any case a suspect and provocative activity. Officials and gentry did not forget that popular rebellions were also usually inspired and organised by the followers of some esoteric sect of Buddhism, and the T'ai P'ing rebellion itself had been strongly influenced by the quasi-Christianity of its leaders and founders. Chinese converts tended to seek the protection of the foreign missionary when in conflict with their neighbours: their new religion forbade them to join in the community festivals which the village or trade guild subscribed to. The converts refused to pay such dues. They refused, also, to accept the direction of their unconverted senior relatives in such matters as marriage and the education of children. They were therefore regarded as subversive of the family system, the linch-pin of Chinese society.

The educated class, the provincial gentry, whether in or out of office, objected to the Christian missionaries and converts on rather different grounds. They saw, dimly perhaps, yet truly, that Christian teaching, however spiritual and unworldly, was basically subversive of the whole Chinese culture. It set up a new orthodoxy, other than that of Confucianism. It introduced a new, alien learning, strange to the classical tradition of China and wholly unfamiliar to those educated in that arduous school. It was foreign, and preached by foreigners. This last objection was still felt against Buddhism nearly two thousand years after it had been introduced to China. It was still thought that Chinese Muslims, however long assimilated, were of a different race as well as of a different faith. With these well-established prejudices in mind it was not easy for a Chinese scholar to accept the Christian converts or approve of Christian, foreign missionaries. The fact that these missionaries had only won the right to live and teach in China as a consequence of China's defeat in the war of 1839–42, called the Opium War, was never forgotten. Foreign trade and foreign ways promoted the rise to wealth and influence of a new class, the city merchants, and especially those among them who were associated with the foreigners, known to these latter from a Portuguese word as 'compradors'. This new class was also obnoxious to the provincial gentry, especially since very many of its members were Cantonese, coming from the city and province which had a well-established reputation as being the most subversive, anti-dynastic and troublesome region in the empire.

Thus the T'ung Chih Restoration was frustrated by the failure of the rulers of China to grapple decisively with their two greatest problems, the need to modernise China and thus ward off the threat of foreign aggression, and the parallel need to give the people that clear leadership which could have overcome the forces of reaction and bigotry and directed their energies towards the reconstruction of the country. This failure in China occurred in the very decades when similar problems confronting Japan were met by the bold, almost revolutionary, policies adopted by the Meiji regime; among the great statesmen of the T'ung Chih period were men at least as able and as patriotic as the Japanese ministers of the Emperor Meiji, but at the top, at the supreme level of the throne, the Manchu dynasty was unable in these crucial years to provide a sovereign with the assured authority of mature age, the intelligence to understand what had to be done, and the prestige to enforce reform policy.

The dynasty had in any case to overcome a grave handicap, its alien origin. The Manchu people, although deeply influenced by the civilisation of China before they conquered the empire, were still a foreign race. They had set up, at the conquest, a system of government which clearly revealed their mistrust of their Chinese subjects, and if this system had become in the course of two centuries smoother in its operation and less objectionable to the Chinese of the educated class, it still gave to the small Manchu minority a wholly disproportionate share of power and privilege. It had already been shown, both in the Opium War against Britain and in the T'ai P'ing rebellion, that the old Manchu military organisation was useless. The dynasty had been saved by loyal Chinese officials commanding Chinese armies. Yet during the Restoration period and subsequently no attempt was made to modify the restrictions imposed on Chinese, who could compete for only half of the civil-service posts, and the Manchu aristocracy, idle, incompetent and ignorant as they often were, retained their privileges intact.

The dynasty had been challenged in the T'ai P'ing movement by a rival which claimed to be liberating China from alien rule. This appeal met with a profound response in the southern provinces which had resisted the Manchu conquest for nearly forty years after the submission of the north. The T'ai P'ing leadership weakened its cause by adopting a form of Christianity, unfamiliar and unwelcome to the mass of the people and positively repellent to the provincial gentry, who had therefore rallied to the dynasty. The T'ai P'ings also made grave military mistakes when victory was within their reach; their movement had been shaken by internal dissensions, and had failed to secure the recognition of foreign powers. Yet it had won the widespread support of the common people of south China and had, in the earlier period of its power, made genuine and well-conceived attempts to remedy some of the miseries of the peasants and reform the Chinese system of government. Its long continuance, its great local victories, and the support it had received from the people should have been a pregnant warning to the court. Following victory a policy of decisive and sweeping reform led and inspired by the throne could have saved the dynasty, and set the course of Chinese history for a century. But the throne was occupied by a child and the regency exercised by women who wholly lacked the vision and the knowledge for such leadership.

I Hsin Prince Kung was the most capable prince of the imperial family in its later years. But in a subordinate position, not even having the powers of regent, the weakness of his character prevented him from asserting himself, and permitted the steady growth of the power and ambition of the emperor's mother, the Empress Dowager Tz'u Hsi. In the first years of the regency Prince Kung had held preponderant power; he held the new title of Prince Counsellor, was head of the newly founded Tsungli Yamen, the first Chinese ministry of foreign affairs in the empire's history, head of the Grand Council (a position equivalent to Prime

Minister in some respects), and also commanded the Peking Field Force, one of the few corps equipped with modern firearms. But in 1865 these powers were suddenly and seriously diminished. Abruptly dismissed from all his offices on vague charges, he was by the intercession of the leading officials of the empire reinstated as head of the Tsungli Yamen and Grand Council, but not to the rank of Prince Counsellor. Thus the empress dowager won an important victory, demonstrating that her power as co-regent was sufficient to overshadow that of the senior prince of the imperial family.

Throughout the period of the First Regency of the two empress dowagers, 1861–73, a great part of the empire was still ravaged by the rebellions which had started in the Hsien Feng reign. The Muslim rebellion in the north-western provinces continued until 1878, although the province of Kansu was pacified by the capture of Suchou in 1873. In effect, therefore, the provinces of China proper, as distinct from such outer dependencies as Sinkiang, were not completely pacified until the end of the regency. The long continuing disorder did not encourage the T'ung Chih statesmen to embark on profound and disturbing reforms, they sought instead to pacify the provinces and restore the traditional form of government.

Few of the great officials of the period, however able and conscientious, had any training in or understanding of economic affairs. They considered that such specialised knowledge was not desirable in senior officials, but should be confined to advisers of low rank; it was a cardinal tenet of the Confucian system that men trained in commerce and industry could not be expected to have the pure and lofty principles of the classical scholar. Few if any of the high officials therefore really learned the lessons of the great rebellions; they did not appreciate that the great rise in population during the long peaceful reigns of K'ang Hsi and Ch'ien Lung in the previous century had increased pressure on the agricultural land to a point never before experienced. The least failure of harvests, the occurrence of a severe flood, was bound to inflict vast misery, while the absence of any modern communications made it impossible for the most benevolent and competent government to provide any appreciable relief. The great rebellions had been sparked by the misery resulting from such catastrophes, the only practical means of guarding against a recurrence was to improve communications and develop industry. But the building of railways, the opening of mines and mills were all foreign innovations which they profoundly distrusted.

During the years 1868–70 the British minister in Peking and the officials of the Tsungli Yamen headed by Prince Kung were negotiating a revision of the Treaty of Tientsin and Convention of Peking, instruments which had brought the 'Arrow War' to an end in 1860. Both sides realised that these treaties did not meet the actual situation and the negotiations for their revision were welcome to both. Unfortunately, whereas Alcock and the British government understood that concessions should be made to China and that real and lasting advantages would accrue from a treaty freely negotiated and signed by the Chinese government without threat of force, the China merchants of Shanghai, Canton and Hong Kong saw nothing but an opportunity for obtaining fresh advantages and extended privileges. Alcock was constantly and violently criticised in the European press in China, and his opponents did not fail to drum up opposition at home. The Chinese negotiators, subjected for their part to the criticisms of the reactionary party, and disturbed at the rising clamour of the foreign press in China, showed themselves very anxious to sign a treaty which, although conceding far less than they had hoped for, yet made some valuable adjustments, and at least admitted the right of China to an equal status. The Convention was signed in Peking on 23 October 1869. The Chinese, not yet fully aware of all the niceties of western diplomacy, formed the mistaken impression that this act was binding, since it had been sealed with the emperor's seal, that of Prince Kung and those of four of the senior ministers. When several months later, in June and July 1870, it became clear that the British government, bowing to the clamour of commercial interests in China and at home, would not ratify, the 'loss of face' suffered by Prince Kung was serious, and gave great satisfaction to his opponents.

Among these, although still covertly, had to be reckoned the Empress Dowager Tz'u Hsi, mother of the emperor (then fifteen years old) and still co-regent. For some years past friction between the empress dowager and the prince had been growing; in 1869 an incident occurred which caused open enmity. Prince Kung tried to check the power of the empress dowager by summarily removing her favourite eunuch, an action which inflicted on her that 'loss of face' which was so serious a matter for the Chinese of that period. She had her revenge when the British refused to ratify the Convention which Prince Kung had negotiated and sealed.

At the very time when this refusal of ratification was about to be announced there occurred an incident which further embarrassed the prince who was responsible for the foreign relations of the empire. Following the 'Arrow War' the French had occupied Tientsin in 1860, and did not evacuate the city and foreign concession until 1863. The inevitable quarrels between foreign soldiery and the populace had led to much ill feeling. The French had also established their consulate in a former imperial villa, and built a cathedral on the razed site of a Chinese temple, all of which had given offence to the local gentry. The populace was at the same time, particularly in the summer of 1870, roused by a number of kidnapping cases, which were attributed to the French Sisters of Charity. These nuns had undertaken the charitable work of rescuing abandoned children, and had further, and most unwisely, offered small rewards for such children if brought alive to the convent. Kidnappers were thus encouraged to snatch children and obtain a reward. An epidemic, common enough in summer, was raging and there were many deaths among the children in the orphanage. Upon these facts becoming known the population was roused to fury and being further provoked by the unwise and violent behaviour of Fontanier, the French consul, killed him, two French priests, ten Sisters of Charity and a number of their Chinese servants. The church, convent and other premises were burnt and sacked.

This event, the Tientsin massacre of 21 June 1870, became a landmark in the relations between China and the western nations on the one hand, and on the other in the internal development of the policy of the court. Only the fact that France and Prussia went to war that year prevented a Sino-French war; all initiatives for further treaty revision came to an end, while China was forced, to avoid a conflict, to send Ch'ung Hou, a high Manchu official, on a mission to France to convey an apology for the murder of Fontanier to the French government. Since the envoy himself had narrowly escaped being shot by the consul, it was not unnaturally felt by the Chinese that this mission was a weak surrender to foreign threats and violence. The memory of the Tientsin massacre lasted long, and embittered both sides. It may be said to linger yet, for the charges of kidnapping and neglecting children in orphanages were persistently maintained through the years, revived by the Boxers, and (in respect of the charge of neglect) endorsed by the present government of China.

There can be little doubt that the two events of the summer of 1870, the rejection of the Alcock Convention by the British government, the Tientsin massacre and its consequences, did much to strengthen the party of reaction in China and diminish the influence of men such as I Hsin Prince Kung. The concurrent rise to power of the empress dowager provided for the reactionary party a leader who shared their prejudices and was by her sex and situation inhibited from gaining that wider knowledge of the world which the officials of the Tsungli Yamen and the provincial viceroys were beginning to acquire.

In 1871 the emperor, whose personal name was Tsai Ch'un, reign title T'ung Chih, was sixteen years old, and by dynastic custom of an age to govern. None the less a petition was organised to implore the empress dowagers to continue the regency for two more years. The complacent acceptance of this violation of the dynastic laws by the court was an ominous indication of the ascendancy which the Empress Dowager Tz'u Hsi had acquired. The next year the young emperor was married to a lady of rank, and his majority formally declared on 3 February 1873. The co-regents resigned, but in fact the empress mother, Tz'u Hsi, continued to dominate the government and her own weakling son.

Outwardly the year of the T'ung Chih emperor's majority seemed

auspicious enough. The Muslim rebels in Yunnan had been finally suppressed, Tso Tsung-t'ang recovered the city of Suchou and drove the
north-western Muslim rebels out of China proper. On 29 June the
emperor accorded the first audience to the ministers of the foreign powers
at which the *k'o t'ou* (the prostration before the throne) was, in accordance
with treaty provisions, dispensed with. But to those who knew what was
passing in the palace the situation cannot have seemed promising. The
emperor was weak physically, idle and dissipated. He succumbed rapidly
to the temptations which corrupt eunuchs put in his way, he disliked and
quarrelled with his formidable mother. He had chosen for his consort a
girl, daughter of a Mongol high official, of whom his mother disapproved.
He quarrelled, too, with his uncle I Hsin Prince Kung because the latter
reproved him for extravagance and loose conduct. In November 1874 the
emperor contracted smallpox, a disease then very common in China, and
regarded as an inevitable ailment of youth. Tsai Ch'un, with his weak
constitution, did not throw off the disease, and on 18 December his continued illness gave the empress dowagers an excuse to resume the regency.
On 12 January 1875 the T'ung Chih reign ended with the young emperor's
death, aged nineteen. He left no son. Thus within less than two years the
hope of mature leadership and an adult sovereign was destroyed, and a
dynastic succession crisis of a most dangerous character arose.

The Ch'ing (Manchu) dynasty had adopted a rule of succession which
differed in one important respect from that which had obtained under
earlier, Chinese, dynasties. To avoid the intrigues which had too often
surrounded the person of a crown prince, it had been decided that the
emperor should write the name of the son he chose to be his successor on
a paper which was kept secret until the sovereign was *in extremis*. In the
event of the emperor having no son he should choose a successor from the
generation lower than his own, a nephew, who could then be officially
adopted as his son, and so enabled to perform the ancestral rites to the
spirit of the departed sovereign, which a brother or cousin of the same
generation could not do, since such a person could not stand in the son–
father relationship. In actual practice no such necessity had ever arisen as
the first seven emperors of the dynasty had all left sons, one of whom had
been nominated as heir. The late Emperor Tsai Ch'un (T'ung Chih), the
first of the dynasty to leave no son to succeed him, had also been the
only surviving son of the Hsien Feng emperor, and consequently had no
nephews. The only possible heirs must be found among the great grandsons of the Tao Kuang emperor, who had died in 1851. This meant that
the only possible candidate was Prince P'u Lun, then a child, the eldest
son of Prince Tsai Chih. But there was here a further difficulty; Tsai Chih
himself was not a grandson of the Tao Kuang emperor, but only the
adopted son of that emperor's eldest son, I Wei. Tsai Chih was by blood
only the great-great-grandson of the Ch'ien Lung emperor, who had died

in 1799. The Tao Kuang emperor had several grandsons, the children of his five younger sons, but these, all young children at this time, were of course of the same generation as the late emperor, and thus, on a strict construction of the succession law, ineligible.

The late emperor's consort was at this time pregnant; some of the Grand Council therefore proposed that a regency be established until it was seen whether she gave birth to a son who could then be proclaimed emperor at birth. The Empress Dowager Tz'u Hsi was not at all in favour of this proposal. If her daughter-in-law did in fact have a son, it would be she, not Tz'u Hsi, who would be the regent through the long minority of such an infant, and Tz'u Hsi greatly disliked her daughter-in-law. Under these circumstances she would have no further standing in the government and would be forced into retirement. She therefore declared that the situation of the empire was too serious to permit a vacancy of the throne, and that an heir must be chosen at once. Prince P'u Lun was then proposed, but the empress dowager at once objected that as his father was only the adopted son of I Wei he could not be considered to be a real heir. This view had no foundation in custom or law, for in China adoption is regarded as constituting a definite and binding relationship. If P'u Lun was to be set aside there remained only the first cousins of the late emperor, and of these the eldest was Tsai Ying, son of I Hsin Prince Kung, then fourteen years old. If he became emperor his minority would be very short, and his father Prince Kung, would be the obvious choice for regent. But the Empress Dowager Tz'u Hsi had no great love for Prince Kung, and knew very well that his regency would be the end of her power.

She therefore proposed Tsai T'ien, then four years old, the son of I Huan Prince Ch'un, seventh son of the Tao Kuang emperor, and younger brother of I Hsin Prince Kung. I Huan's wife, however, was the younger sister of Tz'u Hsi herself, thus Tsai T'ien was her nephew. He was therefore the only member of the imperial family closely related to the empress dowager, his mother was her sister, and she could be assured of the regency for many years yet. The child's father, I Huan, was a weak character lacking the ability of I Hsin Prince Kung. If the latter prince had had more real strength of will, if his prestige had not recently been dimmed by the failures in foreign affairs, he might have resisted this usurpation, which it is known he greatly resented. He yielded to the ambitions of the empress dowager, supported as they were by the sycophantic majority of the Grand Council. In this way, by an open and flagrant violation of the law of succession the Empress Dowager Tz'u Hsi secured a further long lease of power, with consequences which were in the end fatal to the dynasty.

Tsai T'ien was chosen; the two empress dowagers were proclaimed co-regents once more; the consort of the late emperor wholly thrust aside. A few weeks later she died suddenly, as it is said by taking her own life in protest against the usurpation. It is at least obvious that this demise was very convenient to the Empress Dowager Tz'u Hsi, since the birth of a posthumous son to the T'ung Chih emperor would have been a great obstacle to her ambitions. For the next fourteen years those ambitions were to have full rein. The co-regent, the Empress Dowager Tz'u An, died, after a very short illness, on 7 April 1881. Popular tradition has always maintained that she was poisoned by orders of Tz'u Hsi. The death of Tz'u An weakened the position of I Hsin Prince Kung, and prepared the way for his fall.

During the early years of the Kuang Hsü period, under the regency of the two empress dowagers, foreign affairs had continued to be the main problem of the government. The last stage of the internal pacification of the rebellions of the previous decade was completed in 1878 by the final conquest of the Muslim rebels in Sinkiang, or Chinese Turkestan. This event, however, involved the court in a new foreign question of a dangerous character. In 1870, when the rebels were still in full control of Sinkiang, where Yakub of Kokand emerged as the principal leader, and also much of north-west China, Russia had occupied the Ili region of Sinkiang, in order to protect her traders. After a full ten years of foreign occupation it seemed at least doubtful whether China could now recover this territory. Ch'ung Hou, who as a consequence of his part in the Tientsin massacre had been sent on a mission to France, was at that time the only high Chinese official with any direct experience of foreign countries. He was sent to Russia in 1879 to negotiate for the return of Ili.

Ch'ung Hou, after opening negotiations in St Petersburg, followed the Russian court to Livadia on the Black Sea, where on 2 October 1879 he signed the Treaty of Livadia. This provided for the Russian evacuation of one-third of the occupied territory and the payment by China to Russia of a large indemnity, with various trade concessions which also favoured Russia. The treaty was violently denounced in China by many senior officials, prominent among whom was a rising man of brilliant talents, Chang Chih-tung. Largely as a result of his scathing criticism Ch'ung Hou was dismissed and imprisoned, the treaty denounced, and the life of the unlucky envoy spared only upon the intercession of the foreign ministers, who were naturally loath to see the failure of a diplomatic mission punished with the death penalty. The party of reaction claimed great credit for the denunciation of the Treaty of Livadia, but the more favourable terms obtained from Russia by Tseng Chi-tse, in the Treaty of St Petersburg (24 February 1881) were really due to the skill of this envoy. Although he agreed to increase the sum paid to Russia to recompense her 'occupation expenses' he was able to recover a much larger part of the disputed territory including the strategic passes between Ili and Kashgar.

Against the relative success of these negotiations with Russia, by which lost territory was recovered and a threatened war averted, must be set the deterioration of relations with Britain, an outcome of the murder of a British subject, A. R. Margary, on 19 February 1875. Margary had made an overland journey from Shanghai, across south-west China to Bhamo in Burma, where he met a British trade mission which had the task of exploring and opening up a new route for trade between lower Burma, then already annexed by Britain, and the Chinese south-western province of Yunnan. On his way back into China, a little in advance of the British mission, Margary was attacked and murdered in the jungles on the Chinese side of the Burma–Yunnan frontier. The country was (and is) very wild, and the area had been recovered from the Muslim rebels only two years before. During the rebellion a British trade mission had been received by the rebel authorities, but prevented from proceeding farther by imperial troops. There was thus a local prejudice against the British, whose penetration of Burma was at this time rapidly extending. Sir Thomas Wade, the British Minister to Peking, and western opinion generally, attributed the responsibility for the murder of Margary to the governor of the province, Ts'en Yü-ying. Wade demanded an investigation by Chinese and British officials on the spot and the punishment of those responsible. The court called upon Ts'en for a report, but Yunnan was 2000 miles away and neither the request nor the reply could be received for months. In the meantime Wade pressed his demands, left Peking for Shanghai, and threatened war. When Ts'en's report was received it confirmed the Chinese belief that Margary had been murdered by local bandits and discharged soldiery. Ts'en Yü-ying was in no way responsible. Wade refused to accept this report; the Chinese government was equally unwilling to victimise a very high official who had performed most valuable services to the throne and who was certainly in no way to blame.

To dismiss this loyal, able, popular and powerful man at the bidding of foreigners would have been to invite a further and very dangerous rebellion and would have ruined the prestige of the court in the provinces. Rather than take such action Prince Kung advised that the British be bought off by other concessions. The Margary Affair was therefore settled by Li Hung-chang who negotiated with Wade the Chefoo Convention, 13 September 1876, which conceded the opening of further Treaty Ports, gave further trade concessions, and settled the rules of procedure for the reception of foreign envoys. Incidents such as the Margary Affair, where the Chinese court was forced to make concessions to foreign powers under threat of war, for minor causes, for which the senior officials of the empire were blamed, but were not responsible, did much to diminish the authority of liberal officials and inflame the anti-foreign feelings of the people and provincial gentry.

The declining power of the dynasty was to be revealed still more clearly in the years between 1881, when Tz'u Hsi became sole regent, and the majority of the Kuang Hsü emperor in 1889. If the empire was now internally at last peaceful, China's position in her outer dependencies was challenged by French encroachment in the south and the rising power of Japan in the north. For many centuries China had exercised a light suzerainty over the two neighbouring kingdoms which had adopted most thoroughly the Chinese civilisation, Annam in the south, Korea in the north. Both had, in the distant past, been provinces of the Chinese empire under the Han dynasty. In later centuries both kingdoms had established their local independence, but had acknowledged the supremacy of the Chinese emperor, no matter what dynasty came to power in China. The Manchus had succeeded to this suzerainty when they ousted the Ming. But if China exacted only a nominal, ceremonial, tribute, and left the Korean and Annamite kings to govern as they pleased, she also provided no protection, stationed no forces, and had no normal system of defensive alliance with her tributaries. If attacked they would call on the emperor for his aid; it was nowhere laid down whether he in turn was bound to afford it, or what form it should take. In the early 1880's this ancient relationship was to be challenged, and later overthrown, by the aggressive policies of western imperialism, aptly imitated by Japan.

As early as 1862, when China, distracted by the T'ai P'ing rebellion and the 'Arrow War', was in no position to intervene, France had compelled the king of Annam (see footnote, p. 644) to cede the three southern provinces of his kingdom, known as Cochin-China, including the important city of Saigon. After the Franco-Prussian War France resumed her forward policy in Annam, and in 1874 secured further rights, among them that of navigating the Red River in Tongking. China refused to yield her suzerainty or to admit French trade into the neighbouring province of Yunnan. But in 1882 France resumed her pressure, and in April of that year an expeditionary force occupied Hanoi, capital of Tongking, and the northern capital of the kingdom. The Annamite king did not dare to appeal openly to China, and the Chinese government, unwilling to intervene and bring on war with France, resorted to encouraging the resistance of local Tongking patriots organised in a force known as the Black Flag army commanded by an ex-bandit named Liu Yung-fu. The pattern of Chinese assistance to Annamite opposition to France in 1882 thus foreshadowed very closely the manner in which seventy years later China was to support the cause of the Viet Minh movement to regain independence from France. By the middle of 1883, despite the Li–Fournier Agreement by which China agreed to open the Kuangsi and Yunnan provinces to French trade, the situation had degenerated into war between China and France. By the middle of 1884 the Chinese forces had met with several reverses and China's coasts were threatened by the French fleet.[1]

[1] Below, pp. 650-2, for further details.

The empress dowager had for a long time sought an opportunity to rid herself of the competition for power exercised by I Hsin Prince Kung. She now availed herself of the criticisms which several censors of the war party made concerning the inept conduct of the war, and dismissed not only Prince Kung but the entire Grand Council. This change was accepted without protest; it marked the final ascendancy of the empress dowager. As successor to Prince Kung in the post of head of the Tsungli Yamen, the ministry of foreign affairs, the empress dowager chose I K'uang Prince Ch'ing, a great-grandson of the Emperor Ch'ien Lung and the head of one of the collateral branches of the imperial family. Prince Ch'ing was a man of much less talent than I Hsin. He had to some extent a liberal outlook, but invariably gave way to the empress dowager, avoided, so far as he could, involvement in any dangerous issue, and was personally well known to be corrupt and engaged in the lucrative traffic in appointments. This man, then forty-eight, became and remained the chief minister of the empire until the fall of the dynasty. I Hsin had been weak; I K'uang was negligible as a check on the power of the empress dowager; the succession of I K'uang to I Hsin marks a long step downward in the decline of the Ch'ing dynasty.

Meanwhile, although Prince Kung had been dismissed for allegedly bungling the war, the Chinese continued to put up a more creditable resistance to the French than they had done either in the 'Arrow War' against the French and English twenty years earlier, or were to offer to Japanese attacks ten years later. Nevertheless, and in spite of a Chinese victory in Tongking, peace negotiations were reopened through the mediation of Sir Robert Hart, the British head of the Chinese Maritime Customs, and were founded upon the abortive Li–Fournier convention of 1883. Peace was signed on 4 April 1885, and China evacuated Tongking and renounced her suzerainty over Annam. This result was certainly paradoxical; Li Hung-chang's concessions, repudiated by the war party two years before, were now accepted after the policy of that party had unexpectedly been crowned with more success than could reasonably have been expected. One reason for this decision was the danger of a spreading war with France, but perhaps the main cause was the fact that during the same years as the French war, China had had to cope with an equally dangerous crisis at the other end of the empire, in Korea. Li Hung-chang and other high officials were convinced that even if it was possible to win some victories against the French, China could not hope to conduct successful war both with France and Japan at the same time.

Just as the first cause of French expansion into northern Annam had come from China's failure to support her tributary, Annam, in resisting French encroachment in Cochin-China, so it was China's indifference to Korean affairs which now led to Japanese intervention in that country. In 1875 Japan had a dispute with Korea over the treatment of shipwrecked sailors, unfortunates whom the Korean coastal population despoiled and ill-treated. China had declined to take any responsibility for Korean behaviour, and in the next year, 23 July 1876, Japan had come to a direct settlement with the Korean king. This instrument impaired China's claim to suzerainty and weakened her status in the peninsula kingdom. On the other hand, when the internal condition of Korea deteriorated in the next few years Chinese as well as Japanese troops were sent to restore order; and in December 1884, after an engagement between the Chinese and Japanese forces, the Japanese were compelled to withdraw, and the Chinese remained in possession of Seoul.[1]

There was thus a real possibility, early in 1885, that the French, repulsed in Tongking, and the Japanese, driven out of Seoul, would form an alliance against China. The danger was averted by the peace signed with France in April and in the same month Li Hung-chang and Prince Ito met in Tientsin and there concluded a convention by which both sides agreed to withdraw their troops from Korea, and not to send forces into that country without prior notification to the other power. If China avoided, for a while, the loss of all her suzerain rights in Korea, she had in practice conceded to Japan an equal status in that country, an uneasy settlement containing the seeds of further conflict. Unrest in Korea continued for the next eight years until a further crisis brought on the Sino-Japanese War in 1894.

In 1886 the young emperor attained his sixteenth year, and was then of age to assume the government in accordance with dynastic law and the august precedent of the great K'ang Hsi emperor, who had also succeeded to the throne as a minor. Tsai T'ien, the Kuang Hsü emperor, was a promising youth; intelligent, reflective and sober in his habits and life. Unlike his immediate predecessors this penultimate emperor of the Ch'ing dynasty was capable of developing into a competent and liberal-minded ruler. The empress dowager was no doubt well aware of the character of her nephew, and already disappointed with her choice. Instead of terminating the regency the whole court, led by the weak father of the emperor, I Huan Prince Ch'un, petitioned the empress to continue as regent for two more years. She graciously consented.

In 1889 the emperor's majority could no longer be postponed; on 26 February he was married to a lady who was the niece of Tz'u Hsi, a consort for whom he never felt any affection, and who throughout her life acted as her aunt's spy upon him. On 4 March, having thus secured her influence, the empress dowager formally retired to the summer palace near Peking, although she continued to see all decrees and approve those of importance before they were issued. The empress dowager had no intention of living henceforth in obscurity; indeed she was not satisfied with the disrepair in which the remains of the original summer palace had

---

[1] See ch. XXIII.

been left since its partial destruction by the British in 1860. She required that it be renovated and rebuilt, and when other funds were not available, she appropriated the money which had been raised to build and equip a modern navy to replace and expand the fleet destroyed in the French war. The emperor and his ministers, even his own father Prince Ch'un, who had shown especial and genuine interest in the navy, were unable to prevent this malversation.

It was during this period of the Kuang Hsü emperor's partial emancipation that there developed in China an important and growing divergence between the officials from the south of China and those from the north, with whom the Manchu officials usually combined. The danger of such a quarrel had long existed. The dynasty was not only established in Peking, in the far north, which therefore benefited from the patronage of the court, but it had from the first been more acceptable to the northern Chinese, and much less so to those of the south. So long as southern discontent was openly subversive it could be crushed, and exercised no influence on the government. But from the T'ai P'ing rebellion onwards, when the dynasty had owed its survival to southern troops and southern leaders such as Tseng Kuo-fan and Tso Tsung-t'ang, both from Hunan, southern officials loyal to the throne became more influential and began to advocate a more liberal policy than appealed to the Manchu princes and their northern Chinese colleagues. There was, on the whole, a preponderance of ability among the southern men, natives of the wealthy and cultured provinces of Kiangsu, Chekiang, Anhui, Hupei and Hunan; these regions were also more in touch with the western foreigners, and if these were equally disliked in the south, their inventions, their customs and their power were better understood.

Gradually there formed in the Grand Council two parties: the liberals, or more truly cautious modernisers, led by the emperor's tutor Weng T'ung-ho, and the reactionaries, led by Hsü T'ung and Kang I, the latter a Manchu and a fanatical xenophobe. Weng T'ung-ho and his following were southerners, Hsü T'ung and the other reactionaries from the north. The southern party were supported by the tacit backing of most of the great viceroys of the south: Chang Chih-tung, who ruled the twin provinces of Hunan and Hupei in the middle Yangtse, Liu K'un-i who for many years held the corresponding position in the lower Yangtse over Kiangsu, Kiangsi and Anhui, while Li Hung-chang, though not in charge at this time of any southern province, was certainly the leader of the modernising group of high officials.

This group had scored some successes; since the 1880's they had gradually broken down the prejudice against the building of railways, on which a slight start was made in 1881 with a line from the coal-mining town of T'angshan to Tientsin. Telegraph lines had been set up connecting all the major cities with Peking and each other from 1884.

Following the French war a military academy to train officers and men on modern lines was set up by Li Hung-chang at Tientsin in 1885. From this establishment there emerged all the officers who in the later years of the dynasty and early Republic dominated, disastrously, the civil government of China. The railway was extended from Tientsin to Peking and work was begun on the great line from Peking to the south (the Peking–Hankow–Canton railway of later years) in 1898. This project was the special interest of Chang Chih-tung, the viceroy of Hunan-Hupei, who conceived and fostered it.

Unfortunately for the policy of cautious modernisation which was the best that could now gain sufficient support to be practicable, events outside China were moving much faster than the most enlightened official was prepared to go. Japan, her own policy of modernisation a proven success, was ready for expansion, and fearful of Russian ambition in the distracted kingdom of Korea. In 1893 the outbreak of another fanatically anti-foreign rebellion in Korea, the Tong Hak movement, precipitated the Sino-Japanese war of 1894–5. The war was lost by March 1895; and it was obvious that China would be unable to prevent the Japanese advancing to Peking itself. Li Hung-chang was sent to Japan to obtain an armistice. Peace was signed on 17 April. Li had already enlisted the assistance of Germany, Russia and France in order to curb Japanese ambitions; on 23 April the promised intervention took place and these three powers insisted, by joint representations to Japan, that the clause in the treaty giving Japan the lease of the Liaotung peninsula, which included Lushun (Port Arthur) and Talienwan (Dairen), should be waived. By this supreme example of the current Chinese foreign policy of 'playing off one barbarian against another' Li Hung-chang averted, for the moment, the loss of further territory. But suzerainty over Korea was gone; new privileges for Japanese traders, a heavy indemnity, were in themselves sufficient loss of face; and the cession of Formosa, indubitably a part of the territory of the empire itself, sowed the seeds for a continuing cause of conflict which still troubles the Far East.[1]

The indirect consequences of this disastrous war were even more serious. China had now been shown to the world as an impotent, decadent empire, more 'sick' in east Asia than the famous 'Sick Man of Europe'. The unedifying episode known as the 'Battle for the Concessions' swiftly followed. It was now assumed as proved that the dissolution of the empire was at hand; every foreign power determined to carve itself a share of the prize; China was, to use the Chinese phrase, about to be 'melondivided'—suffer a piecemeal partition and multiple annexations. Within two months of the end of the Sino-Japanese War the scramble was beginning, within two years the western powers were in full cry upon their quarry.[2]

[1] Below, pp. 655-7, for further details.   [2] Below, pp. 658 ff. for details.

In answer to this surge of foreign encroachment the Chinese, both court and country, responded in their own fashion. In 1898, while the foreign powers were openly talking of their spheres of influence and taking the initial steps to stake out these future colonies, the emperor, advised by liberals and southern ministers, embarked on a last desperate attempt to reform and modernise the country; the people, still inspired by their ancient pride and xenophobia, rallied to a sect which, drawing upon an ancient popular tradition, promised its followers immunity in battle if they rejected every foreign influence, object and practice. In the same year, 1898, that the Kuang Hsü emperor embarked upon the reform movement known as the Hundred Days Reform, the Boxer sect arose in the province of Shantung, where foreign pressure was currently most acute.

After the event, when the reform movement had failed, many foreign writers poured scorn on its measures, which were described as brash, ill-considered, headlong, and premature. But fifty years later the reform programme appears, on the contrary, as the very minimum which could have been applied to the desperate plight of the nation and dynasty. The Kuang Hsü emperor deserves the credit of realising what that plight was and being prepared to run the enormous risk of alienating the conservative forces, including his formidable aunt, in a last attempt to save the throne. All of the reforms proclaimed in the imperial decrees which were issued in June, July and August of 1898 were to be adopted before many years had passed, and far more sweeping innovations have been accepted with enthusiasm by the Chinese people in later years.

The principal reforms announced were as follows:

1. The abolition of the traditional form of civil service examination by writing stylised essays in classical Chinese.
2. The establishment of an imperial university.
3. The modernisation of the army.
4. Modernisation of the provincial school system.
5. Secularisation of superfluous temples and Buddhist monasteries.
6. Inauguration of a special economic examination.
7. Permission for junior officials and the common people to memorialise the throne directly.
8. Provision for sending students to study abroad.
9. Establishment of a National Board to promote commerce, agriculture, mining and the construction of railways.
10. Reform of the provincial administration, abolition of sinecure ministries and obsolete posts.

This programme was uneven and uncoordinated in the brief period in which it operated, but some at least of these reforms, such as the ninth, contained the germ of the idea of a planned programme of national development which has in modern times transformed the economy of China.

It is not certain whether the empress dowager, nominally in retreat at the summer palace, was from the first determined to suppress the reforms and deprive her nephew of power, or whether she was prepared to see how far he would go before taking action. However she did, at the very beginning of the movement, strike one decisive blow which was no doubt intended to make subsequent reaction easy when the time came. On 15 June, only four days after the issue of the first reform decree, Weng T'ung-ho, the emperor's most trusted adviser and an inspirer of the reform programme, was dismissed from all his posts and retired to the country. The fact that the emperor was unable to prevent this action shows the very real limitations of his authority when it ran counter to the will of his aunt. Without Weng and the prestige which his age, rank and accomplishments conferred upon the reform programme, the emperor and his young, idealistic supporters, K'ang Yu-wei, T'an Ssu-t'ung, and Liang Ch'i-ch'ao, were left isolated at court, exposed to the ceaseless opposition of the entrenched reactionary party, now increasingly alarmed at the trend of events.

Although all the principal reformers were distinguished scholars, and brilliant minds, none at that time had had any experience of administration or occupied senior posts in the civil service. Their sudden rise and influence was therefore very unwelcome to the regular officials who, even if liberal in outlook, were still jealous of their rank and privilege. If the emperor could have called to his side some leading moderate among the senior officials, Chang Chih-tung or Li Hung-chang, it is possible that he might have formed a party strong enough to dominate and outface the reactionaries. He did not do so, and the attitude of the great provincial viceroys was ambiguous. Li was still under the shadow of his recent failures in foreign affairs, the disastrous consequences of the Japanese war which he had always opposed. Chang played a peculiar role; at first supporting the reforms with his pen, but refraining from active political support, possibly because, warned by the dismissal of Weng T'ung-ho, he shrewdly realised that reaction was still potent and apt to triumph. Liu K'un-i, viceroy of the Lower Yangtse provinces with his seat at Nanking, a post he had occupied for twenty years, took no part in court politics. He was almost the last of the T'ung Chih great officials—loyal, competent, moderate—but no reformer in the manner of K'ang Yu-wei.

Early in September 1898, a bare three months after the issue of the first reform decrees, the emperor became aware that he was menaced by a reactionary *coup d'état*, inspired by the empress dowager. Urged on by the more conservative princes and Manchu nobles, backed by such Chinese as Hsü T'ung, Tz'u Hsi had decided that the reform programme must be halted, and this could only be done by virtually deposing the emperor. He was due to pay a first visit by railway to Tientsin, an innovation in itself obnoxious to the reactionaries. It was planned to seize him when out of the capital and place the government once more under the regency of the empress dowager.

The emperor decided that he must forestall this *coup* by removing Jung Lu, the commander-in-chief of the armies in north China, a devoted adherent of the empress dowager, in favour of a general whom he could trust. The new commander was to lead his troops to the summer palace, seize the empress dowager and, there is little doubt, put her to death. But his plans were betrayed. The empress dowager was alerted, and on 23 September 1898 she returned secretly to Peking, accompanied by troops, surprised the emperor and imprisoned him on an island in the Lake Palace adjoining the Forbidden City. On 25 September it was announced that the empress dowager had resumed the regency. The reform movement was suppressed, the reformers hunted down and put to death, with the exception of K'ang Yu-wei and Liang Ch'i-chao, who managed to escape abroad. T'an Ssu-t'ung refused to escape, believing that the sacrifice of his life would demonstrate his loyalty to the emperor and better serve the cause of reform.

During the remaining months of 1898 it was generally believed that the days of the Kuang Hsü emperor were numbered, and that his 'illness' would soon be followed by the announcement of his decease. That this act was deferred was due to the warnings received from the great southern viceroys, especially Liu K'un-i of Nanking, who plainly told the empress dowager that the death of the emperor would be considered in the south as a murder and would probably provoke open revolution. The British minister also told the court that the death of the emperor would be ill-received by the foreign powers, who would not be inclined to credit the story that it was due to natural causes. The empress dowager nevertheless took the unprecedented step of naming an heir apparent, Prince P'u Chün, the young son of Prince Tuan, who was a grandson of the Tao Kuang emperor by his fifth son. P'u Chün thus descended from an elder brother of I Huan, the Kuang Hsü emperor's own father, and this fact served to indicate that the Kuang Hsü emperor was now to be treated as a usurper. Once again Prince P'u Lun, who might well be considered the real heir, was passed over. The father of the new heir apparent, Prince Tuan, was a notorious reactionary and violently anti-foreign. The ministers of the foreign powers signified their disapproval of the appointment of his son by refraining from offering any congratulations. His appointment was indeed a further violation of the dynastic succession law, which had hitherto forbidden the nomination of an heir during the lifetime of the reigning emperor, leaving the announcement of the name of the chosen prince to be the last act of a dying monarch.

In the autumn of the year 1898 the Yellow River burst its banks causing great devastation in the western part of Shantung and adjoining regions; the harvest had been bad, the province was already disturbed by the high-handed actions of the German forces now established in Tsingtao, and with the government once more in the hands of extreme reactionaries, the Boxer sect, or to give it its true name the I Ho Tuan, or Society of the Harmonious Fist, spread rapidly among the starving peasantry. In October the sect made open attacks upon Chinese Christians in several parts of the province, and these disorders were condoned, if not actually encouraged, by the governor, Yü Hsien. In December 1898, following protests from the foreign powers, Yü was removed, but not disgraced, being appointed instead to the governorship of Shansi in March 1900. Yüan Shih-k'ai replaced him in Shantung, and immediately set about a vigorous campaign to suppress the Boxers. The attitude of the court towards this movement was from the first ambivalent. In January 1900 Yüan was warned against too much severity, but continued his campaign of suppression, driving the Boxers out of the province into the neighbouring Chihli (Hopei), the metropolitan province in which Peking is situated. The governor of Chihli, Yü Lu, vacillated, and the court on 11 January 1900, and again on 17 April, issued decrees condoning the movement and deprecating any undue severity. The diplomatic corps protested against the first of these decrees on 27 January and on 2 March, but they were not revoked and the belief spread that the Boxers enjoyed the favour of the court. Soon the Boxers themselves were openly making this claim, and their following rapidly increased.

A strong party at court were now advocating that the Boxers be recognised and enrolled as an official militia, the argument being that they were giving proof of patriotic fervour which the dynasty should take care to enlist in its own service rather than permit the independent growth of such a movement among the people. The senior provincial officials were not at all in agreement with this view. Yüan Shih-k'ai, now governor of Shantung, firmly rejected such an idea, and Yü Lu of Chihli, who had at first permitted the spread of the Boxers in his province, now opposed them. In the month of May his own troops clashed with Boxer bands, and repulsed them, disproving very clearly the legend of their invulnerability. Yet aware of the trend at court Yü Lu did not follow up this action with a decisive move against the Boxers. Late in the month of May, 1900, they renewed their attacks and now began to destroy telegraph lines and damage the railways in north China. The foreign ministers in Peking were seriously alarmed both at the violence of the Boxers in the countryside, from which missionaries and railway engineers were now hastily withdrawing, and at the dubious attitude of the court, dominated as it was by violent reactionaries. On 28 May the Boxers burned down the railway station at Fengt'ai, a junction just south of Peking, and the legations decided to call upon the foreign naval squadrons in China waters to send up detachments to act as legation guards. These forces arrived in Peking on 31 May.

The destruction of the railways aroused the imperial military commanders and provincial officials; on 4 June Nieh Shih-ch'eng, a senior military officer, engaged a large band of Boxers at Huangts'un, on the railway between Peking and Tientsin, and severely defeated them. Yü Lu, governor of the province, now urged the court to permit him to suppress the Boxers by force (6 June). The destruction of the railway from Peking to Paoting, the first section of the Peking–Hankow railway to be built, had aroused the indignation of the viceroy of Hupei-Hunan, Chang Chih-tung, who had sponsored the building of this line. He sent a memorandum to the throne strongly urging the suppression of the Boxer bands.

Jung Lu, the favourite of the empress dowager, and commander-in-chief of the Chinese forces in the north, occupied a key post. If he had thrown his power against the Boxer movement it could still have been crushed as easily as Yüan Shih-k'ai had destroyed it in Shantung. But Jung Lu was very closely in touch with the court, he knew that the reactionary party, led by Prince Tuan, father of the new heir apparent, were ardently pro-Boxer; the empress dowager was wavering, but her dislike of modern ways, which were necessarily foreign, and her hatred of reformers, who were influenced by foreign ideas, impelled her to the support and approval of the extreme anti-foreign party. Jung Lu did not favour the Boxers, he certainly realised the risk of general war with the foreign powers if they were left unchecked, but he was receiving contradictory and conflicting instructions from day to day, and he took refuge in total inaction.

On 7 June the Grand Councillor, Kang I, a violently anti-foreign Manchu, was sent by the court to interview the Boxer leaders at Chochou, some eighty miles south of Peking; whatever his real instructions may have been, the choice of this man made it certain that the Boxers would receive the approbation of the court, and in fact Kang ordered all imperial troops to withdraw and allow the Boxers to move freely forward to the capital. On 9 June the British minister, Sir Claude Macdonald, requested Admiral Seymour, commanding the China station squadron, to land forces to occupy the foreign concessions in Tientsin and reinforce the legation guards in Peking.

The last train from Peking had left on 3 June; by the 5th the railway between the capital and Tientsin had been wholly interrupted and destroyed. Curiously enough the Boxers left the telegraph line in operation until 12 June. By that date Admiral Seymour with five hundred men had landed at Tientsin, and with the addition of some detachments already in that port, set out for Peking on 10 June with a total force of 1945 men. On 13 June the court ordered the imperial generals to resist and repel this expedition. Seymour's force clashed with imperial troops at Langfang, half-way to Peking, on the 13th, and finding himself opposed in great strength, his advance blocked, the admiral was forced into a perilous retreat to Tientsin, which he regained on 26 June. By that date China was at war with the foreign powers. On the afternoon of 13 June the Boxer bands entered Peking in force and immediately started to massacre the Chinese Christians, burn churches and molest foreign residents. A member of the Japanese legation, Mr Sugiyama, had been murdered on the 11th just outside the city. The naval commanders at Tientsin decided that the foreign concessions there and Seymour's force could not be safeguarded unless the forts at Taku, which commanded the entrance to the Hai Ho river on which Tientsin stands, were surrendered. They demanded this of the garrison commander, who, having no orders from Peking, refused. The forts were attacked on the night of 15 June, and captured by naval landing parties.

Up to the capture of the Taku forts the court had still taken the attitude that the foreign ministers should rely on the protection of the Chinese government and that the Boxer movement was an internal affair with which they had no right to concern themselves. It seems possible that the empress dowager still hoped to overawe the foreign powers by following a militant reactionary policy, which yet stopped short of war. On the other hand the out-and-out pro-Boxers, such as Prince Tuan, were determined to stop at nothing. On 16 June an imperial council was held, the emperor, dragged from his confinement, being for once present. Prince Tuan and his faction argued violently for war, the empress dowager inclined to their side, the emperor courageously opposed them and received the support of the Grand Councillor Yüan Ch'ang, one of the last of the moderates still in office. Nothing was decided.

On the next day the imperial council met again, and the empress dowager produced an ultimatum which she said she had that day received from the foreign ministers in Peking. This contained four demands: (1) that a special place be assigned to the emperor for residence, (2) that all revenues be collected by the foreign ministers, (3) that all military affairs be committed to the direction of the foreign ministers, (4) that the rule of the emperor be restored. These demands were a fabrication, almost certainly the work of Prince Tuan, who since 10 June had been appointed head of the Tsungli Yamen or ministry for foreign affairs. The empress appears to have believed them to be genuine. Although Li Shan and other senior members of the Tsungli Yamen were sent next day to interview Sir Claude Macdonald they were not instructed to inquire whether these demands were false or true, although they all believed from the tenor of the meeting that no such demands had been made. Macdonald, on the other hand, rejected a request that he stop the foreign forces from landing and marching on Peking.

On 19 June the court learned of the fall of the Taku forts: regarding this as an act of war the empress dowager instructed the Tsungli Yamen to break off relations with the foreign powers and order their representatives to leave Peking under guard of Chinese troops. This the ministers refused, believing, with every justification, that such protection would be valueless and that to leave would be to invite a general massacre. On 21 June China declared war on the western powers. On the previous day, 20 June, Baron von Kettler, the German minister, set out to pay a call on the Tsungli Yamen to protest against the attacks being made by Boxers upon the legation guards. As he proceeded up the Hatamen street in his official chair he was stopped and murdered by a Manchu soldier acting under the direct orders of Prince Chuang, one of the pro-Boxer imperial princes. On the same evening a general assault upon the foreign legations was begun by the Boxers in Peking. The foreign residents fortified themselves in their legations, taking the large walled enclosure of the British legation, a former Manchu prince's palace, as the centre point of their resistance.

Meanwhile the Boxers were attacking the concessions at Tientsin and an international force drawn from the naval squadrons and leased ports in the Far East was assembling to defend Tientsin and relieve the legations in Peking. Two thousand men were landed at Tientsin on 24 June, and thenceforth the concessions were not really in acute danger. In Peking the foreign residents successfully repelled numerous and continual Boxer assaults. On the other hand the imperial troops, particularly Muslim forces from Kansu commanded by a violent xenophobe general, T'ung Fu-hsiang, himself a Muslim, who had joined in the assault, were un-provided with artillery; although Jung Lu had modern guns at his disposal these were never used against the legations. The circumstances surrounding this strange restraint have never been fully elucidated; Jung Lu could certainly have wiped out the legations had he allowed his artillery to be employed; the court openly supported the Boxers, but the commander-in-chief held back, while at the same time deploring, in tele-grams to the southern viceroys, his inability to influence the policy of the empress dowager (26 June).

A vital decision had been taken by the great viceroys of south China: on 21 June, when the edict declaring war on the powers was received, Chang Chih-tung of Hunan-Hupei, Liu K'un-i of the lower Yangtse pro-vinces, Li Hung-chang who was now viceroy of Kuangtung-Kuangsi (resident at Canton), and Yüan Shih-k'ai, governor of Shantung, con-sulted each other by telegram and agreed to suppress the war edict and maintain neutrality. A very important part in this decision was taken by the Director of Posts and Telegraphs, Sheng Hsüan-huai, an official resident at Shanghai, who had a liberal outlook, and although not holding very high rank, was strategically placed by his post to learn the news and relay it to others. From 24 to 26 June Sheng negotiated with the foreign consuls in Shanghai for the protection of the concessions in that city and the peace of the Yangtse valley. An agreement was arrived at, though never formally signed, by which the southern viceroys and provincial governors undertook to protect foreign residents, suppress Boxer infiltration and maintain normal trade if the foreign powers refrained from landing troops or sending warships up the Yangtse. This virtual secession of the south saved most of China from the consequences of the Boxer rebellion.

The southern viceroys were, indeed, prepared to go farther than this; they urged Yüan Shih-k'ai, who was much closer to Peking, to march on the capital with his army, suppress the Boxers and end the trouble. Had Yüan done so there is little doubt that he could have succeeded, but his own position would have been exceedingly difficult. On 28 June he refused this suggestion, and remained inactive, keeping the Boxers out of Shantung, but also taking no action against the foreign troops then invading the neighbouring province of Chihli. The incoherence and disintegration of the empire could not have been more strikingly illuminated.

On 14 July the allied forces captured the Chinese city of Tientsin and ended the attacks upon the foreign concessions there. This success gave the reactionary party in Peking pause; it was clear that the Boxers were proving a disappointment; no progress had been made in the attack upon the legations, and China was now at war with a number of the most powerful nations in the world, who were preparing invasion. Such a prospect might well have daunted reactionaries even more bigoted than Prince Tuan and the empress dowager, but they did little to avert the catastrophe. Attacks on the legations were indeed suspended between 14 and 26 July. A further attempt was made to get the besieged diplomats to leave the city escorted by Chinese troops, a proposition which was not accepted. Another curious incident at this time illustrates the devious policy of the court, or the independent action of some of its servants. To the relief of the outside world a message was received in Washington from the American minister in Peking, Mr Conger, in which he gave news of the situation of the legations and confirmed, for the first time since the siege had begun, that their defence still held. This message was sent to the Chinese minister in Washington through the Tsungli Yamen, the head of which was the notorious Prince Tuan himself.

Six days later, on 26 July, the empress once more changed her policy, resumed the attacks upon the legations, and two days later had the two remaining moderate and anti-Boxer members of the Grand Council, Yüan Ch'ang and Hsü Ching-ch'eng, executed. On 4 August the allied forces left Tientsin to advance on Peking. In the capital the situation was now one of the utmost confusion. Kansu soldiery and Boxers roamed the streets slaying anyone suspected of foreign sympathies, habits, knowledge or demeanour. The homes of powerful officials were invaded and looted, thousands of the wealthier citizens fled from the doomed city. Yet the court appeared unable either to control the troops or to comprehend the nature of the disaster which had overtaken the dynasty and nation. The advance of the allied army, numbering less than 20,000 men, was rapid and irresistible. Yü Lu, the governor of Chihli, was defeated and his forces dispersed on 6 August; he took his own life the same evening. Another force under the general Li Ping-heng was routed on the 9th, and when the city of T'ungchou, starting-point of the Grand Canal, fell on the 11th, Li committed suicide. The allies were now within twelve miles of Peking.

The debacle could no longer be concealed or evaded; on the same day that T'ungchou fell the court telegraphed to Li Hung-chang, at his distant post in Canton, urging him to come north at once to undertake peace negotiations with the foreign powers. But Li was in no hurry to begin this thankless task: he waited first to see whether there were signs of a real change of heart, realising that so long as Prince Tuan and other pro-Boxer leaders remained around the empress dowager, any negotiations would be a waste of time.

On the afternoon of 14 August 1900 the allied forces reached the walls of Peking, entered the city almost without any resistance and relieved the besieged legations; very early the next morning, 15 August, amid scenes of the utmost panic and confusion, the empress dowager, disguised as a Chinese peasant woman, accompanied by the emperor, P'u Chün the heir apparent, and a handful of attendants, fled in common carts from the palace and the city. Before leaving the empress dowager ordered the emperor's favourite concubine, Chen Fei, the only woman for whom he had affection, and his only friend, to be thrust down a well in the court-yard just inside the north gate of the Forbidden City. The flight of the court took them first to Huai Lai, beyond the Great Wall, which they reached on the 17th, and where they for the first time received some assistance and relief. Continuing westward, since the pursuit of the allies seemed to threaten, they reached T'aiyüan, capital of Shansi, on 10 September, and finally came to rest at Sian, capital of Shensi province, on 26 October. Peking meanwhile was in the hands of the allies, and Li Hung-chang had made his slow way to Tientsin to open negotiations, arriving there on 19 September.

During the course of the next year these negotiations and the aftermath of the Boxer movement determined the status of China for the remaining decade of the Ch'ing dynasty's history. Russia had occupied Manchuria during the autumn months of 1900. In the south the wise policy of the great viceroys at one and the same time restrained the foreigners from fresh incursions and demands, and staved off the revolution which already threatened the discredited dynasty. In distant Sian the court, at first still dominated by the Boxer princes and ministers, was slowly brought to realise that only the repudiation of their policies and their punishment and elimination could appease the foreign powers and prevent the partition of the helpless empire. Early in January 1901 P'u Chün, the son of Prince

Tuan, was deprived of his status as heir apparent, and expelled from the palace. With great difficulty Li Hung-chang managed to save the life of Prince Tuan himself, who was instead exiled for life to the remote parts of Chinese Turkestan. The other pro-Boxer princes, ministers and governors, such as Yü Hsien, were either ordered to commit suicide or decapitated.

On 7 September 1901 Li Hung-chang signed the peace protocol. Two months later the old statesman, the last of the great generation who had fought the T'ai P'ing rebellion and striven, with all their limitations, to save the dynasty, died on 7 November 1901. Half a century was to pass before China recovered from the degradation, weakness and incoherent confusion to which the reactionary policies of the empress dowager and her like-minded supporters had finally brought the empire. That recovery, when it came, was the work of revolutionaries beside whom such reformers as K'ang Yu-wei, the bugbear of the empress, was an archconservative. The programme of reforms which the Kuang Hsü emperor had so ardently embraced, and which had roused so forceful a reaction, was to seem the mildest of moderate conservative progress. The revolution which the policy of the reactionary party had made inevitable swept away not only the throne and dynasty, but the whole social and economic system of old China.

CHAPTER XVII

JAPAN

I T is convenient to regard 1868 as marking a turning-point in the modern history of Japan. In January of that year a group of new leaders seized power in the then imperial capital of Kyoto, men who became, despite subsequent shifts in both policy and personnel, responsible for initiating changes which revolutionised the country's political, economic and social institutions and eventually raised it to a high level of international power and prestige.

Since the beginning of the seventeenth century government had been in the hands of a line of feudal rulers, the Tokugawa family. As shogun, nominally the emperor's military deputies, they had possessed the hereditary *de facto* authority of monarchs, exercising direct control over their own enormous domains and effectively subordinating the lords of the great feudal territories into which the rest of the country was divided. They sought, with remarkable success, to preserve their power by preventing change. After about 1640 Japan was by their decree almost entirely cut off from contact with the rest of the world, while at home political relationships were frozen in their seventeenth-century form, rigid social distinctions developed and were enforced for all classes of the population, and attempts were made to inhibit even economic change.

It was in its economic aspects that this policy was least successful. By the eighteenth century domestic commerce had expanded and the feudal class, the samurai, for the most part resident in castle-towns, had become accustomed to a higher standard of living. They had not, however, secured a commensurate increase in revenue or income. As a result, both domain governments and individual samurai became steadily more indebted to city rice-brokers and financiers. Attempts to secure for the lord a higher proportion of the product of the soil brought peasant revolts. Devices by which domain governments engaged in monopoly trading, in co-operation with the merchants of the towns, alienated the richer farmers and an emerging class of rural entrepreneurs. Nor did these measures benefit the majority of samurai. Most of them derived their income not directly from the land but from rice stipends paid by the fief treasury; and these stipends, far from being increased, were often reduced when the treasury found itself in financial difficulties.

By 1850, therefore, there was widespread recognition in Japan that Tokugawa society was facing a serious crisis. Opposition to the regime existed almost everywhere. A number of the most powerful of the feudal lords continued to resent their subordination to the Tokugawa—indeed, a great part of the machinery of central government was directed to keeping their ambitions in check. Poverty was weakening the loyalty of the lower-ranking samurai, while the more able and energetic of them resented the hereditary system of office-holding which stifled their political ambitions. The wealthy merchants of the towns, though too deeply involved in feudal finance to oppose the regime wholeheartedly, were restive at the inferior social status it imposed upon them. The peasants expressed their hatreds increasingly in violence.

All these elements played a part in bringing about the downfall of the Tokugawa. Motives varied widely, and at no time was the whole welded into a single movement with agreed objectives. On the other hand, there were two factors which tended to provide a basis of co-operation beyond the mere desire for change. During the first half of the nineteenth century there was a growing awareness that Japan's isolation was threatened by western expansion in China and on the mainland to the north. This estimate was apparently confirmed by the appearance of an American squadron demanding treaty relations in 1853. Since Japan's military strength was clearly unequal to the task of enforcing the policy of seclusion, treaties had to be signed; and there were many who argued that this external threat made still more urgent the need for radical reform.

Since the Tokugawa government was responsible for the conduct of foreign relations, it had to assume also the responsibility for unpopular concessions to the west. This fact strengthened the appeal of its only potential rival as a centre of legitimate authority, the imperial court, which remained uncompromisingly hostile to western demands. For a century or more there had been men who urged the desirability of reviving the court's prestige and the emperor now began to fill a double role in the anti-Tokugawa movement: to provide a focus of loyalty which transcended sectional interests, at least superficially, and to give an air of respectability to revolutionary activities carried on in his name.

Thus, by 1868, the so-called 'honour-the-emperor' (*sonno*) movement had made possible an alliance of anti-Tokugawa forces. Power was seized, when the opportunity came, by a loose coalition of forces under the leadership of a group of samurai of middle rank from four great domains of west Japan: from Satsuma, Choshu, Tosa and Hizen. They had already won control of their own domain governments, thereby securing a nucleus of armed force and the co-operation, not always willing, of their feudal lords. They had allies in the lower ranks of the court nobility, vital as a means of access to the emperor. Finally, they could count on the financial support of some of the merchants and the active help of many local leaders in the countryside. These were the elements which were in time to form the ruling class of modern Japan.

In January 1868 troops under the command of anti-Tokugawa leaders seized the imperial palace in Kyoto. Decrees were issued in the name of the boy-emperor Meiji—to use his reign title: his given name was Mutsuhito—depriving the shogun of his power and his lands and re-asserting the emperor's direct responsibility for the conduct of affairs. The former offices of state were swept away and the administration entrusted to new advisers. Almost at once Tokugawa adherents took up arms to defend their privileges, but they were defeated at clashes outside Kyoto in February and thereafter offered surprisingly little resistance. In April the shogun's surrender was negotiated and his capital of Edo was formally occupied. A few months later the imperial court was transferred there and, renamed Tokyo, the city resumed its function as the centre of national government. Meanwhile, scattered fighting continued in the north and north-east. It was not until the early summer of 1869 that the last pockets of Tokugawa resistance were finally overcome.

For this first year and a half of its existence the Meiji government faced immediate problems which left it little time to grapple with questions of reform. It began without finances or administrative machinery, for both had in the past been provided by the Tokugawa from their own resources of men and lands. As the fighting progressed more and more of the Tokugawa territories came under imperial control. So, too, did former Tokugawa officials, many of whom eventually took service under the emperor. Yet in the interval money had to be found and an organisation created with which to fight the civil war. Loans were raised from sympathetic merchants, Tokugawa cash reserves were seized wherever they could be found, and the balance of expenditure was made up by printing notes. An army, the other primary need, was created by summoning contingents from those domains which had rallied to the imperial cause, each unit serving under its own feudal leaders. This army, however, was fully engaged in fighting the Tokugawa. It was not available as a means of bringing pressure to bear on the great majority of feudal lords, enjoying almost complete autonomy within their own boundaries, who were content to await the outcome of the struggle before declaring their allegiance. Hence, for some months at the beginning of 1868, the new government's authority was enforcible only in the vicinity of the capital and in those areas where loyal troops were operating. At this time Japan had no effective central government at all.

It is not surprising that in these circumstances the task of building an institutional framework for the new regime proceeded slowly. The first step, in January 1868, had been to create posts around the emperor's person for members of the anti-Tokugawa coalition. An imperial prince was made nominal head of the administration. Under him were two groups of councillors, the senior comprising several members of the court and a number of feudal lords, the junior (and more numerous) being lesser court nobles and samurai leaders from the allied domains. In February administrative departments were formed, councillors being appointed to the senior offices within them. Their functions, like their staff, were limited. Such rights as they had to intervene in local matters were dependent on the concurrence of feudal lords, even—perhaps especially—in the territories from which the councillors themselves were drawn. It remained so as long as there was any doubt about the outcome of the civil war. In an attempt to meet this difficulty and to widen the basis of support, samurai representatives from all the domains were summoned in March to act as a kind of consultative assembly, while on 6 April the court issued an imperial pronouncement, known as the Charter Oath, setting out in vague but reassuring terms the policies it planned to follow. The cardinal points were a promise to carry out wide consultation on all important decisions, to abolish 'base customs' of the past, and to seek new knowledge 'throughout the world' as the basis of reform.

With the shogun's surrender in April and the occupation of Edo shortly after, the imperial government felt more secure. On 11 June 1868 it promulgated revised arrangements for the central administration, ostensibly in fulfilment of the Charter Oath. These reflected western influence in their enunciation of the principle of separation of powers, but in practice the executive remained supreme and the real function of the legislative, like the samurai assembly which had preceded it, was to act as a sounding-board of feudal opinion. This was still more obvious in the next reorganisation, effected in August 1869, a few weeks after the fighting in the north had ended. The assembly now lost the power of initiating legislation and after a few meetings was adjourned *sine die* in October 1870. It was abolished altogether in June 1873 without having met again. The executive was put under the general supervision of a central board, the Dajokan, subordinate to which were six ministerial departments: Civil Affairs, Finance, War, Justice, Imperial Household, and Foreign Affairs. At the same time, the number of senior posts was reduced and office-holders, regardless of social origin, were given court rank commensurate with their responsibilities.

Yet it was the nature of the appointments made, rather than organisational changes, which reflect the most important development of this period. Initially, while the struggle with the Tokugawa was continuing, it had been necessary both to maintain the alliance and to reconcile as much 'neutral' opinion as possible. Appointments were therefore made not only from the ranks of those court nobles, feudal lords and samurai who had been most active in the anti-Tokugawa movement, but also from other groups (within the same social range) which showed themselves willing to co-operate. As the new government grew stronger, however, the basis of selection narrowed. After June 1868 fewer councillors were appointed from the imperial court, while those of feudal origin came mostly from Satsuma, Choshu, Tosa and Hizen. In August 1869 the remaining figureheads of the Restoration movement, high-ranking court nobles and feudal lords of the original coalition, were removed from the highest offices of state to make way for the small group of men of lower rank who had long determined policy behind the scenes. These included the court noble Iwakura Tomomi and a number of samurai: Okubo Toshimichi and Saigo Takamori of Satsuma; Kido Koin, Ito Hirobumi and Yamagata Aritomo of Choshu; Okuma Shigenobu of Hizen; Goto Shojiro and Itagaki Taisuke of Tosa.[1] These, with their immediate subordinates, men of similar origin to themselves, formed the core of the new leadership.

It would be wrong to suggest that Japan's new rulers possessed from the beginning a detailed plan of the uses to which they would put their power. Their ultimate objective was clear enough: Japan had to be saved from internal disruption and foreign threat. The precise measures to be adopted to this end and the priorities to be assigned them were more difficult to determine, but at least it was clear that, whatever else needed to be done, the government's authority had to be given reality and its decisions made valid for the country as a whole. Feudal separatism was the greatest obstacle to the achievement of this goal. As one of the Meiji leaders wrote some thirty years later: 'The annihilation of centrifugal forces taking the form of autocratic feudal provinces was a necessary step to the unification of the country under a strong central government, without which we would not have been able to offer a united front to the outside forces....'

There is no evidence that the abolition of feudalism had been decided on before the new leaders rose to power, though they attempted from the first to establish a position of supremacy for the imperial government as against any other focus of traditional loyalty. The Shinto religion, with its emphasis on imperial divinity, was given an important place in the new official hierarchy. More directly, attempts were made to gain some measure of control over the affairs of the feudal domains. As early as March 1868, samurai entering the service of the central government were ordered to sever relations with their fiefs, while in the following year the most influential of them were granted imperial stipends and court rank. In June 1868 certain restrictions were imposed on the freedom of action of the feudal lords in their relations with each other. By the end of the year they had been ordered to appoint special officials for liaison with the government and to standardise administration within their territories on a pattern laid down by Tokyo. A similar centralising tendency was apparent in the handling of lands confiscated from the Tokugawa. After a brief period of military government during the campaign, they were designated as imperial cities (*fu*) or prefectures (*ken*) and brought directly under the central administration.

For some this was still not enough. Even before June 1868 Kido had proposed that the lords be required to surrender all their lands, since this

---

[1] In citing Japanese personal names the Japanese order has been followed, that is, family name followed by given name.

was the only means of ensuring effective centralisation. When the proposal was rejected by his colleagues, he turned his efforts to persuading his own lord, Mori of Choshu, and eventually won him over, subject only to the understanding that Satsuma make a similar gesture. Okubo Toshimichi was approached in November and agreed to use his influence with the other Satsuma leaders. By February 1869 they had all given their support, as had also Itagaki of Tosa and Okuma of Hizen. On 2 March the lords of the four fiefs submitted a memorial putting their lands and people at the emperor's disposal. In the discussions which followed in the imperial council there were those who urged that this was an opportunity to abolish the domains and extend the prefectural system, but both Kido and Okubo insisted that the government was still too weak for such a step to be successful. A decision was not reached till July, when the memorial was accepted, the other lords were ordered to take similar action, and the former feudal rulers were appointed as imperial governors of the territories they had surrendered.

This compromise, however disappointing to the more radical thinkers, seems to have been much what the lords and many of their retainers had expected. Some of them, especially in Choshu and Satsuma, resented even this limited degree of central control. On the other hand, the reform was not entirely successful in the government's eyes, since local officials were still local nominees and frequently gave only token allegiance to Tokyo. It became more and more obvious, at least to men like Okubo and Kido, that the process, once begun, must be carried to its logical conclusion. Throughout 1870 they tried in vain to overcome the objections of colleagues in their own domains. Early in 1871, when it began to seem that the whole basis of the regime might be destroyed by continued disagreement on this issue, they invoked imperial intervention and made renewed efforts to effect a reconciliation. This time they were successful. In April arrangements were made to move Satsuma, Choshu and Tosa forces into Tokyo in case of trouble. On 29 August fifty-seven provincial governors, former feudal lords, were summoned to the emperor's presence and informed that the domains were to be abolished, all territory thereafter to be divided into prefectures under direct imperial control.

The removal of political barriers within the country made it possible to solve the urgent problem of providing the government with an adequate and stable revenue. By the abolition of the fiefs, it had fallen heir to their debts and other commitments, greatest of which was the annual cost of samurai stipends. It had also inherited their feudal dues. The disadvantage was that these not only varied widely from one locality to another, but also were paid in kind as a percentage of the crop. They therefore fluctuated with seasonal yield, as well as being difficult to collect. A solution could be found by substituting for them a land tax payable in cash, but before this could be done it was necessary to establish ownership of each piece of land (and hence responsibility for the payment of tax). In February 1872 the Tokugawa ban on alienation of land was abolished. At about the same time the government began to issue certificates of title, beginning with certain types of land in Tokyo during January and extending the process throughout the country from July.

The introduction of land tax itself came in 1873. It was to be a cash payment of 3 per cent of the assessed value of the land, in addition to which local authorities were permitted to levy a maximum of a further 1 per cent. Valuations were so calculated that the total yield was approximately equal to that of the former feudal dues, though the fact that it had to be paid in cash at a fixed date and was unvarying from year to year, whether harvests were good or bad, made it irksome to the majority of farmers. Its importance to the government can be seen from the calculation that it provided on average approximately 78 per cent of ordinary revenue up to 1881, despite its reduction to a $2\frac{1}{2}$ per cent assessment in 1876.

By 1873, therefore, after almost five years in power, the Meiji government had laid the foundations of its own authority. It had created a workable system of central administration, brought local affairs directly under its own control and provided itself with a predictable annual revenue. It had also taken the first steps towards creating a military force which would be free of feudal loyalties. Conscription laws had been announced in 1872 and the training of a conscript army began the following year, eventually providing an effective weapon against feudal revolt and giving invaluable support to the new police force in the suppression of peasant riots. Meanwhile the government had already begun to devote its attention to questions of national strength and international politics.

Almost the first act of the regime in 1868 had been to issue an explicit disavowal of its own former anti-foreign slogans and take steps to suppress those activities of its own adherents which might bring Japan into conflict with the western powers. None the less, there remained a strong element of hostility to the west in Japanese thinking. A major object of this hostility was the treaty system, negotiated in 1858 and expanded in 1866, by which Japan had been deprived of legal control over foreign nationals in her ports and of the right to modify her tariffs on foreign trade. In 1871, after the abolition of the fiefs, Iwakura Tomomi took a mission abroad to explore the possibilities of treaty revision. In Washington it was made clear to the group—which included Okubo, Kido and Ito, as well as Iwakura—that there was little hope of early change; and thereafter the mission became more concerned with the acquisition of knowledge than with diplomatic negotiations. In London, Ito inspected factories. In Berlin, Iwakura was lectured on *real-politik* by Bismarck.

After some eighteen months of travel, this section of Japan's leadership became convinced that only through a programme of domestic reform, far more extensive than they had previously envisaged, could their country achieve the respect of the powers.

Meanwhile, those who had been left behind in Tokyo were taking a different course. The occasion was a series of disputes with Korea, provoked by that country's insistence on maintaining the same policy of national seclusion that Japan had now abandoned, and Japan's caretaker government, of which the most powerful member was Saigo Takamori, decided to back its demands with force in the summer of 1873. News of this decision brought the Iwakura mission hurrying home from Europe. It reversed the decision after an acrimonious dispute with Saigo, who, with a number of others, resigned from the government.[1] The outcome of this crisis determined the pattern of Japanese politics, both at home and abroad, for the following twenty years. The men now driven into opposition made constant attacks on their former colleagues and succeeded, as we shall see, in modifying the course of Japan's constitutional development, but they never won back control. Okubo remained the dominant figure till his assassination in 1878, supported by Iwakura and, less consistently, by Kido. Kido died in 1877 and Iwakura in 1883, but they were succeeded by others of like mind, notably Ito Hirobumi and Yamagata Aritomo. There was no essential change of policy. Japan, until 1893, continued to act with restraint abroad. At home, her government launched a programme of sweeping reform.

A description of reforms in the machinery of government, both central and local, can most conveniently be undertaken in the context of political rivalries and the constitutional struggle, discussion of which follows separately. It is sufficient to emphasise here the general nature of the process taking place in the years after the Korean crisis. There was a gradual tightening of control over administration, accompanied by the growth of a professional bureaucracy, members of which owed their appointment and promotion, in part at least, to a system of state examinations. Simultaneously there was a progressive introduction of western methods and ideas, directed partly towards increasing efficiency, partly towards giving Japan that appearance of 'respectability', as the west understood the word, which was a necessary prelude to treaty revision. In 1875, for example, a committee was formed to draft a new civil code, though it was over twenty years before revision and amendment of its work was finished. The result, finally adopted and enforced in 1898, showed the influence of a variety of western models, French, German and British. At a less formal level, Japanese social habits also engaged the government's attention, especially those which might arouse criticism abroad. Official regulations and exhortations covered subjects as varied as the behaviour

[1] Below, pp. 645-6, for further details.

of Japanese tourists overseas, the sale of girls as prostitutes, pornographic literature, even stage jokes.

The creation of a system of compulsory education was one of the most important achievements of these years. Institutions of higher education established in the Tokugawa period, concerned chiefly with the training of officials, continued for a time under the supervision of the new government. In 1877 a number of these were combined to form Tokyo Imperial University. Several other state universities were added soon after, while some of the private foundations dealing with western studies also acquired university status. Before this, in 1872, the Education Department had announced a plan for primary education, beginning at the age of six, which envisaged the establishment of one elementary school for approximately every 600 of population. Despite a shortage of funds and teachers, expansion was fast enough to enable the compulsory period of attendance to be increased from its original 16 months to three years in 1880 and four years in 1886. By this date 46 per cent of the children of school age were receiving primary education. The figure rose to 61 per cent in 1896 and 95 per cent a decade later. Normal schools, for the training of teachers, had begun in 1872 and high-schools were added in 1894.

The pattern of educational administration was based at first on that of France, but there was a period between 1880 and 1885 when American methods were adopted, including the use of elected school-boards. After 1885, however, with the appointment of Mori Arinori as Education Minister, there was an increase in nationalist influences and a turning towards the German models of government supervision. Much of the curriculum was still devoted to a training in 'practical', that is, western subjects, but there was a new emphasis on the study of Japanese history and literature, accompanied by a deliberate attempt to inculcate habits of loyalty and civic obedience. This trend was reinforced by the issue in 1890 of the Rescript on Education. The wording of the document revealed clearly that a principal object of education was thereafter to be the production of useful and disciplined citizens of an authoritarian state.

Government control was also a feature of the plans to give Japan a modern network of communications. The government postal service, established in 1871, was extended to all major centres of population in 1873, from which date private competition was forbidden. Telegraphs had been made a state monopoly the previous year, the construction of major trunk lines being more or less completed in the following decade, and a similar decision was taken concerning telephones in 1890, soon after their introduction to Japan. Railway development, though not always under state ownership, depended heavily on the government for finance and technical assistance, a fact which enabled officials to determine priorities in building. The first line was that between Tokyo and Yokohama, begun in 1870 and opened in 1872, but this was envisaged as the first stage of a route linking Tokyo with Osaka, the whole of which was not completed till 1888. Thereafter railways were extended rapidly, on both government and private initiative.

The steps taken to ensure facilities for education and communications played an important part in stimulating economic development, as did the provision of a framework of legal security and political order. Yet government intervention in economic matters went far beyond the creation of an environment favourable to growth. This is true particularly in the field of industrialisation. The Meiji leaders took over from their Tokugawa predecessors, as well as from some of the great domains, a number of recently established enterprises of western type. They included shipyards, like that at Yokosuka, and several plants for the manufacture of weapons. Strategic industries of this kind, directly related to military strength, were inevitably of concern to men who saw their country threatened from abroad; and this segment of the economy, like communications, remained subject to direct government control. Similar reasoning prompted government interest in other types of industrial undertaking. Wealth, it was realised, was the basis of military power—the slogan of these years was *fukoku-kyohei*, 'rich country, strong army'. Other motives worked in the same direction. The opening of the ports had brought into Japan a flood of cheap foreign manufactured goods, the demand for which was greater than anything the country could provide by way of exports. The adverse trade balance which resulted in the period 1868–81 caused a constant and disturbing drain of specie. Moreover, the import of foreign goods was ruining a number of domestic handicraft industries on which the heavily taxed farmer depended for cash income. Thus a programme of industrialisation had a number of attractions apart from its relevance to the question of defence. It could cut down the volume of imports by providing substitutes manufactured in Japan, while the new factories, if placed in areas hard hit by foreign competition, could provide alternative employment for surplus rural labour.

This does not explain why the Meiji government chose to initiate, rather than simply to encourage, new types of economic enterprise. The answer lies partly in the need for speed, if Japan were not soon to succumb to foreign pressure, partly in the lack of capital available for investment. The growth of commerce in the Tokugawa period had not been great enough to promote widespread capital accumulation on any scale, while, with few exceptions, such rich financial houses as had emerged were ruined by the collapse of the feudal system on which their operations had depended. In addition, rents and interest rates remained high after 1868, making land and usury a more attractive investment than factories. Hence, to achieve rapid action, the government itself was forced to give a lead. It did so in a wide variety of ways. Foreign technicians were brought in as teachers and advisers—the Ministry of Public Works alone employed as many as 130 by 1879—and Japanese students were sent abroad for training. Technical schools were established and trade exhibitions organised. Foreign goods and equipment were imported for loan to local authorities as models, while the government even bought spinning machinery abroad for resale to Japanese entrepreneurs on the instalment plan. It engaged directly in foreign trade, selling shipments of rice, silk and tea to finance its imports. Finally, it established factories of its own, some of them, such as a cotton-spinning mill in Aichi (1878), to serve primarily as training centres, others, like the Fukugawa cement factory (1875), to provide goods which would otherwise have had to be imported at considerable cost. It has been estimated that total government investment in industry averaged at least $5\frac{1}{2}$ per cent of ordinary revenue in the years 1868–80. At the end of that period there were three shipbuilding yards, five munitions works, ten mines and fifty-two factories listed as state-owned.

The financing of this programme presented many difficulties to a government without reserves. Foreign loans were not a possible expedient, both because of the reluctance of investors abroad to risk capital in Japan and because the Japanese themselves feared they might open the way to foreign control of the economy. Since taxation of the farmer was already at a maximum and the treaties forbade any change in tariffs, a temporary solution was found in the large-scale printing of paper money. For a time the growth in economic activity proved capable of absorbing the larger issue of notes in circulation. After 1877, however, inflation rapidly became serious. Higher prices, especially of rice, brought a spurt of rural prosperity. On the other hand, they sharply reduced the real value of the land tax on which the government depended for the greater part of its revenue. In October 1881, with the appointment of Matsukata Masayoshi as Finance Minister, firm measures were introduced to restore stability to the public finances, including new taxes on rice-wine and tobacco, stringent economy in administration, and the reduction of government grants and subsidies. It was in this context that the decision was taken to dispose of most of the industrial enterprises founded and still run by the state. To sell them would recoup part, at least, of the government's investment in them and relieve it of the continued drain of operating losses. Only the military industries were retained, the others being disposed of as opportunity arose, mostly in 1884; and they went, as a rule, at bargain prices, to men with government connections, thereby playing a part in creating the close relationship between government and the great financial–industrial combines (*zaibatsu*) which was a conspicuous feature of later economic development.

The Matsukata policy was successful in balancing the budget and restoring the value of the currency. Inevitably it did so at some cost in human terms, especially in the countryside, and it must bear responsibility for much of the rural unrest that characterised the next few years.

This fact underlines the value which the Meiji leaders placed on their modernisation programme. Both before and after 1881 they showed themselves willing to maintain it, if necessary, at a sacrifice of rural interests which constituted a considerable political risk. Yet for agriculture, if not agriculturalists, they had a real concern. Much of the government's economic training programme was devoted to improving methods of agricultural production, with the result that the yield of rice and other cereal crops grew steadily, almost keeping pace with the growth of population and the gradual increase in consumption per head. By 1893, in fact, despite the effort the government had made to promote industrialisation, Japan was still predominantly rural. Modern factories were few and small. Foreign trade was modest, important chiefly as a means of technical borrowing. Most of the population still lived in small communities, following agriculture as their primary occupation, and land-tax remained the major source of government revenue. It was not until after the Sino-Japanese War that the economy moved at all rapidly towards new forms.

The same cannot be said of political structure during these same years. Quite apart from administrative changes undertaken for purposes of increased efficiency, there were others—and these the most striking— which arose out of a bitter struggle for power between the government and its critics.

The form of opposition which gave the government most difficulty during the 1870's was that arising from samurai discontent. The policy of conciliating samurai opinion was gradually abandoned as the central authority grew stronger, and was replaced by a series of attacks on feudal privilege. Among the earliest were decrees which established legal equality between the different classes and forbade the samurai to wear distinctive dress or carry swords. The conscription laws, moreover, though not immediately effective, soon threatened to rob them of their status as a military élite. However, it was not until their economic position was endangered that resentment was expressed in large-scale violence. With the abolition of the domains in 1871 the government assumed responsibility for the payment of samurai stipends, but on a reduced scale and with differences between various levels within the class. The lords themselves were treated generously. This, indeed, was an inducement designed to secure their acquiescence in the change. For many of lower rank, however, already suffering hardship under the old system, the reductions now effected brought their incomes below subsistence level. Even so, their loyalty was not entirely destroyed, for in the first half of 1873 they were co-operating extensively with the police in suppressing local peasant revolts, possibly because they still had faith in some, at least, of the new leaders. By the end of the same year this no longer obtained. The victory of Okubo and his colleagues in the dispute over Korea frustrated samurai hopes of overseas conquest and caused the resignation, among others, of Saigo Takamori and Eto Shimpei. Almost simultaneously came a threat to what was left of feudal stipends. Faced with growing expenditures, the government sought to economise by offering samurai the option of taking a capital grant instead of an annual pension. A little less then three years later, in 1876, this was made compulsory. All former samurai were forced to accept a lump sum in interest-bearing government bonds, yielding far less than their original stipends. Some idea of the effect can be gained from the fact that the new bonds bore a total interest of about 11·5 million yen a year, whereas the market value of the 1871 stipends had been some 22·6 million and the estimated annual value of former domain stipends 34·6 million.

These developments led to open samurai rebellion, the more disturbing because it centred in the areas from which the Meiji leaders themselves had come. In February 1874 Eto Shimpei led a revolt in Hizen. Another followed almost at once in Choshu. The most important, however, came in Satsuma three years later. After his resignation from the government in 1873, Saigo Takamori had retired to his home province and busied himself with the organising of 'schools' for samurai, which had the double object of creating a trained corps of military administrators and of providing for co-operative self-help. Within a short time his followers were in virtual control of prefectural administration, able to ignore the orders of Tokyo at will. In January 1877, after much hesitation, the government took the first step towards bringing the area back under its control by ordering the removal of the arms stored at the provincial capital of Kagoshima. Saigo's followers promptly seized the arsenal and broke into open revolt. The campaign that followed lasted six months before Saigo, with the remnant of his force of 15,000 men, was forced back on Kagoshima and took his own life; and the government had to put into the field the whole of its standing army of 32,000, with 10,000 reserves and most of the national police.

The suppression of the Satsuma Rebellion, costly though it was, demonstrated that feudal risings were no longer effective in a modern state, even one as new-fledged as Japan. Samurai continued to resort to violence from time to time, initially as leaders of peasant riots, eventually as political assassins—a type of political action which the events of 1858–68 had made almost respectable—but the main stream of opposition to the government thereafter was found in the so-called 'movement for freedom and people's rights' (jiyu-minken undo). This, too, found effective leadership as a result of the split within the oligarchy in 1873. Whereas men from Hizen and Satsuma, like Eto and Saigo, took up arms to back their views, the Tosa group, notably Itagaki Taisuke and Goto Sojiro, preferred legal agitation to secure the creation of a representative assembly.

The motives, as well as the limitations, of this 'liberal' movement are revealed in two memorials presented by its leaders in 1874. The first, dated 17 January, argued that the arbitrary action of those in office was alienating popular support and thus endangering the state. To establish an elected assembly would enable national unity to be achieved: 'Then and only then will the country become strong.' Though this argument was supported by references to western political philosophy, in essence it was a challenge to the group in power, accepting the objective of achieving national strength and disputing chiefly the means of doing so. It was not an appeal based on the doctrine of individual rights. Indeed, when a supporter of the government criticised the demand for an assembly as premature, on the grounds that 'outside the present government officials, there would be not more than sixty or seventy men of distinguished ability and knowledge in the whole nation', Itagaki and Goto replied that they had no immediate intention of making the franchise universal. 'We would only give it in the first instance', they wrote, 'to the samurai and the richer farmers and merchants, for it is they who produced the leaders of the revolution of 1868.'

Thus the appeal of the movement was made directly to those elements of the anti-Tokugawa alliance which had reason to feel disappointment at the results of the change they had helped to bring about. Its leaders were drawn from those domains, Tosa and Hizen, which resented the growing predominance of men from Satsuma and Choshu in central government. The rank-and-file at first were largely samurai from the same areas. This was evident in the membership of the early political associations formed to give the movement some coherence, such as the Aikokuto (Patriots' party), organised in 1874, and the Aikokusha (Society of Patriots), which succeeded it, still more in the Risshisha, a Tosa group consisting exclusively of samurai. Potentially, however, much wider support was available in the countryside. Landlords and rural entrepreneurs, though they had profited economically from the Restoration, welcomed the prospect of playing a larger part in national politics and were specifically critical of what they regarded as government favouritism of the towns in the matter of taxation. The farmers, too, hated the land-tax. They also had a host of other grievances, ranging from high rents to conscription and such new-fangled amenities as schools and telegraphs. A start was made in bringing such groups into an organised opposition with the formation of Japan's first modern political party, the Jiyuto (Liberal party), in October 1881.

Before this, however, the government had been forced to reconsider its own stand on the question of constitutional development. Kido had advocated representative institutions as early as 1873, but Okubo had argued that the time was not yet ripe, though he agreed that the creation of some kind of written constitution was desirable as a means of ensuring stability and national unity. In fact, the chief difference between the views of Okubo and his colleagues, on the one hand, and opposition leaders, on the other, was that the former sought a constitution which would confirm their power, the latter one which would break it. This is clear from the discussion of various constitutional proposals which took place among government leaders in the period 1878–80. Ito put the point most succinctly. After analysing briefly the nature of existing opposition, he stated: 'it is the responsibility of the government to follow a conciliatory policy and accommodate itself to these tendencies so that we may control but not intensify the situation, and relax our hold over government but not yield it.'

Action was precipitated by a further split within the ranks of the oligarchy. Since the death of Okubo in 1878 the chief rivals for over-all leadership had been Ito, who had the support of Iwakura and the Choshu interests, and Okuma Shigenobu of Hizen. Okuma had not at first committed himself on the constitutional issue, but in March 1881, apparently in an attempt to use popular agitation to back his own bid for power, he came out openly in favour of the immediate establishment of a constitution on British lines. It must, he said, include provision for an elected legislature and for party cabinets depending on a parliamentary majority. In June, at the instance of Ito and Iwakura, this proposal was rejected. In October they succeeded in getting Okuma himself removed from office, whereupon he formed a political party of his own, the Rikken Kaishinto (Constitutional Progressive party), composed of a number of his followers among the younger bureaucrats, a group of city intellectuals, and some of the new industrialists, led by the great Iwasaki (Mitsubishi) concern.

Simultaneously with Okuma's enforced resignation, Ito and Iwakura procured an imperial edict promising that a constitution would be granted —not immediately, as Okuma demanded, but in 1889. This had the double advantage of blunting the opposition's attacks and giving time for preparation. Soon after, in 1882, they formed their own party, the Rikken Teiseito (Constitutional Imperial party), but it proved weak and generally unpopular. Much more effective were the direct measures they took against the rival parties. The Press Law of 1875, which made it a punishable offence to criticise the government, had already been used extensively to muzzle and sometimes suppress the opposition newspapers. In 1880, moreover, Ito had introduced laws putting political meetings under police control and prohibiting political associations from advertising meetings, soliciting membership, or corresponding with similar groups elsewhere. These weapons of suppression, originally devised for use against Itagaki's followers, were now turned against the Kaishinto as well. They were reinforced, often successfully, by attempts to set the two parties against each other. Finally, in December 1887, came the Peace Preservation Law, extending the powers of the police still farther and making it possible to banish political suspects from the capital.

The opposition parties had not the strength to withstand such treatment. Within the Jiyuto, in particular, the effect of government regulations against correspondence and combination was to weaken the control of samurai leaders at the centre and enable power to pass into the hands of local committees, dominated as a rule by landowners. Moreover, the rural depression caused by Matsukata's financial policy after 1881 brought a wave of tenancy disputes, under the influence of which the peasant wing · of the party became increasingly radical in outlook and violent in action, the landowners increasingly conservative. Facing such difficulties, Itagaki and his colleagues decided to dissolve the party in October 1884. At about the same time Okuma withdrew from the Kaishinto, which was thereby rendered harmless.

The government had meanwhile made a start on the positive side of its policy, the preparations for issuing a written constitution. Not all these were due to pressure from its domestic enemies or to a Machiavellian scheme for perpetuating its own authority. In part, at least, they were a logical stage in the attainment of political unity in modern forms, an extension of the attack on local separatism. As Ito described the process, the Japanese people 'were slowly but steadily led to extend their vision beyond the pale of their village communities, to look upon the affairs of their districts and prefectures as their own, until finally they could interest themselves in the affairs of state and nation as strongly as, or even more strongly than, in the affairs of their own villages'. The first step in this direction had been taken in 1874, with the creation of an assembly of prefectural governors. Another came in 1878, with the addition of elected prefectural assemblies to discuss local matters, including taxation, though the electorate was limited and extensive powers of veto and suspension were given to the Home Minister and his subordinates. Similar restrictions were put on the activities of the town and village councils established in 1880. Since the same period saw the tightening of central control over local officials, as well as the strengthening of the latter *vis-à-vis* the population at large, it is clear that these assemblies did not reflect anything more than a superficial relaxation of the oligarchy's hold.

Changes in the structure of central government came after the decision to announce a constitution and were more immediately connected with preparations for it. First was the institution of new orders of nobility in 1884. The avowed object was to provide rewards for loyal service, but the pointed omission of Okuma and Itagaki, despite their distinguished careers in the administration, indicated that the move was also to provide politically dependable members for a future House of Peers. In December of the following year came the introduction of a modern cabinet system on the German model, with Ito as Prime Minister, in charge of over-all policy, and a number of department ministers each personally responsible to the emperor. An appointed Privy Council, created in April 1888, provided yet another stronghold of oligarchic influence.

The general shape of the constitution had already been decided by Ito and Iwakura in July 1881 and a set of 'general principles' written by Iwakura, virtually an outline of the document to be issued eight years later, had been adopted by the Dajokan in October of that year. Hence Ito's famous visit to Europe in 1882–3, undertaken ostensibly to study foreign constitutions, was in fact concerned only with deciding points of detail. Since Iwakura's advice had been 'to form a cabinet with no regard for parliament, on the model of Prussia', Ito naturally spent most of his time in Berlin and Vienna, where the lectures he heard served to confirm his preconceptions. He only made brief visits to Paris and London before his return to Japan in the summer of 1883. Thereafter drafting of the final text proceeded under his personal supervision and the constitution was announced, with due ceremony, on 11 February 1889. It came into force in 1890.

The Meiji Constitution made little concession to the views of Okuma and Itagaki. It was a gift of the emperor, who reserved the right of initiating revisions. Moreover, it confirmed the almost absolute powers of the monarchy, including those of declaring war, making peace and concluding treaties, of control over the bureaucracy and the army and navy, and of issuing ordinances. The duties of subjects, such as those of performing military service and paying taxes, were clear-cut. Their rights (freedom of speech, fair trial, etc.) were subject to the provisions of the law. Even more disturbing to the opponents of the government were the parliamentary sections, for although the emperor exercised the legislative power 'with the consent of the Imperial Diet', ministers were not responsible to the elected House of Representatives, while the House of Peers, inevitably a conservative body, had in effect a veto on all bills. In the matter of finance, all expenditures 'involved in the exercise of the Imperial Prerogative'—subsequently defined as including those on account of the armed forces, as well as much of the civil and military salary list—were removed from the control of the Diet. The annual budget required the consent of the Lower House, but if this were refused the government was empowered to carry out the budget of the previous year. There was little chance that the parties could use this as a means of achieving their ambitions. The constitution, in fact, was the final step in erecting the structure of a modern state, not a concession wrested from the government by its opponents.

The Electoral law of 1890 prescribed tax qualifications for voting which limited the electorate to about 450,000 out of a total population of 40 million. Because of the heavy incidence of the land-tax, landowners comprised the largest single group of voters, a fact reflected in the first elections (1890), when over 90 per cent of the 300 representatives in the Lower House depended on the rural vote. Of more immediate importance was the strength of the political parties, now reorganised. The groups led by Itagaki, Goto and Okuma controlled 160 seats and thus possessed between them a majority over supporters of the government. They sought to use this majority to win acceptance for the idea of party cabinets, a policy to which Yamagata, the Prime Minister, and most of his colleagues were unalterably opposed. The result was a head-on clash between the leaders of the oligarchy and the Lower House of the Diet. From the beginning this centred on the budget. In the first session (1890–1) the Lower House proposed a 10 per cent cut and Yamagata succeeded in effecting a compromise only with the aid of extensive bribery and intimidation. His successor, Matsukata, faced even greater difficulties and dissolved the House in December 1891, attempting to control the elections which followed by the use of police as well as bribery. The result was a casualty list of twenty-five dead and several hundred injured, but no important reduction in the opposition's strength. The struggle over the budget continued. Ito, who replaced Matsukata late in 1892, broke the deadlock temporarily by invoking direct imperial intervention, but even so found it necessary to dissolve the House again in December 1893 and June 1894.

A wave of enthusiasm for the war with China brought a political truce in 1894–5. Thereafter politics began slowly to take on a new pattern. The parties had been disillusioned by lack of success and dismayed by the recurring cost of elections, so that a desire for the fruits of office made them more inclined to compromise than in the past. Similarly, some members of the oligarchy were now prepared to work with, rather than against, the Lower House. Ito set an example by an alliance with Itagaki's Jiyuto in 1895, and when his government fell in 1896 it was followed by a Matsukata–Okuma combination. Both alliances, however, were weakened by disputes over constitutional principles and the allocation of office. As a result there was a brief reversion to the former pattern in 1898, when the Jiyuto and Shimpoto combined to form a single party, the Kenseito (Constitutional party), and, on Ito's initiative, Okuma and Itagaki formed a joint ministry. The experiment was unsuccessful. Attempts at administrative reform were blocked by the bureaucracy; the effort to frame concrete policies brought out conflicts between the landed interests of the Jiyuto and the city interests of the Shimpoto; problems of patronage proved unfailingly divisive. Within a few months, before the government had even had to face the Diet, the coalition dissolved into its component parts. This brought Yamagata back to power in a government without specific party affiliations.

By this time disagreements had developed between Ito and Yamagata and the former set himself to strengthen his position by a much closer alliance with party politicians than had been attempted so far by any member of the oligarchy. In September 1900 he formed his own party, the Rikken Seiyukai (Association of Friends of Constitutional Government), consisting largely of former members of the Jiyuto. Ito's side of the bargain was to ensure his followers some seats in the cabinet and a modicum of influence over policy. In return, as he made clear in his inaugural address, they had to abandon the principle of party government. The upshot was that the Seiyukai, first under Ito and then under Saionji, secured a decade of limited power—though sometimes only at the cost of supporting ministries formed by Yamagata's nominee, Katsura—while the struggle to secure responsible party cabinets was side-tracked for almost twenty years.

Political and constitutional developments after 1890 were less striking, certainly to foreign observers, than the rapid change in Japan's international position and prestige. This was first apparent in the matter of treaty revision. Attempts to secure the abolition of extra-territoriality and tariff control, both embodied in the so-called 'unequal treaties' of the late Tokugawa period, became a major theme of Japanese foreign policy after 1878. In that year the United States agreed to grant Japan tariff autonomy, subject to the consent of the other powers, but British opposition brought negotiations to an end early in 1879. Talks concerning extra-territoriality met a similar fate in 1882. In 1886 agreement was reached in principle on the establishment of mixed courts, with both foreign and Japanese members, to replace consular jurisdiction, but news of the compromise became public in Tokyo and an outburst of popular criticism prevented any final decision. Much the same happened when Okuma, as Foreign Minister, reopened discussions in 1888–9, this time conducting talks in European capitals. News of the agreement was published prematurely in London and again provoked violent reaction in Japan.

After these abortive attempts at compromise the attitude of Japanese negotiators hardened. When Mutsu, Foreign Minister in the Ito government, opened new discussions in 1893, he set himself to secure British agreement to the total abolition of extra-territoriality. His attitude was much more inflexible than that of his predecessors. He emphasised the danger of again offending Japanese opinion, which was now vociferously represented in the Diet, and even hinted that Japan might be forced to renounce the treaties unilaterally. Despite some sharp conflicts of view, agreement was eventually reached and a treaty signed with Britain in July 1894, providing that extra-territoriality would end in Japan one year after promulgation of the new civil code. It took effect, as did the treaties subsequently signed with other powers, in August 1899. Even so, full tariff autonomy was not obtained until 1911, when these treaties expired.

The note of greater confidence evident in Japanese policy under Mutsu was still more apparent in the country's dealings with its neighbours. Before 1890 Japanese governments had acted with studied moderation, especially when there was any danger of provoking conflict with one or other of the powers, though they had successfully pressed minor territorial claims to the Kurile and Ryukyu islands. They had shown considerable patience since 1873 even over the question of Korea. But in 1894 Japanese demands for the reform of Korea under Japan's tutelage were the immediate cause of the war between Japan and China.

The notable contrast between Japan's policy in 1894 and that which was followed in the similar dispute ten years earlier is made all the more marked by the fact that Ito was Prime Minister on both occasions. In attempting to explain the change, historians have disagreed. Some have emphasised the greater stubbornness of Chinese policy in 1894 and the growing importance of Japan's economic interests in Korea during the intervening decade. Others have sought an explanation in the political pressures on Ito resulting from the actions of opposition parties in the Diet. Both arguments have force, but the second, at least, is open to objection. It is true that most party leaders had belonged to the group which had resigned over the Korean dispute in 1873 and that they found criticism of government 'weakness' in foreign policy a ready means of gaining votes: foreign policy, after the fears aroused by western actions in the period 1853–68, remained an issue which was always likely to arouse emotion. On the other hand, there is little evidence that the parties were strong enough to force their wishes on the government. A more extreme form of pressure came from the patriotic groups, whose tastes ran to coercion and whose plans for Japanese expansion involved a complete rejection of that respect for western diplomatic practice to which the Meiji government was committed. Such organisations as the Genyosha, established in 1881 by political malcontents who had been closely connected with the Satsuma Rebellion, sought to win acceptance for their views by a mixture of wire-pulling and intimidation, but it was not until the twentieth century that they and their successors gained an effective voice in the shaping of Japanese policy.

A clearer understanding of Ito's policy towards China can be obtained if it is remembered that the decision not to attack Korea in 1873, which he had supported strongly, was taken on the grounds that an overseas adventure at that time would have been both dangerous and impracticable. Similar reasoning continued to induce caution thereafter. But by 1894 the argument had lost much of its cogency and Japan's leaders could face the world with greater confidence. Japan had attained a fair measure of political and financial stability. She had a growing modern industry and commerce, a small but efficient western-style navy, an army reorganised, especially after 1882, to become an effective instrument for use abroad. With so much achieved, the prospect of a war in Korea could be viewed with less concern and by that very fact became attractive. In this sense the change in Chinese policy and the need to placate domestic opposition were only of secondary importance.[1]

[1] Below, pp. 644 ff., for further details.

The war itself went quickly in Japan's favour. Within a few weeks she had secured naval control of the seas between Korea and North China, thus cutting the best route for Chinese reinforcements to the peninsula, and by the beginning of 1895 had occupied the whole of Korea, Port Arthur and its hinterland in Liaotung, and parts of South Manchuria. China was forced to seek peace terms, eventually sending Li Hung-chang to Japan to negotiate with Ito. By the Treaty of Shimonoseki, concluded in April 1895, China agreed to recognise the independence of Korea; to cede to Japan Formosa, the Pescadores and the Liaotung Peninsula; to open four more Chinese cities to foreign trade; and to pay an indemnity of 200 million taels in silver. But the treaty at once provoked the intervention of Russia, France and Germany, demanding that Liaotung be returned. Reluctantly, the Japanese government complied and the treaty was amended. An increased indemnity was Japan's only consolation.

The Sino-Japanese War opened a new era for Japan, for it had important repercussions in domestic politics and economic development, as well as in foreign affairs. The enthusiasm brought by victory and the outraged feelings brought by the Triple Intervention of the powers, coinciding as they did with treaty revision, gave renewed impetus to the growth of nationalism and made expansion, rather than the attainment of equality, the focus of Japanese aspirations. At the same time, Japan's emergence as an active participant in the international affairs of the Far East involved a complete rethinking of her position. The events of April 1895 had demonstrated that realisation of her hopes would inevitably bring rivalry with Russia, perhaps an open clash. For this she was by no means ready. Much remained to be done before she could afford to reject, if necessary at the cost of war, the 'advice' of one of the powers.

In the building of a strong economy a good deal had already been accomplished. In the textile trades especially, the rapid growth after 1890 owed little to government finance or national economic policy, though the export of textiles was greatly stimulated by the readier access to Chinese and Korean markets resulting from the Treaty of Shimonoseki. Japan's heavy industry, however, was still far from being able to support a major war; and it was to this sector of the economy that government attention was now directed. The foundation of specialist banks, the Hypothec Bank in 1896 and the Industrial Bank in 1900, provided means of channelling investment in the desired directions. So, too, did the postal savings movement. As a result, industrial growth was rapid, though it remained on a small scale by European standards till after 1914. Paid-up capital in the engineering industry, for example, increased from 2·6 million yen in 1893 to 14·6 million yen in 1903 and 61·1 million yen in 1913. In 1896 shipping companies were given subsidies for the use of iron and steel vessels of 700 tons and over, while additional subsidies were granted after 1899 to those using Japanese-built ships. Japan's merchant fleet and the output of her shipyards grew steadily: by 1903 38 per cent of the ships entering Japanese ports were Japanese-owned, compared with only 14 per cent a decade earlier. The iron and steel industry came into being on a significant scale in 1901, when the government-financed Yawata Iron Works began production. It was soon followed by a number of private concerns. Coal production was increased from an annual average of 2·6 million metric tons for the period 1885–94 to an annual average of 8 million metric tons in 1895–1904.

Ten years after the Sino-Japanese War therefore the Japanese economy was already showing significant changes. Silk and cotton textiles, including cotton yarn, accounted for 22 per cent of exports in 1900. There had been a corresponding increase in the imports of raw cotton, a relative decrease in the exports of natural products like rice and tea. Population growth had finally overtaken agricultural production and the country had become a net importer of foodstuffs. Government expenditure had risen threefold in a decade, largely owing to the cost of armaments and of developing new colonial territories, with a consequent increase in taxation and government borrowing. The national debt more than doubled between 1894 and 1903.

In so far as the nature of economic development was determined by government policy, it was linked, both in origin and purpose, with the international situation. On the other hand, rapid though development was, it was not sufficiently so to encourage recklessness in foreign affairs. Nor did the political situation at home: Japan had six different cabinets in the six years following the Treaty of Shimonoseki. Accordingly, her approach to foreign problems remained cautious, designed to avoid embroilment with the powers.[1] It led, eventually, to alliance with one of them. In Korea, which was the focus of interest until early 1898, she made an attempt to collaborate with Russia. During the scramble for China which began with the German seizure of Tsingtao and the Russian lease of Port Arthur in 1898 she found herself in a difficult position. The development threatened her own future trading prospects on the mainland, while the Russian seizure of Liaotung rubbed fresh salt in the wounds left by the Triple Intervention. On the other hand, she knew herself too weak to control events or even enter the competition on her own account. She was therefore forced to tread warily. This was equally true of the situation resulting from the Boxer outbreaks in 1899. Japan, of all the interested countries, was best able to provide forces for the relief of the legations in Peking, but she feared giving offence to the powers and therefore waited until her intervention was invited, withdrawing her troops again as soon as was reasonably possible. Russia's occupation of Manchuria, however, was a different matter, for it directly threatened Japanese interests in Korea, as well as those of the powers in China. Kato,

[1] Below, pp. 658 ff., for further details.

Foreign Minister in the Ito government, registered the strongest of pro-tests with St Petersburg in the spring of 1901, despite his failure to secure effective British co-operation.

It was largely from the Manchurian crisis that there arose negotiations for an Anglo-Japanese alliance. There had been influential advocates of an alliance in both countries ever since 1895 and a number of tentative discussions had taken place. Moreover, there had been co-operation in negotiations concerning China, especially on the question of the Boxer indemnities. All this had created an atmosphere in which some more formal arrangement became possible, but it was still a big step from this to the conclusion of a military alliance, even though the plan had obvious advantages. Britain stood to gain a means of checking Russia's advance in the Far East and a welcome easing of the strain on her naval resources. Japan would immeasurably increase her influence in international affairs. Yet both also had reasons for hesitation, since the implied threat to Russia might make it more difficult to reach a settlement with her and thereby bring new complications. For this reason the talks which opened in London in July 1901 proceeded slowly; Ito continued to sound out the possibility of an agreement with Russia for some time after they had begun; and in the final text of the Alliance the clause promising British support for Japan's position in Korea was carefully worded to avoid giving undue encouragement to Japanese ambitions. Nevertheless the Alliance was finally signed on 30 January 1902 and Japan seems on balance to have had the best of the negotiations. For her, at least, the occasion was one which warranted celebration.

In many ways indeed the Anglo-Japanese Alliance represents the pinnacle of the Meiji government's achievements. From a beginning in uncertainty and civil war it had gradually created an administrative and governmental structure more efficient than Japan had ever known before. A small group of leaders, successfully resisting challenges to their own control of this structure, had initiated far-reaching reforms in the country's society and economy, through which they had at last secured treaty revision, which constituted a recognition of Japan's formal equality in international affairs, and had gained victory in a foreign war. Alliance with one of the greatest of the powers set the seal on their success. Yet it was also, in chronology if not causation, a new point of departure. In the twentieth century Japan was irretrievably committed to playing a major part in the affairs of the Far East; and under the pressure of expansionist sentiment at home, the temptation of opportunity abroad, she launched a programme of empire-building which eventually brought disaster.

CHAPTER XVIII

THE UNITED STATES

DURING the late nineteenth century the United States lost their former place in the imagination of Europe, and by 1900 the accusations of immaturity, materialism and indiscriminate self-praise, formerly the stock-in-trade of conservative critics, had been accepted by the European left. In spite of attempts to treat this as an 'age of enterprise' modern Americans have been inclined to echo these criticisms, and 'the Gilded Age', with its implications of ostentatious wealth and intrinsic worthlessness, remains the popular label. Yet America remained the land of opportunity both for millions of poor European migrants and for well-to-do investors, and Americans themselves moved from the doubts and divisions of civil war to self-confidence, to social stability, and to a surprising uniformity in their fundamental beliefs. Movements of protest and criticism appealed to a traditional stock of American principles; proposals for radical change in the political, social and economic system won little support. For critics and conservatives alike the American utopia remained America.

The period was dominated by the rise of a highly developed industrial and capitalist society in the North and Mid-West. This society experienced internal tensions similar to those of other industrial societies, but avoided the great fissure of politics based on class. Until the last years of the century it did not encounter the problem of dependencies overseas, but it faced comparable problems in its relationship with the less-developed rural regions occupying a greater part of the territory of the United States. The political system gave these 'colonial' areas participation in the national government, encouraged alliances between groups in the different regions, and thus mitigated the effect of overwhelming power concentrated in one part of the United States; but politics which were either meaningless or corrupt often seemed to contaminate rather than to harmonise the diverse sections of the country. In 1888 Lord Bryce in his book, *The American Commonwealth*, remarked of the two great parties that aims and principles seemed to have vanished, 'all had been lost, except office or the hope of it'; and a man such as James G. Blaine, who dominated his party and commanded the devoted loyalty of a personal following, appears in retrospect to have been superficial, careless of public virtue, and associated with no great measure or significant policy. Yet the American Union was a political achievement and only by the art of politics could it be maintained

The Civil War and Reconstruction fostered new loyalties and a new definition of political aims, and the election of 1896 saw party conflict identified with a real clash of interests; the slack intervening period saw both parties trying to broaden their basis by becoming more like each other. After the period of emotional conflict, through that in which parties lived on their past, the organisation of politics could become for politicians an end in itself. What survived when 'all had been lost' were a large number of autonomous local party organisations bound together in a loose alliance with the object of electing a President. It was the business of the successful leader to keep control of these local organisations, staffed by minor professional politicians, and even the dignified national figure could not avoid preoccupation with the hard facts of patronage, influence and political manipulation. Respectable public men might come to tolerate practices which they would condemn in private, and the system could also raise up bosses and 'spoilsmen' or patronage brokers who regarded with cynical indifference the principles which they exploited. This system of professional politics sometimes seemed to stand apart from the real history of America which was being made by business entrepreneurs; but politics were entwined with the economic as with every other aspect of national life. The pattern of power in this democratic society was more intricate than the formal structure of government by the people, and more complex than that of societies arranged upon a hierarchic model.

The Republican party was in origin a movement of protest, irritation and ideals. It emerged from the Civil War as a middle-class party drawing upon working-class support; it included most intellectuals, and combined idealism and reformist zeal with a vast respect for the dynamic economic forces of the age. The Republicans recognised no conflict between welfare and individualism, and this fact, regarded by some future commentators as evidence of weak thinking or deliberate self-deception, was their chief source of strength. The party did not regard itself as the servant of big business but of the small entrepreneur, the hard-working farmer, the decent citizen, and the virtuous poor. As the momentum of the party slackened it came to rely increasingly upon patronage, upon the emotional memories of the Civil War, and upon an appeal to the interests of business. A party formed to prevent the extension of slavery came to place high tariffs in the centre of its platform, and if it began the period with something akin to Gladstonian liberalism it ended close to Lord Salisbury's conservatism. It did not however cease to claim that it was the party of nineteenth-century enlightenment, and it was from good Republican soil that progressivism sprang in the ensuing period.

The late nineteenth century has been associated with the ascendancy of the Republican party, but there was a Democratic majority in the House of Representatives for nine of the eighteen congresses between 1865 and 1901, and though the Republicans had a Senate majority in all but four years this was never greater than three between 1877 and 1891. In the mid-western heartland of the Republican party Douglas had won almost as many votes as Lincoln in 1860, and this great reserve of Democratic strength was now being supplemented by the increasing number of foreign-born Roman Catholics and low-paid city workers. In the South the Republican party was annihilated by 1877, and old Whigs led a revived and monolithic Democratic party. In the North there were reserves of Democratic strength in the cities and amongst the poorer farmers, while a comparatively small number of wealthy men, mostly from New York and affiliated with international banking and overseas commerce, commanded a disproportionate influence in the party. The aims of each group remained fairly consistent, but the shifting balance of power, bringing one or the other to preponderant influence, made for extreme confusion. The Democrat could never be sure whether he would find himself committed to hard money or inflation, to free trade or to modest proposals for tariff revision, to reform or to conservatism. This inconsistency mattered less than might be imagined to a party which made a virtue of political negation, and which, to quote the New York *World*, the leading exponent of Democratic views in the eastern states, tried to adhere to 'the old Democratic doctrine...to permit the town to do nothing which the school district could do as well; the state nothing which the county or city could do; and the federal government nothing the state could as completely and safely accomplish' (7 March 1865). Local autonomy was still attractive to those who, for one reason or another, wanted a free hand; the Democrats might claim to be the party of the common man but their real support came from the small vested interest and the local power group. Thus in New York the Democratic principle of municipal autonomy kept Tammany in the saddle, and in the South the party became an effective weapon in the hands of the upper-class oligarchy. The Republicans were accused of 'centralism' but their real offence, in many Democratic eyes, was to attempt protection of the Negroes against the consequences of Southern home rule. The Democratic party ended the century in alliance with agrarian radicals, but it had shown little sympathy for organised labour, had little attraction for skilled workers, was still regarded as conservative by many of its adherents, and would have to undergo a twentieth-century metamorphosis before it could become the vehicle for reform in an industrial age.

Both parties were trying to capture the same middle-class vote and their national programmes often did no more than find two ways of saying the same thing; yet there were differences of temperament and of principle which convinced contemporaries that they were not fighting sham battles. The Republican was the party of individuals, the Democrat of minorities. The Democrats still believed in States' Rights modified by the abandonment of secession; the Republicans believed that States' Rights did not include the right to do wrong to persons or property. The Democrats were strong in numbers but weak in policy; the Republicans represented education and respectability, but the precariousness of their electoral position forced them to a concentration upon political tactics amid which public virtue languished. Both parties tended to live on the past; but whereas the Democrats really believed in the past the Republicans tried to exploit it.

It would be an error to assume that all men in public life were rascals, or that business drained away all the best talent from politics. Most men who achieved national office were respectable and many were able, while many of those who achieved outstanding success in business would have made poor political leaders. Nor, in anything short of a Platonic republic, can politics expect an exclusive command over the best men. What the United States lacked was a recognised upper class, accustomed to filling public office and maintaining a code of gentlemanly behaviour; the defeat of the South had driven such a class from the central position, and leadership had to come from those who could make a success in the rough school of local politics. As in earlier periods the legal profession was the royal road into public life, but political prominence went most frequently to the small-town lawyer with a bare professional training. Most politicians maintained that their primary duty was to their constituents, but in practice this often meant service to those who were most influential and most vocal. The lobby and the pressure group became more and more significant during the period, and those with a ready-made nucleus of organisation, such as large business interests and the Grand Army of the Republic, had a long start in the race for favours.

Congressional procedure heightened the impression that politics were at the best a compromise of principles and at the worst a scramble for rewards. The middle-class men who filled both Houses of Congress projected upon the political world their own sedate and businesslike habits, and the great oratorical efforts after the style of Webster and Clay went out of fashion. More and more work was done in committee behind closed doors, and though more information was gathered and more business transacted than in any previous period, the public derived from Congress no impression of purposeful leadership. The vital function of initiating policy, left by the Constitution in a void, was performed out of the public eye and in an atmosphere which was liable to generate suspicion. The attention paid to lobbyists could be justified as a necessary part of consultation in the business of government, but it could also confirm the belief that wealth was favoured above commonwealth. What created most alarm was not the occasional scandal but the failure to prevent its repetition and the apparent impossibility of reconciling disinterested government with the requirements of party organisation. State legislatures were particularly susceptible to pressure, and some states won an unenviable reputation for rule by the pocket-governments of great corporations. The prestige of the House of Representatives declined, thanks partly to rigid rules of debate which made men prefer government by committee. There was some gain in the reputation of the Senate; but looking at Congress as a whole there was a widespread impression that its members were not living up to their responsibilities.

The period began with a decided bid for legislative supremacy which would have relegated President and Supreme Court to secondary roles in government. The Republicans inherited the Whig tradition of Congressional government—with Lincoln's extensive powers explained though not always justified by the exigencies of war—and the seizure of the initiative by the Congressional majority from President Johnson in December 1865 was not the innovation which some have deemed it. The Joint Committee on Reconstruction might have broken new ground as a Congressional cabinet, without executive authority but charged with the task of digesting, preparing and proposing legislative measures. The Tenure of Office Act of 1867 was a more direct bid for legislative supremacy. It reversed a decision of Congress in 1789 that though the Constitution required the Senate to confirm appointments in the Federal Service, including cabinet ministers, it left the power to dismiss with the President. If its main provisions had not been repealed in 1869 it would have set up the least stable feature of the eighteenth-century British constitution—the dual responsibility of ministers to the executive and the legislature—without suggesting collective responsibility which had solved the British dilemma. Finally, the impeachment of President Johnson, though ostensibly for a breach of the Tenure of Office Act, was really for his persistence in a policy condemned by Congress and the electorate; if successful it might have set the precedent for a far greater degree of executive dependence upon and responsibility to Congress. Nevertheless, the one vote which saved Johnson from conviction by the Senate deflected the drive for legislative supremacy, and with the accession of President Grant the majority was ready to let relations between the two branches slip back into their customary lack of definition. Congressional policy, so far as it was aimed at legislative supremacy, suffered because it evolved as a series of reactions to particular situations, with little consideration of the general problem, and produced no definitive statement of constitutional theory.

As the head of the administration and responsible for all Federal appointments the President had powerful weapons with which to influence Congress and to make his party what he thought it should be. For a time this power was circumscribed by the overmighty influence of the great 'spoilsmen', but it was to prove far easier for a President to break their hold upon the party than anyone had imagined. The veto remained as a great reserve of power in the President's hands, and the threat to use it could be effective in influencing legislation; few Congressmen would waste laborious hours upon a measure which they knew to be doomed, and this was a power which could be defeated only on the rare occasions when two-thirds of both houses were opposed to a particular veto. Thus the President had resources which would be very effective when fully exploited. In 1892 Cleveland, who had begun with a very modest conception of the presidential function, used all the means at his disposal to secure from a doubtful Congress the repeal of the Silver Purchase Act. McKinley, a skilled political tactician, did not use such challenging methods but was able to get most of what he wanted from Congress. Between 1865 and 1868 the Republicans cut the President down to the size which their traditions and political interests required; but by the end of the century it was clear that Congress had reached and passed the zenith of its authority and that the Presidency had great latent powers which awaited development.

In 1865 the Republicans had a poor opinion of the Supreme Court, and resented the idea that the Court could, by the invalidation of laws, interfere with Congressional policy. There had been only two precedents for the voiding of a Congressional Act, and the second (Dred Scott) hardly contributed to the prestige of the Court in 1865. The decision of the Court in *ex parte Milligan*—that neither the President nor Congress had the power to order military trials out of a theatre of war—cut at the root of Congressional policy in the South where military courts were the main safeguard for Negro civil rights. The *Nation* observed editorially (vol. IV, p. 30) that in the Dred Scott and Milligan cases the Court had departed from its settled practice of leaving political matters to Congress and added that 'we cannot believe that the attempt will be repeated. If it should be, the people will have to meet it not merely with contempt but with punishment.' In March 1868 Congress deprived the Court of jurisdiction over appeals from military tribunals, and in 1869 the size of the Court was enlarged to nine, which enabled President Grant to appoint two new justices and reverse a decision which conflicted with Congressional currency policy. The Court's acquiescence in the act of 1868 may have saved it from more drastic curbs, such as the requirement of a two-thirds majority for the invalidation of a Congressional act or provision for the re-passage by Congress of an invalidated act. Nevertheless, the constitutional shift of the ensuing years was to be towards judicial legislation and not away from it.

Even during the tenure of Chief Justice Chase (1864–73) ten acts were invalidated. More judicial vetoes followed, and in 1895 the Court threw out a Federal Income Tax law which was a major item of national policy. Upon the Court fell the responsibility of deciding what Congress had really meant by the Interstate Commerce Act of 1887 and the Anti-Trust of 1890, and when it had done so the result was far from that intended by the ardent supporters of these measures. The most important piece of legislation of the period, the fourteenth amendment, was given meanings which few of its sponsors had envisaged and subjected to limitations which they had certainly meant to override. During the same period the Court imposed drastic restrictions upon the social and economic legislation of the states. These encroachments upon legislative freedom were possible because powerful interests feared the unfettered operation of majority rule. In the Constitution, and in the Court which interpreted it, the dominant groups in the industrial capitalist society saw a guarantee for security and stability; the Founding Fathers had begun by making a government of laws not men, but their successors now wanted laws beyond the reach of men, and the Supreme Court, not Congress, rose to the occasion.

If the fundamental law was to be taken out of politics there seemed to be an equally good case for doing the same with administration. The weakness of the central civil service and the rise, in local politics, of party machines were largely products of early nineteenth-century democracy, and late nineteenth-century reformers set themselves the task of checking these manifestations of majority rule. Civil service reform, which aimed to recruit by examination and promote on merit, became a favourite objective for middle-class reformers and received growing support from business men. It had to contend with the ingrained suspicion of anything which looked like an aristocracy and with the needs of practical politicians; an academic élite could easily be pictured as the worst form of aristocracy, and one need not be a cynic to suggest that patronage was less harmful than other means by which power in politics might be sustained. Nevertheless by 1883 the pressure for civil service reform had become so great that Congress passed and President Arthur (himself a reformed spoilsman) signed the Pendleton Act 'classifying' a large number of posts which were to be filled by examination and held so long as the duties were efficiently performed. President McKinley removed a number of posts from the classification, but by the end of the century the United States had gone far towards the creation of a professional civil service. They were still, however, far from the British model which inspired many reformers: the high departmental posts remained political appointments and there was little incentive for men of distinguished attainments to compete for the lower positions; the hold of the politicians upon a segment of the public service had been weakened, but the patronage system had not been broken and was perhaps stronger because less likely to produce the more outrageous administrative scandals.

At the other end of the political scale middle-class reformers pressed the idea of efficient, economical and honest municipal government against the rule of bosses, rings and party machines. These local reform movements sometimes achieved an early and striking success, but seldom prevented the restoration of boss rule as soon as the political temperature was lowered. The attempts of 'good citizens' to effect reform left some impression, and there is a direct link between the civil service and municipal reformers and the progressives of the next generation, but their refusal to participate regularly in the rough and tumble of local politics, and the limitations of their social philosophy, made their efforts sporadic and the results superficial.

The triviality of much which passed for political controversy does not detract from the magnitude of the real political problems. At either end of the period—in Reconstruction and the Populist revolt—stand two great conflicts which settled the relationship of the industrial capitalist society to the agrarian regions of the country. Reconstruction raised two basic problems: the future of the Negro and the future of the Union. Should the victorious North revolutionise Southern society by insisting upon equality between the races? Could the Union be preserved without such a revolution? In the North President Johnson and the Democratic minority maintained that the object of the war, the preservation of the union, had been achieved when the South surrendered, and that the only remaining problem was the restoration of normal government in the South and of normal relationships between the states and the Union. This view ignored the experience of war, the emotions generated on both sides, the great social revolution initiated by the emancipation of the slaves, and the emergence of a Northern conviction that the purpose of war was not merely to restore but also to create a more perfect union. Amongst a religious people the war had had an apocalyptic significance: blood had been necessary for the remission of sins, the great sacrifice had transcended legalistic argument, and after the long dominion of unrighteousness the elect of God were once more on the march. In secular terms Lincoln had interpreted the struggle as one for free government, and in its first issue of 5 July 1865 the *Nation*, which was to become the principal organ of the Northern intelligentsia, declared that 'we utter no idle boast when we say that if the conflict of ages between the few and the many, between privilege and equality, between law and power, between opinion and the sword, was not closed on the day on which Lee threw down his arms, the issue was placed beyond doubt'. These mystical rhapsodies were far more important than the economic aims of northern businessmen, which some historians have stressed, though for Republicans of this generation the extension of Northern economic interests was identified with the extension of Northern enlightenment. Even for Northerners who experienced neither enthusiasm nor economic ambition there remained a puzzling and inescapable obligation: four million slaves were free and their future as American citizens depended upon whatever dispositions the North might make.

During the summer of 1865 Johnson proceeded with his policy of restoration. Once the war was over it was not difficult to gather a majority in each Southern state ready to take an oath of allegiance to the United States, and upon this basis Johnson invited them to set up new governments. Though leading Confederates were exempted from his proclamation of amnesty, he mitigated this by a generous issue of pardons. He demanded ratification of the thirteenth amendment abolishing slavery, but asked no guarantees for Negro civil rights. Under this generous but incautious policy governments were set up and hope revived among Southerners that, after all, they would be able to control their own future. Meanwhile alarm was growing in the North and this was confirmed by the election, as proposed members of Congress from the Southern states, of prominent ex-Confederates, and by the passage of 'black codes' which combined some needed social regulation for the freedmen with the assumption of perpetual Negro inferiority. The political atmosphere when the momentous thirty-ninth Congress met in December 1865 was anxious and angry. Southerners and their Northern Democratic allies saw restored power almost within their grasp; on the other side the old abolitionists were profoundly shocked by the abandonment of the Negroes to their former masters, moderate Unionists were perturbed by the prospect that Southerners (with increased representation since a Negro would no longer be counted as three-fifths of a man for the purpose of Congressional apportionment) might resume their former dominance in the nation, and good party men feared that Republicans might become a minority in the country. Not all these fears were inspired by high motives, but all were human and comprehensible, and it is unnecessary to predicate a bitter measure of Northern vindictiveness to understand Republican policy. This policy was to wrest control of reconstruction from the President, and to formulate a programme which would incorporate the safeguards which were deemed necessary.

The situation brought to the fore the Radical Republicans who had some of the characteristic of that determined minority which is necessary to the success of all revolutions. Charles Sumner, who had represented the New England conscience since 1850 and who combined an ardent love of humanity with a very imperfect understanding of human beings, led the Radicals in the Senate. In the House Thaddeus Stevens, a man of narrow but dominant personality, established an extraordinary ascendancy. Stevens knew all the arts of politics and used them without stint, but a contemporary, Whitelaw Reid, found the secret of his strength 'in that source to which mere politicians so seldom look—his high, all-embracing devotion to a noble idea'.

The 'noble idea' of the Radicals was racial equality; but they had to work with colleagues who lacked the same conviction, and the first phase of Congressional Reconstruction, leading up to the fourteenth amend-ment, was a compromise. The amendment attempted to drive from leader-ship the old ruling class of the South by disqualifying from public office all those who had once taken the oath of allegiance to the United States (as office-holders or legislators) and subsequently joined the rebellion. It met the vexed question of suffrage and apportionment by leaving the right to enfranchise with the states, but reduced proportionately their Congressional representation if any group of adult males were disenfranchised. It was, however, the first clause in the amendment which effected a constitutional revolution by placing civil rights under national protection; it prohibited the states from making any law which 'abridged the privileges and immunities of the citizens of the United States', or deprived 'any person of life, liberty, or property without due process of law', or denied 'to any person within its jurisdiction the equal protection of the laws'. Congress was given the power to enforce this amendment, and cases arising under it could be heard in the Federal courts. Charles Sumner believed that the National government had always possessed such power (though prevented from using it by the slavocracy); others derived it from the thirteenth amendment which in abolishing slavery also gave to Congress the 'power to enforce this article by appropriate legislation'; but the fourteenth amendment removed all doubts by nationalising civil rights. The wheel had swung a full circle from the time when the states were regarded as the natural protectors of individual rights against national authority; and federalism, as the old constitution had understood it, was dead.

Acceptance of the amendment by the Southern legislators would probably have been considered by the Congressional majority as sufficient ground for their readmission; but in every Southern state save Tennessee it was rejected by overwhelming majorities. The first phase of Congressional reconstruction was thus brought to a dead halt, but Republican objectives remained unchanged and the instrument for their realisation lay at hand. Pressed by the old abolitionists, rejected by the moderates, Negro suffrage had been waiting in the wings for exactly this opportunity. The intransigence of Southern whites, together with an overwhelming victory for the Republicans in the Congressional 'elections of 1866, confirmed Radical leadership and inaugurated the second phase of Congressional reconstruction. The Reconstruction Acts passed in 1867 ended the existing Southern state governments, restored military rule, and instructed the military commanders to call constitutional conventions elected by all adult males save those whom the fourteenth amendment had intended to disqualify from office. The conditions on which a state could be readmitted to the Union were the inclusion of adult male suffrage in its constitution, the ratification of the fourteenth amendment by the legislature, and the passage of the amendment into law by the consent of a sufficient number of states. The work of reconstruction was crowned by the fifteenth amendment which enacted that the right to vote could not be abridged 'on account of race, color, or previous condition of servitude', thus enacting not universal suffrage but what contemporaries called impartial suffrage, leaving the state free to impose any voting qualifications which applied equally to all races. Technically the programme sketched by the Reconstruction laws was a success. New constitutions were written upon the best Northern models; Negroes took their places as state legislators, as executive officers, and even as Congressmen; by June 1868 seven states had qualified for re-admission and by June 1870 all the former rebel states were restored to the Union. The renaissance of secessionist power had been checked, colour-blind democracy had been introduced, the Republican party and the Union rested upon a solid and devoted Negro vote, and the whole structure was knit together by a new grant of national power. All that had been left out of account was the attitude of the Southern white people.

The completeness of the political revolution, which brought colour-blind democracy to the South at a time when the English agricultural labourer had no vote, concealed serious weaknesses. Thaddeus Stevens had hoped to build Negro democracy upon the sound Jeffersonian basis of freehold land, but Congress had ignored his proposal for the confiscation of rebel estates and their distribution among the freedmen. The majority of Negro farmers ended as share-croppers; occupying land but committing half their crop to the landowner for rent, and probably mortgaging the rest to a merchant in payment for supplies. Thus the economic ascendancy of the upper class was assured at a time when it was politically alienated by disqualification from office and the taxation of property by the representatives of the propertyless. While the mass of Negroes remained low-grade peasants the emergence of a small Negro middle class intensified the resentment of the poorer whites and the threat of racial amalgamation played upon deep-seated emotions. The history of Reconstruction also became entangled with a grim economic struggle which brought speculative business into the political arena without attracting to the new governments the support of stable interests. Ruined planter families grasped at whatever opportunities offered; a few linked their fortunes with the Reconstruction regime, but the majority preferred to bet upon a restoration of white supremacy; and whatever course they took brought them into competition with the speculative Northerners who came South to investigate stories of undeveloped resources, dirt-cheap labour, and favours to be won from state legislatures. A candid study of the Reconstruction governments would probably reveal more goodwill and sounder notions of public responsibility than has usually been credited to them—what has survived is the story which white Southerners wanted to believe—but there was petty pilfering, a few major scandals, and much inexperience. Negro suffrage had been defended in a traditional American way as the protective device by which a poor man could secure his rights, and against such an argument the ignorance of Negro voters had little relevance; but it became obvious and important when Negro democracy was called upon to fulfil the functions of positive government. The circumstances of the times forced these untried administrations to act more like modern governments than anything which the South had known before; they had to tax, borrow and spend; to underwrite economic recovery and attract capital; to provide for relief and inaugurate systems of public education. Much of their work, like the constitutions under which they existed, lived on after their downfall, and the 'new' South owed more than it cared to admit to the stimulation of 'carpet-bagger' activity; but the responsibilities were too great for inexperienced men pulling against the tide of tradition. Southern reconstruction was to become a classic example of a revolution which failed.

War and reconstruction had weakened the cohesion of Southern society, and for the time being there was only force—wielded either by Federal troops or by illegal white-protection societies such as the notorious Ku-Klux-Klan—to impose order upon anarchy. Out of the ruins of the old a new society had to be created, and for its new social compact two opposed bodies of ideas were presented: one based upon racial equality and the promises of the Declaration of Independence; the other based upon white supremacy and an idealised picture of the old South. Yet while one half of the Southern mind looked resolutely backward, the other half welcomed an economic revolution which would enable the South to recover what it had lost on the field of battle. With the restoration and extension of the railway system, the revival of cotton culture, the increase in the number of cotton mills, and the development of iron, steel and coal the South entered upon an industrial revolution which was unique in attracting the enthusiastic support of both old landed families and white labour. With the coming of this economic revolution certain of the old leaders added to their family prestige the power to bargain and to direct. As early as 1870 the counter-revolution was under way in most Southern states, and once the 'redeemers' united popular support with economic influence the problem of Negro suffrage was comparatively easy to solve. The threat of force, economic coercion, and social pressure kept the Negroes from the polls or forced them to vote Democratic. Old planter Whigs and back-country farmers sank their traditional antipathy and joined their forces to sweep the Democratic party to victory. By 1876 Republican governments survived in only three states, and each of these depended upon Federal troops. Their withdrawal in the following year ended Republican rule in the South.

'Redemption' in the South, though spontaneous and indigenous, depended for its success partly upon the waning of Northern enthusiasm. Though the Ku-Klux-Klan outrages kept indignation alive and facilitated the passage of laws to enforce the fourteenth and fifteenth amendments, radicalism became less confident and drifted into division. In 1872

Sumner and other of the old abolitionists were found in the Liberal Republican movement which favoured reconciliation with the South, though not at the expense of the Negro, and without them Radicalism tended to become merely the political strategy of the Republican party. As the prospects of success receded there was less and less willingness to reinforce failure. In 1875 Congress did pass a Civil Rights Act (for which Sumner had fought until his death in the preceding year), but the debates indicated the reluctance of Congress to regulate individual behaviour in the only way which would make civil equality a reality. In 1883 the Supreme Court confirmed these doubts by invalidating the Act; and in 1896 it decided that the 'equal protection of the laws' of the fourteenth amendment was compatible with racial segregation, provided that the facilities were 'separate but equal'. In 1890 the Senate refused to pass an act to enforce the fifteenth amendment. The Radical experiment in colour-blind democracy had failed, and the Southern white majority had won 'home rule'. Behind the liquidation of radicalism lay the formation of a conservative alliance, which was to be of great significance for the future. Northern business, finding that reconstruction was a losing bet, turned to Southern business; Southern leaders anxious to preserve the counter-revolution turned to Yankee conservatives. In politics Northern conservatives would cease to agitate upon the race question, while Southern conservatives would stifle agrarian attacks upon business leadership; in business local autonomy was given to Southern leaders but ultimate control would rest with the great entrepreneurs and financiers of the North. This unwritten conservative alliance, which was to dominate Congress and particularly the Senate for many years to come, may seem materialistic, calculating and often inhumane, but it is fair to remember that it succeeded where Radicalism had failed, in making a significant contribution to the restoration of national unity.

For the remainder of the century Southern domestic politics made little impact upon the national scene, for, whatever happened, the Southern states continued to be represented by Democrats, and outside his own section only a crudity of manner distinguished the Southern radical from the upper class or 'bourbon' leader of redemption. The memory of Reconstruction sublimated normal economic and social conflicts, and when agrarian radical movements gathered momentum in the later years of the century the key to their success was the alliance of political discontent with racial extremism. It was the victory of back-country farmers under rural demagogues within the Democratic party which led to the imposition of rigid and legalised segregation and to the virtual disenfranchisement of the Negro. After 'redemption' Negroes continued to vote in some numbers, 'bourbon' ascendancy in the 'black belt' depended in part upon the Negro vote, and there were a few Negro members of state legislatures. This situation was ended by the imposition of suffrage qualifications which did not contravene the fifteenth amendment, but which were administered with the intention of defeating its objects. Literacy, property and tax-paying qualifications were applied at the discretion of state authorities to disenfranchise Negroes while permitting poor whites to vote; as Ben Tillman of South Carolina remarked at the Constitutional Convention of South Carolina in 1895, the registration officer 'is responsible to his conscience and his God; he is responsible to nobody else.... It is just showing partiality, perhaps, or discrimination.'

Thirty years after ruin and defeat the Southern whites had recovered their self-respect, the economy was more diversified than ever before, and the Northerners had ceased their efforts to rearrange society. For this achievement a price had to be paid. The new order depended upon evasion of constitutional amendments which represented reasonable deductions from the American political tradition; and this created an unhealthy atmosphere. The glorification of the past prevented Southerners from facing the real problems of the future. In reaction against reconstruction activity the state governments were niggardly and limited in their activities. The public education systems created by the reconstruction governments made some headway, but not without the stimulation of private charity, and the results were still meagre compared with the well-established systems of northern and western states. None of the Southern states had compulsory school-attendance laws and illiteracy was still common among both races. As in earlier periods the South attracted few immigrants. Amid the disease, poverty and ignorance of backward rural areas many Southerners still lived in an eighteenth-century world, uncontaminated by factories, schools, or modern medicine, and the state governments had done very little to remedy these conditions. Inevitably the heaviest price was paid by the Negroes whose poverty and degradation seemed to justify racial inequality. Yet no one could seriously maintain in 1900 that the Negroes had been better off under slavery, and harsh discriminatory laws were often mitigated by kindly relations between the races. A small Negro middle class had been slowly emerging, and it was here that the greatest of Negro leaders, Booker T. Washington, saw the best hope for his race. He argued against political agitation, and for education, enterprise and the accumulation of wealth. A passionate desire for equality had never animated more than a small minority of Negroes, and it was more in keeping with their temperament and with practical possibilities to show that a Negro was just another kind of good American. Like other groups with cause for discontent the Negroes appealed to American traditions and not away from them; there is perhaps no more convincing proof of the attractive force of American ideals.

Unlike the South the other great rural region, the Great Plains, accepted the intellectual assumptions of Northern society but tried to reject economic control. The migrants who flooded west in great numbers after the Civil War went in quest of independence; yet no region was more dependent upon the resources of a developed capitalist civilisation. The great plains were arid, contained few natural communications and were remote from their markets. Not only prosperity but even subsistence depended upon railways, large-scale marketing organisations, banking facilities and manufactures. Whatever dreams the Homestead Act of 1862, which gave 160 acres free to bona fide settlers, might have inspired, the farmer found himself caught in the network of capitalist economy and at the mercy of forces which he could neither understand nor control. If small farming was precarious, considerable profit could be made from large-scale wheat or cattle farming, and this provided a powerful incentive for the evasion of those provisions in the Homestead Act which limited ownership to 160 acres and conveyed a freehold title after five years' occupation and cultivation. The railway land grants already formed an exception to the homestead rule and these with land won through evasions of the act contributed to great land-holdings often owned and controlled by capitalist interests outside the region. At the same time the western farmer had the numbers, if they could be politically organised, to oppose the intrusive power of large-scale capitalism, and a national association for farm education and co-operation, known as the Grange, moved into politics with considerable success. The main target for agrarian agitators were the great railway corporations which had been liberally endowed with land, made districts in which they held a monopoly subsidise with high freight rates the long-distance competitive runs, and often showed a more lively interest in quick profits than in the long-term development of the regions which they served.

Regulation of the railways became one great theme of agrarian radicalism; the other was currency reform. The spectre of Wall Street and hard money stood behind high interest rates, the refusal to lend, foreclosures, and the transformation of the independent freeholder into the tenant of some remote corporation. Moreover the attack upon the gold standard was symptomatic of a profound difference between the agrarian west and the industrial east, for the real debate was over the means by which capital could be supplied. Western farmers had good ground for believing that the financial system unduly restricted the flow of capital to their rural section—hindering expansion and magnifying distress—but there was equal force in the argument that industrial expansion depended upon the supply of foreign capital, which would be repelled by inflationary policies. Thus there was a real clash of interest which imparted passion and emotional significance to the debate: on the one hand agrarian radicals saw 'sound' money as a symbol of the mysterious external forces which they were trying to control, on the other adherence to gold came to stand for all that was civilised, rational and progressive, and currency reform was linked in the timid eastern mind with violence, anarchism and retrogression.

The demand for easy money had deep roots in American history but its immediate antecedents were found during the war and after, and in the east rather than the west. The Civil War had been financed in part by the issue of greenbacks, an inconvertible paper currency, and despite depreciation they were popular with those who did well out of the war— with manufacturers, commercial farmers and speculative businessmen— and unpopular with New York bankers, import merchants, and men on fixed incomes. Henry Carey, the best-known of American economists, favoured the continuance of government-managed paper currency as an element in a national economic system isolated by a protective tariff from the competition of cheap labour; and immediately after the war the greenbacks had the powerful support of radicals such as Thaddeus Stevens, William Kelley and Ben Butler. The question was confused with that of the National Debt, and easy money was somewhat discredited in Republican eyes by the Democratic adoption, in 1868, of the 'Ohio Idea' for the payment of the debt in paper currency. In spite of this, Republican majorities in Congress refused to sanction an immediate contraction of the greenbacks, which would have restored them to par and paved the way for resumption of specie payments; instead they adopted a compromise by which the currency would become convertible when the increased volume of business brought the greenbacks to par. The onset of depression in 1873 postponed the realisation of this policy and created a demand for new paper issues as a measure of relief; but Grant vetoed a bill embodying such a measure and in consequence the Republicans became more firmly committed to resumption, which finally took place in 1879.

Meanwhile the centre of gravity for currency reform had shifted west, and it was in the western states that the short-lived Greenback-Labor party, formed in 1877, found most of its support. This movement coincided with a period of modest agricultural prosperity from 1879 to 1884; but in the latter year a fall in prices began which was not checked until 1896, and in 1887 began a prolonged drought which brought ruin to many western farms. This period saw the rise of the greatest movement of agrarian discontent, which culminated, in 1892, with the formation of the Populist party at Omaha, Nebraska. In the preamble to the Populist party platform of 4 July 1892, Populism drew together all the strands of western discontent and challenged the dominant forces in American society with the statement that 'we meet in the midst of a country brought to the verge of moral, political and material ruin....The fruits of the toil of millions are boldly stolen to build up colossal fortunes for a few.... From the same prolific womb of governmental injustice we breed the two great classes—tramps and millionaires.' Populism did not stop short at rhetoric but proposed the public ownership of railways, a graduated income tax, the direct election of senators, democratic control through local initiative and referendum, and the restriction of immigration in the interests of labour. The greatest attention was however focused upon the currency question and upon a demand for the unlimited coinage of silver. Before the war the United States had been on a bimetallic standard, but as the official ratio had over-valued silver it had not gone into circulation and in 1873 the coinage of silver was dropped. In the following years production from the new western silver mines brought down the price and it would have been profitable to sell to the mint at the old silver/gold ratio of 16 to 1. The use as currency of a precious metal which was also an American asset seemed to avoid the disadvantages of an inconvertible paper currency, and provided an inflationary theory which could easily be expressed in terms of popular jargon. Congress proved responsive to silver agitation and in 1890 passed the Sherman Silver Purchase Act, which fed silver into the currency without adopting it as a standard. The measure was bitterly criticised by orthodox sound-money men, who protested that any approach to bimetallism would be disastrous so long as London, the world's money market, was wedded to gold.

At the height of the Populist agitation a Democratic President, Grover Cleveland, sat in the White House. The Democrats had for long been torn between sound- and easy-money men, but thanks to the influence of New York in the party all the presidential candidates had been sound-money men and Cleveland was no exception. In 1893 a sharp economic crisis precipitated a drain of gold from the country. This was intensified by the operation of the Silver Purchase Act, under which men could bring silver to the mint, sell it for legal-tender paper, and convert the paper into gold, which could then be exported at a considerable profit. Cleveland forced the repeal of the act through Congress, and concurrently made a deal with J. P. Morgan to replenish the country's gold reserve; this reversion to hard money and the alliance with high finance split the Democratic party and led to a revolution in policy. At the National convention of 1896 the party made an abrupt jump into agrarian radicalism by nominating William Jennings Bryan of Nebraska on a 'free-silver' platform. Bryan's oratory had carried the day, and it was in a fit of splendid emotion that the assembled party delegates responded to his exhortation that 'you shall not crucify mankind upon a cross of gold'. With some reluctance the Populists endorsed Bryan who had committed himself to none of their demands save free silver, and the stage was set for the most momentous and exciting election since 1861. Agriculture was arrayed against industry, agrarian demagogues against bankers, and the less-developed dependencies against the highly developed 'homeland'. The Republicans closed their ranks in defence of a policy initiated by an eastern Democrat, and the Democrats gathered the fruit of discontent propagated by the homestead policy of western Republicans.

The Republican candidate, William McKinley, said little and won unprecedented and enthusiastic support from business interests. Bryan spoke much, rousing passionate response in rural areas, losing conservative eastern Democrats, and making little impression upon skilled industrial labour. Business propaganda, coupled with some economic coercion, cannot alone account for the Republican victory. Bryan carried every purely rural state by great majorities, but in all those where industry was significant he lost votes which had gone to Cleveland in 1892. Opposition to Bryan united intellectuals with businessmen, and it was claimed that the university faculties were solid for McKinley; most of those who subsequently became prominent in the Progressive movement voted Republican and so, probably, did a majority of trade unionists. Republican victory settled the future course of American history, for never again would agrarian radicalism capture a major party or seek to control the nation. If populism had anticipated some of the characteristics of later liberalism it was also provincial, anti-intellectual, anti-semitic, opposed to foreign immigration, and impregnated with romantic intolerance. It had stabbed away at many of the problems which perplexed America, but it had evolved no coherent philosophy for a country in which industry was essential and in which urban population grew every year.

On 16 January 1865 in the House of Representatives that vigorous radical William G. Kelley, old abolitionist, friend of labour, greenbacker and ardent protectionist, spoke to Congress about the new age which was dawning. 'History', he exclaimed, 'is not repeating itself. We are unfolding a new page in national life. The past has gone forever.' Written upon this new page Kelley saw the popular press, the telegraph, the railway, industrial invention, homestead laws, the welcome given to destitute immigrants, the American Missionary Society, the emancipation of the slaves, the common school, and the dissemination of knowledge by cheap printed books. This was as good a summary as any of the things which convinced members of the Northern and Mid-western society that they were riding in the van of progress. The suspicion that the American experiment had failed when it plunged into civil war hardly penetrated the minds of this buoyant generation, and if some were aware of the deficiencies of American culture, only a tiny minority developed nostalgic yearnings for Europe. Nor was American culture failing to develop its own resources: despite the poor reputation of the press every region possessed newspapers which were informative and responsible; periodicals such as *Harper's, Century, Forum* and the *Atlantic Quarterly* were among the best in their respective fields; and American universities were beginning to create a system of graduate training which was to be a focal-point of twentieth-century scholarship.

In this new society the centre of the stage was taken by the emergent class of businessmen. Seen at their worst in association with politics, their real strength lay in small towns where they were the creators of prosperity, local benefactors, and organisers of communal activities. The apparent contradiction, which a later generation delighted to discover, between sharp practice and pious charity, was hardly noticed; a man was despised for acting against his own interest in a business transaction but he was also expected to give time, energy and money to voluntary and charitable work. Whether these social activities sprang from natural altruism or from social pressure, they led to surprising results. The harsh structure of economic power was underwritten by a network of social obligations, and even the fraternal associations, in which businessmen began to enjoy their separate existence as a class apart, were ostensibly devoted to humane and charitable objectives. If the ordinary businessman was expected to act in this way, the man of great wealth was expected to give munificently. Hospitals, universities, museums, public parks, and finally the philanthropic foundations of the modern times were by-products of nineteenth-century wealth and the projects of nineteenth-century businessmen. Andrew Carnegie's *Gospel of Wealth*, published in 1889, provided a rational justification for habits of giving which sprang from American communal behaviour; convinced that men of great wealth were inevitable in and beneficial to a healthy society, Carnegie was nevertheless disturbed by the price paid for their ascendancy. His remedy was that the rich man should regard himself as the trustee of wealth for the community, with the duty of organising its redistribution into those channels, such as medicine, education and culture, where it would contribute to the permanent betterment of mankind. Pious admonitions addressed to powerful individuals have been placed at a discount in twentieth-century thought, but it is impossible to understand late nineteenth-century America without realising the effect which they had upon plutocratic behaviour. To European critics, and to many subsequent writers, the American businessman appeared narrow, crude, and aware of no value save that of the dollar; to his fellow townsman he could be a benevolent oligarch and the pride of the community in which he had risen.

Engaged upon their separate pursuits members of this business civilisation were nevertheless conscious of a common purpose. The guiding Providence of Protestant Christianity, classical economics, and the new theory of evolution merged together in the belief that there was a natural order, that within it the dynamic forces of mankind were utilised and harmonised, and that competitive struggle led to the betterment of mankind. This complex of moral, political and economic ideas has been tied together with the generic title of *laissez-faire*, though the economic doctrine of non-interference by the state was only one aspect in the thought of a generation which was mesmerised and constantly reassured by man's effort to improve his condition. Reassurance was sometimes needed, for there were intellectual and practical difficulties to be overcome. If the natural equilibrium ensured that a man unconsciously served humanity in serving himself, did this mean that avarice and a ruthless use of power ought to be condoned? If the natural order was the automatic and irresistible regulator of human destiny, must men abjure that portion of their reason which taught men collectively to control their environment? Must politicians endowed with the power to act voluntarily abstain from its use? Was individualism compatible with the survival of the fittest? Ultimately these questions would drive intellectuals either to an acceptance of collectivism, exercised by the state or by the great corporations, or to angry exhortations and gloomy prediction as men rebelled against the tyranny of a theory which seemed as wasteful and as callous as the biological struggle for existence upon which it depended for its analogies.

Intellectual orthodoxy tended to invest with the attributes of nature the hypotheses of economic science, and even so artificial a contrivance as the gold standard became a part of the natural law. Most intellectuals acclaimed the dogmatic optimism of Herbert Spencer even while his assumptions were being challenged by events. After the great depression began in 1873 it was difficult to believe wholeheartedly in the beneficence of uncontrolled economic activity, and after the strikes and attendant violence of 1877 it was difficult to believe in the natural harmony of society. In rural slums and great cities the numbers of the very poor increased and their condition seemed to become more degraded. The small businessman complained of unfair competition from monopolistic giants, and John D. Rockefeller, reflecting in later life upon the formation of his Standard Oil Trust in 1882, observed that 'The day of combination is here to stay. Individualism has gone, never to return.' If self-made magnates could still be reconciled with a society of equal opportunity, it was more difficult to justify John Pierpont Morgan, who exercised enormous financial power from a remote upper-class world. But the pressure exerted by economic change produced less dramatic results than it did in other industrial societies; the 'safety valve' of American society, which some have seen in the existence of unsettled western land, was the range of opportunity offered by technological revolution, vast untapped natural resources and a rapidly expanding home market. For the ambitious American there was always some pursuit more profitable than political agitation. Nevertheless, the problems fed anxieties which lay beneath the surface of this self-confident society.

The most influential critic of the new American order was Henry George, whose *Progress and Poverty* was published in 1879. George forced attention upon 'the great enigma of our times', which was the persistence of poverty despite wonderfully increased productivity. Here was a problem which economic theory ought to solve but had evaded. George retained an ardent belief in the benefits of competitive capitalism provided that its defects could be isolated and cured; his own analysis led him to the conclusion that the root of the evil lay in the private ownership of land, which he believed to be the source of all wealth. As a remedy he proposed not confiscation but a tax on land values replacing all other forms of taxation, transferring to the treasury the increment in value won by labour and skill, and making government 'merely the agency by which the common property was administered for the common benefit'. His ideas attracted many followers and form a strong though often unacknowledged undercurrent in modern social thought, but the force of his passionate attack upon unnecessary poverty tended to become lost in technical arguments over the single tax. More profound but less influential was *Dynamic Sociology*, the work of a civil servant and scientist named Lester Ward, which appeared in 1883. Ward distinguished between human and natural evolution and maintained that human reason should control society and not submit to its irrational forces. He placed the human power to direct and control within the natural order, and thus provided a solution to the dilemma of evolution.

The *laissez-faire* model received a more damaging blow from the political pressure of interests and organised numbers. The history of the protective tariff, having been written by free-traders, has been represented as the imposition of an unpopular and unsound policy by vested interests. In fact the tariff had a long history in several regions as a popular vote-winning policy, and its popularity increased with the rise of industry; organised labour generally supported it, and even the farmer wanted equal protection rather than no protection. Clearly some interests were not well-served by high tariffs, but it is necessary to discount the moralistic tone with which their case was presented. If the Americans wished to monopolise the benefits of the world's largest free-trade area, there was no particular reason why they should not do so provided that they were prepared to pay the price. The success of protectionists is indicated by the average level of duties on specific articles which rose from 47 per cent in 1869, to 49·5 per cent in 1890 and, after some relaxation during Cleveland's administration, to 57 per cent in 1897.

If non-intervention broke down at one end, an idea that capitalism ought to be regulated crept in at the other. Distrust of monopoly was an old American tradition, and the older generation of Americans saw no limit to the economic activities of the state save those expressly laid down in the Constitution. The school of thought which held that the Constitution ought to provide for the inviolability of free enterprise had to have time to mature, and at first the drive by western Grangers to regulate the activities of corporations aroused some sympathy outside their own section. The Granger laws were brought to a test case in 1876 in Munn *v.* Illinois, when a majority of the Court agreed with the opinion of White, C.J., that 'property does become clothed with a public interest when used in a manner to make it of public consequence, and affect the community at large'. This doctrine permitted a wide range of state regulation, but an opposing view gained ground, and for the remainder of the century the Court was concerned to close the door which it had opened. In 1873 the Court resisted the argument that the privileges and immunities protected by the fourteenth amendment included the right to pursue a trade without legislative interference, but by 1890 it had come to accept the view that regulation might amount to deprivation of property without due process of law which the amendment forbade to a state. In 1886 the Court decided that a corporation as a 'person' was entitled to the protection of the amendment. Another blow at state regulation rested upon an interpretation of the commerce clause, giving Congress exclusive jurisdiction over interstate commerce, and thus making it difficult if not impossible for states to regulate the activities of great corporations operating in several states.

From the outset there was confusion in defining the aims of regulation. The objective might be the protection of the consumer against monopoly or of the small businessman against 'unfair' competition. For the first a straightforward process of supervision and regulation would be sufficient, but the second would require the enforcement of a code of fair competition; either public authority was to be introduced as arbiter of the price mechanism without dictating the form of capitalist enterprise, or free competition was to be made compulsory by the abolition of monopoly. Late nineteenth-century policy took both roads ineffectively and with inadequate administrative agencies, but the precedents created were of great significance for the future.

The Interstate Commerce Act of 1887 followed the first principle of regulation, and brought the Federal government into the field from which the states had been excluded by the Supreme Court. It set up a Federal Commission with the duty of supervising interstate railways, but it did not specifically confer the power to fix rates and this was quickly denied to it by judicial interpretation. The judges were suspicious of a constitutional innovation which combined executive, judicial and legislative power, and by the end of the century the commission had been confined largely to the collection and publication of railway statistics. The Sherman Anti-Trust Act of 1890 wrote into the law the enforcement of competition. Its passage was stimulated by the publicity given to Rockefeller's Standard Oil Trust, which had come to control most of the country's oil-refining, and it declared flatly that 'every contract, combination in the form of trust or otherwise, or conspiracy, in restraint of trade or commerce among the several states, or with foreign nations, is hereby declared to be illegal'. The Act was constructed on a quite different principle from the Interstate Commerce Act; it made a change in statute law, left its enforcement to the courts, and placed the responsibility for prosecution primarily with the law officers of the Federal government. It had respectable antecedents in the old common law principle that contracts in restraint of trade were void, but the difficulty lay in language which was at once too precise and too vague. A literal outlawry of all combinations in restraint of trade might embrace normal business agreements to which no one could object, while the prosecutor was forced to prove restraint against the plausible defence that combination had been followed by expansion and greater efficiency. There was therefore a genuine difficulty in the interpretation of the act and the Court need not be blamed for giving defendants the advantage of the most favourable interpretation. There was also a reluctance, on the part of Cleveland's and McKinley's administrations, to prosecute, and during this period big business found more effective methods of organisation. A traditional obstacle to combination was the provision, normal in state charters, that a corporation could not hold the stock of another corporation; the Trust, by which the stockholders in nominally separate companies yielded their interest to a body of Trustees, was at the best a cumbersome device, and when the state of New Jersey rescinded the old provision in its charters, the business magnates were able to incorporate holding companies which then acquired the stock of operating subsidiaries. The first decade after the Anti-Trust Act saw an acceleration rather than a check to consolidation, and a paradoxical effect of the act was that small companies which executed a trade agreement might be successfully prosecuted while an industrial giant could escape. Despite the disappointing history of these two great measures for the regulation of capitalist enterprise, important principles had been established: the acts were on the statute book and could be implemented or extended; Congress had decided and the courts had admitted that there ought to be rules for the conduct of business; and an important step had been taken towards the definition of these rules by public authority.

Regulated capitalism was an attempt, shared between agrarian radicals and small businesses, to restore the world of the small entrepreneur, but at one stage the whole employer class was almost forced on to the defensive, and in 1886 an observer who believed in the coming class-struggle might have predicted that it was about to be fought out on American soil. In that year a great labour organisation known as the Knights of Labour, claiming over 700,000 members and embracing both skilled and unskilled, had just won some spectacular struggles with employers, and showed signs of moving into the political field. At the same time recent German immigration had brought many socialists and anarchists, whose influence seemed to be on the increase. However, the strength of the Knights concealed the real difficulties of organising labour in a country where education and opportunity drained off potential leaders, where small property owners preponderated politically, where the gap between skilled and unskilled was widened by racial and religious differences, and where agitation was seen as a threat to society against which all the resources of the law must be mobilised. In this situation the influence of foreign agitators was particularly unfortunate for respectable unionism, and this was dramatised when a bomb outrage at Chicago in 1886 discredited the whole labour movement. The over-ambitious organisation of the Knights was too weak to stand up against these difficulties, and they were of diminishing influence after a rapid decline from the zenith of their power.

As the Knights withered away the American Federation of Labor, founded in 1885 under its first and perennial President, Samuel Gompers, came to the fore. Here was a masterful personality prepared to devote his life to the cause of labour, but only on the terms which he himself dictated. Unionisation should aim at the skilled, not the unskilled; the effort to improve wages and working conditions for this restricted group would be unremitting, but it would work for immediate gains within the capitalist system not for its overthrow; in politics the unions would reward friends and punish enemies but would commit themselves to no party or political creed, and association with intellectual radicals would be avoided. Skilled labour would win middle-class status and accept the conventions of a middle-class world, and the successful labour leader would establish himself as a useful member of the community who could offer industrial discipline in return for employer concessions. The labour history of the late nineteenth century was far from untroubled: there was a shocking incident at the Homestead Steel works when first a private army of Pinkerton detectives and then the state militia of Pennsylvania were used against strikers who had occupied the factory, and in 1894 Federal troops were used in force against railways strikers in the Chicago area. It was also at this period that judges sympathetic to employers began to make extensive use of injunctions ordering strikers to cease and desist from actions which threatened property, and to punish breaches of this injunction as contempt of court without jury trial. These events drove a small minority of labour leaders to socialism, but they also demonstrated the wisdom of the cautious policy of Gompers, which was deliberately framed to avoid clashes between labour and the organised forces of law and order. Even more conservative were the Railway Brotherhoods drawing upon the skilled cream of the labour force. By 1904 the American Federation of Labor claimed over three-quarters of the 2,000,000 union members, and though engaged in perpetual propaganda warfare with the recently founded National Association of Manufacturers it had become even more dogmatically anti-socialist.

With all their harshness and crudity the raw centres of industrial civilisation seemed vigorous and hopeful, but the same could hardly be said of the greater cities, which seemed to add to the vices of the old world some which were peculiarly American. In 1890 a Danish-American journalist,

Jacob Riis, published a revealing book on New York's densely populated tenement districts entitled *How the Other Half Lives*. It attracted widespread attention and challenged the easy assumption of religious and evolutionary thought that bad social conditions were the consequence of depravity, not its cause. To nineteenth-century reformers the more apparent evil of urban society was government by bosses and rings, clearly one of the worst political abuses in the world, which seemed to be impregnably based upon the mass vote of the very poor. In cities almost entirely devoid of public social services, and in a country with a traditional distrust of those who were huddled together in towns, the slum dweller received from the boss and his henchmen small charities, protection, jobs, and above all human contact with the bewildering world of power and consequence. Unacknowledged by the good citizens the boss performed an important service for them in preventing the spread of revolutionary ideas in this soil of discontent, but there could be little doubt that the need for his existence pointed to a major failure in American civilisation. The slums and the evils of city government blinded most intelligent Americans to the obvious fact that the city rather than the countryside was the standard-bearer of the new American civilisation, that they were centres of culture and higher education as well as of social evil, and that, especially in the Mid-west, it was the city which provided the outlet and opportunity for depressed or redundant rural population. To one group of Americans this was obvious, and the period saw the beginning of the great migration of Negroes from the South to northern cities.

The problem of the city merged into that of the foreign-born. These continued to arrive in formidable numbers; there was a marked shift away from those to whom English was a native language; the vast majority of them went to the great cities. But their assimilation had long been a matter of pride to patriotic Americans and in general American society maintained its attitude of welcome. Wherever the American educational system could reach the immigrant it performed a remarkable work of indoctrination, which was facilitated by the immigrant's acceptance of Americanisation as necessary for the success of his children. In most areas which received immigrants the tradition if not the consistent application of free elementary education was established, and most of them enacted compulsory attendance laws. A great deal of local pride and communal effort went into the elementary school system, and during this period the free high-school was also striking roots in many areas. Though educational progress was a spontaneous achievement and followed the course set by earlier trends, its aims and methods were influenced by the need to educate new Americans in American citizenship, and a study of school curricula would form a useful indication of the picture which Americans wished to present to themselves and to the world. Lacking the mystical trappings of ancient monarchy, with a short history devoted to the attainment of middle-class ideals rather than to military glory or genteel chivalry, and with the raw memory of the Civil War in the immediate past, the American of the late nineteenth century might have a difficult task when he sought to celebrate or explain his national existence. Yet by 1900 no people were more conscious of national identity or more self-conscious about its merits; American patriotism transcended diverse racial origins and flourished under a government which seemed to offer no focal-point for loyalty.

The war with Spain in 1898 is sometimes represented as the opening of a new era in American nationality; at one bound it seemed to heal sectional discord and turn the Americans from an introvert into an extrovert people. Yet national feeling was latent and released by the war, not created by it. It was not fought because the leaders of the developed capitalist society wished to fight it, and it was bitterly opposed by many keepers of the Northern conscience; but it aroused the enthusiasm of those who had been least associated with American progress: Southerners, westerners and ordinary newspaper readers whose passions were stirred by patriotic journalism. Nationalism which had seemed lost in the morass of sectional discord had retained its powerful appeal and, once its latent forces were released, the self-confidence which had characterised the North and Mid-west swept across the country.

First among the factors which aided the regeneration of American nationalism in the late nineteenth century was material achievement. Despite the recurrent crises it was apparent that most Americans were better off than ever before and that the country was leaping ahead of her industrial rivals. For the ordinary American material progress was not merely a matter of wealth and production, but a romantic concept which transformed the ugliness of the late nineteenth-century civilisation into a symbol of man's triumph over both nature and the ancient bonds of aristocracy and monarchy. Nothing struck the imagination more forcibly than the conquest of the continent; vast wheat fields covered land which earlier geographers had marked as the dead heart of the continent, five great railway routes spanned the west, and on the shores of the Pacific a thriving new American society had come into being. Fraudulent railway promotion, Homestead Act failures, armed warfare between settlers and cattle barons, wars of extermination and savagery against Indians, and the lawlessness and materialism of western society were all transformed into an epic of achievement which came to count for more than the reality. Could not the vigour of western expansion and the breakdown of old social restraints be productive of much good? The civilisation of the Mid-west seemed to supply an affirmative answer for here was a region which owed little to the traditions of the Old World, which was a purely American creation, and in which great differences in wealth were reconciled with social mobility, neighbourliness seemed compatible with the acquisitive instinct, men of different races were blending to produce a new type of man, and democratic politics were freely and vigorously conducted. Even eastern academics could become excited by this western achievement, and there was a ready response when F. J. Turner, a young Mid-western historian, enunciated his 'frontier thesis' in 1893. For Turner American civilisation was distinct and not a mere imitation of Europe; it owed its distinctiveness to a unique historical experience, and it was the moving frontier which had moulded the American character. Turner's theory might be given a pessimistic twist, for it was occasioned by the 'closing' of the frontier discovered by the census of 1890 with the implication that this expansive and creative phase in American history was now past, but for most people the impact of the theory lay in its explanation of national character. Nor need one forget the Old World if one remembered the changes wrought by the American climate, and in the same year 1893 another young academic, destined to wield an even greater influence than Turner, Woodrow Wilson, wrote that 'every element of the old life that penetrated the continent at all has been digested and has become an element of new life. It is this transformation that constitutes our history.'

Though the idea of nationality fed upon economic success and western expansion, Americans inevitably found the most telling symbols of the national existence in politics. Turner saw American democracy as the culminating effect of American experience 'rising stark and strong and full of life from the American forest'. The American tradition had emerged as a political tradition and it was to a body of political doctrine that allegiance was given; particular interest therefore attaches to those forces which sustained ideas and institutions formulated in the rural world of the eighteenth century. The practice of politics did less than might have been imagined to damage these beliefs, for with all its faults the political system was resilient, retained its capacity to absorb discontents, and provided the formulae by which diverse interests could be harmonised. The acceptance by the South of its new and subordinate position in the nation can be largely explained by the major role which it played in one of the main parties. The grievances voiced by agrarian radicals were offset by the share which agrarian representatives obtained in the parties and in the national government. The great Populist upheaval passed away without effecting a permanent disruption of the nation because it was first absorbed by a major party and then defeated in a normal electoral battle. At the same time the localism of politics left a field of action for those who failed to impress their views upon the nation. Though grievances might be exploited at election time, the whole tendency of party politics was to blunt the edge of discontent and to harmonise divergent groups. The less commendable aspects of politics worked in the same direction. The services of the city bosses in immunising the city masses against revolutionary infection have already been noticed. At a higher level the developing use of pressure groups held out to special interests the hope of obtaining what they wanted, led them to work with politicians rather than against them, and ensured that those with power and the ability to organise would not become alienated from representative government. In the same way the nature of politics had much to do with the reconciliation of organised labour to life in a capitalist world. Thus politics reflected and emphasised the characteristics of a society in which there were still great opportunities, in which class prejudice or accent did little to embarrass the man who made himself, and in which social and geographic mobility allowed a very large number of men to get what they wanted out of life.

The course of events revealed the strength of a political tradition based upon revolutionary principles, yet incorporating the checks and balances dear to conservative minds. The discontented could appeal to the tradition without being branded as heretics, the dominant groups could appropriate from it so much as coincided with their economic and social needs. When the divisive character of politics in other countries is remembered, the function of the maligned American political system assumes a greater significance and helps to explain the social stability which the United States had achieved by 1900. It was within this established framework, and using familiar slogans and remedies, that the ferment of progressivism was beginning to move at the end of the century; its three great incentives—anti-trust, anti-boss, and anti-slum—were variants on accepted themes, and reforming intellectuals did not develop that profound sense of alienation which influenced so many of their European counterparts.

The reconciliation of a conservative social order with a still-radical political creed necessarily caused doubts and divisions amongst the leaders of American thought, and there was a perceptible shift away from the old assumptions. The radical Republican concept of national power riding upon equal rights lost its hold, and the failure of Reconstruction democracy and the evils of city government spread disillusionment amongst the educated upper classes. A few intellectuals moved from the advocacy of impartial suffrage which would disenfranchise the ignorant of all races to a profound distrust of democracy. Henry Adams in his novel *Democracy* and in his *Education of Henry Adams* expressed this alienation from the popular creed in marked form. Anti-democratic feeling was seen in a less overt way in the legal profession and especially in the higher courts where the protection of property against democratically elected majorities became a major theme. Public men gave public praise to democracy, whatever their private reservations, but if white democracy had to be endorsed black democracy was abandoned. By the end of the century an influential minority stressed the importance of race, and of leaders within the race. Captain Alfred Mahan believed in the mission of the Anglo-

Saxons and argued for the naval power with which it could be fulfilled. Rudyard Kipling abjured the Americans to take up the white-man's burden, and the young Theodore Roosevelt was infected with a mystical notion of racial destiny. The changing mood was reflected in changing emphasis upon the traditions and symbols of American history. Nation-building replaced revolution as the great theme of early American history; the star of Jefferson waned slightly despite the conventional loyalty of the Democratic party, and the star of Hamilton shone forth more brightly; above all the Founding Fathers, a convenient description which could embrace men of varying beliefs, came to occupy first place in the American pantheon, while the Declaration of Independence, manifesto of a revolution, yielded its place at the centre of the American stage to the Constitution, symbol of ordered and balanced government.

CHAPTER XIX

THE STATES OF LATIN AMERICA

At the end of the seventh decade of the nineteenth century two generations had passed since the continental American colonies of Spain and Portugal had won their independence. During these years these new states had maintained their independence, expanded their commercial and cultural relations with Europe and progressed toward political stability. The half-dozen larger Spanish American units, roughly coincident with the colonial viceroyalties and captaincies-general which had emerged from the struggle against the mother-country, had split into sixteen separate republics, and within each of these national feeling had grown and increasingly justified a political map which at the outset had not set off really separate peoples from each other. Portuguese America, in contrast, had successfully weathered centrifugal tendencies, and in 1870 the empire of Brazil was the largest, the most powerful, and the most stable state in Latin America. In the West Indies, the political pattern remained colonial: Cuba and Puerto Rico remained under Spanish control; the lesser Antilles were subject to their various European metropolises; and isolated Haiti and the precariously sovereign Dominican Republic alone represented the republican principle in the Caribbean.

After 1870 the chief source of changes in this area was the unprecedented development of its connections with the outside world. Expanding industry in Europe and in the United States required ever larger amounts of raw materials such as hides, cotton, and wool; the new chemical and electrical industries required more and more rubber, copper, zinc, lead, and other metals. New concentrations of urban population also needed increasing amounts of imported food: sugar, wheat, meat, coffee, and cacao. At the same time capital funds and engineering skill became available in the economically advanced countries for the purpose of expanding production to meet these new demands. Of equal significance is the greatly increased flow of immigration from southern Europe—Portugal, Spain, and Italy—to the countries in the temperate portions of South America.

European investors had been quick to see possibilities of profit in Latin America immediately following the achievement of independence there, but the loans floated in London by the new governments had practically all gone into default. The high hopes of those who invested in mining enterprises in Chile and Mexico in the 1820's were also dashed. Since then, there had been a slow movement of funds into the area, but after 1870 there was a rapid change in the situation. Overall figures are not available, but it has been calculated that by 1880 Latin American securities with a par value of £179,490,261 had been floated in London. About £70,000,000 represented Latin American government bonds in default, but £56,412,255 consisted of direct investments in business enterprises in Latin America. By 1900 these sums had vastly increased, though most of the new funds were invested before the economic depression of the 1890's. At the end of the century total par value of Latin American securities traded on the London Stock Exchange was £540 million and more than half of this sum represented direct investments rather than Latin American government bonds. Of course many investments were made that were not listed on the London exchange. By 1897 the United States investments in Latin America, chiefly consisting of mines and railroads in Mexico and sugar interests in Cuba, totalled $300 million. There were also French, German, and other European investments of considerable importance, though the British share in the total was the greatest. In 1913, after a decade of rapid investment expansion, British investments were still more than double those of the United States and four times the value of French and German investments. It is almost certain that British pre-eminence in this field of activity was even greater in 1900.

Of the direct investments in Latin America, a very large part of the British share consisted of railroads, about 70 per cent in 1890. Mining enterprises, public utilities, and the Chilean nitrate industry accounted for most of the rest of the British direct investments.

The transforming effect of this flow of capital, by far the greater part of which went to Brazil, Uruguay, Argentina, Chile, Peru, Mexico, and Cuba, can hardly be overestimated. It brought about modernisation of public services: gas, electricity, water, and public transportation by street railways in the major Latin American cities. It made possible railroads that connected mines and agricultural hinterlands with seaports, capital cities with interior provinces and with ports. In addition, machines, steam-engines, generators, and motors brought about changes in the labour force because of their requirements of new mechanical skills. This created the beginnings of an industrial proletariat in countries that had previously been inhabited almost exclusively by peasants and landholders—the *peón* and the *patrón*.

The influence of European immigration was much more selective than that of foreign investment. Though colonies of European business and professional men, managers and technicians appeared in all the larger urban centres in Latin America, the numbers involved were negligible as far as any influence on the ethnic pattern of population was concerned, except in three countries. Almost all the European immigrants to Latin America in this period went to Argentina and Brazil. Overall figures compound many errors and do not take into account the reverse current of emigration which was at times very considerable. However, more than four million Europeans migrated to Latin America during the three decades from 1870 to 1900. There was a steady increase in the current during these years. From 1870 to 1879 less than half a million immigrants arrived; in the next decade, almost a million and a half; from 1890 to 1899 over two million.

Apart from the massive movement to Argentina and Brazil which accounted for most of these immigrants, Uruguay was also involved. As early as 1860 over 20 per cent of its population was of European birth. In 1900, there were close to 150,000 European-born living in the country. Chile received a smaller number of immigrants. The fact that a considerable number of these were concentrated on the southern frontier and that many of these were German or Swiss made them somewhat more conspicuous than if they had been more widely distributed, but the total number, including both colonists brought by the government and free immigrants, was less than 100,000 from the beginnings of colonisation to the end of the century.

The largest group of immigrants was the Italian, followed at some distance by the Spaniards and Portuguese (mainly to Brazil), and then there came a great variety of much smaller groups: German, French, British, Jewish, and a few Slavs. In the areas in which they settled they overwhelmed the native creole population. Brazil from São Paulo to the South became predominantly European, as did Montevideo and its environs in Uruguay, and most of Argentina, except for the far north and western provinces.

Closely related to the investment of capital and the migration of people were the improvements in transportation and communication between Europe and Latin America and between the United States and the northern Caribbean part of the area. Submarine cables were laid between 1865 and 1890, connecting first Mexico and Central America and eventually the whole of South America via the Pacific coast with the United States. Other lines connected the east coast of South America with Europe. Even more conspicuous was the improvement in maritime transportation brought about by the general introduction of steel steamships, both for passenger and freight service. The area served best was the east coast of South America, where the greatest volume of traffic existed. All the maritime nations of Europe competed in this area. There were British, French, German, Spanish, and Italian passenger lines serving Brazilian and Río de la Plata ports, to say nothing of freighters of a still wider variety of nationality.

In the Caribbean, American lines served Central America, Mexico, and the West Indian islands of Cuba and Hispaniola. On the Pacific coast British services were the most important for South America but the American Pacific Mail Company connected the west coast of Central America and Panama with United States Pacific ports. The lack of any direct passenger service from the United States to Brazil and Argentina is clear indication of the relative unimportance of commercial relations between the United States and this part of Latin America in the latter nineteenth century.

Complementary to shipping and telegraphic communication as an adjunct to trade was the service provided by banks. The first corporate banking institutions devoted to the financing of foreign trade were the British institutions in Argentina: the London and River Plate Bank and the British Bank of South America, both founded before 1870. The London and Brazilian Bank dates from the same period (1862). Between then and the end of the century banks were founded by Italian, French, and German interests to finance trade between those countries and Buenos Aires. In time branches were established in Uruguay, Chile, and elsewhere.

To get a clearer picture of economic changes in this period it is necessary to review the developments in various countries, for there was much variety in the experience of the different nations.

It was in Argentina that economic growth was most marked. This country, one of the least developed and most underpopulated parts of the Spanish empire at the beginning of the century, outdid all other Latin American states in rapidity of population growth, volume of immigration, mileage of railroads constructed and in expansion of foreign trade during the last three decades of the century. Immigration had begun shortly after the fall of Rosas in 1852, but it remained small until after 1860. Between 1870 and 1900 over 2,200,000 immigrants entered the country. Some of these settled in agricultural colonies in the provinces of Santa Fé, Entre Rios and Buenos Aires; many others became tenants on lands of Argentine *estancieros*, now increasingly devoted to agriculture; others remained in the growing cities of Buenos Aires, Rosario, and Bahía Blanca. The greatest single group was that of the Italians. Next, at some distance, came the Spaniards. These two nationalities comprised the great majority of all immigrants admitted. Partly because of this flow of new blood, but also because of rapid increase of the creole population, the census of 1897 showed more than double the number of inhabitants in 1869. The city of Buenos Aires grew at an even more rapid rate. Railway construction had begun in the 1850's, but in 1870 there were but 458 miles of track in operation. These had grown by 1880 to over fifteen hundred miles and by 1900 to ten thousand miles. The Argentine rail network surpassed that of all other Latin American countries. Between 1880 and 1900 the nominal value of British investments alone rose from £20 million to over £200 million.

Railroads and immigrants together made possible for the first time the large-scale production of wheat and other cereals for export. The area of cultivated land in the country increased from one million and a half acres in 1870 to over 17 million acres in 1901. From being a net importer of cereals, Argentina in thirty years reached a point at which 100 million bushels of wheat and maize were exported in 1899. Meanwhile, the export of meat products was revolutionised by the advent of refrigeration. The first refrigerated steamer took a cargo of frozen mutton to Europe in 1877. In 1883 the first modern packing plant or *frigorífico* was built near Buenos Aires. By the end of the century thousands of tons of frozen mutton and beef were being shipped yearly to Europe. This development brought with it a transformation of the traditional cattle industry which had only produced hides, horns, tallow, and jerked beef for export. The market for frozen meat encouraged the importation of pure-bred Durham and Hereford bulls and the consequent upgrading of the native stock. To take care of more valuable herds it became necessary to fence pastures, to control insect pests and diseases of cattle, to grow artificial pasture of alfalfa and other forage crops, to provide better water supply, and to use more labour than had been customary. As a result of this economic growth the value of Argentine foreign trade (the sum of exports and imports) almost tripled between 1870 and 1900.

No other Latin American country could rival Argentina during these years in rapidity of material progress. Each of the others lacked one or more of the combination of favourable conditions which presented themselves in Argentina.

In Brazil, which had overshadowed Argentina in development, as in area, before the 1870's, development, though considerable, was now less pronounced. Here again immigration was a major transforming factor, though it brought change primarily to the south, from São Paulo to Rio Grande. It had begun earlier than in Argentina but it remained small until the eve of the abolition of slavery in the 1870's. When a wage system of labour was introduced in the coffee industry and slave labour disappeared the inflow of European immigrants became important. From less than two hundred thousand in the 1870's, immigrants increased to over half a million in the decade of the 1880's and to well over a million in the 1890's. Portuguese were most numerous until the end of the imperial era in 1889 but were surpassed in number by Italians thereafter. The great majority of the immigrants went to the rapidly growing state of São Paulo. The production of coffee boomed in São Paulo, just as cereal production did in Argentina, under the combined stimulus of immigration and railroad construction. Brazil, in terms of miles of track in operation, was not far behind Argentina. Over 6000 miles were in use by 1889 and by 1904 the 10,000 mile point had been reached, but, of course, these lines served less adequately a vastly larger country. Most of the construction was in the state of São Paulo with trunk lines connecting it with Rio Grande to the south and Rio de Janeiro and Minas to the north and east. Coffee exports rose from 400 million pounds, the average for the years 1870–5, to 1130 million pounds, the average for the last five years in the century. Unlike Argentina, however, which could depend on a variety of export staples, Brazil's foreign trade depended heavily on coffee, which was responsible for about two-thirds of the total value of exports. It was double that of Argentina in 1870, and three times that of Chile, Peru or Mexico, but thereafter it did not grow at the rate of Argentina's. For a while rubber seemed to be bringing about a desirable diversification. Exports from the Amazon Valley rose from 10 million pounds in 1870 to 52 million pounds in 1900. However, this was a short-lived boom soon to collapse. Cacao, meat products, lumber, and forest products were only minor items among exports.

In one respect Brazil forged ahead of Argentina during the final decade of the century. The cotton textile industry expanded until in 1905 over 100 mills employed about 40,000 workers and produced almost a quarter of a million metres of cloth. There was a rush of investment in industry in the years immediately following the fall of the empire and the establishment of the republic in 1889. These establishments were, apart from textiles, devoted to the production of hats, shoes, and clothing, and the processing of various kinds of foodstuffs. An industrial complex in São Paulo was stimulated by the capital gains of coffee-plantation owners, the availability of labour, and the existence of water-power which at the end of the century was harnessed in hydro-electric plants.

Despite these promising economic developments in Brazil, there can be no doubt that the pace of progress was not so rapid as in Argentina. Population growth was slower, the total moving between 1870 and 1900 from 10 to over 17 million inhabitants, but failing to double itself as in Argentina. Again, if the British capital investment can be taken as an indication of the rate of growth, Brazil lagged in this respect. In 1870 British investments in Brazil had been larger than those in Argentina. In 1900 they were less than one-half the value of investments in the River Plate republic.

In Chile we have another example of a country which made some spectacular economic gains, but which was not as greatly changed as Argentina. Immigration was not heavy. Investment of foreign capital was also smaller than in either Argentina or Brazil. In 1900 the total sum, more or less evenly divided between mining property (including nitrate works), railroads, and government bonds, was not much more than one-third the figure for Brazil. Railroad construction, though considerable in relation to area, was far behind Argentina and Brazil in total mileage, amounting in 1900 to about 3000 miles, equally divided between state-owned and privately owned lines. Chilean agriculture, though it was diversified and based on extensive irrigation, did not expand and population growth was far slower than in either Argentina or Brazil. From about two millions in 1870 the total number of inhabitants had only increased to a little less than three millions in 1900.

Chile did experience extraordinary progress in these years in the nitrate industry in the northern deserts acquired from Bolivia and Peru as a result of the Chilean victory in the War of the Pacific. In 1870 Chile had produced no nitrates; in 1880 a quarter of a million metric tons; in 1900 one million four hundred thousand metric tons, and approximately three-quarters of the total world production. This had an enormously stimulating effect on government revenues, public works and railroad construction, and the growth of industry. By 1900 Chile was manufacturing an extraordinary variety of consumer goods: hats, shoes, cigarettes, flour, lard, textiles, leather, furniture, cordage, paper, tin and earthenware, cement, matches, soap, candles, fertilisers, and industrial chemicals. There were also important machine and metal-product works which could repair railroad and industrial machinery and make spare parts. Chilean businessmen were already organising a national association of manufacturers and had achieved sufficient influence to induce the government to adopt a frankly protective tariff.

It was only in mining, therefore, that Chile could be said to surpass Argentina and Brazil in 1900, but if some of the statistical data are presented in terms of *per capita* figures or figures per square mile the result is much more favourable to Chile. In short, Chile was making excellent progress but on the smaller scale natural to a country with a much smaller area and population than its neighbours on the Atlantic coast.

Uruguay must also be included among the countries making substantial economic gains in this period, though in scale these were even smaller than those of Chile. Only about a million people lived in this republic in 1900, though growth had been steady from about 600,000 in 1870. The same forces that led to the expansion and transformation of the Argentine livestock industry were at work in Uruguay, bringing about an extraordinary growth in the number of sheep and cattle in the country. The former increased from less than a million at mid-century to over 18 million in 1900; the latter in the same period moved up from less than two million to almost seven. The export of dried beef was important and, in 1900, there were twenty-one establishments engaged in producing *charqui*. In Uruguay, too, were the pioneer factories for the production of meat extract dating from the establishment of the original Liebig plant at Fray Bentos in 1863. Uruguayan railroad progress was considerable in relation to the size of the country. Over a thousand miles of track were in use by 1900 and 11 of a total of 36 million pounds invested in the country represented railroads. The foreign trade of the republic doubled in value between 1870 and 1900. It will be noted, however, that there was no important growth of Uruguayan agriculture except in the livestock industry. Growing prosperity was therefore somewhat more precarious than where it had a broader base.

In 1870 Peru would have had to be included among the countries showing significant economic growth. This had been due almost entirely to the export of guano from the rocky coasts and offshore islands where the excrement of countless birds for thousands of years had created deposits of great value as fertiliser. Government revenue derived from guano shipments made possible large expenditures for public works and railroads; it also led to waste of money and the undue enrichment of those private interests associated with the government in these varied activities. What was worse, perhaps, was the expansion of the foreign debt beyond all reason. To cope with the threat of bankruptcy the administration of President José Balta created a monopoly of guano operations, eliminating for the future the many *consignatarios* who had served as agents for the sale of guano in European and colonial markets. A contract was made with a French banking firm, Dreyfus et Cie, according to which it was granted the guano monopoly and in return agreed to pay the interest on the foreign debt and advance funds to Peru in addition. This might have permitted an orderly liquidation of the financial difficulties of the republic, but the Balta administration began spending and borrowing, recklessly mortgaging future guano shipments. The American promoter and railroad builder Henry Meiggs was at this time engaged in his spectacular construction programme. On the surface, then, Peru seemed to be forging ahead rapidly, but this apparent progress was based rather insecurely on guano. A fall in the price or in the demand for the product would bring disaster.

When this era of speculative prosperity was followed by the defeat of Peru in the War of the Pacific (1879–83), which was accompanied by widespread looting and destruction of property in enemy-occupied areas, the result was bankruptcy and stagnation. After 1890 there was a beginning of recovery, but even in 1900 total Peruvian trade was smaller than in 1870. In thirty years the population had increased only from 3,200,000 to 4,000,000 inhabitants. There was no appreciable European immigration and in its stead the earlier introduction of Chinese coolies before 1870 was supplemented in the 1890's by Japanese workers. The chief new elements of strength in the Peruvian economy in 1900 were the expanding commercial, large-scale agriculture of the irrigated coastal areas, which produced large quantities of sugar and cotton, and the revival of mining under new, technically advanced foreign management, which was making Peru an important producer of copper and other metals. Large sums had been spent on railway construction, which was carried on in the teeth of enormous engineering difficulties and at high cost, but the total mileage in operation was considerably less than that of Chile. In Peru the influences working toward economic progress were neutralised by contrary factors.

Only two countries in northern Latin America can be said to have made economic gains at all comparable to those of Argentina, Brazil and Chile. These were Mexico and Cuba. In 1870 Mexico, with over nine million inhabitants, was second only to Brazil in population among Latin American countries, but its general economic progress was not comparable to its population. The only railroad in the country was that linking Mexico and Veracruz. The foreign trade of Mexico was less valuable than that of Peru or Chile and far behind that of Argentina. The great majority of Mexicans were engaged in subsistence agriculture. Even the large estates were primarily run to supply local markets. Mining, which accounted for most of the value of exports, had expanded only slowly in normal times and was affected adversely by the many civil wars. After 1876, however, the dictatorial regime of Porfirio Díaz adopted policies favourable to the entry of foreign capital and this led to extensive railroad building and the connection of the Mexican lines with those of the United States. During the 1880's, too, a new era of mining based on modern technology and capable of using lower grade ores came into existence. Though silver mining was still important, copper and other metals previously neglected were now produced on a large scale. Coal mining also became important in the 1890's. Foreign capital also went into the public-utilities field and on a smaller scale into manufacturing, establishing jute and linen factories, soap and vegetable-oil works, a cement plant, and other enterprises. The first beginnings of the Mexican oil industry came in 1890 with the founding by United States' interests of the Mexican Petroleum Company. Measured in some ways, Mexican economic progress was considerable. The credit of the government was good. By 1900 the annual value of the foreign trade of the republic had increased fourfold since 1870. On the other hand there was no real advance in Mexican agriculture; the mass of the peasantry were living in an even more depressed state than in 1870 and the growth of population was very small. Mexico and Brazil in 1870 had almost the same number of inhabitants, but Brazil in 1900 had three and a half million more than Mexico. Mexico has been estimated to have received by 1900 approximately £67 million of British capital in addition to over $200 million from the United States. Foreign investment, therefore, was roughly equivalent in Mexico and in Brazil, a clear indication that over-all economic progress depended on many other factors.

Cuba may be included with the countries which made marked progress during the latter decades of the nineteenth century, but this progress was neutralised, as in the case of Peru, by war—in the case of Cuba there were two successive wars of independence, 1868–78 and 1895–8. In both of these conflicts there was very great damage to the sugar plantations which were the chief base of Cuban wealth. In addition, the country was a colony until 1898 and it is therefore difficult to compare with independent countries. However, it is clear that Cuba represented one of the areas of economic progress. The population of the island grew with sugar prosperity and received immigrants both from Spain and from Jamaica and other West Indian islands suffering from under-employment. Over $50 million of United States capital was invested in Cuban sugar. British capital invested included about £10 million in railroads and manufacturing. In 1900 the country had not yet recovered from the terrible losses incurred during the struggle for independence. In spite of that fact, Cuba's trade at that time was of greater value than that of nine other Latin American countries. As a major source of sugar Cuba was important to the rest of the world.

The countries which have not so far been mentioned are those located in the American tropics from Guatemala to Paraguay. It cannot be said that these countries were completely stagnant economically, but their progress was relatively slight. In all of them economic growth was chiefly due to the expansion of production of one or two export crops or minerals for which the markets of the world exhibited an uncertain demand. This made difficult any steady progress. Coffee production began to expand notably in the last years of the century in Colombia and in several Central American countries. Cacao prospered in Venezuela and Ecuador as well as in Brazil. Peru, Bolivia, Colombia and Venezuela all shared to some extent in the rubber boom which was on the march in 1900 in Amazonia. Toward the close of the 1890's Bolivian mineral production increased, replacing in importance the nitrates lost to Chile in the War of the Pacific. The production of tin, later to be so important in Bolivia, began at this time. Paraguay also saw some recovery as the century waned. The value of its foreign trade doubled between 1880 and 1900, but the total value remained small in comparison to nearby Uruguay.

It is an indication of the regional contrasts which had developed in Latin American economic life that the value of the foreign trade of Venezuela and Colombia combined was less than that of Uruguay. There were more miles of railroad in operation in Chile than in ten of the tropical republics.

Changes in political life in Latin America showed a tendency to correlate with the different rates of economic progress. In the period between the achievement of independence and 1870 certain characteristic forms of political behaviour had appeared in Latin America, manifesting themselves to a greater or a lesser degree in the various countries. Among these were: political instability evidenced by failure to create a workable constitutional order, by frequent civil wars and *coups d'état*; the primacy of personal loyalty to charismatic leaders over ideology, and the consequent prevalence of regimes of force based on the prestige of *caudillos*; political conflicts taking the form of clashes between liberals, who were above all anti-clerical, but also were upholders in theory of democracy and of local autonomy or federalism, and conservatives who upheld the concept of a hierarchical aristocratic political and social order and a close collaboration of the state with the Roman Church. All these tendencies continued after 1870, but in some countries they came to be modified in important particulars. In certain countries political stability increased greatly. It was based on the growing strength of 'enlightened' oligarchies who governed either through political machines operating under a constitutional system or through co-operation with an 'enlightened' dictator. Parallel to this greater stability came a great expansion of the bureaucracies and a professionalising of the military service. At the end of the era it is also possible to see the dawn of a protest against the selfish rule of the few over the many.

As in the case of economic change, one of the countries which best exemplified the growth of political stability was Argentina. By 1870 the sporadic revolts of *caudillos* of the interior had all been put down, but the country was still disturbed by conflict within the city and province of Buenos Aires between those who favoured and those who opposed the 'federalisation' of the city. This question led to fighting in 1874 and again in 1880, but on the latter occasion the matter was definitively settled by the creation of a federal district and the separation of the city from the province of Buenos Aires. The national point of view had triumphed, and though the form of the Argentine constitution was federal the power of the federal government grew rapidly at the expense of the provinces. The old unitary and federal parties which had dominated Argentine politics since 1820 disappeared. A conservative, business-minded oligarchy governed the country. The government was carried on, superficially at least, according to the constitution and elections were held regularly. Electoral laws, however, made possible the control of elections by the ruling conservatives as there was no provision for a secret ballot.

In Chile political evolution took a somewhat different form. Constitutional stability had been the achievement of an earlier age, beginning in 1830. The years from 1870 to 1890 were marked by the progressive weakening of the executive power, which had previously been almost all-powerful and able, through the ministry of the interior and the police, to control the results of congressional elections. In a process of transition from the earlier strong presidential regimes towards a system in which political parties or factions in the congress played a greater part, the executive came to be more and more the creature of shifting coalitions between the factions of the major conservative and liberal parties in which the nationalists (a smaller intermediate group) and the left-wing radicals played a lesser role. Though the Constitution of 1833 did not prescribe it, it became customary for presidents to govern through ministries which enjoyed the support of congressional majorities. This trend had gone so far that when it was challenged by a headstrong chief executive, José

Manuel Balmaceda, in 1891, a revolution broke out which succeeded after severe fighting in deposing the president. The failure and subsequent suicide of Balmaceda firmly established the parliamentary system in Chile until the constitutional changes of the third decade of the following century. On the other hand, although the conservative party was no longer dominant and although the liberal party, which represented primarily a tendency to limit the power of the Church, was increasingly powerful, both parties supported the interests of the landed aristocracy. Congress, dominating the executive, but ruling according to all the forms of constitutional law and government, was the stronghold of an oligarchy.

In Brazil, the only monarchy in the New World, the major development of the late nineteenth century was the downfall of the empire and the establishment of the United States of Brazil. In spite of the personal popularity of Dom Pedro II republicanism began to make gains after 1870. It was in harmony with the positivist philosophy which became dominant in intellectual circles and with the movement for the abolition of slavery which was stirring the country. At the same time, the enthusiasm of the slave-holding aristocracy for the imperial system was weakened by the emperor's acceptance of a policy of gradual emancipation. The clergy, meanwhile, had been alienated from the monarch by the interposition of the emperor on regalist grounds to prevent the ecclesiastical castigation of freemasons. The economic balance of power was shifting, also, from the old plantation areas of the north-east to the new coffee-producing areas in São Paulo and to other provinces farther south, to which the bulk of the European immigrants were going and whose business leaders sympathised less with tradition than those of Pernambuco and Bahia. New forces increased the power of the liberals who campaigned against a system in which, while a national assembly decorously debated public issues and provided an appearance of parliamentary government on the English model, as liberal and conservative ministries succeeded each other in orderly manner, the emperor jealously guarded his prerogative, and the lives of ministries depended on his will rather than on the parliamentary majorities which were regularly manufactured to support the ministers he called to power.

The crisis began in 1888 when, after years of violent agitation, the government yielded to demands for immediate emancipation of all remaining slaves. The legislation providing for abolition made no provision for compensation of slave-holders for their losses and antagonised conservatives who might otherwise have supported the empire, but who remained aloof when a military revolt in 1889 proclaimed a republic. The revolutionists were able to take possession of the government with practically no bloodshed. The whole country accepted the new regime and Dom Pedro and his family were sent into exile in Europe.

The disaffection of the armed forces was in part the result of positivist indoctrination in the military academy, in part due to the civilian bias which Dom Pedro had exhibited. It was also caused by the political ambitions of higher officers. For some years after the declaration of the republic military and naval men held the highest offices in the new government. In 1893 there was fighting between military and naval forces for supremacy. However, the form of the new republican constitution was federal and provided great freedom for the growing business interests of the country. As these interests came increasingly to control the governments of the most powerful states, São Paulo and Minas Gerais, they were able finally to dominate from behind the façade of military leadership. After Deodoro da Fonseca, the first president, and his successor, Floriano Peixoto, succeeding chief executives were civilians.

The achievement of constitutional order in Argentina after 1880, the implanting of parliamentary government in Chile, the adoption of republican institutions by Brazil, though they seemed to be disparate developments, brought into power governments which gave free rein to oligarchical interests. At the same time these countries were acting in harmony with the vogue throughout the western world of constitutionalism, republicanism, and representative government. In other Latin American countries governments responsive to the interests of the landowning and business classes took a somewhat different form: the 'dictatorship of order and progress'. These dictatorships differed from earlier personal regimes in that they were all professedly liberal and anti-clerical. Their liberalism, however, was much modified by their acceptance of the positivist political philosophy. Even if the ultimate goal was to be liberal democracy, the positivist emphasised the necessity for gradual progress through work and education. He had no faith in revolution or in the preaching of liberal principles as means to secure democracy or progress. In practice these regimes frequently used the same repressive and cruel methods to keep themselves in power and to eliminate opposition that had been made familiar by earlier dictatorships with fewer ideological pretensions. They governed with the support of part of the landholding aristocracies and enjoyed, in addition, the favour of commercial and industrial interests and frequently that of foreign capitalists.

In Mexico the Díaz regime evolved from the liberal republic restored by Benito Juárez after the collapse of Maximilian's empire. Díaz, one of the principal heroes of the war against the French, having failed to achieve the presidency via the ballot box, succeeded in his second attempt via the *pronunciamiento* in 1876. He retained his liberal label throughout his long career, but it was not long before he had established a highly authoritarian political order. The army, the landholders, foreign investors, businessmen, ambitious young politicos, even the Church, were all given things they badly wanted in order to keep them friendly. Anyone who opposed the regime found himself facing extremely disagreeable situations.

The army had faith in Díaz (one of their own) and generals were extensively employed in lucrative political and administrative positions. Landowners were given *carte blanche* in dealing with discontented debt-ridden peons; found the way made easy for them to purchase public lands at low prices; appreciated the efficiency of Díaz' *rurales* in maintaining order in the countryside. Foreign capitalists admired Díaz' re-establishment of Mexican government credit and gladly lent him money. Those who wished to invest in railways, mines, or *haciendas* found the government co-operative. Díaz, in spite of his anti-clerical traditions, gradually relaxed the enforcement of laws disagreeable to the Church, though they remained on the statute books. It is not surprising therefore that the hierarchy found that it could live with the dictator. Díaz gathered around himself a group of young, able, and ambitious men, imbued with the positivist ideas of the times, the so-called *científicos*. Education lagged, agriculture remained static, but in other respects Mexico showed economic progress unknown at any time since independence.

Antonio Guzmán Blanco's two decades of power in Venezuela from 1870 to 1888 were in many ways parallel to the Díaz regime in Mexico. Like Díaz he had a liberal tradition behind him, even though it was that of the successful revolt of liberal *caudillos* against the old aristocracy and the conservative party which had been its political expression; and even more than Díaz he continued while in power to retain certain shibboleths of liberalism. He patronised the Masonic Order, achieved separation of Church and state, established civil marriage and secular primary education, and suppressed religious orders. At the same time he was a patron of economic progress, borrowing money in Europe for elaborate and decorative public works and for the building of railroads. His policy produced stability of a sort. Behind the façade of liberalism, however, it is easy to recognise the tyrant who denied his people political freedom, persecuted his political rivals and made constitutions and elections a farce.

There were a number of similar regimes in Latin America in the final years of the century. Justo Rufino Barrios, who ruled in Guatemala from 1871 to 1885, also exemplifies the liberal revolutionary who, in office, becomes the benevolent despot. He followed an economic policy favourable to business, landholders, and to foreign capital. He initiated a programme of aid to agriculture and commerce, railroad building, and other public works. Unfortunately, less was accomplished along these lines than might have been expected, owing primarily to Barrios' preoccupation with the idea of reconstituting the political union of Central America. It would be possible to include other rulers in this group, but none of them held power long enough to create a regime that can really be identified as a dictatorship of 'order and progress'.

Except where the new developments of the type described above occurred Latin American politics continued to follow the pattern established earlier. Paraguay, especially, had suffered so extraordinarily in the course of its valiant last-ditch defence of its territory against overwhelming odds that it was not able to recover for decades. In 1870 it was still occupied by foreign troops and final settlement of the peace terms was in the future. The casualties of war, hunger, and disease had reduced the population of the country from approximately one million prior to the outbreak of war to less than half that number. Almost all men capable of bearing arms were killed or disabled during the conflict. From 1870 onward Paraguay, no longer able to play a major or an independent role in the politics of the Río de la Plata region, tended increasingly to become a satellite of rapidly growing Argentina, through whose territory alone communication between the rest of the world and Paraguay was possible. In Uruguay, the forced ally of Argentina and Brazil in the war against Paraguay, the war did lead to a reaction against the domination of politics by military chieftains. In 1870 a movement was inaugurated by young civilians of both traditional parties to bring about a new political alignment based on principles. The movement was short-lived, however. The attachment of Uruguayans to their traditional parties and to men on horseback proved too powerful to overcome. The Colorado party which had been placed in power through the successful revolution headed by Venancio Flores remained in power, supposedly. In actuality power was exercised by a series of generals, mainly in the interest of themselves and their associates. It would not be worth while to chronicle the succession of wars, revolutions and dictatorships which succeeded each other in Bolivia, Ecuador, Peru, Colombia, Central America and the Dominican Republic and Haiti.

Any discussion of Latin American politics in this era, however, cannot be closed without mention of the beginnings of protests against oligarchical rule and dictatorship. These movements of protest grew out of democratic idealism, socialism, anarcho-syndicalism, and the labour movement. None of these could point to important achievements before the turn of the century, but their beginnings must be noted for they all became significant shortly after 1900.

Liberal democratic idealism achieved the most conspicuous growth in Argentina. The mismanagement and corruption of the administration of President Miguel Juárez Celmán led to the formation of a protest group, the Union Cívica, headed by the idealistic Leandro Além, with whom many men later to play major roles in Argentine politics were associated; Hipólito Irigoyen, Marcelo Alvear, Lisandro de la Torre and others. An uprising in 1890 organised by the Union Cívica failed, but succeeded in so weakening the position of the president that he resigned. Some leaders of the Union Cívica accepted a compromise political settlement, but Além and Irigoyen held out against this and founded the Union Cívica Radical, later to be known as the Radical party. The Radicales campaigned against the regular use of fraud and violence in elections. Electoral reform, they believed, was the key to the solution of all problems. They revolted again in 1893 and, though again put down, increasingly won the support of public opinion. Early in the following period they were to become the dominant political party in Argentina.

Except in Argentina liberal democratic ideas did not lead to organised political activity, unless the left wing of the Chilean Radical party might be considered to hold such views. Nevertheless, many individual figures of importance spoke out against prevailing abuses. In Mexico Ignacio Altamirano, the celebrated poet, spoke out against the official positivist doctrine which denied the rights of man. In Cuba and in exile Jose Martí was forging with his pen the democratic doctrine that was to become the ideology of the future Cuban republic. In Peru Manuel González Prada, a great patriot and liberal, called upon all his countrymen to work for the national welfare with honesty and with discipline. In Uruguay, José Batlle y Ordóñez from the columns of his newspaper and in his speeches in the national congress called for policies that would transcend the traditional party politics of his country. These men are only a few of many individuals who in journalism and politics stood out in many countries for liberalism and democracy. It could hardly be said, however, that they had by 1900 achieved many important results.

Equally scattered and even more lacking in concrete results were the early beginnings of left-wing radicalism in Latin America. In the 1890's anarcho-syndicalist agitation and the organisation of labour unions under the auspices of leaders of this persuasion began in several countries. In Mexico the chief propagandist of this viewpoint was Ricardo Flores Magón whose activities, with those of his brother Enrique and others, date from 1892. In 1891 a syndicalist federation of labour unions came into existence in Buenos Aires. Pedro Abad de Santillán was the chief exponent of this ideology in Argentina. At the very end of the century, after 1897, syndicalist unions and periodicals appeared in the nitrate fields of northern Chile. It was natural that anarcho-syndicalism should have been one of the first forms taken by proletarian discontent in Latin America in view of the importance of anarchist doctrines in Spain. Socialism, the chief rival of syndicalism hardly got a foothold anywhere in Latin America before 1900 except in Argentina. The Argentine Socialist party was founded by Juan B. Justo and Alfredo Palacios in 1896. This party was not a doctrinaire Marxist party. It was a reformist organisation favouring political action through legislation, somewhat along the lines of the English Fabian Society.

Apart from the above-mentioned types of radical thought and organisation in the interest of the working class there were scattered examples of more limited and moderate labour organisation. In Mexico a union of railway workers was organised as far back as 1890. In Argentina the earliest instance seems to have been that of leather workers in 1874. Most unions, however, were affiliated with either socialist or anarchist organisations. In Buenos Aires there were federations after 1891 of both syndicalist and socialist unions. Those of Cuba and of Chile before 1900 were chiefly under syndicalist influence. The labour movement and working-class agitation were delayed in Latin America long after they achieved importance in Europe and in the United States. Their first beginnings, naturally enough, were in those countries which had been most fully affected by capitalistic progress: Argentina, Chile, Cuba, and Mexico. Brazil, however, lagged behind, unaccountably, in this movement.

A survey of Latin American government in this era must also take account of the appearance of a new member of the family of Spanish American republics—Cuba. Though the 'Pearl of the Antilles' had remained in Spanish hands when continental Spanish America became independent, it had rested there uneasily. Soon after the close of the American Civil War the discontent of Cubans with the discriminatory and exploitative Spanish colonial regime brought on the first powerful movement for the independence of the island. In 1868 a revolutionary assembly had declared for independence, the end of slavery, and the establishment of a liberal and democratic republican regime. Led by the aristocratic Carlos María de Céspedes and other men of rank and station, the rebels appealed to Cubans of all classes. Some Latin American republics recognised the Cuban republic but the United States did not. Failure to secure recognition made it hard to secure munitions and the war degenerated into guerrilla operations. The Spanish authorities were unable to suppress the guerrillas and the war hung on for ten years. Finally, the exhaustion of both sides led to a compromise 'Pacto del Zanjón' with the Spanish governor and commander-in-chief, General Martínez Campos. Not all the promises made at this time were kept by the Spaniards and revolutionary unrest continued to smoulder. The Cuban spirit of nationality was fanned during these years by the writings and by the example of José Martí who, in prison and in exile, personified the yearnings of Cubans for freedom. In 1895 the revolution broke out once more. Martí was killed early in the initial campaign, but, in death as in life, his career unified the Cubans and the revolt became increasingly formidable. The rebel guerrilla policy of burning cane fields was paralled by the Spanish policy of placing the rural population in concentration camps. The widespread destruction of life and property and the hardships and sufferings of Cubans were publicised throughout Europe and America.

The story of the eventual intervention of the United States, three years after the beginning of the revolution, is outside the scope of this chapter.

The outcome of the ensuing Spanish-American War was the total destruction of Spanish power in America. This fact is well known. It should also be realised, however, that Cubans believed that they had won their own freedom. Even during the period of hostilities with Spain there had been friction between Cuban and American military authorities. When the United States set up a military government in Cuba the islanders were dismayed. At the outset of United States intervention Congress had formally announced that the United States harboured no annexationist plans and that it desired an independent Cuba. At the close of the war annexationist feeling appeared to be growing. It was not sufficient to bring about a reversal of the earlier stand, but the United States did force on Cuba the famous limitation on the sovereignty of the new republic known as the Platt Amendment. Firmly embedded both in the permanent treaty between the United States and Cuba and in the Cuban Constitution, the Platt Amendment provided among other matters that the United States might intervene in Cuba for the preservation of 'Cuban independence, the maintenance of a government for the protection of life, property, and individual liberty'. When the Cubans reluctantly accepted these conditions under duress the American military government was withdrawn and the Cuban Republic assumed control of the island in 1902. The end of the Spanish empire in America was significant in many ways but not least because there no longer remained any barrier to the re-establishment of cordiality between Spain and her one-time colonies, and the *rapprochement* between Spanish and Spanish American artists, writers, and intellectuals was to be a major cultural fact of the ensuing age.

Conflict and rivalry among the Latin American states had a significant effect upon their political and economic life in the later nineteenth century. Conflicts often grew out of boundary disputes, a large number of which remained unsettled owing to the nationalistic intransigence of the parties and the difficulties created by the lack of exact geographical knowledge concerning the unsettled and remote areas usually involved. In addition, more powerful states sought to dominate weaker neighbours and by such policies awoke the hostilities of still other countries. In the course of time there came to be a kind of balance of power, centring on the more powerful South American states, into which most of the other countries of the continent were drawn. In Central America the same process was apparent in miniature, but remained unrelated to the system of South American relationships.

This continental system evolved from earlier local conflicts in the Río de la Plata area and among the republics of the Pacific coast. In the former region the elements of conflict were the rival ambitions of Argentina and Brazil. Both attempted to influence the political affairs of their smaller neighbours, Uruguay and Paraguay, to their advantage. In 1870 the destructive Paraguayan War had come to an end with the exhaustion of that small but warlike country and the death of its ambitious dictator, Francisco Solano López, after almost five years of struggle against the combined forces of Argentina, Brazil, and Uruguay. Both of the two larger victorious countries sought territorial cessions and indemnities from Paraguay and both tried to check the designs of the other to draw the defeated country into its sphere of influence. It had also become traditional for Brazil and Argentina to favour opposing factions in the constantly disturbed politics of Uruguay. Largely as a result of these antagonisms Argentina and Brazil were drawn into a competition for military supremacy. Both nations began to develop more highly trained professional army officers (the Argentine military academy was founded in 1870). By purchasing vessels abroad both Brazil and Argentina laid the foundations for modern navies.

On the Pacific coast international relations at the beginning of the decade of the 1870's had been harmonious. Only a few years earlier Chile, Ecuador, and Bolivia had made common cause with Peru in the latter's resistance to Spanish naval intervention. However, beneath the surface, there was a tradition of jealousy between Chile and Peru. In the colonial period Peru had been the seat of Spanish viceregal authority and had usually been favoured over the outlying province of Chile. These ancient rivalries, which might otherwise have remained dormant, were revived by the rise of the nitrate industry in the arid coastal region of southern Peru and Bolivia. Chilean businessmen were active in the exploitation of this new form of mineral wealth and the Chilean government began to press its previously inactive claims to part of this desert territory now suddenly of enormous value. Bolivia, weak and misgoverned, gave ground before Chilean diplomatic pressure and in 1866 signed a treaty ceding territory south of latitude 25° S. and agreeing to a sort of condominium with Chile for the territory between latitude 23° S. and 25° S. in which both countries would be free to exploit such resources as guano and nitrates and would share the revenue derived from such activity. But there followed in 1873 an alliance between Peru and Bolivia. Chilean historians explain this as a step toward a common policy of monopoly prices in the nitrate industry on the part of the two countries and as an attempt to check Chilean participation in it. Peruvian and Bolivian writers interpret the alliance as a purely defensive measure against an apparently aggressive neighbour and deny the existence of any secret articles or accompanying agreements.

The 1866 treaty between Chile and Bolivia had not worked satisfactorily. The countries did not find it possible to agree about the sharing of revenue. Chilean protests led to the signature of a new treaty in 1874 which settled the boundary at 24° S. and provided that for twenty-five years Bolivia would not increase the taxes levied by her on Chilean nitrate firms operating within her jurisdiction. The Bolivian president, Daza, caught between the pressures exerted by his two stronger neighbours, elected to co-operate with Peru. He raised export taxes levied on a Chilean nitrate company at Antofagasta. In spite of the protests of the company and of the Chilean government the Bolivian authorities persisted and, upon non-payment of taxes, seized the properties of the Chilean concern. Chilean forces then immediately occupied Antofagasta in February 1879. The Peruvian government attempted to mediate the dispute between Chile and Bolivia, but Chile, believing that Bolivian policy had been arrived at in connivance with Peru, refused to accept the offer and demanded the immediate dissolution of the treaty of alliance between Peru and Bolivia of 1873. War followed the refusal of the allies to meet this demand.

The War of the Pacific, as it was called, went through various stages. In the first of these Chile seized the Bolivian littoral, but further advance was checked by the inability of the Chilean fleet to control the sea-lanes until they were finally able to put out of action the speedy Peruvian cruiser *Huascar*. In the next stage a Chilean force defeated allied forces and occupied the province of Tarapacá. The disastrous course of the war at the end of 1879 brought about a political crisis in Peru. President Mariano Prado disconcerted the nation by suddenly leaving the country for Europe, ostensibly on a mission to buy arms. Shortly after this extraordinary event Nicolás de Piérola led a successful uprising and with the united support of the whole nation attempted to organise the continued defence of the country. The Chilean army, however, succeeded in defeating the Peruvians first at Tacna and later at Arica. By the middle of 1880 both of these provinces were completely in Chilean hands. Peace negotiations attempted at this time failed, as did the clumsy and badly directed efforts of the United States to exert its good offices or to mediate. At the end of 1880 Chilean forces moved north against Lima. In January 1881 the Peruvian capital was captured after severe fighting in the outskirts of the city. The Piérola regime collapsed and resistance was only maintained by certain guerrilla forces in the interior. Peace negotiations were made difficult by the hostility created by the looting and destruction of property by the occupying army. None of various Peruvian leaders was able to secure general support or to find a basis for negotiation with Chile. Finally, however, General Miguel Iglesias accepted the inevitable and signed the Treaty of Ancón, which ceded the province of Tarapacá to Chile and provided for Chilean occupation of Tacna and Arica for a ten-year period to be followed by a plebiscite to decide the ultimate disposition of the two provinces.

The War of the Pacific had repercussions apart from its effects on the belligerents. One of these was in the relations between Chile and Argentina. For decades the two nations had been involved in a dispute over boundaries in the southern extremity of the continent in an area which had been uninhabited except by a few Indians until Chile founded the town of Punta Arenas at mid-century, but which both countries began to regard as increasingly important. The claims of both countries were far apart and neither was willing to compromise. Argentina favoured delay in the hope that its more rapid growth in wealth and population would eventually give it the advantage. Chile unsuccessfully tried to get Brazilian support for its claims. A crisis came during the War of the Pacific. Chile could not afford to maintain a strong position during that conflict as this might dispose Argentina to intervene in the war. A treaty was accordingly agreed to in 1881 which surrendered most of the disputed territory in Patagonia to Argentina and gave Chile control only over the Straits of Magellan.

The years which followed the War of the Pacific saw a heightened international rivalry among Argentina, Brazil and Chile. Chile had achieved recognition as the foremost power on the Pacific coast of South America. Its military success led Argentina, which still had pending a dispute with Chile as to the exact location of the mountain frontier between the two countries, to improve the size and effectiveness of its army and navy. The tension between Brazil and Argentina was relieved in 1889 when they agreed to accept arbitration of their dispute in the territory of Misiones on the upper Paraná, and demarcation of the frontier was complete by the end of the century. In 1896 Argentina and Chile submitted to arbitration their dispute as to whether their boundaries should follow the peaks of the cordillera or the continental divide. Between 1899 and 1902 the decisions under this agreement were handed down. Talk of war which had grown insistent for a while died down and there came a marked improvement in the relations of the two nations. Most of the unsettled boundary questions of Brazil which remained in 1900 were successfully dealt with during the first decade of the twentieth century by the celebrated diplomat and statesman, the Baron de Rio Branco. Between Venezuela and Colombia, Peru and Ecuador, and among various Central American countries these stubborn boundary controversies hung on to create difficulty throughout the first half of the ensuing century.

In the cultural life of Latin America new elements which appeared in the period 1870–1900 came from the assimilation of European ideas and movements, especially those of France and England. In those aspects of civilisation which depended in part on the availability of funds, as, for example in the fields of public education, the improvement of university libraries and facilities, the establishment of libraries and museums, and the development of monumental architecture, the countries which were making the greatest advances in wealth took the lead, as might be expected. In the field of literature and the arts, however, there was no correlation with economic progress and works of genius were produced in poor and undeveloped countries.

The supremacy of French influence and the primacy of French taste were unquestioned in this era. The cultivated classes read French books and university students wrestled with text-books in that language. The new avenues and boulevards in the greater Latin American cities were to a large extent replicas of the Parisian boulevards: the Avenida de Mayo in Buenos Aires, the Paseo de la Reforma in Mexico City, and the Avenida Rio Branco which followed the pattern a few years later in Rio de Janeiro. The improvement of communications and of wealth made it possible for the women of the upper classes to dress according to the mode of Paris.

In the field of public education German and United States influence was important. Though all the Latin American countries recognised the importance of a literate citizenry and had provided by law for some kind of public education, it was only in a few countries that real progress was made in combating illiteracy. The greatest progress was made by Argentina where Domingo F. Sarmiento, under the inspiration of studies and travels in Europe and in the United States, was responsible during his presidency (1868–74) for the establishment of normal schools and the establishment of standards and plans for an educational system under the control of the provinces but supervised and encouraged by the national government. Improvement of teaching was made possible by bringing in foreign experts and establishing publications in the field of education. Progress of a similar type on a much smaller scale was made by Uruguay after 1880 under the leadership of Sarmiento's admirer, José Pedro Varela. In Brazil Pedro II had done much to further education, especially after 1870. By the end of the imperial period there were over six thousand primary schools and secondary schools in all the provinces, including the Collegio Imperial Dom Pedro II in Rio de Janeiro.

Except in the countries mentioned, little was done to extend education to the masses; but progress was made in many other countries in higher and special education. The University of Chile, established early in the republican period, was in many ways a model in Latin America. In the latter decades of the century most of the countries expanded and improved curricula and facilities in their leading institutions. These remained everywhere, however, teaching and professional schools devoted very largely to law and medicine. The research function of the university was not as yet developed. Nevertheless, in all the more important countries the establishment or the improvement of national libraries and of museums of natural history provided materials for future study.

In spite of the great tradition of Spanish art on which they could draw and in some countries the existence of an Amerindian artistic inheritance of great value, the Latin American nations achieved little that was important or original in the arts during the later nineteenth century. Music was almost entirely derivative and consisted of efforts to achieve skilful execution in the approved French and Italian manner of the works of such romantics as Liszt and Verdi. Sculpture was limited to the production of commemorative pieces for public squares in the academic manner and much of this was actually done in European studios. In painting there was more variety. Though there was a great deal of academic portraiture of wealthy worthies and production of battle pieces and other historical works of nationalistic inspiration for the decoration of public buildings, there was also work that went beyond this. The Uruguayan painter Juan Manuel Blanes, who did much of his work in Argentina, was an excellent portraitist and also produced dramatic canvases somewhat in the manner of Delacroix. One of the most powerful artists of nineteenth-century Argentina was Prilidiano Pueyrredón, most of whose work was done before 1870, but who lived on into the later period. He produced notable portraits in which the artist's handling of colour was remarkable; he also produced genre scenes of great interest. Somewhat later, toward the end of the century, the most eminent Argentine painter was Eduardo Sivori in whose work it is possible to trace the influence of Courbet and Manet. In Mexico the most distinguished painting of the period was done by José María Velasco, a landscapist with remarkable gifts. His studies of scenes in Mexico rivalled, if they did not surpass, the work of artists in the United States in this period who painted the Rocky Mountains and the American West. Velasco, who was himself taught by an Italian master, was later the teacher of Diego Rivera who distinguished himself in later years as one of the greatest artists of the twentieth-century Mexican school.

It was in literature that Latin Americans achieved the most distinguished and original work in this period. Two movements stand out as major aspects of the literary history of the later nineteenth century: the evolution of the novel from earlier romantic forms through the transitional form of the regionalist schools to the fully developed realistic, and later to the naturalist, style. Brazil was the most important country in the field of the novel. Joaquim Maria Machado de Assis is almost universally recognised as the greatest novelist of Latin America. His work bridges the entire period of transition to realism. At the close of the century Euclydes da Cunha with his remarkable literary–philosophical–sociological book *Os Sertões*, and José Pereira da Graça Aranha with his study of clashing peoples in a frontier environment, *Chanaan*, ushered in the naturalist school. Though a similar movement took place in Spanish American prose, it came to fruition somewhat later than in Brazil with the work of Gallegos, Rivera, and a host of others in the early twentieth century. Before 1900 the romantic vein had, however, been exhausted and realism introduced through the medium of the *costumbrista* sketch, the *gaucho* literature made popular by José Hernández and others, and most of all by the novels of Alberto Blest Gana of Chile. Naturalism appears at the beginning of the twentieth century in the work of the Mexican, Federico Gamboa, whose work seems to have been patterned on that of Zola.

In poetry Spanish American literature went through a period of great richness and originality beginning in the 1890's. The *modernista* movement owed something to the inspiration of French poets like Verlaine and Baudelaire, but it was even more an American declaration of independence from Spanish traditional limitations, both in poetic form and in vocabulary. The greatest exponent and the founder of the movement was Rubén Darío of Nicaragua. The freedom and sensitivity to all kinds of sense impressions exemplified in Darío's verse and prose and his ingenuity in inventing new ways to express them met an immediate response in the work of other young poets: Leopoldo Lugones in Argentina, José Santos Chocano in Peru, and Amado Nervo of Mexico, who are only a few of the most renowned members of this school. From Latin America *modernismo* spread to Spain and became a major force working upon all subsequent writers in the Spanish language.

These young men who were revitalising Latin American letters at the close of the century were not, however, as well known in 1900, nor did they have as much influence on the nineteenth century as a number of older men, more frequently politicians, newspaper men, teachers, or professional men. In the Caribbean Martí's influence went far beyond his beloved Cuba. More than any other one person he was responsible for the growth of a sense of brotherhood among literate Spanish Americans. Other intellectuals also exerted influence beyond the borders of their own countries. At the beginning of the period under review that could be said of Domingo Faustino Sarmiento, Argentine enemy of tyrants and enthusiast for education. His early exile led him to Chile and his subsequent travels for study and in diplomatic service took him far and wide. His influence on Varela in Uruguayan education has been noted. He also did much to draw together educators in the United States and Argentina. At the end of the century the Uruguayan José Enrique Rodó achieved great influence on young people throughout Spanish America. His famous essay *Ariel* (1900), which preached Spanish American spiritual unity and warned against the supposed materialism of civilisation in the United States, became the bible of idealistic university students and literary men during the next generation. In the Caribbean area Eugenio María de Hostos of Puerto Rico, as reformer and later as revolutionary, travelled far and wide in the New World and always as a propagandist for the anti-imperialist cause—against Spain, or against the United States. He also worked manfully for the improvement of education in his own country and in the Dominican Republic. Enrique José Varona exercised a very similar influence in Cuba as patriot, philosopher, educator, and poet.

The versatility of many of these men was a peculiarly Latin American trait. Many of them are difficult to classify because they combined so many different kinds of activity. Two examples must suffice to illustrate this many-sidedness. Bartolomé Mitre's name is outstanding in three different fields. He was the outstanding political leader of Buenos Aires in the critical period of Argentine national organisation. He fought with varied success in civil wars from the campaign against the dictator Rosas (1852) to a fruitless rebellion against Sarmiento's administration (1874) but he also was the leader of the Argentine forces in the Paraguayan War and successfully led his troops in battle. Mitre must also be remembered as the first journalist of his age in Argentina. He founded *La Nacion*, from his day to the present, one of the outstanding newspapers of Argentina. In still a third field of activity Mitre became perhaps the most able historian of his country and one of the small number of Spanish American historians of his day who are still read today. His major works, *La historia de San Martín y de la independencia americana*, and *La historia de Belgrano y de la independencia argentina*, were works of Mitre's old age which appeared in the 1880's, but which combined a vivid narrative style with a respect for documentary evidence. Nationalist that he was, he could not situate himself coolly outside of his theme, but he produced a kind of history comparable to that of Macaulay in England or of George Bancroft in the United States.

The other example of versatility among Latin American men of letters is primarily a historian, the Chilean, Diego Barros Arana. He is most widely known for his monumental *Historia general de Chile* which covered the history of his country from before the Spanish conquest to the close of the era of its political independence, a work which is the most important and the most workmanlike Latin American product of that type of professional historical research that used to be referred to as scientific of the nineteenth century. In addition to his work as an historian Barros was also a figure of the first magnitude in the history of Chilean education. A doctrinaire liberal, he worked throughout his long career to create a strong secular system of public education. As a teacher in the celebrated Instituto Nacional in Santiago and as a professor in the University of Chile he was personally a vital influence on two generations of young Chilean intellectuals. As rector of the university he influenced policy toward the organisation of higher education. A third kind of activity led him to serve his country in the national congress, where he was a staunch liberal, and as a diplomat. He put his historical talents to work in the building of Chile's case against Argentina for the ownership of Patagonia and was the negotiator of the treaty in which Chile finally surrendered its claim in 1881 during the War of the Pacific.

Looking back on the Latin America of the latter decades of the nineteenth century it is possible to understand the optimism and the belief in progress which so many Latin Americans felt at that time. Economic and material progress did occur, though much of this was distributed very unevenly. Political stability in some countries increased; a high price, however, was paid for this in terms of oligarchical rule that disregarded broad public interests; in many countries where civil wars and dictatorial regimes seemed to have become endemic it was hard to see any improvement. Another decade and a half was to pass before a new era would set in. The effect of the world upheaval that accompanied the first World War would be felt in Latin America, changing traditional relations as Russia became revolutionary and the United States world position was transformed. Only in that newer era would movements for political and social reform take place in Latin America paralleling the increasing pace of economic change and offering hope of a better life to the submerged millions of the continent. But, as we have noted above, major factors in twentieth-century Latin American history—the organisation of labour and its political activity; industrialisation and the growth of a middle class in some areas; revolutionary movements, nationalist and proletarian— were foreshadowed in this period which was on the surface as stagnant in social reform as it was dynamic in economic progress.

CHAPTER XX

INTERNATIONAL RELATIONS

THE last thirty years of the nineteenth century saw the European balance of power at its most perfect: five great powers (with a doubtful sixth), each able to maintain its independence, none strong enough to dominate the others. The irreconcilable antagonism between France and Germany, and the equally irreconcilable, though less persistent, antagonism between Austria-Hungary and Russia in the Balkans, prevented the creation of any preponderant combination. The balance of power took on the appearance of a natural law, self-operating and self-adjusting; Europe enjoyed the longest period of peace known in modern times; and the powers turned their energies outwards to 'imperialist' expansion. All acquired empires; some at their own backdoor, the others overseas.

The Franco-Prussian War, which broke out in July 1870, created this exceptional balance. It began as a French attempt to arrest the progress of German unity; instead it freed Europe from the shadow of French predominance without putting German predominance in its place. It was the last war fought solely in Europe and confined to European great powers. It was indeed confined to two powers. This was unexpected. Great Britain was genuinely neutral once Belgium was secured. But Austria-Hungary prepared to intervene on the French side, though only after French victories. Russia first talked vaguely of threatening Austria-Hungary into neutrality; then, with equal vagueness, planned to compete with her for French favour. These calculations came to an abrupt stop as the campaign developed. The first battles on the frontier went against France. On 3 September the main French army was defeated and compelled to surrender at Sedan. Napoleon III became a prisoner. The French empire was overthrown, and the Republic proclaimed in Paris.

Sedan ended the war as a struggle for mastery in Europe. The long centuries of French predominance were over. Germany was free to arrange her own destinies. The war was prolonged by the German demand for Alsace and Lorraine. The ostensible reason for this was military security; the deeper cause was a desire to satisfy national feeling. The new Germany should get off to a good start by recovering the lands of the old Reich. The French raised the standard of national defence; and the war which had begun in the cabinets became a war of peoples. Thiers toured Europe, seeking allies. In vain. Neither Austria-Hungary nor Russia feared a German victory. The Austrians hoped for German backing in the Near East; the Russians calculated that a resentful France would keep

Germany in check. Only Gladstone, the British Prime Minister, wished to protest against the transfer of Alsace and Lorraine without consulting the inhabitants, on grounds of morality, not of power; and he received no support from his cabinet.

Besides, the Russians twisted international relations eastwards by denouncing the neutralisation of the Black Sea, imposed by the Treaty of Paris in 1856. The British threatened war or, at any rate, a revival of 'the Crimean coalition'. Bismarck did not want a situation which might provide France with allies or at least enable her to air her case before an international meeting. He solved the crisis neatly by paying Russia and Great Britain with the same cheque. He proposed a conference, confined to the Black Sea clauses and pledged in advance to their abolition. Thus Russia got freedom from her servitude; the British vindicated the principle that treaties could be changed only by international agreement; and Bismarck was rewarded by a general promise that the conference, which met in London in January 1871, should not mention the war between France and Germany.

The French had therefore to rely on their own strength. This was not enough to reverse the verdict of Sedan. Gambetta sounded the Jacobin appeal of 1793—the *levée en masse*, and the country in danger. Though he brought new armies into the field, these could not defeat the Germans nor prevent the fall of Paris. At the end of January 1871 the French had to accept the German terms; and these became the definitive peace of Frankfurt on 10 May. France lost Alsace and Lorraine, though retaining Belfort at the last moment; paid an indemnity of five milliard francs (a sum exactly proportioned to the indemnity which Napoleon I had imposed on Prussia in 1807); and had to support a German army of occupation until the indemnity was paid. This was certainly a victor's peace on the Napoleonic model. Yet Bismarck did not attempt to bind the future. France remained a great power. The Treaty of Frankfurt did not limit her armed forces or control her foreign policy. The path of revenge was open if she wished to take it. She could not do so. Sedan and its outcome did not so much change the balance of power in Europe as symbolise that it had changed; and the balance went on turning against France. Germany continued to increase in population and economic resources. France remained almost static.

Few contemporaries appreciated this. They expected an early war of revenge. Though the French, under the leadership of Thiers, followed a policy of 'fulfilment', they also introduced universal military service on the German model, and reorganised their armed forces. Bismarck made isolation of France the mainspring of his foreign policy. In 1873 he brought Austria-Hungary, Germany, and Russia together in the League of the Three Emperors—ostensibly a conservative Holy Alliance against the moribund socialist international which Karl Marx had just shipped off to an early death in New York; in fact no more than mutual abstention from a French alliance. The League carried within itself the germs of a mortal sickness: Austria-Hungary and Russia did not renounce their rival ambitions in the Balkans. Instead, their agreement contained the strange provision that, even when they fell into dispute there, they would not allow the conflict 'to overshadow the considerations of a higher order which they have at heart'. Like the Holy Alliance, the League of the Three Emperors was a fair-weather system, which would be blown away in a Balkan gale.

The Balkans were however still quiet, and France the likely storm-centre. In 1873 Thiers was driven from office; and his monarchist successors wished to restore French prestige by an active foreign policy. Dreaming nostalgically of a Catholic League, they first patronised the pope—prisoner in the Vatican since the Italian occupation of Rome on 20 September 1870. Then, abandoning this course in 1874, they flew at higher game and patronised the German Roman Catholics in the *Kulturkampf*. Bismarck, always ready to perceive widespread conspiracies against himself, detected—or so he claimed—the hand of international clericalism. At least, this seems to be the most reasonable explanation of the 'war-in-sight' crisis which he unleashed in April 1875. It is unlikely that Bismarck actually planned a preventive war; such a course was against his deepest instincts. But he hoped to frighten the French out of their clericalism and perhaps out of their rearmament. Instead, Decazes, the French Foreign Minister, exploited the crisis to his own profit. Simulating alarm, he appealed for protection to the other powers; and they responded. Though Austria-Hungary remained silent, both Russia and Great Britain expostulated at Berlin. Bismarck shammed surprise and repudiated all aggressive intention. The crisis died away. It had been a score for France, though of a peculiar kind. Great Britain and Russia had combined to protect France and save the peace, but the peace they saved was the peace of Frankfurt. Neither wished to reverse Sedan, only to ensure that it should not be repeated. Both were satisfied with the existing balance. Both opposed a German attack on France; neither would support a French attack on Germany. Hence the 'war-in-sight' crisis paradoxically determined that there would be no war in Europe for more than a generation.

With relations between France and Germany thus stabilised, only the Balkans remained as a topic of conflict. In July 1875 they burst into flames. The Turkish province of Bosnia broke into revolt. Neither Russia nor Austria-Hungary wished to open the Eastern Question; but once it was opened, Russia could not abandon the Balkan Slavs, Austria-Hungary dared not let them succeed. Both tried to observe the pledge which they had given in the League of the Three Emperors. They sought to avert the crisis by a programme of Balkan reforms. Andrássy, the Austro-

Hungarian Foreign Minister, first proposed that the consuls of the powers should settle the Bosnian revolt on the spot. Then he devised the note of 30 December 1875, containing reforms which the powers should recommend to Turkey. Next, at a meeting with Bismarck and Gorchakov, the Russian Chancellor, he produced the Berlin Memorandum of 13 May 1876, which contained not only reforms but a grudging hint of 'sanctions' to enforce them. All these schemes broke on the obstinacy of the Turkish government which held, with some justification, that reform would lead to the disintegration of the Ottoman empire.

Russia and Austria-Hungary were drifting apart. Andrássy would not go beyond advice, given to Turkey by the Three Emperors. Gorchakov wished to impose reforms in the name of the Concert of Europe. He brought France into the negotiations; and this inevitably brought in Great Britain also. The British had once been the great proponents of the Concert of Europe; but, since their failure over Schleswig in 1864, they had withdrawn from European affairs. Isolation was the keystone of British policy; and the counterpart of isolation is isolated action. Lacking allies and repudiating diplomacy, the British had only the choice: all or nothing. Either they turned their backs on a problem; or they appealed to force. There was no middle course; and it is no accident that between 1871 and 1904 Great Britain was alone in using the formal threat of war against another great power—in 1878 and 1885 against Russia, in 1898 against France. The British government had swallowed the consular mission and the Andrássy note, though principally in order to guard Turkish interests. The Berlin memorandum was too much for them—particularly as it reached London at the weekend. They rejected the memorandum and sent the fleet to Besika Bay, thus encouraging the Turks to defy the powers.

This the Turks were always willing to do. The suppression of the revolt was beyond their strength. In June revolt spread to Bulgaria; and the Turks answered with the 'Bulgarian horrors'—the worst atrocities of the nineteenth century, until eclipsed by the Armenian massacres twenty years later. The Russian government, though still shrinking from war, was driven on by the groundswell of Slav sentiment within Russia. At first Gorchakov hoped that the Ottoman empire would collapse of itself; and at Zakupy (Reichstadt) in July, he reached agreement with Andrássy that they would allow this to happen. His hope was disappointed. There was deadlock in the Balkans: more revolts, more massacres, but no collapse. Russian intervention drew nearer, Alexander II himself foreshadowing it publicly in November. Gorchakov was desperately anxious to save Russia from repeating the isolation and failure of the Crimean War. He called on Bismarck to repay the supposed Russian service in 1870 by holding Austria-Hungary neutral. Bismarck refused. He claimed later that he would have gone with Russia 'through thick and thin', if the Russians in return had guaranteed Germany's tenure of Alsace and Lorraine. This was a red herring. The survival of Austria-Hungary as a great power was an essential part of Bismarck's system, both at home and abroad; and, while he had no objection to Russia's success in the Balkans, this must be in agreement with Austria-Hungary, not achieved against her. Bismarck's 'great refusal' was a decisive moment in European relations. From refusing to support Russia against Austria-Hungary it was a short step to supporting Austria-Hungary against Russia. In 1879 Bismarck took this step; and so set the pattern for the future.

Failing Germany, Gorchakov tried France. Here, too, he was disappointed. The French pleaded that they had not recovered from the defeats of 1870—a convenient, though genuine, excuse which enabled them to sidestep the Eastern crisis without offending Russia. The last Russian resource was the Concert of Europe; and this did not altogether fail them. Even Great Britain moved towards the Concert. The Bulgarian horrors had produced a passionate campaign of protest in England under Gladstone's leadership; and the Conservative government had to favour the reform of Turkey. In December 1876 a conference of the great powers met at Constantinople—of all the many gatherings which wrestled with the Eastern Question, the only one to meet on the spot. Once more sweeping reforms were devised; once more the Turks evaded them—this time by the ingenious trick of first proclaiming a constitution and then insisting that all changes must be referred to a constituent assembly which never met. Yet the conference served Russia's purpose. Though the powers would not impose the reforms which the conference had devised, they could not object when Russia set out to do so. The Concert, having failed to reform Turkey, would not now protect her.

Even the British were now willing to stand aside. They insisted that nothing must be done to disturb Egypt—a remote speculation where Gorchakov at once met their wishes. They also declared that they would not tolerate a Russian occupation of Constantinople, 'even temporary'. Here, too, Gorchakov replied sympathetically. He had no desire to see Russia saddled with responsibility for Constantinople. But if Turkey collapsed, who could guarantee the outcome? And Gorchakov left it open whether he would then cheat the British or the victorious Russian generals.

From Austria-Hungary Russia needed something more positive than tolerance. She needed a firm promise of neutrality if her armies were to pass safely through the bottleneck of Roumania. Andrássy was ready for a bargain. In the last resort, he preferred a limited Russian success against Turkey to a great European war which would shatter the existing set-up in the Habsburg monarchy, almost as much by victory as by defeat; and Gorchakov on his side, cool towards Pan-Slav ambitions, was ready to limit Russia's prospective gains. The Budapest conventions, signed on 15 January 1877, laid down that there should be 'no great compact state,

Slav or other', if Turkey fell to pieces. In return Austria-Hungary promised to observe benevolent neutrality in a war between Russia and
Turkey, and to disregard the triple guarantee of Turkey in which she had
joined after the Crimean War. This was a great stroke by Gorchakov
despite the restriction. The Crimean coalition was dissolved; and
Andrássy in fact kept his promise of neutrality right up to the Congress
of Berlin. Besides, who could tell what would happen in the Balkans if
Turkey really fell to pieces? Here too Gorchakov could decide whether
to cheat Andrássy or the Pan-Slavs. The immediate gain was what
mattered. Thanks to Gorchakov's diplomacy, Russia was free—as never
before in the nineteenth century—to settle the Eastern Question by her
own armed strength.

Here was the great surprise. Russian armed strength proved inadequate
for the purpose. On 24 April Russia declared war against Turkey,
ostensibly to enforce the recommendations of the Constantinople conference. Russian armies advanced through Roumania and crossed the
Danube. There they were arrested by the fortress of Plevna, and battered
themselves into exhaustion against it before it fell on 11 December. The
prolonged engagement of Plevna—battle rather than siege—foreshadowed
the grinding trench-warfare of the First World War. But unlike those
battles, it changed the course of history. In June, when the Russians first
ran against Plevna, Turkey-in-Europe seemed doomed. By December the
Russian armies were worn down; and, equally important, British opinion
had swung round. The heroic defence of Plevna obliterated the Bulgarian
horrors; and the Conservative government could revert to its original
policy of supporting Turkey. The Russian armies staggered to the gates of
Constantinople by the end of January 1878; but the Ottoman empire did
not collapse. Though the Turkish armies had almost melted away, the
Russians could not give the final push. It only needed first the rumour and
then the reality of the British fleet before Constantinople to bring the war
to an end.

The Russians had assumed that the Ottoman empire would fall of
itself, once war started. It had not done so; and the Russians were now
stuck for peace terms. They first thought of demanding the opening of the
Straits; but, since Russia had no Black Sea fleet, this—though a theoretical gain—would be a practical disadvantage. They therefore fell back
on inflating the principal proposal of the Constantinople conference and
demanded autonomy for a 'Big Bulgaria'. This had no Machiavellian
intent. A national state seemed the only alternative to Turkish rule; and
the Russian peacemakers drew the frontier according to the best ethnographical knowledge of the time. But the Turks realised that Big Bulgaria
would provoke opposition from other powers; and therefore accepted the
peace of San Stefano, signed on 3 March, with every confidence that it would
soon be overthrown. A general war seemed in the offing. The British kept

their fleet at Constantinople, and demonstratively moved Indian troops to Malta. Andrássy, though evading British requests for an alliance, also evaded Russian requests for a promise of neutrality in a further war. No one has divined his real intent, which was probably unknown to himself. But the Russians dared not risk a renewal of war without firm assurance of Austro-Hungarian neutrality, nor perhaps even with it. The British were ready to face war without allies and even in fact without armed forces of any size. It was a contest of nerve; and the British won. On 30 May the Russians agreed to submit the Treaty of San Stefano to an international Congress, with the understanding that Big Bulgaria should disappear. Salisbury, who had become British Foreign Secretary at the beginning of April, rounded off his achievement with two other agreements. He guaranteed Turkey-in-Asia, receiving a lease of Cyprus in exchange; and he secured the belated backing of Austria-Hungary against Big Bulgaria.

The Congress of Berlin which met on 13 June 1878 was a grandiose assembly of European statesmen—the German and Russian Chancellors, the Prime Minister of Great Britain (the first ever to attend an international meeting), and the Foreign Ministers of the great powers. Big Bulgaria dissolved into three: a quasi-independent principality; an autonomous province of eastern Roumelia; and a remnant called 'Macedonia', which was pushed back under Ottoman rule. Austria-Hungary undertook the administration of Bosnia and Hercegovina, where the revolts had started. Unexpectedly, the Congress also produced a grave challenge to the rule of the Straits. Salisbury had agreed on 30 May that the Black Sea port of Batum should go to Russia; but British opinion was outraged when this became known. To calm opinion at home, Salisbury announced that henceforth Great Britain would only regard herself as bound to respect 'the independent decisions' of the sultan in regard to the closing of the Straits. In British eyes the sultan was independent only when he was pro-British. Hence they claimed to be free to pass the Straits whenever it suited them. This was a terrifying prospect for Russia; and the spectre of a British fleet in the Black Sea haunted Russian policy for almost twenty years.

The Congress claimed to have averted a great war and to have settled the Eastern Question. There was not much in either claim. War had been averted long before the Congress met—in fact when the Russian armies faltered in front of Constantinople. On the other hand, the Congress could not revive the Ottoman empire as an independent great power. The events of 1875–8 ended its real strength; and though it tottered on for another thirty-odd years, this was largely because the great powers were busy elsewhere and shrank from the turmoil which would follow its overthrow. The practical results of the Conference were of little effect. The British fleet never entered the Black Sea until after the collapse of the

Russian empire; and two out of the three parts into which Bulgaria had been divided were united within a few years, to the applause of the powers which had insisted on their separation in 1878. The Congress did a bad day's work when it put Macedonia back under the Turks, and a worse when it put Bosnia under Austria-Hungary. The first act caused the Balkan war of 1912; the second exploded the world war of 1914.

Such blunders occur at the best-ordered gathering. The deeper puzzle is why the Congress made such a fuss about the Balkans at all. Gigantic changes had taken place on the continent of Europe; still more gigantic were to happen outside it. Italy and Germany had been united; France had lost her primacy and two provinces; the pope had lost his temporal power. Soon Africa was to be partitioned; the empire of China was to be disputed between the powers. Here were all the greatest statesmen of the age, assembled in unparalleled number and encompassed by these events. Yet all they could find to discuss was the fate of a few Balkan villages. What is more the Eastern Question continued to dominate international relations for many years after the Congress of Berlin. It shaped the alliances which shot up like mushrooms after summer-rain. Every foreign minister revolved his policy around it. Yet nothing happened. The interminable Eastern crises seemed so many manœuvres, where great skill was displayed and everyone went home unhurt in the evening.

Why did it all go on? The diplomatists pointed to the deadlock as evidence of their sustained skill. Cynical radicals retorted that nothing happened because nothing serious was at stake and that the Eastern Question was kept going to provide 'out-door relief' for members of the foreign services. There was something in these explanations. The working of the balance checked any activity; and the Eastern Question had indeed become a question of habit. Men had regarded it as of vital importance for so long that they had forgotten why it was important, if they ever knew. Perhaps the decisive reason, however, is that the Eastern Question had become essentially a negative affair. When two powers have rival ambitions, a compromise between them is often possible. A deal is more difficult when each merely wants to keep the other out. In the first case, possession is the actual guarantee of the bargain; the second demands reliance on the other's good faith—and in the Eastern Question this was lacking. The Russians, apart from a few Pan-Slav hot-heads, merely wanted to keep the British navy out of the Black Sea; the British merely wanted to exclude the Russians from Constantinople. But each was convinced of the aggressive designs of the other. Similarly the Austrians merely wished to prevent any hostile power from controlling the route to Salonika; and the French wished to preserve their investments in the Ottoman empire. All of them in fact wanted an independent Turkey; but each of them interpreted this to mean that Turkey should be subservient to itself. A modicum of mutual trust or even of indifference; and the

Eastern Question would vanish from the international agenda. This happened some twenty years later when all the powers turned their backs on the Balkans, much to their own astonishment.

Bismarck, the wisest diplomatic head of the day, always advocated this course. He described the inhabitants of the Balkans as 'sheep-stealers'; and held that the Balkans were not worth the bones of any grenadier, let alone a Pomeranian. This was certainly true so far as material gain was concerned. The Balkans were a miserable prize, compared to almost any other part of the world; and have remained so to the present day. Only prestige and strategy were at stake; but these count for more than profit. Bismarck constantly urged the other powers to ignore the Near East; or, if they would not, to share it out—Constantinople with the east Balkans to Russia, Salonika with the west to Austria-Hungary, and Great Britain in control of Egypt and the Suez Canal. Hence his advice to Salisbury during the Congress: 'Take Egypt.' Hence his encouragement to the French that they should find their share of the bargain in Tunis. The powers did not welcome his advice. For one thing, each hoped to acquire its share without yielding anything to others, as the British did four years later in Egypt. More deeply, the negative nature of their aims stood in the way. None of them wanted the trouble which partitioning the Near East would involve.

More deeply still, the powers lacked a common interest or loyalty. This was the age when the anarchy of sovereign states was at its height; and when men believed that in international affairs, as in economic relations between individuals, unchecked liberty for each automatically produced the best results for all. Gladstone alone preached the Concert of Europe. This was a noble aim, but how can there be a Concert unless the players follow the same score? No great principle or belief held Europe together. Monarchical solidarity had ended; the solidarity of peoples had not taken its place. There was not even a common fear—whether of revolution or of some infidel invader. Instead there was only a universal confidence that each power could stand on its own feet without bringing European civilisation, or even itself, to disaster. Bismarck himself judged the Concert contemptuously: 'Whoever speaks of Europe is wrong. It is merely a geographic expression.' And again: 'I only hear a statesman use the word "Europe" when he wants something for himself.' Bismarck accepted the international anarchy, but was confident that he could control it for his own end. This end was peace. Certainly Germany directed the 'system' so far as there was one; but in Bismarck's time her only object was negative—to prevent war, not to make gains. Since the other powers too had this negative aim, though less consciously, they acquiesced —with some grumbles—in Bismarck's direction.

Before the Congress of Berlin Bismarck had helped Russia and Great Britain towards agreement. In the months after the Congress this agreement seemed farther off than ever. The British, invigorated by success, thrust towards new achievements. Salisbury planned to revive the Ottoman empire under British protection. British military consuls swarmed in Asia Minor; British agents harassed the sultan with advice which he usually disregarded. In the Balkans, Austria-Hungary and France supported what they took to be the winning side. The Crimean coalition which had disappeared during the recent crisis seemed to be resurrected. The Russian empire was exhausted by the war. Its rulers were exasperated and alarmed by these new threats. They appealed to Bismarck for support; and this time he responded. The Crimean coalition was as unwelcome to him as it had been to the rulers of Prussia during the Crimean War itself. On the other hand the prospect of co-operating with Russia against it was equally unwelcome. Bismarck's solution—though also anticipated by Prussian policy during the Crimean War—was at first sight surprising. Instead of supporting Russia against Great Britain, he concluded on 5 October 1879 a defensive alliance with Austria-Hungary against Russia. He gave a variety of explanations then and thereafter. Sometimes he alleged that Germany was in imminent danger of attack from Russia and needed Austro-Hungarian backing; sometimes he claimed that he was restoring the old greater German union of the Holy Roman Empire. At one time he proposed making the alliance a fundamental law of the German Reich; at another he advised his successors to get rid of it at a convenient opportunity. Historians, both German and foreign, have added theories of their own.

It is fairly easy to solve the problem of why Bismarck acted as he did in October 1879 by asking: what was the alternative? The Crimean coalition would have grown stronger; it would have pressed harder against Russia; and then there would have followed a new war or else—more likely— such a humiliation of Russia as would upset the balance of power. Austria-Hungary and France, the two powers whom Germany had defeated, would have recovered prestige; and after Russia, it would have been Germany's turn. As it was, Austria-Hungary, secured by Germany's support, grew cool towards the British; and affairs in the Balkans drifted towards oblivion. Bismarck made this clear himself when he said to the Russian ambassador concerning Austria-Hungary: 'I wanted to dig a ditch between her and the western powers.' He made it even clearer when he went on from the Austro-German alliance to revive the League of the Three Emperors, which he succeeded in doing some two years later.

There are deeper problems not so easily solved. The Austro-German Alliance makes sense as the temporary answer to an immediate difficulty. But why did Bismarck give it such a rigid permanent form? Precise alliances, defined in writing, had gone out with the *ancien régime*, except as the early prelude to war. No great power had a fixed commitment of this kind between the Congress of Vienna and the Congress of Berlin.

Now the Austro-German alliance began an era in which every power, except Great Britain, gave formal pledges of action to support some other. Yet Bismarck was himself contemptuous of such attempts to bind the future. Every alliance, he said, had an unwritten clause: *rebus sic stantibus*. Perhaps Bismarck, having now become a conservative statesman, not only wanted things to remain the same, but assumed that he could make them do so. Perhaps, too, he overlooked that alliances by this time were made not between monarchs, but between nations. The alliances of the eighteenth century were family compacts, private bargains between kings and emperors. The new alliances were absorbed by public opinion even though their precise terms were unknown—except for those of the Austro-German Alliance which were published in 1888. Indeed Bismarck's own rule worked against himself. The elaborate clauses, with their reservations and restrictions, were short-lived in their effect. The great names of Triple Alliance and Franco-Russian Alliance shaped men's minds, and determined the pattern of events. Bismarck had meant to preserve his freedom of manœuvre when he made the Austro-German alliance. Instead every great power, including Germany, was taken prisoner by the system of alliances which he inaugurated.

The contrast between the precise terms of an alliance and its general significance was shown as soon as the Austro-German Alliance was signed and throughout its history. Its essential clause was the promise by the two powers to resist any Russian attack. Bismarck meant precisely this, and no more. He would not allow the destruction of Austria-Hungary as a great power, but he would not support her activities in the Balkans. The Austrians never took the reservation seriously: they always assumed that Germany was now committed to them 'through thick and thin'. There began a tug-of-war between Vienna and Berlin which lasted until the Austrians pulled Germany into war in 1914. All Bismarck's diplomacy from October 1879 until his fall was an answering tug: an attempt to escape the inevitable consequences of an alliance which he had himself brought into existence. The simplest way out in his eyes was to reconcile Austria-Hungary and Russia; whenever this broke, as it often did, on Austrian reluctance, he sought to provide other allies for her so that Germany need not be involved. His unrivalled skill enabled him to perform these conjuring tricks with success; but none of them would have been necessary if the Austro-German Alliance had not existed.

The Russians presented no difficulties. They asked only for security in the Near East—the Straits closed to British ships of war, and the Balkan states left in harmless independence. They were eager to revive the League of the Three Emperors; and Bismarck agreed with them once the Austro-German Alliance was signed. The Austrians resisted obstinately; their policy was 'the permanent blocking of Russia' with British assistance. In April 1880 the bottom fell out of this policy. The British Liberal party, under Gladstone's leadership, defeated the Conservatives at the general election. Gladstone hoped to inaugurate a new age in international relations, based on the Concert of Europe instead of individual action. He succeeded only in negation. He abandoned Salisbury's Turkish policy; withdrew the military consuls from Asia Minor; and disregarded the guarantee to Turkey, though he did not return Cyprus, which had been its *quid pro quo*. But the Concert of Europe never came to life. The statesmen of Europe, apart from Gladstone, lacked a common conscience. They relied on the balance of power and thought only of their national interests. Still, Gladstone's acts left the Austrians high and dry. They were driven into the League of the Three Emperors, for lack of anything better.

The new League took another year to come into formal existence. First, the Austrians resisted; then the assassination of Alexander II provoked further delays. The League was finally signed on 18 June 1881. Its predecessor of eight years before had been a declaration of monarchical solidarity; this was a practical bargain with nothing sentimental about it except its name. The three emperors promised each other neutrality; they also asserted 'the European and mutually obligatory character' of the rule of the Straits—a double repudiation, in fact, of the policy of working with Great Britain which Austria-Hungary had previously favoured. Germany was freed from having to choose between Russia and Austria-Hungary. Russia got security at the Straits, short of an isolated action by Great Britain in defiance of all the continental powers. But where was the gain for Austria-Hungary? The Austrians refused to trust Russia's word and grumbled ceaselessly at the position into which Bismarck had forced them. He found an odd way of satisfying them. Italy had been beating about on the fringe of great-power status ever since her unification in 1861. Her quest for alliances was really a quest of recognition as an equal; and this recognition had been rarely obtained. At the Congress of Berlin Italy had ranked rather below Turkey and slightly above Greece. She had come away empty-handed; and in angry resentment ran after predominance in Tunis. This provoked French competition. The French would have much rather left Tunis alone; but they could not tolerate an Italian outpost on the frontier of Algeria. On 12 May 1881 Tunis became a French protectorate.

The Italians were more humiliated than ever; and the monarchy itself seemed threatened. The house of Savoy, once the ally of revolution, now sought conservative respectability. In October 1881 King Humbert went on a begging mission to Vienna. The Austrians refused his proposal for a mutual guarantee. Early in 1882 the Italians had a stroke of luck. There was a short-lived revival of Pan-Slav feeling in Russia. Bismarck feared that Russia might not remain faithful to the League of the Three Emperors. He took up the negotiations with Italy as a precautionary measure. The outcome was the Triple Alliance, concluded on 20 May

1882. The only clause of practical importance in this was Italy's promise to remain neutral in a war between Russia and Austria-Hungary, hence freeing four Austro-Hungarian army corps for the front in Galicia. The Austrians got this benefit for nothing. Germany paid the price by agreeing to defend Italy against France. This was on paper a considerable liability for Germany, though less—in Bismarck's eyes—than the alternative of supporting Austro-Hungarian expansion in the Balkans. In any case, he always assumed, in true Napoleonic fashion, that whatever he wanted to do he would succeed in doing. He would somehow keep the peace between France and Italy; and thus never be called on to discharge his liability.

Bismarck's calculation proved correct. Triple Alliance and Emperors' League between them so tied up the European powers that none could move without his permission; and this was always withheld. Changes took place only outside Europe, the greatest of them in Egypt. Here Great Britain and France had been wrestling for years, in an uneasy condominium, with the chaotic finances of a spendthrift khedive. In 1882 nationalist disturbances broke out against the Europeans in Egypt. Joint intervention was planned. At the last moment the French government drew back, because of opposition in the Chamber. The British intervened alone; and in September 1882 established a protectorate over Egypt (at first unavowed) which was to last for seventy years. This was a great event; indeed the only real event in international relations between the battle of Sedan and the defeat of Russia in the Russo-Japanese War. All the rest were manœuvres which left the combatants at the close of day exactly where they had started. The British occupation of Egypt altered the balance of power. It not only gave the British security for their route to India; it made them masters of the Eastern Mediterranean and the Middle East; it made it unnecessary for them to stand in the front line against Russia at the Straits—ultimately indeed unnecessary to stand against her at all. It also, as a more temporary though still important consequence, disrupted the 'liberal alliance' between Great Britain and France; and thus prepared the way for the Franco-Russian Alliance ten years later.

This however was not the immediate consequence. Instead Bismarck, playing on the French resentment over Egypt, attempted to round off his 'system' by a reconciliation between France and Germany. In the long run the attempt came to nothing; and it is therefore impossible to decide how seriously the attempt was taken by either party—the failures in history have no memorial. Certainly there were reserves on both sides. The French, because of Alsace and Lorraine, could never follow Bismarck's prompting 'to forgive Sedan as after 1815 they came to forgive Waterloo'. Nor would Germany's partners in the Triple Alliance turn wholeheartedly against Great Britain, whose support they might one day need—the Austrians against Russia, the Italians against France. Moreover the colonial disputes which blew up in Africa between France and Germany on the one side, and Great Britain on the other, have led most historians to suppose that the Franco-German co-operation was an accidental product of these disputes, not the other way round. This was probably true so far as France was concerned; but Bismarck, as he himself said, was never 'a man for colonies', and his sudden claim for African colonies seems to fall into place as a move in his European policy—not, of course, that he repudiated the popularity which these claims brought him in Germany.

At any rate, the result is beyond doubt, whatever the cause. Not only was Great Britain isolated—this was her own choice—but her two principal rivals for empire, France and Russia, were for once unhampered by anxieties for their European security; and, more than that, could often count on backing from the other powers. This backing was of a limited kind. No power, except possibly Russia, ever seriously contemplated war against Great Britain. The great disputes which raged from Egypt to the Far East were fought in diplomatic terms, with loans, notes, and railway concessions as the instruments. Armed power receded into the background, an ultimate sanction that was almost forgotten. Egypt illustrates this. The British army controlled Egypt; the British navy dominated the Mediterranean. The British could have annexed Egypt at a moment's notice; and the French could have done nothing to stop them. But the British claimed to administer Egypt in the interests of the bondholders; and the Egyptian question was disputed at the *caisse de la dette*, not between armies and navies. As a result international relations ran on two levels. On one were the formal alliances, which gave promises of support in some hypothetical war which never happened; on the other were the combinations of bankers and committees. On the first level Great Britain was the most isolated of the powers; on the second, the most involved. She had no alliances; but, as the power with the most world-wide interests, innumerable *ententes* and, of course, innumerable quarrels.

Even on this diplomatic plane, Great Britain had a rough time during 1884 and the early part of 1885. French and German colonial advances against her ran together, for whatever reason. In July 1884 a conference to settle the Egyptian question broke up without result. Bismarck held out to the French the prospect of a maritime league directed against England. To others he boasted that he had revived the continental system of Napoleon I, though this time with Berlin as centre. The high point of this continental solidarity came in September 1884 when the three emperors met at Skierniewice—the last such meeting ever to take place. Later in the autumn an international conference met at Berlin to settle the affairs of central Africa, and particularly of the Congo basin. Again the Franco-German partnership against Great Britain was displayed, in principle if not in achievement. The Berlin Act was a great stroke in international affairs. It laid down the rules for 'effective occupation' of uncivilised lands; and so ensured that the partition of Africa should take place without armed conflict between the powers. The Berlin conference has another incidental point of interest; it was the last international conference on any concrete subject for more than twenty years—telling evidence indeed that the Concert of Europe was dissolved. Each power served the common good by pursuing its individual aims, and peace seemed secure without any conscious effort.

The worst moment of British isolation came in April 1885. On 30 March a Russian force defeated the Afghans at Pendjeh on their northern frontier; and so seemed to threaten Afghanistan, India's buffer-state. The British, lacking allies, could rely only on force; and on 21 April the pacific Gladstone secured a vote of credit from the House of Commons as the preliminary to war. The British planned to operate Salisbury's doctrine of 1878 and to send an expeditionary force through the Straits. Bismarck's system worked, as he had intended, for Russia's protection. Every great power—not only Germany and Austria-Hungary but France and Italy also—warned the sultan to keep the Straits closed against the British. It was the most formidable display of continental solidarity on an anti-British basis between Napoleon I's time and Hitler's. Its very success dissolved it. The Russians had felt insecure at the Straits and had therefore sought in Afghanistan a counter-threat against the British. Once convinced that the Straits would remain closed, they lost interest in Penjdeh and agreed to send the dispute to arbitration—quite a score in its way for Gladstone's high principles. Afghanistan remained a buffer-state, as it is to this day: one of the few countries that has always preserved its independence from the competing great powers.

The peaceful outcome of the Penjdeh affair was not the only improvement for the British. The Franco-German *entente* gradually crumbled during the summer of 1885, rather from a French revulsion against colonial expansion than from a pronounced hostility towards Germany. Moreover the Eastern Question caught fire again in September; and Bismarck had to treat the British with more consideration for the sake of Austria-Hungary. The new Eastern crisis centred, like its predecessor, on Bulgaria. But the positions were now reversed. In 1878 Russia had set up a Big Bulgaria which Great Britain and Austria-Hungary insisted on dismembering. In 1885 two out of the three parts of Bulgaria came together—eastern Roumelia joined the existing principality. Russia sought to dismember Bulgaria or, at the very least, to force it back into subordination. Austria-Hungary and Great Britain defended Bulgaria's unity and independence. The crisis lasted in various forms from September 1885 until March 1888. First, Russia tried to undo the unification that had taken place; next to impose a Russian general as governor; finally to prevent the election of an anti-Russian prince. All these moves failed.

The Russians received a barren satisfaction in March 1888 when the sultan, theoretical overlord of Bulgaria, declared the election of Ferdinand of Coburg illegal. But nothing happened. The crisis died away without war.

In retrospect it is tempting to say that nothing vital was at stake. Though it was no doubt humiliating to Russia that Bulgaria had repudiated her patronage, there was no fundamental change in the Near Eastern situation. Was it really worth Russia's while to fight a great war merely for the pleasure of appointing the prince of Bulgaria? In any case, Russia had not the strength to fight a great war even if she wished to do so. All this was less obvious to contemporaries; and the Bulgarian crisis caused an upheaval in international affairs. The League of the Three Emperors was an immediate casualty. The Austrians were determined to resist Russia, despite Bismarck's promptings to the opposite course; and they called for German support. Bismarck referred them to London, where Salisbury, once more in power, was equally reluctant. The two competed in reserves and evasions: both anxious to avoid war or even commitment, both doubtful—in the last resort—whether war was really imminent. Bismarck had a stroke of luck during 1886 when there was a febrile revival of nationalism in France under the nominal leadership of General Boulanger. Bismarck could make out that Germany was too menaced by France to have any forces to spare for the support of Austria-Hungary. This was an adroit and unanswerable excuse. In Bismarck's own words: 'I could not invent Boulanger, but he happened very conveniently for me.' Salisbury, though caring little about Bulgaria, dared not altogether estrange Austria-Hungary and Italy because of the Egyptian question. The result was the first Mediterranean agreement of March 1887 by which Great Britain, Austria-Hungary and Italy promised each other diplomatic support—certainly a gain for Austria-Hungary so far as Bulgaria was concerned, but more immediately an end of the isolation over Egypt with which the British had previously been threatened.

The competition between Bismarck and Salisbury was not yet resolved. The British promise of diplomatic co-operation was almost as non-committal as any promise could be; and Bismarck was himself somewhat compromised by having to agree to the renewal of the Triple Alliance. Both men sought to recover their freedom. Salisbury tried to settle the Egyptian question; and he actually concluded a convention with the sultan (Egypt's nominal overlord) for British withdrawal on conditions. Then Russian and French protests frightened the sultan; and he withdrew his consent. It is easy to understand Russian objections. But the principal French motive was to secure Russian backing in Egypt; yet this would have been unnecessary to them if the British had withdrawn. Such are the confusions of international policy. At all events, the failure of the convention had decisive effects. Salisbury was pushed farther on the path of co-operation with Austria-Hungary and Italy. The French had no alternative to Russia's friendship; and the Franco-Russian Alliance was now only a matter of time.

Bismarck did better. He rescued the Russians from isolation in the Near East at little cost to himself. On 18 June, when the League of the Three Emperors technically expired, he concluded with the Russians a new agreement—the Reinsurance Treaty. This renewed the promise of neutrality with two significant exceptions: it would not apply in case of a Russian attack on Austria-Hungary, nor in case of a German attack on France. Neither signatory projected such an attack; and these two reserves had always existed by implication. The other part of the treaty had more practical application: Germany would give Russia diplomatic support in Bulgaria and at the Straits. Russia was still in a minority, but at least she was not alone; and this moral satisfaction perhaps helped to keep her on the peaceful track. The Reinsurance Treaty contained nothing new. It merely formalised policies which Bismarck, and for that matter the Russians, had defined again and again. Its terms would not have surprised or offended the other powers, if they had become known; but they would have outraged German opinion. It was for this reason that Bismarck kept it secret: he was conducting a policy which ran counter to German sentiment. Germany had no conflict of interest with Russia; yet German feeling was more antagonistic towards her than to any other power. Most Germans wished to be 'western' and liberal; while the threat of cheap Russian grain estranged the Junker landowners who had been the one pro-Russian group. Moreover, Russia was the one continental power which remained obstinately independent even at her moments of greatest weakness; and unconsciously the Germans resented this. Bismarck knew how to moderate his mastery; other Germans were less controlled.

Bismarck got his way for the time being. The autumn of 1887 saw the Bulgarian crisis apparently at its height. Bismarck's reserve once more forced Salisbury's hand; and in December Austria-Hungary, Great Britain, and Italy concluded the second Mediterranean agreement. This went beyond diplomatic co-operation and envisaged common action against any 'illegal enterprise' in the Near East. It was more nearly an alliance with other powers than any agreement that Great Britain had made in peacetime, certainly more binding than the *ententes* made with France and Russia twenty years later. But nothing dramatic happened. The Russians did not attempt any 'illegal enterprise'; and the crisis died away. This peaceful outcome was the greatest success ever achieved by the balance of power; but perhaps it was the general wish for peace which made the balance of power work.

Bismarck would, no doubt, have liked to make his 'system' permanent—Russia checked by the three 'Mediterranean' powers, yet appeased by the Reinsurance Treaty, and France thus safely isolated; and in fact the system ran on until his fall, over domestic issues, in March 1890. Then a general shake-up seemed to follow. Bismarck's successors, the men of 'the new course', were impatient with his complicated pattern of checks and balances. Far from recognising that German reserve pushed Great Britain forward, they believed that she would become a full member of the Triple Alliance if Germany too backed Austria-Hungary without restrictions. They therefore refused to renew the Reinsurance Treaty, and promised to back Austria-Hungary in the Balkans. They sought British favour by renouncing any German attempt to reach the head-waters of the Nile. In their zest for resolute action, they even promised to back Italian ambitions in Tripoli against the French. Things worked out just as Bismarck had expected. The British, far from being tempted into the Triple Alliance, were delighted to see the Germans shouldering their responsibilities and withdrew towards isolation. The Balkans were fortunately quiet; and the German promises to Austria-Hungary therefore had no practical result. But the Italians boasted of their strong diplomatic position; and this alarmed the French. Reluctantly they turned to Russia for support and alliance.

Reluctance was indeed the keyword of the Franco-Russian Alliance on both sides. Not only were republic and despotic monarchy antipathetic; neither had the slightest sympathy with the other's practical concern. Russia had no desire to recover Alsace-Lorraine for France; and France, on her side, was—of all the powers—the most anxious to maintain the independence of Turkey. Their only common interest was security from any German threat, so that each could pursue aims elsewhere. But here again there was no coincidence of policy. Though each was the rival of Great Britain, the rivalries did not overlap. France wanted to get the British out of Egypt; the Russians wanted the Egyptian conflict to continue, so that France and Great Britain should remain estranged. Russia's ambitions centred on north China, where the French had nothing to gain. The Russians had no serious resentment against Germany, despite the failure to renew the Reinsurance Treaty, and thought of the alliance as a general anti-British combination all over the world. The French hoped ultimately to be reconciled with Great Britain, so as to strengthen their position against Germany.

There was conflict even over the military objectives of the two prospective allies. The French wanted to ensure that a considerable part of the Russian army would march against Germany in the event of a general war; the Russians wanted to defeat Austria-Hungary, and were inclined to think that even a German capture of Paris would not be a disaster if they themselves took Budapest and Vienna. Not surprisingly, therefore, the negotiations took long to reach a conclusion: first a general *entente* in August 1891; then a military convention in August 1892; and finally confirmation of this convention by the political heads in January 1894. The French President was allowed to refer to 'the alliance' only in 1895; and the tsar waited until 1897 before acknowledging it in public. Technically the Franco-Russian Alliance was never more than a pledge for common action in case of a war against Germany. This made it impossible for Germany to threaten first one, then the other, and so forced on her the peace which she had kept willingly in Bismarck's time. Ostensibly the alliance was a great defeat for Bismarck's successors. Its practical result was to restore his system in a different form. His overriding object had been to prevent a war between Austria-Hungary and Russia. Now the French, being committed to support Russia, had the same object. The Balkan conflict was dying away in any case; the influence of both France and Germany accelerated the process. The new balance of power offered only the choice between general war and general peace; and all the continental powers chose peace for many years to come. Triple Alliance and Franco-Russian Alliance alike became defensive combinations; and any power that was tempted towards adventure was restrained as much by its allies as by its opponents.

This restraint applied only in Europe; and the very security there made it easier for the European powers to pursue 'imperialist' aims elsewhere. The European stalemate and the expansion outside Europe were two different aspects of the same situation: each produced the other. The loser was Great Britain with her world-wide interests; and the Franco-Russian Alliance began the period of true British 'isolation'. Previously the British had assumed that others were more in need of help than they were. As Salisbury said: 'Great Britain does not solicit alliances; she grants them.' Now however a continental power would endanger its security, instead of increasing it, by an alliance with Great Britain. The British had assumed, too, that their overseas rivals—particularly France and Russia—would always be distracted by anxiety for their European frontiers. Now these frontiers were secure. France challenged the British in West Africa and Egypt; Russia moved ruthlessly forward in the Far East; and the Germans too entered the imperialist competition. Yet this competition had an unavowed limit. All the European powers had chosen peace in continental affairs; therefore they would make imperialist gains, too, only so long as these could be achieved peacefully. If the French would not fight for Alsace and Lorraine, how much less would they fight for Egypt or Siam? And similarly with the others. The British were the one exception: having nothing to lose (or gain) in Europe, they were prepared to fight for their imperial position and, with the steady expansion of the British fleet, could fight successfully. Isolation began as an embarrassment; later, freedom from European commitments left the British untrammelled elsewhere.

The new balance of power took some little time to display its effects. It seemed at first that the Near East might again become a centre of conflict, particularly when the Armenian massacres of 1894 and 1895 raised new demands for the reform, or for the partition, of the Turkish empire. The Russians supposed that they had improved their position in the Near East by making an alliance with France. So they had, but only in a negative way. That alliance certainly made it impossible for the British to act on the old assumption of the Mediterranean agreement, that France would remain neutral while the British resisted Russia at Constantinople. Now that France was Russia's ally, the British dared not pass the Straits with a potentially hostile French fleet behind them. The British proposed that Germany should impose neutrality on France. This, in its turn, asked too much; for a German threat to France would bring her Russian ally into action. Germany and Great Britain demanded the impossible of each other. The British threatened to withdraw into isolation; the Germans answered by threatening Great Britain, as Bismarck had done, with a continental league.

The British threat was the more effective of the two. The Straits ceased to be important to them as their control of Egypt hardened; and in November 1895 the British fleet finally withdrew from Aegean waters. A month later, the Germans used the excuse of the Jameson raid to demonstrate their support of the Boer republics by a patronising telegram to President Kruger; and implied that German, Russian, and French challenges to the British empire would be knit together. This was empty show. Bismarck had no ambitions outside Europe and no objections to those of France or Russia; his continental league therefore had perhaps some sense. Now the Germans expected support from France and Russia without allowing them much gain in return. Yet the two were not even supporting each other in their imperial enterprises; how much less would they support Germany? Besides, the British navy was now a more formidable force than it had been ten years before; and the British answered the Kruger telegram by setting up a 'flying squadron' to show that they could take on all comers.

Yet just at this moment, when Germany and Great Britain had reached deadlock, the Russian danger at the Straits—so far as it had ever existed— was dispelled; not by Austria-Hungary or Great Britain, but by France. The French had tried to avoid this; but, failing anyone else, they had to act. For, just as Russia offered France security on the basis of the Treaty of Frankfurt, so the French offered Russia security within the framework of the Treaty of Berlin. When the Russians talked in December 1895 of seizing Constantinople, the French replied: 'only if the question of Alsace and Lorraine is opened as well'. This price was too high for the Russians to pay. Moreover, their concern for the Straits was essentially defensive; and, as it gradually became clear to them that the British had abandoned any idea of passing the Straits, the Russians too were prepared to leave well alone. The Austrians would still have liked to follow an anti-Russian course; but, failing support from Germany or Great Britain, they also had no choice. In May 1897 the League of the Three Emperors was renewed in weaker form. Russia and Austria-Hungary agreed to freeze the Near East; and 'on ice' it remained for the next ten years. Every European question had thus reached a temporary stability, so much so that even in the early days of 1914 one good judge held that the existing states and frontiers were fixed 'for ever'.

Every great power behaved as though it enjoyed the geographic security which had enabled the British to build their empire in 'splendid isolation'. This had another curious consequence. The opinion long held by English radicals, on an isolationist basis, that foreign policy was unnecessary and wars caused by the wickedness of the governing class, spread to continental countries. In earlier times revolutionary socialists, for instance, had condemned the existing international order and had denounced Metternich or Tsar Nicholas I as peace-mongers, upholding an unjust *status quo*. The new socialist international, revived in 1889, taught that the working classes had no country and proposed to organise a general strike against war, assuming that any war could have only a selfish 'governing-class' motive. Even the governing class had twinges of conscience against war; and the first Hague conference, held in 1899, aired projects of international disarmament, though the only practical outcome was the Hague court on a voluntary basis. This court could only settle casual disputes. It could not handle such questions as Poland or the future of the Ottoman or Habsburg empires; and the creation of the Hague court was, in fact, evidence that men had forgotten the existence of such questions.

The delusive stalemate in Europe opened the short-lived era of 'world-policy'. Men supposed that the powers had abandoned their disputes in Europe because the prizes elsewhere were so much greater, whereas the truth was the other way round. The powers had dropped their disputes in Europe because they were too hot to handle. Russia and France had always tried to combine Europe and empire. Germany was the new entrant into the field. Her economic strength now put her in the front rank of the powers, ahead of any except Great Britain and the United States. It seemed reasonable that like them she should become a world-power. But there was also a political cause for this development. Bismarck had held that Germany's central position in Europe debarred her from expansion overseas. He said to an enthusiast for expansion in Africa: 'Here is France; and here is Russia. That is my map of Africa.' His successors assumed that the danger from France and Russia had ceased to exist. Indeed, these two powers were regarded as a positive advantage by Germany. For, given their fierce competition with the British, Germany could safely pursue world-aims without arousing British, or for that matter Franco-Russian, hostility. Where Germany had once been the pivot in a system of alliance, she now became the exponent of 'the free hand'; rejoicing at the conflicts of others, and collecting rewards from both sides.

The calculation was correct. Germany never had colonial disputes with France. Her project for a railway to Baghdad was less of a menace to Russia than was the world-wide opposition from Great Britain. Most of all, Germany was a lesser danger to the British empire than was France or Russia, at any rate until the plans for a great German navy came to fruition—and realisation of that had to wait until 1909. Though there were colonial disputes between Germany and Great Britain—over a hypothetical partition of the Portuguese colonies and over Samoa—these were relatively trivial; and all were easily settled, even without the fraudulent hope held out by the Germans that they might, if appeased, become Great Britain's ally.

The decisive centre of conflict in the era of world-policy was the Far East. Here too, as in the Near East, a decrepit empire was breaking up under European penetration. Unlike the Near East, however, there was no question of security—no Russian fear for the Black Sea or British anxiety for the route to India. The sole prize was trade, or rather the expectation of trade with a vast hypothetical China market which, in fact, never became real. The British had long held a near-monopoly of what trade there was; but they had no grave objection to sharing this trade with others so long as these others maintained the open door. Hence they did not complain seriously when the Germans entered the Far East by seizing Kiao-Chow in 1897; and they were positively delighted when the United States, in a short burst of imperialism, conquered the Philippines from Spain in 1898. British antagonism was against Russia; for the Russians, being weaker economically, used their military power to close the Chinese door, not to open it.

The Far East was a tougher problem for the British than the Near East had been. Sea-power was less effective, and allies harder to find. The Russians could approach northern China by land; and, with the French in Indo-China, the British could risk their fleet in the China seas even less than at Constantinople. Even worse, there seemed no Far Eastern equivalent of Austria-Hungary: no power whose need to resist Russia was as great as the British. In the early days of 1898 there was an alarm that the partition of China had begun; and the Russians indeed acquired a long lease of Port Arthur, dominating the Yellow Sea. The British beat about for allies. They tried Japan, who had herself staked out an abortive claim to Port Arthur in 1895; they tried the United States. Both evaded entanglement. Most of all the British tried Germany, proposing an alliance which would call a halt to Russian expansion. The proposal was plausible from the British point of view. Great Britain and Germany were modern industrial powers. Both wanted to preserve the Chinese empire and the open door. The scheme broke on the fact, so easily ignored, that Germany—unlike Great Britain—was still in Europe. A Far Eastern war would be for the British a war in the Far East; for the Germans it would be a continental war for survival. This price was too high to pay for the China market. The Germans had to stand aside, and consoled themselves that they were bound to gain from the inevitable war between Great Britain and Russia.

The British were forced back on their own resources. Since they could not resist Russia, they played for time; and of this the Russians were always generous. As usual, the Russians planned more ambitiously than they performed. They were short of money; their railway across Siberia was not completed; their energy was exhausted once they had acquired Port Arthur. Meanwhile, the British improved their position elsewhere. In 1896 they had begun the reconquest of the Sudan. In September 1898 they destroyed the dervish army at Omdurman. At almost the same moment a French expedition under Marchand arrived at Fashoda, farther up the Nile. It arrived two years late. The expedition had been designed as a move in diplomacy. Its object was to reopen the Egyptian question and to bring the British to the conference table. Once the British army advanced up the Nile, diplomacy ended; armed strength took its place. The British refused to negotiate. They demanded Marchand's unconditional withdrawal. The French had no choice but surrender. The British army could destroy Marchand's tiny force; the British navy controlled the Mediterranean. Neither Germany nor Russia would aid France. Fashoda was a triumph for 'splendid isolation'. The British established their domination of the Nile valley entirely by their own strength—indeed with allies they would have had to share. Moreover Fashoda made British isolation still more secure. The British no longer needed the votes of associates now that their hold over Egypt rested on military strength; and the British navy at Alexandria could forget about the Straits.

British self-confidence was at its height, and overreached itself. The British, having routed the French on the Nile without war, thought that they could do the same with the Boers in South Africa; and the triumph of Fashoda led straight to the outbreak of the Boer War a year later. This turned out to be a tougher affair than the British had expected; and the war absorbed all their resources for three years instead of finding them in Pretoria by Christmas. Yet the Boer War too displayed the virtues of splendid isolation. All the continental powers sympathised with a small nation struggling rightly to be free, as powers usually do when the small nation is not struggling against themselves. All of them would have liked to humiliate Great Britain, and to exploit her embarrassment. Yet the talk of a continental league came to nothing. The underlying European conflicts reasserted themselves. The Russians proposed mediation in the Boer War by the powers. The French tactfully replied that they would agree to anything which the Germans agreed to. The Germans, however, would co-operate only if the powers 'mutually guaranteed their European possessions for a long period of years'—in other words, a French renunciation of Alsace and Lorraine, but (given the restriction to Europe) no backing for Russia in the Far East. The negotiations collapsed. In any case, they were futile. The British navy dominated the seas—so much so that the entire army could be sent to South Africa without any fear that the British Isles would be invaded. If all the armies of Europe had mobilised, not a single soldier would have reached the Boers.

The Far East continued to be Great Britain's one weak spot; and the Boer War offered Russia the chance of easy success. The British were saved unexpectedly by the Chinese themselves. The Boxer rising of June 1900 was the greatest repudiation of the West by a non-European civilisation since the Indian Mutiny. The legations at Peking were besieged, the German minister killed. This humiliation forced Germany into the lead. An international force was sent out under the German field-marshal Waldersee: the only time in history when troops of all the great European powers served under a single commander. Intelligent observers had some excuse when they expected that European unity would be achieved in a 'consortium' for the exploitation of China. Of more practical importance, the Germans concluded with Great Britain an agreement (16 October 1900) to maintain the integrity of the Chinese empire. The Germans were only concerned to prevent the British grabbing a 'sphere' for themselves; the British, however, thought that the agreement could be turned against Russia. For a few months, the British seemed to have turned the corner and to have manufactured a Far Eastern equivalent for the Mediterranean Agreements.

The Anglo-German agreement was however a bluff against Russia and the bluff was soon called. The Japanese were eager to resist further Russian expansion; but, if they were to fight a war overseas, they must be secure from the French navy. In March 1901 they asked the British to keep France neutral. The British were still at war in South Africa; they had no ships to spare for the Far East, and passed the Japanese inquiry to Germany. The Germans equivocated. They offered 'benevolent neutrality'; then explained that this meant 'strict and correct neutrality', no more. The myth of Anglo-German co-operation in the Far East was exploded. The British tried to resurrect it by offering to Germany a formal alliance; but no offer could be high enough to involve Germany in a great European war. There was no formal estrangement between Great Britain and Germany. Politicians in both countries continued to talk of the 'natural alliance'; but after March 1901 it was clear that this alliance could not be translated into effective action so long as France and Russia remained independent powers.

The British continued to rely on time. The Japanese were less patient.

They resolved to clear their position one way or the other: either a pact with Russia to share the Far East and exclude all others, or an alliance with Great Britain to keep France neutral. They opened both negotiations in November 1901. The Russians were generous of words; they offered nothing. Their only serious proposal was that Japan should be excluded from the Far East like everyone else. The British were more forthcoming, particularly when threatened with the alternative of a Russo-Japanese combination. The war in South Africa was ending. The British had now ships to spare for the Far East. On 30 January 1902 Japan and Great Britain reached agreement on mutual aid if either were attacked in the Far East by two powers. In practical terms, this meant that Japan could stand up to Russia without fear of being taken in the rear by the French navy. The alliance did not necessarily imply war with Russia. Indeed both parties to it hoped that it would make compromise with Russia easier, now that they could not be played off against each other.

Nor did the Anglo-Japanese agreement imply any British estrangement from Germany. On the contrary, the British assumed relations would be more cordial now that they did not have to plague the Germans with requests for help. Indeed the alliance strengthened British isolation from a European point of view. Previously they had often sought the help of one member or other of the Triple Alliance against the Franco-Russian Alliance, though always in vain. Now they could rejoice, like every other power, that the two alliances cancelled out. Yet, against all expectations, the Anglo-Japanese agreement ultimately turned international relations upside down. Not only did it eliminate the inevitable war between Great Britain and Russia on which the Germans had counted. Assisted by fantastic Russian blunders, it led to a great war in the Far East which shook the balance of power in Europe and so ended the deadlock which had given Europe a peace of unparalleled duration.

CHAPTER XXI

RIVALRIES IN THE MEDITERRANEAN, THE MIDDLE EAST, AND EGYPT

BY 1870 it was plain that in the great area, at once a crossroads and a frontier, which is bounded by the waters of the Mediterranean, of the Red Sea, of the Arabian and Indian Oceans, of the Persian Gulf, and by those of the Caspian and the Black Seas, the influence of the European powers was becoming ever more widely extended.

The capitals of St Petersburg, Paris, and London, rather than those of Constantinople, Cairo, or Teheran, had of course long been the centres wherein Near and Middle Eastern policies were decided.[1] If something unforeseen, something spontaneous and native to the area, actually happened, then steps had at once to be taken in those centres to bring the consequences of any such 'untoward events' under control. One concert of Europe had, in 1840–1, curbed one such disturber of the Levantine peace, the ambitious Mehemet Ali of Egypt. Another concert had, in 1854–6, taken the measure of a more formidable innovator, someone who was not supposed to be a native of the area at all—Tsar Nicholas I of Russia. In 1856, too, the British had sent gunboats into the Persian Gulf to stop the Shah of Persia from absconding with his Afghan neighbour's property of Herat. The existence of peculiar 'spheres of interest' was mutually recognised by the powers: it was their expansion that was objected to. No one went to the assistance of the Circassian leader Shamil in the Caucasus, or to that of Sher Ali in Kabul, of the Bey in Tunis, or of Ahmed Arabi in Egypt, although there have been causes worse. Everyone admitted the plight of the Armenians in Turkey: no one did anything to relieve it. It was not this but a later generation of British officials that adjudged the Hashemites of the Hejaz worthy of support against their overlords. Revolt, or even innovation, anywhere along the route to the East was a danger to all the European powers whose interests anywhere abutted on that route. There were always better strategic arguments for maintaining the *status quo* than for change.

Whether in the last thirty years of the nineteenth century this would continue to be so, was the question now set. Whether the Middle East would continue to be merely a chequerboard for the exercise of European

[1] The term 'Middle East' is an anachronism throughout. Although Valentine Chirol published his *Middle Eastern Question* in 1903, the term was not commonly used in England until after 1917. It apparently originated as a Service designation with the staff of General Maude, commanding in Mesopotamia. It is still used confusedly. American writers in particular often prefer the older term 'Near East', or, when they do use 'Middle East', include India in it. The still older term, 'the Levant', deserves rehabilitation.

diplomacy, or whether it was to become an actual theatre of military operation for European soldiers, was the problem that this generation of statesmen had to decide. A like puzzle faced them simultaneously in Africa. It says much both for the statesmen and for the temperate climate of the public opinion in which they did their work that, although Europe irrupted at will into the two great continents of Asia and Africa, neither a Middle Eastern nor an African dispute was taken by any power as the pretext for breaking the peace.

Of all the powers, it was Great Britain to whom the stability of the Middle East was of greatest importance. The British attitude reflected that of Lord Palmerston, who, having noted Mehemet Ali's control of Crete and his imperialism in Greece and Syria as portents, always believed that the Turk was a better occupier of the road to India than an active Arab sovereign would be. Although later Foreign Secretaries disliked the necessity of keeping intact this ramshackle structure of a barbarous Ottoman empire, none of them altered course; not until, in 1914, catastrophe occurred and the sultan threw in his lot with an enemy coalition, did the British finally bring themselves to take over the freehold of his dismembered domain.

Palmerston had fought dour battles against the construction both of a canal at the Suez isthmus under French auspices and of a railway leading from a Levantine sally-port down the valley of the Euphrates under British auspices, on the single ground that it was not in the interests of England that the Levant should be disturbed by the revolutionary technology of the civilised powers. A canal at Suez, he told Stratford Canning in 1851, must change, and not for the better, 'the relative position of some of the maritime powers of Europe towards each other'. A railway through Mesopotamia would require the prop of a government guarantee, and must inevitably involve interference with Turkish internal administration. He lost his battle over Suez, and won it over the Euphrates—leaving it to the Germans to take up the scheme, thirty years away; but he had a point of which his successors felt the sting. Although Lord Salisbury by 1896 looked on the defence of Constantinople as an 'antiquated standpoint', and was wishing that England had listened to Tsar Nicholas I in 1853, when the tsar had had that thoughtful conversation with Sir Hamilton Seymour on how best to partition the Ottoman empire in a spirit of mutual accord— England taking Egypt, for instance—the Palmerstonian tradition was too strongly entrenched. In that tradition, Russia was the power always to be watched; a rogue power, a comet power, the only one free enough of the European state-system to be able to envisage its overthrow. The Russophobia of the British public was the more acute because of this very solitariness, this splendidly sinister isolation of the potential foe.

To the British, Middle Eastern policy was a matter of communication. England had an empire in India and the Far East: it was essential to be able to reach it. Essential, too, to have speedy news of it, for in 1857 forty days had elapsed before the Court of Directors of the East India Company heard of the mutiny at Meerut. It was essential, therefore, to control the foreign policies of the countries that bordered the direct route to India— although this might indeed be the 'monstrous claim' that Gladstone characterised it to be in the Midlothian election campaign in 1880. In some places the claim was easily asserted. England, the dominant sea-power, was the immediate neighbour of every country that had a coastline, and the direct route to the East was well supplied with coastlines. Countries so endowed might be left to their own internal management, disgraceful by civilised standards though this might be, as they had no power, if it came to a crisis, to resist persuasion by the British navy. Elsewhere complication loomed. The Straits of the Dardanelles and the brand-new Suez Canal (1869) were dangerous bottlenecks, while countries impenetrable by the British navy presented even worse difficulties. Persia indeed had its southern Gulf, where all the trucial sheikhs could be brought into line, but it was not possible to command policy in the distant northern capital of Teheran from Mohammerah or the Karun. Afghanistan was locked away amid mountain fastnesses, and who could know what went on there? These countries, too, were 'inns on the way' to India. Might it become necessary to own them? Or, at least, to put in reliable tenants? But how was one to judge the reliability of an oriental magnate? Amirs at Kabul, the Shah at Teheran, were to exploit these British dubieties in a fashion that was never open to the sultan of a far greater state at Constantinople.

In a dispatch of 6 May 1877 Derby as British Foreign Secretary reviewed for the Russians' benefit British interests in the East. These included the continuing inviolability of the Straits, of Constantinople, of the Suez Canal and of the Persian Gulf. In contrast, it is not at all clear that the Russians ever worked out a consistent attitude towards their own Eastern policy. They were certainly determined that no strong power should be allowed to control the Straits, and 1870 saw Russia dispensing with the hampering 'Black Sea clauses' of the Treaty of Paris of 1856. But, although the Russian story between the fall of Tchemkend (1864) and the battle of Tshushima (1904) is one of expansion, it lacks a common-sense basis. Defeated in the Crimea, Russia turned away from Europe to Asia to appease her military *amour-propre*, but none of the social and economic problems that beset the tsardom were ever to be solved in Turkestan. The Russian foreign office hoped to use Central Asian conquests as a lever with which to offset and deflect objectionable British policies in the Balkans and in Asia Minor. But the relations between St Petersburg on the one hand, and Tiflis and Tashkent on the other, where ambitious governors-general sat spinning schemes of their own, were always tenuous if not hostile; and the blank ignorance of St Petersburg, when charged by an indignant Whitehall with duplicity over an advance in central Asia, was often genuine.

To an outside eye, the very inefficiency of the Russian bureaucracy invested Russian policy with a mysterious menace. In 1889 Curzon in his book *Russia in Central Asia* put the matter more succinctly than ever Gorchakov or Giers managed to do: 'To keep England quiet in Europe by keeping her employed in Asia—that, briefly put, is the sum and substance of Russian policy.' Yet Russian diplomatists could take the hint, and were happy to capitalise on British unease. Nine years later, Witte at St Petersburg was seeking to apply this doctrine to a broader area still. 'He suggested', Sir Nicolas O'Conor apprised his chief, 'that instead of thinking of a useless maritime combat, Russia should prepare to strike the British Power in a vulnerable part. This could be effected by a railway from Merv [in Turkestan] to Kushk [on the Afghan border], which would enable Russia to attack Afghanistan in case of complications with England in respect to the Chinese question.' China or the Transvaal, by then the particular issue hardly mattered: to immobilise British policy all over the world, wrote Tsar Nicholas II at the time of the Boer War in 1899, he had only to telegraph the order for the mobilisation of the Russian forces in Turkestan.

If, north-east of Suez, the Russian menace disquieted the British, west and north of Suez the French irritant was to become ever more acute. In 1870 the French hold on Algeria was only recently consolidated, and the Tunisian and Moroccan flanks lay open: British naval estimates could safely stand at £9½ million. But the French line of communication now lay directly athwart the British in the Mediterranean, and by 1888 France had fifteen battleships in that sea to Britain's eight. Next year the British adopted their celebrated 'Two-Power standard', and by 1898 had added a further twenty-nine battleships and twenty-six first-class cruisers to their entire naval strength. None the less, by the 1890's the French bases at Toulon and at Bizerta in Tunisia together surpassed the British facilities at Gibraltar and Malta. In the long run the British fleet could crush the Toulon fleet, but in so doing it could leave itself no margin to frustrate a Russian *coup* on Constantinople (which must, after the 1877–8 failure by land, be expected by sea). Once the *Franco-Russe* was in being, from 1894—a year when the combined French and Russian naval estimates outstripped those of England, at £17½ million—British naval opinion was firmly convinced that in time of war the Suez Canal would have to be closed; and when the Black Sea had become a Russian lake with the Straits as a safe outlet for the Russian fleet, Russian influence would extend throughout Asia Minor and Syria, thus separating England from India and the East by the distance of the Cape of Good Hope route. The British squadron in the Aegean, symbol of a British naval preponderance that no longer existed, was withdrawn in 1895.

Facts of this kind combined to make it necessary, at long last, for the dangerously extended British empire to get itself a European ally that owned an army—necessary either to fight the French or to make friends with them. Realising this, Salisbury after 1895 would have given the Russians Constantinople itself, if he could have got the Triple Alliance to work with him in a general partition of the Ottoman empire; agreement with Russia, and *par ricochet* with France, was a matter both he and Joseph Chamberlain long considered. British isolation in an imperialist age had become perilous to every British policy.

In 1870, although the French, holding half of the Ottoman empire's public debt, were ubiquitous in the Levant, with a sphere of influence in Syria and the Lebanon that seemed likely to expand, and with everything in Egypt, including its khedive Ismail, geared to the power and attraction of the franc, nothing of this future could be foreseen. Even had it been, no British statesman would have opted for a firm French alliance.

Italy, in contrast, was not a great power, but its geographical position made it a remarkably useful one. It was at once an anteroom to Bismarck's Europe and a springboard to the Levant. The key of the present situation in Europe, Salisbury advised Rosebery when the latter succeeded him at the Foreign Office in 1892, 'is our position towards Italy and through Italy to the Triple Alliance'. It was a notion derived from Disraeli, who in March 1878, among other plans, had advocated constructing a Mediterranean League of Italy, France, Austria, and Germany, 'to secure the trade communications of Europe with the East from the overshadowing influence of Russia'. Moreover, of all the European nations Italy was the most vulnerable to a hostile fleet. Co-operation with England was thus a cardinal article of faith with the Italians, who long recalled that it had been Palmerston and Russell, standing as it were four-square on British ships-of-the-line, who had obviated any possibility of European intervention in the protracted processes of *risorgimento*. In pursuit of this policy Italians had to swallow a pill or two. They saw, for example, their Tunisian ambitions scotched by the French in 1881, since the French had taken care to get British approval beforehand. On the other hand, the Italians could take comfort from the Anglo-Italian 'Mediterranean agreement' (12 February 1887), and knew they could always rely on England, who was determined to keep the French out of the Nile valley, to support them on the Red Sea and in their ambitions in the north-east African hinterland.

The Italian peninsula had its diplomatic parallel across the Adriatic. Balkan turbulences could not become actively dangerous to the sea-powers so long as there existed a friendly Italy on their flank and a friendly Greece to their south. Only once in this period did a new factor emerge in this area—but it was one that galvanised almost to convulsion British policy in the Levant. The 'Big Bulgaria' which the Russians had imposed upon the defeated Turks by the Treaty of San Stefano (3 March 1878) was given a coastline on the Aegean that would have by-passed those Straits into the Marmara whose security so obsessed the British Admiralty. San Stefano thus gave to Russia her first intoxicating draught of 'warm water'. It was indeed a great achievement for British foreign policy that the subsequent Treaty of Berlin (13 July 1878), whatever else may be said about it, disposed of 'Big Bulgaria' and locked its successor, 'Eastern Roumelia', securely away from the southern sea.

The Russo-Turkish War, which ended with the Russian armies occupying Turkish provinces south of the Caucasus, had set England a further problem. It was part of that wider issue which had so troubled the British government when fighting Russia in 1854: how was the whale to get to effective grips with the bear? They had found eventual battleground in the Crimea; but there had been a powerful school of thought, mustered by 'Anglo-Indian' strategists, which held that the chief aim of England's policy should have been the deliverance of the Caucasus from the Russians. Indeed, when the English did in fact penetrate to the Sea of Azov and occupied some coastal towns (May–June 1855), the Russians had been greatly alarmed, and had determined to pin down the Anglo-French invasion in the Crimea at all costs. In this they had succeeded. Since then they had utterly subjugated the Circassians and built a great military depot at Tiflis in Georgia. In 1877–8, when a second Anglo-Russian encounter seemed inevitable, British war plans were still unco-ordinated. Disraeli could talk of sending the Indian army into Turkestan on the one flank and throwing British troops into Tiflis on the other; he could send the fleet up to Besika Bay twice over; and he could summon seven thousand soldiers from India to Malta in April 1878—but just how this clarified the matter, and how these troops could be gainfully employed if the occasion arose, was plain neither to Disraeli himself nor to his admiring viceroy in India, Lytton, who lodged a mild protest even as he sent the troops as requested. War was avoided: but the Russians remained at Kars and Batum, casting their shadow far, and causing Persia, Mesopotamia, and Syria 'to turn their faces northwards'. Obviously England could not throw a competitive shadow across so great an area from a base so distant as Malta. It was essential, therefore, to obtain another watch-tower, or lighthouse, or *place d'armes*, close at hand, in the Levant itself.

As early as October 1876 Salisbury had dispatched an agent, Colonel Home, from Constantinople to look at possible 'material guarantees' of future Turkish security: in other words, to find the likeliest place on Turkish soil where the British might make themselves quickly available. Home had examined the Gallipoli peninsula, in which Disraeli was interested, but advised against it as it did not command 'the very country, Syria and Mesopotamia, that it was requisite to retain control of'. He had gone on to inspect the islands of Mytilene, Lemnos, Crete, and Rhodes in the Aegean, and ultimately Cyprus. Cyprus he considered the best strategic site. It commanded the Turkish entry-port of Alexandretta, and was only 66 miles from Syria. The others were, like Gallipoli, too remote. Crete indeed had some advantages, but these were countered, in Home's opinion, by the existence in the island of a strong *Enosis* (union-with-Greece) movement, which would give an alien governor a deal of political trouble. Now, in 1878, Home's report was brought out of its file. Five days after San Stefano was signed the British cabinet adopted his view of Cyprus, and while Disraeli's plan of transferring troops from India to the Mediterranean was under discussion, it was suggested that these might be disembarked at Cyprus or at Alexandretta itself. In the event, they came to Malta. At the Congress of Berlin, however, Salisbury laid so much stress on the importance to the British empire of a new base in the eastern Mediterranean that he made it clear to the sultan, prior to the publication of the Cyprus convention (4 July 1878), that England was prepared to occupy the island whether or not the sultan issued his permissive *firman*. The conference was shocked, but not moved, by this piece of tactics: the only power likely to obstruct, France, Salisbury had deftly squared by indicating to her representative, Waddington, that no British hindrance of any French plans concerning Tunisia need be expected in the future.

Cyprus proved almost immediately a sad disappointment. What height of hopes was set on it is illustrated in the person of the first British high commissioner sent there. This was no less than Sir Garnet Wolseley, the empire's foremost soldier (who at once set a subaltern, Kitchener, to make the first accurate survey of the island). But Wolseley was called to other and more urgent imperial duties, and no one of similar standing, then or later, succeeded him in Cyprus. It was never suitable as a *place d'armes*: the climate was bad and the harbours inadequate. Nor could it act as a light-house of British influence. It really was not feasible to stalk the Russians at Kars from Cyprus. While British military consuls were in Asia Minor, as a consequence of the Berlin Treaty, it retained some value; but when in 1881 these consuls were withdrawn, it was left with none. Only the dictates of imperial prestige excused its retention. Cyprus was to remain as a useful illustration of a marriage between bad politics and worse strategy.

It was symbolic of its time that a treaty arranged in a suburb of Constantinople should have been torn up and something quite otherwise substituted in a conference at a European capital. But the area over which Europe held this strategic sway was never as entirely passive as European diplomatists would have liked. The Levant indeed contained a civilisation which, in Salisbury's words, 'hung back from the general movement of the world', but it did not lack for princes in whom a quickness of political acumen had been sharpened by long experience of public and personal hazard. Owning no power of any effective weight in a European scale, they resorted to a guile that came naturally. The British *Raj* in India paid one Amir in Afghanistan £200,000 a year between 1857 and 1863 and in 1879 it promised another Amir £120,000; from 1881 it disbursed to a successor £80,000, raising this from 1893 to £120,000 again. But loyalty to an alien system was hardly something that could be so bought; and Cromer, greatest of all the alien proconsuls in this period in the Middle East, always insisted, to quote his book *Modern Egypt*, that British officials must try to remember 'that they are not dealing with the inhabitants of Kent or Norfolk', and that it was ridiculous to apply in indignation the term 'disloyal' to those who displayed either a lukewarm acquiescence only or a frank hostility. The Russians could not afford subsidies, and paid none; and although they recruited members of the conquered Muslim races of central Asia into their frontier armies, they spent little time in trusting them and accordingly felt the less surprise when revolt broke out in Khokand or Turkestan. The French did their utmost to present the Muslims of the southern Mediterranean littoral with an alternative civilisation, but as Islam was incapable of divorcing its culture from its faith, these Levantine *évolués* were not the men to whom the illiterate peasantry beneath could ever give its trust. Asian opinion, of whatever kind, wore whatever mask it thought best suited to the situation. 'Ses victimes', observed a Sherif of Mecca of British imperialism, 'sont condamnés à vivre.' The fate of Arabi in Egypt, whose military *coup* of 1882 rested on genuine nationalist and radical foundations, served notice to more than his own generation of Egyptians, Arabs, and Persians that it was dangerous to lay the mask aside.

An eastern ruler in power would naturally concur with the foreign theory concerning the value of the *status quo*. But his conservative outlook was never enough to ensure his own personal survival: even Shah Nasir-al-Din, who ruled in Persia for forty-eight years, was to die under the knife in 1896. The foreigner might genuinely wish to 'protect' the client state beneath its pliant prince, and, while doing so, keep clear of the state's internal affairs. But three things were likely to happen which made it impossible for him to continue any such policy of 'masterly inactivity'. The prince might either turn traitor to his protector, as Sher Ali was supposed to have done in Afghanistan between 1875 and 1878; or he might succumb in his weakness to the pressure from a rival protector, as both Russia and Great Britain feared might happen to the Shah of Persia at any time. Alternatively, his government might dissolve through sheer ineptitude, and thus leave a vacuum in a vital region which some power of Europe would assuredly take it upon itself to fill. Egypt illustrates the best example of this contingency; but indeed it was only the innate mutual suspicion of each other's ambitions that prevented the powers from dissolving, on exactly similar grounds, the Ottoman empire itself.

The history of the Middle East in this period thus centres on this problem: how to ensure the good government of 'backward areas' which were vital to European commerce, strategy, and communication but whose inhabitants had few interests that corresponded with those of the Europeans themselves. To this problem, the soldiers of the three European powers directly involved produced a similar and a simple answer. Their solution was, to garrison the area in strength. But only the Russians, who had no manpower shortage, found this a practicable policy. Politicians of the Third French Republic always distrusted those aristocratic clericals and monarchists to whom they had, in an unguarded moment, consigned the development of the French empire, and they were accordingly loath to see the sway of such anywhere extended. The British, even before they had it confirmed to them by an American naval historian, harked back to a romantic tradition of storm-beaten ships on which grand armies never looked, and preferred a theory of remote control and the glamour of an imperial prestige. In practice, however, behind all their dealings in areas east of Suez stood the very tangible reality of their Indian army, units of which were to be found in these decades in places as remote from India as Malta, the Sudan, Somaliland, and Malaya.

In the Middle East, indeed, the conjuncture of the British navy with the Indian army gave the British a system of power—well described by Lord Rosebery as one of 'authoritative advice'—that no rival in the area could match. Disraeli, having been the first to recognise this fact of power, always underlined it. It was not a question, he exclaimed in 1878, when the Indian government's invasion of Afghanistan was under fire, of the Khyber Pass merely; it was a question that concerned the character and influence of England in Europe. Nor was it a question of upholding the Turks: the true issue was, as Queen Victoria agreed, whether there should be a British or a Russian supremacy in the world. In taking Cyprus, the movement and the motive were not Mediterranean, but Indian. A great power, after all, was one that had a certain freedom of movement, one that could control and direct events. When the interest of Europe, Salisbury pointed out, centred in conflicts that were waged in Spain, England had occupied Gibraltar. When matters were grave in Italy, England took Malta. When it seemed likely that the interest of Europe would centre on Asia Minor or on Egypt, England occupied Cyprus. Soon after this statement England occupied Egypt also, as if to underline his point.

Three cases of Middle Eastern complication, which unavoidably affected the policies of the European powers, display similar characteristics.

The crisis in Afghanistan formed itself out of the simple desire expressed by the British and Indian governments to find out what Russia had set on foot in central Asia. Between 1864 and 1869 the Russians had made great strides. In 1864 they occupied Tchemkend, in 1865 Tashkent. In 1866 they went forward into Khojend and broke the power of the Khan of Khokand. In 1867 they invaded the khanate of Bokhara, and established fortified posts far to the south of the Syr Daria (Jaxartes) river; they also constituted their new province of Turkestan, making it a viceroyalty for General Kaufmann with his headquarters at Tashkent. In 1868 they captured Samarkand, capital of Bokhara, and made it clear that the Amir henceforward lived as their satellite. In 1874, despite assurances from the tsar's personal representative in London, Peter Shuvalov, that no such thing would happen, the same fate befell the khan of Khiva. It was impossible to argue that the disappearance of the sovereign power of these Central Asian khanates was a blow to human progress, as their best-known attributes were slave-raiding, slave-trading, and a general condition of fanatical barbarism. Gorchakov's declarations that Russia's mission in the east was one of civilisation was therefore hard to dismiss as mere bombast by the British, who had long asserted the selfsame doctrine in regard to their own relations with the native states of India.

In this missionary competition lay the key to all British unease about the Russian forward movement in Asia, that must bring it, inevitably and finally, to the Indian border. Those 'Anglo-Indian' soldiers and civilians who advocated that the British, too, should go forward to meet the advancing Russians, so that the line of actual contact, when made, should be as far distant as possible from India itself, did not do so because they feared direct attack from Russian military might, or had exaggerated notions about the value of Afghan assistance or Persian friendship. Sir Henry Rawlinson, a very influential member of the Secretary of State's Council for India, who kept insisting for years that the British should move into Quetta in Kelat, into Kandahar in southern and into Herat in western Afghanistan, so that they might be supplied with 'a series of first-class fortresses in advance of our present territorial border and on the most accessible line of attack', urged as his reason the fact that India was a conquered country. Therefore, there must always be a 'certain amount of discontent' smouldering, which would be fanned into a chronic conflagration by the contiguity of a rival European power. Every Indian prince and chief, his colleague Sir Bartle Frere warned the India Office in June 1874, would see in the Russians 'a possible alternative claimant for empire in India', and all the disaffected there, all the dangerous and criminal classes, would be on the *qui vive* ready to strike at a moment's notice. Sir Richard Temple classified the malcontents who might be tempted to become pawns in the Russian game: they were the princes, the priests, the soldiers, and the mob. A foreign reader of Temple's book *India in 1880* (and he had many) might well have wondered who in India remained to be 'loyal'. General Roberts, commanding-in-chief in India in 1888, took an even gloomier view of the extent of the 'loyalty' of all these subjects of the queen. They were all agreed that once Russia was arrived on the Indian frontier, both the physical and the psychological security of the British *Raj* would have vanished. India would no longer be an 'island'. It would no longer be possible to propagate a 'Monroe Doctrine' concerning it. And, as a direct consequence, England herself would become a continental state like any other.

To Asians, therefore, Russia presented herself as the great alternative, the other imperial protector. It was this, and not any calculation as to the efficiency of Russian armies or to the extent of the ambitions of the generals, that formed the solid foundation for that 'Central Asian Question' which bedevilled the British Foreign Office during the eighty years that spanned between the Russo-Persian treaty of Turkmanchai and the Anglo-Russian convention of 1907.

As Russell put it in 1860, England did not want to begin a struggle with Russia for influence in Central Asia—'but what we aim at is that Russia shall not take advantage of her relations with Persia and her means of pressure on the states of Central Asia to encroach upon countries which it concerns us should remain in the possession of native rulers, and be undisturbed by foreign intrigue'. Consequently Afghanistan had to stay alive, as a buffer-state between the Russian and the British empires in Asia. But it must also be more than that: and the breakdown of the Anglo-Russian negotiations between 1869 and 1873 to make of the country a genuinely 'neutral zone' between the two empires illustrated the peculiar British interpretation of the words 'foreign intrigue'. Sher Ali, the Amir in Kabul, was too important to the Indian government to be allowed by it to enjoy the privileges and the status of a neutral, as the Russians had suggested. The Amir must certainly be 'independent'—but he must also agree to live in friendly relations with the *Raj*. Facts of life in Asia had to be recognised for what they were. It did not serve to make any firm treaty with Russia on the grounds of *uti possidetis*, both powers promising not to cross certain limits. All limits in Central Asia were unreal, as Gorchakov had already found out after publishing his hopes in November 1864 that Russian armies could stop at Tchemkend. Moreover, neither the Russians nor the British could afford to tie themselves down to fixed positions of which the march of events might make geographical nonsense. In 1873 the two powers agreed only to fix a northern border for Sher Ali's country, and Russia indicated that she considered Afghanistan outside of her sphere of political influence. She considered that this agreement left her a free hand elsewhere in Central Asia, and was genuinely annoyed when she discovered after the fall of Khiva that England thought otherwise. But at least one boundary had been traced, and a pattern was set. Central Asia thus early provided Europe with the problem that was later to face it in Africa: there came a time when some kind of international *imprimatur* on frontiers had to be obtained, unless one party or the other was determined to bring an issue to the point of war.

The facts of life in Asia were of course unpalatable to Asians themselves. Sher Ali, although he wanted its money and its recognition, wanted to be left alone by the *Raj*, which he did not forget had deserted him during the five years (1863–8) he had battled his way to his throne, and which had handed over to his Persian enemies a large part of his frontier province of Seistan (1872). But isolation was not allowed him: what would he do with it? His refusal to allow the Viceroy to station British 'observers' in his country provoked the crisis. Salisbury, the Conservative Secretary of State for India, felt it impossible to continue to 'leave the keys of the gate in the hands of a warder of more than doubtful integrity, who insists, as an indispensable condition of his service, that his movements shall not be observed'. He did not propose to send a British mission into Afghanistan against the wishes of the Amir, but he did propose 'to tell the Government of India to make the Amir wish it'. In Lytton as Viceroy he had a ready agent. Lytton took the view that Sher Ali was an unreliable savage who would play politics between England and Russia if he had the chance; his correspondence with Kaufmann at Tashkent, begun in 1870, should now cease. Lytton first consolidated his frontier in Baluchistan and Kelat, and made Quetta a base before he began his abortive parleys with Sher Ali. Simultaneously the Russians increased their pressure. Expecting war with England in the spring of 1878, they sent columns of troops to the Afghan borders from Samarqand and their Caspian base, Krasnovodsk. On the very day that the European congress convened at Berlin, Kaufmann sent from Tashkent a military mission to Kabul, where, six weeks later, Sher Ali received it with honour. Lytton determined that a British mission should be similarly received, thus putting the Amir, once and for all, to the test. This mission Sher Ali caused to be rebuffed at the frontier, although no shot was fired; and, despite alarm within the British cabinet that no genuine *casus belli* existed, in November 1878 Lytton sent the Indian army into Afghanistan, for the second time in forty years.

Sher Ali fled, to die mysteriously in Russian Turkestan (February 1879). A pliable successor at Kabul signed a treaty in May, accepting British agents and putting his foreign policy at the *Raj*'s disposal in return for a handsome salary. But the British Resident and his staff were murdered in Kabul (3 September); the new Amir threw his hand in, and Afghanistan was left to the marching armies of robber barons before the boldest of these, Abdur Rahman, arrived from Turkestan and consolidated the position as he wanted it. He made a similar deal with the *Raj*, but at a lesser wage as he was that much less to be trusted. The experiment of putting British agents into his country was now called off. The Liberals, who when in opposition had condemned the entire Afghan policy as a piece of piracy, decided to pull the Indian army out of the province of Kandahar, and in April 1881 Afghanistan was left in the control of its new and distinctly dubious ruler.

Critics asserted that nothing had been resolved: the keys of the Indian gate were still in the hands of a warder of doubtful integrity, still insistent that his movements should not be observed. They were answered that the nature of the problem was such that it could not be solved by the exercise of military tactics alone. It was not merely a question of Kandahar, Liberals declared—thus maliciously paraphrasing some of Disraeli's earlier *dicta*—it was a question affecting the entire course of England's policy in Asia. Could England garrison the entire perimeter of her Indian empire —when it could be said (indeed, it frequently was said) that that perimeter extended from Quetta to Gibraltar in the west, and from Burma to Hong Kong and Wellington in the east? Clearly not: and thus the defensive security of half the world must depend not on British soldiers nor even on British sailors, but on the respect and confidence that British policy commanded, on the degree of assurance felt by other nations that British policy marched with the interest of humanity at large, that it was a policy designed to promote peace and commerce among men. If England forgot this, and went in for a policy of aggression or of confiscation of other people's property, she would at once make enemies on every side, and the Russians would not have far to look for assistance in their work of subverting the British empire.

The truth of this diagnosis was soon proved to Liberals themselves, when next year their government bombarded Alexandria and occupied Egypt—an imperialist action which was to cripple British foreign policy *vis-à-vis* that of both France and Germany for the next twenty years. Liberals were to spend nearly all of these years in the political wilderness, but they continued to assert their original view, put with his usual common sense by Campbell-Bannerman. 'The truth is,' he remarked, 'we cannot provide for a fighting empire, and nothing can give us the power.'

Indeed, it was pointless to try to get it. Russia itself was far from being a 'fighting empire'; while the most efficient militarist state in contemporary Europe, Bismarck's imperial Germany, was profoundly pacific in its external policies. It was therefore a waste of time both for the Russians and the British to base their diplomacy on military machines which would inevitably—as was ultimately proved to the British in South Africa and to the Russians at Tshushima—fail to meet whatever tests were placed upon them. Thus, while the British decision to evacuate Kandahar considerably puzzled Giers at St Petersburg, it ushered in a period of mutual compromise in the affairs of Central Asia. This policy was to stand a number of tests with success, two of which—the Penjdeh incident of 1885 and the increasing Russian penetration of Persia—contained as much political dynamite as had the mission of 1878 to Kabul.

It is in its Persian aspect that this phase of European diplomacy is best examined. Matters in Persia never came to that point of danger reached in Afghanistan because the two powers concerned took care not to let them do so. This was not because the Persian situation presented a lesser degree of complication than the other. From the British standpoint, Persia was an ante-room to India far more readily accessible to a hostile invader than Afghanistan. After the fall of Khiva in 1874, the whole region to the north of Persia (and Persia had no defined northern frontier) was placed under the administration of the Russian general Lomakin, who described himself as 'chief plenipotentiary' of the area. With Khiva secure, the Russians were able to establish themselves on the lower Oxus river, thus solving what had been their severest problem of supply and communication. Previously, Tashkent and the province of Turkestan had had to be supplied from Orenburg, 800 miles away over the desert from the Syr Daria river. But, from the Caspian through Khiva and beyond, the Oxus was navigable, and it was simple to plan new overland communication by road or rail that would connect with Samarqand and Tashkent on the one flank and with Krasnovodsk on the other. The Persian flank, the undemarcated regions of Khorassan, roamed by Turkoman tribes, lay exposed. The new Russian incursion had therefore made of Herat the 'key' not only to western Afghanistan, to Kabul, and so to India, but also to Kandahar and the Persian Gulf. The fall of Khiva had thus swung the true centre of gravity, as far as the security of India was concerned, away from the Afghan mountains to the Persian and Turkoman plains.

The shah was prepared to assert his sovereignty over the northern Turkomans could he have got British support: but although from 1874 the name of Merv (often thought to be a great city, but in fact a mud village with an oasis) was often talked of by British statesmen and publicists, since it lay only twelve days' march from Herat, Whitehall was not prepared to commit itself. British military agents in Khorassan—there 'for the love of adventure peculiar to Englishmen', as Giers was assured by the British ambassador at St Petersburg—continued to report on the growth of Russian influence. The shah visited St Petersburg in 1878, and brought back to Teheran General Kosagovsky, who set about organising a Cossack Brigade—'one of the main arms of Russian influence in Persia for the next forty years'. Salisbury, now transferred from the India to the Foreign Office, wished some counteracting British influence to be established quickly; for 'it might very well be that at a later period the imperious exigencies of her position towards Russia' might force upon England the necessity of obtaining, at far greater cost, the alliance or the neutrality of Persia. He thought to offer the shah Herat itself, which Persia had long coveted, and a convention to that end was actually drawn up (8 November 1879). But the cabinet disliked the idea, for if once

England installed a protégé in Herat she would be committed to keeping him there, and this entailed a British garrison, as Persian forces would make no sort of show against the Russians if the latter objected. The shah sought to bargain, and advised the Russians of what was afoot: England promptly dropped the convention, and the shah with it. The incoming Liberal government was anxious to work with Russia, and stood back while Russia and Persia negotiated a boundary for part of the northern area (21 December 1881). A secret clause of this Akhal-Khorassan convention contained a Persian renunciation of any claim over the Turkoman territory, which still stretched from the limits of the newly agreed frontier at Sarakhs some 200 miles north-east towards the Oxus river.

It was to the British, though not to the Russian, interest that this remaining gap in the Indian perimeter should be closed. It was still the Afghan rather than the Persian situation that obsessed the India Office; for if Russian forces, advancing to their new limits, displaced bands of Turkomans into Afghan territory and pursued them, as well they might, there was a very serious possibility of a resultant Russo-Afghan clash. But no British suggestion that he should claim Merv and its dependencies for himself, and so interpose his sovereignty as a buffer between the oncoming Russians and the open Afghan flank, could now win the shah. Merv submitted to the Russians in February 1884. At once the Indian government urged on the Foreign Office the absolute necessity 'to come to a clear understanding with Russia as to the exact line of the north and north-west frontiers of Afghanistan', and an Anglo-Russian negotiation began on how best to draw a line from Sarakhs to the Oxus. For every solution London presented St Petersburg had a difficulty, and not until 1888 was the line actually drawn. The Russians by that time could afford to waive their objection, as their Transcaspian railway from Krasnovodsk had been brought by Annenkov's military engineers to within 100 miles of Herat.

The rancorous frontier debate was interrupted, on 30 March 1885, by the celebrated incident at Penjdeh, an Afghan village from which Russian forces displaced the inhabitants—an event that threw the issue of peace or war between the European powers in Central Asia to the whim of the amir Abdur Rahman at Kabul, for if he had chosen to declare this a *casus belli*, it would have been hard for the official protectors of his foreign policy, the Indian government, to gainsay him. The British government, isolated in Europe, its regular forces in Egypt and the Sudan, drew up hasty war-plans for attacking Vladivostock and the Caucasus—long considered by Anglo-Indian strategists the key to all Russian power in the Middle East—but the Caucasus could not be reached without a penetration of the Straits, and Bismarck was not disposed to grant the consent of Europe to any such action. Fortunately, the amir let the matter go—but another such incident might prove too much for everyone's strained nerves, and England's need to keep Persia friendly grew more pressing than ever. While the Afghan frontier was being demarcated, Russian pressure increased at Teheran, and in August 1887, Russia won a signal victory: the shah agreed to consult the tsar before he granted to foreign companies any concessions to build roads, waterways, or railways. It appeared that Russia was intending to make all Persia her sphere of influence, a policy which could take her one day to the Persian Gulf. The shah knew this too, and he threatened to throw in his lot entirely with 'the good-tempered tiger' in the north unless the English did something concrete for him.

What the shah wanted was an alliance. This of course he could not have. The Conservative government had necessarily fallen heir to the Liberal programme of Anglo-Russian amity, and Salisbury was resolved to pay no heed to the shah, who would inevitably compromise British foreign policy if he got the chance. In October 1887 Sir Henry Drummond Wolff was sent to Persia to inaugurate a new era of Anglo-Russian harmony in that country. Surely both powers were entitled to their legitimate share in the markets of Persia? But, behind such a suggestion, inevitably loomed a policy of an ultimate partition of Persia into joint spheres of influence. Salisbury might dislike the idea equally with Giers, but Wolff went on promoting it and attracting the attention of Europe to it until Lansdowne as Viceroy of India pointed out to him that any encouragement to Russia to build railways in northern Persia, while the British busied themselves building railways in the south, flatly contradicted every principle of security on which the *Raj* had ever depended. Wolff's main achievement was in inducing the shah to open the Karun river in southern Persia to the mercantile marine of all countries. 'C'était là', was Giers' comment, 'une manière de parler.'

Russia was indeed more alarmed by the thought of some new and concentrated financial exploitation of Persia by the British than by any Anglo-Indian scheme concerning Herat. It was the age of economic imperialism, and of all the great powers Russia was the worst-equipped to play a hand in the game. Since she had no capital with which to build railways in Persia, she determined that no one should build them. In October 1890, therefore, the shah further agreed not to entertain any scheme for railway construction, from whatever quarter it came, for fifteen years; and this agreement was kept, for Persia had no railway within its borders when war struck Europe in 1914. Till then, Russian influence remained dominant at Teheran, the Russian Bank supreme, and to Russia fell the preponderance of Persia's trade. 'The independence of Persia', Edward Grey justly observed in 1903, 'is a phrase.'

Thus, although the British were unable to erect a fool-proof system of 'elaborate palisades' around Afghanistan and Persia, the balance of power between themselves and the Russians maintained diplomatic equilibrium, and with it a condition of peace. Moreover, in an age of imperialist competition the problem became overlaid: after 1887 the attention of the tsar and his military advisers turned to the Far East, to Manchuria and to the warm water obtainable at Port Arthur. Russia by so extending herself naturally increased her own degree of vulnerability, and Britain, by allying at the close of this period (1902) with Japan, did not omit to underline this point. Russia was by then, what she had not been in Palmerston's time, too intricately involved in the European state-system to be able to indulge in eastern buccaneering: and from a British standpoint, the Russians in Teheran might well be preferred to the Germans with a railway terminus on the Persian Gulf, the Russians even at Constantinople to a German economic penetration of Turkey. By 1899 it was Russia, not Britain, who was most loudly affirming a deter-mination to keep the territorial integrity of the Ottoman empire intact. But Britain, too, was by then tied to other powers' policies, and she, like Russia, never managed to break this chain.

This had come about because of the stake she had put down in Egypt. After 1882 what Grey was to call 'the logic of an imperial posi-tion'—a phrase he used when he found himself constrained in 1915 to promise Constantinople as a war-trophy to the tsar—was positively forced on the attention of British governments, to such a degree that after 1895 Salisbury was eager for accommodation with both France and Russia on almost any terms short of the evacuation of Egypt. The logic of an imperial position had made it unsafe to move of one's own will in any direction at all. Except for the Boer war, the occupation of Egypt in 1882 was the last unilateral step ever taken by the British empire.

'What we want', said Derby when Foreign Secretary in 1876, 'is an uninterrupted passage through Egypt and the absence of any foreign control over that country.' But this was to want a very great deal, because Egypt was already a European colony. In 1870 there were seventeen foreign consulates in the country, representing about 100,000 foreigners concentrated in Cairo and Alexandria, foreigners who until 1876 paid no taxes to the Egyptian government at all. Egypt at this time, as Cromer later put it, 'must have been an earthly paradise for all who had money to lend at usurious rates of interest, or third-rate goods of which they wished to dispose at first-rate prices'. The Suez Canal, the main line of steam communication to the East, was owned by French interests, and France as a result held an unchallenged ascendancy over the khedive Ismail and his government. Up to 1873, the total interest paid on account of sums borrowed by the Egyptian government in connection with the costs of the canal's construction amounted to £6 million. The interest on Egypt's foreign loans amounted to almost £5 million a year, a sum greater than the whole of her annual revenue during the reign of Ismail's predecessor, Said. European bondholders thus had a great stake in Egyptian insolvency; in 1876 the report of Stephen Cave, the British paymaster-general, emphasised that Egypt could not go on 'serving floating debts at 25 per cent and raising loans at 12 to 15 per cent to meet additions to her indebtedness which do not bring a single piastre into her exchequer'. Ismail's necessity to raise money inevitably made him gamble with his country's greatest asset, the Suez Canal itself (paying its first dividend, of 5 per cent, by 1875). In 1874 he gave an option to a French banker for the purchase of the Egyptian government's holding of 40 per cent of the ordinary shares, at a price of £3¾ million. Disraeli in 1875 bought through Rothschilds these 176,602 shares, as is well known, for over £4 million.

Although he quite correctly described this transaction in the House of Commons as political rather than financial, it was not such a sweeping triumph as his 'You have it, Madam' implied: no voting power accompanied these ordinary shares, as Ismail had been deprived of this by the Canal Company in 1871. In negotiation, de Lesseps as President of the Company did grant back to Great Britain the missing ten votes, but he allotted to her three seats only, on the council of twenty-four members. Disraeli's *coup* nevertheless compelled the British government to take a greater interest in Egyptian finance, and Cave's mission of investigation (January–March 1876) was the immediate result. But France still held the preponderance, of political as well as of financial interest. It was significant that at the Berlin Conference in 1878 she would not permit Egypt—or, for that matter, Syria, the Holy Places, or Tunis—to appear on the agenda.

On 8 April 1878 Ismail was forced to suspend payment on his Treasury bills. On 2 May he issued a decree providing for the establishment of an international *Caisse de la Dette Publique*, to consist of one French, one Italian, one Austrian, and one British national (Evelyn Baring, appointed by the British bondholders, not by the government). There now began an unedifying series of financial squabbles, many of which were taken to extra-territorial courts whose unannounced principle was to recognise only the claims of their own nationals. The European bondholders objected when the *Caisse* funded the entire bonded and floating debt at £91 million, at 7½ per cent interest. Their representatives, Joubert and Goschen, reorganised the funding, and recommended the appointment of two Controllers, one to collect and one to control expenditure. An international board was also instituted to manage the railways, the telegraph, and the harbour of Alexandria, revenues from which were already earmarked in advance. To this arrangement the 'floating' debt-holders—mainly British—further objected; and between these millstones the administration of Egypt ground to a standstill.

In March 1878 the British and the French governments took their first official step. They appointed an Anglo-French commission of inquiry. By August this commission had transformed itself into the responsible ministry of the Egyptian government: Ismail was now a prisoner in the hands of his creditors. Naturally, he was calculatedly unhelpful to his own ministers, all Christians—Nubar Pasha, Rivers Wilson, and de Blignières —and, after organising two popular demonstrations against them, managed by April 1879 to get rid of them. It was too successful an action. On 18 May Bismarck surprisingly made himself spokesman for the European bondholders, and the powers put pressure on the sultan at Constantinople. The latter, on 26 June 1879, sent Ismail a telegram addressing him as 'ex-Khedive of Egypt'. From September his successor Tewfik was made firmly subordinate to an Anglo-French 'Dual Control', as personified by Baring and de Blignières. Although they passed a 'law of liquidation' of the debt (17 July 1880) interest charges on it continued to absorb 37 per cent of Egypt's revenue; even by 1913 this figure still amounted to 22 per cent. Another of their economies was the sale to the *Crédit Foncier* in 1880, at a bargain price of £880,000, of the Egyptian government's preference shares in the Canal Company, entitling it to 15 per cent of the profits. In consequence, from then until 1936, Egypt was to draw no revenue at all from the Canal.

The Controllers also reduced the Egyptian army from 45,000 to 18,000 officers and men, thus giving discontent its leaders. Ahmed Arabi was however more than a disgruntled colonel, representative only of disgruntled colonels: anti-Turkish, anti-foreign, radical views had been gaining ground in Egypt among the intelligentsia for ten years or more. But whatever Arabi was, the foreign governors of Egypt could not brook his rivalry in the matter of control of the khedive and his country. His victory over Tewfik in September 1881, when he forced the khedive to accept the nationalists' demands for representative government and a larger army, ultimately brought a sharp Anglo-French Note (8 January 1882), conceived mainly by Gambetta. This emphasised support for Tewfik and menaced any opposition to him. Its main result was to annoy the sultan, alarm the powers, and alienate opinion in Egypt itself even further. From a foreign viewpoint the local situation continued to deteriorate, and when Tewfik appealed to the powers to rescue him from Arabi and his machinations, an Anglo-French naval squadron appeared off Alexandria in May.

England still hoped to get the Turks to rectify the situation in what was, after all, one of their subject-provinces; but the Turkish contribution to the problem of sending two commissioners to Cairo, one of whom negotiated with the khedive and the other with Arabi, was unhelpful. The French, once Gambetta was gone, found no consistent policy to pursue; their British colleagues found none either, swithered between joint action and internationalisation, lost their balance and tumbled, as Dilke put it, into Egypt. The conference of ambassadors at Constantinople (23 June), sandwiched as it was between a first outbreak of anti-foreign riots in

Alexandria and a second, reached no concrete conclusion. Further riots brought about a British naval bombardment (11 July), from which the French squadron absented itself on instruction. There followed, after a month's delay, the mobilisation of a British army corps under Sir Garnet Wolseley and its dispatch to Egypt, where on 13 September it routed Arabi's forces at Tel-el-Kebir. The British were masters of Egypt. By this action, as John Morley pointed out, England had made herself, at long last, a territorial power in the Mediterranean. Palmerston's worst fears concerning the menace that lurked within the whole concept of a canal through Egypt had been remarkably realised.

Granville from the Foreign Office circularised the powers on 3 January 1883 that the British occupation was only temporary. But, having overturned the only administrative system that Egypt possessed, it was not possible for the uneasy Liberals—128 of whom had abstained from voting credits for Wolseley's expedition—to walk away, washing their hands. They wanted to reform the administration and evacuate Egypt, for continuing to *govern* Egypt must lay an unwarrantable burden on an already overtaxed British empire. But their policy, as their own agent-general, Baring (later Lord Cromer), acidly put it, was not one 'capable of execution'. If one reformed an oriental state, one had to stay to guard the reformation. Dufferin reported in 1883 that even the germs of constitutional progress were absent in Egypt. The introduction of European skills was therefore pointless unless they were backed with European authority.

For getting out of Egypt, Baring pointed out to Granville, was a very different matter from getting out of Afghanistan. No one, after all, was interested in the internal business of Afghanistan but the Afghans themselves. Such a quasi-barbarous people could well be left to the mercies of their own quasi-barbarous governors. To be sure, in Egypt the moral and material conditions of the people were scarcely less barbarous than in Afghanistan. But on these foundations was built 'a top-heavy and exotic superstructure, such as an enormous external debt, Western law courts, complete liberty of contract, and, in fact, all the paraphernalia of European civilisation, with some of its worst and not many of its best features'. He did not suppose, he added, that Europe would stand by and let this superstructure fall to pieces. England thus stood guardian hereafter for the interests of Europe in Egypt; but she could expect no applause for the role, as no European consul-general in Cairo could fail to observe that his British colleague alone had an army at his back—still 4700 men in 1888—with which to support whatever he might suggest for the European good. The Egyptian deficit was a continuing European question; England could follow no independent policy. Lord Lyons from Paris noted 'the natural disposition of almost all Europe to side against us on the Egyptian question'. To Baring fell the task of maintaining his country's authority while at the same time concealing the fact as best he could that he was maintaining it at all. When, in 1892, a new young khedive, Abbas II, thought to assert himself and insisted on changing the personnel of his own ministry, he at once had the length of his political chain made clear to him. Rosebery backed Baring's insistence that Her Majesty's government 'expected to be consulted in such important matters as a change of Ministers'. Baring disliked the incident, complaining that it 'brought him out of his hiding-place', and that this was enough to shatter the system.

To the French, the hiding-place was never hard to discover, the system was always a usurpation. Any khedive of Egypt must necessarily be, in Freycinet's words, 'souverain à la mode anglaise'—a comment Baring considered ironical, when he looked enviously over towards the French position in Tunisia, where no law was valid unless signed by the French resident-general. Disappointed of their rather sanguine expectation that, after the battle of Tel-el-Kebir, the Dual Control would be re-established, the French had 'reserved their liberty of action in Egypt', an expression signifying that henceforward France would do her best to hamper British administration in the country and British foreign policy in general. This loss of an *entente* that had operated for over forty years made Britain more and more dependent on the goodwill of the one important European power with whom she had as yet no direct cause of quarrel— Germany. It was a situation Bismarck was able to exploit to the full.

The British found no way out of the impasse into which they had stumbled in Egypt. They could not take over Egypt and govern it according to sensible colonial or Indian methods, for that would have given the signal for the general partition of the Ottoman empire, and this was not to be risked. For what would not France, what would not Russia do, and how could England, already bailiff in two Turkish dependencies, object? Unlooked-for complication arising in the Sudan—an area which was either Turkish or ownerless, but was certainly not British—made the Penjdeh incident really dangerous. When this dispute with Russia developed, the five thousand troops that had been sent to the Sudan to rescue Gordon had to be summoned home, and Khartoum was visited only to be left again, and the Sudan handed over to the Khalifa and to anarchy for another ten years. The centre of gravity in Egyptian affairs was not Cairo, nor even Paris, but Berlin. Egypt was the only place where Bismarck could successfully apply pressure on British policy, after the Russian mode in Central Asia. Of this pressure repercussions were felt from Angra Pequena to New Guinea; while the conference that was convened at Berlin in 1884, to lay down a programme and a methodology for the partition of Africa, was controlled entirely by Bismarck and Jules Ferry, and its decisions as a natural result cut across many a 'sphere of influence' marked out in that continent by optimistic Britons.

Salisbury like Gladstone tried to retire from this impasse. He likened England's position in Egypt to the difficulty 'a man has in getting credit from the neighbouring tradesmen when he is only staying at an hotel', and he assured the French ambassador, Waddington, that he was only looking 'for the means of withdrawing with honour'. This he never found. As the international code of the day was constituted, it was not possible for one imperial nation to withdraw 'with honour' under pressure from another: John Bull would not leave Egypt as long as France bade him to. Salisbury followed Gladstone, moreover, in his hope that the Turks might still be induced to take up their own responsibility, both in Egypt and in the Sudan. Drummond Wolff, prior to his Persian adventures, was in Cairo in August 1885, under instruction to accept the principle of evacuation, without however arranging a date for it, or binding the British government to obtain the consent of the European powers to anything it might decide to do. These negotiations were ultimately transferred to Constantinople, and there, on 22 May 1887, Drummond Wolff presented a masterful convention for the sultan's ratification.

Under this convention, the British pledged themselves to withdraw from Egypt within three years. There was however a clause that allowed the British the right of re-entry 'upon the appearance of danger from without'; of this appearance of danger, the British themselves were to be the judge. Salisbury had already made it clear to Waddington that this was the point on which Her Majesty's government most insisted, and that the British had no intention of leaving Egypt unless this right of re-entry were conceded. Moreover, in the fifth article of Drummond Wolff's convention it was stated that if the khedive misbehaved, and disorder ensued in Egypt, both the Ottoman empire and the British government would have the right to send troops to keep order; and, even if the Turks did not avail themselves of this right, the British might still do so. As if this was not enough, Wolff added that, if one of the Mediterranean powers did not accept this convention and would not ratify it, that refusal in itself would be considered as 'the appearance of a danger from without', sufficient to prevent the departure of a single British soldier from the Egyptian shore.

The terms of this convention caused a major diplomatic explosion, and ushered in a period of the most bitter Anglo-French colonial rivalry. The sultan was mercilessly browbeaten by the French and Russian ambassadors, and was told that, if he consented to ratify this baleful instrument, France and Russia would consider that they had thereby been given the right to occupy provinces of his empire like Syria and Armenia, and to leave them only after a similar convention had been concluded. This right of reoccupation of Egypt given to the British was such that, for all practical purposes, the government of the Ottoman empire was being divided between England and the sultan. France could never entertain the idea that Egypt should pass once and for all into the control of a single great power. Nelidov, the Russian envoy, was as vehement: by this convention Russia would lose the possibility of making Egypt, as she had made Turkestan, a pawn to be used in return for English concession to Russian ambition in the Balkans. Here a principle was certainly involved. 'Eh bien', was the cheerful comment of his German colleague, Radowitz, 'alors vous garderez votre principe et les Anglais garderont l'Égypte.' The English did so. The only concrete result of Wolff's convention, left unratified by the sultan and by everyone else, was the dispatch of a Turkish high commissioner to Cairo, with a corresponding increase in the number of international problems which beset Baring there. Evacuation of Egypt, like the execution of Scheherazade, was indefinitely postponed.

It was the existence of the Suez Canal that had brought the British to Egypt: solicitude for bondholders, although a part of their attitude, would never by itself alone have galvanised a Liberal government to such action as it took. The Suez Canal continued to keep the British in Egypt. The Canal Company remained a French organisation, operating under a Turco-Egyptian charter: but everything to do with its physical property was done beneath the diplomatic aegis of the British government. The use by Wolseley, in his expedition of 1882, of the canal as a military base had already attracted the attention of the powers before Granville referred to it in his placatory circular of January 1883. In this circular, Granville proposed that the powers should combine to declare that the canal must remain unfortified and free to the passage of all shipping; that no troops or munitions should be disembarked in it; and that no hostilities should take place in the canal or in its approaches, or anywhere in Egyptian waters, even in a case where Turkey itself was a belligerent. But these two last conditions were not to apply to any measure which 'might be necessary for the defence of Egypt'. This was either meaningless or sinister, and the powers not surprisingly thought it the latter. It was France who took the initiative in summoning an international commission to consider the business further, and by June 1885 an instrument had been drafted that incorporated proposals from both Britain and France. But the British representative tacked on a reservation, the effect of which was to suspend the application of the clauses drawn up by the international commission for so long as British forces occupied Egypt. In 1888 the convention was indeed signed by Britain, in company with France and all the powers of Europe, but it did not become operative as Britain continued to insist on her reservation of 1885. The stout British view, well expressed by Dilke in the House of Commons, was that this was a 'crazy and insane convention', under which Russian ships might pass through the Canal on their way to attack India. Not until the negotiation of 1904, when the French goad was finally removed from the British side in Egypt, did the British abandon this attitude. 'The freedom of the seas' had long been a loudly proclaimed British interest: but the Suez Canal, though full of salt water, could not be considered by the masters of Egypt as an international channel.

Thus, British power was asserted successfully, in an area where it was essential for Britain so to assert it. The wider significance of the instructions that Salisbury had given to Lytton, when in 1876 pressure was due to be increased upon the Amir at Kabul, was clearly illustrated. 'Territories', Salisbury had then written, 'ultimately dependent on British power for their defence must not be closed to those of the Queen's officers or subjects who may be duly authorised to enter them.' Nevertheless, the anti-imperial tradition in British political thought, always a powerful factor in drawing back a forward policy, operated in this case, and because there was so much unease in England about the assertion of this power more and more was made of the 'duty' laid upon the English to stay in Egypt for the sake of the Egyptians themselves: the *fellaheen*, and not the bondholders, must become the object of imperial solicitude. Although the Liberal party henceforward concentrated their emphasis on this aspect of 'Cromerism' Gladstone himself always denied that any such duty had arisen, which cancelled all pledges to retire from Egypt. The government of Egypt remained, as he characterised it in May 1893, 'a burden, a difficulty, and a risk'. The introduction of this new missionary element, however, into the British attitude towards Egypt, could only further alienate the French, and give further argument to those who made it their business to collect material for the record of *perfide Albion*.

The Central Asian complication had at least one virtue: it was a matter within the purview of two powers only. But in Egypt everyone had a right to have a say, and everyone said it: it was his bitter experience of listening to its being said that caused Cromer to take particular care that in the 'Anglo-Egyptian Sudan', which he invented for the occasion in 1899, no rights or privileges similar to those they enjoyed in Egypt should be acquired by foreigners. It was this common dislike of British policy in Egypt that assisted other powers to come together, to British detriment, in Africa, in the Far East, and indeed anywhere in the world where the British empire had a frontier. In 1892–3, while Russian agents were penetrating the Pamir plateau to the north of Kashmir, the French were advancing into Siam from their base on the Mekong in Indo-China. It was fanciful to see this as one vast 'pincer movement' on India, but its implications were alarming enough for Rosebery's government to make an accommodation with Russia on the Pamir question in 1895, at a speed that no other Central Asian problem had yet had applied to it.

Other illustrations of the weakness of the British position were to be found in the Levant itself. In December 1894, when the troubles of the Armenians were again forcing themselves upon the unwilling attention of the European powers, Rosebery was disposed to allow Russia to occupy the Armenian provinces of Turkey, in return for Russian recognition of Britain's 'special position' in Egypt, and with, perhaps, some compensation for the French in Syria. So far had Britain abandoned her dogma of a Levantine *status quo*. In Asia Minor, moreover, there was a new factor to be coped with. Since 1888, when the first train from Vienna reached Constantinople, German companies had been interesting themselves in the further railway development of Anatolia, and by 1892 had completed a line from the Bosporus to Ankara. In this age, a railway was looked on as the tentacle of the advancing imperialist octopus, and with good reason: H. N. Brailsford was to note sardonically in his *War of Steel and Gold* (1914) how railways in Anatolia meander for miles over a level plain, making so much extra per mile for the promoter. Yet the British, so sensitive on Persian railway questions, were unable to obstruct this foreign thrust, which must inevitably take it on rails to a region where no other imperial flag had yet been seen—the Persian Gulf. The Germans had their position of advantage made plain to them: for when in December 1892 the British ambassador in Turkey of his own accord showed signs of hindering further German railway schemes, Germany threatened to withdraw support of British policy in Egypt. Cromer, his hands then full with the intransigence of Abbas II, and anxious to get consent to an increase in the Egyptian army, prevailed on Rosebery to see to it that there was no further annoyance of the Germans in Anatolia. Even in their traditional diplomatic battleground in Central Asia, England had to yield ground. When the Russians in February 1900 abandoned the Anglo-Russian agreement of 1873, which had contained a Russian stipulation that Afghanistan lay outside the sphere of Russian influence, the unease caused in 'Anglo-Indian' circles was deepened by the sense of bafflement that things could come to such a pass.

The German incursion, however, set the older members of the Middle Eastern 'club' a common problem. When the German emperor paid his second visit to the Levant in October 1898, and announced in Damascus that 300 million Muslims could count him their friend, the Russian and the French as well as the British empire had reason to feel irritation. An Ottoman empire revivified by German zeal would be a standing menace to a secure future for all three. Curzon as Viceroy of India was able to induce both the sultan of Oman and the sheikh of Kuwait in the Persian Gulf— the latter place the likeliest terminus for any railway down the valley of the Euphrates—to sign treaties with the *Raj* in which they stipulated that they would cede no territory and receive no foreign agent without the sanction of the British government. This they did in the first two months of 1899: but nevertheless, it was in November of that year that the sultan granted his formal approval of a concession to a German company to build a railway across his empire to Baghdad and Basra.

Thus, as this period in Middle Eastern history closed, it appeared to be to the interest of both Russia and Great Britain to decide whether to make an individual accommodation with Germany, or to come to an accommodation with each other. Nothing could now be done in the Middle

East unless each power kept open its line to Berlin; and as it turned out, neither St Petersburg nor London had anything to offer Berlin that made the Germans think it worth their while to keep this line in repair. The British, although painfully slow to take the measure of this problem, did finally make their move. Having countered any menace to the Far Eastern *status quo* by the alliance with Japan, which included a reciprocal recognition of each power's 'special positions' in Korea and in India, they were successful in restoring the *entente* with France (1904), receiving at last the French recognition of the British 'special position' in Egypt in return for approval of the establishment of French paramountcy in Morocco. (This was done, in extreme unwisdom, without German co-operation.) Three years later, another British government came to terms on Central Asia with France's ally, Russia (1907).

This meant that, to keep their stance in Egypt, the British in effect were prepared to jettison their traditional foreign policy of non-commitment to any European *bloc*. As a natural result, they ended by entering a war in 1914, whose primary cause was an Austro-Russian quarrel of a kind that had never previously concerned Whitehall, at the side of those who had for so long been the rivals of their own imperial power in the Middle East. Nor was there any reason for the British to suppose, in 1914, that the French and the Russians would not take up these roles again.

But since, at the turn of the century, they were African and Far Eastern questions that held the attention of European chancelleries and public opinion alike, the Middle East fell out of sight while Cromer continued to present his annual reports on Egypt to the British Parliament. Arthur Balfour was able to hold to his opinion, first expressed in 1896, that a defeat of the Indian army on the Indus would be a trifling disaster for India and the British empire in comparison with a defeat of the fleet in the English Channel. The danger in South Africa passed, and Tsar Nicholas II did not in fact order the mobilisation of his troops in Turkestan: the British empire took heart again, and promoted the Royal Navy to an even higher place in its collective esteem. But whatever other preoccupations came, and wherever else Europe extended its frontiers, the security of the entire Middle Eastern bridgehead between the continents remained a vital matter for every power with extra-European interests. The Middle East was therefore to remain, in the twentieth century as in the nineteenth, an area where outsiders had the greatest say. That 'active Arab sovereign' whose emergence Palmerston had feared was not yet in sight: but his eventual arrival on the scene would, while complicating it, make no difference to the essential issue that confronted the great powers of the world.

CHAPTER XXII

THE PARTITION OF AFRICA

SINCE the nineteenth century began, the Europeans had been strengthening their hold over those parts of the world selected during the era of mercantilism. Australasia, India, South-east Asia, above all the Americas—they were either temperate regions peopled with white immigrants or tropical countries already under white rule. Step by step the mode of white expansion had altered: liberalism and industrial growth shifted the emphasis away from colonies of formal empire to regions of informal influence. But whatever the form it had taken, the groundwork of European imperialism had been truly laid long before the cartographical exercises in partition at the end of the century. Africa was the last continent to win the interest of the strategists of expansion; it seemed to them that here they were scraping the bottom of the barrel.

Dividing Africa was easy enough for the Europeans. They did it at that moment in history when their lead over the other continents was at its longest. Economic growth and technical innovation gave them invincible assurance and force. Their culture and political organisation gave them a carrying power to match their iron ships and high-velocity guns. That Europe had the capacity to subjugate Africa was self-evident; but had her rulers any firm wish to do so?

Twenty years were enough to see the continent carved into symmetries devised by the geometers of diplomacy. By the end of the century only Morocco and Ethiopia were still independent, and their turn was coming. But the statesmen who drew the new frontier lines did not do so because they wanted to rule and develop these countries. Bismarck and Ferry, Gladstone and Salisbury, had no solid belief in African empire; indeed they sneered at the movement as something of a farce. A gamble in jungles and bush might interest a poor king such as Leopold II of the Belgians, or a politician on the make such as Crispi, but the chief partitioners of the 1880's glimpsed no grand imperial idea behind what they were doing. They felt no need of African colonies and in this they reflected the indifference of all but the lunatic fringe of European business and politics. Here their historians must follow them. For all the hindsight of social scientists, there was no comprehensive cause or purpose behind it. In all the long annals of imperialism, the partition of Africa is a remarkable freak. Few events that have thrown an entire continent into revolution have been brought about so casually.

Why then did statesmen bother to divide the continent? It used to be supposed that European society must have put out stronger urges to empire in Africa at this time; and all sorts of causes have been suggested to support the supposition. One and all, however, they suffer from a tiresome defect: of powerful new incentives there is remarkably little sign. Only after the partition was long over and done with did capital seek outlets, did industry seek markets in tropical Africa. As late as the end of the century the European economy went on by-passing these poor prospects in favour of the proven fields of America and Asia. Neither is it realistic to explain the movement by some change in the temper of the European mind. The pride and pomps of African empire did not suit the popular taste until late in the 1890's when the partition was all but completed. Only after Africa lay divided and allotted did European opinion embrace the mythology of empire. Defined as a movement of white men to transform African society, as they had transformed the societies of India or Java, imperialism was not the cause of partition. It was one of the side effects.

This is not to say that there is no rational explanation. It is only to suggest that no single, general cause underlay a movement to which so many things contributed at random. All of them must be included, for it was their concatenations that brought on the partition. And these cannot be revealed unless the view is wrenched away from the standpoint that has obscured it hitherto. Scanning Europe for the causes, the theorists of imperialism have been looking for the answers in the wrong places. The crucial changes that set all working took place in Africa itself. It was the fall of an old power in its north, the rise of a new in its south, that dragged Africa into modern history.

From these internal crises, erupting at opposite ends of the continent, there unfolded two unconnected processes of partition. That in southern Africa flowed from the rise of the Transvaal on its gold reefs, from a struggle between colonial and republican expansion that reached from Bechuanaland to Lake Nyasa. It eventually drove South Africa into the Jameson Raid and the Boer War. The second crisis was the breakdown of the Khedivate in the Egyptian revolution of 1879–82. Their misdealings with this new proto-nationalism brought the British stumbling on to the Nile and trapped them there. This was crucial. It led to bad blood between them and the French in a quarrel that was to spread over all tropical Africa before being settled at Fashoda in 1898.

Hence Europe became entangled in tropical Africa by two internal crises. Imbroglios with Egyptian proto-nationalists and thence with Islamic revivals across the whole of the Sudan drew the powers into an expansion of their own in East and West Africa. Thousands of miles to the south, English efforts to compress Afrikaner nationalists into an obsolete imperial design set off a second sequence of expansion in southern Africa. The last quarter of the century has often been called the 'Age of imperialism'. Yet much of this imperialism was no more than an involuntary reaction of Europe to the various proto-nationalisms of Islam that were already rising in Africa against the encroaching thraldom of the white men.

Muslim rebellion drew Ferry into the unplanned occupation of Tunis which was the prelude of the partition; Muslim revolution in Cairo drew Gladstone into his Egyptian bondage and set off the partition proper. The peoples of this part of North Africa had much to protest about. By 1880 consuls, money-lenders, engineers and philanthropists from over the water had organised both these countries into chaos. Since Egypt commanded a route to British India, since Tunis counted in French Mediterranean policy both the khedive and the bey had been playthings of Anglo-French expansion for three-quarters of a century. Although neither power could be indifferent to the fate of these areas, neither wished to turn them into colonies. Anxious to keep the Ottoman empire intact, the British chose to watch over Suez from Constantinople. Enjoying the fruits of unofficial hegemony in Tunis and Cairo, the French felt no desire for another Algeria. But European investment and trade had increased since the 1830's and it was from investment that the crash came in the 1870's, that golden age of Islamic insolvency when the Commander of the Faithful at Constantinople was himself hammered into bankruptcy. In Cairo and Tunis the financial advice of Europe hardened into something like dictation. Debt commissioners took charge of the revenues so blithely mortgaged by their rulers; payment of the coupon became the first charge on their governments; in the eyes of their peoples the two potentates had become mere debt collectors for the infidels. Inevitably they went from financial catastrophe to political disaster. Their armies, as the least rigid and most westernised group in these states, threatened a *putsch*; or the tribes of the marches talked of revolt. The more they squeezed money from landlord and peasant, the nearer came revolt against their rapacity. By 1881 Egypt and Tunisia were sliding into the ruin which overtook almost all the non-European polities in the nineteenth century that essayed a programme of European-style development. Islam provided neither the law nor the ethos nor the institutions for such work, and the rulers discovered that they could not modernise without loosing their authority or their independence.

In spite of the bankruptcy, the French were far from anxious to occupy Tunisia. But with Italian encouragement after 1877 the grand peculator, Mustapha ben Ismail, replaced Khérédine, the tool of France, as first minister and set about rooting up the concessions which gave Paris the option over the economic and political future of the country. Here was a new situation. Making good these options would require more than gunboats and peddlers of contracts.

Many in Algeria, but few in France, called for a punitive expedition.

There were admirals and generals who looked forward to adding Tunis to their domain in Algeria, there was rubbing of hands among speculators at the prospect of the *coup de Bourse* which would come if their government ended by guaranteeing the debts of a defeated bey. But most French politicians saw more risk than gain. 'An expedition to Tunis in an election year?', the premier, Ferry, exclaimed to his Foreign Minister. 'My dear Saint-Hilaire, you cannot think of it!' But Gambetta, the President of the Chamber, was for intervention, and this was decisive. Assured of his aid, the government at last unleashed the army. On 22 April 1881 the military promenade into Tunisia began.

How large were the French intentions? They were remarkably small for the so-called age of imperialism. Gambetta, defining the expedition's aims, wrote: 'We ought to extort a large reparation from the bey...take a large belt of territory as a precaution for the future, sign a treaty with effective guarantees, and then retire...after having made a show of force sufficient to assure for ever a preponderant position there, in keeping with our power, our interests and our investments in the Mediterranean.' With Ferry also, the aim was to reassert external sway rather than to acquire a new colony and these limited aims were mirrored in the Treaty of Bardo, extorted from the bey on 12 May 1881. It merely announced a French protectorate. By itself this meant only long-range control of his external relations; and even so mild a commitment as this was ratified in the Chamber with a hundred and twenty abstentions. The French occupation of Tunisia was not a matter of forward policy-making in Paris. It came in response to the deepening crisis inside Tunisia itself. The Treaty of Bardo was merely an arrangement with a discredited Muslim ruler whose surrender to France could not bind his subjects.

Within his kingdom, as in Algeria, preachers of the *Sanusi* religious order were whipping up rage against the Christian invaders; a rebellion in Oran was followed by another in the south around the holy city of Kairouan. Holy war was proclaimed, a Khalifa was recognised, the tribes farthest from Tunis flocked to join the movement. Here in essence was the same situation as that which had produced the savage wars of Abd-el-Kader in Algeria during the 1840's and was to produce the Muslim theocracy of the Mahdi in the Egyptian Sudan—lightning explosions of fanaticism against the overlordship of the foreigner and the unbeliever.

Crushing the rising offered no difficulties to the generals, but it presented thorny problems to the politicians. One thing was now clear. The basis of the old system of informal control had gone for good, swept aside by political and religious revolt from below. By the summer of 1881 France had to make the same hard choice in Tunisia as Abd-el-Kader had presented her with in Algeria. She had either to get on or get out. Either the paper protectorate had to be made good, or it had to be torn up. Making it good would entail yet more criticism from the Chamber. In October the rebellion was broken. But the general dislike of African adventures in the Chamber meant that its endorsement would be oblique and ambiguous. Gambetta induced the new Chamber to resolve on the 'complete fulfilment' of the Treaty of Bardo. Behind this dexterously vague draftsmanship, the reality was quite different. The invaders of Tunisia were now compelled to conquer and rule a people whom they could no longer dominate from outside.

So devious an occupation was far from marking the start of a new imperialism. It was not the result of a profound impulse in French society to enlarge the empire in Africa. It was electorally risky. It brought obloquy upon its sponsors. It struck no spark of that Gallic love of *gloire* so often brought in by historians when the problems surrounding French expansion become too puzzling. The protectorate was no more than a continuation of the old move into Algeria, a conclusion of the old informal expansion into Tunisia.

The partition of the African tropics which began two years later was not the result of the Tunisian mishap, or of Leopold's schemes and Bismarck's wiles, or of the squabbles of white merchants and explorers on the spot. What drove it on was the Suez crisis and the repercussions of that crisis.

A recognisably modern nationalist revolution was sweeping the Nile Delta by 1882; its leaders are much more familiar figures today than the pro-consuls who put them down. The Egyptians were reacting against increasing interference over the past six years by Britain and France. Anxious to renovate the crumbling state on which their amicable dual paramountcy and their security in India and the Mediterranean in large part depended, they had acted with a high hand. At their behest, the Khedivate had been clothed in the decencies of constitutional monarchy, the army cut, and the landlords obliged to pay their dues; the khedive Ismail had been sent packing, Tewfik raised in his place and two-thirds of the revenue sequestrated to satisfy the bondholders. Small wonder that the Notables were using the constitution to break their foreign fetters. The mulcted peasantry was at the point of revolt. Muslim gorges were rising against Christians; the army had mutinied to recall dismissed comrades, and the pashas were defending their fiscal privileges in the guise of patriots ridding the country of the foreigner. By January 1882 all were uniting against the Anglo-French Financial Controllers and the khedive who did their will. The French consul reported that Tewfik had lost all prestige; the British that Arabi and his colonels had practically taken over the country.

What was afoot in Egypt was far more serious than the collapse of the bey had been. Here also was 'an anti-European movement...destined to turn into fanaticism';[1] but this time it had the professional army at its

---

[1] French consul in Cairo to Freycinet, 21 February 1882: Archives du Ministère des Affaires Étrangères [henceforth, A.É.], Égypte 72.

head. Gladstone, then prime minister, anticipated 'with the utmost apprehension a conflict between the "Control" and any sentiment truly national, with a persuasion that one way or the other we should come to grief.' 'Egypt for the Egyptians [was] the best, the only good solution to the Egyptian question.' This was true. But as the 'union between [Britain and France] on that...question was the principal symbol' of their overall *entente*, both gave priority in the crisis to keeping in step. Each might grumble at going it together, neither desired to go it alone. The unpopularity of the Tunisian adventure was enough to deter Freycinet's ministry from another promenade in North Africa. Gladstone's Liberals, who had just retired from the Transvaal and Afghanistan and washed their hands of Tunis and Morocco, still had their scruples about meddling abroad. Yet something had to be done. Clearly the ideal solution, the only one as Gladstone had said, was to come to terms with Arabi. This was tried. Paris offered him a paid holiday to study European armies; London tried to reconcile him to the khedive. But Egyptian feelings were too heated for Arabi to agree to the one condition that seemed indispensable: abiding by the Financial Control. So long as he refused this, the British feared a foreign thrust at the jugular vein of Suez, and the French feared Turkish intervention which would bring the aid of Islam nearer to their dissident subjects in Tunis and Algeria. On 6 January 1882 the joint note announced the conclusion of Gambetta, unwillingly subscribed to by Gladstone. The khedive must be supported and the Control upheld. What was not announced was the equally emphatic conviction of the two governments that landing an army in Egypt for this purpose would defeat its own object. Freycinet could not move because the Chamber was opposed, and so an invasion would hand Egypt to the British on a plate. Gladstone's cabinet too was in a dilemma. Intervening single-handed would mean a breach with France. A joint invervention would give France a half-share in the route to the East. Granville at the Foreign Office listed the objections: 'Opposition of Egyptians; of Turkey; jealousy of Europe; responsibility of governing a country of Orientals without adequate means and under adverse circumstances; presumption that France would object as much to our sole occupation as we should object to theirs.' The official case against going into Egypt was overwhelming. As Disraeli had said, 'Constantinople [was still] the key to India, not Cairo and the Canal'. At few times in the century had Anglo-French rivalry in the Mediterranean been so composed. Added to that, the late-Victorian pessimism about the possibilities of making English gentlemen of 'Orientals' made another strong argument against conquering new Indias. All the plans therefore were for staying out and solving the problem from outside.

But effective as the arts of 'moral influence' had been hitherto in bending pashas and mandarins to European whims, they were to prove worse than useless against Arabists, Mahdists and Boxers whose mass defiance signalled the political awakenings of Islam and the Orient. Instead of sobering the colonels and saving the Control, the pressures of gunboat diplomacy and the European Concert only added to the charismatic appeal of Arabi, *el Misr*, the 'Egyptian'. The Anglo-French naval demonstration of June provoked a massacre of Europeans at Alexandria. This destroyed Arabi's credit with the English Liberals, and although the French squadron sailed away, Beauchamp Seymour was allowed to bombard the Alexandrian forts to show that Britain at least was in earnest. This old-fashioned device proved the critical blunder, the point of no return. Arabi proclaimed a *jihad* against the British, rioting spread to the interior. According to the dogmas of strategy, if Suez was in jeopardy, it must be protected at any cost. According to Anglo-Indian orthodoxy, the *jihad* challenged imperial prestige throughout the Muslim East. Hence for Gladstone's ministers, 'the question [was] no longer what form of intervention is... most unobjectionable, but in what form it can be most promptly applied'. No chance of French or international co-operation was left. But in applying their conventional routine of threat and bluff to cow the Egyptians, the British had raised the stakes so high that now they had to win by any means. On 16 August Sir Garnet Wolseley and the redcoats landed on the Canal for another small colonial war. They routed the Egyptian army at Tel el Kebir, imprisoned Arabi and reinstated Tewfik. Gladstone's government pledged its word that as soon as the Canal was safe and Tewfik strong, it would bring the troops home and leave the Egyptians 'to manage their own affairs'.

There is no doubt that this is what the Liberals meant to do. Like the French in Tunisia, they simply intended to restore the old security through influence without extending their rule. The expedition was to be a Palmerstonian stroke of the kind that had brought the Turk to reason in 1839–41, had chastened the Chinese in two Opium wars, the Ethiopians in 1869 and the Ashanti in 1874. Many months passed before they realised that, having rushed in, they could not rush out again; that they had achieved the occupation which above all they had wanted to avoid. By 1884 they had to confess privately that 'the theory on which we originally undertook [to go in]...however plausible, has completely broken down'. The models for intervention proved as outdated as the Crystal Palace. From start to finish the British had miscalculated. They had gone to restore the *status quo ante Arabi*, and discovered that it no longer existed. They had come to restore a khedive and found him a cypher without the authority of British bayonets. And so they had gone in and they could not get out.

What first opened their eyes was another crisis in Africa. After Mehemet Ali had conquered the eastern Sudan for Egypt, the khedive Ismail had laid heavy tribute upon its people. At the same time, he had put down the slave trade, thus depriving them of their chief means of staving off the tax-collector or his bastinado. He had employed white governors to impose Christian ethics on his Muslim subjects. Detesting the imperialism of Cairo, the Sudanese struck back at the Egyptians once they had been disarmed by revolution and invasion. As so often in Muslim Africa, the liberation movement took the form of a puritan revolution against the religious latitudinarianism of the foreign ruling class. In 1881 the Mahdi, Mohammed Ahmad, began his preaching and the revivalist Dervish orders forged the politically discontented sheikhs and deposed sultans, slave traders and tribes, into an army and a state. At first the implications of the *Mahdia* were hidden from the British in Egypt behind a curtain of sands, until news came in November 1883 that the Mahdists had cut the Egyptian troops in the Sudan to pieces. Without soldiers or money, Tewfik could not hold Khartoum. There was no resistance left between the Mahdi and Wadi Halfa. Just as the British were handing back Tewfik a much qualified independence and withdrawing their troops from Cairo, the Mahdi's advance compelled them to stand in defence of the frontiers of Lower Egypt. At last the sinister truth dawned in London. As ministers complained: 'we have now been forced into the position of being the protectors of Egypt'. As with Arabi, so with the Mahdi, there was no chance of striking a bargain of the old mid-Victorian sort. Against fierce Egyptian opposition Gladstone ordered Tewfik to abandon the Sudan and stop the drain on his exchequer, while Gordon was sent to his death at Khartoum attempting the impossible. In enforcing the abandonment, Baring practically had to take control of the khedivial government and, the tighter he gripped it, the deeper the British became involved in its financial difficulties. By this time the unpopularity of the Egyptian fiasco matched that of the Tunisian affair in France. It was increasingly clear that Gladstone's ministry had made fools of themselves. They had hoped to set up an independent Egyptian government; but hampered by the *Mahdia*, the loss of the Sudan, the bankruptcy and the Control's unpopularity with the proto-nationalists, they found no Egyptian collaborators to whom they could transfer power with safety. Nor could they retire so long as the infuriated French refused to admit the exclusive paramountcy in Cairo which they claimed as their due reward. For if they left, the French would upset their influence, or the Egyptian nationalists or Sudanese invaders might upset the financial settlement, and all the dangers of the Suez crisis would arise again.

In the event, the *Mahdia* had trapped the British in Egypt in much the same way as the southern rising had caught the French in Tunisia. No sooner did a European power set its foot upon the neck of the Ottoman rulers of the coastal cities than the nomads of the inland steppes and deserts seized their chance of throwing off the pashas' yoke. Hence the Europeans found the regimes which they had come to discipline or restore falling about their ears and they had to stay and pick up the pieces. Gladstone wearily summed up the result of dealing as if they were politically uninhabited with an Egypt in revolution and a Sudan in religious revival: 'we have done our Egyptian business; we are an Egyptian government.'

The longer the British garrisons remained, the stronger grew the arguments for staying. By 1889 the 'veiled protectorate' had become a necessity for imperial security in the world. As Salisbury said, 'the appetite had grown with the eating'. Sir Evelyn Baring and the Anglo-Indian officials who governed in the name of the khedive, brought from Calcutta to the Nile their professional distrust of nationalists. It became inconceivable that the Egyptians could be trusted to govern themselves. Arabist sentiment still smouldered. In taking over the country, the English had stopped its politics in a state of betwixt and between. Its obsolete Turkish rulers had fallen, but its rising liberal leaders had been put down. So Baring had to rule until native authority revived, but native authority could hardly revive while Baring ruled. If evacuation was impossible for internal reasons, it soon became impracticable on external grounds. Eventually the occupation drove France into the arms of Russia; and this combined menace in the Mediterranean, together with the further crumbling of Turkish power, enhanced Egypt's importance to Britain. After 1889 therefore, the resolution was to stay and keep the lid on the simmering revolution, rather than withdraw and invite another power to straddle the road to India. Henceforth England's statesmen were to be bewitched with the far-fetched fancies of the Nile-valley strategy. To be sure of the canal and lower Egypt, they were to push their territorial claims up the Nile to Fashoda and from the Indian Ocean to Uganda and the Bahr-al-Ghazal.

On an Olympian view, the taking of Egypt might seem to have been the logical outcome of two great movements of European expansion since the end of the eighteenth century. One was the long build-up of British trade and power in the East; the other was the extension of Anglo-French influence which had so thoroughly disrupted Ottoman rule in Egypt and the Levant that the routes to the East were no longer safe. Certainly this long-term logic set limits to the problem. But what determined the occupation of Egypt in concrete terms was not so much the secular processes of European expansion as the Arabist and Mahdist revolutions against its encroaching mastery. When they baffled the customary informal techniques of France and Britain, it was too late to find any other solution but conquest and rule.

The shots of Seymour at Alexandria and Wolseley at Tel el Kebir were to echo round the world. It transpired in the end that their *ricochets* had blown Africa into the modern age. The onslaught on Arabi opened the long Anglo-French conflict over Egypt which more than anything brought on the division of East and West Africa. Up to the 1890's it was merely a partition on paper. The politicians in the European capitals at least intended it to go no farther than that. Hitherto they had ignored the clamour of their merchants, missionaries and explorers for advances in tropical Africa. They had done so with good reason. Communications were difficult; the tribes of the hinterlands seemed lost in chaos; there were grave doubts whether the African could be persuaded to work, or whether he could work at anything worth producing; prospects of trade or revenue seemed gloomy indeed. If governments had sometimes bestirred themselves to help private traders and sent frigates along the coasts to atone for the sins of the slave trade, such acts were not intended as commitments. Since large or stable authorities were few and far between, even the simplest methods of informal expansion worked badly in tropical Africa. Clearly then, this was no place for colonies. For decades before 1882, therefore, a gentlemen's agreement between the powers saw to it that the petty quarrels of their merchants and officials on the coasts did not become pretexts for empire.

But when Gladstone stumbled into Egypt that era ended. To the French, the veiled protectorate was the worst humiliation since Sedan. Their canal and the country which they had nursed since Napoleon's landing had been snatched away under their very noses. This broke the Liberal *entente* and kept Britain and France at odds for twenty years. Once in Egypt, moreover, Britain became highly vulnerable to continental diplomacy. To set Egyptian finances in order, she needed German support against French vetoes in the Debt Commission, if her ministers were to avoid asking their critical Parliament to subsidise the khedive. By altering European alignments thus, the Egyptian occupation for the rest of the century gave the powers both incentive and opportunity to break the traditional understandings about tropical Africa. While Baring played the puppet-master in Cairo, the French sought to force him out by loosing their pro-consuls against exposed British interests in unclaimed Africa; while the Germans did likewise to extort more British aid in their European affairs. Once the powers began to back their nationals' private enterprises for diplomatic purposes, commerce south of the Sahara ceased to be a matter of restricted influence over coasts; it became a business of unlimited territorial claims over vast hinterlands. In this roundabout fashion, Arabi's revolution and Gladstone's blunder exaggerated the importance of intrinsically tiny disputes in tropical Africa and brought the diplomatists to the auction rooms.

On the western coasts before October 1882 there were few signs that the *modus vivendi* was to end so abruptly. Wars between producers and middlemen chiefs along the unpacified lines of supply were strangling the British and French trading stations on the Bight of Benin. For twenty years past, the Colonial Office had been thinking of giving up the Gambia, the Gold Coast, Lagos and Sierra Leone. The French government had left the Ivory Coast and in 1880 it was thinking of moving out of Dahomey and Gabon 'because of the trivial scale of French interests there'.[1] With the turmoil in the hinterlands, the unofficial *pax* rigged up by the palm-oil traders was ceasing to work; but London and Paris refused to replace it with the extravagant order of colonial rule.

The only regions where Europeans had broken through the middlemen chiefs who closed all ways inland, had been along the three great rivers. On the Senegal by 1865 General Faidherbe had carried French influence up-river to Kayes. Sixteen years later their men in the field had visions of going on to bring the formidable Muslim states of the western Sudan under their sway and of building a trans-Saharan railway between Senegal and Algeria. This scheme went back into a pigeon-hole. In 1881, however, an Upper Senegal Command was formed and Colonel Borgnis-Desbordes was instructed to throw a chain of posts from Bafoulabe to Bamako on the Upper Niger. But as soon as the soldiers ran into trouble, the politicians of Paris cut their credits and talked of scrapping the command. The statesmen in London and Paris refused to quarrel about this expansion of Senegal which pointed no threat to the chief centre of British trade three thousand kilometres away on the Lower Niger.

Nor were there the makings of a West African 'scramble' here, where Liverpool merchants throve without the aid of colonial government. By 1881 George Goldie had amalgamated the most enterprising of the Niger firms into the National Africa Company, the better to monopolise the up-river traffic and drive out French competitors. This was Anglo-French rivalry of a sort, but only at the level of private traders cutting each others' throats in the ordinary way of business. So long as the Anglo-French *entente* lasted, their governments had no wish to become involved, as Goldie discovered when he was refused a royal charter for his company. They were as uninterested in the merchants and explorers jostling in the no-man's-land along the Congo river. Disraeli's ministers had rejected the Cameron treaties which offered them a political option on the inner basin. Leopold II of the Belgians was to be more reckless. Under cover of the International African Association which he floated in 1876, this inveterate projector was plotting a private Congo empire under the innocent device of a free state. In 1879 Stanley went out to establish its claims. To preserve a hinterland for its poverty-stricken posts on the Gabon, the French government asked Brazza to pick up counter-treaties that would 'reserve our rights without engaging the future'. All this was but the small change of local rivalry that had gone on for decades. Brazza's was a private venture of passing interest to his government. Leopold's Congo scheme had as little chance of being realised as a dozen others he

[1] Minister of Marine to Foreign Minister, 6 January 1874, A.E., Mémoires et Documents, Afrique (henceforth, A.E.M.D.), 58. Foreign Minister to Minister of Marine, 31 January 1880, A.E.M.D. Afrique, 77.

had hatched for concessions in China, the Philippines, Borneo and the Transvaal. The Belgian government would have nothing to do with it. Nor, as the king admitted, would investors subscribe a centime until the powers recognised his rights in the Congo. But what was the chance that they would then be so generous as to endow his house with a great estate which he was too puny to seize for himself? As long as France and Britain could agree, his hopes of becoming an African emperor were exceedingly thin.

But immediately the British ejected the French from the Dual Control in October 1882, these minor intrigues in West Africa were drawn into their quarrel over Egypt. In Paris there was less talk of jettisoning outposts and more speculation about extending claims to strengthen the diplomatic hand against the English. Treich Laplène was allowed to expand French influence on the Ivory Coast. More important, the French consul on the Lower Niger started a flurry of treaty-making, menacing the chief British trade on the coast. Early in 1883 Granville tried to renew the old self-denial arrangements by offering the French exclusive influence on the Upper Niger if they would respect the *status quo* on the lower river. But the time for such happy understandings had gone. As the ambassador reported, the breaking of the Egyptian gentlemen's-agreement had so outraged the French that a West African standstill was now out of the question. So by November the Foreign Office could see nothing for it but to send out consul Hewett to bring the Niger districts under treaties of protection and 'prevent the possibility of our trade there being interfered with'. His sailing was delayed for six months. Neither the Treasury nor the Liverpool traders could be persuaded to pay his fare!

At the same time, the Anglo-French estrangement overturned the hands-off arrangements on the Congo. Paris scorned Granville's efforts to renew them. In November 1882 the Chamber ratified Brazza's treaty of claim to the right bank of the river instead. A month later, Granville countered by accepting Portugal's ancient claims to the Congo in return for guarantees of free trade. To the French this treaty seemed West African insult added to Egyptian injury; 'a security taken by Britain to prevent France...from setting foot in the Congo Delta'; a violation of an undertaking that went back to 1786. In riposte, Ferry mounted a diplomatic onslaught against the Anglo-Portuguese agreement. Once she had obtained a pre-emptive right over Leopold's holdings, France pressed the counterclaims of the Congo Free State as if they were already her own. At the end of March 1884 the most powerful statesman in Europe took a hand. His own metaphor for it was much more revealing: he would take up his 'Egyptian baton'.

With Egypt dividing them, France and Britain both courted German favour; Granville needed Bismarck's help to extricate his government from their financial troubles in Cairo; while Ferry solicited it in resisting the Anglo-Portuguese Treaty and English ambitions in Egypt—'a consideration which dominated all others' in Paris. The Chancellor could sell his support to the highest bidder; or if need be, he could encourage the weaker contender against the stronger, and so keep the Egyptian issue from being settled. In any case there would be something for Germany; Heligoland might be recovered from England; a number of colonial trifles could certainly be picked up; better still, an isolated France might be diverted from allying with Russia or rejoining Britain into a healing *rapprochement* with the conquerors of Alsace-Lorraine. In March Bismarck began to try out these ideas. He hinted at German help for France if she pressed her rights in Egypt. But Ferry, suspecting that Bismarck did 'not want to do anything to annoy England, but...[would] be delighted to see her opposed by others, especially by [France], negotiated an Egyptian agreement with Britain. In June the English were promising to evacuate the country in 1888, if the French would agree to neutralise it on Belgian lines thereafter.

With the Egyptian baton falling from his grasp, it was time for Bismarck to stiffen the French with offers of German support, if they would raise their terms to Granville. Time also to remove Ferry's suspicions by proving that Germany had serious reasons of her own to act with France against Britain. There were none in Egypt, as the Chancellor had often declared. So for verisimilitude, he blew the petty Anglo-German trade disputes around the African coasts into a noisy anti-British demonstration. In May he pressed the German government's protection over Lüderitz's concession at Angra Pequena, on the barren south-west coast of Africa. A month later, he denounced the Anglo-Portuguese Treaty and demanded an international conference to decide the Congo's future. At the beginning of July he proclaimed Togoland and the Cameroons to be German protectorates. There was no popular cry for African colonies inside the Reich; and as Bismarck always insisted, he himself was 'against colonies...which install officials and erect garrisons'. But paper claims to protectorates cost nothing, and they were good bait to draw France away from Britain into an *entente* with Germany. Surprisingly, this devious diplomacy succeeded. At the London Conference of July, Bismarck, together with the French Chamber and bondholders, contrived to wreck the Anglo-French agreement over Egypt. To drive the wedge home, he proposed a Franco-German *entente* on West African questions. In August the French accepted. 'After the bad treatment inflicted on us by England', wrote de Courcel, 'this *rapprochement* is essential to us under penalty of utter and most dangerous isolation.' To show good faith, the Germans joined France in backing Leopold's Congo Free State. By October 1884 the two powers had agreed to settle the fate of the Niger as well as the Congo at an international conference in Berlin; and the British, who had conceded all Bismarck's African claims and dropped the Portuguese treaty lest 'a breach with Germany...make our chances of honourable extrication from the Egyptian difficulty even less than they are', were compelled to attend.

To strengthen their governments' hands in the coming negotiations, consuls and merchants were now treaty-making wherever they hoped to trade on the west coast. Astonished ministers in London observed that 'the attention of European Powers is directed to an unprecedented extent to...the formation of Settlements on the African coast'. Forestalled by Nachtigal in the Cameroons, Hewett rushed around the Niger Delta bringing the chiefs under British protection to block the Germans and French there. On the Lower Niger, Goldie bought out the *Compagnie du Sénégal* and the *Société française de l'Afrique Equatoriale*, and sent Joseph Thomson to outrun a German expedition for treaties with the northern Nigerian emirates of Sokoto and Gandu. Meanwhile, the French, who had no great hopes of the Lower Niger, were advancing down the upper river from Bamako, occupied by Gallieni in 1883, and were extending their treaties along the Ivory and Slave Coasts. Governments had let the local expansionists off their leashes, now that the Egyptian occupation had merged territorial claims in Africa with power-politics in Europe. How high the symbolic importance of these trivial African clashes had risen was shown when the French and English went meekly to their little Canossa at Berlin. The two leading naval and colonial powers in the world were bidding for West African commerce under the hammer of a third-rate naval person who hitherto had had no colonies at all.

In strange contrast to the zealots on the coasts, the statesmen who met in Berlin at the end of 1884 found each other reasonably accommodating. The conference in fact was something of an anti-climax. Before it had ever met, it had served its main purposes. The Egyptian baton had thwacked Gladstone back into line. The Franco-German *entente* had been formed; and it had kept Granville from declaring a protectorate in Egypt and from taking exclusive charge of its finances. Toward the end of the meeting, indeed, Ferry and Granville were agreeing in the London Convention to pump an international loan into the Khedivate and to continue international control of its revenues. Though they were left pining for the British to leave Cairo, the French had at least prevented them from digging-in any deeper. Hence the West African disputes which had served as outer markers for these evolutions of grand diplomacy were easily dismissed in Berlin. And public opinion in Europe took scant notice of the manner of their going.

The diplomats dealt briskly enough with the outstanding trivia. Who should be saddled with the responsibility for free trade and navigation on the Niger; and on the Congo? How little the powers cared, they showed by recognising the legal personality of the Congo Free State. It was Leopold's year for a miracle. The lions agreed to toss him the lion's share of the Congo basin, while contenting themselves with the scraps. Ferry took for France a much more modest sphere; the region around Brazzaville on the north bank was to be the Gabon's hinterland. For the rest, the Congo river was placed under an international regime and its conventional basin, covering most of Central Africa, became a free-trade area. Having conceded the Congo, Granville was able to keep international authority out of the Niger. Control of the lower river went to Britain, that of the upper river to France, arrangements which merely preserved the *status quo*. Though the Berlin Act laid it down that territorial claims on African coasts should depend on effective occupation, this magical phrase was left so vague that it meant almost nothing.

Far from laying down ground rules for the occupation of Africa, the statesmen at Berlin had no intention of playing that game. Despising colonial ventures in tropical Africa, they had extended their hands-off arrangements largely in order to avoid it. The last thing they wanted was to commit themselves to administering such comparatively unimportant places. Once these countries had been saved from foreign clutches by adjusting their international status, the diplomats planned to wash their hands of them. Except in the Cameroons and Togoland, where the traders refused such gifts, Bismarck gave over his paper protectorates to the Germans trafficking in them. The British hastened to do the same with the Lower Niger. In June 1886 Goldie at last got his monopoly chartered under the title of the Royal Niger Company; this was 'the cheapest...way of meeting' the obligations accepted at the Berlin Conference. Until 1891 the Foreign Office hoped to saddle the Liverpool firms with the governance of the Niger Delta, just as it had fobbed on to Goldie the costs of administering the lower river. But these merchants refused the privilege. There was nothing for it but to put the Niger Coast protectorate squarely under the rule of London. Throughout the British attitude to the Niger had been negative: 'so long as we keep other European nations out, we need not be in a hurry to go in.' Whatever this dictum rings of, it does not sound like imperialism.

The politicians of Paris were equally averse to colonising their new spheres. True, Ferry was saying by 1885 that France must have colonies for all the usual reasons—investment, markets, prestige, the civilising mission—but he had been swept out of office in March by the critics of his colonial adventures: the Freycinet who had followed him in office did not wish to follow him out again. Plainly, the French Congo was a new white elephant. The Gabon was an old one. The French government treated both of them with scorn. In 1887 it stopped its annual subsidy to the Gabon[1] and loftily warned Brazza, the administrator of the Congo, that 'we cannot stay indefinitely in a period of costly exploration'.[2] Until the 1890's there

---

[1] Head of West African Mission to Décazes, 19 October 1885, 25 March 1886, Archives du Gouvernement-Général, Afrique Équatoriale Française (henceforth A.E.F.), 2 B, 28.

[2] Freycinet to Brazza, 12 April 1886, A.E.M.D., Afrique, 94.

were only fifteen French officials in the region. Its annual export was only worth £1500.[1] Paris was no less sceptical about its possessions in the Gulf of Benin. All the Quai d'Orsay could find to say in their favour was that 'even if we admit that they are of small value...[they] are bargaining counters which...may be useful for our interests elsewhere'. The heads of the Ministry of Marine 'show[ed] themselves very lukewarm, not merely to the development, but to the maintenance pure and simple of the French holdings in West Africa'.[2] On the Upper Niger too, they felt no enthusiasm for turning their sphere into a full-blown colony. At the Berlin Conference, neutralisation of the river and free trade along its entire course had been the most they had wanted.[3] But when the British made the Niger Company the monopolists of free trade on the lower river, they may have fooled themselves, but they did not fool the French. The glaring paradox behind this goaded Freycinet into declaring a protectorate over the Upper Niger in 1887 to forestall an extension of so bizarre a theory of free trade.[4] Politically, he meant to go no farther than a vague network of alliances with the Muslim rulers of the area, and early in 1887 Galliéni signed treaties with Amadu Shehu and Samori, by far the most powerful of them. His agreements did not commit France, he explained, neither would they cost her anything. They were simply meant 'to enlarge the limits of our future commercial empire and to close these regions to foreign designs'. Trade was supposed to bind these Muslim states to France:[5] but there was not enough of it. 'It is only retail business,' Galliéni's successor reported, 'the means of transport are lacking for anything larger.'[6] All that Paris had envisaged on the Upper Niger was a small, cheap and conditional option on the region.

If the diplomats and commercial travellers after the Berlin Conference had been deciding these West African affairs on their merits, things would have gone no farther than that. But as usual they had reckoned with an Africa without the Africans. So their intentions were one thing; the outcome on the spot was another. Driven on by the Egyptian crisis, the West African 'scramble' could no longer be halted at will. The old stand-still arrangements could no longer stand. In the end, even paper protectorates were to perform that special alchemy which makes one people regard the remote lands of others as 'possessions' and itself as responsible for their well-being. But it was not working strongly yet; imperial sentiment in Europe was the least of the reasons for the

[1] Memo. no. 70, 24 January 1890, A.E.F., Rapports sur la Situation Intérieure, October 1886–February 1890.

[2] Foreign Ministry memo., 15 April 1887, A.E.M.D., Afrique, 83.

[3] Memo. by Services des Colonies, 17 July 1885, Archives de Ministère de la France d'Outre Mer (henceforth M.F.O.M.), Afrique, IV, 12 B.

[4] Under-Secretary of Colonies to Freycinet, 1 March 1886, M.F.O.M., Sénégal, IV, 84.

[5] Memo. by Galliéni, 24 September 1887, M.F.O.M., Sénégal, IV, 90; Galliéni to Under-Secretary for Colonies, 30 July 1887, ibid.

[6] Memo. by Archinard, 19 August 1889, M.F.O.M., Sénégal, IV, 93 A.

scramble. They are rather to be found in West Africa itself. The diplomatic flurry had compelled governments to back their traders' efforts to break through the middlemen chiefs and trade up-country. So a rivalry for commercial options was spreading as a result from the coast to the interior, with every port competing against its neighbours for a hinterland and its officials plunging deeper into the politics of the African bush. Even so, most of the powers held these local tendencies in check. Germany ceased to extend her claims once the diplomatic manœuvres of 1884 and 1885 had been completed, content to take diplomatic advantage of the Anglo-French dissension to improve her position in Europe. No more ambitious were the British, on the west coast at least. Not only were they wary of going too far in their dealings with powerful Muslims in the backlands, they parsimoniously reined back all advances until local trade and colonial revenue had developed sufficiently to pay for them. What they had on the Niger, they held; but elsewhere the English usually let West Africa go.

It was to the French that it went. For the next fifteen years they made all the running in the western parts of the continent; but not altogether by choice. It would be puerile to argue that they were driven on by a search for glory—most Frenchmen had no idea of the whereabouts of Bafoulabe. Admittedly, the established influence of the military in their colonial affairs made the politicians prone to give their army in Africa its head. But what necessitated their headlong conquest of the middle Niger, the northern Ivory Coast and the western Sudan after 1887 was a series of involuntary imbroglios with the fighting Muslim theocracies of these regions. The hapless policy-makers of Paris had designed no more than a vague paramountcy over them. It was bad luck that, like the Egyptians, the Mahdists and southern Tunisians, the theocrats preferred the *jihad* to working with the French and so dragged them into vast imperial conquests instead. The paper partition had set the French army to grips with a reviving and recalcitrant Islam. In subjugating it, the paper empire had to be occupied.

In the history of Africa, the long expansion of Islam since the eighth century dwarfs the brief influence of Europe. From this western Sudan between the Senegal and Lake Tchad, between the coastal forests and the Sahara, the puritanic Almoravides had set forth to rule over Spain and the Maghreb. Here the golden empires of Mali and Ghana had risen and fallen; here Muslims and animists had struggled for centuries. Yet the difficulty of assimilating tribes into nations had foiled the making of enduring states. By the seventeenth century, Islam here was at best the cult of aristocracies lording it over a mass of pagan subjects. But from the later eighteenth century, the creed was on the march once more. United by the spread of Muslim brotherhoods with their calls for religious reform, the Tokolor and Fulani peoples rose in holy war upon their decadent Muslim rulers, riveting new empires upon the animists. At the end of the nineteenth century, when the British bumped into them in what is now northern Nigeria, their force was spent, and the Fulani emirs who had inherited the disunited provinces of the Sokoto empire were unable to resist British suzerainty. But the French had no such luck with the Tokolor and Manding empires to the west. By 1864 El Hadj Omar at the head of the *Tijani* order had brought the western Sudan from Futa to Timbuktu under his sway. When the French confronted this empire, Amadu Shehu, his successor, was imposing conformity to his version of Islam, and so overcoming the cleavage between rulers and ruled to forge a unified power. It was in the nature of such empires, founded in holy war, bound together by theocracy and the brotherhood of all believers, that their commanders could no longer command if they co-operated with a Christian power. Amadu and Samori were the prisoners of their own systems of leadership, unable to work their treaties with France without destroying their own authority. Both chose to fight rather than to abdicate. By 1889 Paris found out that Galliéni's loose protectorate meant a far-reaching military conquest.

All the traditions of the Ministry of Marine were against it. 'It is the negation of all our policy', the governor protested, '. . .it means starting a holy war...poor Senegal.'[1] But covered by Étienne, the Algerian Under-Secretary for Colonies, the local army commanders seized their chance.[2] In 1890 Colonel Archinard broke the power of Amadu. Thenceforward protests from Paris could not stop the sand-table thinkers of the Upper Senegal Command from encompassing and crushing the embattled Muslim aristocracies one by one. In 'absolute violation of orders',[3] Archinard next invaded Samori's empire. For the next eight years that potentate and his mobile, Sofa hordes kept the French army in hot pursuit from the Upper Niger to the Ivory Coast. Grappling with him and other disaffected Muslim leaders, the French were to end by occupying the entire western Sudan. Having gone so far against their will in the 1880's, logic brought them to rationalise these haphazard conquests in the 1890's. French Africa was to be all of a piece; Senegal and Algeria to be joined with the hinterlands of the Guinea, Ivory and Dahoman coasts; these in their turn to be linked with the French Congo at the shores of Lake Tchad.

For the most part, the British looked on and acquiesced. As Salisbury put it ironically, 'Great Britain has adopted the policy of advance by commercial enterprise. She has not attempted to compete with the military operations of her neighbour.' Her priority in Africa lay in protecting the position in Egypt and, from 1889, in closing off the Nile valley for this purpose. In hope of damping down the Egyptian quarrel, Salisbury saw no harm in offering another round of West African compensations to France

---

[1] Vallon to Under-Secretary for Colonies, 22 March 1890, M.F.O.M., Sénégal, IV, 95 C.
[2] Memo. by Archinard, 19 August, 1889, M.F.O.M., Sénégal, IV, 93 A.
[3] Étienne to Governor of Senegal, 14 April 1891, M.F.O.M., Sénégal, 91 B.

between 1889 and 1891. This vicarious generosity cost nothing either to give or to take, so Paris accepted it. The Gambian hinterland was signed away to French Senegal; that of Sierra Leone to French Guinea. But it was the Convention of August 1890 that gave the French their largest windfall; and once again the Egyptian priorities of the British shook the tree. To compensate Paris for the Heligoland–Zanzibar Treaty of 1890, in which the Germans gave him a free hand at Zanzibar and over the Nile, Salisbury cheerfully consigned to France the 'light soils' of the Sahara and the western Sudan between Algeria, Senegal and the Say–Barruwa line resting on Lake Tchad. This enormous paper concession of other people's countries the Quai d'Orsay accepted with the same irony with which it was given: 'Without any appreciable effort, without any large sacrifice, without the expense of exploration..., without having made a single treaty...we have induced Britain to recognise...that Algeria and Senegal shall form a continuous belt of territory....Political access to Lake Tchad *seems* important....It may become the nodal point for trade routes.... But in striving to extend our activity towards central Africa, there is a more important consideration, bound up with more pressing and concrete interests. We want to get it recognised once and for all that no European nation can ever resist our influence in the Sahara and that we shall never be taken in the rear in Algeria.'[1] For the colonial zealots, there may have been enchantment in such a view. But for the technicians of national security these large but unconsidered trifles were worth picking up only so far as they improved French security in North Africa, and so in the Mediterranean. Like their counterparts in London, it was not so much a new empire as the future of their old interests in Europe and the East that they were seeking in Africa. For the French this meant security in Algeria's hinterland. But it also meant security in Egypt. So Salisbury's bargains could not end the scramble for Africa. France would take all she could get in the west. But she could not afford thereby to be appeased along the Nile.

On the east coast, the Egyptian occupation had also shattered the old *modus vivendi*. Up to 1884 naval power had given Britain the leading influence from Port Natal to Cape Guardafui—an influence exerted through the puppet sultan of Zanzibar, partly to keep other powers off the flank of the route to India, chiefly to put down the Arab slave trade. Unlike West Africa, the east coast had no large states on the mainland. Neither was there any large trade. Ivory was hauled by slaves, cloves were grown by slaves, caravans were stocked with slaves; commerce of this sort had fallen foul of European prejudices and it was being snuffed out. In doing this the powers kept on good terms with each other. In 1862 the British

---

[1] Foreign Ministry memo., 'Considérations sur le projet d'arrangement franco-anglais', 13 August 1890, A.É.M.D., Afrique, 129.

and French had made one of their gentlemen's agreements to respect the sultan's independence. True, his regime was failing. Europe had used him to impose the anti-slavery ethics of Christendom upon his Muslim subjects, and this was over-stretching his authority as their religious head. Yet no government wanted a colony where there was so little to colonise. In 1878 the Foreign Office had refused to back the shipowner William Mackinnon in developing a concession of Zanzibar's mainland possessions. Four years later it turned a deaf ear to the sultan's pleas for what amounted to a British protectorate. London and Bombay considered that this would call for expenditure 'out of all proportion to the advantages to be gained'. Towards the end of 1884 Karl Peters could tout his blank treaty forms around Tanganyika acting as commercial traveller for the struggling *Kolonialverein*; yet Gladstone's ministry would not hear of a Kilimanjaro protectorate.

But in February 1885 a new factor upset this equilibrium. Bismarck recognised the agreements of Peters—the man he had previously called a mountebank. As the Berlin West African Conference was disbanding, the Chancellor rigged up a paper protectorate for the German East Africa Company. Britain and France were reaching agreement on Egypt's finances. The time had come to pick another small African quarrel with Granville and to give another boost to the *entente* with France. Once again the Egyptian baton did its work. London accepted Bismarck's claims and bade the sultan of Zanzibar do the same. As Gladstone put it: 'it is really impossible to exaggerate the importance of *getting out of the way the bar to the Egyptian settlement*...[and] wind[ing] up at once these small colonial controversies.' Just the same, the Indian and Foreign Offices did not wish to be ousted from the entire coast, for the harbours at Mombasa and Zanzibar had some bearing on the security of India. The upshot was another paper partition. In their East African agreement of October 1886, Salisbury and Bismarck divided the mainland, giving the northern sphere to Britain, the southern to Germany. But the governments meant to keep out of the lands they had earmarked. Here at last was Mackinnon's chance. London chartered his British East Africa Company, so as to put a sentry on its claim; to the south Berlin placed the German company in possession.

These paper insurances, casually fobbed off on traders, left the old political hands elegantly bored. Granville and Derby agreed that 'there [was] something absurd in the scramble for colonies'. They were 'little disposed to join in it'. Gladstone welcomed Germany's protectorates. Salisbury did not mind either, so long as they guaranteed free trade. German support in Cairo and Constantinople was cheap at the price. In Berlin and Paris the statesmen were taking their new possessions just as lightly. But here, as in West Africa, they were committing themselves to more than they bargained for. By 1889 the German company was at war with Bushiri and the Swahili slaving chiefs; and the Berlin government had to rescue and replace its penniless caretaker so as to save face. Mackinnon's company was heading for ruin as well, so little did British investors value the attractions of East Africa. This was far more serious. By this time, the hinterland of the British sphere had become entangled with the security of the Nile valley and Salisbury's plans for the safety of India in Egypt.

Baring's failure to come to terms with Egyptian nationalists was partly responsible for this far-fetched design. The continuing occupation had directly shifted the Mediterranean balance. In 1887 Salisbury had sent Drummond Wolff to Constantinople to make what was probably his last serious offer to evacuate the Nile Delta. The troops would sail away within three years if the powers would agree that they could sail back again in case of need. The Porte accepted. But French and Russian diplomacy combined to wreck the agreement. Salisbury pondered the meaning of this debacle. British influence at Constantinople was not what it had been. Plainly the chances of patching up and packing up in Egypt had dwindled since 1885. Despite Bismarck's manœuvres, France was now moving out of isolation and into the *Franco-Russe* toward the end of the 1880's. Worse still, Salisbury found that there were not enough ironclads to fight their way through the Mediterranean against such a combination. How then could the Turk be propped up against Russia? As the margin of security shrank at Constantinople, Salisbury saw the need of broadening it at Cairo. To be safe in Egypt he adopted the policy of keeping other powers out of the Nile basin. Fear lay behind this policy, the alarmist calculation that 'a civilised, European power...in the Nile valley...could so reduce the water supply as to ruin [Egypt]'. So from 1890 the British ran up their bids, claiming a sphere along the whole river and its approaches, from Mombasa and Wadi Halfa to Lake Victoria Nyanza. To gain as much as this, they were ready to tout compensations over most of the continent. As the British pivot began to swing from the Asiatic to the African shores of the eastern Mediterranean, the second phase of partition spread from Uganda and Ethiopia to the Zambezi river, from the Red Sea to the Upper Niger. By 1891 there was little more of Africa left to divide. The partition was all over, bar the ultimatums.

Without much cavil, Berlin agreed to stay out of the Nile basin. Haunted by her nightmare of coalitions, Germany was more trapped by European circumstances than any other of the partitioners. In March 1890 William II and Caprivi had decided to abandon the Reinsurance Treaty with Russia. They made no difficulty about scrapping many of their options in East Africa in return for a visible *rapprochement* with Britain in Europe. Gaining Heligoland and the extension of their sphere from Dar-es-Salaam westward to Lake Tanganyika and the northern end of Lake Nyasa, they agreed to a formal British protectorate over Zanzibar; they gave up their claims to Witu, which would otherwise have blocked British access to Lake Victoria from Mombasa; and they cut back their claims in the north, so conceding Uganda to the British and shutting themselves out of the Upper Nile valley. For Salisbury, things could not have been better. 'The effect of this [Heligoland-Zanzibar] arrangement', he congratulated himself, 'will be that...there will be no European competitor to British influence between the 1st degree of S[outh] latitude [running through the middle of Lake Victoria] and the borders of Egypt.' On paper, at least, his chief purpose had been achieved. This entailed scrapping Rhodes's romantic idea of a Cape-to-Cairo corridor between the Congo Free State and German East Africa. But Salisbury was no romantic. And in any case he had also cleared all German obstacles out of the way of the British South Africa Company's advance into what is now Rhodesia. After Berlin, he dealt with Lisbon. By the Anglo-Portuguese Treaty of 1891, Salisbury threw back the musty claims of Moçambique in Matabeleland to secure the company's claim there. This was partition with a vengeance. But Salisbury had not finished yet. Next it was the turn of the Italians.

No European nation had moved into Africa with less authority or less enthusiasm than they. In 1882 their government had bought the Bay of Assab from an Italian firm; three years later it had occupied the Red Sea port of Massawa with British encouragement. Better the Italians than the French or the Mahdists. This brought the new Romans into contact with the Ethiopians. Questioned about the possibilities of the new sphere two years later, di Robilant, the Foreign Minister, refused 'to attach much importance to a few robbers who happen to be raising dust around our feet in Africa'. But things were to be different. The old system of ministries living on the freedom-fighting of the *Risorgimento* gave way to a confusion that Francesco Crispi contrived to dominate from 1887 to 1896. Before he came to office he had opposed imperialism. After the old Redshirt had reached the head of the regime of which he had once been the critic, he had to find a new field for his extremism. He found it in African expansion. For successful radicals this was not unusual at the end of the century. The new brand of full-blooded imperialism was occasionally the resort of *arrivistes* moving from left to right; for in joining the old oligarchs, they gave up much of their former domestic stock-in-trade. Chamberlain forgot about his unauthorised programme; Gambetta's heirs turned their backs on the *nouvelles couches*: Crispi passed laws against the socialists. As the least disturbing issue for the transitional ministries to which they belonged, they were all permitted to express overseas the nonconformism they had to muffle at home.

The empty wharves of Massawa gave Crispi his chance for originality. Without a hinterland they would continue to crumble. To avenge the Italian defeat at Dogali at the hands of the Ethiopian Ras Alula, Crispi launched a punitive expedition whose gains were organised into the colony of Eritrea in 1890. More than that, he embarked upon a design for informal paramountcy over Ethiopia. It was full of conundrums, but when the negus Yohannes was killed in battle with the Mahdists in 1889, the Italians imagined that their erstwhile protégé, Menilek, Ras of Shoa, would continue to be their man as negus. He seemed to be a westerniser. He looked like a client. By the treaty of Ucciali, signed on 2 May, Rome claimed that he had accepted its protection; Menilek denied it—after taking delivery of the four million lire and thousands of rifles with which the Italians had endowed him. For the moment, Eritrea seemed to have a bright future of trade with Ethiopia. A year later the di Rudini ministry in pursuit of more trade pushed their colony's frontier westwards to Kassala, which lies on a tributary of the Nile, flush inside the Dervish country.

Fecklessly, the Italians were being drawn into the dangerous vortices of Dervish and Ethiopian politics, as the British had been drawn into those of Egypt, and the French into those of Tunis and the western Sudan. They were rushing in to meddle with two African societies ferociously united through a species of proto-nationalism against the unbelievers; but their catastrophe was yet to come. What concerned Salisbury and Baring in 1890 was that these Roman inroads into Ethiopia and the eastern Sudan had brought them closest to the sacred serpent of the Nile. Italian expansion into the realms of the King of Kings was not unwelcome in London. It had the merit of blocking any French advance on the Nile valley from the Red Sea ports of Djibouti and Obok. But the thrust on Kassala was a different story. Salisbury was not shutting the French and Germans out of the valley to let the Italians in. Early in 1891 therefore, he brought them to sign a treaty in which they agreed 'to keep their hands off the affluents of the Nile'; and rewarded them by recognising their claim to preponderance over much of the Horn of Africa.

By edging towards the Triple Alliance and signing away huge stretches of unoccupied Africa, Salisbury had bought safety in Egypt from the Germans and Italians. But it was not to be bought from the French. All the donations of 'light soils' in West Africa would not soothe them into letting bygones be bygones in Egypt. Instead of consenting to leave the Nile alone, Paris, with increasing support from St Petersburg, demanded evacuation. More and more firmly, London refused. Egypt was still the deep rift between France and Britain. The way to the Nile still lay open from the west. Hence the partition of Africa went furiously on into the 1890's.

It is familiar enough, the diplomacy which contrived the astonishing partitions of the 1880's; but the motives behind them are stranger than fiction. As they drew their new map of Africa by treaty, the statesmen of the great powers intended nothing so simple or so serious as the making of colonies there. There were traders and missionaries who clamoured for imperial aid for their enterprises; but it was not they, it was the politicians who decided: and the politicians had no time for the notion that state action should develop the tropics in the interest of national prosperity. Trade, and the political influence that went with it, might expand in Africa; or again it might not. In either case the statesmen were happy to leave the matter to private energies. For tropical Africa at the end of the nineteenth century this meant that next to nothing would be done, for private business was as yet utterly unready to do it. Then were 'claims for posterity' the objects? There is a grain of truth in this old view, but it was more a rationalisation after the event. As they sliced up more and more of the continent, the politicians found it easier to explain their actions in terms of new markets and civilising missions than in terms of the more sophisticated and less high-minded concepts on which their minds were privately running.

Those who presided over the partition saw it with a cold and detached view. It was not Africa itself which they saw; it was its bearing on their great concerns in Europe, the Mediterranean and the East. Their preoccupations were tangential to the continent to a degree possible only in the official mind. They acted upon their traditional concepts of national interests and dangers. They advanced, not the frontiers of trade or empire, but the frontiers of fear.

From a European point of view, the partition treaties are monuments to the flights of imagination of which official minds are capable, when dealing with a blank map of two-thirds of a continent. The strategists anticipated every contingency: the diplomats bargained for every farthing of advantage; while the geographers showed them the whereabouts of the places they were haggling over. From an African standpoint, the main result of their efforts was to change the international status of territory on paper. Turning *res nullius* into *res publica* made work for lawyers. It was to be a long time before it made work for Africans.

This perpetual fumbling for safety in the world at large drove the powers to claim spheres, to proclaim protectorates, to charter companies; but in almost all cases this was done with no purpose more positive than to keep out others whose presence could conceivably inconvenience a national interest, no matter how speculative or unlikely. So Bismarck had laid out a paper empire in 1884–5 mainly to make a Franco-German *entente* look plausible. Caprivi had added to it in 1890 to make an Anglo-German *rapprochement* feasible. So Gladstone had moved into Egypt to protect Suez; Salisbury had laid out the ground-plan of British East Africa to be safe in Egypt and Asia. In the main, British Africa was a gigantic footnote to the Indian empire; and much of the long struggle between France and the Muslims was an expensive pendant to her search for security in the Mediterranean. Perhaps the only serious empire-builders of the 1880's were Crispi and Leopold, and they merely snatched at the crumbs from the rich men's tables. For the rest, there was indeed a 'scramble in Africa'. But it was anything but a 'scramble for Africa'.

Yet if the procedures of the partition were diplomatic and European rivalries affected it, this is far from saying that it was caused chiefly by the workings of the European power balance. Had this been so, these new empires would have ended as they began—on paper. Anglo-French competition, which had given the Germans their chance in Africa, had sprung from the English fiascos with Egyptian revolutionaries and Mahdists; it was to quicken as these imbroglios merged into those of the French with the Muslims of the western Sudan and into those of the Italians with the Christian nationalists of Ethiopia. The European pretensions provoked new African resistances, and these compelled further European exertions. So the partition gained a new momentum. The quickening occupation of tropical Africa in the 1890's, as distinct from the paper partitions of the 1880's, was the double climax of two closely connected conflicts: on the one hand, the struggle between France and Britain for control of the Nile; on the other, the struggle between European, African, Christian and Muslim expansions for control of North and Central Africa. Having embarked so lightly on the African game, the rulers of Europe had now to take it seriously.

What was the nature of this continent into which Europe was spreading? If 'Africa' is merely a geographical expression, it is also a sociological shorthand for the bewildering variety of languages, religions and societies that occupy it. At one end of the scale in aptitude and achievement, the white men found peoples organised in minute segmentary groups, lacking any political authority at the centre, and finding their social cohesion in the unity of equals, not in the unity imposed by a hierarchy. These merged into a second type, the segmentary states where kingship had made little lasting impression upon the particularism of tribal kinships, where the forces of assimilation had been baffled. At the other end of this range came the sophisticated Muslim states and the military confederacies of the most dynamic Negro and Bantu nations. As the Europeans began to deal with Africa, they met trouble from societies of all these types. But their scuffles with the warriors of the segmentary systems have no great significance from the standpoint of the partition: for the rivalries of the kinships and tribes within them almost always provided collaborators, as well as rebels against alien control. But in the case of the organised African states things were very different. Their reception of the white man had a profound effect on the partition of the nineteenth century, just as it left a fiery legacy for the African nationalism of the twentieth.

They reacted in different ways. Some began by resisting, but went down before the first whiff of grape-shot, and have remained passive until only yesterday. Others accepted their new overlords only to rebel within a decade. Others again were flatly opposed to white influence in any shape or form, and were beaten down only after years of savage guerrillas. Yet there were other peoples who came easily to terms with the European, signing his treaty forms, reading his Bibles, trading with his storekeepers. How are these differences to be explained? What led Africans to bare the teeth or to smile a welcome, to come to school or to fight a war to the death? It depended perhaps upon the kind of unity they possessed and on the state of its repair.

From what little is known about it, African political history has shown an extremely high turn-over of regimes. Like the kingdoms of Europe in the Middle Ages, they were chronically short of reserve power at the centre against the overmighty subject and the turbulent priest. Much more than the medieval governments of Europe, they lacked the binding principles of political association which could assimilate conquered neighbours into loyal subjects. This seems to have been particularly true of animist Africa. An animist people, bound together by the web of kinship and by an ancestral religion, could hardly extrapolate these points of union to those it had conquered. In the states which they created, rulers and ruled tended to remain divided. In organisation, the empires which they founded were but tribes writ large; and as kinship loyalties loosened down the generations, their provinces split off and their centres fell into disorders. So much of the history of African policies runs through very-short-term cycles of expansion and contraction, like the heavings of a diaphragm. Hunting for gold or salt or slaves, they might enlarge their territories, but this geographical expansion usually led in the end to political crack-up. How they reacted to the inroads of Europe, therefore, was partly determined by the point they had reached in their cycle of growth and decay. At a time of down-turn, their rulers would have strong reasons for striking a bargain with the new invaders. But challenged during a period of upswing, they might choose to fight it out to the end. Yet again, the more urbanised, commercial and bureaucratic the polity, the more its rulers would be tempted to come to terms before their towns were destroyed. On the other hand, the more its unity hung together on the luxuries of slave-raiding, plunder and migration, the less its aristocracy had to lose by struggling against the Europeans.

Here then were two of the many variables in settling the issue of co-operation or resistance. Not a few animist states whose economy was predatory and whose expansion was in progress fought for their independence. Both the Matabele and the Dahomians did so; but once they were beaten they stayed beaten. Perhaps the low generality of their creeds made them highly vulnerable to the culture of their conquerors. The work started with powder and shot could be completed with the New Testament, and many who came to fight remained to pray. Within a decade of the running up of the Union Jack, the Baganda and Nyasa had taken avidly to the new learning and were staffing the government offices of East and Central Africa. In French Equatorial Africa the Bacongo became the agents of white administration, just as the Baluba were to do in the Katanga.

Such docility was possible among the Muslims, too, when it was a question of dealing with settled Islamic states which had flowered into bureaucracies and passed their peak. For their staid and venerable sultans and *almamys* there was as small an attraction in calling a *jihad* as there was for the Bey of Tunis. Yet apparently religion had much to do with the issue. In many other Muslim polities the harsh imperatives of the Koran were readily obeyed. The plain fact is that the longest and bloodiest fighting against the forces of Europe was carried out by Muslims. No European blandishments could charm them into becoming good neighbours. The task was one for fire-power, not philanthropy.

Robber empires, still expanding into black Africa, still mobile, still led by prophets of the faith—there were good reasons why they could not yield. They were incomparably better fitted to defy and resist than the animists. Islam's insistence on the equality of all believers under one law, together with its extensive brotherhoods and orders, provided firmer strands of unity which transcended the bonds of mere kinship and ancestral religions. Moreover, it postulated a principle of universal Godhead above any of the local deities and fetishes which divided black Africa. Supratribal Muslim institutions and discipline sometimes presented a coherent and continuous resistance. They also made surrender to Christian powers impossible without dissolving the forces of Muslim authority and empire. For many of these fierce foes had fashioned their power out of a sort of Muslim protestantism—attempts to purge Islam of scholiast accretions by moving back to the pristine purity of the Koran of the desert and rejecting the authority of the corrupted Caliphate at Constantinople. On the frontiers of the faith, it was new prophets who combined this stern, unbending fundamentalism with the thirst of tribes for independence and conquest. Muhammad al-Mahdi in the Sudan, Sayyid al-Mahdi among his Sanusi, Amadu Shehu and Samori of the Sofas, Rabih—all of these were prophets or caliphs of prophets and local theocrats. They were no less leaders of independence movements. Independence in African terms meant expansion and the dependence of others upon them, so they became conquerors of infidels for the true faith. After all, it is only armed prophets who have not been destroyed.

To survive, embattled theocrats of this sort had to be proof against the politics of influence practised by invading Christendom. The new dispensations which they preached had made obsolete all the cities and kingdoms of this world. They called upon all to return to God according to their revelation or be destroyed by him. If they compromised with the enemy after such preachings, they would be digging their own graves. Something of this adamantine attitude to unbelievers still rings in the Mahdi's message to the Christian emperor, Yohannes of Ethiopia: 'Become a Muslim and peace will be unto you.... If on the other hand you choose disobedience and prefer blindness... [have] no doubt about your falling into our hands as we are promised the possession of all the earth. God fulfils His promises. ... Let not the Devil hinder you.'[1] African Christianity, at least in Ethiopia, produced the same unyielding toughness. Shadowy and bizarre though the monophysite creeds of the Coptic church might be, they helped to rally national solidarity behind the emperor when the Italians brought the time of troubles.

The deadliest enemies of European expansion into Africa were those states suffused by Islam or Christianity, both of them supra-tribal religious organisations capable of forging tribes into national unities. Believing that the white man was an infidel as well as an invader, these Copts and Muslims faced him, strong in the knowledge of a righteous cause. Meeting with so complete a self-confidence, the white men were pushed into choices they would have preferred—indeed, that they expected—to burke. There was no sensible negotiating to be done with theocrats, still less any converting. Their opposition raised local crises which could not be glossed over. Once the theocracies had been aroused by the challenge of Europe, it became a matter of everything or nothing. Dragged ever deeper into reactions which their own coming had provoked, the powers were forced in the 1890's to occupy the claims which they had papered on to the African map in the 1880's. The spectacular expansion that resulted has often been called imperialism. But at a deeper level it was a reflex to the stirrings of African proto-nationalism.

Whether they liked it or not, the white men were now committed to making sense out of the abstract dispositions of the 1880's. The harsh facts of Africa compelled it. For the French, lured on by British acquiescence and the dashing strategies of their colonial soldiers, there was no escape. In pursuit of Amadu the army had been drawn westward to Timbuktu. It was soon to go on to Gao, and the Upper Niger Command modulated into *Soudan Français*. In Paris the politicians had had enough. In 1891 and 1893 they called a halt to the soldiers, announcing that 'the period of conquest and territorial expansion must be considered as definitely over'.[2] Already the problem was how to make their new acquisitions pay; but the colonels, with one hand on their Maxims and the other on their next set of proofs, were bent on routing out Muslim resistance yet farther afield, in Futa Jalon and the Upper Volta. Paris turned up its nose at the new provinces. But the very fact of pacification gave them

---

[1] Mahdi to Negus Yohannes, 1884–5, quoted in Sanderson, G.N.: 'Contributions from African Sources to the...History of European Competition in the Upper Valley of the Nile': Leverhulme Conference Paper, University College of Rhodesia and Nyasaland, 1960.
[2] Delcassé to Grodet, 4 December 1893, M.F.O.M., Soudan, I, 6 A.

a fictitious value—since hard-won territory could hardly be given up. So step by step the army eventually involved Paris in the economics of development. When Trentinian took over the Sudan in 1895 the era of the sabre had ended. With the coming of government investment to push the railway up to the Niger, closer administration became possible and the battlefield was turned into a colony.

Gradually, the French grew more entangled in Dahomey and the Congo. In 1890 General Dodds, covered by Étienne in Paris,[1] slipped the leash and crushed the pagan slave-raiding confederacy of Dahomey, which had proved an impossible neighbour to the French on the coast. The way was open for a thrust inland. By 1894 French agents were reconnoitring Nikki; they were poised to invade the undefined western flanks of Goldie's monopoly on the lower Niger; what was more, they had seen a chance of uniting Dahomey with their fields of influence on the Senegal, Ivory Coast, Upper Volta and Upper Niger. Since 1889 the colonial zealots had been pressing the government to go one better still. Belatedly they would rationalise all the incongruous advances of the past decade by joining these territories to the starveling French Congo. The junction and symbol of this geographical romanticism was to be Lake Tchad.

After ten years in which their diplomats and soldiers had played ducks and drakes with West Africa, there emerged a group in Paris who demanded that the French empire should be taken seriously for its own sake. In 1890 their private subscriptions sent Crampel from Brazzaville to establish French sway in the regions of Lake Tchad and so ensure 'the continuity of our possessions between Algeria, Senegal and the Congo'.[2] So little did this pipe-dream charm the Quai d'Orsay that in August they signed away the Tchad corridor to Britain. In protest Crampel's supporters toward the end of 1890 organised the *Comité de l'Afrique française*—the first serious pressure group in favour of a tropical African empire; but at no time did it attract any powerful business interests; and though it had the blessing of Étienne, its direct political influence was not spectacular. There was a certain grandiloquent appeal in the *Comité*'s idea of turning Tchad into the linch-pin of French Africa, but it was the risks, not the rhetoric, which moved the politicians. Coming down to the lake from the north meant striking across the Sahara, but this was clean contrary to the policy of the Government-General at Algiers. Since the slaughter of the Flatters expedition by the Touareg in 1880, Algiers had turned down project after project for Saharan penetration on the ground that it would be 'too dangerous'.[3] There were equally sharp objections against moving on Tchad from the west. If the thrust went along the Upper Niger,

---

[1] Étienne to Governor of Senegal, 4 December 1891, M.F.O.M., Sénégal, i, 91 B.

[2] Crampel to Under-Secretary for Colonies, 12 March 1890, M.F.O.M., Afrique, 5. Dossier Crampel, 1890–1.

[3] Governor-General, Algeria, to Colonies, 19 May 1896, M.F.O.M., Afrique, 10. Dossier Foureau, 1896.

it would have to fight its way through Muslim opposition, which might have awkward repercussions in the newly organised French Sudan; as late as 1898 the Government-General in Saint-Louis was against such an advance.[1] The only practicable route seemed to be from the south. In 1891 the *Comité* sent Dybowski, and Brazza sent Foureau, on missions towards the lake from the Congo. Both were hurled back. Once more, French expansion had contrived to entangle itself with Muslim resistance. The wreckage of the Arab slaving state in the Bahr al-Ghazal had driven its survivors into the Wadai country. Here they were reorganised by Rabih into a strong, predatory state, which saw the Europeans as dangerous rivals. Another theocracy was in the making. Rabih 'found in religion more support and strength than a mere desire for loot would have given to a band of adventurers';[2] and after he had moved on to the Bagirmi country by the shores of Tchad, the support of the Sanusi, coupled with the military skills he brought from Egypt, made him a formidable opponent.

For Brazza, the Commissioner-General of the Republic in the Congo, the *Comité*'s drive on Tchad was doubly welcome. It pushed out his frontiers, and it attracted the interest of Paris towards his neglected colony; it remained for him to associate the minority enthusiasm of the Lake Tchad school with a serious national interest that would appeal to the cynics of the Quai d'Orsay. In 1891 he was suggesting to Paris that the expeditions towards Tchad 'can...produce a situation for us which... will allow us to start negotiations with Britain about reciprocal concessions over the Egyptian question...'.[3] This was the germ of the French Fashoda strategy. In August 1891 Liotard was sent to the Ubanghi-Shari country, the western gateway to the Nile valley, with instructions to use the well-tried Brazza methods of influence on the small sultans there. If Paris were to take the plunge into reopening the Nile question, here was a possible method of doing so, and here were the means to hand.

Paris was to take the plunge. Like all the crucial moves in the struggle for tropical Africa, this was decided by a turn in the chronic Egyptian crisis. Salisbury had taken some of the heat out of it by simply refusing to discuss it. The French had hoped for better times when the Liberals came back in 1892, but Rosebery, the new Foreign Secretary, told Paris point-blank that the Egyptian issue was closed. In January 1893 the khedive timidly tried an anti-British *coup*. Cromer shouldered him back into subservience; but the crisis had its bright side for Paris. It showed that the revolutionary situation in Egypt was far from played out. It suggested that the nationalists inside the country might be usefully allied with pressure

[1] Governor-General, French West Africa, to Colonies, 12 July 1898, M.F.O.M., Afrique, 11. Dossier Mission Voulet au Lac Tchad.

[2] Clozel to Colonies, 26 August 1895, M.F.O.M., Afrique, 9, Dossier Clozel.

[3] Brazza to Colonies, 18 April 1891, A.E.F. (unclassified); same to same, 6 June 1891, A.E.F., 2 B.

from outside to turn the British out of their citadel. The chances of external action were brightening as well. By 1893, with the *Franco-Russe* all but consummated, the strategic position in the eastern Mediterranean looked much more secure to the Ministry of Marine, once the tsar's warships had visited Toulon. The politics of deference were over.

Paris therefore had good reason to take a higher line in the Egyptian affair. From the diplomats' viewpoint, the partition of Africa was a large-scale example of game-theory. One of the rules of the game was that control of a river's course amounted to a forcing bid for territory. So it had been on the Niger. So it had been on the Congo. Why not install a French force on the Upper Nile? The Nile was Egypt, as everyone knew. Once the *infanterie de Marine* had straddled the river, the famous Egyptian question could be reopened with a vengeance. In May 1893, Carnot, President of the Republic, revived the Brazza scheme. A task-force could follow the old route towards Tchad, filter north-west through Liotard's empire of influence in Ubanghi-Shari, and then strike hard for the Nile. They would have to join it south of the Mahdists' country, since the Dervishes did not welcome visitors. But one theocracy was as good as another. Striking the river south of Khartoum would allow the French to work with Menilek, who was hunting for European rifles and sympathy. A handful of Frenchmen on the Nile would be picturesque; but joined by an Ethiopian army they would be portentous.

The contest for Egypt and the Mediterranean was speeding up again. As it did so, one remote African polity after another was enmeshed into its toils: the starveling colony of the Congo, the theocracies around Tchad, the petty Muslim oligarchies of Ubanghi-Shari, the wanderers in the marshes of the Bahr al-Ghazal, the Coptic state of Ethiopia, the stone-age men living around the sand-bank at Fashoda. As for the two European powers whose rivalry had provoked this uproar, they each strained every nerve to race the other to the dingy charms of the Upper Nile. There had been a time when light soils were booby prizes. Only the remarkable insights of late nineteenth-century imperialism could have seen them as pearls beyond price.

But the Fashoda scheme was risky. The Quai d'Orsay could not assume that the British would sit smoking their pipes in Cairo while the French were pitching camp by the banks of the Nile; and so the policy-makers in Paris held back the colonial *enragés*. To their minds, the scheme of planting the tricolour on the Nile was not a colonial scheme but a diplomatic weapon; they hoped to use it as a *bâton soudanais* to thwack the British into an Egyptian negotiation. Hence the Fashoda plan went in stops and starts, to be dragged out of the pigeon-holes whenever London grew refractory. Before Paris had summoned up the nerve to carry it out, London was taking precautions against it. On their side, the British were hard at work building up positions of strength in the valley of the Nile.

It was in Uganda that they were building. Goaded by the Foreign Office, Mackinnon's company had sent Lugard inland to Buganda, to tighten Britain's hold on the headwaters of the river. The country was in uproar, through the struggles of rival factions, goaded on by British Protestant, French Catholic and African Muslim missionaries. Early in 1892 Lugard managed to set the Protestants into precarious authority: but vindicating the principles of the Reformation had exhausted Mackinnon's finances, and he ordered Lugard to withdraw from Uganda. This alarmed the government. Already, military intelligence in Egypt was predicting that once the company moved out of Uganda, the French forces in Ubanghi would move in; and the Africanists in the Foreign Office conjured up French threats on all sides. To them, and to Lord Rosebery, the best defence lay in going forward. Formally occupying the country would shut out the French from the sources of the Nile; linking it by rail with Mombasa would make it a base for shutting them out of the upper valley as well. But the Gladstonians in the Cabinet would not go so far as Rosebery. The best he could do was to send Portal to Uganda to report on the pros and cons of holding it.

Both London and Paris were to find that their insurance premiums were too low, for now another partitioner, and one much suppler and subtler than Carnot or Rosebery, declared an interest in the Nile. To a remarkable extent, Leopold II of the Belgians combined the unction of a monarch with the energy of a businessman. For all their modest beginnings, it is Rockefeller, Carnegie and Sanford who offer the closest parallels with this royal entrepreneur. Like them, he gambled on futures; like them, he formed cartels out of chaos; like them again, he was careless of the consequences. Leopold had been given the Congo since his Independent State was the regime which divided the powers least. It was his own money and not the taxpayers' which was used for embellishing the new royal demesne. But since Leopold's African flutter was not an act of state but a private venture, it had to show a cash return—no easy matter this, in the Congo, where there seemed to be no minerals and where the population showed no great zest in working for the market. To keep his private empire going, Leopold badly needed something to export. There was ivory; there was ebony; but these trades were in the hands of the Arabs, especially those of the eastern regions of the Congo. Leopold would have come to terms with them if he could, but his treaties of trade and friendship had no attraction for these oligarchs and oligopolists lording it over the Negro. So it came to war, and this drove the Congo Free State deep into the Arab territories which lay between it and the Nile. In 1891 its missions were setting up posts in Ubanghi, in 1893 in the Bahr al-Ghazal, and in the same year the forces of Van Kerckhoven struck as far as Lado on the Upper Nile itself.

Such spirited advances were welcome neither in Paris nor in London.

They were especially awkward for the French. Leopold's men were undoubtedly spilling north of the rough frontier proposed in 1887 between his sphere and theirs on the Congo; but when they tried to draw the frontier with some precision in 1892–4 the negotiations showed that none of the diplomats had the faintest idea of the lie of the land. What was more, these probings by the Free State showed how weak French authority was on the ground in the Ubanghi-Shari, scheduled as the launching-site for a move on Fashoda. Rosebery too had his troubles. He could order Portal to extend the British sphere from Buganda to the north; after the Liberals had succeeded at last in dropping their pilot, Gladstone, he could bring Uganda proper under a formal protectorate. But in the unreal game the powers were playing for the Upper Nile, the paper bargains of diplomacy still seemed the best insurances. In May 1894 Rosebery clinched two agreements. In the first place, the Italians became a holding company for British interests in Ethiopia. By recognising a Roman hegemony over Ogaden and Harar, Rosebery could take it for granted that the negus would not be of much use to French plans, so long as the Italians were sitting on his border. Secondly, the British tried to neutralise Leopold. By the Anglo-Congolese agreement he was assigned Equatoria and much of the Bahr al-Ghazal, so as 'to prevent the French who are about to send an expedition to [the Bahr al-Ghazal] from establishing themselves there, and to settle with the Belgians who are there already.... The presence of the French there would be a serious danger to Egypt.'

Elegant as this paper-work might be, it was all in vain. Rosebery's ill-judged attempt to settle the Egyptian issue on the Upper Nile only provoked the French to greater exertions. In Paris the Colonial Minister thought that the Anglo-Congolese Treaty 'seems to call for new measures on our part'.[1] One of these was to revive, with £70,000 worth of credits, the scheme of going to Fashoda by way of Ubanghi-Shari. But even now Hanotaux at the Quai d'Orsay managed to pour water into the Colonial ministry's wine. The expedition was to advance along the Ubanghi; but it was ordered 'to avoid breaking into the Nile valley'.[2] By August the second counter-measure was complete. The Anglo-Congolese treaty had been broken by the classic method of a joint Franco-German denunciation. Much to Hanotaux's relief, the Ubanghi striking-force could now be side-tracked out of harm's way, to try conclusions with Samori on the Ivory Coast.[3]

Rosebery was forced into direct negotiations with Paris. He was reported as saying 'Take all you want in Africa, provided that you keep off the valley of the Nile',[4] and like Salisbury before him it was in West

[1] Minister of Colonies to Monteil, 13 July 1894, M.F.O.M., Afrique, III, 16–19 (dossier 19 B).
[2] Idem; revised draft, with emendations by Hanotaux.
[3] Minister of Colonies to Monteil, 22 September 1894, ibid.
[4] French chargé in London to Hanotaux, 22 September 1894, A.E. Angleterre, 897.

Africa that he hoped to give his generosity full play. The hinterlands of the Gold Coast and the borderlands between the French and British spheres on the Lower Niger might all go in return for safety in Egypt. But since the French no less than the British thought much more highly of Egypt than they did of the west coast, there was no basis for a bargain. So the exchanges over the Nile and the Niger grew angrier, until in March 1895 Grey publicly warned the French that any advance into the Nile valley would be taken as an 'unfriendly act'. Sabres were beginning to rattle.

If the contention for Egypt and the Nile had been kept on the diplomatic level hitherto, it was now to burst into active conquest and occupation. As it neared its climax, the partition, which had begun almost frivolously, became hectic. It had been going on for so long that some of the new generation of politicians—the Delcassés and Chamberlains, had come to take it seriously, not only as a matter of old-fashioned power-politics but as a question of African colonies. The partition had brought them to a kind of geopolitical claustrophobia, a feeling that national expansion was running out of world space, and that the great powers of the twentieth century would be those who had filched every nook and cranny of territory left. Yet it was not ambitions or rivalries of this sort which drove France and Britain into carrying out their Nile strategies. It was the defeat of the Italians by the resurgent proto-nationalists of Ethiopia.

How this quasi-feudal, monophysite realm of the Lions of Judah survived the onslaughts of Islam and the Galla nomads through the centuries is a question. From the mid-eighteenth century, the emperors had been shadows, the king-makers all powerful. But after the accession of Teodros II in 1855 the emperor and his feudatories slowly reunited to meet the growing menace of foreign invasion. Their disunity had prevented any effective resistance when Napier's columns marched to Magdala in 1867 to release the imprisoned British consul. When Crispi, hoping to buttress his divided ministry with colonial success, occupied Tigré and ordered the Italian army forward into the Ethiopian highlands in 1896, he relied on the same weakness. His General, Baratieri, knew better. Italian expansion, he observed, was provoking among the Ethiopians 'a kind of negative patriotism'.[1] The negus Menilek was not only equipped with modern fire-power through the courtesies of white-man's diplomacy, he also had the great Rases of Tigré, Gojam, Harar and Wollo behind him. At Adowa on 1 March 1896 these Ethiopian proto-nationalists crushed the Italians. It meant the freedom of Ethiopia and the fall of Crispi. It also meant the first victory of African proto-nationalism. The Mahdists as well as the Ethiopians were moving against Italian Eritrea. The Italian outposts of Kassala on the Atbara tributary of the Nile looked like being cut off altogether.

[1] Rubenson, S., 'Ethiopia in the Scramble', Leverhulme History Conference Paper, University College of Rhodesia and Nyasaland, 1960.

Adowa so sharply transformed the politics of the Nile basin that twelve days later Salisbury ordered the Egyptian army under Kitchener to invade the eastern Sudan. This decision, so he informed Cromer, 'was inspired specially by a desire to help the Italians at Kassala;...to prevent the Dervishes from winning a conspicuous success which might have far-reaching results; and to plant the foot of Egypt rather farther up the Nile'. It is true that the plight of the Italians seemed fortunate to the British. The Kaiser urged Salisbury to do something to help his unhappy partner in the Triple Alliance; and this meant German help in unlocking the Egyptian treasury to pay for the invasion. But if the Italian defeat gave the opportunity of attacking the Mahdists, the Ethiopian victory made it necessary to do so. Hitherto the English had done everything possible to keep out of the Egyptian Sudan. 'If the Dervishes have occupied the valley of the Nile', Salisbury had told Cromer in 1890, 'they do not pledge the future in any way...they can destroy nothing, for there is nothing to destroy.' Without engineering skills, they could not tamper with the Nile flow. 'Surely...this people were [sic] created for the purpose of keeping the bed warm for you till you can occupy it.' Even in 1897 Cromer was opposing the advance on Khartoum, as it would only lead to the acquisition of 'large tracts of useless territory which it would be difficult and costly to administer properly'. Plainly then they were not hastening to conquer another colony. They cautiously ordered the invasion, to forestall the French *coup* on the Upper Nile which Menilek's victory seemed to have made practicable.

This calculation was wrong but reasonable. English complacency about such a *coup* had rested hitherto on the hope that a French force from the west would be unable to fight its way through to the Nile; or if it did, that it would get no help from Menilek under the Italian heel; or if it did get such help, that the Egyptian army could conquer the declining Dervish state before any dangerous Franco-Abyssinian combination could take place. Adowa transformed Salisbury's view of these possibilities. Rid of the Italians, the Ethiopians were much more formidable than had been supposed; and if, as Salisbury suspected mistakenly, they were prepared to act as allies of France, they would be formidable indeed.

The disappearance of the Italians seemed to have put new life into the Mahdists as well. It was known that Menilek was angling for an alliance with them. Not only did this make it less likely that Kitchener would be able to break through the Mahdists and forestall the French at Fashoda; it also raised the spectre that the French might launch a Mahdist-Ethiopian alliance against Egypt itself. Here the British stakes were too great to permit such risks. And Salisbury's government decided to take precautions in time. So opened the last great crisis in the partition of tropical Africa. Like its predecessors, it had been generated by the turn of events in Africa itself.

40-2

Predictably the invasion of the eastern Sudan provoked Paris to sub-stantiate Salisbury's fears by invading it from the west.[1] Three months after Kitchener started for Dongola, Marchand left for Brazzaville, *en route* for Fashoda; and Lagarde went back to Addis Ababa to clinch the alliance with Menilek and arrange for the rendezvous with Marchand on the Nile. Whether the Egyptian army, dragging its railway from the north, could beat down the Khalifa and reach Fashoda ahead of the French seemed increasingly doubtful. So Salisbury was forced to try forestalling them from the south. He pressed on the building of the rail-way from Mombasa to supply the base in Uganda, and in June 1897 Macdonald was ordered to march from there along the Nile to Fashoda 'before the French get there from the west'. So the Anglo-French struggle for the Nile had set in motion four invasions of the Egyptian Sudan. French forces were now toiling towards it from east and west, British forces from north and south.

For long Salisbury was much more worried about the threat from Ethiopia than that from Marchand's expedition. Early in 1897 Rennell Rodd, the British envoy to Menilek, reported that he seemed very much under French influence; there seemed to be Frenchmen occupying high posts and assuming higher titles in the Ethiopian administration. In October the emperor appeared to be co-operating in sending Bonchamps's Franco-Ethiopian expedition along the river Sobat to Fashoda. In fact, Menilek merely intended to play off the French against the British who seemed a greater threat to his independence. Unknown to them, he had already made an agreement with the Mahdists. As for the joint expedition from Addis Ababa to the Nile, Bonchamps complained that 'the Ethiopians did not help the mission; they did all they could to stop it from heading towards the Nile'.[2]

If Salisbury had known all this, he need not have troubled to conquer the rest of the Sudan. But, on the evidence to hand in London, things looked gloomy indeed. Having reached Berber, Kitchener found the Mahdists much stronger than expected, and remembering Hicks Pasha's catastrophe in the desert, he asked for white troops. Ministers were most reluctant to send the redcoats. But Macdonald's force which was to have covered Fashoda from the south had not even set out, because his troops had mutinied and the Baganda had rebelled. Like the French strategy in the east, British strategy in the south had gone astray. There was nothing for it but to press the conquest of the Sudan from the north. In January 1898, perhaps as much from fear of a mythical Dervish counter-attack as from fear of the French moving on Fashoda, the British sent Kitchener his white reinforcements with orders to capture Khartoum. So at last the

---

[1] Memo. by Archinard, 20 January 1896, M.F.O.M., Afrique, 14.

[2] Memo. by Bonchamps, 'Reasons why Junction with Marchand was Impossible', n.d., M.F.O.M., Afrique, III, dossier 36 A.

English army's imbroglio with the Dervishes dragged them into vast conquests of unwanted territory in the eastern Sudan, much as the French army since 1889 had been drawn into the western Sudan by their entanglements with the fighting Muslim theocracies of Amadu and Samori. In the event the fanaticisms of proto-nationalism had done far more to bring European imperialism into Africa than all the statesmen and business interests in Europe.

All these threads came together in the summer of 1898. On 2 September Kitchener's machine-guns proved stronger than the Khalifa's Mahdists at Khartoum. An Anglo-Egyptian condominium was soon riveted upon the Sudan. Six weeks earlier a sorely-tried Franco-Ethiopian expedition had struggled up to the confluence of the Sobat and the Nile near Fashoda, expecting to find Marchand. He was not there. After a Russian colonel had planted the French flag on an island in the Nile, they went away. Three weeks later Marchand himself reached Fashoda. It was deserted. But not for long. On 19 September Kitchener's regiments came up the river in their gunboats and sent him packing.

At first sight it looks as though a British steam-roller had been sent to crush a peanut at Fashoda. Salisbury had spent millions on building railways from Lower Egypt and Mombasa through desert and bush to Lake Victoria and the Upper Nile; he had launched a grand army into the sands and gone to the verge of war with France—and all to browbeat eight Frenchmen. Was the Nile *sudd* worth such exertions? No less an architect of expansion than Queen Victoria herself opposed a war 'for so miserable and small an object'. Yet this anti-climax at Fashoda brought the climax in Europe. For two months it was touch and go whether France and Britain would fight each other—not simply for Fashoda but for what that lonely place symbolised: to the British, safety in Egypt and in India; to the French, security in the Mediterranean. It was Paris that gave way. In the turmoil of the Dreyfus Affair, Brisson's ministry accepted the necessity of avoiding a naval war which they were in no state to undertake, even with Russian help. By the Anglo-French Declaration of March 1899 France was excluded from the entire Nile valley. In return she received the central Sudan from Darfur in the east to Lake Tchad in the west. This decided the Egyptian question in a way that the Anglo-French *entente* of 1904 merely ratified. With that settled, the drawing of lines on maps might have ended as it had begun, with Egypt; but it was too late. By this time there was no more of tropical Africa left to divide.

This central struggle for Egypt and the Nile had produced a series of side-effects elsewhere in Africa, collateral disputes which had twitched into a life of their own. Of these much the most virulent was the Anglo-French rivalry over the middle Niger. During the early 1890's this affair was as hollow as it had been during the first decade of the Scramble, with tempers on the Niger still blowing hot and cool according to the state of negotiations over the Nile. Until Kitchener invaded the Mahdist Sudan and Marchand struck towards Fashoda in retaliation there was little substance in the West African quarrels. But after 1896 they were more fiercely contested, as Lugard and the other filibusters scuffled around the chiefdoms in the Niger bend. From London's standpoint, this flurry of claims and expeditions was a tiresome business, for it had little bearing on the crucial question of the Nile except as a way of marking up bargaining points for the inevitable settlement there. But the struggle for the middle Niger had much more meaning for the official mind in Paris, since its connection with France's Nile strategy was direct. If the Fashoda operation were to succeed, there would have to be solid communications from the West African bases across the Bahr al-Ghazal to this new position on the Nile. As usual, such calculations decided that all roads must lead to Lake Tchad. 'Our chief requirement', wrote the Minister for Colonies, 'must be to bind together our possessions in [French] Sudan with those in the Ubanghi, and the latter with the Nile. Between the Nile and the Ubanghi matters seem promising... between the Ubanghi and the Sudan we must rely on [fresh] missions if the desired result is to be won.'[1] Two ways were tried of carrying out these directives. Pushing up from the Congo, one force strove to come to terms with Rabih, still the man in possession of the eastern and southern sides of Tchad. But they found him far from placable, and in any case the French Congo was too poor to throw much weight behind the thrust. On the other axis of advance, Cazemajou was sent from French Sudan to make his way across the Niger bend to the west side of the lake. But this line of march took him into Sokoto, trampling down the paper barriers erected in 1890 between the French and British spheres. At the same time, a support group from Dahomey threatened to pull Nikki and Borgu out of Goldie's ramshackle empire in northern Nigeria.

Briefly, the long line of British surrenders in West Africa was now to be interrupted. At the Colonial Office, Chamberlain was one of the few powerful politicians anxious to build an African empire for the sake of a new imperialism. Whereas the old school approached the partition on the principle of limited liability which governed all their foreign policy, Chamberlain believed that a bankrupt rival should be hammered. To push forward on the Nile, they were ready to fall back on the Niger; but Chamberlain played for everything or nothing. Having annexed Ashanti in 1896, he jostled the French for possession of the Volta chiefdoms beyond. It was not long before this new forcefulness was warming up the quarrels on the Niger. To defend Borgu and Sokoto, he screwed up Goldie's company into a belligerence as damaging to its dividends as it was distasteful to the diplomats. Cazemajou was to be thrown out of Sokoto by

[1] Colonies to Commissioner-General, French Congo, 15 April 1897, A.E.F. 3 D.

force—a work of supererogation this, since the explorer was already dead. But for all this fire-eating, there was a treaty. Both sides had their eyes cocked elsewhere. Salisbury overruled his Colonial Secretary with the argument that 'if we break off negotiations...it will add to our difficulties in the Nile valley'. Hanotaux calculated that an agreement would stop Britain employing 'a policy of grievances and compensations to block our claim over the Egyptian question'. So on 14 June 1898 they came to terms, France gaining the Upper Volta and Borgu, while its neighbours, Ilorin and Sokoto, were reserved to Britain.

So far as London was concerned, this was the end of the West African affair. Brought to life at the onset of the Egyptian crisis, it could now be tidily buried before the consummation of that crisis. For Paris, however, West Africa remained unfinished business, and its consummation was a necessary part of keeping the Egyptian issue alive. The Lake Tchad strategy had gone all awry. Settling with the British offered a chance of securing the Timbuktu–Fashoda route without the interference of Chamberlain's West Africa Frontier Force. While the Anglo-French negotiation was in full swing, Paris was already organising a force to settle the Tchad business once and for all: with a certain felicity of timing, this group sailed for Africa the day after the agreement had been signed. Organised on a larger scale than the Marchand mission itself, the Voulet–Chanoine mission was to move east from Timbuktu to Tchad, where they would at last give Gentil and the Congo government the chance to impose their will on Rabih. Another expedition, led by Foureau and Lamy across the Sahara, was also converging on Tchad: it was no part of the main scheme, but as things turned out, this group was to decide the issue.

Marchand's fiasco on the Nile knocked the heart out of these plans. After Fashoda, French opinion was far from favourable to more adventures in the African bush. Fearing trouble with the Chamber, the politicians were now inclined to leave Rabih to stew in his own juice. Even less inclined to take risks, the commissioner-general in the Congo recommended that France should make a loose agreement with him, leaving him to do 'whatever he likes on the left bank of the Benue'.[1] The news that Voulet and Chanoine had gone mad and shot it out with their brother officers and then wandered off to found a private empire in the wastes of the western Sudan made Paris even less anxious to try conclusions with their Muslim enemy. But it was the local situation, not the calculations of Paris, which decided the matter. There was no way of coming to terms with Rabih; one by one he attacked Gentil, the Sahara mission and the remnants of the Voulet–Chanoine party. On 21 April 1900 the three groups joined forces. The following day they fought the battle which settled the Tchad issue, which overthrew Rabih, and which

[1] Commissioner-General, French Congo, to Colonies, 24 November 1899, A.E.F. 3 D.

clinched the union of Algeria, the French Sudan and the French Congo. It was the end of a long story.

In Morocco, Libya and the Congo there were to be further adjustments; but these were part of the prelude to the first World War, not of the scramble. By 1900 the directors of the partition had done with tropical Africa. It remained for the administrators to make sense of their paperwork and to make their conquests pay. There could be no going back now. They had embroiled the nations of Europe and the peoples of Africa in such a fashion that their destinies were not to be disentangled.

In the 1880's the policy-makers had intended nothing more ambitious than building diplomatic fences around these territories and hamstringing their rulers by informal control. But such methods would not work with the proto-nationalists of Egypt and Ethiopia, the Muslim revivalists of Tunisia and the Sudan, the Arab slavers of Nyasaland and the Congo, the large animist kingdoms of Buganda and Dahomey. They would not collaborate. They had to be conquered. Once conquered, they had to be administered; once administered, they had to be developed, to pay the bills for their governance. Slowly this development was translated into the idiom of progress and trusteeship, as the new tints of blue or red or yellow or green on the African map awakened feelings of pride or shame among the European voters.

The conversion of the paper empires into working colonies came about from nothing so rational or purposive as economic planning or imperial ardours. The outcome of Salisbury's Nile-valley strategy was as strange as it had been unforeseen. To pay for the occupation of Egypt and its Sudan in the early twentieth century, government had to spend public funds in damming the river and developing Gezira cotton. To recover the money spent on the Uganda railway, government had to provide it with payable loads, and this was the sharpest spur for bringing white settlers into Kenya, as it was for turning the Baganda into cash-crop farmers. Elsewhere the sequence was the same. The development of French West Africa under Roume and Ponty did not come until the Government-General was reorganized to attract capital from France. The German colonies, acquired as by-products of Bismarck's tacking towards France, remained derelict until Dernburg after 1907 carried out a total reconstruction.

So African territories were launched into a development which had not been envisaged at the time they were occupied. What was more, government itself was forced to take the lead in this. Businessmen were still unwilling to plunge into African enterprises, and so most of the capital and the technical services had to be drawn from the public sector. By now the manœuvres and blunders of the partition had been rationalised into apologias for African empire. But the crux of this imperialism lies in its sequence. It was not businessmen or missionaries or empire-builders who launched the partition of Africa, but rather a set of diplomats who thought of that continent merely as a function of their concerns elsewhere. But once started off, this paper partition was turned into occupation and colonisation by the clashes between the Europeans and the proto-nationalists, the religious revolutionaries of Africa. Only at the end of the process did the businessmen arrive—when Europe had to foot the bill for having dealt with Africa as though it was uninhabited. The sequence is quite the reverse of that postulated in the traditional theories. Imperialism was not the cause of the partition. It was the result.

As the Egyptian crisis was giving rise to the devious geometry of partition, an independent process of expansion reached a climax in the southern sub-continent. Unlike the rest of Africa, the temperate south was being settled by white men who since the Great Trek had pushed their homesteads northward from the Orange and the Vaal to the Zambezi and beyond, subjugating the Bantu as they went. Here, moreover, during the last quarter of the nineteenth century investors and merchants were bringing the industrial energies of Europe to develop the colonial economy on a scale unknown elsewhere in Africa. Colonisation grew dramatically deeper and wider after the gold discoveries, which brought a swift inflow of new capital and settlers. Hence the crisis in the south stemmed from the rapid growth of white colonial society and not, as in the rest of the continent, from the decay of an oriental empire and its concatenation of effects. Moreover, it arose from conflicting national aspirations among the colonists, not from rivalry between the powers. The Anglo-French quarrel over Egypt, so fateful for the rest, hardly affected this part of Africa. Occasionally the Germans made as if to intervene, but at most their contribution to the crisis was marginal. This partition was essentially an affair of Boer and Briton in South Africa—even more than it was a matter between the imperial government in London and the colonists—with the silent Bantu looking on. Yet the South African and Egyptian emergencies were alike at least in this: neither was set off by new imperial ambitions; in both the late-Victorians, striving to uphold an old system of paramountcy against a nationalist challenge, fell almost involuntarily into conquering and occupying more territory. Between their vision and reality, between the intent and the outcome of their actions, fell the shadow of imperialism in South, as in North and Central, Africa.

Until the 1870's official London had been content to secure the Cape route to India through colonial control of the Cape and Natal, leaving the inland republics of the *Trekboers* in the Transvaal and the Orange Free State their ramshackle independence. But with the diamond discoveries at Kimberley and the beginnings of investment and railway-building, the British aim became specifically imperial, as it was not in Egypt or tropical Africa. Colonisation, which the Colonial Office had tried first to prevent and then to ignore, had gone so far that there was now nothing for it but to bring the dependencies and the republics together into a self-governing dominion. There were successful models for this kind of imperial architecture in the Australian responsible governments and the Canadian Confederation of 1867. Once united under the Union Jack and relieved of formal Downing Street control, surely the South African colonists' community of interest with Britain in trade and freedom, if not in kinship and culture, would keep them also loyal to the empire. Certainly this technique of collaborating classes worked well in the case of the Cape Dutch who, as the most anglicised and commercial of the Afrikaners, were given responsible self-government in 1872. It might have worked with the Boers of Trans-Orangia. Those of the Transvaal proved far less amenable. Their trading and cultural links with Britain were of the slightest. As they had moved farthest to escape imperial rule in the Great Trek, so were they the most anti-British and inveterately republican of the Boers; and they had a propensity for inviting foreign powers into South African affairs. Happily, or so it seemed to Disraeli's Colonial Secretary, Carnarvon, these twenty thousand Calvinist frontier farmers from seventeenth-century Europe, bankrupt and ringed round with hostile Bantu, were too few to hold up the march of nineteenth-century progress. In 1876 he annexed their country in an attempt to force them into an imperial federation dominated by the far wealthier, more populous and more reliable Cape Colony. But like the Egyptians and Tunisians, the Transvaalers rose three years later to fight the invaders for their independence; and the illusion of federation was consumed in the smoke of the first Boer War of 1881. More than that, the image of imperial aggression awakened among the Afrikaans-speaking South Africans a feeling of racial solidarity with their brothers beyond the Vaal. Gladstone's ministry realised that 'the Boers will resist our rule to the uttermost...if we conquer the country we can only hold it by the sword...the continuance of the war would have involved us in a contest with the Free State as well as the Transvaal Boers, if it did not cause a rebellion in the Cape Colony itself'. Colonial loyalty had been shaken. Afrikanerdom seemed to be uniting behind Kruger's rebellion. To avert a 'race war' between Boer and Briton, the Liberals wisely swallowed the humiliation of Majuba and gave back the Transvaalers their republic.

Out of these reactions of Carnarvon's rough-hewing emerged the modern Afrikaner national movement, with the annals of the Great Trek as its myth and 'Africa for the Afrikaners' as its slogan. Hofmeyr's Farmers' Protection Association at the Cape coupled with the spread of the Afrikaner Bond in the Free State and the Transvaal showed how the Boers' political consciousness was solidifying. Similarly, the Afrikaans language movement of S. J. du Toit and the predicants of the Dutch Reformed Church showed how they were preparing to defend their cultural heritage against anglicisation. Afrikaner nationalism, faced with an empire whose liberality toward the Bantu threatened the colonists' position as a white aristocracy, was bound to be anti-imperialist; yet its leaders were for the most part moderates, by no means unwilling to collaborate with the British authority. But in the Transvaal after the foiled annexation there developed a nationalism more self-assured and much more extreme. Increasingly, the Transvaalers turned from the need of South African unity to the assertion of a romantic particularism, from building a new nation to wrecking an old empire.

It was not going to be easy for British statesmen to turn this balkanised South Africa with its militant nationalists into another Canada. There was no United States on its borders to persuade the Boers that the empire was the best guarantee of their national identity, as the French Canadians had been persuaded. And whereas it was the English-speaking majority who were carrying Canadian colonisation westward to the Pacific, it was the Afrikaans-speaking majority which was expanding into South Africa's hinterland. Downing Street had so much to do in upholding paramount influence over three Afrikaner-dominated, autonomous governments that it could only make haste slowly toward making a dominion. Until 1895 it waited for its colonial collaborators, helped by the inflow of British capital and immigrants, to bring about an imperial union from within. It accommodated its policies to the Cape Ministry's views, so as to avoid offending its chief ally. The Transvaal was handled with kid gloves lest open quarrels with its nationalists should unite Afrikanerdom against the empire, as it had threatened to do in 1881. In conciliating the colonies and republics alike, the 'Imperial Factor' in South Africa was progressively dismantled in favour of the politics of 'moral influence', in all respects but one: London intervened to help the colonies' expansion and to hinder that of the republics, so as to ensure a preponderance of imperial elements in the ultimate federation.

Everything therefore depended on keeping the South African balance favourable to the Cape Colony's future. When Bismarck disturbed it in 1884 by proclaiming his protectorate over Angra Pequena, the British listened to the pleas of Cape Town and quickly brought Bechuanaland and St Lucia Bay under imperial control, thus blocking a German junction with the Transvaalers. Ironically, however, it was not German diplomacy but British capital, pouring into the Transvaal to exploit the gold rushes on the Witwatersrand, that turned the balance against the Cape in favour of the republic. Toward the end of the 1880's the turn was already visible. As the centre of South African prosperity began to shift from the ports to the republic's gold-mines, the colonies frantically pushed their railways northward to catch the new Eldorado's trade. It was plain that their revenue and their farmers would soon depend mainly upon the Transvaal market. Kruger's government on the other hand preferred to apply its new economic power to the strengthening of republicanism throughout

South Africa. At the cost of antagonising the Afrikaner Bond at the Cape, he shut the Cape railway out of the Rand, while using his new riches on building a line to Delagoa Bay that would release the republic from the thraldom of colonial ports and dues. Out of this economic revolution, there followed the long struggle for survival, fought with tariffs, railways and territorial claims, in which the Cape financial and mercantile interests extended their system northward in search of a future. Encircled with colonial railways and new English-speaking settlements, the Transvaal was to be forced or cajoled into a favourable commercial union.

It was this surge of colonisation and capital, this commercial civil war in the south, that drove the scramble for territory northward to the Zambezi, and onwards to Lake Nyasa and the southern boundary of the Congo Free State. Here was empire-building with a vengeance, whose like was to be found nowhere else on the continent. Yet if not cyphers, the men of Whitehall were little more than helpless auxiliaries in it. They were denied by Parliament the price of a protectorate or a colonial railway. The idea, the millions, the political fixing in London and Cape Town, in short the main impetus, was supplied from the craggy genius of Cecil Rhodes. With the impregnable credit of Rothschild's, De Beers and the Consolidated Gold Fields at his back, he knew as well as Leopold II himself how to put big business to work in politics and politics to work for big business— without putting off the shining armour of idealism. He thought big without thinking twice, and yet carried out schemes much larger than his words. A financier with no time for balance sheets but with time for dreams, awkwardly inarticulate, but excelling as a politician, passing as an Afrikaner in South Africa, an imperialist in London, his passionate belief in himself and the destiny of South Africa left him innocent of inconsistency.

When his prospectors told him in 1887 that the gold of Matabeleland would prove as rich as that of Johannesburg, he set about acquiring it—as a way of 'get[ting] a united S. Africa under the English flag'. 'If', he decided, 'we get Matabeleland we shall get the balance of Africa.' That was characteristic. And he persuaded Salisbury's government of it. That was characteristic too. Hope of another Rand and a strong British colony in Lobengula's kingdom which would offset the rise of the Transvaal moved ministers to charter Rhodes's South Africa Company in 1889. Part of the bargain was that he should extend the Cape railways through Bechuanaland and relieve the burden of this pauper protectorate on the Treasury; its essence was that Rhodes under one or other of his twenty different hats should do and pay for everything. Fearful of an anti-imperialist Parliament, suspecting the loyalty of Cape ministries under the shadow of the Bond, the imperial authorities saw no alternative but to play the King of Diamonds. Only Rhodes could make the imperial counterpoise in the north: he alone, first as Hofmeyr's political ally and soon as Cape premier, could keep the Bond faithful in the struggle for supremacy in South Africa. The intransigence of Kruger and his nationalist burghers forced Rhodes to pay the piper but it allowed him to call his own tune. At his insistence Salisbury elbowed aside Portugal's claims and Queen Victoria's protests, taking northern as well as southern Rhodesia for the South Africa Company in 1890, instead of letting it go as he first intended. Moreover, it was Rhodes's cheque-book that enabled Salisbury to throw a protectorate over Nyasaland in 1891 and save the land of Livingstone from the Catholic Portuguese advance. Henceforward Whitehall clung to the coat-tails of the Colossus who had become almost an 'independent power' in southern Africa. For them the problem was not one of promoting British trade and investment, but of shaping to their fixed imperial design the intrinsically neutral movement of colonists and capital. The danger of provoking Afrikaner nationalism stopped them from doing this directly, even if they had had the money. Rhodes not only had the purse, he was the leading Cape Afrikaner. He must do it for them.

But by 1895 all the Cape premier's projecting looked like failing. The fabled gold of Matabeleland had not materialised, but in the Transvaal the deep levels had proved profitable and practically inexhaustible. The settlers who might have colonised Rhodesia were joining the Uitlanders of Johannesburg instead. For a long time to come, the counterpoise across the Limpopo would be a mere featherweight in the imperial scale. Shares in the Bechuanaland railway and the South Africa Company slumped, while Witwatersrand issues boomed. After forty years in which the empire-builders had been working for a dominion founded upon Cape colonial supremacy, it was now certain that the real stone of union lay out of reach in the Transvaal republic. In 1894 Kruger opened his Delagoa Bay railway and, though the Cape now had a line running to the Rand, the Colony's share of the traffic and trade dwindled, as the lion's share went increasingly to the Transvaal and Natal. A year later, the battle of railways and tariffs almost brought the Colony and Republic to blows in the Drifts crisis, but no threat could force the Transvaalers into a commercial union on Rhodes's terms. Kruger held every advantage and he knew it. The true Rand together with the Delagoa Railway was raising him to be arbiter over the colonies' commercial future. Rhodes and Chamberlain suspected that he would arbitrate for a republic of South Africa. They set out to topple him.

Toward the end of 1895 Rhodes organised a rising of the Uitlanders in Johannesburg, It was a fiasco. Worse than that, Dr Jameson's Raid exposed the conspiracy and implicated the imperial authorities. Throughout South Africa, Afrikaner nationalists came together once more against British aggression. At Cape Town, Rhodes fell from office and the government came into the grip of the antagonised Bond. In the Free State, the moderates were replaced by sterner nationalists who soon made a far-reaching alliance with the Transvaal. Afrikaners in the Cape, the Orange

Free State and the Transvaal stood united in defence of republicanism. Germany was giving Kruger cautious diplomatic support, hoping to lever Britain closer to the Triple Alliance. If the Rand had turned the economic balance, Rhodes had swung the political scale against an imperial future.

This cataclysmic view was not that of Rhodes alone. The High Commissioners, Robinson and Milner, and the Colonial ministers, Chamberlain and Selborne, shared it. Early in 1896 the latter were persuaded that the Transvaal must be absorbed quickly into 'a Confederacy on the model of the Dominion of Canada...under the British flag'; otherwise it would 'inevitably amalgamate [the Colonies]...into a [republican] United States of South Africa'. About this vehement thesis the rest of the cabinet were highly sceptical. Recalling the reactions of Afrikaner nationalism to the first Boer War, they suspected that, however low colonial fortunes had fallen, a second war would lose the whole of South Africa for the empire. Such a struggle, moreover, would be extremely unpopular in Britain. The Salisbury ministry resolved to bring Kruger to reason through external pressure alone—perhaps by obtaining possession of Delagoa Bay; perhaps by squaring the Germans; perhaps by using threat and bluff to get the vote for the Uitlanders; by any means short of war to bring the Rand into a South African commercial union. Their efforts to avert a crash repeated Gladstone's over Arabi. But once more events took charge, and the outcome belied the intent. In using the severer weapons of 'moral suasion' called for by Rhodes and the extreme colonial party in South Africa, whose loyalty as their last remaining collaborators they dared not lose, the British government followed them over the edge of war. And like Arabi before him, it was Kruger who finally declared it. Gladstone's ministry had not realised their blunder in Egypt until after the event; unhappily Salisbury's knew theirs in South Africa beforehand. Hicks-Beach protested: 'I hope Milner and the Uitlanders will not be allowed to drag us into war.' Ruefully the Prime Minister admitted that they had. He foresaw with pitiless clarity the vengeance that Afrikaner nationalism would take upon the imperial cause. On the eve of the second Boer War in August 1899 he predicted: 'The Boers will hate you for a generation, even if they submit....If they resist and are beaten, they will hate you still more....But it recks little to think of that. What [Milner] has done cannot be effaced...and all for people whom we despise, and for territory which will bring no profit and no power to England.'

Hence the taking of the Rhodesias and the conquest of the Transvaal came about from a process of colonisation in which the struggles between Afrikaners and British nationalists had receded beyond imperial control. Once economic development had raised the enemies of the imperial connection to preponderance over the colonial collaborators, the government in London attempted diplomatically to switch back South Africa on to imperial lines. But in trying to make it into another Canada, they only created another Ireland. From this standpoint it was a case of mistaken identity. But the mistake went deeper than this: in the end they went to war for the obsolete notion of imperial supremacy in a Dominion—for a cause which was already a grand illusion.

Despite the astounding games of partition it played with the maps of Asia and Africa at the end of the nineteenth century, the so-called new imperialism was merely a second-order effect of the earlier work of European expansion. Colonising the Americas and the other white dominions had been a durable achievement, constructed out of the man-power, the capital and the culture of the lands on the Atlantic seaboard. By this time their growth in self-sufficiency was throwing them outside the orbit of European control, whatever relics of that overlordship might still exist on paper, or might still be fleetingly reasserted by force of arms. Yet far from this being a period of decay for Europe, its energies were now developing their maximum thrust. The potential of the old colonies of settlement had matured so far that they were generating local expansions of their own. The Canadians and Brazilians had organized their backlands. The Americans and Australians had spilled out into the Pacific. The South Africans had driven north of the Zambezi. Whatever the flag, whatever the guise, the expansive energies of Europe were still making permanent gains for western civilisation and its derivatives.

None of this was true of the gaudy empires spatch-cocked together in Asia and Africa. The advances of this new imperialism were mainly designed to plaster over the cracks in the old empires. They were linked only obliquely to the expansive impulses of Europe. They were not the objects of serious national attention. They have fallen to pieces only three-quarters of a century after being thrown together. It would be a gullible historio-graphy which could see such gimcrack creations as necessary functions of the balance of power or as the highest stage of capitalism.

Nevertheless, the new imperialism has been a factor of the first im-portance for Asia and Africa. One of the side-effects of European expansion had been to wear down or to crack open the casings of societies governed hitherto by traditional modes. Towards the end of the nineteenth century this had produced a social mobility which the westerners now feared to sanction and did not dare to exploit by the old method of backing the most dynamic of the emergent groups. Frontiers were pushed deeper and deeper into these two continents, but the confident calculus of early nineteenth-century expansion was over and done with.

It is true that the West had now advanced so far afield that there was less scope for creative interventions of the old kind. The Russians had as little chance of fruitful collaboration with the Muslim emirs of Khiva and Bokhara as the French and British were to have with the theocrats of the

Sudan. When the time of troubles came to the peoples of China or Tong-king or Fiji, their first response was to rally around the dynasty, just as in Africa the Moroccans and Ethiopians were to group under the *charisma* of the ruler. Movements of this sort were proto-nationalist in their results, but they were romantic, reactionary struggles against the facts, the passionate protests of societies which were shocked by the new age of change and would not be comforted. But there were more positive responses to the western question. The defter nationalisms of Egypt and the Levant, the 'Scholars of New Learning' in Kuang-Hsü China, the sections which merged into the continental coalition of the Indian Congress, the separatist churches of Africa—in their different ways, they all planned to re-form their personalities and regain their powers by operating in the idiom of the westerners.

The responses might vary, but all these movements belonged to a common trend. However widely the potentials might range between savage resistance and sophisticated collaboration, each and every one of them contained growth points. In cuffing them out of the postures of tradition and into the exchange economy and the bureaucratic state, western strength hustled them into transformation. One by one, they were exposed to rapid social change, and with it came conflicts between rulers and subjects, the rise of new élites, the transforming of values. All that the West could hear in this was distress signals. But just as its ethnocentric bias has obscured the analysis of imperialism, so its Darwin-ism has stressed the signs of decrepitude and crack-up in these societies at the cost of masking their growth points.

In dealing with these proto-nationalist awakenings, Europe was lured into its so-called age of imperialism; from them, the modern struggles against foreign rule were later to emerge. But the idiom has hidden the essence. Imperialism has been the engine of social change, but colonial nationalism has been its auxiliary. Between them, they have contrived a world revolution. Nationalism has been the continuation of imperialism by other means.

CHAPTER XXIII

EXPANSION IN THE PACIFIC AND THE SCRAMBLE FOR CHINA

I N the first place and for a long time the increasing pressure for expansion in the Pacific and China areas which was so prominent a feature of the last third of the nineteenth century did not come from the European governments. Before 1894 it came almost entirely from Asian governments and their foreign advisers or from European settlers and officials in Australia and New Zealand, the Pacific islands and Asia. For special reasons the latter received strong official support from Europe for a brief period between 1882 and 1885; but apart from this the European governments remained reluctant to extend their responsibilities and their rivalries to this area until the last few years of the century.

Among the earliest problems to arise in the area were those created by the expansion of European trade and settlement in some of the Pacific islands. Clashes between Europeans and between Europeans and natives were becoming serious as early as 1870 in consequence of the growth of trade and plantation agriculture, the improvement of communications and the effect of these developments in dislocating native social and political systems. In Fiji the British Colonial Office had already rejected, twelve years before, a suggestion from the British settlers, who were also afraid of annexation by France, that these problems should be solved by annexation by Great Britain. It had felt reluctant to risk a quarrel with France. Since then the number of settlers, predominantly British, engaged in trade and cotton production had continued to grow despite the lack of effective government and increasing disorder. In 1870 several hundred British subjects living there again petitioned that England should annex the islands. At the same time native chiefs petitioned England to establish a protectorate and help them set up a modern native government, as the United States had done in Hawaii. Native offers of cession were also made to the United States and Germany. There was no response to these appeals; all the home governments still had the same desire to avoid the expense and responsibilities of additional colonies.

The Australian and New Zealand colonies were more familiar with the growing disorder in the islands, more fearful of the expansion of other major powers in the south Pacific and less concerned than Great Britain with problems in Europe. Many of the Australians were frankly imperialistic. The Reverend John Lang of Sydney, the author of a book urging the establishment of British sovereignty over most of the islands of the south-west Pacific, had already advocated that the legislative assembly of

New South Wales should annex Fiji without authority from Britain. Many Australians feared that other powers might act before Britain, to the detriment of Australian and New Zealand interests, and many were also convinced that trade in the islands required effective government to protect it and halt abuses by British adventurers. An intercolonial conference of the Australian and New Zealand colonies, meeting in Melbourne in 1870, resolved in favour of a British protectorate for Fiji. The resolution was forwarded by the governor of Victoria. Like the petitions from Fiji itself, it was rejected by the British Colonial Office. The Colonial Secretary added that he might support a proposal for the administration of Fiji by New South Wales, but the New South Wales cabinet, while strongly urging annexation by Britain, was itself opposed to any such proposal.

Political changes in Fiji then provided an escape from the situation. A modern native government in which British merchants were dominant was set up in 1871 after four unsuccessful attempts in the previous six years. The British government gave this, the Woods government, *de facto* recognition in order to ward off the necessity of intervention. This move was deplored by New South Wales, which considered annexation essential; the British consul was himself hostile toward the Fijian government; many settlers resisted its authority. The continued unrest threatened the copra and cotton enterprises in which Australian interests were considerable. Meanwhile the missionaries, who were influential in English politics, came to support annexation as a means of protecting native welfare, particularly against the abuses of labour recruitment which were inciting anti-European outbreaks in the neighbouring islands. By 1873 for all these reasons the impotence of the Woods government became patent, and conditions were so bad that, although it was especially unfavourable to colonial expansion, the Liberal government in England sent a commission of inquiry to Fiji in 1874. Contrary to instructions the commissioners accepted from the native chiefs another offer of cession to Britain. At about the same time there was a change of government in England and the new, Conservative, cabinet finally decided on the acquisition of Fiji as the only means of restoring order to an area invaded by English capital and English lawlessness. Although the chiefs were reluctant to accept unconditional cession, their earlier offers were taken up without regard to their conditions and Fiji became a British Crown Colony on 2 January 1875.

New Zealand was even more imperialistic with regard to Samoa than Australia had become over Fiji. The problems in the two areas were similar, but the existence of extensive German and American interests made a unilateral solution of the Samoan problems impossible. Germans had the largest land-holdings, mainly devoted to copra production, and Samoa had been the site of their first overseas development. New Zealand had neither trade nor investment in Samoa, but in 1872 Julius Vogel, the

Premier, recommended that Samoa be annexed by Great Britain as vital to New Zealand's safety, and pointed to an American attempt to obtain a naval harbour at Pago Pago as proof of the danger from rival powers. In 1874 he proposed a New Zealand government development company for Samoa. His suggestions found no favour with the British Colonial Office. This did not diminish New Zealand's interest in annexing Samoa with British assistance, although her aspirations were to remain unfulfilled for another half-century.

American interest in Samoa was not a figment of Vogel's imagination. In 1872 Commander Meade of the United States navy was persuaded to conclude a treaty with a local chief by a Californian promoter who had acquired land-rights on Pago Pago harbour, the best in Samoa. In return for American protection the chief conferred on the United States the exclusive privilege of establishing a naval station. This treaty had not been authorised by the American government, but President Grant approved it. Another Californian acquired land-rights around the harbour and persuaded local chiefs to petition for annexation to the United States. Because of the President's interest in a protectorate, the Secretary of State sent Colonel Albert Steinberger to Samoa on a confidential basis to report on conditions. When Steinberger arrived in 1873, he was warmly welcomed by both natives and foreigners, who both hoped for annexation. He assisted in drafting a constitution to set up a modernised native government.

In America, as in Great Britain, there was little sentiment for intervention in Samoa. The Senate rejected the Meade treaty, the offers of annexation were refused, and while Congress affirmed the policy of non-intervention, the press strongly criticised the President. Yet Steinberger was permitted to go again to Samoa at his own expense with some gifts to the chiefs from President Grant and to become the king's chief minister. He organised a relatively efficient government which was able to keep peace. But it soon grew unpopular because it was accused of being too favourable toward the natives, and when they discovered that Steinberger had no American governmental support, the British and American consuls secured his deportation through their influence on the Samoan king. Civil war again broke out and the king was deposed in the disorder resulting from this intervention against Steinberger, which was as unauthorised as his own activities had been.

Hitherto, Germany had also withheld official support from private ventures overseas, in Fiji, Samoa, New Guinea and elsewhere. But the Chancellor, Bismarck, began to be dissatisfied with the treatment of German interests when the British refused to entertain any German claims arising from the annexation of Fiji. When a Samoan delegation went to Washington in 1878 and there negotiated a treaty for the cession of Pago Pago in return for American good offices, the Germans were

41-2

again disagreeably impressed; and they sent two warships into two Samoan harbours to help them to obtain a favourable treaty for themselves. Great Britain then felt compelled to negotiate a treaty with the faction in Samoa which happened to be dominant in 1879. All these treaties provided for jurisdiction by consuls over their own nationals as well as giving rights to establish naval stations and coaling depots. The German, American, and British consuls also set up a neutral area by a convention which they signed in 1879 and which gave them control of the principal town of Apia. These steps failed to solve the problem of disorder and civil war. Partial intervention by foreign governments proved an obstacle to native administration or reform, and the presence of several foreign contingents, while preserving the nominal independence of Samoa, meant that no one foreign country could exercise control. Civil war continued among the natives in which foreigners often actively intervened. The political structure of the islands was such that disputes among rival claimants to the paramount chieftaincy offered ample scope for rivalry between European supporters of the various pretenders.

The German government's new willingness to support its nationals in Samoa received a sharp setback in the German parliament. A bill to enable the government to subsidise the large German company Godeffroy and Sons was defeated, and the company had to be hastily reorganised to save it from the hands of English creditors. Although imperialistic sentiment was beginning to appear among German overseas settlers and officials, party and public opposition in Germany to colonial commitments continued, and the German government did not oppose a new move for the annexation of Samoa by Great Britain which was made by British settlers in 1880. The British Foreign Office, for its part, again concluded that annexation would be inexpedient. British, like American and German, expansionist sentiment was still held within narrow limits by popular opposition to overseas responsibilities and expense and by official reluctance to incur either the expense or the risk of friction with other powers.

Even while these difficulties were arising in the islands, more serious problems had emerged on China's borders, the consequence of the decline of the Chinese state, of the revolution in Japanese society and of the anxiety of both China and Japan on the score of European penetration into the Far East. China was surrounded by lands which had formed almost a system of states. In Korea, the Ryukyu Islands and Vietnam[1] the rulers were still confirmed in their titles by the Chinese emperor, and they still sent periodic missions to Peking bearing tribute in acknowledgement of

---

[1] Until recently, usually referred to as Annam or included in the area called Indo-China. The name 'Vietnam' has been used by the people since early times; it is the most accurate and inclusive designation for the country. For the divisions of the country, including Annam, see p. 650.

China's superiority. These missions offered an opportunity for trade and exchange of information and reinforced cultural and sentimental ties. In reality, however, the tributary states had become independent, managing their own affairs. Partly for this reason but mainly because she was increasingly alarmed by the expansion of foreign countries both into these neighbouring tributary states and into border areas not firmly held by her, China now felt compelled to send military aid, claim sovereignty or expand her own control there in the vain attempt to check hostile rivals. Her motives in the north Pacific resembled those of Australia and New Zealand in the islands of the south Pacific: she was trying to anticipate or prevent the expansion of other powers.

Japan, the other power most immediately concerned, had also for a long time watched the steady expansion of the European powers and the United States in her direction. Soejima Taneomi, who took office as Foreign Minister in 1871, thought Japan would be in a better strategic position if she controlled an arc of territory from Formosa and the Ryukyus to Japan and Korea. Like China and like Australia and New Zealand, Japan sought control of neighbouring territories in order to gain a good position for defence and to deny them to rivals. The territories flanking Japan also provided a strong position from which she might influence China and the continent.

Her opportunity to control the Ryukyu Islands arose as a result of Japanese political reforms. The Ryukyu king was accustomed to send tribute to the Japanese feudal lord of Satsuma as well as to the Chinese emperor, although the islands were really quite independent and preferred to stay so. When the Japanese central government enforced the surrender of the fiefs and reorganised the country into prefectures in 1871, the Ryukyus were placed nominally under the emperor, the king was given a pension and a mansion in Tokyo, and the United States, France and Holland, who had signed treaties with the islands, were told that Japan would assume the obligations incurred by the treaties. By this means, and without opposition, Japan began the process of establishing sovereignty in the modern sense over the islands.

The problem of the Ryukyus became involved with that of Formosa, which was administered as a part of China, when Ryukyu fishermen were shipwrecked in the less settled part and killed by the natives. One of the factions in the government of Japan decided to send an expedition to punish the natives and occupy their part of the islands, which was lightly held by China. Le Gendre, a former member of an American punitive expedition to Formosa, was introduced by the American Minister in Tokyo to Soejima. The Japanese Foreign Minister hired his services, even promising to make him a general and governor if Japan occupied the island permanently, and took him with him on a mission to China in 1873. The ostensible purpose of the mission was to exchange ratification of the long delayed Sino-Japanese Treaty of commerce and friendship and to congratulate the Chinese emperor on his marriage and accession to the throne. Soejima's real purpose was indicated in a report to the throne: 'I shall not let the foreigners who covet Formosa deter me, but shall persuade the Chinese to concede the native territory. We shall develop it and win the hearts of the people. If I cannot do it, it probably cannot be done.' But he does not seem to have discussed the matter of an expedition to Formosa, let alone to have gained Chinese agreement to Japanese occupation of the island. He raised the question of the Ryukyus but the Chinese officials insisted that they were still under Chinese sovereignty.

Before the Formosan question was resolved, the matter of Korea became of extreme importance in Japan. Increasingly bad relations with Korea had roused nationalistic elements in Japan to a fever pitch. The Koreans were, if anything, more anti-foreign than the Vietnamese, the Chinese and the Japanese themselves. They were therefore suspicious of Japan's reforms and her good relations with foreign powers, and they also held it against Japan that she had permitted France to use troops garrisoned in Japan for an attack upon Korea in 1866. On Japan's side many of the leaders were influenced by the feeling that expansion in China and Korea would strengthen the country against the encroachment of the West. They were adopting European methods and institutions not from any love of foreigners but to safeguard themselves from foreign control. In addition, the abolition of the Japanese feudal system had left a large number of former military retainers without the resources or skills to adjust to the new society that was being created, and some of the government leaders, themselves opposed to the speed of Japan's modernisation, sympathised with their distress. A faction led by Saigo Takamori advocated military conquest as a means of strengthening Japan, utilising the former warrior class and making rapid reform much less necessary. Saigo proposed to go as an envoy to Korea and to get himself murdered there in order to provide a cause for war. This plan for war with Korea was substantially approved in 1873, but its implementation was delayed until the return of the Iwakura mission, which had gone abroad to investigate world conditions.

News of the decision to attack Korea brought the mission hurrying home from Europe and its return precipitated a crisis. Its members, the heads of another faction, felt that an expansionist policy was impracticable in view of the overwhelming superiority of the foreign powers and Japan's financial weakness. In one of the most crucial policy decisions of modern times, on 14 October 1873, Iwakura and his chief ally, Okubo Toshimichi, succeeded in cancelling the attack upon Korea. Saigo and the war party, which included Soejima, resigned. The new policy, like that of Germany after 1870, was to be conciliation abroad and concentration on internal unification, development, and reform.

The expedition to Formosa proved more difficult to cancel. The new Foreign Minister did his best to postpone it. The American government recalled the American Minister in Tokyo for his part in encouraging Japanese expansion in Korea and Formosa; it sought to withdraw American citizens such as Le Gendre from the enterprise and to prevent American ships from being used. But the younger brother of Saigo Takamori, Saigo Tsugumichi, who had been made commander of the Formosan expedition, continued to prepare it in the south of Japan, where the expansionists were most influential; and although Okubo Toshimichi, who became the leading member of the internal development faction, even went to the south in an attempt to halt it, Saigo Tsugumichi sailed off after declaring that the government could consider him a free-booter if it wished. Okubo went to China to solve the difficulty caused by Saigo's expedition. Only after mediation by the British Minister to China was he successful in obtaining a settlement in 1874. He obtained a money payment for the families of the Ryukyu fishermen killed in Formosa and also the expenses of the expedition. With this solution he was able to persuade Saigo to withdraw from Formosa after some rather inconclusive operations against the natives.

Since the Ryukyu sailors were referred to as Japanese subjects in these negotiations with China, Japan had taken an important step in strengthening its claim to the Ryukyus. The islands continued to be the subject of sharp dispute with China, who maintained that she was sovereign there, but China was unable to assert herself. Japan eventually incorporated the islands into her local government system in 1879, and Chinese protests proved ineffective.

Japan also succeeded in expanding and fixing her boundaries elsewhere. In 1875 an agreement was reached with Russia whereby Japan abandoned her claims to Sakhalin Island to the north and Russia acknowledged Japan's title to the Kurile Islands. In 1873 the United States abandoned her claims to the Bonin Islands directly south of Japan, as did Britain, in Japan's favour.

During the 1880's, although expansionist forces from within the Pacific area were far from having spent themselves, more serious interest in the area was shown by European governments, if only for a brief period and if only because conditions in Europe temporarily favoured England's rivals and encouraged them to clash with her. In the Far East, as in the increasingly sharp struggle in Africa, Bismarck's diplomatic successes—the renewal of the Three Emperors' Alliance of Germany, Russia and Austria and the Triple Alliance of Germany, Austria and Italy—strengthened Germany. France was led by a strong premier, Jules Ferry, who was convinced of France's need for new colonies, indignant at the British occupation of Egypt and, more important, willing to co-operate with

Germany. England had problems in Egypt and had been so tardy in modernising her fleet that France and Germany probably outnumbered her in first-class ships.

It was for these reasons that Germany clashed with Australian and New Zealand interests in the Pacific islands and that Great Britain was in a weak position when the clash occurred. The trouble began over New Guinea. New South Wales had strongly recommended the annexation by Great Britain of the unclaimed portion of New Guinea on several occasions. The Colonial Office had refused to consider this proposal in 1875, 1878, and again in 1882. After 1880 German planters had begun to develop the north-east coast and an intense local struggle had set in between them and British settlers. On 4 April 1883 the colony of Queensland proclaimed possession of eastern New Guinea despite the fact that as late as the previous January the German government had disclaimed any plans for occupation or political control. With the support of the other Australian colonies the governor offered to pay the expenses of administration. This move was immediately disallowed by England as illegal and as offensive to Germany. Great Britain's action in its turn prompted the New Zealand parliament, with its eye on Samoa, to pass a federation act to facilitate 'steps for the establishment of its rule over such islands of the Pacific as are not already occupied by or under the protection of a foreign power, and the occupation of which by any foreign power would be detrimental to the interests of Australasia'. The British government invalidated this act by withholding the royal assent. Queensland then proposed an intercolonial conference which met in November and December 1883 to consider federation with a view to exerting more influence upon the home government and to discussing the annexation of Pacific islands. Fiji as well as New Zealand and the Australian colonies sent representatives. The conference resolved that 'the further acquisition of dominion in the Pacific south of the equator by any foreign power would be highly detrimental to the safety and well-being of the British possessions in Australasia and injurious to the interests of the empire'.

Germany, or at least German settlers, took alarm at all this activity. The German New Guinea Company was organised in May of 1884; its representatives sought to obtain land in New Guinea. German settlers there then raised their flag on 20 August and their claims were supported by Berlin. The German ambassador in London urged the desirability of a German protectorate for the sake of trade in New Guinea. The British government also took a stand in reply to Germany's. It had deplored the hasty activities of the governments of its own colonies but could not let the German initiative go unopposed. The British Foreign Secretary informed Germany that Britain was not opposed to German colonisation of unoccupied South Pacific islands, but that part of New Guinea, of interest to the Australian colonies, would be claimed by Great Britain.

While discussions were proceeding in Europe, the German government permitted its company to act as though the territory were to be German in October.

The Australians were upset by the German steps toward annexation, and so was the British government. But the Liberal cabinet in London, surprised by the danger of the continental coalition with which Bismarck now threatened it and in need of German goodwill in the matter of the Egyptian debt, had been caught off its guard. It had to give way in New Guinea. Bismarck on his side was prepared to compromise: although he was incensed by the British persistence in opposing Germany's colonial aims, he had overestimated the extent to which colonial pressure could force Great Britain to meet his wishes in Europe, which was more important to him than colonies, and became wary of driving her too far. On 6 April 1885 a joint declaration fixed the limits of the spheres of influence of Great Britain and Germany in the western Pacific. German territory in north-east New Guinea and nearby islands and British territory in south-east New Guinea were mutually recognised. Britain did, therefore, obtain some territory, but not all that the colonies desired, nor did she prevent the expansion of Germany into their vicinity, which was what they had most feared.

Meanwhile in November 1884 the Samoan chiefs had again petitioned for annexation by either Britain or New Zealand, and New Zealand had asked London to permit her to annex Samoa and Tonga. She also offered to take over responsibility for Fiji as well. Unfortunately, the general British–German settlement which was just being reached stipulated that neither power would interfere in Tonga or Samoa, and it could not be upset. Later, in 1889, the Berlin Act signed by Britain, Germany and the United States reaffirmed Samoan independence except for American rights at Pago Pago. The islands continued under the joint protectorate of the three powers, a system which worked badly in practice. It offered too much scope for two of the protecting powers to line up against the third. The alignment was usually Britain and the United States against Germany, primarily because Germany, with the largest share of the commerce of the islands, claimed a supremacy which the other powers had a common interest in denying her; but this alignment was modified by the desire of Britain not to offend Germany, and of the United States not to be seen in co-operation with Britain. Many Americans disliked even this degree of involvement. The Tripartite protectorate was regarded by them as a first, and unnecessary, departure from the good old principle of avoiding entangling alliances.

The same complication did not arise in connection with the increasing American interest in Hawaii. In 1875 the United States had concluded with the king of Hawaii a reciprocity treaty which gave both nations exclusive trading privileges and guaranteed the independence of the islands against any third party. The guarantee was hardly a real one. Although Hawaii had been under British rule for a few months in 1863, and although both Britain and France retained an interest, the real challenge to the islands' independence came from the United States herself. American money poured into their sugar industry, and their trade was virtually pre-empted to the United States. In 1887 the United States leased Pearl Harbour as a naval base. American commercial dominance continued until Queen Liliuokalani, who came to the throne in 1891, attempted to challenge it. Her efforts produced a swift reaction in the shape of her deposition by a provisional government of public safety in January 1893, which began to negotiate for annexation to the United States.

Benjamin Harrison was in the last months of his presidency. He favoured annexation, but before a treaty could be ratified he had been replaced by Grover Cleveland. Cleveland had himself admitted the importance of the islands to the United States, but he was a staunch anti-imperialist, suspicious of the whole affair, and doubly suspicious of anything in which Harrison had had a hand. He withdrew the treaty of annexation from the Senate; but he could not reverse the Hawaiian revolution. He was forced in time to recognise the provisional government of Hawaii as permanent. It was the prelude to annexation, which finally took place in 1898.

Meanwhile, in 1882, another European government had begun to show an increased interest in the China area. France had conquered the southern portion of Vietnam, known as Cochin-China, in the 1860's, when the central part, Annam, and the northern part, Tongking, had remained independent and tributary to China. Subsequent activity by Europeans in Tongking had been mainly the result of the initiative of Frenchmen on the spot. In March 1873 Vietnamese officials had sought to prevent the illegal export of salt into China from Tongking by the French merchant Jean Dupuis. With his company of one hundred and seventy-five men he had seized the port of Hanoi and appealed to Admiral Dupré, governor of Cochin-China, for aid. Dupré had written at this time: 'To establish ourselves in the rich country bordering on China is a question of life and death for the future of our rule in the Far East.' Though cautioned by Paris not to cause international complications in Tongking, he had sent a small force to Hanoi in August in order, as he told the Vietnamese emperor, to evict Dupuis. As soon as the French troops saw how weak the Vietnamese were, they had seized Tongking. When Dupré was killed in December by the forces of Liu Yung-fu, a former Chinese rebel leader, employed by the Vietnamese to keep order in the north, Paris had asserted itself and ordered withdrawal from Tongking. But a treaty had been signed with the Chinese emperor on 15 March 1874 which permitted the French to trade and maintain small garrisons in the trading ports in Tongking; and in an attempt to dissolve the link with China it had provided that Vietnam would apply to France for protection when needed.

In 1882 the French government permitted 400 men secretly to reinforce the small French garrison in Tongking for the purpose of pacifying the pirates there. These troops seized Hanoi in April. Under the prodding of Admiral Jaureguiberry, an officer formerly stationed in Vietnam and now Minister of the Navy and Colonies, the French cabinet next sent three thousand men to Tongking to set up a protectorate over Vietnam. The Chinese government also sent troops to the border where they assisted the Vietnamese.

Early in 1883 the Chinese government decided that the risk of war was too great and ordered Li Hung Chang to negotiate a settlement with France. On 11 May he signed an agreement with the French minister, Fournier, which recognised French interests in Tongking and opened Kuangsi and Yunnan provinces to French trade. He agreed to withdraw all Chinese forces from Tongking by the end of June but, fearing the hostile reaction of the war party at court, he did not make this article of the agreement public. On 19 May 1883, only a week after the Li–Fournier convention, Liu Yung-fu, whose force was now organised as the Black Flag army, defeated the French at Hanoi. The war party in Peking thereupon forbade Chinese forces to evacuate Tongking. The French reinforced their troops, forced the Black Flags to retreat and pushed on to the Chinese frontier, but were again repulsed near Bac Lé on 23 June. They then demanded a large indemnity for the breach of the Li–Fournier agreement. Under the influence of the war party, stimulated by success, China refused and declared war on France. On 25 August the king of Annam, doubtful of Chinese protection, accepted a French protectorate.

During March and April 1884 the French advanced in Tongking, winning several encounters with Chinese forces, and early in the summer they began to threaten the Chinese coasts with their fleet. China fought back. Off Foochow in August the French totally destroyed the obsolete Chinese squadron. In the same month, however, a French attack with landing forces against Kedung in Formosa was repulsed; and although the French made another descent on Formosa in October, and captured Tansui and Keelung, they failed to take the capital, Taipei, which resisted all attacks until the end of the war. In Tongking in the next year they took Liangshan (Langson) and reached the Chinese frontier in February. But they were heavily defeated there on 23 March 1885. By 29 March the Chinese had recaptured Liangshan and all the territory lost in Tongking during 1884.

Ferry, the French premier, was overthrown as a result of these setbacks. But China was not successful in preventing France from expanding in her neighbourhood. In spite of her successes, Li Hung Chang signed a peace treaty in April 1885 by which China withdrew from Tongking and recognised the French protectorate over Vietnam (Annam). He did so partly because of the dangers that would follow if the war with France was allowed to spread, but mainly because China was simultaneously threatened by Japanese activity in Korea.

Japan had abandoned her plans for the conquest of Korea but she had managed in 1876 to conclude with Korea the Treaty of Kanghwa, which provided for trade and diplomatic relations. The treaty stated that Korea was independent and opened three ports to trade; it was in fact modelled upon the treaty concluded by France two years before in connection with Tongking. But the Chinese Board of Foreign Affairs, which had helped to persuade Korea to receive the Japanese envoys, did not accept the denial of Chinese suzerainty over Korea which was implied in the treaty, and Korea continued to be loyal to China. She even sent some Korean students to be trained at the arsenal, and a Korean representative took up permanent residence in Tientsin when the Chinese government shifted control of Korean affairs from Peking to Li Hung-chang in Tientsin. Li's policy was that Korea should enter into treaties with the western powers as a protection against Russia and Japan; and he felt that 'Korea's observance of the usual ceremonies towards our dynasty is not likely to be changed by treaties with western powers'. It was Li who persuaded the Koreans to conclude treaties with the Americans at Chemulpo on 6 May 1882 and with England and Germany soon afterwards.

Against this uneasy background violent feuds between pro-Chinese conservatives and pro-Japanese radicals divided the Korean governing class and in July 1882 the conservative faction, led by the Taewongun, father of the king and former regent, attacked the Japanese legation and tried to seize control of the capital, Seoul. The Japanese Minister was forced to flee. Both China and Japan sent troops to restore peace. The Chinese seized the Taewongun, sent him into exile in China, and restored order. Chinese officials advised the Koreans in their negotiations with Inoue Kaoru, the Foreign Minister of Japan, who went to Korea to try to settle the dispute. The Chinese and Japanese consulted freely between themselves as well as with the Koreans in the settlement. The Chinese urged the Koreans to make fewer concessions, but felt satisfied with the resulting Korean–Japanese agreement. It extended trade and residence privileges as well as giving an indemnity to Japan, and it arranged that, while Chinese troops should uphold the moderate conservatives in Korea, Japanese legation guards should protect the pro-Japanese radicals.

Japan withdrew her troops after gaining the right to use legation guards. Her policy now aimed at independence for Korea, to prevent China or any other power from dominating it and thus threatening Japan, not at dominating the Koreans directly. Even the aggressive elements in Japan had Korean independence as their goal. The Japanese liberals gave support to the most progressive faction in the hope that Korea could follow Japan's example and reform and strengthen herself. The recent Chinese intervention, on the other hand, had represented a stronger policy towards Korea than China had displayed for hundreds of years; and the forward party at court in China now wanted openly to grasp control of Korea and to attack Japan in order to recover the Ryukyus. But Li Hung-chang preferred to station a commercial agent in Seoul, who would give advice to the Korean king. He opposed war with Japan on the ground that greater preparedness was essential. Li's policy was followed. He was bent on increasing China's influence in Korea and keeping Korea free of rival powers without wars.

During the Sino-French hostilities in 1884 another *coup d'état* was carried out by the progressive Korean faction on 4 and 5 December. Takezoe, the Japanese Minister, exceeded his instructions and took an active part in their attempt to seize control. The pro-Chinese officials fled and the chief minister was killed. The king was forced to seek the aid of Takezoe and his legation guards. After two days of hesitation the Chinese engaged the Japanese troops, seized the king, compelled the Japanese to withdraw and re-established the Chinese faction in control. In the clash Chinese troops were joined by Chinese-trained Koreans and Japanese troops by Japanese-trained Koreans.

Japan concluded a relatively mild treaty with Korea in settlement of this affair, despite the patriotic excitement it had aroused at home; and Japan did not seek to gain advantage by combining with France against China. On the contrary, Ito Hirobumi, who exercised a dominating influence on Japanese policy to the end of the century, went to Tientsin to settle the dispute over the clash of Chinese and Japanese troops in Seoul. The convention with China, concluded on 18 April 1885, provided for mutual withdrawal of forces, including legation guards, but both countries kept the right to send troops back to Korea upon notifying the other. This put China and Japan on an equal footing from the strategic point of view although China came to play a more important role politically than she had previously done. The two outbreaks in Seoul involving Japan, together with the new threats from the European powers, had enabled Li Hung-chang to expand China's influence in the peninsula with Japan's acquiescence.

Only three weeks after the Tientsin convention, England, less expansionist than some of the European powers, suddenly occupied Port Hamilton, a harbour formed by two islands off the Korean coast. The reason for this was the outbreak of the Penjdeh crisis between Great Britain and Russia over Afghanistan. As war seemed likely the Admiralty made up its mind to occupy the port as a naval base. Naval vessels were sent there in the first week of April; when a Russian ship visited the harbour in the second week of May the British flag was hoisted. Tseng Chi-tse, the Chinese Minister in London, inquired about this occupation on 8 April. He was informed on 26 April that it was a temporary occupation to prevent seizure by another power, and the Foreign Office indicated its readiness to reach agreement with China on the matter. Li Hung-chang used this as an opportunity to propose an Anglo-Chinese alliance, but there was little response in England or even in China. The Chinese government's proposal that Great Britain should guarantee Korea's independence similarly received no support from England. The Japanese Minister in Peking proposed an international guarantee of Korea by the powers, but again there was no response in London. An informal *entente* of England and China did, however, grow up from this date and they co-operated against their common rivals, Russia, France, and Japan, until the Sino-Japanese War of 1894, when England deserted China.

Almost as soon as Port Hamilton was occupied in April 1885, the Afghanistan tension began to ease between Britain and Russia. At the same time China's war with France and her strained relations with Japan were brought to an end. But tension persisted in the area because of the growing suspicion by other powers of Russia's intentions. Russia's expansionist interest had shifted toward East Asia ever since the territory north of Manchuria was taken and Vladivostok founded in 1860. Since the harbour there was closed by ice four months of the year, the Russians wanted an open harbour suitable as a naval base. Korea had excellent harbours. Russia had even occupied Tsushima, a Japanese island off the south coast of Korea, in 1861, until warned away by English naval vessels. She now brought pressure on China, tempted the Koreans with offers of aid and threatened to seize a Korean port in retaliation for the British occupation of Port Hamilton. At the same time she began negotiations with Li for a joint guarantee of Korea's independence. But the opportunity for an international guarantee was lost because the Chinese failed to appreciate its value. The Russians insisted on the *status quo* in Korea and an arrangement by which the regime could only be changed by joint agreement. Li feared the loss of Chinese freedom of action in Korea as a result of what would have been in effect neutralisation of the peninsula. The matter was not pursued farther.

England withdrew from Port Hamilton on receiving Russia's assurance, at the end of 1886, that she had no territorial ambition in Korea. The Chinese then intervened more actively in the country to oppose the king's attempts to send representatives abroad and to pay off the Korean debts to other countries. China made loans to replace these and assumed the control of Korean customs and telegraphs as security. China succeeded by these means in expanding her political influence in Korea and in excluding any other rivals. She did so with the acquiescence of Japan: the country was under a joint Sino-Japanese protectorate. But the danger of Russian expansion persisted. Li Hung-chang made great efforts to have a modern Chinese fighting-force created, but he was dependent on the resources of his own province, the other provinces being reluctant to finance the weak and corrupt central government. As a counter to Russian expansionism England lent him instructors and helped him to start a modern fleet and to set up a military and naval establishment at Port Arthur in Manchuria. Li secretly sent an English engineer to investigate a railway route north to the Russian border in 1890. This was found out by Russia and the alarm stimulated St Petersburg to carry out the plan for a trans-Siberian railroad, construction of which began in 1891. The inevitable increase of Russian power which would result deeply disturbed the Chinese and Japanese leaders who began to feel that urgent action might be needed to forestall its consequences.

Japan's position was by now quite different from China's as a result of twenty years of internal progress. To a large extent the programme of strength through internal development had been successful. Modern legal codes and courts as well as a parliament were in operation; a modern education system had been established; and Japan was able to revise her treaties with the great powers and to abolish the foreign consular jurisdiction and the fixed tariffs which hampered other oriental countries. In addition to a navy, a modern conscript army had been created. These advances created a greater confidence in the military and diplomatic instruments upon which the Japanese leaders had lavished their efforts for twenty years. At the same time, parliament and the political parties, who gave expression to the discontent resulting from the social and economic consequences of this rapid change, voiced their criticism particularly against the weak and pacific foreign policy pursued for so long.

The Chinese leaders completely misjudged the situation in Japan when a new crisis arose over Korea from the demand of the Tonghak party, or 'party of Eastern learning', for the end of misgovernment and corruption. This party was nationalistic, anti-western and anti-Japanese and it appealed to Korean conservatism, which hated modern and particularly western innovations. The Tonghaks seized control in many Korean provinces and defeated the government troops sent against them. The Korean king asked for Chinese troops to suppress the rebellion. Li, dispatching them, thought that the Japanese government was too absorbed in internal affairs to care much about Korea. Even the Chinese Minister in Tokyo, noting the fury of the political battles in parliament, was of the opinion that no action by Japan was to be expected. But anti-Korean feeling was particularly great in Japan at this time: there had been Korean attempts to stop rice exports to Japan and a pro-Japanese progressive Korean, Kim Ok-kyun, had been killed. The situation was not unlike that of 1873. It is not surprising that the Japanese leaders promptly sent troops, as they had done under less tense conditions in 1882 and 1884.

When the Japanese troops reached Korea the Tonghaks dispersed. The Chinese troops were held at Yashan near the Chinese border to avoid any clash. With their troops in the field the Japanese leaders were inclined to force a solution to the troublesome Korean problem after years of inconclusive efforts. Li Hung-chang and the Chinese court, dismayed by the prompt Japanese intervention, requested a simultaneous withdrawal as the rebellion seemed to be over. The Japanese Prime Minister, Ito Hirobumi, decided not to withdraw but to insist that the two countries should join in carrying out internal reforms in Korea. This would have put Korea under a real condominium and ended the freedom of China to influence her alone. The Chinese leaders were not prepared to accept. The forthright Yüan Shih-k'ai, China's resident in Seoul, asked to have Chinese troops moved forward and reinforcements sent from China. Li asked Japan to withdraw, since her recognition of Korean independence precluded intervention in internal affairs. Li hoped Russia would intervene. Japan went on to occupy Seoul and announced that she would reform Korea on her own. When she expelled Chinese officials from Seoul Li asked for reinforcements to be sent to Pyongyang. On 25 July 1894 the Japanese navy sank a Chinese troop-ship. On 29 July Japanese forces attacked and routed a concentration of five thousand Chinese troops stationed on the west coast of Korea. War was declared by Japan on 1 August.

The Chinese reinforced their army in Korea until it numbered 13,000 men, but no more troops were available in the adjoining provinces of Manchuria and no preparation to bring up larger numbers from China had been made. In addition the Japanese mastery of the sea, secured by the defeat of a Chinese squadron off the mouth of the Yalu river on 17 September 1894, made the use of the only rapid means of communication impossible for the Chinese. Two days before this naval battle the Japanese army attacked the Chinese forces, which they outnumbered, before Pyongyang (P'ingjang), the capital of northern Korea, defeated them and drove them back to the Chinese frontier, the Yalu river. During October and November the Japanese continued their advance into South Manchuria, winning a number of engagements. On 21 November they captured Lushun (Port Arthur), the best harbour on that coast. In February 1895 the remains of the Chinese fleet were destroyed at Weihaiwei, and that port captured; in March the conquest of South Manchuria was completed by a victory at Yingkou, near the Treaty Port of Newchuang.

Japan tried to mollify Great Britain and Russia by assuring them that she would seize no Korean territory: only reforms, not Japanese control, would be undertaken. Britain had first thought that China would win easily, but when China's prompt collapse threatened the balance of power she proposed a joint intervention to several powers. Germany and the United States refused although Russia agreed. The British Cabinet then came to the conclusion that China was too ineffective and that diplomatic efforts to assist her would be useless. British public opinion also turned away from China. But while Great Britain was withdrawing her proposals Russia approached France and Germany in February and March 1895 with proposals for co-operation to secure the independence and integrity of Korea. Germany hesitated; fearing that China was about to be partitioned she inquired if England would support her in securing the Chusan Islands at the mouth of the Yangtse river. But she finally fell in with the Russian proposals and there developed a triple combination of European powers that was to prove a great threat both to Japanese and to British interests.

At the peace negotiations in April 1895 Japan insisted on the complete independence of Korea and demanded the cession to herself of Formosa, the Pescadores Islands and the southern tip of Manchuria containing Port Arthur. Her continental territorial demands went beyond the policy of Soejima twenty years before. An indemnity, the opening of new ports, freedom of navigation on the Yangtse and the right to set up factories in China were also included in her peace terms. A treaty with these provisions was signed by Li Hung-chang on 17 April at Shimonoseki in Japan. Great Britain was satisfied with these terms: the new commercial privileges obtained by Japan would be automatically extended to the other powers; Japan represented a much better obstacle to Russian ambitions than did China. At the same time Korea was to be fully independent and kept out of Russian hands. But Russia, who was too weak to seize Chinese territory before the Siberian railway was finished, France, who was Russia's ally since the negotiation between 1892 and 1894 of the Franco-Russian convention, and Germany, who feared that the partition of China would otherwise be attempted without her, joined together in 'inviting' Japan to give up South Manchuria. If Japan refused, Russia was prepared to bombard Japanese ports and thus to pose as saviour of China.

The Russian, French, and German notes were presented on 23 April. On 1 May Japan offered to return all but Port Arthur but on 5 May she capitulated completely by agreeing to return all her conquests on the continent after the treaty was ratified and if she were given a larger indemnity. The treaty was ratified at Cheefoo on 8 May under the guns of the Russian fleet stripped for action.

The three friends of China fell out over the opportunity to lend money to China for the payment of the Japanese indemnity. Negotiations began between China and bankers in London and Berlin. France, fearing to be left out, offered alternative funds, and Russia agreed to back them with a government guarantee. China accepted this offer and in an agreement with Russia on 6 July agreed to furnish additional security in case of default and undertook to give no foreign power rights to supervise or administer her revenues without granting similar rights to Russia. Russia thus gained a privileged position which marked the start of her preponderance in China. Germany was resentful that her bankers had been jostled aside from a lucrative loan, but she welcomed Russia's diversion from European affairs to the Far East and so made little protest.

Japan retained some of the spoils of her victory. She gained Formosa and the Pescadores as well as destroying China's influence in Korea. But she had failed to expand on to the continent at a time when the great weakness of China, now made clear, combined with the effects of the recent Franco-Russian Alliance on international alignments to stimulate a scramble for Chinese wealth and territory by the European powers. The scramble for China was characterised by the gaining of spheres of influence—areas in which foreign powers obtained concessions for railways, mines and telegraphs, secured favoured positions for trade and leased areas for naval bases or commerce. France was the first to make such demands. As early as 20 June 1895 she forced upon China a border settlement concerning Tongking. Three new frontier stations were opened to trade and reductions were made in China's tariffs. China agreed to apply first to France for help in exploiting mines in the three neighbouring provinces. Later an agreement was made by which French railways and telegraphs would be extended into China.

Great Britain, who possessed the bulk of the trade and influence in south China, was the power most threatened by the French move, but was also well placed to counter it. As soon as it was made she negotiated a separate arrangement with France by which the two powers agreed to share any privileges gained in the southern provinces of China. In February 1896 she obtained China's agreement to her proposals regarding the border between China and Burma. She also gained the right to extend a railway into China from there. This was in compensation for the Chinese concession to France. France then demanded compensation for the English compensation; in June 1897 she received the right to extend her Chinese railway and priority to exploit mines in the southern provinces. Her demands were accompanied by threats to stop payment on the Japanese indemnity loan to China.

On 6 April 1896 a most important demand came from Russia for railway rights in north Manchuria. She wanted a more direct line for the trans-Siberian railway. Since this was a line the Chinese preferred to build themselves, Li Hung-chang was offered an alliance when he went to St Petersburg for the tsar's coronation. A secret defensive alliance against Japan covering Korea and other territories was signed on 3 June 1896, in return for which China agreed that the railway should be built by a Russo-Chinese Bank on an eighty-year lease, though reserving the right to buy it back after thirty-six years. A so-called private company, the Chinese Eastern Railway, was organised by the Russo-Chinese Bank and the Chinese government. It was provided with some Chinese officers, but these had little influence: the bank's shares were all owned by the Russian government and the organisation was used by Russia to develop Russian control in the north.

Japan, dissatisfied with the situation in Korea, also decided to reach agreement with Russia. She offered to divide Korea at the thirty-eighth parallel into Russian and Japanese spheres. An agreement—the Yamagata–Lobanov agreement—reached on 9 June 1896 established what was really a joint protectorate. Neither Russia nor Japan yet felt strong enough to antagonise the other over Korea. They pledged joint support to the Korean king to enable him to establish order, build up his military and police and prevent financial collapse. They renounced separate action in Korea and agreed on arrangements for sending troops into the country, if this became necessary. The two powers were thus temporarily assured that neither would seize territory in Korea, although Japan was free to continue the commercial penetration of that area as Russia had become free to develop the area farther north.

China and Korea were protected from Japan, but there was no one to protect China against Russia, France or England, whose commercial and industrial penetration in separate spheres in north, south and centre was already proceeding, or against Germany, whose demands now began the second stage of the scramble. The German emperor was eager to gain a naval and commercial base since his country was dependent in the Far East upon British Hong Kong for coal and supplies. In August 1897, after careful consideration, the German emperor personally discussed with the tsar the leasing by Germany of the port of Kiao-chow in Shantung. On 1 November two German missionaries were killed by bandits in Shantung. A German squadron was sent to Kiao-chow to occupy it and threaten reprisals. The emperor declared that he was 'firmly determined to give up our over-cautious policy which is regarded as weak throughout eastern Asia, and to demonstrate through the use of sternness, and if necessary of the most brutal ruthlessness towards the Chinese, that the German emperor cannot be trifled with'.

The Russians protested strongly against the German move. Great Britain, on the other hand, to whom Germany was ready to make concessions in return for support, was not only not opposed to the step, but was pleased to see the Germans and Russians competing in the north of China away from the British sphere. The Russians backed the Chinese in resisting the German demands, but at the end of the year abandoned them in order to pursue a different plan. By March 1898 Germany had received a ninety-nine-year lease of Kiao-chow Bay, where she soon built the major military and naval base of Tsingtau. Extensive if ill-defined rights to build railways and develop mines in the whole province made Shantung in all but name a German protectorate.

When the Germans had shown themselves determined not to give way over Kiao-chow, Russian fleet orders for opposition to this occupation had been withdrawn. Russia's alternative policy was to demand an ice-free port in north China for herself. She hesitated before doing so both from fear of precipitating the partition of China and because of the risk of British and Japanese opposition. Britain and Japan opposed any control by Russia of a Korean port for fear it would give her naval predominance in East Asia. A squadron of nine English cruisers and some Japanese ships was now sent to Korea to emphasise their opposition to any moves in that direction. The Japanese also began a naval expansion programme which was to be completed in 1904 and which the Russian minister in Tokyo reported to be aimed at war with Russia. These dangers led to divisions in the Russian government. The Russian Foreign Minister, Count Michael Muraviev, urged the taking of Port Arthur on the tip of Manchuria from which the Japanese had been driven only two years before; all the other Russian ministers were opposed. The Finance Minister, Witte, thought it unnecessary to take anything when China was on such excellent terms with Russia. On the contrary, he still thought the Germans should be ejected from Kiao-chow. Nevertheless, Muraviev managed to win over the tsar, who told the German emperor on 14 December 1897 that on the invitation of the Chinese a Russian squadron would anchor 'temporarily' at Port Arthur, and who expressed the hope that Russia and Germany would work together in the Far East. This decision marked the abandonment of the Russian policy of protecting Chinese territory in favour of participation in the scramble for territorial partition.

When China approached Russia for a loan to finance the third instalment of the Japanese indemnity, she was asked to lease Russia a harbour on the Yellow Sea with connections to the Siberian railway. Russia demanded, in other words, a port and connections to the Manchurian coast, the very territory which she had forced Japan to relinquish. China tried to evade the pressure by turning to Britain for finances. In return for her support Britain asked for rights which would enable her to counter France in south China and to safeguard the British sphere in central China. As the lesser of two evils the loan was awarded to the British Hong Kong and Shanghai Banking Corporation with some concessions to Britain.

The British government, alarmed by the threat of Russian penetration in the north, hoped to off-set it by co-operation, and opened talks with Russia. In order to keep open her access to the trade and industrial development of the whole of China, it wanted a guarantee of equal commercial opportunity in any new Russian sphere. Russia refused to give adequate reassurances on this point and in addition, on 3 March 1898, caused a crisis in Anglo-Russian relations by demanding Port Arthur, Talien, and railway rights from China. England approached the United States, Germany and Japan with the suggestion for a joint protest against the lease of Port Arthur. On 17 March she suggested joint action to the Japanese minister in London. Kato Takaaki recommended an alliance to his own government. This was rejected, and Kato resigned in protest, because the Japanese Prime Minister, like the British, preferred, if possible, to reach agreement with Russia. On 25 April the Nishi–Rosen agreement was signed by Japan and Russia which reaffirmed that both powers would abstain politically and militarily in Korea, and that Japan would have a free hand economically. By making slight concessions to Japan's interest in Korea, Russia was gaining Japanese acquiescence with her penetration in Manchuria. Japan for her part did not like to see any extension of Russian influence, but the Prime Minister thought that war with Russia was inevitable in due course and that this accommodation would serve until military preparations were complete and German and French support of Russia less likely.

England had sent warships to Port Arthur in January at the time of the Russian occupation, and the occupation caused a strong outcry against Russia in England. For some weeks a clash seemed possible. But when it was reported that Li Hung-chang and the other negotiators were yielding —on 27 March China agreed to a lease of Port Arthur to Russia—the British government decided that a war over Port Arthur was not justified, especially since the German and American governments had proved as reluctant as Japan to collaborate. Instead it decided to ask for a lease of Weihaiwei, a port in Shantung opposite Port Arthur. The Japanese had occupied it since the war of 1894, but were willing to hand it over to Britain, who assured both Japan and Germany that it would not be used against them. In the end, her reaction to the Russian move had been the same as Russia's to Germany's. Nor were other powers willing to be excluded. France demanded a coaling station; insisted upon a guarantee that China would not cede provinces in the French sphere of south China to any other country; and asked for further railway construction rights. These demands were granted and France took Kuangchow Bay in the south on 22 April 1898. In 1899 the Italians demanded Sanmen Bay in Chekiang. But by then the Chinese temper had changed. The Italian demand was rejected. Italy threatened war and recalled her minister. But China stood firm and nothing more was heard of Sanmen.

The rivalry of Russia, Britain, France and Germany in China was inspired by fears of the advantages that might be gained by competitors in the exploitation of the country. The spirit animating the powers was well expressed by Lord Salisbury, the British Prime Minister, when he said in his 'Dying Nations Speech' at the Albert Hall on 4 May 1898, 'The living nations will gradually encroach on the territory of the dying, and the seed and causes of conflict amongst civilised nations will speedily appear. Of course, it is not to be supposed that any one nation of the living nations will be allowed to have the profitable monopoly of curing or cutting up these unfortunate patients, and the controversy is as to who shall have the privilege of doing so, and in what measure he shall do it.'

As a result of the war with Spain in 1898 the United States government, too, began to show increased support for expansion in the Far East. American settlers had pressed for the annexation of Hawaii for years; now, on account of the war with Spain and because growing Japanese emigration made it possible that Hawaii might be lost as a naval base, it was annexed on 6 July 1898.

The Americans defeated the Spanish fleet in Manila Bay on 1 May 1898, and the defeat of Spain brought up the question of the future of her colonies. Germany hoped to obtain them. England, opposed as usual to German expansion, urged the United States to take the Philippines for herself. Her arguments were assisted by the dispatch of a German squadron to Manila, for this led to bad feelings between Germany and the United States. The German government had hoped at first for a German protectorate and then for the neutralisation or partition of the Philippines. The violently hostile American reaction to the presence of German ships confirmed the United States in her decision to obtain the Philippine Islands herself, and overcame her earlier hesitation. The final decision to demand all the islands reversed the earlier decision to ask for Luzon only. The islands, besides giving a good strategic position in the Pacific, would also give the United States a territorial base near to China and its valuable trade. The European powers already had such bases and it was clear that they and Japan would scramble for any such area that was not firmly held. These were the arguments underlying the American decision. For similar reasons the United States also had her title to the island of Guam confirmed by Spain.

Germany did not go entirely empty-handed. By secret agreements with Spain in September and December 1898 she was able to purchase the Caroline, Mariana and Pelew Islands, tiny and unproductive islands which were to provide naval and coaling stations. But she was severely disappointed about the outcome in the Philippines, as also by the outcome of an agreement she had reached with Great Britain concerning Portugal's colonies in Africa. She was accordingly the more determined to gain territory when the Samoan problem came up again. The much deposed and restored Samoan king died in 1898, and civil war was resumed. The American Chief Justice of Samoa fled to a British warship when his choice of the king's successor put him in jeopardy. A British ship landed marines to support the American protégé early in 1899. When an American admiral arrived in Samoa in March of 1899, his intervention in local politics caused new outbreaks. American and British ships damaged the German consulate in the course of the disturbances. Incensed by these events Germany pressed with increasing determination proposals which she had made in August 1898 for the partition of the Samoan islands. These would have given two islands to the United States, two to Germany, and Tonga to the British. Great Britain had rejected them, urging the objections of both New Zealand and Australia. In May 1899, however, under German pressure and against a background of worsening Anglo-German relations, she agreed that the three protecting powers should send commissioners to Samoa. Subsequently, partly because of her growing difficulties with the Boer Republic, England became disposed to settle the Samoan issue in a manner satisfactory to Germany—though Australia and New Zealand remained opposed to German expansion, which made it difficult for Britain to strike a bargain, and Germany still felt bitter at having had to struggle for the place where her first colonisation had occurred and where her interests were very large. Final agreement was reached on 1 November 1899. Germany received Upolu, the principal island, and Savaii. Britain received Tonga and Savage, the lesser Solomons and a disputed area in Togoland in Africa. The United States received the two islands in which she was interested in Samoa.

In China, despite the government's resistance to the Italian demands, the struggle for further foreign rights continued. A Franco-Belgian syndicate backed by the Russo-Chinese Bank obtained railway rights in the British sphere in central China and a British bank obtained railway rights in Manchuria. In compensation for the financial invasion of central China by Russian interests, Britain, by threats and naval demonstrations, also obtained other railway construction rights from China. But in 1899 the growing clash between their interests led Great Britain and Russia to sign an agreement to respect each other's spheres and not to support the entry of other powers into them. Russia did not come to the point of promising equal commercial opportunity to all comers in her sphere, as Britain had hoped and as she was willing to grant in her own area.

American business interests had received some of the concessions for railways in China. But they had been unable to take advantage of them, largely because of American reluctance to invest funds in China, and the United States government had not so far concerned itself directly with events in China. It was thus a new departure of some importance when, in September 1899, Hay, the American Secretary of State, asked England, Germany and Russia to promise equal treatment to foreign commerce in their spheres in China with regard to duties, railway charges, and harbour dues. This suggestion was in line with the British policy of preserving 'the open door' for trade and was particularly aimed at Russia; the American government was beginning to be afraid that American commercial interests would be excluded or discriminated against in Manchuria. Great Britain had previously suggested, in vain, that Russia and the United States should support such a policy. Japan, Italy and France were also asked by Hay to subscribe to the principle of equal treatment in November. All the governments addressed fell in with Hay's proposal, but Russia in fact so qualified her reply as to avoid agreeing to the principle of equal commercial treatment. The immediate effect of the American attempt to neutralise China was small, although it was later to be supported by the major powers. Hay's action indicated that the competition in China had reached serious proportions; but his attempt to find some co-operative method of halting the absorption of the country was premature.

China, meanwhile, was looking to Japan as a model in her effort to save herself from European aggression. She sent many students to study there, and while Japanese influence grew in Peking, that of Russia faded for the moment. But the expansionists in Russia were still busy. They wished to attain a good position in Korea where they would not be blocked, as they would by the British near Port Arthur, and where they could command the approach to Japan and north China. In 1898 a group of diplomats, bankers and business interests in Russia had formed the Eastern Asiatic Company with a dramatic plan to smuggle twenty thousand troops into Korea as woodsmen under a timber concession. The tsar gave his approval but the plan was blocked by Count Witte, the Finance Minister, who objected to the necessary loan. The Russian naval authorities then sought a base at Masampo on the southern tip of Korea. Despite the threats of Russia, the Koreans, backed by Japan, refused the request in the autumn of 1899. On 16 March 1900 a Russian squadron anchored near the capital of Korea and induced the king to permit a coal depot and naval hospital to be set up at Masampo. This created tension with both England and Japan, but neither Japan nor Russia was ready to fight at this time. Japan decided not to challenge Russia when she learned that the lease for Masampo was very restricted in nature.

In the summer of 1900, after the outbreak of the Boxer rebellion in China, although the Russian government had decided not to seize Manchuria and north China, it occupied Manchuria when Russia's small forces there were attacked by the Chinese. The less expansionist of the Russian leaders favoured taking no action to rescue the Peking legations. Eventually, however, a small force was sent, and other elements in the Russian government hoped to use it to gain control over the area near Peking. As soon as the legations had been relieved, Russia proposed that the joint expeditionary force which the powers had sent to Peking should be withdrawn immediately. Some Russians, including Witte, urged this general withdrawal from Peking in the hope of preventing a general partition of

China. Others supported the proposal because the presence of an international force would hamper their plans in the Peking area. Others hoped at least to use it as a means of gaining at least the goodwill of the Chinese in a settlement. England and Germany were dismayed by the suggestion: it appeared to them to be aimed at persuading the Chinese to present Russia with Manchuria in return for her having rid Peking of foreigners.

England and Germany also feared partition. They concluded an agreement on 16 October 1900 by which they would uphold throughout China, 'in so far as they could exert influence', equality of opportunity for all in trade, and by which they would themselves seek no territorial acquisitions. Great Britain hoped that this had assured her of German support against Russia, but Germany, who had, indeed, refused to commit herself regarding Manchuria in the negotiation of the agreement, told Russia that the agreement did not extend to Manchuria, where the Russian government was free to do as it wished. Germany was chiefly anxious to prevent Great Britain from using the crisis to increase her hold on the Yangtse valley, and had signed the agreement for that purpose.

Russia was already negotiating with China to obtain a stronger position in Manchuria and other regions of China adjacent to Russia. A draft agreement was given to the Chinese Minister in St Petersburg on 8 February 1901. It provided for the resumption of Chinese civil administration, but permitted the retention of Russian troops and gave new railway rights and indemnification for various Russian expenses. Even before it was presented to China the Japanese Foreign Minister asked Britain to join Japan in a protest to Russia against it. He met with no success. In February he suggested that Great Britain and Japan should jointly warn China against signing the agreement. Britain was afraid to ignore the Japanese proposals lest Japan finally accept an agreement with Russia for the partition of China, but she was also reluctant to be committed against Russia. Accordingly she tried to enlist German co-operation with herself and Japan against Russia. The Germans joined Great Britain and Japan in sending notes to Peking, but they would go no farther. The Russians, ignoring this step, pressed the Chinese to sign at the end of February. Japan hesitated to attack Russia, who might be supported by the French fleet. She therefore sought English support again, asking if England would hold France in check in the event of a Russo-Japanese War.

Germany hoped that England would accept this commitment to Japan and thus become so involved in difficulties with France and Russia that she would need an alliance with Germany. She had for some years been aiming at such an alliance on her own terms, which would include the demand for a larger share of the overseas possessions monopolised so exasperatingly by England. Approached again by Great Britain and Japan, she promised to be neutral if war broke out in East Asia, but refused to support Britain in demanding equal opportunity to trade—the 'open door'—in Manchuria. This caused strong resentment in England since Germany had seemed to join with her a year before in affirming an interest in maintaining the 'open door' in China. Deterred by the German attitude, the British government continued to hold back. The Japanese alone on 6 April sent a strong protest to Russia. The Russians reduced their demands on China, permitting some Chinese troops in Manchuria in return for a larger indemnity and dropping the request for a special sphere in other areas. Li Hung-chang was inclined to yield but, in the face of protests by other viceroys, the Chinese Board of Foreign Affairs appealed again to the foreign powers for aid. England and Japan again warned China not to sign an agreement with Russia. At this Russia withdrew her demands and insisted that she had never made any demands, only suggestions for temporary arrangements.

The Manchurian crisis was temporarily over, but since Russia remained in occupation of Manchuria the problem persisted for the other powers. This was the setting for the conclusion of the Anglo-Japanese Alliance. This project was again discussed between Great Britain and Japan in London in July 1901, but serious negotiations did not begin until October and even then there was further delay. England desired to include India within the scope of an agreement, but Japan insisted that it could only apply to 'the extreme east'. Another difficulty was that, while Great Britain needed an assurance that she would not be dragged into a Russo-Japanese dispute in which her own interests were not directly involved, Japan wanted to be sure of British support for her ambitions in Korea. Each side remained hesitant, moreover, as to whether it would not be better to reach agreement with Russia than with each other. Eventually, however, they reached agreement. The proposal which finally resulted was for a joint guarantee of the independence and integrity of China and Korea and of equal opportunities there for the commerce and trade of all countries; and it was so phrased that Japan was given a free hand in Korea without, on the other hand, receiving undue encouragement there. In addition each party promised to remain neutral if the other was involved in war with a third party and to go to the other's aid if another power sided against her in the conflict.

The principal value of the agreement to Britain was that it precluded any Japanese–Russian co-operation to partition China to the detriment of British interests. The agreement also had the effect of protecting China. On Japan's part the agreement safeguarded her special interest in Korea. Her main concern was that Russia should not be allowed into Korea, whence she could dominate East Asia and threaten Japan. She had even been willing to concede a free hand to Russia in Manchuria and adjacent parts of China provided she was allowed to dominate Korea. Russo-Japanese discussions had fallen through because Russia had not been willing to go so far. Once the Siberian railway was finished, Russia intended to take Korea whether Japan opposed her or not. But with the Anglo-Japanese Alliance Japan felt confident that she could deal with any Russian move.

Both Russia and France were disagreeably surprised to learn of the new alliance. The effect on Russia was immediate. She announced that she was ready to withdraw from Manchuria, but asked China for a separate agreement with and special concessions to the Russo-Chinese Bank. On 11 February the Chinese, strengthened by a protest from the United States, as well as by the news of the new alliance, rejected the bank agreement. On 13 February in the British parliament the government stated that Manchuria was not excluded from the new alliance's scope. Although Japan and Britain did not intend to get involved in a war over Manchuria, this was technically correct, and the Russians must have been impressed. On 8 April they finally withdrew from Manchuria with nothing to show for all their efforts.

The Anglo-Japanese Alliance, by thus bringing the Manchurian crisis to an end, also brought to a halt, if only temporarily, that process in which, especially since 1894, the European governments as well as Japan and the U.S.A. had engaged in increasingly fierce competition in the Far East.

CHAPTER XXIV

THE UNITED STATES AND
THE OLD WORLD

BY the time of the Civil War the first American expansive drive was over. The most obvious objectives of manifest destiny had been achieved, and the frontiers of the United States were logically satisfying. The country stretched from sea to sea. To the north lay Canada, a region which, it could be argued, must some day inevitably fall to the United States, but whose accession it was neither necessary nor desirable to hasten. To the south lay Mexico, arid and uninviting, and peopled by men whose stock, language, religion and traditions were suspect to most Americans.

Within the United States itself there was ample land to occupy the energies of a vigorous people. Even before the Civil War manifest destiny and the lure of the West had not been the only impulse to expansion. Competition between North and South for the control of the West, as a source of both economic and political strength, had been as important in determining the urgency of the rush to the Pacific. The genuine expansionists had hoped to divert Americans from their sectional quarrel by invoking the imperial dream; but their failure to do so did not slow an advance which the quarrel itself turned into a race. When the Civil War was won and lost, the most obvious goal of expansion had been achieved and the most impelling motive of expansion removed.

If there was nothing in American domestic politics to cause an interest in foreign affairs, there was equally nothing in the outside world to require it. In the thirty years after 1870 it was the affairs of Europe that commanded the attention of the European powers. They were years in which great areas were added to European empires, but it is by now a familiar paradox that empires grow at a rate inversely proportional to the attention they receive. When competition is keen the publicity is enormous and the gains small. Empire-builders flourish in the shadows of indifference. It was already well established that the western hemisphere was no area for colonisation. Apart from the hostility of the United States, the political structure of Latin America was sufficiently advanced to make imperialism there a matter calling for the expenditure of considerable national resources. It would have required government intervention, and that their European preoccupations prevented the governments of Europe from considering. After the abortive French intervention in Mexico, whose abrupt end was dictated by European commitments rather than by American opposition, the United States did not face even the mildest challenge to the principles of the Monroe Doctrine. This, originally enunciated by President Monroe in 1823, made two main points—that the western hemisphere was not to be regarded as an area for colonisation by European powers, and that European intervention in the Americas would be treated as an unfriendly act by the United States—as well as asserting that the United States did not intend to take any part in European affairs. The characteristic attitude was that of Russia, which was not only willing but eager to get rid of Alaska, and sold it to the United States in 1867 for the derisory sum of seven million dollars. American enthusiasm for the purchase was distinctly less than Russian for the sale. 'Seward's icebox'—named after W. H. Seward, Secretary of State under Andrew Johnson, who negotiated the purchase—was widely regarded as a poor buy. True to the imperial pattern, the Americans made their largest acquisition in indifference.

The United States then settled into a period in which the development of the country absorbed the energy of its people, and foreign affairs got little attention. The victory of the North, and the political dominance which victory brought, gave the country unity, superficial at first but nevertheless effective, greater than it had had for years. The growing strength of the United States—and these were years of prodigious growth—made confidence increasingly plausible at a time when the attention of the powers was concentrated on Europe and that of Americans on their own continent. But it was essential to American confidence that Americans did not notice the conditions which made it possible. Their ideas of the outside world were based on experience in the Americas; and within the Americas they had long achieved the position of members of the leading state. It was their good fortune to be able to develop their policies and their political myths within the limits of the western hemisphere.

The necessary conditions were the existence in Europe of a group of large powers of roughly equivalent strength. Potentially, if not in actual military force, the United States could already rank as one of the powers; but her geographical position would have made her less effective in Europe then her peers. While the alignments of the powers there were still flexible, it was unnecessary for any group to try to involve her in Europe, and unwise for all to challenge her elsewhere.

The United States was not, during these years, without contact with the European powers. But the first signs of American expansion were towards the west—in the Pacific. There had never been in the American mind the same antipathy towards contact with the Far East that the 'corruption' of Europe had on occasion inspired. Expansion had always meant expansion to the west; and one powerful element in the myth of manifest destiny had been the idea that the United States, linking East and West, was ideally situated to be the centre of their trade. As early as 1844 the

United States had a trade treaty with China. In 1853 it was the American Perry who opened Japan to the trade of the West. But for long, even in the Far East, the United States shared the belief also held in Britain—that trade was a matter apart from government intervention. For Secretary Seward the purchase of Alaska was part of a larger design. The indifference to his purchase was an indication of how little the design was understood.

The first American imperial enterprises could not but increase American confidence. The domination, and finally in 1898 the annexation, of Hawaii was achieved without intervention from Europe; in Samoa, though European powers were directly interested, the prize was relatively small and the competition relatively mild (ch. XXIII). Elsewhere the United States hardly came into direct competition with Europe before the 1890's. Meanwhile, however, relations with South America were becoming closer. James G. Blaine, Secretary of State under President Garfield in 1881, and again under Harrison from 1889 to 1892, was the leading advocate of what came to be called pan-Americanism. Though himself a strong protectionist, Blaine saw that protection was damaging American influence in South America. The countries of South America were still essentially producers of raw materials, and they sold the bulk of their crops—coffee, sugar, hides, wool and others—to the United States. They found it cheaper, however, to buy their manufactured goods in Europe. The pattern of trade was being distorted, and as European trade with Latin America increased, so, Blaine feared, would European influence. His proposed remedy was an American customs union, under which United States goods would enjoy preference in Latin American countries in exchange for reciprocal preference. As part of his design Blaine hoped to arrange arbitration treaties to cover disputes in Latin America, and pan-American conferences to foster close relations among American countries. Blaine had no opportunity to put his plan into effect during Garfield's short presidency; when, returned to office under Harrison, he called the first International American Conference in 1889, his proposals for a customs union and for arbitration were both rejected. The Latin Americans were suspicious of domination from the north, and, since most of their goods already entered the United States duty free, it seemed to them that Blaine's objects were political, not economic. On the American side the businessmen who dominated Blaine's own party were equally suspicious of treaties which might limit American tariffs. Yet his setback was more apparent than real; though the conference would not commit itself to arbitration, President Hayes had already arbitrated a boundary dispute between the Argentine and Paraguay, and Cleveland later arbitrated another between the Argentine and Brazil. Blaine was too busy too early; overestimating the European challenge, he tried to force an American influence in South America which was inevitably growing.

These were, in short, the years of business diplomacy, when it was still possible to claim that the United States had no interests outside her own shores except the maintenance of standards of international conduct such as would make the world both safe and profitable for her citizens. This may appear a simple premise, which should have made the conduct of consistent policy an easy matter; but, no less than other bases for foreign policy, it had limitations. With so few genuinely national interests that could be described as vital, or even defined, American policy was more than usually open to local or temporary pressures. There was no major rift within the country to dominate politics, and the way was open for a whole series of accommodations among politicians which governments, in the absence of stronger counter-pressures, found it difficult to resist. Not every motive in American foreign policy was merely selfish or parochial; there was plenty of idealism, and the defenders of local interests were not, usually, acting improperly. But the interplay of elements so equally balanced and so liable to temporary unbalance made American policy more variable than that of other countries.

It was not until the 1890's that Americans began to pay much attention to the imperatives of international policy. When they did, it was for two main reasons. First, the steady growth of the United States in population and industrial potential since the Civil War made her now a formidable power. The increasing recognition which the powers of Europe gave to that fact in their calculations brought its implications to the attention of Americans also. It became more difficult to assume the continuance of isolation when others were debating its limitations. Second, at the end of the nineteenth century, when the rivalries of the European powers took their classic imperialist form, when competition in China, Africa and the Pacific caught and held public attention, the United States could not remain unaffected by ideas which were influential in western Europe. There, *Machtpolitik* got new support from the work of Darwinian sociologists, who argued that nations and races, like species in nature, competed to survive, and that the survival of the fittest was a moral process. Strength was not merely necessary for security, but necessary as evidence of the right to survive. This belief was widely shared in the United States, as were the ambitions it fostered. Nevertheless, American policy remained distinctive. Influential though the new ideas were, their effect was modified by the history, the political traditions and the geographical situation of the United States. Imperialism fought a running battle with older ideas; American policy charted the struggle.

It was the Spanish–American War, usually and rightly regarded as a landmark, which brought American policy forcibly to the notice of the world and of Americans themselves. But there were earlier indications of change. The first of the controversies which enlarged American thinking was the Venezuela boundary crisis of 1895. The boundary between

Venezuela and British Guiana had never been adequately surveyed and had long been in dispute. There was a long history of diplomatic exchanges on the subject between Great Britain and Venezuela, and at various times the United States had been used as an intermediary. There had also been earlier independent American expressions of interest, but these had not gone beyond general statements of desire to see the dispute settled, and of readiness to do anything that might help to settle it. The Venezuelans hoped for more. They frequently urged on the United States the merits of supporting a small South American country against a large European one. Their aim, or one of their aims, was American intervention. In 1895 they achieved it. President Cleveland and Richard Olney, his Secretary of State, determined to see the matter settled, if necessary by the direct action of the United States.

The new policy was set out in Olney's instruction to the United States ambassador in London, dated 20 July 1895. It asserted the right of the United States to intervene, and invoked in support of that right the Monroe Doctrine. British activity in South America would be contravening that doctrine, if it could be shown that Britain was extending her territory at the expense and against the opposition of Venezuela. From this it followed, said Olney, that it was the right and duty of the United States to determine the facts and so to judge whether the Monroe Doctrine were relevant or not. Lord Salisbury, then both Prime Minister and Foreign Secretary, took more than four months to reply. In two coolly superior dispatches dated 26 November he denied the right of the United States to intervene, he pointed out that the Monroe Doctrine was a principle of American policy, not a rule of international law, and he held that in any event Olney had extended it to cover matters to which it had no relevance.

The dispute became public in December when, in response to Salisbury's dispatches, Cleveland sent a special message to Congress. In it he claimed that the American government had made repeated efforts to persuade Great Britain and Venezuela to agree, that these efforts had failed through the obduracy of Great Britain, and that it was now time for the United States to determine the correct boundary and impose that line on the disputants, if need be by force. As a start he proposed to appoint an American investigating commission, and he asked Congress to appropriate the necessary funds.

American opinion strongly endorsed Cleveland's action. British opinion was indignant, but above all surprised. As James Bryce wrote to Theodore Roosevelt, 'Not one man out of ten in the House of Commons even knew there was such a thing as a Venezuelan question pending'. The rest of the story is that of the negotiation by which Britain ultimately came to accept American intervention, and not only intervention but replacement of Venezuela as the other party to the dispute. Salisbury abandoned his objection to arbitration of the boundary, obtaining in return only the small concession that occupation or political control of any area for fifty years should establish title to it. The arbitration tribunal consisted of two members from each side and a neutral jurist—a Russian. Two Americans sat on the tribunal, and no Venezuelan. The tribunal substantially accepted the British case.

Though Cleveland had been careful to say that in the first instance he was only setting up a commission to investigate the facts, without prejudice to the merits of the case, it was apparent to many observers on both sides that he only acted at all because he thought that Great Britain was in the wrong. Only that assumption would have made the Monroe Doctrine relevant. Whether rightly or wrongly used, it was not intended to protect European colonies against the encroachment of South American republics. American intervention, then, was not impartial; but apart from any bias which the mere fact of intervention implied, the United States had greatly enlarged the number of disputes in which, if this precedent were followed, she could intervene. From now on any dispute could be regarded as coming within the scope of the Monroe Doctrine, provided only that it involved an American and a European power. For a time the precedent seemed likely to become established. When American policy changed in this respect it did so primarily because of the growing resentment among smaller American republics of this supervision from the north.

President Cleveland was a man of courage and honesty, and one hostile to imperialism. He was one of the last opponents of expansion. He prevented while he could the annexation of Hawaii, and he opposed foreign adventures, naval building and competition with rival powers. It is therefore the more surprising that he should have enlarged the scope of the Monroe Doctrine. Probably he did not realise the full implications of what he was doing; he shared with Olney the belief that Britain was inclined to treat American interests lightly, and was therefore determined to defend them vigorously; nevertheless his action reveals the strong moral element in American imperialism. It was modified, of course, by other elements; it was not always as strong in others as it was in Cleveland; but it was important, and it largely accounts for the violence with which American policy was often expressed. Cleveland and Olney thought that they were righting a wrong. If the verdict of the arbitration commission is to be accepted, they were not, but they thought they were and they spoke with the vigour of that conviction.

At the time of the Venezuela boundary dispute there was a good deal of hostility between the United States and Canada—fed by subjects as diverse as Fenianism and fishing rights. In 1897, when President McKinley succeeded Cleveland, a long-drawn-out dispute began between the two countries over the boundary between Alaska and Canada, which was not finally settled till 1903. The boundary had been defined by an Anglo-

Russian Treaty of 1825. In 1867, when Russia sold Alaska to the United States, the Americans succeeded to all Russian rights under that treaty. The definition of the boundary, however, was one thing; the surveying of it quite another. In practice the definition proved inadequate. The exact location of the boundary was not of any importance until gold was found in the border region at the end of the century, but miners of both nationalities then began to invade the area and there was hope of more permanent development. That made it desirable to mark the boundary accurately. A narrow coastal strip deeply indented by inlets extends southwards from the main body of Alaska. The most important point at issue was whether the boundary properly ran across these inlets. This would have given Canada access to the sea at the head of the inlets, and ports of her own convenient to the goldfields, and would have reduced American territory to isolated headlands. The Canadians argued that this was the proper interpretation of the treaty, the Americans that the Canadian claim had never been raised before 1890 and was indefensible.

There were two possible ways of approaching the problem. Either it could be treated as a political dispute, and therefore open to compromise, or it could be treated as a strictly legal one. The Canadians—represented, of course, by the British government—tried both ways. When the problem first arose a joint commission, on which both Canada and Newfoundland were represented, was already examining certain minor but vexatious issues in dispute between the two countries. The settlement of the Alaskan boundary was referred to that commission, but without success. Ironically, in view of the later history of the dispute, the Americans complained that Lord Herschell, the chief British commissioner, was too insistent on the letter of his case and not ready enough to compromise. At the same time, as will be seen, the two countries were negotiating the terms of the building and control of an isthmian canal. The Canadians tried to connect that question with the Alaska boundary, with equal lack of success. The Americans maintained that the Alaska boundary had no relation with other questions and should be settled as a matter apart. That was undoubtedly sound policy. Americans were settling the disputed region faster than Canadians, and Canada did not in fact have access to the sea. Time was on the American side. A *modus vivendi* was reached in October 1899. Once that had removed the risk of trouble on the frontier, John Hay, now Secretary of State, was quite willing to postpone a permanent settlement.

Accordingly the Canadians had to concede the major American point, that this was a legal dispute, which should be settled by a judicial tribunal and not by negotiation. The appointment of the tribunal, however, proved very difficult. The Venezuela boundary had been settled by a tribunal of five, two from each side and one neutral. Yet in 1897 Britain and the United States had signed a general arbitration treaty providing that each country should find three out of six arbiters, five of whom must agree for a decision. The treaty had narrowly failed to pass the Senate, but after long negotiation this was the form of tribunal agreed in January 1903, without the five-sixths majority rule. It is a measure of how time had been working against Canada that by then Sir Wilfred Laurier, the Canadian Premier, had given up hope of getting a port and was anxious to shift the responsibility for giving way on to a tribunal, while the Americans, who had blocked any other form of tribunal, accepted even this one only with reluctance. It finally consisted of three Americans, two Canadians, and one Englishman.

Once the judicial tribunal was accepted the dispute turned on the proper interpretation of the treaty of 1825. Both sides had a defensible case, though there seems little doubt that the American case was the better. The United States won a complete victory. Canada did not gain access to the sea in the disputed region. But though the result was reasonable enough the means by which it was reached were more dubious. Neither in its composition nor in its procedure was the tribunal truly judicial. Clearly it could only reach a decision if at least one of the members rejected the case of the government which had appointed him, and the confidence given by that knowledge was important in securing American agreement to the tribunal. In the event, the English member, Lord Alverstone, the Lord Chief Justice, voted with the Americans. He maintained that he had considered the case on its merits and had reached a strictly judicial decision. No one, however, either in the United States or in Canada, believed the same of the American members. Theodore Roosevelt, who had succeeded to the Presidency when McKinley was assassinated in 1901, undoubtedly violated the spirit of the agreement in selecting partisans. None was a 'jurist of repute', as the agreement required—though Elihu Root, then Secretary of War and without judicial experience, later became a member of the Permanent Court of Arbitration at the Hague—and each had committed himself in public on the subject before the hearings began. The choice was the more unnecessary because Roosevelt had stated publicly that he had no intention of accepting an adverse decision.

In these circumstances the setting up of the tribunal was itself evidence of American victory. The manner of the triumph was Roosevelt's. Hay, gentle and anglophile, would have been content with the maintenance of the *modus vivendi*; when the tribunal was set up he recognised that Roosevelt's nominations were needlessly offensive. Roosevelt, however, regarded the American case as unassailable, and saw the tribunal as merely a means of allowing the British government to escape from an untenable position, and American agreement to it as a concession. He was not prepared to risk any compromise in its conclusions, or even to seem to do so. 'Speak softly and carry a big stick' was one of Roosevelt's favourite maxims. In the conduct of politics, his failing was not that he carried a big stick but that he was quite incapable of speaking softly. He was unable to understand, or even to notice, Canadian resentment of his action.

Some time before the settlement of the Alaskan boundary, the Hay–Pauncefote canal treaty had brought to an end the negotiations with which the Canadians had once tried to connect it. The possibility of cutting a ship canal through the Central American isthmus had been discussed for many years, and the control of such a canal accepted as important. Rivalry between Britain and the United States in Central America in mid-century had been allayed by the Clayton–Bulwer Treaty of 1850. This provided that any isthmian canal that might be built should be jointly controlled, should not be fortified, and should be neutralised for the benefit of all nations.

After the Civil War, American interest in a ship canal grew, and the Clayton–Bulwer Treaty came to be seen as a limitation on the United States. While the arguments for the canal were commercial, there were opposing interests—railroad interests for example—whose opposition, together with the technical difficulties of the task, prevented action; but support for the canal was greatly strengthened by the Spanish–American War. When war broke out, the American battleship *Oregon* had to make the long voyage round Cape Horn in order to reach the Atlantic and take an effective part. The propagandists of expansion and a big navy were not slow to point out that a canal would have been of great use in the war in the Caribbean, and to renew their insistence that it should be built—and not only built, but built and controlled by the United States.

The Clayton–Bulwer Treaty stood in the way. There had been attempts by unscrupulous American politicians to argue that it had lapsed and could be ignored; but that was not the best American opinion. Though there was a good deal of talk about the possibility of the United States abrogating the treaty, Hay and his colleagues were anxious to act with strict legality. Hay put forward his proposals in December 1898. Lord Salisbury's initial response was favourable, and Hay set to work with Sir Julian Pauncefote, the British ambassador, who was a lawyer by training, and who had earlier had special experience of a similar problem while working on the Suez Canal Treaty. Hay and Pauncefote worked fast— by the middle of January they had produced a draft treaty. The pressure for change was solely American. The British government were perfectly satisfied with the Clayton–Bulwer Treaty. They saw, moreover, that a concession to American interest in the matter of a ship canal might well be worth a concession to Canada elsewhere, and they were aware of the objections to the building of a canal while an important dispute with the United States was continuing. Hence their attempts to connect the canal with the Alaskan boundary question, which delayed the new treaty for a year. These attempts were abandoned in the face of American refusal to consider them, and the first Hay–Pauncefote Treaty was signed in February 1900.

The new treaty modified the Clayton–Bulwer Treaty in one respect only—it withdrew the British claim to a share in the building and maintenance of the canal. The Clayton–Bulwer Treaty remained in force except as superseded by the new one. But in spite of the care taken by both Hay and Pauncefote to modify the earlier treaty as little as possible, there was no doubt that the United States would be the chief beneficiary. Since the building of the Suez Canal British interest in the Panama route to the East, never very great, had declined. Strategically the advantage of the canal—chiefly the ability to concentrate the Atlantic and Pacific squadrons of her navy in one ocean at need—would go to the United States. The British position would not be strengthened by its building but rather the reverse. Yet for more than a generation it had been accepted that an isthmian canal would be a great work of civilisation. It was difficult to oppose, even without the knowledge that continuing opposition would not be effective unless backed by force. Britain had no intention of sharing in the building of the canal. Even in support of Canada, she could not for long decline to give up her right of veto.

The British government therefore accepted the first Hay–Pauncefote Treaty as drafted; but the American Senate, to which it duly went for ratification, did not. The Senate criticism took two main lines. The first was an objection to the clause in the treaty which invited other European powers to adhere to it. This invitation to help guarantee a treaty effective in the western hemisphere seemed to many Senators at variance with the Monroe Doctrine. The more important criticism, however, was that the existence of a neutralised canal would strengthen as against the United States any power with a navy larger than hers. Such a power could effectively blockade the canal, while the United States, though possessing equal rights, would not be able to prevent larger foreign squadrons from passing it. The canal, said the naval strategists, would be valuable to the United States only if it could be fortified.

Senate opposition to the treaty built up during the spring and summer of 1900. When the Senate adjourned in June it had taken no vote, and during the summer the Boer War, the American election campaign, and, above all, the Boxer rising in China and the prolonged negotiations which followed, diverted attention in both countries from the canal. But before the Senate reassembled in December, William Jennings Bryan, the Democratic presidential candidate, had attacked the treaty, making it a political issue and lining up the Democrats against it. The Senate finally ratified the treaty with three amendments. The first, though it made the supersession of the entire Clayton–Bulwer Treaty specific, was of minor importance. The second and most important added to the clauses neutralising the canal another providing that none of these should 'apply to measures which the United States may find it necessary to take for securing by its own forces the defence of the United States...'. The third struck out the clause inviting other powers to adhere.

The treaty as amended was virtually a rejection of the draft which had gone to the Senate, and the British government in turn declined to accept the amended version. Though Hay and Joseph Choate, the American ambassador in London, did their best to persuade them that the amendments were unimportant, that was simply not true. Hay's anxiety was that if the new treaty were not accepted the Senate would abrogate the Clayton–Bulwer Treaty in defiance of international law. When the new treaty lapsed, however, in March 1901 (since it had not been accepted), the Senate adjourned at the same time without, in Pauncefote's words, 'committing any further enormity'.

The rival drafts of the canal treaty appeared to be irreconcilable. When Lord Lansdowne, now Foreign Secretary, finally offered his comments on the Senate version, he raised objections which, though familiar, were important and valid. Nevertheless, there were already signs that Lansdowne's real objection was to the manner in which the Senate had acted, and not to the substance of the amendments. The draft treaty lapsed; a new one was prepared during the summer of 1901; it was signed on 18 November, and ratified by both countries without difficulty. In that treaty—the second Hay–Pauncefote Treaty—the United States gained everything for which the opponents of the first version had been contending. The Clayton–Bulwer Treaty was specifically superseded; the neutrality of the canal in time of war was not guaranteed; and other powers were not invited to adhere. Lansdowne abandoned his earlier objections. In the negotiating of the new treaty the only concession which he and Pauncefote gained was in ensuring that other powers which were not signatories were placed by the treaty under exactly the same restrictions as Britain. That achieved, they were content that those restrictions should be administered and enforced by the United States. For their part most of the naval party in the Senate were not concerned to place Britain under peculiar disadvantages. The agreement reached reflected the considerable power shift in the Caribbean in the half-century since the Clayton–Bulwer Treaty had been signed. That fact passed almost unnoticed and quite unchallenged in Britain.

Both the Alaskan boundary dispute and that over the control of the isthmian canal were confined to the American continent, and the American attitude to them was therefore simpler, more vigorous and compounded of older emotions than it would have been in more distant conflicts. As an immediate result, the United States determined to treat each negotiation as separate. The conduct and settlement of one did not affect the other. Thus the signing of the Hay–Pauncefote Treaty did not modify the

American stand on Alaska. Nor, though the goodwill for Britain generated by the British attitude to the Spanish–American War was real and marked, did that influence the outcome of the later negotiations with Britain. This fragmentation of foreign policy is not peculiar either to the time or to the United States. It is difficult and not always necessary to combine diplomatic negotiations into a policy. Nevertheless, the absence of any attempt to do so was more obvious than usual in American policy in the 1890's; and its cause was unshaken confidence in American ability to control the western hemisphere together with an equal confidence in American right to do so. These enabled the United States to treat the most trivial dispute as if a vital interest were involved. They go far to account for the violence with which American policy was upheld by men like Olney and Theodore Roosevelt. They largely explain, too, the tendency of these men to cast political issues in legal terms and yet, without any consciousness of inconsistency, to use political pressure to determine their outcome.

While American diplomatic activity was concentrated on the western hemisphere, its limitations were concealed. American confidence in American strength was in fact justified, but it was not achieved by any rational calculation. It was rather a sense of security which had developed unquestioned over seventy years. For a short time Americans were able to support new ambitions and new theories of world politics while still adhering to older principles with which the new ones were inconsistent. Their debate about the terms for the building of the isthmian canal was essentially a strategic one. Yet American navalists made almost no attempt to relate their demand for a fortified canal to any larger policy. Though the demand for a canal implied larger ambitions, those ambitions were not defined. Since the canal was in the western hemisphere its fortification was assumed to be necessary, and justified by the signs of British opposition. Corresponding inconsistencies can be found in American political thought. The Darwinian political ideas which influenced Roosevelt and others, and which undoubtedly exaggerated the violence of their reactions, logically demanded the expansion of American interests and influence; an end, indeed, for which Roosevelt worked with his usual energy. For other Americans, however, hardly less vigorous, the implications of political Darwinism were blurred by older ideas. As Andrew Carnegie, the Scots-born steel king, put it at the time of the Venezuela crisis, '[Great Britain cannot] fairly grudge her race here one continent when she has liberty to roam over three'.

The Spanish–American War provided the first real test of American policy. It lasted only a few months, and never engaged any considerable proportion of American men or resources; but American motives were of more importance than its scale would suggest. The war can be regarded either as a brief aberration, the result of a surge of imperialism which rose quickly and as quickly died; or as a major departure, the abandonment of isolation, the beginning of an involvement in world affairs which was to continue and grow. There is truth in both views. The United States did not become on any scale an imperial power in the sense of achieving formal political control of overseas possessions. The opportunity was already past and the enthusiasm quickly faded. But there are other forms of empire. Power produced in due time the desire to use it. After 1898 isolationists could not assume their case.

The Spanish–American War itself had its origin in the growing American readiness to take charge of the doings of the hemisphere. Its ostensible cause was the failure of Spain to subdue a persistent rebellion against her rule in Cuba. Ultimately the United States determined to end the guerrilla war which was ruining the island. Rebellion in Cuba against Spanish rule had been sporadic throughout the nineteenth century. Though the mixed population contained a sizeable proportion of Cubans of Spanish, or largely Spanish, blood the island was ruled by officials sent out from Spain, and Cuban demands for autonomy were disregarded. Spanish rule was both inefficient and corrupt, and for both reasons was prodigally expensive. The most serious rebellion had been the great ten years war of 1868–78. This was the expression of a demand for reform rather than for separation from Spain, and it was ended by a convention in which the desired reforms were promised. But the Spaniards failed to keep to the spirit of the convention—or even to its letter—and it was that failure, more than anything else, which led to the outbreak of a new rebellion in 1895. In the intervening years, the separatists had become more influential than the autonomists among the Cuban leaders.

Before the American Civil War, many Americans had considered the purchase or annexation of Cuba. The position of the island in the Caribbean gave it a strategic importance, and the value of its tropical crops, especially sugar, was considerable. But enthusiasm for the acquisition of Cuba was confined to the South; and—with justice—it was suspected in the North that the desire to create two new slave states lay behind Southern zeal. At a time when sectional rivalry dominated American politics, that suspicion was enough to prevent American action. By 1898, however, the situation was very different. Slavery had ceased to be a political issue, and in Cuba as well as on the mainland it had ceased to be an institution. If the chief motive for annexation had gone, so had the chief objection to it. Nor was annexation the only possibility, or even the most attractive one. Many Americans disliked the prospect of a Cuban colony, for sound republican reasons, and found equally distasteful the addition of large numbers of citizens of mixed blood. To these men the right and satisfactory solution was the independence of Cuba.

For the first years of the rebellion the United States maintained a proper neutrality, but it was formal and official only. President Cleveland's refusal to intervene was not popular, and with McKinley's presidency began a steady American progress towards intervention. Even before American intervention, however, the Spaniards felt that they had good grounds for complaint. Many Cubans fled to the United States and there formed groups to collect money, arms and men, and to organise propaganda against Spain. The activity of these Cuban juntas was well known, and the Spaniards claimed that the rebellion could not have been maintained without them. They charged that the American government was lax in controlling them. This was secondary to a more fundamental grievance. The Spaniards believed that not even their gun-running was successful enough to give the insurgents any chance of victory, and that they were continuing their efforts only in the hope that the United States would ultimately intervene. A firm statement by the American government that the United States would not intervene would have ended that hope and with it the rebellion. Americans themselves were therefore largely responsible for the evils of Spanish rule which they hypocritically denounced.

It is true that American opinion so far favoured the Cuban insurgents that it would have been difficult for an American president formally to reject them. But the basis of American sentiment was not merely commercial imperialism. The United States had large investments in Cuba and imported almost all the sugar which was much the island's most important crop. But there was no unanimity among American businessmen about the importance of Cuba. Only the sugar companies had a direct interest; and their preferred solution, on the whole, was the restoration of Spanish authority. As for other businessmen and conservatives, they regarded Cuba as likely to prove an expensive distraction from the area in which they wanted to see American government intervention—the Far East. The impulse for intervention in Cuba came from a very different source. It derived from the principles and satisfied the emotions summed up in the term 'the Progressive movement'. Humanitarianism was an essential element in this movement, with, as a corollary, distrust of business motives and distaste for business selfishness. The skill, moreover, with which the opponents of the Progressives had invoked the Constitution and used the courts to block reform had bred in the reformers a disregard for the niceties of law and a readiness to ignore them when that was necessary to get things done. When the object was good it was pusillanimous to let legal technicalities stand in the way of its achievement.

To the Progressives reform at home and reform abroad were indivisible. The same moral impulse was behind the attack on Big Business in the United States and the attack on Spanish rule in Cuba. But there was an obvious difference. Business in the United States was all too successful; the Spanish colonial regime was unsuccessful. Many Americans who would have accepted without question a stable Spanish regime felt that a

Spain which could not pacify Cuba had no right to rule. The Spanish counter-argument, that the United States was largely responsible for Spanish difficulties, nearly all Americans rejected. They did so because they believed that Latin races were by nature inefficient, cruel and corrupt and therefore unfit to rule others. The defects of Spanish rule were inherent, and no improvement was to be looked for. This sense of racial superiority was strong in the Progressives, and it often formed the basis of a coherent philosophy of world politics. When the Boer War broke out, a surprising number of Progressives, in spite of traditional opposition to Britain and enthusiasm for the name of republic, believed that in the interests of civilisation Britain should win. The Cuban war was seen quite differently. It was a struggle among the barbarous or the decadent, much more analogous to the Turkish oppression of the Armenians, something to which the civilised conscience reacted strongly, and which it was the duty of civilised nations to stop. It follows that the Progressive attitude to the Cubans was ambivalent. A real desire that they should be free was complicated by the conviction that they needed the supervision of the United States. By blood and history they were unfit for self-government.

This ambivalence could be concealed while the problem was still that of ending Spanish misrule. A readiness to believe the worst of the Spaniards was fed by the New York press which, in the course of a circulation war, reported, magnified and invented atrocity stories heavily slanted against Spain. For these reasons, far from discouraging the Cubans, the American government increased its pressure on Spain after September 1897. Spanish complaints redoubled; and they were now against American policy, not against American negligence. The Spaniards were ready to make concessions, but they regarded them as made to show goodwill, to deprive the United States of international support and of any excuse for further interference, and ultimately to force the repudiation of the insurgents. The Americans regarded them as steps to autonomy in Cuba or even the ending of Spanish rule. The gulf could not be bridged.

The situation was aggravated when the American battleship *Maine*, on a visit to Havana in February 1898, exploded and sank, a disaster whose cause has never been satisfactorily determined. Though incidental to the real questions at issue, the *Maine* explosion heightened tension in both countries to such an extent that peace became unlikely. Spain, much the weaker power, was anxious for peace, but she could not make all the concessions demanded by the United States without real risk of an internal revolution. Repeated attempts to involve the other powers failed. Though, with the exception of Britain, they all deplored American policy, they were essentially indifferent. Their determination to remain neutral meant that the United States had virtually a free hand, and when that became apparent, Spain, the last concessions made, declared war.

The war itself was short and its engagements entirely successful to the

United States. The only important Spanish squadron, that under Admiral Cervera, was blockaded in Santiago Bay. Although an American attempt to sink a blockship across the harbour mouth failed, Cervera stayed in harbour long enough to allow the American expeditionary force to land unopposed. When that force invested Santiago by land his position became untenable and he put to sea, only to have his squadron quickly destroyed in a battle that was essentially a triumph for superior American gunnery. With the destruction of Cervera's fleet the surrender of the Spanish land forces was only a matter of time.

The speed and ease of the American military victory was, however, surprising. At sea, slight superiority lay with the Americans, but the Spaniards had almost two hundred thousand men on the island with which to oppose some fifteen thousand Americans; yet this small force not only landed unopposed, but was able to reach Santiago in about a week and fought, when it fought, against greatly inferior Spanish forces. The inability to concentrate their forces effectively is the chief charge against the Spanish leaders, since they were neither able nor willing to wage guerrilla war.

The campaign in Cuba was the centrepiece of the war, and indeed the only campaign that followed logically from the long debate that had preceded the war. But attention was diverted from it and the whole scope of the war extended by the exploits of Commodore Dewey at Manila. Dewey commanded the American Asiatic squadron. No sooner was war declared than he set out for the Philippines and, entering Manila Bay, completely destroyed the Spanish fleet. His was the first, the most complete and the most spectacular victory of the war. It raised a problem which, plainly, few Americans had considered before the war began—that of the future of the Philippines. The aroused martial pride of the Americans and the completeness of their victory made the return of the islands to Spain at the war's end impossible. By the terms of the peace treaty, signed at Paris on 10 December 1898, Spain withdrew from Cuba, and ceded Puerto Rico and Guam to the United States; she also ceded the Philippines, for whose loss she was paid twenty million dollars.

There was no serious objection to this transfer from the other powers. The Far East, unlike the Caribbean, was an area in which they took a keen interest. The fate of the Philippines exercised them all. Spain as the ruler of the islands was inoffensive, too weak to do more than maintain herself and that not very effectively. The prospect of American intervention in the Far East was much more disturbing. Nevertheless, if the islands could not be returned to Spain their retention by the United States was the generally preferred alternative. Right of conquest was difficult to challenge, and international rivalry was keen enough to make their transfer to other hands unacceptable. This attitude also indicated the general belief that the United States would not make effective use of her new acquisition. Those observers who foresaw American activity did so usually because they expected co-operation between the United States and Britain; and most were well aware of the difficulties in the way of that.

So far as the Philippines were concerned, this international judgement was proved right. Hardly was the war over than enthusiasm for empire began to weaken in the United States. Its implications were brought home to Americans by an insurrection against their rule in the Philippines which took three years to put down and was much more costly than the war with Spain. But it was not merely the cost of pacifying and administering the Philippines which raised doubts. Many reformers who had been eager to free Cuba from Spain objected, for obvious reasons, to subjugating the Philippines themselves. William Jennings Bryan, the great western Populist leader who still dominated the Democratic party, was one such. Most Progressives, on the other hand, accepted American imperialism without a qualm. The fitness of their race to rule was beyond question. Of that the vigour of their individualism in domestic politics was one sure indicator. It would be merely inconsistent to decline the responsibilities of power abroad. American reformers were faced with the dilemma which foreign policy has always presented to radicals. The near-unanimity which they had shown on the Cuban question began to break down.

Both in the United States and among the other powers, however, interest in the Philippines was primarily a reflection of interest in China, then temporarily the centre of international rivalry. The object of the rivalry was commerce. China traders had long been trying to gain readier access to the interior, and had been demanding government intervention to overcome the obstructiveness of Chinese officials, in Peking and in the provinces. In the later 1890's, for various reasons, their desires briefly found wider support. The importance of the Chinese market for the future was much exaggerated. A new form of competition, for railway concessions, was added to the familiar competition in the sale of consumer goods. Railway concessions were by their nature exclusive; railway building was financed by loans to the Chinese government; both the concessions and the loans could be used to increase the political influence which had been necessary to negotiate them. The Sino-Japanese war had called attention to the weakness of China, seemingly ripe for dissolution. Above all, the rapid advance of Russia towards the control of north China, control whose object was not commercial but political, led many to fear that the dissolution had begun. The situation was one to which the apostles of race competition reacted strongly.

Americans shared these general anxieties. Their interest in China was of long standing, and united very various groups. China traders, like their European competitors, had long wanted more government support. But in the 1890's their special interest seemed less special. American businessmen came to be haunted by the problem of over-production. A sudden export surplus which developed very quickly between 1893 and 1898 argued not only an impressive volume of production but a satiated home market. If the United States produced more than she could consume disaster, it was believed, could be avoided only by finding new export markets. For different reasons, Europe, the British empire, Africa, even South America, all seemed to offer little hope. Only China remained, and to American businessmen as to Europeans it came to have an importance beyond the reality of the trade involved.

The businessmen with an interest in China were not, on the whole, imperialists. What evidence there is suggests that in general they opposed the Spanish–American War. Apart from its cost, they thought that it would divert energies better spent in fostering the China trade. But when, ironically, the result of the war was the taking of the Philippines, they realised how valuable the islands could be to their cause, and redoubled their propaganda. They could see, and were prepared to help others to see, the connection between the Philippines and China.

In this they found allies among the expansionists, who claimed a theoretical interest in trade with the East. Competition in trade was one form of the competition in which nations inevitably engaged. The need to defend trade routes across the Pacific had been used as one argument for the building of a large navy, the acquisition of Hawaii, the control of the isthmian canal. China policy, moreover, since there was no question of any annexation, did not place the same strain on American radicals as had the taking of the Philippines. The protection of China and freedom of commerce against the predatory powers was—even to men who distrusted Big Business at home—unquestionably ethical. Finally, American missionaries in China were many, their dismay at political developments there was growing, and their influence at home was considerable.

From these various groups, then, the pressure on the government to take action in China increased; but before the Spanish–American War it was entirely unsuccessful. President Cleveland was unsympathetic. After McKinley's election the war diverted attention from China; and McKinley's first Secretary of State, John Sherman, was ineffective. When in March 1898 the British ambassador asked McKinley informally whether the two countries could co-operate in the Far East, the answer was a courteous rebuff. The United States, said McKinley, had a well-defined tradition of declining joint action. The British approach was ill timed at the height of the Cuban crisis, but there is no hint of any change in American policy. In John Hay, however, who became Secretary of State in 1898, the China lobby found a spokesman more to their liking. At the end of the war they hoped for a more active policy.

The alliance between China traders and expansionists was not effective. The belief that American trade would quickly expand from its base in the Philippines, with Manila as the American Hong Kong, proved illusory.

Before the building of the Panama Canal most American goods had to be protected by a preferential tariff even in the Philippines themselves. Yet as a commercial base the Philippines were doubtless of some value. Unfortunately the problem in China was political, not commercial; it was essentially that of bringing effective pressure to bear on the Chinese government in opposition to the pressure of other powers. That the United States, even under Theodore Roosevelt, was not prepared to do. In spite of his efforts and those of propagandists for the navy, the United States did not have an effective base in the Philippines. As late as 1902 Congress had not been persuaded to vote the money for defence and facilities. There was, however, a more fundamental weakness in American policy in the Far East. Even with a more effective base it would have had to be conducted under great disadvantages of distance. Only Japan and Russia among the powers did not share these disadvantages. Effective opposition to either—though Russia was then the chief offender—required co-operation among the others. The American tradition of isolation was still too strong to be broken. Moreover, rivalries in China were too closely interwoven with European rivalries to be treated as a thing apart. Involvement in China meant involvement in Europe, and that the United States was not yet prepared to face.

For these reasons, American retention of the Philippines was of small moment in the politics of the Far East. Only the British had seriously hoped for more, welcoming the possibility of support in checking Russian ambitions. Meanwhile, however, the British had taken the port of Weihaiwei, held by the Japanese since the Sino-Japanese War, and had lent the Chinese the money to pay the Japanese indemnity for which it was the security. Salisbury decided on this move reluctantly, considering that he must do something to counterbalance the recent German acquisition of Kiao-chow; but the taking of Weihaiwei seemed to Americans to indicate that Britain had given up hope of maintaining the 'open door'—the policy of equal rights for all powers throughout the whole of China. American suspicions were reinforced by the speeches of British statesmen later in 1898, and still further by the so-called Scott–Muraviev Convention of 1899, in which Britain undertook to seek no railway concessions north of the Great Wall in return for a similar Russian undertaking south of it. The limit placed on Russian advance southwards was welcome enough, but it looked certain to lead to the division of China into 'spheres of influence' for trade as well. American interests were concentrated in north China, where Russian pretensions were most threatening. The occasional British resort of obtaining counter-concessions farther south to offset a Russian gain was not open to the United States. It was essential to American interests that the powers refrain from demanding new privileges.

John Hay's first attempt to achieve this was his famous 'open door' note. On 6 September 1899 he sent virtually identic notes to Russia,

Great Britain and Germany, the powers most immediately concerned, and followed them in November with similar notes to France, Italy and Japan. These were essentially an invitation to the powers to rest content with their existing treaties, and to agree that subjects of all the powers should be equally treated throughout China. The proposal was received with mixed feelings, but all the powers accepted it—on the condition that it was also accepted by the others. Though the Russian reply was so equivocal as to constitute a virtual rejection, Hay contrived to express himself as satisfied. The history of the writing of the note makes it clear that it was chiefly directed against Russian expansion in north China. The Russians were reluctant to subscribe because they realised that; but their decision to do so did not indicate that they intended to modify their policy. It is doubtful whether a policy so essentially negative as that put forward in the note could ever have been imposed on the powers. What is certain is that it could not be imposed by a circular note. The note was clearly an appeal to international public opinion, a device to get the powers to commit themselves in public. In the circumstances it was an admission that the United States would not use force in opposing Russia. There was a logical connection between the self-denying policy which Hay advocated and the means which he chose to support it. Both lacked vigour.

The failure of the 'open door' note was concealed for a time by the outbreak of the Boxer rebellion, three months after Hay announced his acceptance of the European replies on 20 March 1900. Chaos in China produced a situation so out of the ordinary that no power could object to any step that another might take to protect its nationals. Those powers with expansive intentions and those without agreed for different reasons that it was immediately important to damp down the crisis. In this situation the United States played the expected part. Hay's first reaction was to instruct the U.S. minister in China to confine himself to the independent protection of American citizens. When it became clear how serious the position was, Hay was willing to approve joint action. He announced his policy in another circular note, in which he took the opportunity to repeat that American policy was still to preserve the integrity of China and 'the principle of equal and impartial trade with all parts' of the empire. Though this note has often been taken to initiate a new and more active American policy in China, or even a determination to defend Chinese territorial and administrative entity, in fact American policy stayed as cautious as before. Temporarily, during the Boxer crisis, it looked effective, because all the powers—except perhaps Germany—were prepared, temporarily, to be moderate, whether in order to end the negotiations and so free their hands or in order to strengthen the Chinese government. The concert of the powers and the integrity of China were seen to go together. While the powers were anxious to maintain the first they were ready to accept the second.

Their agreement concealed fundamental differences among them and also the weakness of American policy. Only under some such stress, however, could the United States act in concert with other powers, even in defence of her own interests. As Hay remarked on 23 June 1900, 'anything we should now do in China to take care of our imperilled interests, would be set down to "subservience to Great Britain". France is Russia's harlot—to her own grievous damage. Germany we could probably get on our side by sufficient concessions and perhaps with England, Germany and Japan we might manage to save our skins. But such a proceeding would make all our fools throw fits in the market place—and the fools are numerous.' The advance of Russia continued till it was ended by the Russo-Japanese War, when the attention of the European powers returned to Europe, and when the dominance of Japan proved as unwelcome to the United States as that of Russia had been.

The pattern of American policy in the forty years following the Civil War is thus one of growing domination of the western hemisphere together with a continuing reluctance to act outside it. These geographical limits set to American policy did not, however, imply any lack of confidence. Rather they made it possible to maintain the larger confidence which had been bred in isolation. American policy was limited by a distrust of international relations somewhat analogous to the Jeffersonian distrust of government. It derived from American theory and not from diffidence, and was quite compatible with an enlarged sense of dignity and an exaggerated sensitivity to affront. Americans could therefore still retain old notions of the nature of foreign policy which could not—durable though they have undoubtedly proved—survive the test of practice. Their sense of power was the greater because they never explored its limits. They began to develop larger ambitions, but not yet the will to realise them. It is ironical that the Spanish–American War, which did so much for Roosevelt's reputation, did so little to establish the ideas he advocated. Yet in the last analysis the limited, provincial outlook which so annoyed Roosevelt was sound enough. A world policy is not devised because it is something that a great power must have—it develops naturally from national needs and interests. Lacking that basis, American zeal for expansion quickly faded.

In short, the diplomatic relations of the United States with Europe during these years were still marginal. American potential was well recognised, by Americans and others, but so, equally, was American reluctance to engage in world affairs. It would take a great deal to make the United States put forth her strength outside the Americas. But not all the relations between the United States and Europe were diplomatic. The United States had never consistently aimed at economic self-sufficiency, and her commercial links with the rest of the world continued to grow. Though she was still a debtor nation—a position not altered till the first World War—the title was already a misleading one, for the balance of payments was moving in her favour. Foreign investment was increasingly no more than reinvestment. Moreover, American trade was coming to be more important to the countries of Europe than it was to the United States, a fact evident, and diplomatically important, at the time of the Spanish–American War. The reluctance of the continental powers—and of Britain—to place trade and investment in jeopardy by supporting Spain against the United States was one reason for the speed with which agreement on neutrality was reached.

Another link, unique in strength and importance, joined the United States to Europe as no European country was joined to another—that of immigration. From the beginning most immigrants inevitably came, whether freely or perforce, as individuals, removed from the society in which they had had a place. In spite of that, the first settlers quickly recreated a social environment as nearly what they had known as a new land, empty of their kind, would allow. Before long their successors found a society perhaps less rigid than the one they had left, but both cohesive and familiar. This was the society of the eastern seaboard. When a solid base of population was established and settlers moved westward, they met physical conditions unknown in western Europe. They adapted; and the passage of time during which their interests were in the exploitation of the West did more to make Americans different than merely crossing the Atlantic had done. Newcomers now found a society individual, confident, and with conventions of its own. This change was completed even while much of the West was still empty. By the end of the Civil War the United States was a strange land, and those who came to it found themselves strangers. They came, however, in unprecedented numbers. For the first time the interplay of immigrant and native Americans became more important than that of man and environment.

The history of American immigration remained, as it had always been, essentially that of emigration from Europe. Long before the Civil War, with the abolition of the slave trade, Negro immigration had virtually ceased. From about 1854 onwards there was substantial immigration from China. It reached its peak of 40,000 in 1882, but in no other year did it exceed 25,000 and a more typical figure would be 5000 or 10,000 a year. Chinese immigration quickly roused opposition, and it was, in any event, almost confined to the West Coast. Numerically more important was immigration from Canada. The numbers fluctuated widely, touching 125,000 in 1881 but usually very much lower, and falling almost to nothing after 1885, not to recover for twenty years. But immigration from Canada was immigration from Europe at one remove. The Canadians who crossed the border were Europeans at some stage in the process of becoming American, if they had not become American already. These figures con-

trast sharply with those for immigration from Europe. They too fluctuated widely, for a variety of reasons, some European and some American,
but after 1865 they never fell below 101,000—in 1878 when immigration
from Canada was no more than 26,000; and they rose to 974,000 in
1905—the year in which total immigration first reached more than a
million—with an intermediate peak of 648,000 in 1882.

As significant as the rise in the number of immigrants were the changes
in their nationality. As late as 1865, Britain and Germany provided the
great majority of immigrants. The numbers from eastern and southern
Europe were still insignificant. But it was those regions which accounted
for nearly all the increase in immigration towards the end of the century.
The figures are given in the following table:

Immigrants by country of origin (in 000's)

	Total (Europe)	Great Britain	Ireland	Scandinavia	Other N.W. Europe*	Germany	Poland	Austria-Hungary	Russia	Other E. Europe*	Italy	Other S. Europe*
1865	214	82	30	7	8	83	< 1	< 1	< 1	< 0·1	1	1
1870	329	104	57	31	9	118	< 1	4	1	< 0·1	3	1
1875	183	48	38	14	12	48	1	8	8	< 0·1	4	3
1880	349	73	72	66	15	85	2	17	5	< 0·1	12	2
1885	353	58	52	41	14	124	3	27	17	1	14	3
1890	446	70	53	50	21	92	11	56	36	< 1	52	4
1895	250	29	46	27	7	32	< 1	33	36	< 1	35	3
1900	425	13	36	31	6	19	*	115	91	7	100	8
1905	974	84	53	61	25	41	*	276	185	11	221	18

* 'Other N.W. Europe' includes Belgium, France, Luxembourg, the Netherlands and
Switzerland; 'Other Eastern Europe' includes Roumania, Bulgaria and Turkey in Europe;
'Other Southern Europe' includes Spain, Portugal, Greece and other Europe not elsewhere
classified. The blank years for Poland are due to the fact that between 1899 and 1918 the
American immigration authorities listed Poles under Russia, Germany or Austria-Hungary.
Poles made up a high proportion of the enlarged numbers from Austria-Hungary and
Russia at the end of the century, an influx which continued till the outbreak of the First
World War. The figures are condensed from *Historical Statistics of the United States,
Colonial Times to 1957* (U.S. Bureau of the Census), q.v. for their original source.

With certain exceptions the basic tradition of the United States had
always been that of welcoming immigrants. In an empty land they were
needed both for progress and for security. But they were not welcomed
merely because labour was scarce—they were welcomed as participants in
an experiment. The United States early became a peculiarly self-conscious
nation, the embodiment of a political theory. This was a country whose
natural endowments made possible the deliberate creation of a new and
better society, which would in turn breed new and better men. Such a
country attracted the vigorous and adventurous; it attracted many who
were looking for fortune; but it also attracted political idealists. This

attraction was, of course, necessary if the ideal were to be realised; but the ideal provided standards by which immigrants could be judged. Xenophobia was latent in it, for European corruption could all too easily enter with Europeans. Three main strands can be isolated in American nativism—three strands which formed a complex pattern, which were variously important at various times, but which were always there. The first was anti-catholicism, itself a complex of emotions surrounding the suspicion that Catholics were both disloyal and depraved. Paradoxically the second was anti-radicalism, all the stronger because the nation had its origin in the most conservative of revolutions. The French Revolution left its mark on Americans. It became a source of pride to them that *their* revolution had not gone too far, and they saw European radicalism as a greater danger than reaction. The third was acceptance of the Anglo-Saxon or Teutonic origins of the United States. It should be remembered with what reluctance the American revolutionaries had extended their demands from the rights of Englishmen to the rights of man. The tendency to look back to English liberties as the origin of their own remained, defining the American vision rather than limiting it, but inducing a certain suspicion of other stocks.

These attitudes remained latent except when brought out by difficulties within the United States itself. Both because of their numbers and because of their origins the newcomers posed a new problem. Like the Irish before them, Italians or Slavs or East European Jews were more difficult to assimilate because differences of religion and culture were greater; and they also shared the language difficulties familiar to Germans or Scandinavians. Their numbers meant that, even more than earlier immigrants, they settled in groups and clung to their own customs. The growth of large racial ghettos in the major cities made local government much more difficult, and complicated state and national government also. But these difficulties, though real, merely intensified strains whose essential cause was domestic, the development of an industrial society on a scale and at a speed hitherto unknown. The United States could still absorb a great deal of labour—that was the essence of the opportunity—but she was beginning to meet the European problems from which free land, large resources and political democracy had been enough to exempt her till then. *Laissez-faire* was under attack. This was the period of the protest movements which culminated in the Populist revolt. Domestic tensions determined the American attitude to the foreigner, and immigration became an issue in what was essentially a domestic debate.

When it turned to immigration, the debate was no straightforward affair of pro and con. The flow of immigrants was welcomed—and indeed often arranged and subsidised—by those who had lands to dispose of or mines to work, but it was increasingly resented by working men. Immigrants worked for less than the native born; they could be more easily intimidated and managed, and they threatened the benefits which American working men had gained or were trying to gain. The lines, however, were not simply drawn between native born and immigrants. Too many of the most active trade unionists were themselves immigrants. In their efforts to limit later immigration they drew a distinction between those who came under contract to an employer—who alone were deplorable—and those who came independently. For the opponents of labour the issue was no simpler. Immigrants might be welcomed as a docile labour force, or feared as likely dupes of the radical agitators who might easily be among them, as at best fodder for political bosses. Not all conservatives were large employers or their allies. Those reformers who wanted to return to the individualism of an earlier America were hostile equally to Big Business and regimented labour. The economic arguments gained or lost in force with the state of the economy, but they were complicated by a nativism which had other sources. Even in the United States racialists began to debate the likely effects of so large an influx of strange stocks.

The doubts and difficulties must not be exaggerated. It is a tribute both to American resources and to the generosity of the American tradition that there was no effective check on European immigration till after the first World War, though Congress recognised some responsibility for controlling it in 1882. There was no crisis of American confidence. Indeed, the famous lines placed on the base of the Statue of Liberty in 1886—

> Give me your tired, your poor,
> Your huddled millions yearning to breathe free,
> The wretched refuse of your teeming shore...

show a proud certainty that the United States could make something of a mass of unpromising material—not a certainty which the Founding Fathers would have shared. This did not mean that Americans thought of America primarily as a refuge. The idea of America as an example remained dominant; and social Darwinism itself could be adapted to inclusive or exclusive purposes. But common to all the arguments was a growing realisation that the United States was an established society, and that the fitting of large numbers of immigrants into it was a large and difficult task. Opinion differed as to just how difficult the task was, and whether its dangers or its rewards were greater.

None of this seriously weakened the belief of Americans in their national mission, but the belief of Europeans was less robust. Throughout its existence the United States had claimed to be in the van of progress, and the claim had been generally allowed. Whether observers foresaw the American future with enthusiasm or with dismay, they agreed that here was something new and significant. The Civil War itself, however variously interpreted, did nothing to shake that agreement. But the claim to leadership was one that could be made inoffensively only by a small nation, and safely only by a nation remote as well as small. As the power of the United States grew, as her trade expanded, as communications developed, her weight in the international scale became more important than her political example. To Europeans she seemed to behave increasingly like other powers.

Equally important, with the passage of time the United States, once the beacon of radicals, became a conservative country. First in achieving political democracy, she lagged in social reform. By 1890 American industrial legislation was behind that of western European countries. British employers increasingly complained that their American rivals had an unfair advantage from the absence of effective trade unions in America; British working men no longer thought a move to America the easiest way of bettering themselves. It would be difficult to show that the new immigrants were always poorer than their predecessors. Most immigrants had always been poor; if the demand of American industry for cheap labour and the active search of shipping lines for steerage passengers made movement possible for completely new groups, it is also likely that they were induced to come, rather than forced to go by positive hardship in eastern Europe. Nevertheless, poverty was a more important motive for emigration than before—more important because other motives, enterprise or political idealism, were now lacking.

For these reasons European observers looked with less interest at the United States. The skill with which the Constitution has been interpreted during the past fifty years to meet the needs of a changing society was not yet developed; nor would it then have impressed non-Americans if it had been. European reformers had once seen the United States as a land where prosperity naturally followed from sound political institutions; they now saw a land where only large resources made antiquated institutions tolerable. With political dominance and incomparable wealth still in the future, the United States entered the twentieth century diminished from a great experiment to a power among the powers.

INDEX

Bolivia, 525, 530, 534–5

Bolshevism, 110, 120, 272, 371, 373

see also Marxism

Bonchamps, Christian de, in Africa, 628

Bonin Islands, 647

Book-production, 98

Booth, Charles, English shipowner, his *Life and Labour in London*, 402

Booth, William, founder of the Salvation Army, his *Darkest England*, 402

Borgnis-Desbordes, French soldier, 603

Borgu, 630–1

Borneo, British chartered company in, 384

Bosanquet, Bernard, English philosopher, 115

Bosnia, 39 n., 334

under Turkish rule, 328, 330, 333, 342, 544

and Austria-Hungary, 333–5, 336, 337, 339, 340, 342, 343, 344, 348, 548

Boulanger, Georges Ernest Jean Marie, French general, 221, 256, 293, 310–12, 557

Bourgeois, Léon, French Radical leader, 319

Bourget, Paul, French writer, 139

Bournville model village, 69, 164

Bowen, Edward, headmaster of Harrow, 179

Boxer Movement, *see* China

Boyen, Hermann von, Prussian militarist, 214

Bradley, Francis Herbert, English philosopher, his *Ethical Studies*, 115

Brahm, Otto, German theatrical producer, 142

Brahminism, 423

Brailsford, H. N., his *War of Steel and Gold*, 591

Branco, Baron de Rio, Brazilian statesman, 536

Brazil

population, 12, 521, 524; European immigration, 517–18, 520

political structure and developments: fall of monarchy, 25, 527; United States of Brazil established, 527

status in 1870, 516

economic developments: foreign capital investment, 517, 521; banking institutions, 519; economic growth, 520–1; southerly shift of economic power, 527

railways, 520

relations with neighbouring states, 533–4, 670

armed forces, 534

education, 537

see also Latin America

Brazza, Pierre Savorgnan de, French explorer and Commissioner-General of Congo Republic, 603, 604, 607, 622

Brentano, Lujo, German liberal economist, 279

Brialmont, Henri Alexis, Belgian general, 208

Brisson, Henri, French politician, 629

British and Foreign Schools Society, 184

British Association for the Advancement of Science, The, 80, 86, 102

British Bank of South America, 519

British Cotton and Wool Dyers, 72

British East Africa Company, 612, 613

British Guiana, 672

British India Association, 422, 433

British North America Act (1867), 104

British Soap Makers Association, 70

British South Africa Company, 614

Broglie, Jacques Victor Albert, Duc de, 303

Brougham, Henry, 1st Baron Brougham and Vaux, and London University, 180

Brousse, Paul, French Possibilist, 111

his *Fédération des Travailleurs Socialistes de France*, 316

Bruce's type-casting machine, 99

Brunetière, Ferdinand, French critic, 139

Brunner, Mond and Company, chemical manufacturers, 72

Brussels Conference (1874), 241, 254

Bryan, William Jennings, American Democrat, 503–4, 677, 684

Bryce, James, 1st Viscount, 672

his *Modern Democracies*, 406, 408

his *American Commonwealth*, 487

Buddhism, 433

Buganda, 624, 625, 632

Bukovina, 259, 335, 339

Bulgaria, 39 n.

autonomy, 25, 244, 249

Russians and, 208, 212, 348, 556–7; 'Big Bulgaria' project, 547, 556, 571–2

crisis of 1885–8, 223, 233, 347, 556–7, 558

franchise, 260

under Turkish rule, 329–30, 342, 346; 'the Bulgarian horrors', 545, 547

and Pan-Slavism, 335

suppression of Rhodope rising of Muslims, 343

frontier, 343, 361

nationalism, 347

Bullock, William, inventor, 99

Bülow, Prince Bernhard Heinrich von, German statesman, Imperial Chancellor 1900, Secretary of State for Foreign Affairs, 258, 296, 297, 298

Bulygin, A. S., Russian Minister of the Interior, 377

Bunge, N. Kh., Russian Minister of Finance, 367, 370

Bunnerjea, Surendranath, Indian political leader, 435

Fashoda crisis, *see* Sudan

Fauré, Gabriel Urbain, French composer, 322

Fawcett, Philippa, 198

Fénéon, Félix, French critic, 165–6

Ferdinand of Coburg, and throne of Bulgaria, 557

Fergusson, James, Scottish art historian, 434

Ferranti, Ziani de, inventor, and Deptford generator, 87

Ferry, Jules François Camille, French statesman, 187, 305, 306, 311, 587, 593, 595, 596, 604–5, 606, 607, 647–8, 651

Fertilisers, 91–2

Fichte, Immanuel Hermann von, German philosopher, 200

Figaro
and Impressionist painters, 157
and Dreyfus case, 320

Fiji Islands, 385, 386, 393, 401, 639, 641–2, 649

fin de siècle, 121, 159

Finance, international, 6, 55–6

Finland, 29, 201, 248, 372, 374, 381

Fisher, John Arbuthnot, 1st Baron Fisher, British admiral and First Sea Lord, 222, 223
on submarines, 232

Fisk University, U.S.A., 186

Fizeau, Armand Hyppolyte Louis, French physicist, 79

Flatters, Paul-François-Xavier, French African explorer, 621

Flaubert, Gustave, French novelist, 126, 132, 134, 136, 140, 141

Flores, Venancio, Uruguayan political leader, 530

Fonseca, Manoel Deodoro da, first President of Brazil, 528

Fontane, Theodor, German writer, 139, 140, 141, 142

Fontanier, French consul in Tientsin, 437, 444

Formosa
ceded to Japan (1895), 453, 484, 657–8
French attacks on (1884), 651
Sino-Japanese quarrels over (1870's), 645–7

Fortnightly Review, English periodical, 117

Forum, American periodical, 504

Fouillée, Alfred, French social theorist, 117

Fourah Bay College, 180

Foureau, Fernand, French explorer, 622, 631

Fournier, François Ernest, French admiral in China, and Li–Fournier trade agreement, 449, 450, 651

France
trade and industry: industrial development, 3, 57; metallurgic industries, 3,

57, 96, 308; export trade, 7, 56, 57, 63, 307; raw material imports, 54; textiles, 57, 308; coal, 58, 308; years of depression, 307–8

economic structure and developments: capital investment, 4; tariffs, 8, 64, 309; economic decline, 307–9; taxation, 319; banking interests in Latin America, 519; loan to Ottoman empire, 571

population, 12, 48, 245, 246, 247, 308–9

agriculture, 14, 307, 309; disaster of phylloxera, 307; increase of peasant proprietors, 309

social structure and developments: trade unions and workers' associations, 15, 74, 112, 312, 313, 315–16; working conditions and living standards, 21, 309; immigrants from Italy, 247; individualistic and regional tone of public life, 261; class structure, 300; social changes resulting from economic crisis, 309; social reforms, 313–14; idea of General Strike, 317; Bourses de travail, 317; anti-semitism, 321; gulf between intellectual life and rest of nation, 321–2

fall of the Second Empire, 25, 542

political structure and developments: Opportunists, 27, 305–7, 310–14, 315, 318, 321; Liberal Action party, 33; Paris Commune, 104, 105, 301, 315, 322; *Parti ouvrier français* or Guesdists (Marxist), 110, 271, 316–17; Possibilists, 111, 270, 316; relation of church and state, 117, 187, 267–8, 303, 304, 314–15; republican movement, 244, 263, 301–2, 304, 318; constitution, 249–50, 256, 302, 303–4, 306–7; weaknesses of parties, 259, 261–2; franchise, 260, 322; social legislation, 265, 312–14; socialist parties, 270, 271, 314, 315–18, 321; Waldeck-Rousseau cabinet (1899), 272; elections (1871), 301–2; (1876), 303; (1877), 304; (1885), 310, 314; (1889), 312, 314; (1893), 315, 317; royalists, 301, 302, 311, 315, 318; Ministry of Moral Order, 303; granting of fundamental freedoms, 305; Radicals, 305–7, 310, 315, 318, 320; Belleville programme, 306; Conservatives, 310, 312, 314, 317; anti-parliamentary trend, 310; Boulangist movement, 310–12, 313, 314, 315, 316, 322; nationalism, 310, 322, 557; Rally (Catholic) party, 314–15, 318, 321; influence of rural voters, 313, 319; *Fédération des Travailleurs Socialistes de France*, 316; *Parti Socialiste Révolutionnaire*, 316; *Centrale Syndicale*, 316; anarchists, 316, 318; corruption in 'the Panama

French Equatorial Africa, 252, 611, 619, 621-3, 629-31
see also constituent territories
Frere, Sir (Henry) Bartle Edward, British colonial administrator, 576
Freud, Sigmund, psychologist, 113, 115, 120, 125
The Interpretation of Dreams, 120
Freycinet, Charles de, French minister of war, 216, 224, 314, 587, 598, 607
Friendly Societies, 14-16
Froebel, Friedrich Wilhelm August, German educationist, 193
Fu'ād Pasha, Mehmed Kecheji-zāde, Turkish Grand Vezir, 324, 325
Fulani emirate, 609-10

Gabon, 603, 607
Gaj, Croat nationalist, 334
Galicia (Polish Austria), 332, 339
Gallé, Émile, French artist, 171, 173
Gallegos, Latin American writer, 538
Galliéni, Joseph Simon, French soldier, 225, 606, 608, 610
Gallifet, Gaston-Alexandre-Auguste, marquis de, French general, 216
Gallipoli peninsula, 572, 573
Gambetta, Léon Michel, French republican leader, 301, 306, 543, 585, 596, 597, 598, 614
Gambia, 602, 610
Gamboa, Federico, Mexican writer, 538
Gana, Alberto Blest, Chilean writer, 538
Gandhi, Mohandâs Karamchand, Indian leader, 435
Gandu, Nigerian emirate, 606
Gapon, G. A., Russian labour leader, 376
Garden cities, 69, 164
Garfield, James Abram, President of the United States (Republican), 670
Gaudí, Antoni, Spanish architect, 154, 173-4, 175, 176
Gauguin, Paul, French painter, 156, 166-8, 169, 170, 171, 175, 176
Gautier, Théophile, French poet, 130
General stores, development of, 68
Geneva Convention (1864), 241
Gentil, French explorer in Congo, 631
Genyosha, Japanese political organisation, 483
Geography, increased knowledge of, 4
Geology, 2, 4-5
George, Henry, American economist
his *Progress and Poverty*, 108, 506-7
his single tax, 392
George, Stefan, German poet, 143-5
Georgia (Russia), 372
German Association of the Eastern Marches, The, 292, 296

German Colonial Union, The, 296
German East Africa, 252, 292, 612-14, 632
German East Africa Company, 612
Germanisation of Poles, 44, 249, 292-3
Germany
trade and industry: industrial production, 3, 30, 47, 58-60, 285; cotton, 3; iron and steel, 13, 48, 51, 58, 74, 95, 285, 290, 398; mercantile marine, 52; rivalry with Britain, 54, 56, 58-64, 395-6, 398-9, 605; export trade, 56, 60, 285, 295; coal, 58, 285; chemicals, 59, 285, 399; electrical industry, 60, 285; kartells, 72-4, 291; dye industry, 92; Krupp works, 96; engines, 285; food imports, 285; maritime interests, 296
economic structure and developments: capital investment, 4, 51, 285; tariffs and free trade, 8, 9, 10, 62, 64, 264, 290, 396; dependence on primary imports, 54; industrialisation, 58-63, 246-7, 284-6; banks, 62, 74, 292; *per capita* income, 62; economic fluctuations, 284-5, 286; state revenue and taxation, 289-91, 298; boom years, 295; banking interests in Latin America, 519
population, 12, 30, 48, 58, 246, 285-6
social structure and organisation: trade unions, 15, 62, 74, 281; social insurance, 21, 264, 273, 289; working conditions and standard of living, 21, 58, 264, 285, 286, 289; emancipation and influence of middle classes, 191, 286, 297; increase in political-mindedness, 275, 279, 280; class tension, 280; privileges for Prussian aristocracy, 280; strike of mineworkers, 294
political structure and developments: compulsory social insurance, 21, 264-5, 273, 289; state control of public utilities, 22; Social Democratic (Marxist) party, 26, 28, 31, 110-11, 261, 270-1, 273, 280-1, 283-4, 288-9, 294, 296, 298; franchise, 30, 257, 260; liberalism, 33, 34, 263, 264, 278, 279, 280, 289; imperialism, 42, 48, 60, 265; nationalism, 44, 119, 297; non-German minorities, 44, 249, 282, 287; state intervention in economic affairs, 61; unification of Reich, 104, 243, 244, 274; *Machtpolitik*, 107; racial purity and anti-semitism, 108; Marxism, 110-11, 112, 280-1; state socialism, 110, 270-1, 289; Gotha programme, 110, 271, 280; Erfurt programme, 111, 271, 280; *Kathedersozialisten*, 112; *Kulturkampf*, 117, 119, 267, 282, 284, 287-8, 292, 544; Catholic Centre party, 119,

INDEX

Hague Conference (1907), 254
Hague Congress (1872), 269
Hague Court, The, 242, 254
Haiti, 235, 516, 530
Halbe, Max, German dramatist, 142
Hall, C. M., scientist, 89
Hall, Granville Stanley, American psychologist, his *Adolescence, its Psychology and its relation to Physiology, Anthropology, Sociology, Science and Education*, 194
Hamilton, Alexander, American statesman, 515
Hanotaux, Gabriel, French statesman, 625, 630
Hanover, 278, 282
Hardenberg, Carl August, Fürst von, Prussian statesman, 280
Hardinge, Henry Hardinge, 1st Viscount, as Governor-General of India, 414, 421
Hardy, Thomas, novelist and poet, 122–3
Hare, Indian nationalist, 430
Harkort, German engineer, 62
Harmsworth, Alfred Charles William, 1st Viscount Northcliffe, British newspaper proprietor, 68, 406
Harper's, American periodical, 504
Harriman, American businessman, 53, 73
Harris, W. H., American educationist, 193
Harrison, Benjamin, President of the U.S.A., 650, 670
Harrison, Frederic, English lawyer and philosopher, 117
Harrow School, first 'modern' side, 179
Hart, Heinrich, joint editor of *Kritische Waffengänge*, 142
Hart, Julius, joint editor of *Kritische Waffengänge*, 142
Hart, Sir Robert, British Head of Chinese Maritime Customs, 450
Hartington, Spencer Compton Cavendish, Marquis of, and 8th Duke of Devonshire, 227
Hartington Commission, 227, 228
Harvey, Hayward Augustus, American inventor, 230
Hashemites of the Hejaz, 567
Hastings, Warren, English administrator in India, 412
Hauptmann, Gerhart, German dramatist, 142, 143
Havemeyer, Henry O., American patron of art, 157
Hawaii, 35, 641, 649–50, 662, 670, 673, 685
Hay, John, United States Secretary of State, 663–4, 674, 675
  Hay–Pauncefote Canal treaties, 676–8
  'open door' (in China) notes, 686–7
  on China policy, 688

Hayes, Rutherford Birchard, President of the United States (Republican), 670
Hegel, Georg Wilhelm Friedrich, German philosopher, 106, 113, 115
Heligoland, 605, 611, 613
Heligoland–Zanzibar Treaty, 611, 614
Helium, discovery of, 79, 103
Helmholtz, Hermann, scientist, and First Law of Thermodynamics, 103
Henley, William, English poet, 128
Hennique, Léon, French novelist, 136
Henry, Commandant, of the French Intelligence Bureau, 320
Herat, 580, 581, 582
Herbart, Johann Friedrich, German philosopher and educationist, 193, 194
Herbert, Hilary, secretary of U.S. Navy, 238
Herbst, Edward, German liberal in Austria, 337
Hercegovina, 39 n., 330, 334, 335, 336, 342, 361, 548
Heredia, José-Maria de, French poet, 138
Hernández, José, Latin-American writer, 538
Héroult, P. L. T., scientist, 89
Herschell, Farrar Herschell, Lord, British statesman, 674
Hertz, Heinrich von, physicist, 78, 89
Herzen, A. I., editor of Russian *émigré* newspaper *Kolokol*, 359
Herzl, Theodor, *Der Judenstaat*, 119
Hesse, Bismarck's annexation of, 278
Hesse, Grand Duke of, his palace at Darmstadt, 164
Hewett, British consul in Niger territory, 604, 606
Heyse, Paul, German writer, 141
Hicks, William (Hicks Pasha), British officer in command of Egyptian forces, 628
Hicks-Beach, Sir Michael Edward, later Viscount St Aldwyn, British statesman, 638
Hill, James J., American businessman, 50
  in railways, 73
Hindus, 423, 433–4
Hispaniola, 518
History, philosophy and study of, 115–17
Hitler, Adolf, influence of H. S. Chamberlain on, 108
  influence of Austrian racialism, 119
Hobart Pasha (August Charles Hobart-Hampden), commander of Turkish navy, 326
Hodler, Ferdinand, Swiss painter, 170
Hoffmann, Josef, Austrian architect, 174
Hofmannsthal, Hugo von, German poet, 145
Hofmeyr, Jan Hendrik, South African Boer statesman, 634, 636

717

Japan (*cont.*)

    foreign affairs: status as Asiatic power, 239, 449, 482–3, 484, 486; isolation threatened, 465; relations with western powers, 465, 470; treaty revision, 470, 471, 482, 484; claims to Kurile and Ryukyu islands, 483, 645, 646, 647; 'Triple Intervention' against Treaty of Shimonoseki, 484; *see also* relations with individual countries

    and Korea, 374, 450–1, 471, 483–6, 646–7, 652–3; a Sino-Japanese protectorate, 654–5; Russo-Japanese rivalry, 659–61, 664, 666–7

    relations with China, 465, 644–7 *passim*, 652–662 *passim*; aid for legations in Boxer riots, 485; commercial treaty, 646; *see also* Korea; Sino-Japanese War

    relations with United States of America, 465, 470, 482, 647

    Tokyo substituted for Edo as name of capital, 466

    Shinto religion, 468

    communications, 472–3

    agriculture, 475; farmers in opposition to government, 477; population overtakes production of foodstuffs, 485

    Press control, 478

    relations with Russia, 484, 485, 486, 565, 647, 656–8, 661–7, 665, 666; Nishi–Rosen agreement, 661; *see also* Russo-Japanese War

    and Manchuria, 656, 657, 665

    relations with Great Britain, *see* Great Britain

Japanese influence on Western art, 156, 160, 168, 171–2

Jaureguiberry, French admiral and minister of Navy and Colonies, 651

Jaurès, Jean, French socialist, 110, 111, 272, 317

    as Dreyfusard, 321

Jefferson, Thomas, American President, 515

Jenatsch, Jürg, Swiss patriot, 140

Jesuits (Society of Jesus)

    Gerard Manley Hopkins a member of, 129

    forbidden to teach in France, 304

Jevons, William Stanley, English economist, 408

Jews

    anti-semitism, 108, 119, 321, 339, 365–6

    Zionism, 119, 372

    political organisation in Russia, 371, 374

Johnson, Andrew, President of the United States (Democrat), 491, 495, 669

Johnston, Sir Harry Hamilton, British explorer, 384

Joint-stock Companies, development of, 12–13

Jones, Viriamu, Welsh educationist, 181, 190

Jones, Sir William, British orientalist, 433

Jongkind, Johan-Berthold, Dutch painter, 155

Joseph II, Emperor of Germany (1741–90), 249

Joubert, French financier, 584

Joule, James, scientist, 103

Jowett, Benjamin, Master of Balliol College, Oxford, 405

Juárez, Benito Pablo, President of Mexico, 528

Jung, Carl, psychologist, 113

Jung Lu, commander-in-chief of Chinese forces of the north, 458, 460

Justo, Juan B., Argentine socialist, 531

Kahn, Gustave, French poet, 137

Kallay, Benjamin, Hungarian leader, 333, 340

Kang I, Chinese reactionary leader, 452, 458

K'ang Yu-wei, Chinese reformer, 455, 456, 463

Kangwha, Treaty of, 652

Kant, Immanuel, German philosopher, influence, 115

Kapital, Das (Marx and Engels), 101, 112, 268–9

Kardorff, Wilhelm von, German conservative leader, 290

Kars, 572

Kashmir, 590

Kassala, 615

Katanga, 619

Katkov, M. N., Russian nationalist, 360

Kato Takaaki, Japanese statesman, 485–6, 661

Katsura, Japanese official, 482

Kaufman, Constantine Petrovich von, Russian general and governor of Turkestan, 576, 578

Kautsky, Karl, German socialist, 289

    his *Social-Democratic Catechism*, 281

Kekulé, Friedrich, scientist, 84

Keller, Gottfried, Swiss writer, 139, 140–1

Kelley, William G., American radical, 502, 504

Kelvin, William Thomson, 1st Baron, Scottish physicist, 103

Kemāl Bey, Young Turk, 341

Kenya, 632

Kerschensteiner, German educationist, 201

Ketteler, von, bishop, 119

Kettler, Baron von, German minister in Peking, 460

Keynes, John Maynard, English economist, 119

Khair al-Din Pasha, Tunisian minister, 342

Khérédine, Tunisian first minister, 595

Peerage, Great Britain
changing composition of, 31–2
political influence of, 31–2, 393
marriages with American heiresses, 32
Péguy, Charles Pierre, French poet and essayist, 138, 320, 321
Peixoto, Floriano, President of Brazil, 528
Peking, Treaty of, 374
Peking [Alcock] Convention, The, 437, 442–3, 444
Pelew Islands, 662
Pelloutier, Fernand, French trade unionist, 317
Penjdeh incident, 556, 579, 581, 587, 653
Pepper, John Henry, English chemist, 195
Perkin, William, English chemist, 84, 92
Perret, Auguste, French architect, 174
Perry, Matthew Galbraith, American commodore, 670
Persia, 412, 416, 572
Safavid dynasty, 417
and Afghanistan, 567, 578
position on Britain–India route, 569, 577, 580
Russian and British interest in, 579–83
Persian Gulf, 385, 580, 582, 583
British gunboats in, 567
German railway plans, 591
Peru, 517, 523, 525, 530, 531, 534
in War of the Pacific, 523, 533–5
Pescadores, 484, 657, 658
Pestalozzi, Johann Heinrich, Swiss educationist, 193, 199
Peters, Karl, German explorer, 612
Petrol engine, 41, 96, 209, 395
Petroleum, 3, 73, 96–7, 368
Phayre, Sir Arthur Purves, British Chief Commissioner in Burma, 418
Philadelphia Enquirer, rotary printing, 99
Philippines, 35, 239, 563, 662, 683–4, 685–6
Phillips, Peregrine, English manufacturer, 91
Phylloxera, 307
Physics
developments in, 77–80, 103–4
beginnings of atomic physics, 80
Picquart, Colonel, 320
Picric acid, 93
Pierce, Charles, American philosopher, 117
Piérola, Nicolás de, Peruvian leader, 535
Pirandello, Luigi, dramatist, 137
Pisarev, D. I., Russian nihilist writer, 359
Pissarro, Camille, French Impressionist painter, 155, 157, 158, 166
Pius IX, Pope
his *Syllabus Errorum*, 118, 304, 314
end of pontificate, 118
prisoner in the Vatican, 544
Pius X, Pope, accession of, 118
Pixii, Hippolyte, French scientist, 86

Plehve, V. K., Russian police chief and minister of the interior, 373
assassination, 375
Plekhanov, and Swiss Liberation of Labour Group, 110
Plevna, Turkish defence of, 208, 547
Plombières, Pact of, 39
Plunkett, Sir Horace Curzon, Irish agricultural reformer, 397
Pneumatic tyres, 3, 97–8
Pobedonostsev, K. P., Russian, Chief Procurator of the Holy Synod, 363–4, 365, 366
Poe, Edgar Allan, American poet and short-story writer, 132
Poincaré, Raymond Nicolas Landry, French Opportunist, 321
Poland, 25
Poles in Germany, 44, 249, 282, 287, 292–3
nationalism, 44, 249, 282, 287, 292, 360
Russian troops in, 214
emigration, 247
russianisation, 248–9, 366
Poles in Austria (Galicia), 332, 338
land reform, 360
socialists, 371
Polish minority in Germany, 44, 249, 282, 287, 292–3
Political parties
development and character of, 26–7, 30–2, 34, 110–11, 255–64, 270–3
see also under individual countries
Polytechnics, 202–3
Pomak rising, 343
Ponty, French colonial administrator, 632
Popular Science Monthly, 105
Population, increase in, and migrations of, 4–5, 11–12, 14, 30, 245–7, 689–91
in Australasia, 4, 11–12, 393, 401–2
in Austria, 12, 246, 337
in China, 12 n.
in Cuba, 525
in Europe, 245–6
in France, 12, 48, 245–7, 308–9
in Germany, 12, 30, 48, 58, 246, 285–6
in Great Britain, 5, 12, 245–7, 386, 393, 401–2
in Ireland, 247, 388
in Italy, 30, 246
in Japan, 12, 485
in Latin America, 4, 12, 516–19, 520–2, 525
in Poland, 247
in Russia, 12, 30, 48, 246, 354, 369
in South Africa, 4, 11, 393, 401, 633
in Sweden, 245
in the United States and Canada, 4, 11–12, 48, 50, 247, 401–2, 489, 501, 511, 671, 689–91

Russia (*cont.*)

transport and communications: railway development programme, 51, 212, 355, 368; Trans-Siberian line, 51, 212, 368, 564, 655, 658, 666; strategic inadequacy of railways (1876), 214; cost of construction, 224, 240, 564; Transcaspian line, 581; demands for rights in Manchuria, 658–9

education, 188, 358–9, 364–5

relations with Poland, 214, 248–9, 360; Polish socialist party, 371

Baltic provinces, 248, 360, 366; political activity in, 372

Balkan affairs, 323, 336, 337, 342, 345, 348, 360–1, 367, 544–8; Pan-Slavism, 51, 248, 335, 360, 546–7, 553; and Bulgaria, 208, 212, 348, 556–7; Bessarabia ceded to Russia, 342; evacuation of peninsula, 346; proposals for reform in Macedonia, 348; *see also* relations with Turkey

relations with Turkey, 328, 329, 342, 345, 346, 347, 583; *see also* Russo-Turkish War

relations with Austria-Hungary, 336, 361, 366–7, 545, 546–8, 551–2, 557; *see also* Three Emperors' League

agriculture, depression in, 354; land tenure, 367, 370; agrarian reforms, 369, 380–1

judicial system, 356–7, 364

local government reforms, 357; establishment and work of *zemstva*, 357–8, 364, 371, 372–3

Church–state relations, 365; in Baltic provinces, 366

relations with Germany, 366–7, 368, 545–6, 551; Reinsurance Treaty with, 39 n., 40 n., 224, 294, 366, 558, 559, 613; in Far East, 657, 660; *see also* Three Emperors' Alliance

relations with Japan, 484, 485, 486, 647, 656–8, 661–7; *see also* Russo-Japanese War

relations with Persia, 577, 579–82, 583

relations with Great Britain, *see under* Great Britain

see also Armenia; Baltic Provinces; Finland; Georgia

Russo-Japanese War, 35, 42, 212, 240, 374, 554, 566, 688

Treaty of Portsmouth, 374

battle of Tsushima, 377, 569, 579

Russo-Turkish War, 35, 38, 204, 337, 341, 355, 360–1, 547

Treaty of San Stefano, 38, 343, 344, 361, 547–8, 572, 573

Ruthenians in Austria, 332

Rutherford, Mark [i.e. William White], English novelist, 125

Ryukyu Islands, 483, 644, 645, 646, 653

taken over by Japan, 647

Sagasta, Práxedes Mateo, Spanish liberal leader, 188

Sahara, 611

plan for trans-Saharan railway, 603

Said Pasha, khedive of Egypt, 583

Saigo Takamori, Japanese official, 468, 471

leader of samurai revolt, 476

and plan for Korean war, 646

Saigo Tsugumichi, Japanese soldier, 647

Sailing ship, survival of, 52

St Andrews University, 181, 198

Saint-Hilaire, Étienne, French biologist, 80

Saint-Hilaire, Jules Barthélemy, French foreign minister, 596

St Leonards School, 198

St Lucia Bay, 635

St Pancras Station, 154, 163, 175

St Petersburg, Treaty of (1881), 447

Saionji, Japanese official, 482

Sakhalin Island, 647

Salisbury, Robert Arthur Talbot Gascoyne Cecil, 3rd Marquis of, English Conservative statesman, 38

on Hague Conference, 43

on demand for overseas bases, 223

establishes Defence Committee, 228

and parliamentary practice, 255

on Turkish credit, 345

as Prime Minister, 389, 390, 392

and party organisation, 391

on the *Daily Mail*, 406

on security measures in India, 416, 590

and policy in Eastern Europe, 548, 553, 556, 557, 558

on alliances, 560

on defence of Constantinople, 568

on Britain's position in Europe, 571

and security in Mediterranean and Levant, 572–3, 575

on Levantine civilisation, 573

on Sher Ali of Kabul, 578

and relations with Persia, 580, 582

and Egyptian problems, 587–8, 601, 610–11, 613, 615, 622, 628, 631, 632

and African empire, 593, 610–11, 612, 614, 615, 616, 637

and East African railways, 629

orders Kitchener to invade Sudan, 626–7

his 'Dying Nations' speech, 661–2

on Monroe Doctrine, 672

and Panama negotiations, 676

and taking of Weihaiwei, 686

Salt Union (British), 72

Salvation Army, The, 117, 402

Siemens, Frederick, and steel-making, 51, 95

Siemens, Werner von, German scientist, 60, 62

Siemens, William, scientist, 53, 60

Sierra Leone, 602, 611
Fourah Bay College, 180

Signac, Paul, French painter, 165–6

Simon, John, doctor, 20n.

Sino-Japanese Treaty of commerce, 646

Sino-Japanese War (1894), 35, 179, 204, 240, 451, 453, 475, 481, 654, 656–8, 684
defeat of Chinese fleet, 230–1, 656
Korea as cause of war, 483, 655–6
Treaty of Shimonoseki, 484, 485, 657

Sipyagin, D. S., Russian minister of the interior, 372

Sisley, Alfred, Impressionist painter, 155, 157

Sivori, Eduardo, Argentine painter, 538

Skobolev, Mikhail Dmitrievich, Russian soldier, 222

Skoda Works, and armaments, 240

Skyscrapers, 96, 175

Slave Coast, 606

Slave trade, 384–5, 611, 618, 622, 632

Slavonia, united with Croatia, 334

Smiles, Samuel, Scottish author and social reformer, 69

Snow, John, English anaesthetist, 82

Soap industry, 4, 68, 70–2

Social legislation, 14–15, 20–4, 265
in Australia, 404, 408
in Belgium, 15, 265
in Denmark and Sweden, 265
in France, 15, 265, 312–14
in Germany, 15, 21, 264–5, 273, 289
in Great Britain, 14–15, 20–1, 23, 75, 203, 264
in India, 265, 415
in Italy, 265
in the Netherlands, 265
in Russia, 265
in Spain, 15, 21, 265

Socialism, 34, 111, 243, 268–73
see also Marxism; and under individual countries

Sociology, 105–6, 115, 506–7

Soejima Taneomi, Japanese foreign minister, 645–6

Sokoto, Nigerian emirate, 606, 610, 630–1

Solomon Islands, Lesser, 663

Somaliland, use of Indian troops in, 575

Sorel, Georges, French philosopher, 112–13, 120
his *Avenir socialiste des syndicats*, 113

South Africa
population: emigration to, 4, 11; non-European elements, 393, 401; rapid growth of European element, 633

trade and industry, 5, 6; gold, 71, 385, 594, 633, 635, 637; diamonds, 633

Boer War, 25, 35, 75, 120, 204, 239, 251, 385, 410, 564–5, 566, 570, 677, 682; armoured trains in, 212; weakness of British armed forces revealed by, 227, 237, 239; volunteers from Australasia and Canada, 407; outbreak of, 638

Boer Republics: superiority of armed forces, 225; resistance to annexation, 385 (*see also* Boer War); Afrikaner nationalism, 410, 594, 634–5, 637, 638; status of Afrikaans language, 410; Transvaal rising (first Boer War, 1881), 634, 638

British settlements and defence, 226

tribal resistance, 385

German influence, 385, 561, 633, 635, 637–8; the 'Kruger telegram', 43, 561

local government, 391

social problems not faced, 404

British rule in, 410, 633–9; and self-government, 251, 386, 633

Jameson Raid, 561, 594, 637

Bantu, 633, 634

Dutch Reformed Church, 634

the Afrikaner Bond, 635, 636, 637

Delagoa Bay Railway, 637

Drifts crisis, 637

South Africa Chartered Company, 385, 614, 636, 637

Spain
economic development: tariffs, 10
political and constitutional developments: social legislation, 15, 21, 265; monarchy overcomes republic, 25, 244; franchise, 30, 260; Carlist Wars, 244; parliament and parties, 260, 261
education, 188–9
armed forces: influence of military leaders, 219; overseas commitments, 225; navy in war with America, 238
end of empire in America, 533, 662
see also Spanish-American War

Spanish-American War, 35, 120, 202, 204, 238–9, 512, 533, 563, 662, 671, 676, 679–83, 685, 688
Philippines seized by United States, 563, 662
Spanish fleet defeated at Manila Bay, 662, 683
war declared, 682

Spencer, Herbert, English philosopher, 105, 506

Spengler, Oswald, German historian, 162

Spurgeon, Charles Haddon, English Baptist minister, 406

Stalin, Joseph, Russian leader, 120

United States of America (*cont.*)
496; constitutional separation of Church and state, 202; the federal pattern, 251–2; reconstruction problems and policies, 487, 491, 494–8, 499, 513; patronage and political manipulation, 488, 493; Tammany, 489; Tenure of Office Act, 491; President's power of veto, 491–2; Federal Income Tax Law rejected, 492; Interstate Commerce Act, 492; Civil Service reform (Pendleton Act), 493; municipal reform, 493–4; end of Republican rule in South, 498; 'home rule' in South, 499; North–South conservative alliance, 499, 514; the Grange (agrarian association), 501, 507; demand for currency reform, 501–4 (*see also* Populist party); Greenback-Labor party, 502; Sherman Silver Purchase Act, 503; nationalism, 512–13, 692; Constitution established, 515; 'a conservative country', 693

art and architecture, 164–5; skyscrapers, 96, 175; *see also* individual artists

education: universities, 182–3, 186, 197, 504; Morrill Act, 182, 202; Land Grant Colleges, 183; Massachusetts Institute of Technology, 183, 202; National Education Association, 186; of Negroes, 186, 202; state control, 186–7, 511; compulsory education, 187, 511; of women, and co-education, 199; adult education, 202; Church contribution, 202; Southern backwardness, 500; education in American citizenship, 511

Negroes: education of, 186, 202; Republican protection of, 489; civil rights (the Dred Scott and Milligan cases), 492; principle of racial equality, 494–8, 499; suffrage, 496, 497, 498; emergence of Negro middle class, 497, 500; measures to disenfranchise, 499–500; migration from South to northern cities, 511

armed forces (1): military thought, 206; army: size and organisation, 239; and disarmament proposals, 241

armed forces (2): naval affairs, 228, 231; strategic considerations, 235; expansion, 237–8; overseas bases, 238

relations with Great Britain: hostility to Britain engendered by Irish immigrants, 388; trade rivalry, 395–6; in Latin America, 672; and Canada–Alaska boundary, 673–6, 679; and Panama Canal, 676–9

relations with Japan, 465, 470, 482, 647, 670, 688

philanthropic activities, 505

relations with Latin America, 516–19; International American Conference, 670

interests in Latin America, 517, 518–19, 524, 670; relations with Cuba, 238, 239, 532–3, 680–3; and War of the Pacific, 535

interests in Pacific, 641, 647, 669; in Samoa, 642–3, 649, 662, 670; in Formosa, 646; in Hawaii, 649–50, 662, 670, 673

relations with Germany in Pacific, 662

relations with China, 663–4, 669–70, 684–8

Alaska, 669, 670, 673–9

political thought, 671, 679

Alaska–Canada boundary dispute, 673–6, 679

Universities, 180–4, 197–8, 203
in Africa, 180
in Canada, 181
in Germany, 182
in Great Britain, 180–3, 196–8, 200, 202–3, 404–5, 409
in India, 415, 428, 431
in Ireland, 183, 197–8
in Japan, 474
in the Netherlands, 183
in New Zealand, 183
in Russia, 358–9, 364–5
in the United States, 182–3, 186, 197, 504

Unwin, Raymond, English architect, 164

Upolu (Samoa), 663

Upper Niger, 603, 604, 606–8, 620–1

Upper Volta, 620, 621, 630–1

Uranium, discovery of radiation, 80

Urbanisation, 11–12, 17, 19, 58, 246–7, 510–11, 691

Uruguay, 517, 518, 519, 522, 530, 531, 533–4, 537

Utilitarianism, 101, 114–16, 119

Valéry, Paul, French writer, 132

van de Velde, Henri, French painter and architect, 165, 166, 171, 172, 174

Van Gogh, Vincent, Dutch painter, 156, 166, 167, 168–70, 175, 176

Van Kerckhoven, Belgian general, 624

Van 't Hoff, J. H., scientist, 84–6

Varela, José Pedro, Uruguayan leader, 537, 539

Varona, Enrique José, Cuban writer, 539

Vatican, The
and papal authority, 104, 118
Vatican Council, The (1870), 104, 118, 266, 282
conflict with Italian state, 117–18, 266, 544
attacks Liberalism and Nationalism, 118
change of attitude, 118–19, 314–15